The**G**reen**G**uide

Alsace Lorraine Champagne

Shop sign on rue du Général de Gaulle, Kaysersberg © Nicolas Thibaut/Photononstop

MICHELIN

THE GREEN GUIDE **ALSACE LORRAINE CHAMPAGNE**

Editorial Director	Cynthia Clayton Ochterbeck
Editor	Sophie Friedman
Principal Writer	Terry Marsh
Production Manager	Natasha George
Cartography	Stéphane Anton, Andrew Thompson
Picture Editor	Yoshimi Kanazawa
Interior Design	Chris Bell
Layout	Natasha George
Cover Design	Chris Bell, Christelle Le Déan

Contact Us

Michelin Travel and Lifestyle North America
One Parkway South
Greenville, SC 29615
USA
travel.lifestyle@us.michelin.com

Michelin Travel Partner
Hannay House
39 Clarendon Road
Watford, Herts WD17 1JA
UK
☎01923 205240
travelpubsales@uk.michelin.com
www.viamichelin.co.uk

Special Sales

For information regarding bulk sales,
customized editions and premium sales,
please contact us at:
travel.lifestyle@us.michelin.com

HOW TO USE THIS GUIDE

PLANNING YOUR TRIP

The blue-tabbed PLANNING YOUR TRIP section at the front of the guide gives you **ideas for your trip** and **practical information** to help you organize it. You'll find tours, practical information, a host of outdoor activities, a calendar of events, information on shopping, sightseeing, kids' activities and more.

INTRODUCTION

The orange-tabbed INTRODUCTION section explores **The Region Today** including religion, economy and cuisine. The **History** section spans from Prehistoric times through to the Revolution and World Wars. The **Art and Culture** section covers architecture, art and literature, while the final section explores **Nature** in the region.

DISCOVERING

The green-tabbed DISCOVERING section features Principal Sights by region, featuring the most interesting local **Sights**, **Walking Tours**, nearby **Excursions**, and detailed **Driving Tours**. Admission prices shown are normally for a single adult.

ADDRESSES

We've selected from the best hotels, restaurants, cafés shops, nightlife and entertainment to fit all budgets. See the Legend on the cover flap for an explanation of the price categories. See the back of the guide for an index of hotels and restaurants.

Sidebars

Throughout the guide you will find blue, peach and green-colored text boxes with lively anecdotes, detailed history and background information.

🕮 A Bit of Advice 🕮

Green advice boxes found in this guide contain practical tips and handy information relevant to your visit or a sight in the Discovering section.

STAR RATINGS★★★

Michelin has given star ratings for more than 100 years. If you're pressed for time, we recommend you visit the ★★★, or ★★ sights first:

★★★ **Highly recommended**
★★ **Recommended**
★ **Interesting**

MAPS

🕮 National Driving Tours map, Places to Stay map and Sights map.
🕮 Region maps.
🕮 Maps for major cities and villages.
🕮 Local tour maps.

All maps in this guide are oriented north, unless otherwise indicated by a directional arrow. The term "Local Map" refers to a map within the chapter or Tourism Region. A complete list of the maps found in the guide appears at the back of this book.

PLANNING YOUR TRIP

INTRODUCTION TO ALSACE LORRAINE CHAMPAGNE

DISCOVERING ALSACE LORRAINE CHAMPAGNE

CONTENTS

Welcome to Alsace Lorraine Champagne

A source of much contention between powerful neighbours, these regions witnessed bitter battles that left deep marks on their soil and soul. Occupied or annexed by foreign armies, they managed to protect their architectural heritage and preserve their natural environment, while developing a warm sense of hospitality which is cherished by visitors.

Place du Marché, Obernai, Middle Vosges

© Hoffmann Photography/age fotostock

ALSACE LORRAINE

Argonne and the côtes de Meuse *(pp114–135)*

Background to famous battles such as 18C Valmy and WW I Verdun, this area keeps a faithful watch over the fallen. Nature lovers will appreciate the Regional Park of Lorraine, set in a vast expanse of preserved forest and ponds, home to a bewildering array of wildlife.

Metz and industrial Lorraine *(pp136–151)*

Capital of the Austrasian kingdom, cradle of the Carolingian dynasty, Metz dominates the Lorraine Iron Industry Country. Former high furnace cities such as Thionville and Longwy are slowly recovering from economic downfall and successfully putting forward their architectural heritage.

Nancy and the Lorrain plateau *(pp152–175)*

Walk around Nancy's 162ha architectural preserve, and do not miss its iconic 18C Stanislas Square. Also consider visiting neighbouring Baccarat and its world-famous crystalworks showcasing delicate, sparkling artefacts.

Épinal and the Vôge plateau *(pp176–189)*

Straddling the Moselle river, the charming garden-city of Epinal is home to a famous popular imagery style. While in the area, indulge yourself in a relaxing stay in one of the thermal towns of the Vôge plateau, like Vittel or Plombières-les-Bains.

The Southern Vosges *(pp190–219)*

Stretching over half of the southern Vosges mountain ranges, the Ballon des Vosges Regional Park has many walking trails in store for you, as well as a wealth of spectacular viewpoints. Local wildlife includes chamois, beaver, grouse and peregrine falcon.

Saverne and the Northern Vosges *(pp220–241)*

Start from Alsatian Saverne, on the Marne to Rhine Canal, and head north to discover the first transfrontier biosphere preserve in Europe, composed of France's Northern Vosges and Germany's Pfälzerwald. Abundant wildlife and a wealth of mysterious castles are among the local attractions.

The Maginot Line *(pp242–249)*

Built between 1929 and 1938 along France's border with Belgium, Luxembourg, Germany and Italy, and named after the French Minister of War André Maginot, this massive defensive system failed to stop German invasion during WWII. It has left many concrete fortifications, obstacles, weapon installations and shelters in the region, particularly around Metz and Thionville.

Strasbourg and the Middle Vosges *(pp250–289)*

Seat of the European Council, Strasbourg is a warm, lively city built around a celebrated Gothic cathedral. Enjoy its picturesque Christmas market and the timeless charm of its half-timbered houses reflected in the peaceful waters of the Ill river. Further south, the 11C Haut-Kœnigsbourg castle proudly stands vigil over the Alsatian plain.

Colmar and the Alsatian vineyard *(pp290–323)*

From Old Thann to Marienheim, the charming Alsatian Wine Road winds through vineyards and colourful villages. You may want to have lunch in lovely Colmar, and for a wonderful taste sensation, have dessert served with a touch of Late Harvest Riesling.

Mulhouse and the Alsatian Jura *(pp324–339)*

Head south from Mulhouse, a city with an original past as a former independent republic, and a strong industrial tradition. You will explore the Sundgau, a colourful region in the foothills of Jura, which harbours fine examples of karstic landscapes carved by rivers.

CHAMPAGNE-ARDENNE

Ardennes *(pp342–363)*

The frontier town of Sedan is home to the largest fortress in Europe, while Charleville-Mezières, birthplace of French poet Arthur Rimbaud, boasts a remarkable Louis XIII Place ducale, complete with its stone-clad brick pavilions and arcades. Leave town and follow the sinuous course of the Meuse river. Its wide meanders will lead you through dense forests and by mountains averaging around 350–400m in height, but rising to almost 700m in the Hautes Fagnes region of south-east Belgium.

Marne *(pp364–421)*

Walk through Reims' maze of medieval palaces and basilicas, dominated by its beautiful 13C gothic cathedral. Visit the Champagne cellars of world-famous producers of sparkling wine before discovering Reims Mountain, a major wine-growing area towering above town, which produces some of the best champagnes.

Aube *(pp422–443)*

Former capital of Champagne, Troyes offers a wealth of medieval churches, half-timbered houses and quaint lanes. A stone's throw from the city and its popular factory outlets, the woods and lakes of the Forêt d'Orient Regional Park are home to wildlife observation areas and a bird sanctuary for waterfowl.

Cathédrale St-Mammes, Langres, Upper Marne

© Franck Guiziou/hemis.fr

Upper Marne *(pp444–461)*

The spring of the Marne River rises from the Langres plateau, not far from the city of Langres, one of the three capitals of Burgundy under the Gauls. This is a rich agricultural region, and farms are large, capital-intensive and highly mechanised. Cereals are widely cultivated, along with large quantities of champagne and table wine. Further north, crowds of visitors come to Colombey-les-Deux-Eglises to honour the memory of Charles de Gaulle, who rests in the village cemetery.

Cross-country skiing on the Champ du Feu, the Vosges
© Denis Bringard/hemis.fr

Michelin Driving Tours

The following is a brief description of each of the driving tours shown on the map on the inside back cover.

1 THE ARGONNE REGION AND FOREST

200km/124mi starting from Ste-Menehould

Located at the border of Champagne and Lorraine, the Argonne region has distinctive geographic characteristics. The hilly, wooded land is a lovely place for long walks or cycling trips; horse riding and off-road biking are also great ways to enjoy the natural setting and see things you can't see from inside the car.

Ste-Menehould is a good starting point for these adventures. You'll be rewarded with constantly changing terrain with ridges and plateaux and deep rivers in narrow gorges.

Break your journey at the Château de Braux-Ste-Cohière, home to the Champagne-Argonne cultural association, which sponsors many events to promote the region, and home to an interesting regional museum. The conflicts that have ravaged the Argonne at different times over the centuries have left their scars and trenches from the First World War are still visible in the forest outside Varennes, at the historic site of Haute-Chevauchée.

2 THE GOLDEN TRIANGLE

120km/74.5mi starting from Reims

Between Reims, Châlons, Épernay and Château-Thierry, the vineyards stretch along the sunny hillsides. Villages seem to float and bob like ships on a sea of green in summer months.

The 'gold' in this tour is bottled and bubbly: many fine cellars await you in the regions of the Montagne de Reims, the Marne valley and the Côte des Blancs. The vintners will welcome you and tell you all about the methods behind the magic. Many have set up interpretation centres and museums devoted to the fine art of champagne-making. Of course, you will want to taste a little (☺ *but not if you're driving!*). No doubt you can be persuaded to pick up a few bottles to take home.

3 BRIE CHAMPENOISE

165km/102.5mi starting from Provins

Between the regions of Île-de-France and Champagne, the landscapes of Brie are adorned with historic towns set along the rivers and streams like the beads of a necklace. Nogent-sur-Seine, Villenauxe-la-Grande, Montmirail and Verdelot are all good places to stop. The singular jewel in this setting is Provins, a medieval city standing on a hilltop that has been occupied since Roman times. You can easily spend a very pleasant afternoon (or longer) strolling along the high ramparts and in summer there are all sorts of activities here including a jousting tournament and falconry demonstrations.

While Provins is famed for its red roses, the gardens at Viels-Maisons are famous for their myriad varieties of fragrant flowers, herbs and shrubs. Divided into gardens both formal and "English-style", the park is a feast for the senses.

4 THE LAKES OF THE DER REGION

170km/105.6mi starting from Brienne

Outdoor types will want to make special note of this excursion. Whether you prefer the peace and quiet of secluded natural sites for observing wildlife or fishing, or you would rather join in lively sports and games at the beaches and recreation areas, there's a destination that matched your holiday wish list. Swimming, boating and fishing are just some of the activities on the agenda on the large lake at Der-Chantecoq. Birdwatchers will want to be sure to pack their binoculars to study the many species of migratory

Grey cranes, Lac du Der

© gilles_oster/iStockphoto.com

waterfowl (including the *grue cendrée,* grey crane). The Maison de l'Oiseau et du Poisson, with exhibits on the local ecosystem, is a good place to stop before setting out to observe the inhabitants of the lake and its shores. As you drive around the region, notice the local half-timber style of architecture, which extends its churches.

Farther north, the Forêt de l'Orient is a lovely forest that also has several lakes devoted to recreational uses. The Parc de Vision Animalier, in the eastern part of the Regional Nature Park, includes hides where with a bit of peace, quiet and patience you can observe animals in their natural state.

The Lac d'Orient is a bird sanctuary, but its appeal is not limited to those with ornithological hobbies. It also offers opportunities for scuba diving, sailing and swimming. The road that runs around it offers a pretty drive and a good overview. Anglers and canoeists should visit the Lac du Temple. The smaller Lac Amance is reserved for motorised craft.

5 CHAMPAGNE: FROM BAR TO BAR

225km/140mi starting from Troyes
The title of this excursion is not meant to encourage you to drink and drive (far from it ...). It is a reference to the region known as the Côte des Bars. The towns of Bar-sur-Aube and Bar-sur-Seine derive their names from the old Celtic word *barr,* signifying summit. This route passes through beautiful landscapes of vineyards, forest and fields thanks to those summits.

The town of Riceys is the only *commune* in all of France to produce three wines labelled *appellation d'origine contrôlée,* including the delightful rosé for which it is best known. Children will enjoy an afternoon at Nigloland amusement park 👫👤 (🕐*see p424*).

6 ARTS AND CRAFTS IN HAUTE-MARNE

200km/124mi starting from Langres
Begin your journey in the old town of Langres and enjoy the view from the ramparts.

Carry on to Fayl-Billot, where there is a national school of wickerwork. You ought to look for a basket in which you can put the rest of your souvenirs. But there are a number of artisans who give demonstrations in their shops; you may leave wanting to take up a new hobby. In Bourbonne-les-Bains, you may be tempted to ease your aches and pains in a warm mineral water bath or go for a massage (particularly if you have taken advantage of all the walking in the area). In Nogent, the Musée de la Coutellerie is devoted to the cutlery trade, and includes an old-fashioned workshop with a large wheel dating from the 18C.

7 REMEMBERING TWO WORLD WARS

272km/169mi starting from Verdun
Although the First and Second World Wars are increasingly distant memories for older travellers, and may seem like ancient history to the young, this tour brings the events that rent Europe asunder into sharp focus. A trip here reminds you of the absurd tragedy of war.
Verdun is famous for its fortifications and as the site of numerous battles, but the peaceful old town is well worth a visit, too. In the national cemetery there is a memorial to seven unknown soldiers. The Douaumont ossuary is the resting place of soldiers who once fought under different colours. The fort and the "bayonet trench" are startling reminders of the violence of the First World War.
The once-vaunted, later taunted Maginot Line (built to stop the Germans in the Second World War but was in fact easily circumvented by them) is still marked by several forts and defensive works: Fermont Fort and its military museum, the Immerhof defensive works, the Zeiterholz shelter and Fort Guentrange.

In Longwy, you should stop to admire the works of enamel artisans, and in nearby Thionville the Château de la Grange is worth seeing.
Continue the tour of military installations at Hackenberg, impressive in its size. In the busy city of Metz, visit the cathedral and the old town.
Complete the tour via Briey, where the visionary architect Le Corbusier built one of his *cités radieuses,* and Étain, which was entirely rebuilt after 1918.

8 BETWEEN MEUSE AND MOSELLE

261km/162mi starting from Metz
This drive leads you between the banks of the two rivers, and through different periods of French history. Begin in Metz, where the past is associated with wars and religion, but with culture and fine architecture as well. (Metz is especially lovely at night under the many lights installed to accentuate the features and proportions of buildings.)
In Pont-à-Mousson, the old abbey dates from the 18C. Nancy is the former capital of the dukes of Lorraine. The beautiful monuments and public squares are evidence of its rich cultural and artistic heritage.
Vaucouleurs and nearby Domrémy-la-Pucelle are forever linked to the most famous of all French heroines, Joan of Arc. Born in Domrémy, the peasant girl

Old town house façade, Bar-le-Duc

© Franck Guiziou/hemis.fr

Thermes Napoléon, Plombières-les-Bains

© Charlotte Defarges/Vosges Méridionales

first took her quest to the governor of Vaucouleurs, whose condescension did nothing to dissuade her fervour. Commercy is reputed to be the best source of the soft cakes favoured by Marcel Proust, madeleines. On your way back to Metz, visit the Château de Stanislas, the old town of Bar-le-Duc and the 17C church in St-Mihiel.

9 SPA RESORTS IN THE VOSGES

219km/136mi starting from Vittel

The French are very fond of their spa treatments, or cures, which are prescribed for a variety of ailments. For good reason. In addition to the therapeutic values of the waters, the spa experience is said to improve overall health and well-being in other ways, such as enabling patients to take a break from medication, reducing stress, improving sleeping and eating habits and encouraging outdoor exercise. A full course of treatment generally runs for three weeks, but some spas offer short stays for a quick programme of revitalisation. Casinos, racetracks, facilities for tennis and golf are among the options most of these resorts to have to entertain *curistes* and their families. They are oft located in accessible natural settings.

This tour takes you through Vittel, Contrexéville, Bourbonne-les-Bains, Luxeuil-les-Bains, Plombières-les-Bains

and Bains-les-Bains, which combined, seem to treat just about every ailment known to man (and woman). For information on spa treatments, contact the local tourist office or log on to www.vosges.fr.

10 THE VOSGES FOREST

377km/234mi starting from St-Dié

Lace up your walking shoes as you leave St-Dié and head out to the enchanting hills and dales of the beautiful Vosges forest.

After visiting the cathedral and cloisters in St-Dié, head to the old town of Senones. The Donon range begins here, defining the border of Alsace and Lorraine and providing photo-worthy views of the Vosges mountains. There are a number of good walks to take starting from Schirmeck. By way of contrast, the former concentration camp of Struthof is open to visitors interested in learning more about this tragic chapter of the history of the Second World War.

For more extreme outdoor excursions, you could climb the Neuntelstein peak, discover the Hohwald or (in season, of course), ski on the slopes at Champ du Feu. Ste-Marie-aux-Mines is the ancestral home of the Pennsylvania Dutch, where you will find fabric displays in the textile museum which echo Amish designs. Travel the high passes on the Route des Crêtes, including Col du Bonhomme and Col de la Schlucht. Stop at Munster to taste its eponymous (and delicious) cheese, then it's on to the Petit Ballon and the Markstein ski resort. Catch the view from the Grand Ballon.

Thann is at a lower altitude, which your lungs may appreciate, and you can admire the church there before climbing to the highest point in the range, the Ballon d'Alsace.

Around St-Maurice-sur-Moselle and La Bresse there are many ski areas. In Gérardmer, you can ski in winter, or take a pedal boat out on the lake in warmer weather.

11 THE ALSATIAN WINE ROAD

277km/172mi starting from Strasbourg

Begin your wine tour in the European capital of Strasbourg. The city has long been an economic, cultural and intellectual magnet for the region and is now a city break in its own right. At nearby Haguenau you can trace the fortifications of this historic town. Bouxwiller, once home to princes and princesses, seems to huddle for warmth at the base of Mt Batsberg, a legendary haunt of sorcerers and witches. Then it is on to Saverne to visit the marina and château.

The wine begins flowing in earnest in Molsheim, where the nearby hillsides are covered in Riesling grapes. Obernai is a lovely wine-growing town surrounded by vineyards. Climb to the top of Mont Ste-Odile for a visit to the old convent. This is one of the most popular tourist attractions in Alsace. Some come for the view (all the way to the Black Forest on a clear day), others for sacred inspiration, while many more are drawn by the mystery of the "pagan wall" Iron-Age fort.

Following along the wine road, you will pass by the ruins of Andlau Abbey, guarded by a stone bear. The fortifications of Sélestat, storks' nests and a castle at Ribeauvillé mark your route as you continue to the village of Riquewihr, the capital of Riesling. Kaysersberg is another picturesque hamlet. It seems to have sprung straight off the pages of a book of fairytales with its ruined medieval castle, half-timbered houses, pots of bright geraniums and fortified bridge. Continue through charming Niedermorschwihr and the towers of Turckheim on the way to the city of Colmar. This is the capital of the wine-growing region; the old town and the area known as la Petite Venise are particularly attractive. Return to Strasbourg by way of the Rhine valley.

Hunawihr, Alsatian Wine Road

© Nigel Blythe/Cephas/Photononstop

When and Where to Go

WHEN TO GO

CLIMATE

In Alsace, Lorraine and Champagne, weather patterns vary appreciably with the landscapes. The Ardenne uplands are known for heavy precipitation, low clouds, fog and frost; a bleak climate, which may partly explain why this area has one of the lowest population densities in Europe. The lower plains of Champagne form part of the Paris Basin and share its milder climate. Temperatures occasionally drop below freezing between November and March; the hottest days are in July and August.

In Alsace, comparable variations can be observed between the plain and the Vosges mountains. The average annual temperature in Colmar, for example, is 10.3°C, while the Grand Ballon (the highest summit) averages just 3°C. Prevailing winds arrive from the west or southwest, carrying rain and snow. When these weather systems run up against the Vosges, they result in precipitation, leaving the eastern plain fairly dry. Indeed, Colmar holds the record for the lowest annual rainfall in France.

While the uplands are generally wetter and cooler throughout the area, visitors travelling on mountain roads may experience a curious phenomenon of temperature inversion, which occurs when atmospheric pressure is high. At such times, while thick mist swathes the plain, the mountains bask in bright sunlight; temperatures may be 10°C higher than in the valley below. The luminosity and extensive views from here are magnificent.

SEASONS

Visitors will enjoy the **summer** months for holidays, but other seasons have their charms, too. In the **autumn**, the vineyards and forests are rich with colour and harvest time livens

Place de la République in spring, Strasbourg

© SGM/age fotostock

up the villages, as the cool evening air brings red to your cheeks. Hunting season in the Ardenne forest opens in November. **Winter** resorts in the Vosges are especially attractive to cross-country skiers and snowshoe enthusiasts, who appreciate the largely unspoiled beauty of the forest, and the traditional mountain villages. Many areas have satisfactory downhill runs as well, and are equipped with snow-makers. The main resorts are Le Bonhomme (700m), La Bresse-Hohneck (650m), Gérardmer (750m), Saint-Maurice-sur-Moselle (560m) and Ventron (630m). **Spring**, of course, brings the hills, plains and forests into bloom after winter.

WHAT TO PACK

As little as possible! Cleaning and laundry services are available almost everywhere; most personal items can be replaced at reasonable cost. Take the weather and climate into consideration, as you may visit several microclimates in one holiday. Comfortable shoes are essential if you plan on taking advantage of the region's beautiful walks and parks, as is a rain jacket and an extra sweater. Try to pack everything in one suitcase and a tote bag. Porter help may be in short supply, and new purchases will certainly add to the original weight

Vosges forest at La Bresse - Route des Crêtes

© Bertrand Rieger/hemis.fr

(and you will want souvenirs). Take an extra tote bag for packing new purchases, shopping at the open-air market, carrying a picnic, etc.

As is the case anywhere you travel, be sure your luggage is clearly labelled and old travel tags are removed.

Do not pack medication in checked luggage; keep it and other valuables with you at all times.

WEATHER FORECAST

National forecast: ☏ 32 50 (€2.99 per call + network charge). Information about the weather is also available online at www.meteofrance.com.

SUGGESTED ITINERARIES
TOURIST ROUTES

In the areas covered by this guide, there are numerous *routes touristiques* plotted out for motorists who wish to explore a particular aspect of the area in detail. The best-known routes in Alsace are the **Route des Crêtes**, running along the ridge of the Vosges from the Col du Bonhomme to Thann, and the **Route des Vins**, or wine road, both described in this guide (remember: these trips do not advocate drinking and driving; quite the opposite!).

Motorists will notice many other itineraries signposted in the region: for example, the **Route du Rhin** from Lauterbourga to St-Louis along the River Rhine; the **Route de l'Amitié** from Paris to Munich, taking in the Lorraine region, both sides of the Vosges, Strasbourg, the Black Forest, etc.; the **Route du Cristal**, with visits to the principal crystal works in Lorraine; and the **Route des Potiers**, featuring the pottery workshops of Soufflenheim and Betschdorf.

In Champagne-Ardenne, you may like to take the **Route Touristique du Champagne** through the Marne, Aisne and Aube *départements*, the **Route des Légendes de Meuse et Semoy, Route des Fortifications** or the **Route des Forêts, Lacs et Abbayes**, to name but a few.

CITY BREAKS
Strasbourg

Strasbourg is the capital and major city of Alsace. To some it once seemed to be the capital of Europe, with a cosmopolitan culture on a par with that of Paris. Strasbourg is rarely, if ever, confused with Paris these days, but thanks to culinary experimentation, rich museums, strong universities and sports teams, it provides all the things that an urban-dweller (or holidaymaker) demands. In some ways, it is the large student population that keeps Strasbourg hopping after the sun goes down. Bars typically stay open until 4am and, unlike Paris, New York and other major cities, dress code is rarely a requirement for admittance.

Nancy

Amongst the Art Noveau and the botanic garden and other historical and quaint attractions in Nancy there are brasseries; opulent, mansion-lined streets and a nightlife worth noting. Bars and clubs in Nancy have very distinct images and areas of focus. One club even has fire-eaters and jugglers weaving their way through the crowds as the music plays. Cuban, Jazz and Latin music are frequently heard on the streets of Nancy.

Reims

Some count Reims, Champagne's largest city, as the centre of the best after-dark action of any town in the region. There are a number of dance clubs, brew pubs and Irish pubs. A large student population keeps things interesting. Métropole, the public transport network is efficient, which is perfect if your night on the town includes champagne-sipping.

Châlons-en-Champagne

Châlons-en-Champagne is the capital of the region, despite the fact it is just a quarter the size of Reims. But small doesn't mean sleepy. The city offers evening activities to keep urban tourists entertained. Discos, sporting events and nightclubs are among the options.

ONE WEEK

If you have just one week in the region, and you want to see a little bit of everything, here's one way you can do it. But start off with a good night's rest, because you'll be on the go for seven great days!

Day 1: Start in Reims and get ready to take in the heart of the Champagne region. Spend the day immersing your-self in Reims' rich history and art and architectural highlights.

Day 2: Hit the Champagne trail. Reims and Epernay are dotted with Champagne cellars, open for tastings.

Day 3: Art Nouveau comes alive in Nancy. Spend the day exploring the art and architecture of Lorraine's major city.

Day 4: The capital of Alsace, Strasbourg, has long incorporated the best of both France and Germany. Explore the pleasures of Alsatian culture through food, architecture, art and music.

Day 5: All of Strasbourg and its surrounds cannot be seen in a day. Spend your second day here on the canals or explore La Petite France's neighbourhoods, cobblestone streets and charming restaurants.

Day 6: Hit the Alsatian Wine Road, learning about Riesling and all the other grapes and vineyards that dot these hillsides.

Day 7: More art, Alsatian culture, breathtaking views and wine wrap up your last day in Colmar.

TWO WEEKS

Even two weeks is not enough time to see everything this region has to offer. An easy approach to the perfect fortnight itinerary is to double the time spent in each location on the one-week itinerary. This approach allows you to get a big picture sense of the many sights, sounds and tastes of the region, but also to have more quality time to explore the atttactions in each town.

Or, there's another simple formula for a relaxing two-week sojourn to the area: Book a two-week stay at one of the healing mineral springs or hot springs (⎈*See pp27–28*).

THEMED TOURS
HISTORY

Routes historiques are heritage trails mapped out by the Fédération Nationale des Routes Historiques (*www.routes-historiques.com*). These guide motorists to towns, villages, châteaux, manors, abbeys, parks and gardens of architectural and historical interest. Among others, they include the **Route Historique des Marches de Lorraine**, running through the Moselle, the Meuse and the Vosges, and the **Route du Patrimoine Culturel Quebécois** in the Champagne region, retracing the history of the French who settled in Québec.

CULTURAL HERITAGE

Focusing more specifically on the cultural heritage of the Champagne region are the **Route des Églises à Pans de Bois**, specialising in timber-framed churches and the **Route de la statuaire et du Vitrail**, taking in stained glass and religious sculpture in the Aube *département*.

The **Route Romane d'Alsace** offers a choice of more than 120 sites, from the more prestigious to the less well known ones.

The **Route de la Musique en Lorraine; route des Orgues en Moselle**, takes visitors across the Moselle *département* where a wealth of organs can be seen and heard (more than 20 concerts are organised during the holiday season).

TRADITIONS AND NATURE

Routes gastronomiques

As you may expect, these itineraries are dedicated to unearthing rich regional culinary specialities, cheeses, beers, trout, *choucroute*, etc.

These and other special itineraries are the subject of brochures that can be found in most local tourist offices. More information on food-related tours can be found at www.route-des-vins-alsace.com and www.tourisme-colmar.com.

Parcs et Jardins de Haute-Marne

Every summer, more than 20 parks and gardens throughout the *département* welcome visitors. A brochure is available from tourist offices and further information can be obtained by applying to **Conseil d'Architecture, d'Urbanisme et d'Environnement**, ✆03 25 32 52 62.

"Jardins sans Frontières"

This programme presents a selection of themed gardens in the Moselle département and across its borders into the neighbouring Sarre and Luxemburg. Information is available from the **Comité Départemental du Tourisme de la Moselle**, 4 rue du Pont-Moreau. ✆03 87 37 57 80.

Animal parks

There are many animal parks in the region, some offering entertainment in the form of shows and demonstrations, many keeping their animals in semi-captivity:

- ◆ **Parc Animalier de St-Laurent**, near Charleville-Mézières (several tours available) ✆03 24 57 39 84.
- ◆ **Parc Animalier de la Bannie**, near Bourbonne-les-Bains ✆03 25 90 14 77.
- ◆ **Parc de Vision Animalier in the Forêt d'Orient Nature Park** ✆03 25 43 81 90.
- ◆ **Parc Animalier de Ste-Croix, Lac de Madine** ✆03 87 03 92 05.
- ◆ **Centre de Réintroduction des Cigognes (storks) et des Loutres (otters) in Hunawihr** ✆03 89 73 72 62.
- ◆ **Jardin des papillons exotiques** (butterfly conservatory) in Hunawihr ✆03 89 73 33 33.
- ◆ **Montagne des Singes** (monkey mountain) in Kintzheim, near Sélestat ✆03 88 92 11 09.
- ◆ **Volerie des Aigles** (eagle aviary) in Kintzheim ✆03 88 92 84 33.
- ◆ **Zoo and Botanical Gardens** in Mulhouse ✆03 69 77 65 65.
- ◆ **La Pépinière (plant nursery), gardens and zoo** in Nancy ✆03 83 36 59 04.
- ◆ **Tropical Aquarium** in Nancy ✆03 83 32 99 97.
- ◆ **Les Naïades Aquarium** in Ottrott ✆03 88 95 90 32.
- ◆ **Zoo de l'Orangerie**, opposite the Palais de l'Europe in Strasbourg ✆03 88 61 62 88.

Verzenay vineyards and Musée de la Vigne - Route du Champagne

WINE AND BEER COUNTRY

Roaming the vineyards 🐝

In Alsace, the **Route des Vins** carries travellers from Marlenheim to Thann, linking up the charming little wine-growing villages of the region and incorporating the seven officially recognised (*appellation d'origine contrôlée*) grape varieties in the area. A number of small towns have waymarked tracks winding through the heart of the vineyards, punctuated by information boards explaining work on the vines and the different grape varieties. These *sentiers viticoles* can be found in Soultzmatt, Westhalten, Pfaffenheim, Eguisheim, Turckheim, Kientzheim, Bennwihr-Mittelwihr-Beblenheim-Zellenber-Riquewihr-Hunawihr (Grands Crus itinerary), Bergheim, Scherwiller, Dambach-la-Ville, Epfig, Mittelbergheim, Barr, Obernai, Dorlisheim, Molsheim, Traenheim, Dahlenheim and Marlenheim.

🔖 Information about wine in general is available from the following:

🐝 **Maison des Vins d'Alsace**, 12 avenue de la Foire-aux-Vins (north of the town), 68012 Colmar Cedex. ☎03 89 20 16 20. www.vinsalsace.com. This organisation publishes a number of brochures on the wines of Alsace, including a guide-directory with details of wine cellars open to the public.

🐝 The **Espace Alsace Coopération** (☎03 89 47 91 33), in Beblenheim, on the wine route, has a good selection of regional wines produced by Alsace's 18 different cooperatives, along with other local products to taste.

🐝 The castle in Kientzheim (☎03 89 78 21 36) houses the **Musée du Vignoble et des Vins d'Alsace** (www.musee-du-vignoble-alsace.fr), with exhibits explaining various interesting aspects of vines and wines. It also has a monumental winepress.

In the Champagne region, take the **Route du Champagne**, where frequent signposts show you the way to vineyards, Champagne houses and cooperatives. There are a number of courses available, both for novices and enthusiasts who wish to learn more:

IN ALSACE:

🐝 **Centre de Formation, Lycée Viticole**, 8 Aux-Remparts, 68250 Rouffach, ☎03 89 78 73 07.

21

IN CHAMPAGNE:

- **Comité Départemental du Tourisme de l'Aube**, 34 quai Dampierre, 10000 Troyes ℘03 25 42 50 00. www.aube-champagne.com. A brochure lists wine-growers who offer wine-tasting courses.
- **Chambre d'Agriculture de la Marne**, Complexe agricole du Mont-Bernard, route de Suippes, BP 525, 51009 Châlons-en-Champagne Cedex ℘03 26 64 08 13. Several wine-growers offer half-day wine-tasting courses.
- **Institut International des Vins de Champagne**, Villa Bissinger, 15 rue Jeanson, 51160 Ay ℘03 26 55 78 78. www.villabissinger.com. Offers courses in wine-tasting, gastronomy and tours of different cellars.

Wine Festivals

Harvest festivals are held in October throughout Alsace; other celebrations take place from April to October:

- April: **Ammerschwihr**
- 1 May: **Molsheim**
- Ascension: **Guebwiller**
- Mid-July: **Barr**
- 4th weekend in July: **Ribeauvillé**
- 1st half of August: **Colmar**
- 1st weekend in August: **Turckheim**
- Last weekend in August: **Eguisheim**
- September: **Riquewihr**

Breweries

Your beverage education is not limited to wine and champagne: beer is on the schedule, too. Guided tours are available at the following:

- **Heineken**, 4 rue St-Charles, 67300 Schiltigheim. ℘03 88 19 57 55; free guided tour by appointment only.
- **Kronenbourg**, 68 route d'Oberhausbergen, 67000 Strasbourg. ℘03 88 27 41 59. Free guided tour, booking essential.
- **Schutzenberger**, 8 rue de la Patrie, BP 182, 67304 Schiltigheim,

℘03 88 18 61 00. Free guided tour on Tuesdays and Thursdays at 2.30pm by appointment only.

- **Monks on the Web**. If you love Trappist beer and would like to know more about how it is made, take a virtual tour of the abbey where Chimay is brewed: www.chimay.com.

LOCAL CRAFTS AND INDUSTRIES

A brochure is published by the regional chamber of commerce (℘03 88 52 82 82) to help you to discover the people and trades of the region; information is also available from the Comités départementaux du tourisme (*see Addresses in Know Before You Go*).

Free guided tours are offered by PSA Peugeot-Citroën, Bugatti Royale, Météo France or La Poste as well as by small traditional businesses such as the slipper and carpet factories in Sedan (*information from the CDT des Ardennes. ℘03 24 56 06 08*).

Favourite local crafts you might want to explore include basket-making at a national school of wickerwork, textiles and wallpaper.

CULINARY COURSES

Visitors with a good command of French, and a desire to get 'hands-on' with culinary skills, will find that a few restaurant owners in Alsace offer culinary courses with complimentary or discounted accommodation. Courses are usually held in winter, outside the busy tourist season. Information on cookery classes can be found at www.tourisme-alsace.com, but it would also be profitable to contact the local tourist office in advance if you are keen to follow this topic.

What to See and Do

OUTDOOR FUN

WATER SPORTS

The entire region covered by this guide is dotted with lakes, canals and rivers, providing many opportunities for recreational activities.

Fishing

The **Fédération de Pêche** or angling union (*www.federationpeche.fr*) is a good source of information for local fishing. You need to buy a permit, or *carte de pêche,* and familiarise yourself with national and local regulations. Permits can usually be obtained locally, and are available from tourist offices, and in cafés where you are likely to pick up a few tips from the regulars.

Canoeing-kayaking

This sport is popular on the majority of rivers in the Champagne and Ardenne regions.
The more challenging courses are on the Blaise, Saulx, Rognon and Aire. Gentler waters are the Meuse (at Sedan), the Aube and the Marne.
The **Fédération Française de Canoë-kayak**, 87 quai de la Marne, 94344 Joinville-le-Pont, ℘01 45 11 08 50. www.ffck.org (*French only*) is a good source of information.
In the Aube, canoeing or kayaking can be practised on the Seine, Aube and Ource rivers or the lakes of the Forêt d'Orient. Information can be obtained from local tourist offices.

Bases de loisirs are signed recreational areas with sports and recreation facilities (picnic areas, trails, etc.).

Rafting

Adrenalin-seekers often prefer white-water rafting to other water sports, with the challenge of the rapids and speed of the river getting their blood pumping. The region offers a number of opportunities for rafting, but you must go through a tour operator. Most have three-to-six-man rafts, with experience guides, to show you the way. Ask in the tourist office for recommendations for tour operators. For more rafting outings and advice in the area, try www.ubaye-rafting.fr.

CYCLING

Even non-cyclists know France is bike-friendly. For general information about cycling in France, contact the **Fédération Française de Cyclotourisme** (℘*01 56 20 88 88. www.ffct.org*, in French only). Off-road and mountain bike (*VTT* in French) enthusiasts will find the **Fédération Française de Cyclisme** (℘*08 11 04 05 55, www.ffc.fr*, in French only) a useful source of information.
The IGN (*www.ign.fr*) offers Map 89024, *Routes des Grandes Alpes*, which covers routes open to cyclists. Map 924 covers *Voies vertes et Véloroutes de France*, which covers 250 cycling routes across the whole of France.
Regional tourist offices (Comités Départemental du Tourisme. ♿*See Know Before You Go*) can provide information on special mountain-bike itineraries in their area, and local tourist offices usually have a list of cycle hire firms.
The **Association Française pour le développement des Véloroutes et des Voies Vertes** is an excellent resource for planning cycling trips around France (*www.af3v.org*), and their website gives a region by region breakdown of routes.

The website of the **Parc naturel régional des Ballons des Vosges** (*www.parc-ballons-vosges.fr, French only*), has a whole page dedicated to VTT and cyclotourisme, with depart-mental breakdowns.

LAKE/RESERVOIR	Nearest town	Acreage	Swimming	Boating	Fishing
Alfeld	Kirchberg	25	✓	✓	✓
Amance	Troyes	1 236211	✓	✓	✓
Bairon	Le Chesne	297	✓	✓	✓
Blanc	Orbey	7270	–	–	✓
Blanchemer	La Bresse	1423	–	✓	✓
Charmes	Langres	487	✓	✓	✓
Corbeaux	La Bresse	2523	–	✓	✓
Der-Chantecoq	Vitry-le-François	11 861	✓	✓	✓
Folie	Contrexéville	25	✓	✓	✓
Gérardmer	Gérardmer	284	✓	✓	✓
Gondrexange	Sarrebourg	1 730902	✓	✓	✓
Hanau	Falkenstein	44	✓	✓	✓
Lauch	Le Markstein	27	–	✓	✓
Liez	Langres	717	✓	✓	✓
Longemer	Gérardmer	188	✓	✓	✓
Madine	Hattonchâtel	2 718	✓	✓	✓
Mouche	Langres	232	–	–	✓
Noir	Orbey	35	–	–	✓
Orient	Troyes	5 6836 177	✓	✓	✓
Pierre Percée	Badonviller	692988	✓	✓	✓
Retournemer	Gérardmer	14	–	–	–
Temple	Troyes	4 522	–	–	✓
Vieilles-Forges	Revin	371	✓	✓	✓
Vert	Hohrodberg	556	–	–	–
Vingeanne	Langres	487492	✓	✓	✓

Based in the UK, **Cycling for Softies** organises a number of cycling holidays to the region, and elsewhere in France (*www.cycling-for-softies.co.uk*).

GOLF

Golf is increasingly popular in France, and the area covered in this guide is well equipped with courses, particularly Lorraine, where both regular players and novices are welcome.

The Comité Régional du Tourisme (*www.tourisme-alsace.com*) publishes a free, downloadable brochure with detailed information about gold in the region (in English). For more information, contact the

Stepping Smart

Choosing the right equipment for a walking expedition is essential: the wrong gear can ruin a trip, the right gear can make it a joy. Among the must-haves are flexible walking shoes with non-slip soles, a waterproof jacket, an extra sweater, sun protection (hat, glasses, lotion), drinking water (1–2l per person), high energy snacks (chocolate, cereal bars, etc.), and a first aid kit. Of course, you'll need a good map (and a compass if you plan to leave the main trails). Plan your itinerary well, keeping in mind that while the average walking speed for an adult is 4kph, you will need time to eat and rest, and some walkers may not keep up the same pace. Leave your itinerary with someone before setting out (for example, an innkeeper or fellow camper).

Respect for nature is the cardinal rule and includes the following precautions: don't smoke or light fires in the forest, which are particularly susceptible in the dry summer months; always carry your rubbish out; leave wild flowers as they are; walk around, not through, farmers' fields; close gates behind you.

If you are caught in an electrical storm, avoid high ground, and do not walk along a ridge top; do not seek shelter under overhanging rocks, isolated trees in otherwise open areas, at the entrance to caves or other openings in the rocks, or in the proximity of metal fences or gates. Do not use a metallic survival blanket. If possible, position yourself at least 15m from the highest point around you (rock or tree); crouch with your knees up and without touching the rock face with your hands or any exposed part of your body. A hard-top car is a good refuge, as its rubber tyres ground it and provide protection for those inside.

Ligue de Golf Grand Est (13 rue Jean Moulin, 54510 Tomblaine. &03 83 18 95 34. www.http://ligue-golfgrandest.org).

HORSE RIDING

The **Comité National de Tourisme Équestre** (9 bd MacDonald, 75019 Paris. &01 53 26 15 50, www.ffe.com) publishes several brochures relating to horsse riding:

- *Cheval Nature, l'Officiel du tourisme équestre en France*
- *Le Tourisme Équestre en France*
- *L'Estafette.*

Also consult Terre Équestre (&09 67 68 21 14 / &06 82 12 75 96, www.terre-equestre.com), which produces an annual list (free) of horse riding, and horse related, establishments across France.

Alsace

- **Comité Régional de tourisme équestre d'Alsace.** 6, Route d'Ingersheim, 68000 Colmar &03 89 24 43 18 / &06 03 89 23 15 08. www.chevalsace.com.

Lorraine

- **Comité Régional de Tourisme Équestre de Lorraine,** 13, rue Jean Moulin, 54510 Tomblaine. &03 83 18 87 52.

Champagne-Ardenne

- **Comité Régional d'Équitation Champagne Ardenne,** 3, rue Ampère, 51000 Chalons en Champagne. www.equitation-champagne-ardenne.com.
- **Conseil des Chevaux de Champagne-Ardenne**, Haras National, Rue Saint Berchaire 52220 Montier en Der. &03 25 05 58 12. www.chevaux-champagne-ardenne.com
- The **Relais de la Largue**, 3 rue Ste-Barbe, 68210 Altenach. &03 89 25 12 92, organises trips in Sundgau and the Alsatian Jura by pioneer-style covered wagon.

WALKING

There is an extensive network of well-marked footpaths in France for rambling (la randonnée). Several

Hiking above Lac Blanc, réserve naturelle Tanet-Gazon du Faing, parc naturel régional des Ballons des Vosges

© Denis Bringard/hemis.fr

Grande Randonnée (GR) trails, denoted by the red-and-white horizontal marks on trees, rocks, and in town on walls, signposts, etc., go through the region. Along with the GR, there are also the **Petite Randonnée (PR)** paths, which are usually blazed with blue (2h walk), yellow (2h15–3h45) or green (4–6h) marks. To use these trails, get the *topoguide* for the area published by the **Fédération Française de Randonnée Pédestre** (&01 44 89 93 93. www.ffrandonnee.fr).
Another source for walking maps and guides is the **Institut Géographique National** *(www.ign.fr)*.
Cicerone Press in the UK publish a number of guidebooks for walkers and cyclists in the Alsace-Lorraine-Vosges region *(www.cicerone.co.uk)*.

Le Club Vosgien
Founded in 1872, this is the oldest walkers' association in France (&03 88 32 57 96. www.club-vosgien.eu, in French only) and also the largest, with more than 34 000 members. The walkers have joined forces to protect natural and historic sites, and maintain the marks on around 16 500km/10 000mi of trails. The club sponsors a quarterly publication, *Les Vosges*, and publishes detailed maps and guides to paths on the Lorraine plateau, in the Jura mountains of Alsace, in the Vosges

and on the Alsatian plain. Check with local tourist offices for the dates of scheduled group rambles.

Grande Randonnée trails
◆ **GR 2** – Across the Pays d'Othe, through a hilly landscape and along the River Seine.
◆ **GR 5** – From the border of Luxembourg to the Ballon d'Alsace, through the Lorraine Regional Nature Park.
◆ **GR 7** – Across the Vosges from the Ballon d'Alsace to Bourbonne-les-Bains, and continuing into the region of Burgundy.
◆ **GR 12** – A section of European footpath No. 3 (Atlantic-Bohemia), cutting across the French and Belgian Ardennes.
◆ **GR 14** – Follows the Montagne de Reims through vineyards and forest, then continues across the chalk hills of Champagne to Bar-le-Duc before turning towards the Ardennes.
◆ **GR 24** – The loop starts at Bar-sur-Seine and goes through the Forêt d'Orient Regional Nature Park, vineyards and farmland.
◆ **GR 53** – From Wissembourg to the Col du Donon, through the northern Vosges Regional Nature Park.
◆ **GR 654** – Links Northern Europe to Santiago de Compostela via Rocroi, Signy-l'Abbaye and Reims.

Sleighing on the summit of the Ballon d'Alsace

- **GR 714** – From Bar-le-Duc to Vittel, linking GR 14 and GR 7.
- **GR 533** – Sarrebourg to the Ballon d'Alsace.

HUNTING

The Ardenne forest, thick and sparsely populated, is a good place to hunt deer and wild boar. For more information, contact the **Fédération départementale des Chasseurs des Ardennes** (℘*03 24 59 85 20; www. fdc08.com*); the **Fédération Départementale des chasseurs de l'Aube**, (℘*03 25 71 51 11; www.fdc10.org*), or the **Fédération Nationale des Chasseurs** (℘*01 41 09 65 10. www. chasseurdefrance.com*).

One-day and weekend hunting parties are organised on the estate of the **Maison Forestière de Germaine** in the hamlet of Vauremont (*8 rue de la Croix-Verte, 51160 Germaine, ℘03 26 51 08 27*), including hunting from an observation tower, in a 400ha park, or in a 1 200ha wooded area. In the Ardennes the **Pavillon du Territoire du Sanglier** (*Office de Tourisme des 3 Cantons, ℘03 24 29 79 91*) offers introductions to wild boar hunting, as well as a tavern and a play area for the kids. Open only in season.

SKIING

The Vosges mountains are perfect for skiers. In the pine forests, gentle landscapes unfold between 600m–1 400m. Resorts offer downhill and cross-country trails, snowboarding, biathlon, ski-jumping, snowshoeing, dogsledding, toboggan riding or simply peaceful walks through the wintry countryside.

Downhill skiers have 170 lifts from which to choose and many stations are equipped with snow-making machines and lighting for night skiing, including Gérardmer, La Bresse, Le Markstein and Lac Blanc. Schnepfenried is appreciated for the panoramic view of the crests forming the blue line of the Vosges. Cross-country skiers can enjoy more than 1 000km/621mi of marked and groomed trails.

For information and reservations, contact local tourist offices, or visit www.france-montagnes.com for the latest update on snow conditions; some sites also list available accommodation.

SPAS

The Vosges mountains on the Lorraine side and the region of Lorraine itself are particularly blessed with natural spring waters that have given rise to spa resorts. The Alsatian side of the range also has its share of resorts. None of the waters are sulphurous, but all other types of spring water are found and used in treating various chronic affections.

MINERAL SPRINGS AND HOT SPRINGS

Natural springs result when water filters through permeable layers of the earth's surface until it meets resistance in the form of an impermeable layer of rock. The water flows along this impenetrable layer until it breaks through to the open air, and the water surges forth.

A mineral spring can be water surging forth in the same way, or water rising from deep within the earth, collecting mineral substances and gases with therapeutic properties as it flows towards the surface. Hot springs

produce water which hits the air at a temperature of at least 35°C.
Springs are found in zones where the earth's crust is fairly thin, where boulders have been thrown into place by eruptions or cracking. Hot springs are found along the Lorraine plateau fault line or near crystalline mountain ranges and outcrops.

Water, water everywhere

Water from mineral or hot springs is usually unstable, and contact with the air changes its properties. This is why its therapeutic virtues are best enjoyed at the source, and spa therapy is based on this principle.
The two geographic zones in the Vosges, the "plain" to the west and the "mountains" to the east and south-east, have different types of springs, each with its own special qualities.

Cold springs

The plains are dominated by cold springs, water which has filtered through the earth's crust and re-emerges enriched with calcium and magnesium and, in some cases, lithium and sodium.
The best-known resort in the area is certainly **Vittel**; the waters were reputed in Roman times, then forgotten, only to be rediscovered in 1845. In 1854, the Bouloumié family began actively promoting and marketing the spring water.
Vittel and the neighbouring spa at **Contrexéville** treat kidney and liver ailments; Vittel also specialises in metabolic diseases. In conjunction with therapeutic activities at the spa, the water is bottled for sale, and many tourists visit the plants each year (with Évian, it is one of the world's largest bottling operations).

Hot springs

The springs found in the mountainous region are quite different from those in the plains. Of volcanic origin, their properties depend less on mineral content and more on temperature and radioactivity.

These waters have a long-standing reputation: they were known to the Romans, who appreciated warm springs, as did the Celts and the Gauls.
Plombières, with 27 hot springs, some of which reach as high as 80°C, is reputed for the treatment of rheumatism and enteritis.
Bains-les-Bains is a spa specialising in the treatment of a number of heart and artery disorders, whereas **Luxeuil-les-Bains** treats gynaecological ailments.
A relatively recent arrival on the scene is **Amnéville**, where *curistes* come to relieve the symptoms of rheumatism and respiratory problems, using the therapeutic waters of the St-Éloy spring, which emerge at 41°C.
Bourbonne-les-Bains, located on the border of Lorraine and Champagne, boasts warm, radioactive water with a slight chlorine content. Louis XV created a military hospital on the site, for the treatment of soldiers with shot-wounds. Today, the spa is prescribed for the purposes of healing bones, arthritis, rheumatism and respiratory problems.
In Alsace, **Niederbronn-les-Bains** is recognised for the treatment of digestive and kidney afflictions and arteriosclerosis. **Morsbronn-les-Bains** is a small spa specialising in rheumatic disorders.

Roman baths at Bains-les-Bains

© J.-P. Clapham/MICHELIN

HYDROTHERAPY AND TOURISM

The benefits of spa treatments were rediscovered in the 18C to 19C.

At that time, "taking the waters" was a past-time reserved for wealthy clients with time to spare. Today, the French national health system recognises the therapeutic value of many spa treatments, and patients' stays are provided for, all or in part, by different social welfare organisations.

Treatment occupies only part of the day, so spas offer their guests many other activities to pass the time pleasantly – sports, recreation and various forms of entertainment. More often than not, the beautiful natural settings provide the opportunity for outdoor excursions.

Besides the traditional courses of treatment, which usually last three weeks, many resorts offer shorter stays for clients with a specific goal in mind, such as stress relief and relaxation, fitness and shaping up, giving up smoking, losing weight or simply do not have the time to devote to a three-week stay.

The **Villes d'eaux des Vosges** publishes brochures with information on Bains-les-Bains, Contrexéville, Plombières and Vittel. Copies can be downloaded from www. villesdeauxdesvosges.fr.

You can also get information by contacting the following:

♦ **La Medicine Thermale**, 1 rue de Cels, 75014 Paris. ℘01 53 91 05 75. www.medecinethermale.fr *(French only)*.

♦ **Chaîne thermale du Soleil**, 32 avenue de l'Opéra, 75002 Paris. ℘0800 05 05 32. www. chainethermale.fr *(French only)*.

The spas and their specialities

♦ **Amnéville:** rheumatic disorders, post-traumatic injury treatment and respiratory problems. Open: February to December.

♦ **Bains-les-Bains:** cardiovascular ailments, rheumatic disorders, post-traumatic injury treatment. Open: April to October.

♦ **Bourbonne-les-Bains:** rheumatic disorders, osteoarthritis, respiratory ailments, bone fractures. Open: March to November.

♦ **Contrexéville:** kidney and urinary problems, excess weight. Open: April to October.

♦ **Luxeuil-les-Bains:** phlebology, gynaecology. Open: March to November.

♦ **Morsbronn-les-Bains:** rheumatic disorders, post-traumatic injury treatment. Open: year round.

♦ **Niederbronn-les-Bains:** rheumatic disorders, post-traumatic injury treatment, physical rehabilitation. Open: April to December.

♦ **Plombières-les-Bains:** Digestive ailments, nutritional problems, rheumatic disorders, post-traumatic osteo-articular therapy. Open: April to October.

♦ **Vittel:** Liver and kidney ailments, rheumatic disorders, post-traumatic injury treatment, nutritional problems. Open: February to December.

ACTIVITIES FOR KIDS 👥

This region has a lot to offer children, from having fun in leisure parks such as Nigloland, to visiting zoos, safari parks, aquariums, museums and castles (&*see Sightseeing*). Throughout the *Discovering* section of the guide, places and activities particularly suited to children are denoted by the KIDS symbol (👥).

FEAST OF ST NICHOLAS
The legend of St Nicholas

St Nicholas, bishop of Myra in Asia Minor in the 4C, is known for offering a dowry to three impoverished girls. He is also said to have prevented the execution of three unjustly accused officers.

Perhaps because of images relating to the number three, he has also been associated, since the 12C in France, with the miraculous resurrection of three young children, who had been brutally cut up and set to cure by a butcher.

These different legends have created a popular figure who, on the night of 5 December, distributes gifts to good children in the countries of northern Europe (Lorraine, Germany, Belgium, the Netherlands, Switzerland).

Fête de la St-Nicolas

The Feast is celebrated either on the eve of or on the 6 December, or sometimes the following Saturday or Sunday. Many towns in Lorraine have celebrations, especially St-Nicolas-de-Port (torchlight procession in the basilica), Nancy (parade and fireworks), Metz (musical parade), and Épinal (floats in a parade).

SHOPPING
OPENING HOURS

Most of the larger shops are open Monday to Saturday from 9am to 6.30 or 7.30pm. Smaller, individual shops may close during the lunch hour. Food shops – grocers, wine merchants and bakeries – are generally open from 7am to 6.30 or 7.30pm; some open on Sunday mornings. Many food shops close between noon and 2pm and on Mondays. Bakery and pastry shops sometimes close on Wednesdays. Hypermarkets are usually open until 8pm or later. People travelling to the USA cannot import plant products or fresh food, including fruit, cheeses and nuts. It is acceptable to carry tinned (canned) products or preserves. (*See p58 for a note on Value Added Tax*).

SIGHTSEEING
TOURIST TRAINS (CHEMINS DE FER TOURISTIQUES)

In Alsace steam and diesel locomotives offer visitors a charming ride through the countryside. All services operate regularly at weekends in the summer, see their websites for timetables.

At the southern end of the Route des Crêtes, you can enjoy a ride along the **Vallée de la Doller** from Cernay to Sentheim (*Train Thur Doller Alsace, BP 90192, 68703 Cernay. 03 89 82 88 48. www.train-doller.org*), travel aboard the **forest train** from Abreschviller to Grand Soldat in the Massif du Donon (*03 87 03 71 45. http://train-abreschviller.fr*) or take a combined boat and steam train trip along the **Rhine** between Neuf-Brisach and Baltzenheim (*2 rue de la Gare, Volgelsheim, 03 89 45 29 84. http://cftr.evolutive.org*).

In Champagne-Ardenne, the **Train touristique de la Forêt d'Orient** (*departure from Mesnil-St-Pierre, 03 25 41 20 72; www.lacs-champagne.fr*) takes its passengers on a charming ride through the regional nature park.

The **Train touristique du Der** runs north from Wassy to Éclaron or south from Wassy to Dommartin-le-Franc and Doulevant-le-Château (*www.lacduder.com*).

The **Train touristique du Sud des Ardennes** (*cour de la Gare, Attigny, 03 24 71 47 60; http://cftsa.fr*) steams down part of the Aisne valley from Attigny to Challerange, passing through Vouziers (31km/19mi); or from Attigny to Amagne-Lucquy (9.5km/6mi).

Draisines

In the past, pedal cars, handcars and trolleys (known collectively as *draisines*) were propelled by railroad workers maintaining or inspecting the track. Today, this mode of locomotion can be used to explore the **Vallée de la Mortagne**. Energetic travellers can pedal along 20km/12.4mi of otherwise unused railways, starting from Magnières, west of Baccarat (*www.trains-fr.org*). Similarly in the **Vallée de la Canner**, you can pedal the 11km7mi from Vigy to Budange.

FROM ABOVE

Balloon rides – For a spectacular view and memorable experience, consider a hot-air balloon ride:

♦ **Aérovision** – 34 Chemin de la Speck, 68000 Colmar. 03 89 77 22 81. www.aerovision-montgolfiere.com (*French only*).

- **Pôle aérostatique Pilâtre de Rozier** – 11 boulevard Antoine de Saint-Exupéry, 54470 Hageville. ℘03 82 33 77 77. www.pilatre-de-rozier.com.
- **Flights in light aircraft** – Flights in small planes are arranged by the Aéroclub du Sud Meusien, BP 10184, 55005 Bar-le-Duc. ℘03 29 77 18 30. www.aeroclub-sudmeusien.fr *(French only)*.
- **Helicopter flights** – Flights on the outskirts of Nancy are offered by Proteus Hélicoptères: Aéroport de Nancy-Essey. ℘03 83 29 80 60. Flights over the Lac du Der-Chantecoq start from Vauclerc airport. ℘03 26 74 28 18.

EXCURSIONS TO NEIGHBOURING COUNTRIES

The region is bordered by Germany to the north and east, Switzerland to the southeast, Belgium and Luxembourg to the north.

Visitors to Alsace will naturally be drawn to the other side of the River Rhine and lovely towns including Freiburg im Breisgau, Belchen and Baden-Baden in the Black Forest. Consult the **Green Guide Germany** for tourist information, and the red-cover **Michelin Guide Deutschland** for hotels and restaurants.

Basel, in Switzerland, is also a popular tourist destination, especially at carnival time. The three days before the beginning of Lent mark the only Catholic ceremony to have survived the Reformation; a festival of parades and costumed revelry. The **Green Guide Switzerland** is useful for visiting Basel and the surrounding region. The red-cover **Michelin Guide Switzerland** makes it easy to choose where to spend the night and to find a special restaurant.

The Ardennes forest covers most of the Belgian provinces of Luxembourg, Namur and Liège and part of the Grand Duchy as well as the French *département*. The valley of the River Meuse meanders to the North Sea by way of **Dinant**. This picturesque town is just 60km/37mi from Charleville-Mézières. Travellers can enjoy local honey cakes (known as *couques*), baked in decorative wooden moulds, and may like to take advantage of a boat trip on the river (board in front of the town hall). Carry on to **Bouillon**, nestled in a bend of the River Semois and dominated by its medieval fortress. **Chimay** is known for its castle, but is also a familiar name to beer-lovers; the Trappist monks have their brewery at the abbey of Notre-Dame-de-Scourmont, just a few miles south of the town. Round

Rathausplatz, Freiburg im Breisgau, Germany

© Reinhard Schmid/Sime/Photononstop

off the excursion with a stop at **Orval Abbey**, in the Gaume Forest. Founded in 1070 by Benedictines from Calabria in southern Italy, it became one of Europe's wealthiest and best known Cistercian abbeys.

The tour includes a visit to the ruins, which date from the Middle Ages to the 18C. From Dinant to Orval, the distance is 99km/61mi.

For further information, see the red-cover **Michelin Guide Benelux**.

RIVER AND CANAL CRUISING

There are numerous navigable waterways in the region, where you can enjoy a cruise or hire your own boat. **Voies Navigables de France** (www.vnf.fr) can provide information on travelling the waterways, or you may like to contact the regional tourist office for information (&see Know Before You Go).

Nautical maps guides and services

◆ **Éditions Grafocarte-Navicarte**, Champagne-Ardenne in English; order online at www.stanfords.co.uk or www.bookharbour.com.
◆ **Éditions du Plaisancier**, 43 porte du Grand-Lyon, 01700 Neyron. &04 72 01 58 68.

Self-skippered holidays

The following hire fleet agencies and bases offer boats accommodating 2–8 people:

◆ **Ardennes Nautisme** – Bases: Pont-à-Bar and Namur (Belgium). &03 24 54 01 50. www.ardennes-nautisme.com.
◆ **Le Boat** – &04 11 92 04 04. www.leboat.fr and &023 9280 1625. www.leboat.co.uk.
◆ **Locaboat Plaisance** – Port au Bois, BP 150, 89303 Joigny. &03 86 91 72 72. www.locaboat.com.
◆ **Nicols** – Base: Saverne. &02 41 56 46 56 (France), or &02392 401 320 (UK). www.boat-renting-nicols.co.uk.

Cruises

These can last from a few hours to two weeks, travelling along the Rhine, Moselle, Sarre, Neckar, Main, Danube, Meuse, Marne or Seine.

The brochure *Lorraine au fil de l'eau* contains information on boat trips in the area and can be obtained from the **Comité Régional du Tourisme de Lorraine** (&see Local Tourist Offices, pp39–40).

CroisiEurope-Alsace Croisières, (www.croisieurope.co.uk. &0208 328 1281), offers many trips out of Strasbourg. From March to December, you can tour the city in the care of **Batorama** (18 place de la Cathédrale 67000 Strasbourg. &03 69 74 44 09. www.batorama.com).

Take a trip on the **River Marne** aboard the *Champagne-Vallée* (&03 26 54 49 51. www.champagne-et-croisiere.com) leaving from Cumières.

For an extended, 6-night cruise on the River Meuse, try **Merganser itineraries** (&01992 550 616 (UK), www.bargedirect.com/mergitin2013.html).

BIRDWATCHING AND NATURE PARKS

Birdwatching

The many lakes in Champagne-Ardenne attract a sizeable feathered population. Part of the **Lac de Bairon** has been set aside as a **bird refuge** and includes a nature discovery centre in Boult-aux-Bois (*Maison de la Nature 5, Rue de la Héronnière, 08240 Boult-aux-Bois &03 24 30 24 98. www.maison-nature-boult.eu*).

So too has part of the Lac d'Orient in the Forêt d'Orient Nature Park (information from the Maison du Parc in Piney (&03 25 43 81 90. www.pnr-foret-orient.fr). The **Lac du Der-Chantecoq** (&03 26 72 54 47. LPO, Ligue pour la protection des oiseaux, http://champagne-ardenne.lpo.fr) and nearby ponds have observatories and discovery trails. Here, the **Ferme aux Grues** is devoted to cranes, their migratory habits, how to observe them and conservation measures. The **Maison de l'Oiseau et du Poisson** is devoted to birds and fish and has exhibits and displays explaining the lake's ecosystem. More information on the area's bird population is available from the **Musée du Pays du Der**, 51290 Sainte-Marie-du-Lac-Nuisement. ✆03 26 41 01 02. www.villagemuseeduder.com *(French only)*.

Nature parks
There are five regional nature parks in the region described in this guide:
Two in Champagne-Ardenne, the **Parc naturel regional de la Montagne de Reims** (between Reims in the north and Épernay in the south) and the **Parc naturel regional de la Forêt d'Orient** (east of Troyes).
Three in Alsace-Lorraine, the **Parc naturel regional des Ballons des Vosges** (west of the Rhine between Sélestat in the north and Mulhouse in the south), the **Parc naturel regional des Vosges du Nord** (west of the Rhine, between Wissembourg in the north and Saverne in the south) and the **Parc naturel regional de Lorraine** split into two sections situated east and west of the Metz-Nancy motorway.
They are all described in the *Discovering* section of the guide. For websites and contact details visit www.gites-refuges.com.

Nature conservatories
Devoted to the safeguard of natural sites, they organise a variety of nature discovery tours:
♦ **Conservatoire des Sites Alsaciens**, Maison des espaces naturels, Écomusée, 68190 Ungersheim, ✆03 89 83 34 20; www.conservatoire-sites-alsaciens.eu *(French only)*.
♦ **Conservatoire des Espaces Naturels de Loraine**, 3, rue Robert Schuman, 57400 Sarrebourg. ✆03 87 03 00 90; www.cren-lorraine.com *(French only)*.

BOOKS
HÉLOÏSE AND ABÉLARD
Latin scholars can enjoy the beautiful **Letters** written by these medieval lovers, and thankfully there are also various modern translations available:
♦ **Peter Abélard**, by Helen Waddell, was first published in 1933 and has had more than 30 reprints (Constable and Co Ltd, 1968). This slim volume is a novel but reads like a true account, moving in its simplicity.
♦ **Stealing Heaven: the Love Story of Héloïse and Abélard**, by Marion Meade (Soho Press, 1979), tells the story from a woman's perspective. This sensuous historical novel of epic proportions is an immersion in 12C France.
♦ **Abelard: A Medieval Life**, by M T Clanchy (Blackwell Publishers 2000). This is the first new work to come out on Abelard in 30 years. The author paints a vivid and clear portrait of the 12C scientist (master of Latin, logic and philosophy), monk and controversial theologian. The book defends a new concept: it was Heloise who inspired many of Abelard's most profound ideas.

POETS FOR EVERY PURPOSE
♦ **The Complete Fables of La Fontaine**, edited and with rhymed verse translation by Norman B Spector (Northwestern University Press, 1988). No verse is unturned in this collection, which presents the French text opposite its translation, keen wit intact. Illustrated children's editions and paperback editions of the Fables are also available.
♦ **Paul Verlaine**, a seminal Symbolist and critical author, left an extensive body of work. Readily available in translation (ie by Jacques LeClerque, Westport Conn., Greenwood Press, 1977) are such famous books as *Songs Without Words, Yesteryear and Yesterday, The Accursed Poets* and *Confessions of a Poet*.

Musée Rimbaud, housed in the old mill over the Meuse, Charleville-Mézières

- **One Hundred and One Poems by Paul Verlaine: A Bilingual Edition**, translation Norman R Shapiro (University of Chicago Press, 1999) presents exciting new translations of works spanning the poet's entire life.
- **Arthur Rimbaud** got quite a few stanzas out before putting down his pen at age 20. His best-known works available in translation include *A Season in Hell* and *The Drunken Boat*.
- **Rimbaud and Jim Morrison: the Rebel as Poet**, by Wallace Fowlie (Duke University Press, 1994), was inspired by a letter written to the author by the Doors' founder and lead singer, thanking him for publishing his translations of Rimbaud. The illustrated volume is a twinned tale exploring the symmetry of two lives and the parallels between European literary tradition and American rock music.
- **Rimbaud: A Biography**, by Graham Robb (Norton & Company, 2001) takes a long look at the volatile youth, the outrageous behavior and the poetic genius of Rimbaud and his influence on contemporary cultural icons such as Bob Dylan and other rebellious artists who have rallied to his call for "derangement of the senses".

THE RAVAGES OF WAR

- **The Franco-Prussian War: The German Conquest of France in 1870–1871**, by Geoffrey Wawro (Cambridge University Press, 2003), is a concise account of a war that violently changed the course of European history. The author analyses innovative tactics, weaponry, logistics and organisation as well as the characters of the leading generals, from the bloody battles at Gravelotte and Sedan to the last murderous fights on the Loire and in Paris.
- **The Other Battle of the Bulge: Operation Northwind**, by Charles Whiting (History Press, 2007), is a fast-moving account of the battle that took place around Colmar and Strasbourg in early 1945. it was a battle fought by two contrasting armies: the Allies, who were primarily made up of raw recruits, while the Germans had a collection of battle hardened divisions that were under-strength and lacking in reserves.
- **The Debacle**, by Émile Zola (translated by LW Tancock. Penguin, 1972) takes place during the Franco-Prussian War of 1870 and describes the tragic events of the defeat at Sedan as well as the uprising of the Paris Commune. The author carried out extensive research (arms, strategy, tactics) to produce this remarkably factual novel depicting the battle and its aftermath.
- **The Pity of War**, by Niall Ferguson (London: Allen Lane, 1998). This radical, readable reassessment of the powers driving nations and individuals into the terrible conflict

of the First World War focuses on life in the trenches.

- **A Balcony in the Forest**, by Julien Gracq (translated by Richard Howard. London: Harper Collins, 1992), is set in the Ardennes Forest in the winter of 1939–40, during the so-called Phoney War. Following a winter of solitude and contemplation of nature, a young officer on the Maginot Line must face attacking Panzer divisions.
- **A Time for Trumpets: The Untold Story of the Battle of the Bulge**, by Charles B MacDonald (New York: Morrow, 1984). The author was one of the 600 000 American soldiers who fought against Hitler's vanguard troops in the mists and snow of the Ardennes Forest on 16 December 1944 – Germany's last desperate gamble and the turning point of the war.
- **Memoirs of Hope: Renewal and Endeavour** by Charles de Gaulle (New York: Simon and Schuster, 1971). Written in Colombey-les-Deux-Églises, the General's memoirs also include descriptions of the landscape of the Champagne region beyond the windows of his study.
- **Alamo in the Ardennes**, by John C McManus (J Wiley & Son, 2007). The untold story of the American soldiers who made the defence of Bastogne possible.

WORDS ON WINE

Among the many books on wines of the region:
- *The Wines of Alsace* Tom Stevenson (London: Faber and Faber, 1994)
- *Touring In Wine Country: Alsace* (Hubrecht Duijker, 1996)
- *Oz Clarke's Wine Companion Champagne and Alsace Guide* (David Cobbold, 1997)
- *Alsace Wines* Pamela V Price (London: Sotheby Publications, 1984)
- *Alsace: The Wine Route* Jacky Blind and Jean Claude Colin (L'Edition, 2007)

- *Wines of Alsace: Guide to wines and top vineyards* Benjamin Lewin (CreateSpace Independent Publishing, 2016)

Michelin Guides
The Wine Regions of France (2018) An in-depth guide to the wine-producing regions of France.

... ON CHAMPAGNE

- *The Wine Lover's Guide to Champagne and North East France* Michael Busselle (New York: Viking, 1989)
- *The Glory of Champagne* Don Hewitson (London: MacMillan, 1989)
- *Champagne for Dummies* (Ed McCarthy, 1999)
- *Tom Stevenson's Champagne & Sparkling Wine Guide* (Tom Stevenson, 2002)
- *Champagne: How the World's Most Glamorous Wine Triumphed over War and Hard Times* Don Kladstrup and Petie Kladstrup (2005)
- *Champagne for the Soul: Celebrating God's Gift of Joy* (Mike Mason, 2006).

...AND ON FOOD

- *Alsace Gastronomique, Sue Style (Conran, 1996)*
- *The Pâtissier: Recipes and Conversations from Alsace, France* Susan Lundquist, Hossine Bennara, and Frederic Lacroix (2006)
- *Champagne Cookbook: Add Some Sparkle to Your Cooking and Your Life* (Malcolm R. Hebert, 2007)

FILMS

Champagne (1928). One of Alfred Hitchcock's last (and least iconic) silent films centres on the fortunes made in a champagne business.
L'inconnu de Strasbourg (1998). A story of amnesia with Strasbourg as the setting.
Indigenes (2006). A tale about French Algerian troops in Alsace in the Second World War.

Calendar of Events

Regional tourist offices publish brochures listing local festivals and fairs and details of forthcoming events are to be found on websites.
Nearly all cities, towns and villages hold festivities for France's National Day (14 July), and many organise events on *Assomption* (15 August) also a public holiday.

MUSIC

APRIL–MAY

Épinal – Floreal Music: Festival of classical music. ✆03 29 82 53 32 (Tourist office). www.lorraineaucoeur.com.

ASCENSION (odd numbered years)

Nancy – International festival of choir singing (200–300 choristers). ✆03 83 27 56 56. www.chantchoral.org.

MAY

Vandœuvre-lès-Nancy – Musique Action, festival of contemporary music and theatre. ✆03 83 56 15 00. www.musiqueaction.com.

JUNE

Strasbourg – Music festival. ✆03 88 60 90 90. www.en.strasbourg.eu.

JUNE–AUGUST

Reims – Summer music festival. Jazz and classical music. ✆03 26 36 78 00. www.flaneriesreims.com. (*French only*).
Châlons-en-Champagne – rock, jazz, blues and world music festival. ✆03 26 68 47 27.

JUNE–SEPTEMBER

Fénétrange – International festival of music and gastronomy. ✆03 87 07 54 48. www.festival-fenetrange.org.

JULY

Colmar – International music festival. ✆03 89 20 68 97. www.festival-colmar.com.
St-Dizier – Music festival: pop, rock, world. ✆03 25 07 31 31. www.ville-saintdizier.fr.

LATE SEPTEMBER–EARLY OCTOBER

Strasbourg – Le Festival Musica: Musica, international contemporary music festival. ✆03 88 23 46 46. www.festivalmusica.org.
Nancy – Nancy Jazz Pulsations. Jazz and world music. ✆03 83 35 40 86. www.nancyjazzpulsations.com.

CULINARY AND WINE FESTIVALS

SATURDAY OR SUNDAY FOLLOWING 22 JANUARY

In all wine-growing towns – St Vincent festival, honouring the patron saint of wine-growers.

THURSDAY BEFORE EASTER

Les Riceys – Grand Jeudi wine fair. ✆03 25 29 15 38.

APRIL

Rethel – Boudin Blanc festival. ✆03 24 38 03 28.

JUNE

Revin – Bread festival. ✆03 24 40 20 91.
Reims – Independent Winemakers Fair. ✆03 26 77 45 00. www.reims-tourism.com.
Ribeauvillé – Kugelhopf festival. ✆03 89 73 20 00. www.ribeauville.net.

AUGUST

Erstein – Sugar festival. ✆03 88 64 66 33.

LATE AUGUST–EARLY SEPTEMBER

Metz – Mirabelle festival: Flower-decorated floats, parade and fireworks. ✆03 87 55 53 76. http://metz.fr.

Geispolsheim – Choucroute festival. www.geispolsheim.fr.

SEPTEMBER
Baccarat – Pâté Lorrain festival. ☎03 83 75 17 20. www.lorraineaucoeur.com.

Pays d'Othe – Cider festival. ☎03 25 80 81 71. www.tourisme-othe-armance. com.

Brienne-le-Château – Choucroute de Champagne festival. ☎03 25 92 80 31. www.ville-brienne-le-chateau.fr.

OCTOBER
Renwez – Mushroom festival. ☎03 24 54 82 66 or 03 24 54 93 19

Launois-sur-Vence – Ardenne festival of food and drink. ☎03 24 35 06 36. www.launoissurvence.com.

OTHER EVENTS

FEBRUARY
Gérardmer – Fantasy film festival. ☎03 29 60 98 21. www.festival-gerardmer.com.

MARDI GRAS (MARCH–APRIL)
Strasbourg – Carnival. www.otstrasbourg.fr.

APRIL
Gérardmer – Daffodil festival (every other year; next 2019): Parade floats decorated with daffodils. ☎03 29 63 12 89. www.societe-des-fetes-gerardmer.org.

APRIL–NOVEMBER
Provins Storming the ramparts (June). Eagles on the ramparts (Oct). Jousting tournament (Nov). www.provins.net.

MAY
Grand Jardin de Joinville – Plants and gardens festival (early May). ☎03 25 94 17 54. www.haute-marne.fr/culture.

Parc naturel de la Forêt d'Orient – Water sports festival. ☎03 25 41 53 19. www.pnr-foret-orient.fr.

Château-Thierry – Jean de la Fontaine festival of music theatre and dance. ☎03 23 69 20 27. www.festival-jeandela fontaine.com.

Reims – Fêtes Johanniques historical pageant and folklore festival (Johan Festival and Folkloric Coronations). ☎03 26 82 45 66. www.reims-fetes.com.

WHITSUN
Wissembourg – Opening of the annual fun fair (until the following Sunday). Folk dancing, parade of traditional costumes, horse races. ☎03 88 94 10 11. www.ot-wissembourg.fr.

JUNE
Châlons-en-Champagne – Furies Festival of street theatre and circus. ☎03 26 65 90 06. www.festival-furies.com.

Provins – Medieval festival. Sound and light. ☎01 64 60 26 26. www.provins.net.

Saverne – Rose festival. ☎03 88 71 83 33. www.roseraie-saverne.fr.

JUNE-JULY
Reims – Musical Summer Strolls (Flâneries musicales de Reims). Almost 100 concerts by the greatest names in classical music and jazz. ☎03 26 77 45 00. www.reims-tourism.com.

JULY
Seebach – Streisselhochzeit (Traditional customs festival plus rock and pop music). ☎03 89 94 70 94. www.uas.fr.

LATE JULY–EARLY AUGUST
Chambley, near Metz – Biennale Mondiale de l'Aérostation, the world's second-largest

JULY–AUGUST: Biennale Mondiale de l'Aérostation, Chambley

© OSTILL/iStockphoto.com

international balloon festival.
(odd-numbered years).
☏ 03 82 33 77 77.
www.pilatre-de-rozier.com.

JULY–AUGUST
Vendresse – Open-air theatre plus
sound and light show at the
Cassine Château.
☏ 03 24 35 44 84 or 03 24 56 67 76.

AUGUST
Sélestat – Corso Fleuri, flower-
decorated floats on parade.
☏ 03 88 58 87 20.
www.corso-fleuri.fr.
Gérardmer – Music and light show,
dragon boats and fireworks over
the lake. ☏ 03 29 60 60 60.
www.ville-gerardmer.fr.

*DECEMBER: Christmas market,
Place Kléber, Strasbourg*

© René Mattes/hemis.fr

Haguenau – Hops festival, world
folklore festival. ☏ 03 88 73 30 41.
Eguisheim – Wine-growers festival.
www.ot-eguisheim.fr.
Provins – Harvest festival.
☏ 01 64 60 26 26.
www.provins.net.

SEPTEMBER
Ribeauvillé – Fête des Ménétriers or
Pfiffer Daj (minstrels): Historical
parade, wine flows freely.
☏ 03 89 73 23 23.
www.alsace-dvestination-tour-
isme.com.
Troyes – 48-hour vintage car rally.
(even-numbered years)
☏ 03 25 40 02 03.

OCTOBER
Troyes – Nuits de Champagne.
Major choral festival (inc. rock pop,
folk and blues bands).
☏ 03 25 72 11 65.
www.nuitsdechampagne.com.
Reims – Paths of Light at Notre Dame
Catherdral (inc. organ music)
☏ 03 26 47 15 79.
www.reims-tourism.com.
Provins – Fair of Saint Martin (inc.
carnival and champagne history).
☏ 01 64 60 38 38.

DECEMBER
Throughout Alsace and Lorraine –
Christmas markets.

Know Before You Go

USEFUL WEBSITES

http://uk.france.fr
The French Government Tourist Office site has practical information and links to more specific guidance, for American or Canadian travellers, for example. The site includes information on everything you need to know about visiting France.

www.visiteurope.com
The European Travel Commission provides useful information on travelling in 30 European countries, and includes links to commercial services, rail schedules, weather reports, etc.

www.ViaMichelin.com
This site has maps, tourist information, travel features, suggestions on hotels and restaurants, and a route planner for numerous locations in Europe. In addition, you can look up weather forecasts, traffic reports and service station location, particularly useful if you will be driving in France.

www.france-travel-guide.net
A practical and developing website for the traveller, written by a Francophile travel writer. Includes essential information, as well as a wide range of regional and local content.

Tourism Alsace operates www.tourisme-alsace.com, another one-stop-shopping type of website with information on hotels, outdoor activities and events in the area.

www.ambafrance-uk.org
www.ambafrance-us.org
The websites for the French Embassy in the UK and the USA provide a wealth of information and links to other French sites (regions, cities, ministries).

TOURIST OFFICES
FRENCH TOURIST OFFICES ABROAD

For information, brochures, maps and assistance in planning a trip to France you should apply to the French Tourist Office in your own country:

Australia
French Tourist Bureau, 25 Bligh Street, Sydney, NSW 2000, Australia
℘(0)292 31 62 77;
http://au.france.fr.

Canada
Maison de la France, 1800 av. McGill College, Bureau 1010, Montreal, Quebec H3A 3J6, Canada
℘(514) 288 20 26;
http://ca.france.fr.

South Africa
Block C, Morningside Close
222 Rivonia Road, MORNINGSIDE 2196
– JOHANNESBURG
℘00 27 (0)10 205 0201.

UK and Ireland
Lincoln House, 300 High Holborn, London WC1V 7JH. ℘0207 061 66 00;
http://uk.france.fr.

USA
825 Third Avenue, New York, NY 10022, USA ℘(212) 838 78 00;
http://us.france.fr.

LOCAL TOURIST OFFICES
The best online source of information is the local tourist office, but you can also contact them in advance to receive brochures and maps.
The addresses and telephone numbers of tourist offices can be found in the orient panels in the *Discovering* section of the guide.

Départements
Address enquiries to the **Comité Départemental du Tourisme (CDT)**:
♦ **Ardennes** – 24 place Ducale, BP419, 08107 Charleville-Mézières. ℘03 24 56 06 08. www.ardennes.com.

River Moselle viewed from Château des Ducs de Lorraine, Sierck-les-Bains, Moselle

- **Aube** – 34 quai Dampierre, 10000 Troyes Cedex. 📞03 25 42 50 00. www.aube-champagne.com.
- **Bas-Rhin** – 4 rue Bartisch, 67100 Strasbourg. 📞03 88 15 45 80. www.alsace-destination-tourisme.com.
- **Haute-Marne** – 4 cours Marcel-Baron, Chaumont 52902. 📞03 25 30 39 00. www.tourisme-hautemarne.com.
- **Haut-Rhin** – Alsace Destination Tourisme, 1 rue Camille Schlumberger, 68000 Colmar. 📞03 89 20 10 68. www.alsace-destination-tourisme.com.
- **Marne** – Agence de Développement Touristique de la Marne, 13 bis, rue Carnot, 51006 Châlons-en-Champagne. 📞03 26 68 37 52. www.tourisme-en-champagne.com.
- **Meurthe-et-Moselle** – 48 Esplanade Jacques Baudot, 54035 Nancy. 📞03 83 94 51 91. www.tourisme-meurtheetmoselle.fr.
- **Meuse** – 33 Rue de Grangettes, 55012 Bar-le-Duc. 📞03 29 45 78 40. www.tourisme-meuse.com.
- **Moselle** – Moselle Attractivité, 2-4 rue du Pont-Moreau, BP 80002, 57003 Metz. 📞03 87 37 57 80. www.moselle-tourisme.com.

- **Vosges** – 8 rue de la Préfecture, 88000 Épinal. 📞03 29 82 45 03. www.tourismevosges.fr.

Régions
At regional level, address enquiries to:
- **Alsace** – 20A, rue Berthe Molly BP 50247, 68005 Colmar. 📞03 89 24 73 50. www.tourisme-alsace.com.
- **Lorraine** – Abbaye des Prémontrés, 54704 Pont-à-Mousson Cedex. 📞03 83 80 01 80. www.tourisme-lorraine.fr.
- **Champagne-Ardenne** – 5 Rue de Jericho, 51000 Châlons-en-Champagne. 📞03 26 21 85 80. www.tourisme-champagne-ardenne.com.

ENTRY REQUIREMENTS

Passport – Nationals of countries within the European Union entering France need only a national identity card; in the case of the UK, this means your passport. Nationals of other countries must be in possession of a valid national **passport**.

😕 *In case of loss or theft, report to your embassy or consulate and the local police.*

😕 *You must carry your documents with you at all times; they can be checked anywhere.*

Visa – No **entry visa** is required for Canadian, US or Australian citizens travelling as tourists and staying less than 90 days, except for students planning to study in France. If you think you may need a visa, apply to your local French Consulate.

US citizens – General passport information is available by phone toll-free from the Federal Information Center (item 5 on the automated menu), ℘800-688-9889. US passport forms can be downloaded from http://travel.state.gov.

CUSTOMS REGULATIONS

In Britain, go to the Customs Office (UK) website at www.hmrc.gov.uk for information on allowances, travel safety tips, and to consult and download documents and guides. There are no limits on the amount of duty and/or tax paid alcohol and tobacco that you can bring back into the UK as long as they are for your own use or gifts and are transported by you. If you are bringing in alcohol or tobacco goods and UK Customs have reason to suspect they may be for a commercial purpose, an officer may ask you questions and make checks.

Australians will find customs information at www.border.gov.au/Trav; for **New Zealanders** Advice for Travellers is at www.customs.govt.nz.

HEALTH

First aid, medical advice and chemists' night service rota are available from chemists/drugstores (pharmacies) identified by the green cross sign. It is advisable to take out comprehensive travel insurance cover, as tourists receiving medical treatment in French hospitals or clinics have to pay for it themselves.

Nationals of non-EU countries should check with their insurance companies about policy limitations. Remember to keep all receipts.

British and Irish citizens, if not already in possession of an EHIC (European Health Insurance Card), should apply for one before travelling. The card entitles UK residents to reduced-cost medical treatment. Apply at UK post offices, call ℘0845 606 2030, or visit www.ehic.org.uk. Details of the healthcare available in France and how to claim reimbursement are published in the leaflet Health Advice

EMBASSIES AND CONSULATES IN FRANCE		
Australia	Embassy	4 rue Jean-Rey, 75015 Paris ℘01 40 59 33 00. www.france.embassy.gov.au
Canada	Embassy	37 avenue Montaigne, 75008 Paris ℘01 44 43 29 00. www.international.gc.ca
Ireland	Embassy	12 ave. Foch, 75016 Paris ℘01 44 17 67 00. www.embassyofireland.fr
New Zealand	Embassy	103, rue de Grenelle, 75007 Paris ℘01 45 01 43 43. www.mfat.govt.nz
South Africa	Embassy	59 quai d'Orsay, 75343 Paris ℘01 53 59 23 23. www.afriquesud.net
UK	Embassy	35 rue du Faubourg St-Honoré, 75008 Paris ℘01 44 51 31 00. www.gov.uk/world/france
	Consulate	16 rue d'Anjou, 75008 Paris ℘01 44 51 31 01 (visas). www.gov.uk/world/france
USA	Embassy	2 avenue Gabriel, 75008 Paris ℘01 43 12 22 22. http://fr.usembassy.gov
	Consulate	2 rue St-Florentin, 75001 Paris ℘01 42 96 14 88. https://fr.usembassy.gov

for Travellers, available from post offices. All prescription drugs taken into France should be clearly labelled; it is recommended to carry a copy of prescriptions.

Americans and Canadians can contact the International Association for Medical Assistance to Travellers (*www. iamat.org*):

- USA: 1623 Military Rd. #279 Niagara Falls, NY 14304-1745 ℘(716) 754-4883
- Canada: 67 Mowat Avenue, Suite 036 Toronto, Ontario M6K 3E3 ℘(416) 652-0137

ACCESSIBILITY &

The sights described in this guide that are easily accessible to people of reduced mobility are indicated by the & symbol.

On French TGV and Corail trains there are wheelchair spaces in 1st-class carriages available to holders of 2nd-class tickets. On Eurostar and Thalys special rates are available for accompanying adults. All airports are equipped to receive physically disabled passengers. Disabled drivers may use the EU blue card for parking entitlements.

Many of France's historic buildings, including museums and hotels, have limited or no wheelchair access. Older hotels tend not to have lifts.

Tourism for All UK (*Pixel Mill, 44 Appleby Road, Kendal, Cumbria LA9 6ES. ℘0845 124 9971; www.tourismforall. org.uk*) publishes overseas information guides listing accommodation that they believe to be accessible but haven't inspected in person. Information about accessibility is available from French disability organisations such as **Association des Paralysés de France** (*17 bd. Auguste-Blanqui, 75013 Paris; ℘01 40 78 69 00; www.apf.asso.fr*). Useful information on transportation, holidaymaking, and sports associations for the disabled is available from the French-language website www.handicap.fr. In the UK; www.disabilityrightsuk.org is a good source of info and support, and the US website www.access-able.com provides information on travel for mature travellers or those with special needs.

PETS

Recent regulations make it much easier to travel with pets between the UK and mainland Europe. All animals must be microchipped, vaccinated against rabies (at least 21 days prior to travel) and have the EU Pet Passport. Full details are available from the website of the **Department for Environment, Food and Rural Affairs** (*www. gov.uk/take-pet-abroad*).

Getting There and Getting Around

BY PLANE

Various international and other independent airlines operate services to **Paris** (Roissy-Charles de Gaulle and Orly airports) and there are regular air links to **Strasbourg** International Airport, **Basel-Mulhouse** (EuroAirport) and **Metz-**

Nancy-Lorraine Airport from Paris and a host of other, mainly European, cities. There is a frequent shuttle bus service into Strasbourg from Monday to Friday, and when planes arrive at weekends (journey time of 30min). The shuttle service from EuroAirport to Mulhouse train station also takes 30min. Metz-Nancy-Lorraine Airport is situated between Metz and Nancy. The AÉROLOR shuttle runs from the airport to Metz (30min) or Nancy (40min) train stations.

Practical advice

Practical advice for travelling by plane, specifically as regards carrying liquids, gels, creams, aerosols, medicines and food for babies is provided on www. francetourism.com. Some countries impose restrictions on liquids bought in duty-free shops when transferring to a connecting flight.

BY SHIP

There are numerous **cross-Channel passenger and car** ferry services from the United Kingdom and Ireland. To choose the most suitable route between your port of arrival and your destination use the Michelin Tourist and Motoring Atlas France, Michelin Map 911 (which gives travel times and mileages) or Michelin maps from the 1:200 000 series.

- **Brittany Ferries** ☎0330 159 7000 (UK). www.brittanyferries.com. Services from Portsmouth, Poole and Plymouth to Caen (Ouistreham) from where it is a three-hour drive to Angers.
- **Condor Ferries** ☎0345 609 1024. www.condorferries.co.uk. Services from Weymouth, Poole and Portsmouth.
- **DFDS Seaways** operate routes between Dover and Calais, Dover-Dunkerque Portsmouth-Le Havre and Newhaven-Dieppe. ☎(UK) 0871 574 7235 and ☎0800 917 1201. www.dfdsseaways.co.uk.
- **P&O Ferries** ☎0800 130 0030 (UK). www.poferries.com. Service between Dover and Calais.

BY TRAIN/RAIL

Eurotunnel operates a 35-minute rail trip for passengers with a car through the Channel Tunnel between Folkestone and Calais ☎08705 35 35 35 (in the UK) or ☎08 10 63 03 04 (in France); www.eurotunnel.com. **Eurostar** runs from **London** (St Pancras) to **Paris** (Gare du Nord) in under 3hr (up to 20 times daily). In Paris it links to the high-speed rail network (TGV) which covers most of France. From Paris (Gare de l'Est), the French national railways **SNCF** *(www.sncf.fr)* operates an extensive service to the region.

Bookings and information

☎08705 186 186 (£3 credit card booking fee applies) in the UK, www. eurostar.com.

Ⓢ*All rail services throughout France can be arranged through Rail Europe in the UK online (www.voyages-sncf.com), by telephone ☎0844 848 4070, or call into the Rail Europe Travel Centre at 198 Picadilly, London W1J 9EU. Rail Europe can also book Eurostar travel.*

Citizens of non-European Economic Area countries must complete a landing card before arriving at Eurostar check-in. These cards can be found at dedicated desks in front of the check-in area and from Eurostar staff. Once you have filled in the card, please hand it to UK immigration staff.

France Rail Pass and Eurail Pass are travel passes which may be purchased by residents of countries outside the European Union. In the US, contact your travel agent or Rail Europe 44 South Broadway, White Plains NY 10601, ☎1-800-622-8600 (US) and ☎1-800-361-7245 (Canada).

If you are a **European resident,** you can buy an individual country pass, if you are not a resident of the country where you plan to use it.

At the SNCF (French railways) site, **www.sncf.fr,** you can book ahead, pay with a credit card, and receive your ticket in the mail at home.

There are numerous **discounts** available when you purchase your tickets in France, from 25–50 percent below the regular rate. They include discounts for using senior cards and youth cards, and seasonal promotions. There are a limited number of discount seats available during peak travel times, and the best discounts are available for travel during off-peak periods.

Ⓢ Tickets for rail travel in France must be validated *(composter)* by using the (usually) automatic date-stamping machines at the platform entrance (*failure to do so may result in a fine*). The French railway company SNCF operates a **telephone information, reservation and prepayment service in English** from 7am to 10pm (French time) ☎08 36 35 35 39.

BY COACH/BUS

www.eurolines.com has information about travelling by coach in Europe.

BY CAR

Planning your route

The area covered in this guide is easily reached by motorways and national routes. **Michelin map 721** indicates the main itineraries as well as alternate routes for avoiding heavy traffic during busy holiday periods, and gives estimated travel times. **Michelin France Tourist & Motoring Atlas** details French motorways, indicating tolls, rest areas and services along the route; it includes a table for calculating distances and times. The latest Michelin route-planning service is available on the Internet at **www.ViaMichelin.com**. Travellers can calculate a precise route using such options as shortest route, route avoiding toll roads, Michelin-recommended route, and gain access to tourist information (hotels, restaurants, attractions). The service is available on a pay-per-route basis or by subscription. The roads are very busy during the holiday period (particularly weekends in July and August) and, to avoid traffic congestion, it is advisable to follow the recommended secondary routes (signposted as *Bison Futé – itinéraires bis*). The motorway network includes rest areas *(aires de repos)* and petrol stations *(stations-service)*, usually with restaurant and shopping complexes attached, around every 40km/25mi.

Driving Licence

Travellers from other European Union countries and North America can drive in France with a valid national or home-state **driving licence**. An **international driving licence** is useful because the information on it appears in nine languages.

Registration papers

For the vehicle, it is necessary to have the registration papers (logbook) and an approved nationality plate.

Insurance

Many motoring organisations offer accident insurance and breakdown service schemes for members. Check with your insurance company with regard to coverage while abroad. Because French autoroutes are privately owned, European Breakdown Cover service does not extend to breakdowns on the autoroute or its service areas – you must use the emergency telephones, or drive off the auto route before calling your breakdown service.

ROAD REGULATIONS

The minimum driving age is 18. Traffic drives on the right. All passengers must wear **seat belts**. Children under the age of 10 must ride in the back seat. Headlights must be switched on in poor visibility and at night; dipped headlights should be used at all times outside built-up areas. Use sidelights only when the vehicle is stationary. In the case of a breakdown, a **red warning triangle** or hazard warning lights are obligatory, as are **reflective safety jackets**, one for each passenger, and carried within the car. it is now compulsory to carry an in-car **breathalyser kit**, too; you can be fined if you do not. UK right-hand drive cars must use headlight adaptors.

In the absence of stop signs at intersections, cars must **give way to the right**. Traffic on main roads outside built-up areas (priority indicated by a yellow diamond sign) and on roundabouts has right of way. Vehicles must stop when the lights turn red at road junctions and may filter to the right only when indicated by an amber arrow.

The regulations on **drinking and driving** (limited to 0.50g/l) and **speeding** are strictly enforced – usually by an on-the-spot fine and/or confiscation of the vehicle.

Further regulations – It is obligatory to carry spare lightbulbs; yellow fluorescent jackets in case of breakdown, one for each passenger, and accessible from within the car; in-car breathalyser kit. UK right-hand drive cars must use headlight adaptors.

Speed limits

Although subject to changes, speed limits are as follows:

- Toll motorways *(autoroutes)* **130kph/80mph** (110kph/68mph when raining);
- Dual carriageways and motor ways without tolls **110kph/68mph** (100kph/62mph when raining);
- Other roads **90kph/56mph** (80kph/50mph when raining) and in towns **50kph/31mph**;
- Outside lane on motorways during daylight, on level ground and with good visibility – minimum speed limit of 80kph/50mph.

Parking Regulations

In urban areas there are zones where parking is either restricted or subject to a fee; tickets should be obtained from the ticket machines (*horodateurs* – small change necessary) and displayed inside the windscreen on the driver's side; failure to display may result in a fine or towing. Other parking areas in town may require you to take a ticket when passing through a barrier. To exit, you must pay the parking fee (usually there is a machine located by the exit – *sortie*) and insert the paid-up card in another machine which will lift the exit gate.

Tolls

In France, most motorway sections are subject to a **toll** (*péage*). You can pay in cash or with a credit card.

RENTAL CARS – RESERVATIONS	
Avis	www.avis.co.uk www.avis.fr
Europcar	www.europcar.com
Budget France	www.budget.com
Hertz	www.hertz.com
SIXT	www.sixt.com

CAR RENTAL

There are car rental agencies at airports, railway stations and in all large towns throughout France. European cars have manual transmissions; automatic cars are available in larger cities only if an advance reservation is made. Drivers must be over 21; between ages 21–25, drivers are required to pay an extra daily fee; some companies allow drivers under 23 only if the reservation has been made through a travel agent.

Car hire and holders of UK driving licences

In 2015, changes to the UK Driving License came into force which mean that because details of fines, penalty points and restrictions are now only held electronically you are going to have to enable a car hire company to access your online driving record by means of a DVLA-issued pass code. Full details are available at www.gov.uk/view-driving-licence.

PETROL/GASOLINE

French service stations dispense:

- *sans plomb98* (super unleaded 98)
- *sans plomb95* (super unleaded 95)
- *diesel/gazole* (diesel) – many with high-grade diesel
- *GPL* (LPG).

Prices are listed on signboards on the motorways, although it is usually cheaper to fill up before joining or after leaving the motorway.

The website www.prix-carburants.gouv.fr collects information on current fuel prices around the country.

Where to Stay and Eat

☾For Hotel and Restaurant selections, see the Addresses within the Discovering section of the guide.

WHERE TO STAY

Turn to the **Addresses** within individual Sight descriptions for a selection and prices of typical places to stay (**Stay**) and eat (**Eat**). The key at the back of the guide explains the symbols and abbreviations used in these sections. Use the map of **Places to stay** (*overleaf*) to identify recommended places for overnight stops. To enhance your stay, hotel selections have been chosen for their location, comfort, value for the money, and in many cases, their charm, but it is not a comprehensive listing. Prices indicate the cost of a standard double room for two people in peak season. For an even greater selection, use the red-cover **Michelin Guide France**, with its well-known star-rating system and hundreds of establishments throughout France.

The **Michelin Charming Places to Stay** guide contains a selection of 1 000 hotels and guest houses at reasonable prices. Always be sure to book ahead, especially for stays during the high season.

A guide to good-value, family-run hotels, **Logis et Auberges de France**, is available from the French Tourist Office (*www.tourisme.fr*). The website gives a list of accommodation for each *département*, as well as links for making reservations, and a list of tourist offices all over France.

Another resource, which publishes a catalogue listing holiday villas, apartments or chalets in each *département* is the **French national family tourism network Clévacances** (*www. clevacances.com*).

For good-value, family-run accommodation, the **Logis** network, is one of the best organisations to contact (*www.logishotels.com*).

Relais & Châteaux (*www.relaischa-teaux.com*) provides information on booking in luxury hotels with character:
UK: ☎0203 519 1967
France: ☎01 76 49 39 39
Australia: ☎1300 121 341
New Zealand: ☎0800 540 008
USA: ☎1 800 735 2478

www.viamichelin.com covers hotels in France, including famous selections from the Michelin Guide as well as lower-priced chains.

ECONOMY CHAIN HOTELS

If you need a place to stop en route, these can be useful, as they are inexpensive and generally located near the main road. Breakfast is available, but there may not be a restaurant; rooms are small, with a TV and bathroom. Central reservation numbers and websites (online booking is usually available):

- **Akena:** ☎0810 220 280; www.hotels-akena.com
- **B&B:** ☎02 98 33 75 29; www.hotel-bb.com
- **Best Hôtel:** www.besthotel.fr
- **Campanile**, UK ☎0207 519 50 45; France ☎0892 23 48 12; www.campanile.com
- **Kyriad**: UK ☎0207 519 50 45; France ☎0892 23 48 13; www.kyriad.com
- **Première Classe:** UK ☎0207 519 5045; France ☎0892 23 48 14; www.premiereclasse.com
- **International Hotels Group:** ☎0871 423 4896; www.ihg.com
- **Best Western Hotels:** www.bestwestern.fr.
- **Ibis and Accor Hotels:** UK ☎0871 663 0628; France ☎0825 88 22 22; www.ibis.com

COTTAGES, BED AND BREAKFAST

The **Maison des Gîtes de France** lists self-catering cottages or apartments, or bed and breakfast accommodation (*chambres d'hôtes*) at a

reasonable price: ☎0826 10 44 44;
www.gites-de-france.com.

La Fédération des Stations Vertes
(*BP 71698, 21016 Dijon ☎03 80 54 10 50;
www.stationsvertes.com*) lists some
600 country and mountain sites
ideal for families.

There is also **Bed and Breakfast
France** (*12 rue des Tulipes, 85100 Les
Sables d'Olonne; www.bedbreak.com*).

The **Fédération des Logis de France**
offers hotel-restaurant packages
geared to walking, fishing, biking,
skiing, wine-tasting and enjoying
nature (*☎01 45 84 83 84 (English
spoken); www.logishotels.com*).

The adventurous can consult
www.gites-refuges.com, where
you can download a guidebook, *Gîtes
d'étapes et refuges*, listing some 4 000
shelters for walkers, mountaineers,
rock-climbers, skiers, canoe/kayakers,
etc.: *74 rue A. Perdreaux, 78140 Vélizy
☎01 34 65 11 89.*

HOSTELS, CAMPING

To obtain an International Youth Hostel Federation card (no age requirement; senior card also available)
contact the IYHF in your own country.
An online booking service (*www.
hihostels.com*), lets you reserve rooms
up to six months ahead.

The two main youth hostel associations
(*Auberges de Jeunesse*) in France are:

◆ **Ligue Française pour les
  Auberges de la Jeunesse**
  67 r. Vergniaud, Bâtiment K, 75013
  Paris. ☎01 44 16 78 78. www.
  auberges-de-jeunesse.com/en.
◆ **Fédération Unie des
  Auberges de Jeunesse**
  27 r. Pajol, 75018 Paris.
  ☎01 44 89 87 27. www.fuaj.org.

There are numerous officially graded
camp sites with varying standards of
facilities throughout the Burgundy-
Jura region.

The **Michelin Camping France** guide
lists a selection of camp sites. The area
is very popular with campers in the summer months, so it is wise to reserve in
advance.

WHERE TO EAT

A selection of places to eat in the
different locations covered in this
guide can be found in the **Addresses**
appearing in the *Discovering* section of
the guide. The Legend at the back of this
guide explains the symbols used in these
Addresses. Use the red-cover **Michelin
Guide France**, with its famously reliable
star-rating system and descriptions of
hundreds of establishments all over
France, for an even greater choice. If
you would like to experience a meal
in a highly rated restaurant from the
Michelin Guide, be sure to book ahead.

Winstub Pfifferbriader, Strasbourg

© SGM/age fotostock

Places to stay

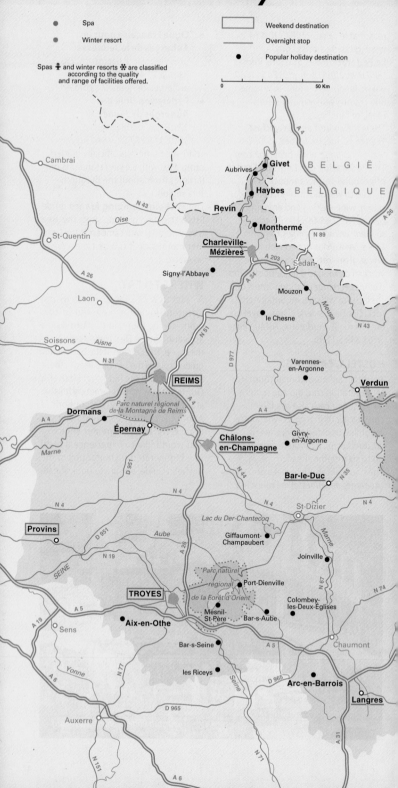

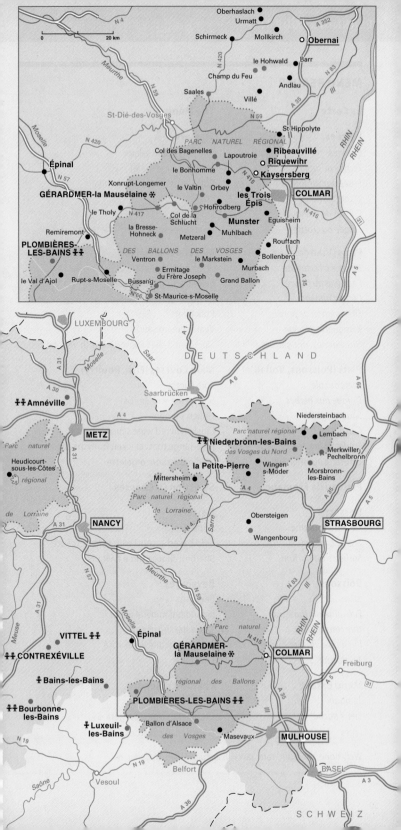

MENU READER

La Carte

Entrées
Crudités
Terrine de lapin
Frisée aux lardons
Escargots
Cuisses de grenouille
Salade au crottin

Plats (Viandes)
Bavette à l'échalote
Faux filet au poivre
Côtes d'agneau
Filet mignon de porc
Blanquette de veau
Nos viandes sont garnies

Plats (Poissons, Voilaille)
Filets de sole
Dorade aux herbes
Saumon grillé
Coq au vin
Poulet de Bresse rôti
Omelette aux morilles

Plateau de Fromages

Desserts
Tarte aux pommes
Crème caramel
Sorbet: trois parfums

Boissons
Bière
Eau minérale (gazeuse)
Une carafe d'eau
Vin rouge, vin blanc, rosé
Jus de fruit

Menu Enfant
Jambon
Steak haché
Frites

The Menu

Starters
Raw vegetable salad
Rabbit terrine (pâté)
Curly lettuce with bacon bits
Snails
Frog's legs
Goats cheese on a bed of lettuce

Main Courses (Meat)
Steak with shallots
Sirloin with pepper sauce
Lamb chops
Pork fillet
Veal in cream sauce
Our meat dishes are served with vegetables

Main Courses (Fish, Poultry)
Sole fillets
Sea bream with herbs
Grilled salmon
Chicken in red wine sauce
Free-range roast chicken from the Bresse
Wild mushroom omelette

Selection Of Cheeses

Desserts
Apple pie
Cold baked custard with caramel sauce
Sherbet: choose three flavours

Beverages
Beer
(Sparkling) mineral water
Tap water (no charge)
Red wine, white wine, rosé
Fruit juice

Children's Menu
Ham
Ground beef/beefburger
French fried potatoes

Well-done, medium, rare, raw = *bien cuit, à point, saignant, cru*

Fête du Kugelhopf, Ribeauvillé

© Denis Bringard/hemis.fr

In the countryside, restaurants usually serve lunch between noon and 2pm and dinner between 7.30 and 10pm. It is not always easy to get something to eat in between those two mealtimes, a snack in a café may fill the gap.

In Alsace, **winstubs and brasseries** are two traditional types of eating house. *Winstubs* were created by the Strasbourg wine producers to promote their wines and provide a convivial setting in which to order a carafe of Alsatian wine to accompany a choice of different local dishes. For those who prefer beer, *brasseries* offer the opportunity to taste food from the region accompanied by a glass of beer brewed on site.

Fermes-auberges (farm-inns) may offer overnight accommodation, but they do serve farm produce and local speciality dishes. The tradition of serving country fare to travellers is centuries old in the Hautes-Vosges, where dairy farmers were known as *marcaires*. The *repas marcaire* proposed by many farms usually includes a *tourte de la vallée de Munster* (deep-dish pie with smoked pork, onions and garlic), followed by a blueberry tart.

The *Guide des Fermes-auberges* in the Haute-Alsace is available from the

Association des Fermes-auberges du Haut-Rhin. (℘*01 53 57 11 50; www.bienvenue-a-la-ferme.com*).

GOURMET GUIDE

The Grand Est region (Alsace-Lorraine) boasts a number of production sites, gastronomic itineraries, fairs and other events of interest to the gourmet traveller. Among those that have been awarded the special distinction of *site remarquable du goût* are the Kronenbourg and Météor breweries for their beer, the sugar festival in the Erstein area (last weekend in August), the fried carp route in the Sundgau, the wine road in Alsace, the Kugelhopf (a local cake) festival in Ribeauvillé (first fortnight in June) and the cheeses of Cornimont (Munster, Géromé and Bargkass).

In Champagne-Ardenne, a number of chefs offering local recipes or products have formed a special group and display a sign with a chef's hat on a red background at the entrance to their establishments. In Ardenne, those who offer at least three or four specialities from the region display a blue-and-red sign.

⌖*For information on local specialities, see Regional Cuisine in the Introduction section, p67.*

Useful Words and Phrases

ARCHITECTURAL TERMS
See Introduction: Architecture.

Sights

	Translation
Abbaye	Abbey
Beffroi	Belfry
Chapelle	Chapel
Château	Castle
Cimetière	Cemetery
Cloître	Cloisters
Colombage	Half-timbering
Cour	Courtyard
Couvent	Convent
Écluse	Lock (Canal)
Église	Church
Fontaine	Fountain
Gothique	Gothic
Halle	Covered market
Jardin	Garden
Mairie	Town Hall
Maison	House
Marché	Market
Monastère	Monastery
Moulin	Windmill
Musée	Museum
Pan de Bois	Timber-framed
Parc	Park
Place	Square
Pont	Bridge
Port	Port/harbour
Porte	Gateway
Quai	Quay
Remparts	Ramparts
Romain	Roman
Roman	Romanesque
Rue	Street
Statue	Statue
Tour	Tower

Natural Sites

	Translation
Abîme	Chasm
Aven	Swallow-hole
Barrage	Dam
Belvédère	Viewpoint
Cascade	Waterfall
Col	Pass
Corniche	Ledge
Côte	Coast, Hillside
Forêt	Forest
Grotte	Cave
Lac	Lake
Plage	Beach
Rivière	River
Ruisseau	Stream
Signal	Beacon
Source	Spring
Vallée	Valley

On the Road

	Translation
Car Park	Parking
Diesel	Diesel/gazole
Driving licence	Permis de conduire
East	Est
Garage (for repairs)	Garage
Left	Gauche
Lpg	Gpl
Motorway	Autoroute
North	Nord
Parking meter	Horodateur
Petrol/gas	Essence
Petrol/gas station	Station d'essence
Right	Droite
South	Sud
Toll	Péage
Traffic lights	Feu tricolore
Tyre	Pneu
Unleaded	Sans plomb
West	Ouest
Wheel clamp	Sabot
Pedestrian crossing	Passage clouté

Time

	Translation
Today	Aujourd'hui
Tomorrow	Demain
Yesterday	Hier
Monday	Lundi
Tuesday	Mardi
Wednesday	Mercredi
Thursday	Jeudi

Friday	Vendredi
Saturday	Samedi
Sunday	Dimanche
Spring	Printemps
Summer	Été
Autumn	Automne
Winter	Hiver
Week	Semaine

Numbers

	Translation
0	zéro
1	un
2	deux
3	trois
4	quatre
5	cinq
6	six
7	sept
8	huit
9	neuf
10	dix
11	onze
12	douze
13	treize
14	quatorze
15	quinze
16	seize
17	dix-sept
18	dix-huit
19	dix-neuf
20	vingt
30	trente
40	quarante
50	cinquante
60	soixante
70	soixante-dix
80	quatre-vingt
90	quatre-vingt-dix
100	cent
1000	mille

Shopping

	Translation
Antiseptic	Antiseptique
Bank	Banque
Bakery	Boulangerie
Big	Grand
Bookshop	Librairie
Butcher's	Boucherie
Chemist	Pharmacie
Closed	Fermé
Cough mixture	Sirop pour la toux
Cough sweets	Cachets pour la Gorge
Entrance	Entrée
Exit	Sortie
Fishmonger's	Poissonnerie
Grocer's	Épicerie
Newsagent	Maison de la Presse
Open	Ouvert
Painkiller	Analgésique
Plaster (Adhesive)	Pansement Adhésif
Post office	Poste
Pound (Weight)	Livre
Push	Pousser
Pull	Tirer
Shop	Magasin
Small	Petit
Stamps	Timbres

Food and Drink

	Translation
Beef	Bœuf
Beer	Bière
Butter	Beurre
Bread	Pain
Breakfast	Petit-déjeuner
Cheese	Fromage
Chicken	Poulet
Dessert	Dessert

"Fourchette" and "Couteau"

©Andrew Johnson/iStockphoto.com

Dinner	Dîner
Duck	Canard
Fish	Poisson
Fork	Fourchette
Fruit	Fruits
Glass	Verre
Grape	Raisin
Green salad	Salade verte
Ham	Jambon
Ice cream	Glace
Jug of tap water	Carafe d'eau
Jug of wine	Pichet de vin
Knife	Couteau
Lamb	Agneau
Lunch	Déjeuner
Meat	Viande
Mineral water	Eau minérale
Mixed salad	Salade composée
Orange juice	Jus d'orange
Plate	Assiette
Pork	Porc
Red wine	Vin rouge
Salt	Sel
Sparkling water	Eau gazeuse
Spoon	Cuillère
Still water	Eau plate
Sugar	Sucre
Tap water	Eau du robinet
Turkey	Dinde
Vegetables	Légumes
Water	De l'eau
White wine	Vin blanc
Yoghurt	Yaourt

Personal Documents and Travel

	Translation
Airport	Aéroport
Credit Card	Carte de crédit
Customs	Douane
Passport	Passèport
Platform	Voie, Quai
Railway station	Gare
Shuttle	Navette
Suitcase	Valise
Train/plane ticket	Billet de train/d'avion
Wallet	Portefeuille

Clothing

	Translation
Coat	Manteau
Jumper	Pull
Raincoat	Imperméable
Shirt	Chemise
Shoes	Chaussures
Socks	Chaussettes
Stockings	Bas
Suit	Costume/tailleur
Tights	Collant
Trousers	Pantalon

USEFUL PHRASES

	Translation
Goodbye	Au revoir
Hello/ Good morning	Bonjour
How	Comment
Excuse me	Excusez-moi
Thank you	Merci
Yes/No	Oui/Non
I am sorry	Je m'excuse
Why?	Pourquoi?
When?	Quand?
Please	S'il vous plaît

Do you speak English?
Parlez-vous anglais?
I don't understand
Je ne comprends pas
Speak slowly, please
Parlez lentement, s'il vous plaît
Where's...?
Où est...?
When does the ... leave?
À quelle heure part ...?
When does the ... arrive?
À quelle heure arrive ...?
When does the museum open?
À quelle heure ouvre le musée?
When is the show?
À quelle heure est la représentation?
When is breakfast served?
À quelle heure sert-on le petit-déjeuner?
What does it cost?
Ça coûte combien?

Where can I buy a newspaper in English?
> Où puis-j'acheter un journal en anglais?

Where is the nearest petrol/ gas station?
> Où se trouve la station d'essence la plus proche?

Where can I change traveller's cheques?
> Où puis-j'échanger des cheques de voyage?

Where are the toilets?
> Où sont les toilettes?

Do you accept credit cards?
> Acceptez-vous les cartes de crédit?

May I have a receipt, please
> Puis-j'avoir un reçu, s'il vous plait

Basic Information

BUSINESS HOURS

Admission to state-owned **museums** and historic monuments is free for travellers with special needs, such as people with disabilities – as well as those accompanying them – but the rules require that you show an identification card. Admission is free in most museums for children under 18 years of age. Admission is sometimes free for all visitors on the first Sunday in every month. Museums and art galleries are often closed on Mondays; municipal museums are generally closed on Mondays.

Most of the larger **stores** are open Mon–Sat 9am–6.30pm/7.30pm. Smaller, individual shops may close during the lunch hour. Food shops – grocers, wine merchants and bakeries – are open from around 7am–7.30pm; some open on Sunday mornings. Open-air food markets usually close on Mondays. Hypermarkets typically stay open until 9pm/10pm.

Banks are usually open from 9am–4.30pm or 5pm and are closed on Mondays or Saturdays; some branches open for limited transactions on Saturdays. Banks close early on the day before a bank holiday.

DISCOUNTS

Almost all attractions offer discounted admission prices for children, seniors, students and (sometimes) family groups; many also offer discounts for advance booking online.
The ages that children's discounts apply to vary, but where these relate to Sights that are noted as specific attractions for children with the 👥 symbol, the price and age range for children are shown. Student discounts tend as a rule to be for French students only, on presentation of a student ID card.

ELECTRICITY

The electric current is 220 volts. Circular two-pin plugs are the rule. Adapters and converters (for hairdryers, for example) should be bought before you leave home; they are sold in most airports. If you have a rechargeable device (mobile phone, video camera, portable computer, battery recharger), read the instructions carefully or contact the manufacturer or shop. Sometimes these items only require a plug adapter, in other cases you must use a voltage converter as well or risk ruining your appliance.

EMERGENCIES

European Emergency Call: ☎112
Police: ☎17
SAMU (Paramedic) ☎15
Fire ☎18

MAIL/POST

Main post offices open Monday to Friday 9am to 7pm, Saturday 9am to noon. However, many post offices, especially smaller ones, close at lunchtime between noon and 2pm, and some may close early in the afternoon; in short, opening hours vary widely. Stamps are also available from newsagents and tobacconists *(tabacs)*. Stamp collectors should ask for *timbres de collection* in any post office.

France has two different stamps which are used for the standard postal service. The red stamp is the one used for a quicker delivery, and letters should take between 1 and 3 days to arrive. This is the equivalent of the first class service in the UK. The green stamps offer a slower service, between 2 and 3 days, the equivalent of second class deliveries in the UK.

Postage via air mail:
UK: letter (20g) €1.20.
North America: letter (20g) €1.30
Australia and NZ: letter (20g) €1.30
Stamps are also available from newsagents and *bureaux de tabac*. Stamp collectors should ask for *timbres de collection* in any post office. A useful website for mailing information and prices is www.tarifs-de-la-poste.fr.

MONEY

The euro is the only currency accepted as a means of payment in France, as in the other European countries participating in the monetary union. It is divided into 100 cents or centimes. There are no restrictions on the amount of currency visitors can take into France. Visitors carrying a lot of cash are advised to complete a currency declaration form on arrival, because there are restrictions on currency export: if you are leaving the country with more than €10 000, you must declare the amount to customs.

BANKS

Bank hours vary from branch to branch, but for typical hours 🕐*see BUSINESS HOURS above.*

One of the most economical ways to obtain money in France is by using **ATM machines** to get cash directly from your bank account (with a debit card) or to use your credit card to get a cash advance. Be sure to remember your PIN number; you will need it to use cash dispensers and to pay with your card in shops, restaurants, etc. Code pads are numeric; use a telephone pad to translate a letter code into numbers. PIN numbers have 4 digits in France; enquire with the issuing company or bank if the code you usually use is longer.

CREDIT CARDS

Visa is the most widely accepted credit card, followed by MasterCard; other cards, credit and debit (Diners Club, Plus, Cirrus, etc.) are also accepted in some cash machines. American Express is accepted primarily in premium establishments. Most places post signs indicating which cards they accept; if you don't see such a sign, and want to pay with a card, ask before ordering or making a selection. Cards are widely accepted in shops, hypermarkets, hotels and restaurants, at tollbooths and in petrol stations.

Before you leave home, check with the bank that issued your card for emergency replacement procedures. At the same time, inform the bank that you will be using your credit card abroad – it may prevent refusal of your card at cash desks. Carry your card number and its emergency phone numbers separately from your wallet and handbag; leave a copy of this information with someone you can easily reach. If your card is lost or stolen while you are in France, call one of the 24-hour hotlines shown in the box above.

🔊 **If your card is lost or stolen** call the appropriate 24h hotlines listed on ***www.totallymoney.com/guides/ lost-stolen-credit-card***.

Better still: always carry with you the correct number to call for your particular credit cards. You must report any loss or theft of credit cards or traveller's cheques to the local police who will issue you with a certificate (useful proof to show the issuing company).

TRAVELLER'S CHEQUES

It may be a good idea to carry a few traveller's cheques in addition to your credit cards, and to keep them in a safe place in case of emergency. A passport is necessary as identification when cashing traveller's cheques in banks or major hotels. Smaller establishments are not likely to cash them. Commission charges vary and hotels usually charge more than banks for cashing cheques.

PUBLIC HOLIDAYS

♿*See the box below for a list of major public holidays in France.* There are other religious and national festivals days, and a number of local saints' days, etc. On all these days, museums and other monuments may be closed or may vary their hours of admission. In addition to the usual school holidays at Christmas and in the spring and summer, there are long mid-term breaks (ten days to a fortnight) in February and early November.

1 January	New Year's Day (Jour de l'an)
Mon after Easter Sun	Easter Monday (Pâques)
1 May	Labour Day
8 May	VE Day
Thu 40 days after Easter	Ascension Day (Ascension catholique)
7th Sun after Easter	Whit Monday (Pentecôte)
14 July	**Fête National** France's National Day (or Bastille Day)
15 August	Assumption (Assomption)
1 November	All Saints' Day (Toussaint)
11 November	Armistice Day
25 December	Christmas Day (Noël)

SMOKING

In France smoking is banned in public places such as offices, universities railway stations, restaurants, cafés, bars, nightclubs and casinos. In 2013 the ban was extended to e-cigarettes.

TELEPHONES
Public telephones

Due to the widespread use of mobile phones, the number of **public telephones** in France is decreasing. Those that remain accept pre-paid phone cards *(télécartes)*, rather than coins. Some telephone booths accept credit cards (Visa, Mastercard/Eurocard). *Télécartes* (50 or 120 units) can be bought in post offices, branches of France Télécom, *bureaux de tabac* (cafés that sell cigarettes) and newsagents and can be used to make calls in France and abroad. Calls can be received at phone boxes where the blue bell sign is shown; the phone will not ring, so keep your eye on the little message screen.

National calls

French telephone numbers have ten digits. Paris and Paris region numbers begin with 01; 02 in northwest France; 03 in northeast France; 04 in southeast France and Corsica; 05 in southwest France.

International calls

To call France from abroad, dial the country code (+33) + 9-digit number (omit the initial 0). When calling abroad from France, dial 00, then dial the country code followed by the area code and number of your correspondent.

Australia	☎61
New Zealand	☎64
Canada	☎1
United Kingdom	☎44
Eire	☎353
United States	☎1

International Dialling Codes

Dial 00 before the country code (*see box above*) minus the first 0, then the full number.

MOBILE/CELL PHONES

While in France, all visitors from other European countries should be able to use their mobile phone as normal. Visitors from other countries need to ensure before departure that their phone and service contract are compatible with the European system (GSM). The three main mobile phone operators in France are SFR, Orange and Bouygues:

Orange www.orange.fr
Bouygues www.bouyguestelecom.fr
SFR www.sfr.fr

A number of service providers now offer the facility to use home-country units rather than paying roaming charges, but make a daily charge for this. If you plan to make regular use of a mobile phone while abroad, this is worth considering.

The EU abolished roaming charges in June 2017, as a result EU citizens won't be charged extra for calls. But for the foreseeable future the application of this decision in practice remains unclear. If necessary, consult your own provider.

TIME

France is 1hr ahead of Greenwich Mean Time (GMT). In France the 24hour clock is widely applied.

WHEN IT IS NOON IN FRANCE, IT IS	
3am	in Los Angeles
6am	in New York
11am	in Dublin
11am	in London
7pm	in Perth
9pm	in Sydney
11pm	in Auckland

TIPPING

Since a service charge is automatically included in the price of meals and accommodation in France, any additional tipping is up to the visitor, generally small change, and usually not more than 5 percent. Taxi drivers and hairdressers are normally tipped 10–15 percent.

Tour guides and tour drivers should be tipped according to the amount of service given: from €2–5 would not be unusual.

VALUE ADDED TAX

There is a Value Added Tax in France *(TVA)* of 19.6% on almost every purchase (some foods and books are subject to a lower rate). However, non-European visitors who spend more than €175 (including VAT) in a single shop on the same day can get the VAT amount refunded. Usually, you fill out a form at the store, showing your passport. Upon leaving the country, you submit all forms to customs for approval (they may want to see the goods), so do not pack them in checked luggage. The refund is usually paid directly into your bank or credit card account, or it can be sent by mail. Big department stores that cater to tourists offer special services to help you; be sure to mention that you plan to seek a refund *(remboursement)* before you pay for goods (there is no refund for tax on services). If you are visiting two or more countries within the European Union, you submit the forms only on departure from the last EU country. The refund is worthwhile for those visitors who would like to buy fashionwear, furniture or other fairly expensive items, but remember, the minimum amount must be spent in a single shop (though not necessarily on the same day). *See www.douane.gouv.fr.*

CONVERSION TABLES

Weights and Measures

1 kilogram (kg) 6.35 kilograms 0.45 kilograms **1 metric ton (tn)**	**2.2 pounds (lb)** 14 pounds 16 ounces (oz) **1.1 tons**	**2.2 pounds** 1 stone (st) 16 ounces **1.1 tons**	*To convert kilograms to pounds, multiply by 2.2*
1 litre (l) 3.79 litres 4.55 litres	**2.11 pints (pt)** 1 gallon (gal) 1.20 gallon	**1.76 pints** 0.83 gallon 1 gallon	*To convert litres to gallons, multiply by 0.26 (US) or 0.22 (UK)*
1 hectare (ha) **1 sq kilometre (km²)**	**2.47 acres** 0.38 sq. miles (sq mi)	**2.47 acres** 0.38 sq. miles	*To convert hectares to acres, multiply by 2.4*
1 centimetre (cm) **1 metre (m)**	**0.39 inches (in)** 3.28 feet (ft) or 39.37 inches or 1.09 yards (yd)	**0.39 inches**	*To convert metres to feet, multiply by 3.28; for kilometres to miles, multiply by 0.6*
1 kilometre (km)	**0.62 miles (mi)**	**0.62 miles**	

Clothing

Women	🇪🇺	🇺🇸	🇬🇧
	35	4	2½
	36	5	3½
	37	6	4½
Shoes	38	7	5½
	39	8	6½
	40	9	7½
	41	10	8½
	36	6	8
	38	8	10
Dresses	40	10	12
& suits	42	12	14
	44	14	16
	46	16	18
	36	6	30
	38	8	32
Blouses &	40	10	34
sweaters	42	12	36
	44	14	38
	46	16	40

Men	🇪🇺	🇺🇸	🇬🇧
	40	7½	7
	41	8½	8
	42	9½	9
Shoes	43	10½	10
	44	11½	11
	45	12½	12
	46	13½	13
	46	36	36
	48	38	38
Suits	50	40	40
	52	42	42
	54	44	44
	56	46	48
	37	14½	14½
	38	15	15
Shirts	39	15½	15½
	40	15¾	15¾
	41	16	16
	42	16½	16½

Sizes often vary depending on the designer. These equivalents are given for guidance only.

Speed

KPH	10	30	50	70	80	90	100	110	120	130
MPH	6	19	31	43	50	56	62	68	75	81

Temperature

Celsius (°C)	0°	5°	10°	15°	20°	25°	30°	40°	60°	80°	100°
Fahrenheit (°F)	32°	41°	50°	59°	68°	77°	86°	104°	140°	176°	212°

To convert Celsius into Fahrenheit, multiply °C by 9, divide by 5, and add 32.
To convert Fahrenheit into Celsius, subtract 32 from °F, multiply by 5, and divide by 9.
NB: Conversion factors on this page are approximate.

The Region Today

21ST CENTURY
REGIONS

In 2014, the French Parliament (the National Assembly and the Senate) passed a law that reduced the number of regions (the largest type of administrative district) in Metropolitan France from 22 to 13. The new regions took effect on 1 January 2016.

Across France, each region is made up of *départements* (numbered 01 to 96 alphabetically – their numbers are used as identification on car registration plates and in post codes). Thus, Alsace includes Bas-Rhin (67) and Haut-Rhin (68); Lorraine is made up of Meurthe-et-Moselle (54), Meuse (55), Moselle (67) and Vosges (88); Champagne-Ardennes includes Ardennes (08), Aube (10), Marne (51) and Haute-Marne (52). The country is further divided into *arrondissements*, which are split into cantons, and finally *communes*, which are managed by an elected mayor. There are over 36 000 mayoralties in France.

This guide covers one of the new regions, one that almagamates the former regions of Alsace, Lorraine and Champagne-Ardenne into the new region of Grand Est.

PEOPLE AND POPULATION

The new name is said to have been inspired by former French provinces disbanded in 1790.

Grand Est has diverse populations with people who celebrate many traditions and heritages. At some point over the years, both France and Germany have claimed the people of Alsace as their own, and that has influenced everything from the food to the music to their livelihoods. In 1900, 86.8% of those living in Alsace-Lorraine spoke German. Today, most residents speak German, French and Alsatian, a dialect which is a combination of the two languages.

Slightly less than half of the life scientists in Strasbourg work in the biotechnology industries, which continually attract recent graduates from France and the Rhineland. Strasbourg hosts the Council of Europe/European Parliament. The European Pharmacopoeia, the European Court of Human Rights and the European Science foundation are major organisations based in the city, some of which have significant effect, which has helped to attract a diverse, well-educated workforce.

Champagne has also seen its share of changes of the years. Because of its proximity to Paris, it has in some ways become like a suburb of the City of Light, despite the fact that the region is one of the least-populated areas in the country.

European Parliament, Strasbourg

© Agence d'Attractivité de l'Alsace/Zvardon

LIFE IN THE CITY

As is the case in most urban centres across the globe, residents of the major cities in this region live both in houses and apartments, generally in close proximity to one another.

With almost one million residents, Strasbourg is a vibrant, 21C urban hub. Part of a larger Eurodistrict that includes very important Rhine industrial communities, the city attracts a fairly mobile population and has a substantially younger population than the European and French average (60% of the population is 40-years-old or under).

Like most big cities, Strasbourg struggles with issues of density, such as pollution. Despite serious pollution from heavy industries in the past, the major source of pollution in Strasbourg today comes from automobile traffic. Recent, stringent environmental regulation has come into effect, and new tram lines are aiding those efforts.

Strasbourg is a cultural wonder: the Opera national du Rhine is a major European opera house, with significant funding; performances have a very extensive repertoire, even by French or Italian standards.

LIFE IN THE COUNTRYSIDE
VILLAGES

Most of the people living outside main urban centres live fairly close to their neighbours in villages. This has been the custom since the first settlers arrived. Rather than a response to a perceived need for protection, this pattern is more likely a result of communal farming and forestry techniques.

In **Alsace**, the houses in a village are generally detached from one another, and may even face different directions. Some villages are little more than a group of farmhouses around a belfry. Traces of a more glorious past may remain: a ruined castle rising above the roof line, a lovely church in an otherwise unremarkable place. In any case, one of the most conspicuous features of the Alsatian village is the pride the inhabitants take in keeping their doorways swept, windows sparkling and geraniums blooming.

In **Lorraine**, the houses in the village are generally attached and stand along both sides of the street in an orderly row. Often, there is an entranceway wide enough to accommodate a tractor or wagon, and a smaller doorway into the building itself. The large entrance opens onto the farmland, and often the farm extends far back beyond the main house, with the usual collection of buildings and equipment scattered about.

On the dry plain of **Champagne**, sizeable villages grew up around fresh water springs, often quite far from one another. While the streets are narrow and confined, through an open gate you might glimpse a spacious courtyard with neatly kept buildings holding presses and other equipment needed to maintain and harvest grapes. In the southern part of the region, around Bar-sur-Aube, Bar-sur-Seine, Langres and the Blaise valley, villages can be seen from afar as the buildings are predominantly made of bright white limestone. In the Argonne forest, the linear look of houses lined up along the road is reminiscent of neighbouring Lorraine.

HOUSES AND FARMS

While houses and farms in rural Alsace have many things in common, there are also many subtle differences from one area to another. Gables, the colour, shape and type of timbers, and the materials, patterns and embellishments used to fill in the frame, all vary from north to south. In the vineyard region, the ground floor, in stone, is used for pressing grapes and storing wine. An outside stair leads to the living areas above. The Écomusée d'Alsace (⟲see p333) is a good place to see various building techniques.

In a typical Lorraine village, the older buildings have gently sloping roofs covered with a kind of hollow tile. The traditional farmhouse held the living area, barn and stables under one roof. The limestone walls are coated to preserve the mortar joints.

Half-timbered houses, Troyes

The **Champagne** region is home to many wine-growers. Their houses are typically low, made of millstone, local chalkstone or brick. In **"dry" Champagne**, the farmyards are generally bordered by the living area (facing the street), the barn (facing the fields) and other buildings for animals. In the south-east, half-timbering appears, filled in with blocks of chalkstone or cob covered with plaster. In the greener or **"wet" Champagne**, timbers are cut from pine and poplar, held with cross beams and daub, or earthen bricks. Around **Troyes**, brick is commonly used in decorative patterns between the timbers. A traditional dwelling in the **Argonne forest** has a dark brick façade on the ground floor and a roughcast plaster storey above. The flat tiles of the roof extend out over the sides of the house.

The region of **Ardenne** is rich in schist and quartzite stone, often used for building; the blue slate quarried here is of excellent quality. These materials make the houses rather gloomy looking. To defeat the rigours of winter, all of the farm buildings are close together, making for a single, long building, in contrast to the rectangular courtyard with outbuildings seen in more clement neighbouring areas.

RELIGION

Martin Bucer (1491–1551) worked from Strasbourg and was influential in the city's adoption of the Reformation and the organisation of its Protestant ecclesiastical structure. Because of this, Strasbourg had a strong Lutheran administration by the mid-16C, and that influenced the future of religious development there. Some of the Lutherans in the region became Anabaptists, and Anabaptist refugees from Switzerland and various German states joined them for another 150 years. After becoming part of France in the late 17C, Lutheranism in Strasbourg experienced significant toleration compared with the remainder of the kingdom; Lutheran presence in city councils, in the university, and other areas of public life continued.

From the late Middle Ages, the Duchy of Lorraine remained fairly intact and thus somewhat insulated from the political fragmentation that arrived with the Reformation, but Alsace split into many politically separate regions. Molsheim, for instance, did not experience the surge of Protestant conversions, and instead remained a bastion of Catholic, Counter-Reformation piety, which increased with the founding of a Jesuit religious school in 1580. In general, the Hapsburg-affiliated parts of the region remained strongly Catholic, while the independent German principalities tended towards Lutheranism.

Champagne was caught almost immediately in French religious conflicts because of its strategic position near rivers and other resources. Since the rise of Calvinism, the region had seen steady conversions. In 1662, The Duke of Guise massacred a gathering of Protestants in Wassy, triggering the first wave of battles in the Wars of Religion (*see box, p76*), causing Huguenots to take up arms and fortify their holdings. Huguenot nobles in Champagne owned considerable amounts of land, while the Guise family pressurised many towns there to join in the Catholic League and provide support for its struggles. These remained part of the Catholic League after the assassination of the Duke. Calvinism in Champagne was shattered by the power of the Guise family and at the repercussions on of the massacres on St Bartholomew's Day, 1572. The War of the Three Henrys effectively ended with this, and the Catholic League was further shaken in the region. Most of the region capitulated to the power of Henri of Navarre after his victory at the Battle of Ivry in 1590 and his conversion to Catholicism in 1593, which solidified his control of Paris. Today the region is more strongly Catholic.

THE ECONOMY

ALSACE

This region has become a symbol of the transnational European economy. For the past 30 years, regional development has centred around this theme. Strasbourg, seat of the Council of Europe, was one of the first "Eurocities" on the continent. Mulhouse expanded its commercial activities through close ties with Basel and Fribourg across the Rhine. Because of its history, language and traditions, Alsace is able to develop privileged trading partnerships with the bordering nations of Germany and Switzerland. The valley of the River Rhine, long a significant communications corridor, has contributed to regional prosperity. As early as the 8C–9C, boats left Strasbourg for the North Sea, where they sold wine to the English, Danish and Swedish. Steam ships made their appearance in 1826. It was the construction of the Canal d'Alsace, begun in 1920, which modernised navigation on the Rhine, while harnessing the considerable energy resources provided by the river between Basel and Strasbourg. A strong local policy for encouraging investment has made Alsace the second most dynamic region in France for capital growth. The fertile plain of Alsace could be used for growing many different crops, but the long strip at the foot of the Vosges is used almost exclusively for the cultivation of grapes: 14 566ha. All of the wines are bottled in the region of production (almost 150 million bottles) and represent more than 18% of total French still white wine production. This activity involves 7 000 wine-growers. Grapes make up more than half of overall crop production in the region (40% of total agricultural output). On the domestic market, one-third of still white AOC wines consumed in France is from Alsace. The export market takes up 25% of the annual production (about 40 million bottles).

LORRAINE

Its reputation as an industrial leader has been tarnished since its most brilliant period in the late 19C. First the textile crisis, then the decline of the **steel industry** and the closure of **coal mines** pushed the area into a deep economic slump. Local policy makers have had to work overtime to find innovative solutions for recovery. These include the creation of "technopoles" in Metz and Nancy, districts zoned for the development of high-tech industries. Subsidies have been allotted to areas around the Meuse Valley, Longwy and Thionville for similar development projects.

Diversification is slowly making inroads where heavy industry once dominated: manufacture of synthetic fabrics for tyre manufacture, paper products, service industries and tourism are expanding. Lorraine is also involved in joint development projects with its neighbours in Germany and Luxembourg.

Approximately 2 000 new jobs were created in Hambach for the manufacture of the innovative Smart Car. A collaborative effort, the mixed diesel/electric or petrol automobile has the design pedigree of Swatch and the motoring quality imprint of Mercedes.

Farms in Lorraine are France's leading producers of rape seed, used for making cooking and salad oil; the flowering plants make bright yellow fields. The region actively promotes "quality labelling" of agricultural products, including beef, cheese and eggs. Wood and wood-processing operations (parquet flooring, panelling, furniture etc) also account for a significant share of French production.

CHAMPAGNE

Clearly the most important export (20% of total) for this region is its namesake, sparkling wine. But it should be noted that in recent years, an accumulation of stock and subsequent lowering of prices have pushed leading traders to rethink their marketing philosophy. Related economic activities include bottling and processing plants and farm machine manufacture. The "Packaging Valley" association brings together 250 businesses specialising in packaging products and processes.

Agriculture, shored up by government subsidies, has also made steps towards increased profitability through diversification. Milk products have taken on an important role; the region produces 25% of all the ice cream in France (mostly in Haute-Marne). Research is underway on the chemical components of natural substances, used in non-food products: biological fuels from rape seed, alcohol and ethanol from sugar beet, paper products and adhesives from wheat starch. The textile industry offers employment to a significant number of people in Champagne-Ardenne, especially in Troyes and the Aube *département*. Among the world-famous manufacturers of knitted goods are Absorba, Petit Bateau, Lacoste, Dior and Benetton.

Ardennes

Foundry and metalworks are leading sources of employment, and many automobile and appliance makers place orders with local plants (Citroën, Ford, Électrolux, General Motors, BMW, Porsche). Various automobile-related industries have also set up shop (automotive textiles, safety parts, machine tools), as well as plants producing parts for high-tech projects such as Ariane rockets, TGV trains, Airbus, Rafale fighter jets and the Channel Tunnel. More recently plastics have taken off, in some instances replacing metal parts and devices, as well as in the packaging field.

Most of the businesses in Ardenne are small and medium-sized firms engaged in subcontracting. The network of companies is supported by the CRITT (Regional Centre for Technology Transfer) in Charleville-Mézières, which works in research and development of new and rare materials, microanalysis, non-destructive controls, thermic and thermionic treatments and other highly specialised testing. In an immense effort to revitalise the region after the damage of the Second World War and the decline of heavy industry, the government offers significant fiscal advantages to companies choosing to locate in Ardenne.

Tourism has become an important economic factor in the region. Local authorities have sought to enhance and promote the value of the many historic towns and sites, natural resources and recreational opportunities they provide. Improvements in the **transportation network** have helped this effort, most notably the launch of the high-speed **TGV Est Européen** train service in June 2007 which began operating at a maximum speed of 320kph/199mph. This has brought the region within commuting distance of Paris. As train speeds increase further (the TGV Est Européen has recorded a speed of just under 575kph/357mph!) the journey time will be even shorter; Paris–Strasbourg will eventually be cut to under two hours.

International airports in Strasbourg and Basel-Mulhouse also provide connections to European capitals. The network of **autoroutes** is dense and practical, making it easy to reach the area by car, from the north or south.

DIVERSIFICATION

Although their traditional coal and steel industries have diminished or disappeared, both Alsace-Lorraine and Champagne-Ardennes have successfully diversified: the former is the third wealthiest region in France. In Alsace, agriculture (high-value crops include hops and tobacco), cars (PSA Peugeot-Citroen), chemicals (Rhône-Poulenc) metal casting, machine and tool construction, oil and gas refining, boatbuilding and banking are key areas, as well as tourism. In Lorraine interesting vestiges of traditional industries that

Making of Munster

have survived include glass-making at Baccarat, violin-making at Mirecourt, and high quality ceramics at Longwy, Lunéville and Sarreguemines.

Champagne-Ardennes, meanwhile, has retained its metallurgic and textile industries. Lacoste shirts are made in Troyes, and the Nogent Basin see the production of fine cutlery, surgical instruments and tools. The area has long been famous for its gastronomy and wine production, and tourism is now a vital part of the economy with much of it based around the eponymous sparkling wine – rare is the trip made to Champagne without at least one visit to its world-famous *caves*.

REGIONAL CUISINE
ALSACE-LORRAINE
Charcuteries

Ham and Strasbourg sausages are featured in the classic *assiette alsacienne*, an array of pork meats; but *foies gras* (fattened livers) hold pride of place. This delicacy has been appreciated since the Roman era; in 1778 a young local chef, Jean-Pierre Clause, created the prototype goose liver *pâté en croûte* (wrapped in a crust). Today there are more than 40 variations on his theme on sale in local delicatessens.

In Lorraine, traditional dishes are loaded with butter, bacon and cream. **Potée** is a pot roast made with salt pork and sausages, white cabbage and other vegetables. Of course, **Quiche Lorraine** is world-famous fare: a creamy tart made with beaten eggs, thick cream

and bacon bits. Pâté from Lorraine is made from veal and pork.

Choucroute

Strasbourg is the capital of this cabbage-based speciality made with white Alsatian wine. The savoury white cabbage is heaped with sausages, pork chops, bacon and ham, and on special occasions a bit of partridge, a few crayfish or a truffle find their way in.

Fish and fowl

Chicken dishes are popular in Alsace, and menus often list *coq* and *poularde* (pullet hen), served with mushroom and cream sauce; local *coq au vin* is made with Riesling wine. Local fish recipes are eels stewed in wine sauce (matelote), fried carp, pike and salmon.

Les marcaireries

Dairy farmers and cheesemakers in the Vosges are known as *marcaires*. Traditionally, they take their herds up to the high pasturelands on 25 May (the old feast day of St Urbain), and bring them down again on 29 September. Today farms that serve country fare to travellers may be called by the more usual French name of *ferme-auberge*, but the local traditions remain the same.

Munster and Géromé

The perfect way to polish off an Alsatian meal is with one of these two cheeses, which are only made in the Vosges. Munster is an unpasteurised, soft fermented cheese. On the Lorraine side, Géromé – a word in dialect which means 'from Gérardmer' – also has a long reputation. It is made with unheated whole milk to which rennet (for solidifying) is added immediately. The cheese is aged for four months in a cool cellar until the crust turns russet and the interior is creamy.

Pastries

There are as many different tarts in Alsace as there are fruits to make them with. Any chef is proud to pull a perfect **Kugelhopf** out of the oven, a delightful puff of flour, butter, eggs, sweetened milk, raisins and almonds. Other special desserts are *macarons de Boulay* (dainty biscuits of egg whites and almonds), *madeleines de Commercy* (soft, buttery cakes), and *bergamotes de Nancy* (hard sweets flavoured with citrus rind).

Waffles *(gaufres)* were traditionally made at carnival time in irons forged with unique designs, both religious and profane. Hot waffles sprinkled with sugar or dripping with chocolate are still a popular treat, but the old-fashioned irons are now rare collector's items. **Meringues** were first served in France at the table of Duke Stanislas, in Nancy.

Beer

Breweries abound in Alsace (Schiltigheim, Strasbourg, Hochfelden, Obernai, Saverne); Stenay is home to the Beer Museum; the Brewery Museum is in St-Nicolas-de-Port. Beer has always been made from the same elements: pure water, barley, hops and yeast. Barley transforms into malt, giving colour and flavour; hops provide the bitterness. Each brewery cultivates its own yeast, which gives each brand its distinctive taste.

Beer has been enjoyed since Antiquity: Egyptians called it liquid bread; Hippocrates defended its use as a therapeutic medicine.

Today, beer production starts with the reduction of malt to flour, the addition of water, and heating at a low temperature. While the mixture is stirred, the starch contained in the grain turns to sugar. In another tank, non-malted grain (such as corn) is prepared in the same way. The two tanks are mixed into a **mash**, which is filtered to become the **stock**. The hops are added to the **wort kettle** where the mixture is heated, then filtered again. Fermentation takes place at temperatures between 5°C–10°C. Pasteurisation stablises the final product, and industrial chilling enables year-round production.

Beer leaves the brew house and has yeast added to it, which turns the sugar into alcohol over a two-week period. The yeast is removed after maturation: a final filtration and it's ready for the bottle.

CHAMPAGNE-ARDENNE

Champagne

Savoury sauces, rich meats and fresh produce are the ingredients of fine cuisine in the region. Sauces made with Champagne garnish many recipes for chicken, pullet, thrush, kidneys, stuffed trout, grilled pike, crayfish and snails. Smoked ham and sausage are used in **potée champenoise**, a popular dish at grape harvest time, served with mounds of fresh cabbage, a vegetable which is at its prime in the fall.

Brenne-le-Château has its own recipe for *choucroute*, Troyes is celebrated for its *andouillettes* sausage and Ste-Menehould is famous for dishing out pigs' trotters and mashed potatoes.

Ardennes

The isolation of this region has contributed to the preservation of local traditions. The cuisine is hearty and fortifying, based on natural products found in the wooded hills. Game and fish are prominent on the menu: young boar, venison, rabbit with sauce *chasseur*; woodcock and thrush roasted in sage leaves or served *en terrine* with juniper berries; rich pâtés of marinated veal and pork meats. Smoked ham cured over juniper and *boudin* sausages are on display in local charcuteries.

Cheese

South of Troyes, the region has specialised in the production of creamy cheeses such as Chaource. This cheese has been served at the best tables since the 12C. It can be enjoyed within five days after it is set out *(frais)* or may be left to firm up for about 20 days *(fait)*. Firmer cheese may be covered with a thin film of white mould. Some other regional cheeses are varieties of **Cendré**, with a powdery dusting of grey ash (Châlons-en-Champagne, Les Riceys and the Marne Valley). **Maroilles** is a fragrant cheese from Thiérache that is typically enjoyed at harvest time. Mostafait is a white cream cheese blended with butter and tarragon. **Rocroi** is from the town of the same name; **Igny** shares its name with the Trappist monastery that produces it; **Troyen** is a regional cheese that resembles Camembert.

Pastries

At carnival time, doughnuts are a festive treat, variously known as *frivoles* or *fiverolles* or *crottes d'âne* (donkey droppings!). At Easter, little tarts *(darioles)* are filled with a flan mixture made from milk and eggs. Gingerbread is still made with a traditional recipe from the 13C.

In Reims, many varieties of delicate biscuits are served with Champagne: *massepains, croquignols, bouchons*.

In the Ardennes region, crêpes are called *vautes* or *tantimolles*; hard sugar biscuits are served with coffee; soft cakes served at wedding banquets were sometimes baked with a silver ring inside, for luck.

WINE AND CHAMPAGNE
VINS D'ALSACE

The vineyards of Alsace stretch from Thann to Wissembourg, over about 100km/60mi, but the main area to explore starts just south of Marlenheim, where travellers join the famous **Route des Vins**. The route meanders through a sea of grape vines and many wine-growing villages; everything is devoted to the production of wine.

Varieties

The wines of Alsace are identified, not by geographical area, but by grape variety. **Riesling** is a bright star in the constellation of white grape varieties. Most of the wine produced in the valley of the River Rhine is made from these grapes, which create a sophisticated, subtle bouquet.

Gewürztraminer is a heady, fragrant wine with an intense bouquet. The wine to choose if you wish to quench a thirst is **Sylvaner**, dry and light, with a fruity note.

Pinot blanc wines are generally considered well-balanced, with a fresh and supple character.

Pinot gris, also called **Tokay Pinot gris**, is a distinguished grape which produces opulent, full-bodied wine.

The flavour of fresh grapes has a strong presence in **Muscat d'Alsace**.

The only red variety is **Pinot noir**. These grapes have grown in popularity in recent years, and go into fruity rosé or red wines marked by a cherry aroma and taste. The red wines are firmer and more complex than the rosés.

Edelzwicker is the name given to the only wine made from a blend of varieties, including the less noble Chasselas.

Vin d'Alsace is an *Appellation d'Origine Contrôlée*, and is always bottled in the region of production. It is generally served in a round glass with a thin green stem. Most Alsace wines are best when fairly young and should be chilled.

Before a meal, a sparkling Crémant or sweet Muscat is a good apéritif; Sylvaner goes well with assorted cold cuts served as a starter. Riesling or Pinot accompany fish, fowl, meats and, of course, *choucroute*. Flavourful cheeses and desserts do well with the rich aroma of Gewürztraminer.

Eaux-de-vie

Cherries, mirabelles and raspberries are used to make sweet liqueurs: Kirsche in the Vosges, *quetsch* and mirabelle in Lorraine. Clear raspberry liqueur is served in a large glass to increase the pleasure of the aroma. The Musée des Eaux-de-vie in Lapoutroie (10km/6mi northwest of Kaysersberg, *www.musee-eaux-de-vie.com*) shows how these liqueurs were traditionally made.

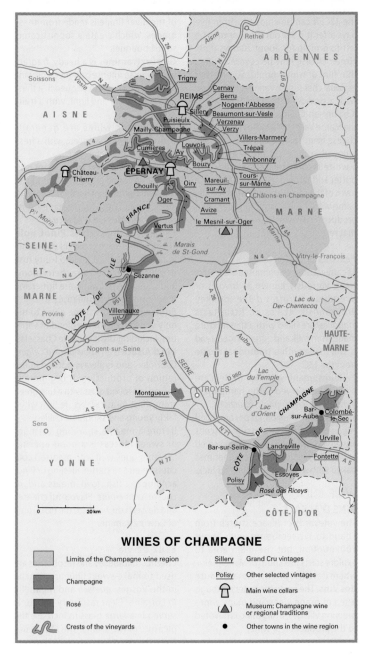

WINES OF CHAMPAGNE

Limits of the Champagne wine region	_Sillery_	Grand Cru vintages
Champagne	_Polisy_	Other selected vintages
Rosé		Main wine cellars
Crests of the vineyards		Museum: Champagne wine or regional traditions
		Other towns in the wine region

CHAMPAGNE

A long and prestigious past

When Roman soldiers arrived in the Champagne region, grapes were already cultivated on the slopes. The first bishops of Reims encouraged this activity. Vineyards flourished around monasteries and the many travellers attending trade fairs or coming to the royal court boosted sales. Even the

A Merry Widow

Veuve Clicquot-Ponsardin is one of France's best-known and best-selling brands of Champagne. The eponymous origin is indeed a Grande Dame, Nicole-Barbe Ponsardin. In 1798, she married François Clicquot in a Champagne cellar (the churches had not yet been restored for worship after the Revolution). He left her a widow eight years later. Twenty-seven years old, with a baby daughter and almost no experience in the trade, she took over the family Champagne house, and ran the business until her death in 1866.

She revolutionised the art of blending (assemblage) when she developed the technique known as *remuage*. Previously, the wine had to be decanted into new bottles after the second fermentation, an inefficient process that was necessary to remove the sediment, but which reduced precious effervescence. Nowadays, using her technique, the bottles are twisted and tilted so that the dregs settle around the cork, which can then be popped open briefly. A small bit of wine is removed (dégorgement), then the bottle is quickly topped off.

"Champagne," wrote Madame de Pompadour, "is the only wine which leaves a woman beautiful after drinking it. It gives brilliance to the eyes without flushing the face." Good news for merrymakers.

popes favoured Champagne, starting with Urbain II, a native of the region. During the Renaissance, Pope Leo X had his own vineyard to keep him supplied. St Bernard, in Clairvaux, introduced the arbanne stock, which created the basis for Côte des Bars vintages.

Champagne has been called the 'nectar of the gods' and the 'wine of kings'. Henri IV, impatient with the Spanish ambassador's recitation of his master's aristocratic titles, interrupted him by saying, "Tell His Majesty the King of Spain, Castille and Aragon that Henri, lord of Ay and Gonesse, is master of the greatest vineyards in the world...".

At that time, Champagne was a still wine with only a hint of sparkle. That sparkle caught the eye of **Dom Pérignon**, who carefully studied the wine's characteristics and developed blending. The popularity of Champagne grew throughout the centuries, admired and imbibed by kings and their courts and figures of romance such as Mme de Pompadour and Casanova.

Political revolutions came and went, but Champagne remained. Napoleon was a faithful client, and Talleyrand plied the participants at the Congress of Vienna with Champagne in hopes of gaining a better settlement. The Prince of Wales, the future Edward VII, speaking of the Most Honourable Order of the Bath, is reputed to have said, "I'd rather have a bath of Champagne".

The Vineyards

The vineyards cover about 30 000ha, in the *départements* of Marne, Aube and Aisne. The most famous areas of production are the Côte des Blancs, the Marne valley and the Montagne de Reims, where the great vintages originate. The grapes grow half way up the limestone slopes, above the chalky bedrock and in the sandy clay soil of the Côte de l'Île de France. The only varieties allowed are Pinot noir, Pinot Meunier and Chardonnay. The vines are planted close together and pruned low.

A delicate process

Champagne is created through a series of carefully executed steps which take place in the vineyards and in the cellars, where a steady temperature of about 10°C must be maintained.

Harvest

In October, bunches of grapes are picked and set down in flat trays; they are then sorted and carried to the press.

Pressing

The entire grapes are pressed, which results in a white must, even when dark grapes are used. Only the juice

Storing the bottles at an angle, Champagne Ruinart, Reims

obtained by the first pressing (about 2 550l from 4 000kg of grapes) is used to make true Champagne wine.

Fermentation
The juice is stored in barrels or vats and fermentation is under way by Christmas.

Vintage and blend
In the spring, the maître de chais creates the vintage by blending different still wines, produced by various vineyards in various years. Each Champagne house has its own vintage that respects quality standards. Blendings include wines from the Montagne de Reims (hearty, full-bodied), the Marne valley (fruity, aromatic wines), the Côte des Blancs (fresh, elegant wines) and the Côte des Bars. Red and white grapes are used in proportions that may vary but are generally about 2/3 to 1/3. Blanc de Blancs sparkling wine is made with only white grapes. Champagne labels bear the vintage year when the blending includes only wines of the same year.

Second fermentation and foam
The second fermentation is brought about by adding sugar and selected yeasts to the wine. The wine is drawn and put in very thick bottles that withstand pressure. Under the effects of the yeast (in the form of powder collected from the grape skins), the sugar is transformed into alcohol or carbonised into gas which, when the bottle is uncorked, creates foam. The bottles are set on racks in a cellar for 15 months to three years or more.

Settling and removing sediment
Over time, a deposit forms and must be eliminated. It is forced to settle in the bottle neck by storing the bottles at an angle, upside down. Each day, one person alone gives a slight turn (⅛ rotation) to as many as 40 000 bottles, and adjusts them for gradually increasing verticality. After five or six weeks, the bottle is fully vertical and all of the sediment has settled around the cork. The cork is then removed and the sediment with it. This process is called *dégorgement*. The bottle is topped off with more of the same wine, which may have had sugar added to make the final product sweeter.

Finishing
The corks need to be wired down to contain the pressure of the gas within; then the bottle can be labelled and shipped. Champagne will not improve any more in the bottle after three or four years and should be consumed.

Marketing
Nearly 120 Champagne houses, mostly family-owned, and many dating back to the 18C, produce 70% of all Champagne shipped, with the remaining 30% in the hands of récoltants-manipulants, who blend their own wine; there are a few cooperatives as well. Financial backing is necessary for successful operations, because Champagne must be stored and cared for for an average of three years before it can be marketed, thus involving keeping a lot of stock on hand. Every year, more and more Champagne leaves the region for sale elsewhere. Production of the region's sparkling wine accounts for around 4% of total French wine production, but because of its value generate about 33% of France's earnings from wine exports.

History

TIMELINE

PREHISTORIC INHABITANTS

Human settlements in Champagne and the Ardenne had developed into small villages by the Neolithic Era (4500–2000 BCE). By the Bronze Age (1800–750 BCE), the region had already established what would become a long tradition of metalworking.

BCE 58–52 Roman conquest. In Champagne and Ardenne, the people lent their support to Ceasar's troops. In Alsace, the Germanic tribes were forced to retreat to the east of the Rhine.

27 Under Emperor Augustus (27 BCE–14 CE), Champagne was part of the province of Belgium. A sophisticated civilisation developed under the *Pax Romana;* villas were built, trading centres grew and roads improved communication.
The area's thermal springs were appreciated for their curative powers.

CHRISTIANITY AND MONARCHY TAKE ROOT

CE 69–70 Following the death of Nero, the Roman Empire weakened. Assembly held in Reims.

3–5C Missionaries travelled the region; Germanic invasions: Alemanni, Vandals and Huns successively carried out raids.

486 The regions of the Meuse and Moselle came under the control of the Merovingian king Clovis, establishing a Frankish kingdom. While the **Franks** were not numerous, they became the ruling class of the territories conquered.

498 St Remi persuaded Clovis to convert on Christmas Day.

511 Death of Clovis. Champagne was divided into incoherent parcels, constituting several small kingdoms.

683 Étichon, father of St Odile (♿*see p101*), ruled as Duke of Alsace. After his reign, the land was divided into Nordgau and Sundgau, each ruled by a count.

774 Charles Martel seized church property for the secular state. At the same time, the region was organised into parishes, and the power and authority of the church grew stronger; a balance of powers developed.

800 The title of emperor was revived and conferred upon **Charlemagne**. The

Tympanum on the north façade of Cathédrale Notre-Dame in Reims depicting Clovis being baptised

©Xavier de Tarade/iStockphoto.com

Holy Roman Empire was a complex of lands in Western and Central Europe ruled by Frankish then German kings for ten centuries (until renunciation of the imperial title in 1806). The empire and the papacy were the two most important institutions of Western Europe through the Middle Ages.

816 Louis I (known as The Pious and also The Debonair), son of Charlemagne and Hildegarde the Swabian, was crowned emperor in Reims by Pope Stephen IV; a forceful French monarchy began to take shape.

817 Louis I, in accordance with his father's will, divided Charlemagne's realm among three sons from his first marriage: Bavaria to Louis the German, Aquitaine to Pepin, and Lothair he named co-emperor and heir.

829 Louis' second marriage to Judith of Bavaria had produced a son (Charles the Bald), to whom he granted the realm then known as Alemannia. From this time on, the sons formed and dissolved alliances, overthrew their father twice, and territories were passed back and forth or seized outright by the brothers who continued fighting for decades after their father's death.

839 With Pepin dead, another attempt at partition divided the empire between Lothair and Charles, with Bavaria left in the hands of Louis the German. The following year, Louis I died.

843 Under the Treaty of Verdun, Lothair received *Francia Media* (today, parts of Belgium, the Netherlands, western Germany, eastern France, Switzerland and much of Italy); Louis the German received *Francia Orientalis* (land east of the Rhine); Charles received *Francia Occidentalis* (the remainder of present-day France). This treaty marked the dissolution of Charlemagne's empire, and foreshadowed the formation of the modern countries of Western Europe.

870 Lothair left the land of Lotharingia (Greater Lorraine) to a son (Lothair II), who died without a legitimate heir. By the Treaty of Meersen, Charles received western Lorraine and Louis the German saw great expansion of his territories west of the Rhine. The region today known as Alsace remained separate from the rest of the French kingdom for the next seven centuries.

911 Louis IV died, the last of the east **Frankish Carolingians**. The many dukes controlling the feudal states in the region elected Conrad, duke of Franconia, as successor; he was followed by Henry (918) and thus began more than a century of **Saxon** rule in the region.

959 Lotharingia was divided into two parts: Upper Lorraine (Ardennes, Moselle valley, Upper Meuse valley) and Lower Lorraine (northern part of the realm, including parts of modern Belgium and the Netherlands).

Late 9C and 10C Raids by northmen destabilised Charles' reign; power struggles continued as rival dynasties emerged and the feudal system took hold of the people. In France, the Carolingian dynasty waned.

THE MIDDLE AGES

987 Hugues Capet was crowned, the first of 13 French kings in the **Capetian** dynasty, which lasted until 1328.

11C The domains of Tardenois, Château-Thierry, Provins, Reims, Châlons and Troyes, through marriage agreements, came under the authority of the counts of Blois (the king's immediate vassals, but also his most dangerous rivals).

1098 Robert de Molesmes founded the abbey at Cîteaux.

25 June 1115 Clairvaux abbey was founded by St Bernard.

1125–52 Thibaud II, count of Blois, strengthened the economy by creating sound currency and cashing in on trade between Italy and the Netherlands. Communication routes improved, many trade fairs (Lagny, Provins, Sézanne, Troyes, Bar-sur-Aube) were the meeting place for Nordic and Mediterranean merchants.

1015 On the site of a temple to Hercules, a Romanesque cathedral was begun in Strasbourg. St Bernard said Mass there in 1145, before it was destroyed by fire.

1152 French King Louis VII repudiated Eleanor of Aquitaine, who later married Henry Plantagenet, bringing western France under the English crown. For three centuries, the French and English remained 'hereditary enemies'.

1176 The new cathedral at Strasbourg was begun, inspired by the Gothic style.

1179–1223 Philippe Auguste reigned as the 'king of France' rather than the 'king of the Franks'.

1210 Construction started on the cathedral at Reims.

1284 The brilliant court and unified counties of Champagne joined the French crown with the marriage of Jeanne, Countess of Champagne and Navarre, to Philippe le Bel.

1337 Beginning of the Hundred Years' War.

14C In Alsace, ten cities formed the Decapole, to resist the excesses of the feudal system; gradually these cities (Strasbourg, Colmar, Haguenau, and others) freed themselves from their overlords.

1429 Joan of Arc, aged 17, led the French armies to victory over the English at Orléans, thus opening the way for the coronation of Charles VII at Reims.

1434 **Gutenberg** settled in Strasbourg and formed a partnership with three local men for the development of a secret invention. Their association ended acrimoniously in a court of law; in 1448, in Mainz, his printing press saw the light of day.

1480 The Upper Duchy of Lorraine (Lower Lorraine was no longer a unified duchy) united with Bar and Vaudémont, and became known as Lorraine.

THE RENAISSANCE

Late 15C After a century of strife in Champagne, trade flourished anew during the reign of Louis XI.

The Wars of Religion – 1562–1598

This 36-year-long crisis was marked by complex political as well as religious conflict. During the latter half of the 16C, the French monarchy was in poor shape to withstand the looming hegemony of Spain, with political life in chaos and debt reaching incredible dimensions. The stand taken on religion by Spain and Italy and by the Protestant countries on the other was missing in the France of Catherine de' Medici's regency, where a policy of appeasement applied.

The nobility took advantage of the situation, seeking to bolster their power base in the provinces and, under cover of religion, to grasp the reins of government. The Catholic League was formed by the Guise and Montmorency families, supported by Spain and opposed by the Bourbon, Condé and Coligny factions, Huguenots all, with English backing.

Though historians distinguish eight wars separated by periods of peace or relative tranquillity, the troubles were continuous: in the country, assassinations, persecutions and lawlessness; at court, intrigues and volte-faces. Actual warfare, threatened ever since the Amboise Conspiracy, began at Wassy in 1562, following a massacre of Protestants. Dreux, Nîmes, Chartres, Longjumeau, Jarnac, Montcontour, St-Lô, Valognes, Coutras, Arques, Ivry follow in bloody succession.

The Peace of St-Germain in 1570 demonstrated a general desire for reconciliation, but only two years later came the St Bartholomew's Day Massacre, in which some 20 000 Huguenots died.

The States General were convened at Blois at the request of those who were opposed to the centralisation of power into royal hands. Fearful of the power of Duke Henri of Guise, head of the Catholic League and the kingdom's best military commander, King Henri III had him assassinated in the château at Blois one cold morning in December 1588, only to be cut down himself the following year.

This left the succession open for the Huguenot Henry of Navarre, the future Henri IV. By formally adopting the Catholic faith and by promulgating the Edict of Nantes, this able ruler succeeded in rallying all loyal Frenchmen to his standard.

The Wars of Religion affected Alsace with refugees and political intrigues, but it was not until France entered the Thirty Years' War that the impact of religious conflict really hit Alsace. The French army ravaged the region while attempting to cut off Spanish supply roads crossing from Italy and the Alps toward the Netherlands. The region was invaded many times during the War, and suffered constantly until the Peace of Westphalia (1648) ended the War and stabilised European religious conflicts.

1507	In St-Dié, the *Cosmographiae Introductio*, a work by several scholars, first gave the name America to the continent discovered by Christopher Columbus, in honour of the navigator Amerigo Vespucci.	**1562**	The massacre at Wassy signalled the beginning of the Wars of Religion in Champagne, which devastated the region for the following century (*see box*).

1515-59   Uprisings against the house of Austria in Mézières, Ste-Menehould, St-Dizier and Vitry.

1525   The revolt of peasants (*Rustauds*) ended with their massacre in the town of Saverne.

THE UNIFICATION OF LORRAINE AND ALSACE WITH FRANCE

1552–53   Henri II occupied Metz, Toul and Verdun, defeating Charles V.

1572   The St Bartholomew's Day massacre undermined the power of Protestants in the regions of Champagne and Ardenne.

1635–37 An outbreak of plague in Lorraine killed half of the population; the Thirty Years' War, plague and famine ravaged the entire region.

1648–53 The period was marked by serious unrest caused by the far-reaching peasant revolt known as *La Fronde,* and persistent Spanish offensives in Champagne.

1678 The Nijmegen peace agreement confirmed the unification of Alsace and France.

1681 Louis XIV revoked the independence of Strasbourg.

1738 **Stanislas Leszczynski**, former king of Poland, father-in-law of Louis XV, was named duke of Lorraine.

1766 After the death of Stanislas, Lorraine was definitively annexed by France.

REVOLUTION AND THE TRANSFORMATION OF EUROPE

1785 Napoleon Bonaparte became an officer of the French army.

1789 The French Revolution toppled the king, proclaimed the rights of man and destroyed the Ancien Régime.

1791 Louis XVI and his family were arrested in Varennes-en-Argonne.

1792 Rouget de Lisle sang the *Marseillaise,* the future French national anthem, in Strasbourg.

1794 Near Saverne, Chappe's telegraph began operation.

1798 Mulhouse, the last independent town in Alsace, united with France.

1799 Napoleon instituted a military dictatorship and named himself First Consul.

1804–15 Napoleon had himself crowned emperor after victories in Austria and Russia, and successfully consolidated most of Europe as his empire until about 1810.
The revived Allied coalition and his defeat at Waterloo led to his final exile.

1814–15 The Congress of Vienna reorganised Europe after the Napoleonic Wars. It began in September 1814, five months after Napoleon's first abdication, and completed its 'Final Act' just before Waterloo and the end of the Hundred Days of his return to power.

1815–71 France was ruled by a limited monarchy, with the exception of a brief Republican period (1848–52).

1870–71 At the end of the Franco-Prussian War, Alsace and part of Lorraine were in German hands.

1885 Pasteur administered the first rabies vaccine to a young Alsatian shepherd.

1906 Captain Dreyfus, a native of Mulhouse, was reinstated and decorated with the Legion of Honour, the conclusion of the scandalous 'affair' of 1894.

THE WORLD AT WAR

1914–18 The violent conflicts of the First World War lasted four years; at the end, Alsace and Lorraine were once again in French territory.

1928 Construction of the Grand Canal of Alsace.

1930–40 Construction of the Maginot Line.

1940–44 Germany invaded France; Alsace and Lorraine occupied.

Late 1944 Lorraine liberated by French and Allied armies.

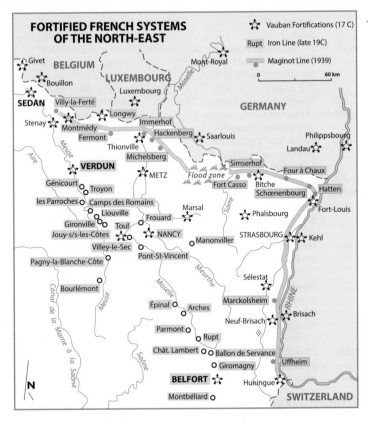

FORTIFIED FRENCH SYSTEMS OF THE NORTH-EAST

☆ Vauban Fortifications (17 C)
Rupt Iron Line (late 19C)
Maginot Line (1939)

0   60 km

BELGIUM
LUXEMBOURG
GERMANY
SWITZERLAND

Givet
Bouillon
SEDAN
Villy-la-Ferté
Stenay
Montmédy
Fermont
Thionville
Michelsberg
VERDUN
Génicourt
Troyon
les Parroches
Camps des Romains
Liouville
Gironville
Jouy-s/s-les-Côtes
Toul
Villey-le-Sec
Pagny-la-Blanche-Côte
Bourlémont
Épinal
Arches
Parmont
Rupt
Chât. Lambert
Ballon de Servance
Giromagny
BELFORT
Montbéliard
Mont-Royal
Luxembourg
Longwy
Immerhof
Hackenberg
Saarlouis
Simserhof
Four à Chaux
Philippsbourg
Landau
METZ
Flood zone
Fort Casso
Bitche
Schœnenbourg
Hatten
Fort-Louis
Marsal
Frouard
NANCY
Manonviller
Phalsbourg
STRASBOURG
Kehl
Pont-St-Vincent
Sélestat
Marckolsheim
Brisach
Neuf-Brisach
Uffheim
Huningue
Meuse
Aire
Canal de la Marne à la Saône
Saône
Meuse
Moselle
Meurthe
Sarre
Moselle
RHINE

N

1945 Final German retreat from Alsace, Armistice signed in Reims.

1949 The Council of Europe established headquarters in Strasbourg.

1950 Formation of the Coal and Steel cooperative between France and Germany.

1952 Dr Albert Schweitzer, of Kaysersberg was awarded the Nobel Peace Prize.

1963 Canalisation of the River Moselle.

1962–99 The decline of the area's traditional heavy industries, notably Mines and metalworks meant some 178 000 workers left the region to find employment elsewhere.

1974 Works were completed on the Rhine in Alsace, with the inauguration of the hydroelectric plant at Gambsheim.

1976 Paris–Metz–Strasbourg motorway opened.

1977 The Palais de l'Europe (European Economic Community) buildings were inaugurated in Strasbourg.

1991 Creation of ARTE (*Association Relative à la Télévision Européenne*), a joint Franco-German TV station based in Strasbourg.

1993 Strasbourg confirmed as seat of the European Parliament.

1995-96 Nuclear power plant Chooz B begins operating on the Meuse.

1999 Total solar eclipse observed in Reims.

1 500th anniversary of the baptism of Clovis.
The striking New European Union Parliament Louise Weiss building opens in Strasbourg.

2001 Provins, Town of Medieval Fairs, is placed on the UNESCO World Heritage List, *see p396*.

2004 Closure of potassium mines with a loss of 2 000 jobs.

2007 The new high-speed *TGV Est Européen* train service cuts train times between Strasbourg and Paris to 2h20.

2009 Rioting in Strasbourg before the 60th anniversary NATO summit forces several dignitaries and heads of state to cancel or change plans.

2012 François Hollande, who was born in Rouen, is elected President of France.

2016 On 1 January, the number of mainland regions in France was reduced from 22 to 13.

2017 Emmanuel Macron is elected President of France, representing his "La République En Marche!" centrist political party. He beat the far-right National Front's Marine Le Pen. He appointed Le Havre mayor Édouard Philippe to be Prime Minister. His party wins an overall majority in parliamentary elections.

THE FRANCO-PRUSSIAN WAR

From July 1870 to May 1871, the war also known as the Franco-German War came to mark the end of French hegemony on the continent and formed the basis for the Prussian Empire.

Napoleon III's ambitious plans appeared to Prussian chancellor Otto von Bismark as an opportunity to unite northern and southern German states in a confederation against the French. Within four weeks, French troops had been effectively bottled up in the fortress at Metz. The rest of the army, under Marshal Mac-Mahon and accompanied by Napoleon, was surrounded and trapped at Sedan on 31 August. By 2 September, they had surrendered. French resistance fought the desperate odds under a new government of national defence, which had assumed power and deposed the emperor on 4 September 1870, establishing the Third Republic. With Paris under siege, negotiations were stalled while Bismarck demanded Alsace and Lorraine. Léon Gambetta, a provisional government leader, organised new armies after escaping from Paris in a balloon. Despite their valiant efforts, and the Paris insurrection which declared the independence of the **Commune de Paris**, capitulation was at hand. The Treaty of Frankfurt was signed on 10 May 1871: Germany annexed all of Alsace and most of Lorraine, with Metz; France had to pay a heavy indemnity. Thus French influence on German states came to a halt and the Prussian domination of Germany was ensured.

For the next 40 years, until the First World War, an uneasy peace held sway as further consequences were felt: the papacy lost power and Italian troops entered Rome; the Russian government repudiated the Treaty of Paris and began an aggressive campaign in Eastern Europe.

THE FIRST WORLD WAR (1914–18)

The Germans planned a six-week campaign to conquer France by way of an invasion of Belgium and a northern attack, bypassing France's solidly defended eastern flank. Once victory in France had been achieved, the plan called for transporting German troops to the Russian front, where the northern giant would be beaten in a few short months.

AUGUST–SEPTEMBER 1914

French troops crossed the border on 7 August and entered Mulhouse the following day, but had to withdraw to Belfort under the enemy's counter-

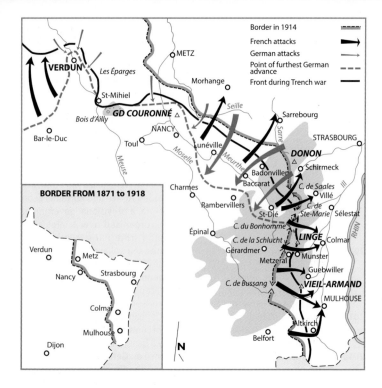

Border in 1914
French attacks
German attacks
Point of furthest German advance
Front during Trench war

BORDER FROM 1871 to 1918

attack. On 19 August, after grim combat, Mulhouse was captured anew and the Germans retreated towards the Rhine. Preparing an offensive, the French took control of mountain passes in the Vosges. Meanwhile, on 14 August, the First and Second French Armies had penetrated occupied Lorraine.

An assault launched on 20 August was met with such a violence of firepower that the French troops were decimated and forced to pull back to the Meurthe. The defensive line between Badonviller and Nancy formed a funnel shape, with the town of Charmes at the narrow end. The Germans took advantage of this position to attack Charmes, but met with resistance. From 26 August to 9 September they brought their force to bear on the eastern front, the line of the Vosges towards Upper Meurthe and on to Nancy. Yet German commander **Moltke** spread his infantry too thin, and hesitation cost him the **Battle of the Marne** (5–10 September 1914) along with his

military command. Marshal **Von Kluck** pushed the German troops towards the Seine. For the French, **Joffre** and **Gallieni** attempted a bold attack on the German's right flank. Four thousand reinforcement troops were carried to the front in the famous **Marne taxis**. British soldiers were able to drive into the opening thus created in the German line, forcing a retreat as far as the Aisne valley. A terrible war of attrition settled in along the front from the Jura mountains to the North Sea, through the heart of Alsace and Lorraine.

TRENCH WARFARE (1915–18)

After the Battle of the Marne the German position stabilised along the pre-war border in Lorraine, the Vosges and Alsace. Fierce localised combat pitted the armies against each other as they strove to take and hold strategic positions (Les Éparges, Ailly woods, Le Linge, Le Vieil-Armand). In February 1916, the Germans concentrated their efforts on **Verdun**; the stakes were high

regions of France after the first war. This siege mentality, coupled with the old guard's refusal to modernise offensive and defensive weapons or to develop new strategies, proved poor preparation for the onslaught to come. In May 1940, a German offensive drove the Dutch to surrender within days. Meanwhile, armoured units made their way through the supposedly impenetrable Ardennes Forest – simply bypassing the Maginot Line, France's illusory defence. By 20 May, the Germans had reached the coast. Not until D-Day, 6 June 1944 was the Norman peninsula wrested from German occupation by American, British and Canadian troops.

As the Allies advanced to liberate France however, on 16 December 1944 the Germans launched the **Ardennes Offensive**, better known as the **Battle of the Bulge**. Their plan was to split the British and American lines (causing a bulge on the battle map, which gave it the popular title) then encircle and destroy them.

During one of the coldest, snowiest winters the area had known this came to be one of the fiecest battles of the war, fought between half a million Germans, 600 000 US troops and around 55 000 British. It was one of the greatest tank battles of the war. By the time it finished a month later on 15 January 1945, with victory for the Allied Forces, there were 100 000 German casualties (killed, wounded or captured), and 81 000 American casualties (23 554 captured, 19 000 killed) – the bloodiest campaign the USA had ever fought up to that point. The Battle of the Bulge was also renowned for its brutality, culminating in the **Malmedy Massacre**, when around 86 American soldiers

as the site became a giant battlefield which was to determine the outcome of the war.

The **Second Battle of the Marne** began with a German incursion in June 1918; Foch led the French forces in powerful resistance. Under pressure from all sides, the Germans fell back to the so-called Hindenburg Line. On 26 September of the same year, Marshal **Foch** launched a general offensive, which finally brought about German defeat and the Armistice of 11 November 1918, executed at Rethondes.

THE SECOND WORLD WAR (1939–45)

The Second World War was in ways a continuation of the disputes left unresolved at the end of the First World War. France expected that if another war occurred, it would resemble the last one, and so built up a continuous defensive front, the Maginot Line, which also responded to the very low demographics of the eastern

Desirable Location

Due to the geography of Alsace-Lorraine as part of the greater industrialised Rhine valley, Nazi war leadership kept close watch on the region and clung to it until late in the war. There was significant destruction of historical monuments during the war; the prominent synagogue of Strasbourg was destroyed by Germans, and Allied bombing toward the end of the occupation damaged urbanised parts of Alsace, particularly Strasbourg. The Cathedral and many medieval and ancient sites were spared.

were murdered – the worst atrocity committed against American troops during the war in Europe.

With the last major Axis offensive overcome the Allied armies raced eastward and northward: Paris was

French 2nd Armoured Division liberated Strasbourg on the 24th November 1944

© Art Media/age fotostock

liberated on 25 August; Verdun at the end of the month. Nancy and Épinal followed in mid September. The fierce German defence did not yield in Metz until 22 November. On 1 January 1945, the Germans rallied and re-occupied Strasbourg. Eventually the Wehrmacht was forced over the last bridge still under its control, at Chalampé, on 9 February. German capitulation was marked by the signature of the Armistice at Reims on 7 May 1945.

EUROPEAN PEACE AND UNIFICATION

On 9 May 1950 Robert Schuman (a former French foreign minister, born in Alsace-Lorraine) proposed the idea of the European Coal and Steel Community (ECSC). Schuman's declaration was inspired by Jean Monnet's idea of "building Europe" step by step. Six States laid the foundations: Belgium, France, Germany, Italy, Luxembourg and The Netherlands. By 1993, the Member States numbered 12, and the Treaty on European Union came into force.

The **European Union**, founded to promote peace and economic stability, freedom of movement, and a unified approach to problems of security, defence, and social welfare, operates through Parliament, which meets in **Strasbourg**, but also other bodies: the Commission makes proposals for European legislation and action; the Council of the European Union is made up of one minister for each Member State government and for each subject; the European Council decides broad policy lines for Community policy and for matters of foreign and security policy and justice; the Court of Justice is the supreme court of the European Union. Among the main aims of the Union, the goal of a single European currency is a reality in many countries, and the euro is now the currency used by banking and financial institutions in most EU nations, and entirely replaced French francs. The UK never adopted the euro, and in 2016 voted in a referendum to leave the European Union, a decision that will take effect from March 2019.

Art and Culture

ABC OF ARCHITECTURE

Religious architecture

I. Ground plan of a church

Axial chapel: in churches which are not dedicated to the Virgin this chapel, in the main axis of the building, is often consecrated to the Virgin (Lady Chapel)

Ambulatory: in pilgrimage churches the aisles were extended round the chancel, forming the ambulatory, to allow the faithful to file past the relics

Chancel, nearly always facing east towards Jerusalem

Arm of the transept, often extending outward

Bay: transverse section of the nave between two pillars

Chevet

Radiating or apsidal chapel

Sanctuary

Transept chapel

Transept crossing

Side chapel

Nave

Side aisles

Narthex

Porch

II. Cross-section of a church

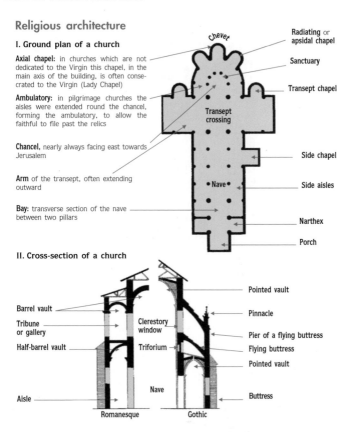

Barrel vault

Tribune or gallery

Half-barrel vault

Aisle

Clerestory window

Triforium

Nave

Romanesque

Pointed vault

Pinnacle

Pier of a flying buttress

Flying buttress

Pointed vault

Buttress

Gothic

III. MÉZIÈRES – Notre-Dame-de-l'Espérance Basilica (15 C)

Keystone pendentive: characteristic of late or Flamboyant Gothic period, embellishments, added in the Renaissance

Lierne: a short, intermediate rib

Tierceron: an intermediate rib between the main ribs

Diagonal rib

Transverse arch: reinforcing arch under a vault

Transverse rib

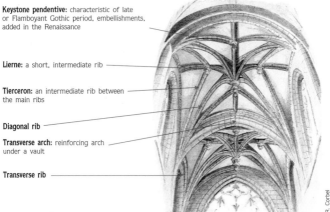

R. Corbel

IV. MARMOUTIER – Romanesque façade of St-Étienne (*c*1140)

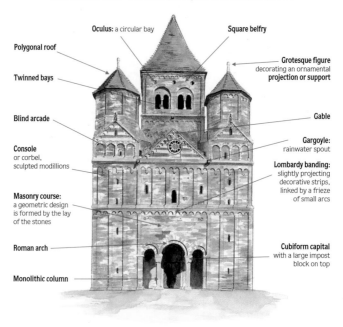

Oculus: a circular bay

Square belfry

Polygonal roof

Grotesque figure
decorating an ornamental
projection or support

Twinned bays

Blind arcade

Gable

Console
or corbel,
sculpted modillions

Gargoyle:
rainwater spout

Lombardy banding:
slightly projecting
decorative strips,
linked by a frieze
of small arcs

Masonry course:
a geometric design
is formed by the lay
of the stones

Roman arch

Cubiform capital
with a large impost
block on top

Monolithic column

V. REIMS – Chevet of the cathedral (1211-1260)

The cathedral in Reims can be compared to Chartres. Both are great works of Gothic architecture, which reached an apogee in Champagne and the Ile-de-France region between the late 12C and mid-13C.

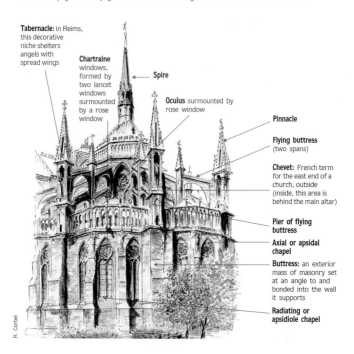

Tabernacle: in Reims, this decorative niche shelters angels with spread wings

Chartraine windows, formed by two lancet windows surmounted by a rose window

Spire

Oculus surmounted by rose window

Pinnacle

Flying buttress (two spans)

Chevet: French term for the east end of a church, outside (inside, this area is behind the main altar)

Pier of flying buttress

Axial or apsidal chapel

Buttress: an exterior mass of masonry set at an angle to and bonded into the wall it supports

Radiating or apsidiole chapel

R. Corbel

VI. Strasbourg – Central façade of Notre-Dame cathedral (12-15C)

The abundant detail of Flamboyant Gothic is evident in the central doorway, richly sculpted and crowned with openwork gables.

Gable: decorative, vertical triangle above certain doorways, here incorporating openwork

Pinnacle

Great rose window, made up of sixteen geminated (split) petals

Sculpted **rose** cornerpieces

Embrasure embellished with statues

Arch: a curved construction which spans an opening; a series of arches forms the **archivolt**

Jamb shaft: vertical member forming part of the jamb of a door

Bronze door leaf

Tympanum made of four historiated bands

Band sculpted ornamental strip

Archivolt: the series of arches

Upright post or bearing shaft of a portal, generally a statue is bonded to it

R. Corbel

85

VII. MOUZON – Interior of the Abbey church (1195-c1240)

The elevation of the nave embraces four storeys (arcades, gallery, Triforium, clerestory windows), typical of primitive Gothic art (second half of the 12C).

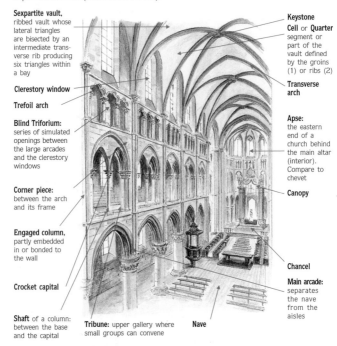

Sexpartite vault, ribbed vault whose lateral triangles are bisected by an intermediate transverse rib producing six triangles within a bay

Clerestory window

Trefoil arch

Blind Triforium: series of simulated openings between the large arcades and the clerestory windows

Corner piece: between the arch and its frame

Engaged column, partly embedded in or bonded to the wall

Crocket capital

Shaft of a column: between the base and the capital

Tribune: upper gallery where small groups can convene

Nave

Keystone

Cell or **Quarter** segment or part of the vault defined by the groins (1) or ribs (2)

Transverse arch

Apse: the eastern end of a church behind the main altar (interior). Compare to chevet

Canopy

Chancel

Main arcade: separates the nave from the aisles

VIII. THANN – Choir stalls in St-Thiébaut (14C-early 16C)

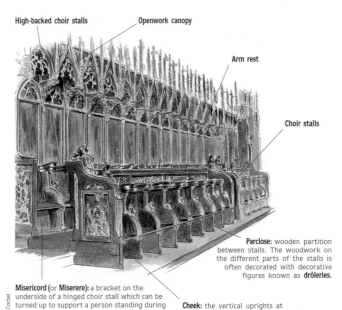

High-backed choir stalls

Openwork canopy

Arm rest

Choir stalls

Parclose: wooden partition between stalls. The woodwork on the different parts of the stalls is often decorated with decorative figures known as **drôleries.**

Misericord (or **Miserere**): a bracket on the underside of a hinged choir stall which can be turned up to support a person standing during long services (from the Latin for "compassion")

Cheek: the vertical uprights at the end of a row of stalls

R. Corbel

Civil architecture

IX. SAVERNE – Katz House (1605-1668), no 76, Grand'Rue

Half-timbered houses, numerous in Alsace, illustrate the skill of local carpenters, especially between the 17-19C.

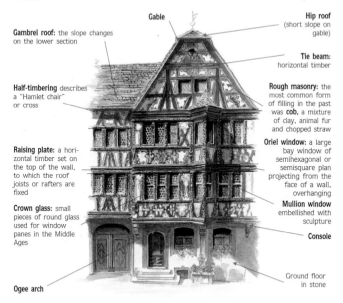

Gable

Hip roof (short slope on gable)

Gambrel roof: the slope changes on the lower section

Tie beam: horizontal timber

Half-timbering describes a "Hamlet chair" or cross

Rough masonry: the most common form of filling in the past was **cob**, a mixture of clay, animal fur and chopped straw

Raising plate: a horizontal timber set on the top of the wall, to which the roof joists or rafters are fixed

Oriel window: a large bay window of semihexagonal or semisquare plan projecting from the face of a wall, overhanging

Crown glass: small pieces of round glass used for window panes in the Middle Ages

Mullion window embellished with sculpture

Console

Ogee arch

Ground floor in stone

X. LUNÉVILLE – Château (18C)

Also known as "Petit-Versailles", this château was designed by the architect Germain Boffrand.

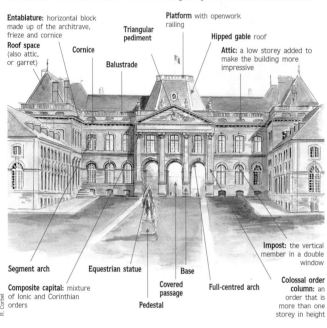

Entablature: horizontal block made up of the architrave, frieze and cornice

Roof space (also attic, or garret)

Cornice

Triangular pediment

Platform with openwork railing

Hipped gable roof

Attic: a low storey added to make the building more impressive

Balustrade

Impost: the vertical member in a double window

Segment arch

Equestrian statue

Base

Composite capital: mixture of Ionic and Corinthian orders

Covered passage

Full-centred arch

Pedestal

Colossal order column: an order that is more than one storey in height

R. Corbel

XI. CONTREXÉVILLE – Thermal springs gallery and pavilion

The design expresses the architectural eclecticism typical of spa town; neo-Byzantine style predominates.

Drum embellished with decorative brick designs

Cupola: metal frame is pierced to let light in

Doric capitals

Concentric peristyle

Circular pavilion above the spring

Large **bay windows**

Gallery-portico

Fluted columns with mosaic embellishments

Military architecture

XII. HAUT-KOENIGSBOURG – Feudal castle rebuilt in the early 20C

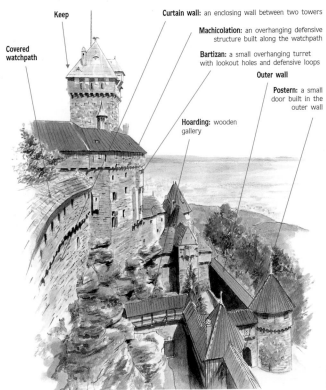

Keep

Covered watchpath

Curtain wall: an enclosing wall between two towers

Machicolation: an overhanging defensive structure built along the watchpath

Bartizan: a small overhanging turret with lookout holes and defensive loops

Outer wall

Postern: a small door built in the outer wall

Hoarding: wooden gallery

R. Corbel

XIII. NEUF-BRISACH – Stronghold (1698-1703)

The polygonal stronghold was developed in the early 16C, as firearms became more common in warfare: the cannon mounted on one structure covered the "blind spot" of the neighbouring position. This stronghold was built by Vauban, opposite the formidable Breisach, handed back to the Hapsburgs under the Treaty of Ryswick (1697).

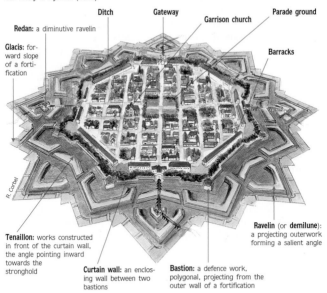

Ditch **Gateway** **Parade ground**

Garrison church

Redan: a diminutive ravelin

Glacis: forward slope of a fortification

Barracks

R. Corbel

Ravelin (or **demilune**): a projecting outerwork forming a salient angle

Tenaillon: works constructed in front of the curtain wall, the angle pointing inward towards the stronghold

Curtain wall: an enclosing wall between two bastions

Bastion: a defence work, polygonal, projecting from the outer wall of a fortification

Other architectural terms used in this guide

Ashlar	Hewn masonry or squared stones lain in regular courses, as distinguished from rubble work.
Bailey	Space enclosed by the outer walls of a castle (also: *ward*).
Barbican	Outwork of a medieval castle, often with a tower, defending a gate or bridge.
Bartizan	An overhanging battlemented corner turret, corbelled out; sometimes as grandiose as an overhanging gallery (illustration XII).
Battlements	Parapet of medieval fortifications, with a walkway for archers, protected by merlons, with embrasures between them.
Buttress	Vertical mass of masonry built against a wall, so strengthening it and resisting the pressure of a vaulted roof (illustration II).
Clerestory	Upper stage of an elevation, consisting of a range of tall windows (illustration VII).
Crenellation	The low segment of the alternating high and low segments of a battlement.
Donjon	French term for the castle *keep* (illustration XII).
Glacis	A bank sloping down from a castle which acts as a defence against invaders; broad, sloping naked rock or earth on which the attackers are completely exposed (illustration XIII).
Machicolation	In medieval castles, a row of openings below the projecting parapet though which missiles could be rained down upon the enemy.
Merlon	The high segment of the alternating high and low segments of a battlement.
Portcullis	A heavy timber or metal grill that protected the castle entrance and could be raised or lowered from within to block passage or to trap attackers.
Postern Gate	A side or less important gate into a castle; usually for peacetime use by pedestrians (illustration XII).
Rustication	Worked ashlar stone with beveled edges defining conspicuous joints.
Wicket	Person-sized door set into the main gate door.

ARCHITECTURE IN ALSACE

RELIGIOUS ARCHITECTURE

Romanesque churches

In Alsace, Carolingian influences persisted longer than elsewhere in France; the flowering of Romanesque art took place in the 12C, lagging a century behind the rest of the country.

Exterior

Most of the churches in Alsace are small or modest, and laid out in the form of a Latin cross with short lateral arms. The 11C church at Ottmarsheim still shows the Carolingian polygonal ground plan, inspired by the Palatine chapel in Aix-la-Chapelle (Aachen).

Among the distinctive local features, **tours lanternes** (lantern towers) are found above the transept crossing (Ste-Foy in Sélestat is a good example). **Belfries**, both square and round, often rise from the angle made by the main body of the church (chancel and nave) and the transept crossing.

The western façade, with or without a porch, is flanked by belfries several storeys high. The east end culminates in a semicircular apse; flattened chevets (Murbach) are the exception. The side walls, gables, apse and façade are embellished with Lombardy banding, slightly projecting decorative strips linked by a frieze of small arcs.

Interior

The architecture is ascetic; arcading and bays without decorative moulding are surmounted by a wall, with one or two windows that flare open wider on the inside. The chancel is not ringed by an ambulatory. Vaulting was not used until late in the 12C. The main supports are Romanesque arches that shape the ribbed vault. They rest on thick rectangular pillars flanked on four sides by engaged columns. The side aisles are covered with groined vaulting formed by the intersection of the long vault of the side aisle and the transverse vaults.

Decoration

The spare decoration is mostly found on doorways, in plain geometric patterns; only the church at Andlau has any interesting sculptures.

The **capitals**, the wide upper portion of columns supporting arches, are an important part of the architectural style. Ribs from more than one vault can rest on a single pillar. In Alsace, the Romanesque churches usually have very simple, cubic capitals, with little variety of sculpted forms – a few rare figures and some foliage.

Gothic churches

Gothic art in Alsace reached a rare degree of perfection: The cathedral in **Strasbourg** is proof enough. Many Gothic buildings, civil and religious, went up between the 13C and the 14C: in **Colmar**, the Unterlinden cloisters, St-Martin Church, the Koifhus (Customs House); in Wissembourg, St-Pierre-St-Paul; St-George in Sélestat, to name but a few. At the end of the 15C, Flamboyant Gothic appeared on the scene in **Thann** (St-Thiébaut) and Strasbourg (St-Laurent doorway on the cathedral).

During the 16C, while the Renaissance was influencing civil architecture, religious buildings remained true to the Gothic spirit. The churches in **Ammerschwihr** (16C) and **Molsheim** (16C–17C) reflect this well.

Traces of the **Renaissance** are more evident in charming private residences and admirable public buildings.

Classical style

In the 17C, a long period of trials and warfare halted nearly all construction of new civil and religious buildings. Under French authority, Alsace rebuilt and embellished monasteries.

Yet there are a few churches dating from this time, including St-Pierre in **Colmar** (Regency style), and Notre-Dame in **Guebwiller**, built by the abbots of Murbach on a strict Classical design.

Baroque influences are apparent in the abbey church at **Ebersmunster**, lavishly decorated with sculptures, mouldings and frescoes.

CIVIL ARCHITECTURE

Town halls

As early as the Middle Ages, Alsatian towns sought a degree of independence. Town halls were built to serve the municipal authorities, a symbol of power and an illustration of architectural preferences of the times.

The lovely town halls in **Ensisheim, Mulhouse** (the covered porch was inspired by Swiss buildings), **Obernai, Rouffach, Kaysersberg, Molsheim** and **Guebwiller** as well as the old town hall of Strasbourg (today the Chamber of Commerce), testify to the intensity of local politics.

Bourgeois and princely manors

Picturesque places like **Riquewihr, Kaysersberg**, the Petite France district of **Strasbourg** and Petite Venise in **Colmar** have a rich architectural heritage of traditional 16C–17C private residences. Overhanging elements mark the façade, and the upper storeys culminate in sharp points. Both stone and wood are used as building materials. During the Renaissance, many amusing details were added: fancy gables, wooden galleries around towers, wrought-iron work, sculpted or painted wooden panelling on the façade. The two most distinctive features of Alsatian manors built in the 15C and during the Renaissance are the gables and the oriel windows.

Gables perch ornately atop buildings. In Strasbourg, the Maison de l'Œuvre Notre-Dame is topped with a gable mounting squarely upwards like a set of stairs; in Colmar, curling scrolls adorn the sloping sides of the gable on the Maison des Têtes.

Oriel windows

These large bay windows with semi-hexagonal or semi-square plans project from the façade, creating an overhang, as on the Maison des Têtes. The oriel window provides a break in the uniformity of a façade and creates a lively play of light and shadow. For a building located on a narrow street, it can be a precious source of light, and

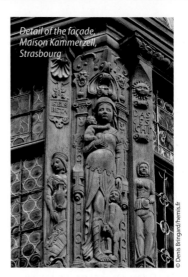

Detail of the façade, Maison Kammerzell, Strasbourg

© Denis Bringard/hemis.fr

a good vantage point for watching the comings and goings of the town. Prestigious residences built for the powerful lords, prelates and financiers in the 17C – once the devastating Thirty Years' War was past and Alsace was in the hands of Louis XIV – and the 18C are distinguished by the increase in French influence on the banks of the Rhine. While 18C residences do not have the imaginative style of Renaissance houses, they are admirable for their graceful balconies, delicate corbels and elegant bay windows, as well as the fine quality of stone.

The luxurious palaces of the Rohan family, in **Strasbourg** and **Saverne**, are splendid examples of Classical architecture.

MILITARY ARCHITECTURE

All along the Vosges hillsides, rising above the plain of Alsace, the vestiges of ancient fortresses and feudal keeps mark the horizon.

More recent vestiges also interest the visitor: magnificent ramparts built and renovated by Vauban; German defences put up between 1870 and 1914; concrete pillboxes and armoured towers from the above and below-ground works that made up the **Maginot Line**; numerous forts and blockhouses left from the Second World War.

Defensive castles

Sentinels in times of war, all of these castles have kept their proud bearing, even those that are little more than an isolated keep or a lone wall crumbling under moss. The reconstitution of the Haut-Kœnigsbourg castle, by the order of Kaiser Wilhelm II, was controversial from the outset. Still today, some prefer the romantic reverie of ruins to the academic demonstration of a pristine reconstruction.

Medieval walled cities

In the Middle Ages, towns and cities built fortifications to defend themselves from both feudal lords and enemies from abroad. A city would build a ring of protective walls, with strategically located towers and just a few gateways that could be closed up and protected. These gateways still stand in many towns (Porte Haute), and towers (Tour du Diable, Tour des Sorcières) mark the line of the old fortified wall.

ARCHITECTURE IN LORRAINE
RELIGIOUS ARCHITECTURE

Romanesque churches

The churches in Lorraine are mostly basilicas, often simplified to the extreme. The smaller churches have only a nave, a chancel and an apse. The doors are crowned with a semicircular tympanum, and the façades are sparsely decorated. Ribbed vaulting is common in Romanesque building. It was introduced in Lorraine in the last third of the 12C. Towers are generally square, and placed atop the square formed by the transept.

Among the most characteristic churches of this period, one is in Mont-Devant-Sassay; part of Notre-Dame de Verdun is also a good illustration of this style.

Gothic churches

Lorraine was slow moving from Romanesque to Gothic architecture.

In **Toul** and **Metz**, the cathedrals bear the marks of French influence. Indeed, they were designed by masters who had already worked in Champagne and Île-de-France, the cradle of the French Gothic style.

The links between Lorraine and France were numerous at that time, and French predominance was felt in many fields: students from Lorraine travelled to the University of Paris; the famous trade fairs in Lorraine made it an economic centre; the dukes of Lorraine were well aware of the ambitious plans of the Capetian kings next door.

Other Gothic edifices worth citing: **Avioth**, where the great ambulatory of the church was frequented by pilgrims, St-Étienne in **St-Mihiel** and the basilica of **St-Nicolas-de-Port**, whose magnificent façade was completed in the 16C.

Renaissance

The most significant works from this period are the Chapelle des Évêques in the cathedral at **Toul** and the church at **St-Gengoult**.

CIVIL ARCHITECTURE

Renaissance

The monumental doorway of the old ducal palace at Nancy, so finely wrought, dates from the 16C. Few châteaux from the period are still standing, but those at **Louppy-sur-Loison**, **Cons-la-Grandville** and **Fléville** are worth seeing.

Cathédrale St-Étienne, Metz

© PocholoCalapre/iStockphoto.com

Classical architecture

The 18C was the heyday of this style. Although there was a pronounced taste for French styles, the traditional Italian influence remained present. Robert de Cotte designed the Château de la Grange and the Verdun bishopric in this style.

Germain Boffrand, a student of Jules Hardouin-Mansart, superintendent of buildings for the French king, drew the plans for Lunéville Château, the "Versailles of Lorraine," for the benefit of Duke Leopold. He also built the lovely Château d'Haroué. But the most impressive examples of Classical architecture are found together in the city of **Nancy**. When he was granted the duchy of Lorraine in 1737, former Polish king Stanislas Leszczynski undertook a plan to beautify his new capital. In particular, he called on Boffrand's disciple **Emmanuel Héré**, and a metalwork craftsman from Nancy, **Jean Lamour**.

Their work still shines on place Stanislas (on the UNESCO World Heritage List), the Arc de Triomphe and place de la Carrière. The ensemble constitutes one of the masterpieces of European urban architecture.

MILITARY ARCHITECTURE

Many defensive castles were erected in the Middle Ages. Today most have been reduced to ruins, or mere vestiges remain: Prény, Sierk, Tour aux Puces (Thionville), Châtel-sur-Moselle. Few of the former fortified towns have kept all of their walls, with the exceptions of **Montmédy** and **Neuf-Brisach**. Most often, it is only the gateways which have remained.

ARCHITECTURE IN CHAMPAGNE-ARDENNE

RELIGIOUS ARCHITECTURE

Romanesque churches

As in Lorraine, most of the works dating from the Carolingian period have disappeared. Of the many sanctuaries built in the 9C, only the chancel of the abbey at Isle-Aumont remains.

Architecture in the year 1000

A period of reconstruction followed the Norman and Hungarian invasions. The East Frankish Ottonian Empire (962–1002) had a strong influence on contemporary artistic style at the time. Churches from the early 11C often look like big basilicas, with sturdy framework allowing for many openings to provide light. There are towers outside, and galleries and sometimes an ambulatory inside. The interior decoration is usually very simple, based on geometric patterns.

Three churches in Champagne illustrate this style: Notre-Dame in **Montier-en-Der** (rebuilt in 1940), St-Étienne in **Vignory** and St-Remi in **Reims**. St-Étienne is one of the most remarkable monuments in the region because it has changed so little over time. St-Remi, on the other hand, has been renovated many times, and yet the Romanesque elements are easily recognisable, in particular the sculpted capitals adorned with foliage and figures.

End of the 11C and 12C

The traditions of the year 1000 continued to grow through the 11C, while at the same time, Gothic influences from the neighbouring Île-de-France were making inroads. Romanesque architecture from this period is mainly represented by a few buildings around Reims and in the Ardenne. Covered porches are common, and because of this are often referred to as *porches champenois*. The Carolingian influence is apparent in the plain decorative effects: capitals and cornices are embellished with rows of geometric designs, palmettos, and notched patterns. Romanesque traces in vestigial monastic buildings hint at the great beauty that must have been there: the cloisters of Notre-Dame-en-Vaux at **Châlons-en-Champagne**, the doorway of St-Ayoul in **Provins**, and the chapter house in St-Remi in **Reims**.

The birth of Gothic

Gothic art originated in the Île-de-France in the 12C and spread quickly to the

Champagne region, where manpower and financing made construction possible. The primitive Gothic style has echoes of the Romanesque: the use of embellished decoration was restrained and structures remained simple. Experimentation was taking place, too, with the building of the abbey church at **Mouzon**, Notre-Dame-en-Vaux in **Châlons-en-Champagne**, St-Quiriace in **Provins**, and the abbey church at **Orbais**, where the architect Jean Orbais designed a remarkable chancel that served as a model for Reims Cathedral. The chancels of Notre-Dame in **Montier-en-Der** and St-Remi in **Reims**, which date from the origins of Gothic art, have a distinctive feature: columns stand in the ambulatory at the entrance to the side chapels, and support ribs of both chapel and ambulatory vaults, forming an elegant and airy colonnade.

The apogee of Gothic art

The golden age of the great cathedrals was the **13C** and **14C**; lit brilliantly by vast bays and vivid rose windows. They are covered in delicately carved sculptures. When the cathedral at **Reims** was built, architects were already seeking to lighten the walls and interiors with immense bays: St-Amand-sur-Fion, the cathedrals at Châlons and **Troyes** and in particular St-Urbain show the accomplished fruits of their labours.

Decline

Gothic architecture then moved into its Flamboyant period (15C–16C), just before it began to wane. The over-abundance of decorative elements tended to mask the essential lines of the buildings. In the Champagne region, the basilica of Notre-Dame de l'Épine is the best example.

The Renaissance (16C)

Most of the architectural achievements of the Renaissance concern civil construction, but a few churches which were enlarged or renovated are worth mentioning: St-André-les-Vergers, Pont-Ste-Marie, Les Riceys, Auxon and Bérulle. Many beautiful windows and statues were produced in Troyes during this period.

CIVIL ARCHITECTURE

Gallo-Roman vestiges

Although not many major monuments are still intact, there are some very interesting vestiges. In **Reims**, remains of the ancient urban settlement include a triumphant arch, the Porte Mars, and a cryptoporticus; in **Langres**, a gateway stands. In **Andilly-en-Bassigny**, archaeological research has uncovered a villa complete with its baths. Museums in Troyes, Reims, Nogent-sur-Seine and Langres have extensive collections.

The Renaissance

Italian influence brought about a major change in style, notable for a renewed interest in forms from ancient civilisation: columns and superimposed galleries lend grandeur to monuments of the period. Niches, statues and medallions are set into the façades; pilasters frame the bays (**Joinville Château** and Renaissance manors in **Troyes** and **Reims**).

Classical architecture

In the Ardennes region this style is best represented by the masterpiece in the Henri IV-Louis XIII style, place Ducale in **Charleville**. There are many similarities with the famous place des Vosges in Paris.

In the 18C, the construction of large urban squares on the Classical model was popular in France. In Paris, place Louis-XV (now place de la Concorde) inspired similar works in **Reims** (place Royale) and **Châlons-en-Champagne**, where the town hall is further evidence of the Parisian influence.

MILITARY ARCHITECTURE

Located on the French border, the Ardennes still boasts a few fortifications, including the impressive château of Sedan, the largest in Europe, which was built between the 15C and the 18C. There are fortified churches in the Thiérache region, dating from the 16C and 17C; a few traditional fortifications

Fortified town of Rocroi

© Arnaud Chicurel/hemis.fr

erected by Vauban; the **Villy-la-Ferté** fort was part of the Maginot Line.

Most **fortified churches** were built up at the end of the 16C and early 17C to serve as refuges. The region, neighbouring both The Netherlands under Spanish rule and the Prussian Empire was rocked by incessant warfare.

Vauban

Sébastien le Prestre de Vauban (1633–1707) took inspiration from his predecessors, and in particular from **Jean Errard** (1554–1610) of Bar-le-Duc, who published a treatise on fortifications in 1600. Able to learn his lessons from the many wars of siege that occurred in his century, Vauban promoted fortifications in the countryside. Vauban's system is characterised by bastions which function with advanced ravelins – projecting, arrow-shaped outworks – all surrounded by deep ditches. One of the best examples of his work is in **Rocroi**. Taking advantage of natural obstacles, using materials found nearby, he also sought to bring some beauty to his fortifications, by bestowing monumental stone entrances upon them. On the northern front in the Ardennes Forest, he set up a system known as *pré carré* ('private preserve'). This consisted of two lines of strongholds located near enough to one another to prevent enemy passage, and to offer help in the case of attack. Although most of these fortified places are in today's Flanders and Hainaut regions, the Ardennes was defended by the **Charlemont** fort on the front lines, and by Rocroi, **Mézières** and **Sedan** on the rear lines.

The Maginot Line

Devised by War Minister Paul Painlevé and his successor, **André Maginot** (1877–1932), this line of defensive fortifications was under study by 1925. It includes a series of concrete works placed at the top of a hill or on the hillside all along the north-eastern border from the Ardennes Forest to the Rhine. The fort of **Villy-la-Ferté** is a good example of the defensive architecture of the line. Unfortunately for the French, this stronghold was without troops at the crucial moment, which meant that the resistance of May–June 1940 was pathetically futile.

Besides the famous series of fortifications, the Maginot Line also has a series of museums and tourist facilities; an educational tour that is easy to undertake. ♿ *See Ligne MAGINOT in the Discovering section of this guide.*

SCULPTURE AND STAINED GLASS
ALSACE

The finest examples of **sculpture** in Alsace are found in the embellishment of churches: statues, low-relief sculptures and funerary monuments. The most famous sculptor to come from Alsace was **Auguste Bartholdi**, from Colmar, who made the Belfort Lion (a copy can be found in Paris, place Denfert-Rochereau) and what may be the world's best-known statue, the Statue of Liberty, which stands majestically in New York Harbour.

Some of the more remarkable **religious sculptures** in the region are found in **Andlau** on the church porch. In the 13C, Gothic artists had a field day on the cathedral of Strasbourg (low-relief sculpture of the Death of the Virgin, the Angels' Pillar); the 14C statuary shows a more fluid style (Virtues and Vices, Wise and Foolish Virgins).

The doorway of St-Thiébaut in **Thann** and St Laurent's doorway in Strasbourg Cathedral illustrate the opulent art of the Flamboyant period (15C). **Hans Hammer** carved the pulpit in Strasbourg Cathedral, which is often referred to as lace tatted from stone.

The best examples of **funerary sculpture** are also found in **Strasbourg**, in St-Thomas's Church: the tomb of Bishop Adeloch (12C), in the form of a sarcophagus, and the tomb of Marshal Maurice de Saxe.

The proudest piece of **sculpture in wood** is no doubt the Issenheim altar in the Unterlinden Museum in Colmar. The paintings are by Grünewald, but some of the glory must go to **Nicolas de Haguenau**, who carved the gilded statues of saints Anthony, Augustine and Jerôme; Sébastien Beychel crafted the lower section which shows Christ in the midst of his Apostles.

Beautiful carved screens and altars are also on view in **Kaysersberg, Dambach** and **Soultzbach-les-Bains**. Elsewhere, there is a profusion of pulpits, organ lofts and choir stalls (**Marmoutier, Thann**), which demonstrates the skill and artistry of local artisans.

The windows in **Strasbourg Cathedral** date from the 12C, 13C and 14C. While they have been damaged over time, they are remarkable in number.

LORRAINE

Romanesque decoration of churches was often rather awkward. The doorway of Mont-Devant-Sassey, dedicated to the Virgin Mary, is in fact an inferior reproduction of statuary in Reims. A better example is Notre-Dame in **Verdun** where the Lion's Door is carved with a Christ in Majesty surrounded by symbols of the Apostles; though some find it lacks elegance, it does have its own original beauty.

In the 16C, **Ligier Richier**, working in **St-Mihiel,** brought new life to the art of sculpture, and his influence is felt throughout Lorraine.

Many mausoleums were embellished with **funerary art** between the 16C and the 18C. Perhaps the most remarkable example of Richer's work is in St-Étienne church (&see BAR-LE-DUC); known as the Tormented Soul, the skeletal figure with one arm raised high, adorns the tomb of René de Chalon. Richier also sculpted the tomb of Philippa de Gueldre in the Église des Cordeliers in **Nancy**; the tomb of René II in the same church is by Mansuy Gauvain. In Notre-Dame-de-Bon-Secours, the tomb of Stanislas and the mausoleum of his wife Catherine Opalinska are the work of Vassé and the Adam brothers, respectively.

St-Étienne Cathedral in **Metz** was built between the 13C and the 16C. The church has been called 'God's lantern' because of the many stained-glass windows. The oldest date from the 13C, and the most recent are contemporary, including some designed by painter Marc Chagall. Other modern stained-glass windows of interest can be found in the church at **St-Dié**. In **Baccarat**, St-Rémy Church has windows made of crystal.

CHAMPAGNE-ARDENNE

Gothic **sculptures** on buildings are made in fine-grained limestone, which is easy to carve, and are both ornamental and figurative. The **Ateliers de Reims** workshops were particularly productive in the 13C, and the masterpieces produced there are visible on Reims Cathedral. The famous smiling angel is a good illustration of the delicate mastery of sculptors from the Reims School. During the **14C–15C**, while the Hundred Years' War raged artists favoured funerary art such as *gisants* (recumbent figures) and monumental sepulchres showing scenes from The Passion.

The first half of the 16C was an exceptionally creative time for sculptors in **Troyes**, as styles segued from Gothic to Renaissance. The treatment of draped fabric and folds in clothing, of embroideries and jewels shows extraordinary attention to detail. Facial expressions suggest a range of emotion, and in particular give an impression of sweetness, sadness or timidity. The great master of this type of sculpture created the statue of St Martha in Ste-Madeleine church (Troyes), the Pietà in **Bayel** and the Entombment in **Chaource**. The Flamboyant altar screen in Ste-Madeleine is from the same period.

The emergence of the Italian style is also evident in St-Urbain, where a statue of the Virgin Mary holding grapes has graceful posture and a gentle expression, marking a departure from Gothic Realism. As of 1540, such manneristic, refined representations had completely invested the Troyes School of Sculpture, and put an end to its distinctive appearance. Churches installed many works by **Dominique Florentin**, an Italian artist who married a native of Troyes and settled there, training students in his workshops.

Some works in **stained glass** have survived the wars, pollution and the 18C practice of replacing coloured windows with milky white ones (making it easier to read the liturgy).

The **13C** saw the creation of the windows in the chancel of Troyes cathedral plus those of Notre-Dame in **Reims** (apse and rose on the façade), a few in St-Étienne in **Châlons-en-Champagne** and finally the great windows of **St-Urbain** in Troyes, which are the most typical of the era. Very colourful, they portray solitary characters (bishops) in the high panels, whereas the lower panels, more easily studied by visitors, illustrate the lives of the saints or episodes from the Life of Christ. The compositions are enlivened by complex backgrounds and the expressive attitudes of the figures;

Stained-glass window depicting the mystical wine press by Linard Gontier, Cathédrale St-Pierre-et-St-Paul, Toryes

some panels reveal details about the daily life of the time.

In the **16C**, painting on glass became popular and many pieces were ordered for donations to churches (the donor's name or likeness often appearing thereon). Cartoons (basic drawing patterns) made it possible to reproduce the same image over and over, which explains the wealth of windows in the small churches of the Aube region. Some of the artists' names are known to us today: Jehan Soudain, Jean Verrat, Lievin Varin. Early in the 16C, colours exploded on the scene, as can be seen in the spectacular upper windows in **Troyes cathedral**, which were installed between 1498 and 1501. In these windows the contours of the drawings are clearly defined and the technical prowess is evident in engraving, pearling, brushed *grisaille*, which creates a three-dimensional illusion, and inlays of different coloured glass, as used in the stars.

As of 1530, polychrome effects were abandoned by the masters in favour of *grisaille* – tones of a single colour – on white glass with golden yellow and blood red highlights. Italian influence is found in the evolution of the drawings. The architectural backgrounds were inspired by the Fontainebleau School.

In the 17C, the tradition of stained-glass craft continued in Troyes with **Linard Gontier**, who brought back polychrome windows with a new technique of enamelling on white glass, which produced bright hues. He is considered the master of monumental compositions, with works such as the Mystical Press, in Troyes cathedral. He was also an exceptional miniaturist and portraitist, working in *grisaille*.

DECORATIVE ARTS AND PAINTING
MEROVINGIAN TREASURES

The Merovingian period refers to the first dynasty of Frankish kings founded by Clovis and reigning in France and Germany from about 500 to 751.

Recently, art historians have become more interested in works from this often neglected time. In the Champagne-Ardenne region, a trove of funerary objects has been uncovered in the many necropolises that once served local communities. In the archaeological museum in **Troyes**, the tomb of Pouan, a prince, reveals much to us about the artistic temper of the times.

Gold and silver work was highly prized. The decorative items on view in the museums include **fibulae** (clasps resembling safety pins), belt buckles, parts of shields and sword handles. The eastern influence is obvious in the designs, in particular the fantastic animal turning its head to look back. Styles and techniques were also adapted by Germanic invaders. The rarity of precious metals led to a preference for gold and silver beaten into fine sheets or pulled into threads. Other metals were also substituted for a precious effect, including copper, tin and bronze.

Arms made during the Merovingian period are another illustration of the prowess of metalwork masters. Various metals, always high quality, were juxtaposed in the forging process. They were welded together and hammered. The layered structure thus created was both resistant and elastic. The most common arms were long double-edged swords, axes and the *scramasax*, a sort of sabre with one cutting edge.

In addition to metalwork, a speciality of Germanic regions, some sculptural works have also survived. In Isle-Aumont, a set of sarcophagi shows the evolution of style between the 5C and the 8C.

ALSACE

In the 15C, great **painting** began to appear in Alsace, with the arrival in Colmar of **Gaspard Idenmann**, creator of a *Passion* inspired by the Flemish style, now on view in the Unterlinden Museum. Another Colmar resident, **Martin Schongauer**, painted the magnificent Madonna of the Rose Bower *(in the Église des Dominicains, see COLMAR)*. Students under his direction painted a series of *Passion* works (also in the Unterlinden), and created other remarkable works, such as the Buhl altar screen. The great German artist **Matthias Grünewald** painted the high altar of the Antonite Church in Issenheim. This screen sets a *Crucifixion* of fearful realism against exquisite figures of the *Annunciation* and a *Heavenly Choir*. Some excellent portraitists (Jean-Jacques Henner) were Alsatian, as were a number of draughtsmen, engravers and lithographers, including **Gustave Doré**, who was from Strasbourg.

In the realm of **decorative arts**, Alsatian craftsmen excelled in woodwork, ironwork, tinsmithing and working precious metals. They have a reputation as skilled watch- and clockmakers, as the astronomical clock in Strasbourg Cathedral proves.

Ceramics made the **Hannong** family, creators of the "old Strasbourg" style, eminent for generations; their production is on view in the Strasbourg Museum. In the second half of the 19C,

Théodore Deck of Guebwiller brought new ideas to ceramic arts and refined techniques.

LORRAINE

The region, with its wealth and as a cosmopolitan crossroads, produced many painters, miniaturists and engravers over the centuries. Some achieved fame beyond the local area. Arts in the 17C were imprinted with the influence of **Georges Lallemand**, a native of Nancy who established himself in Paris in 1601; **Jacques Bellange**, master of Mannerism; **Claude Deruet**, official court painter par excellence; **Georges de la Tour**, known for his remarkable candlelight and torchlight effects incorporating deep black nights; **Claude Gellée**, a landscape painter; **Jacques Callot**, a great draughtsman and engraver (most of his works are shown in the museum of the history of Lorraine in Nancy).

In the 19C, **Isabey** was the leading painter of miniature portraits, and one of the favourite painters of Imperial society, alongside **François Dumont**, from Lunéville.

Mention must be made of **Épinal**. In the 18C and 19C, this town specialised in the production of pretty coloured prints, which were sold around France by street vendors. The pictures became so well known that it is common nowadays to use the expression *image d'Épinal* to refer to any simplistic or naïve representation of life.

Ceramic production in Lorraine was mostly centred around **Lunéville** and **Sarreguemines**; enamellers settled around Longwy.

Crystal

Lorraine has several famous crystal manufacturers, including those in **Baccarat, Daum** and **Saint Louis**. This activity was able to develop, especially in the 16C, thanks to the abundance of wood (to stoke the fires), water and sand in the region. Today, in addition to traditional glassware, as once appreciated by the royal and imperial courts of Persia, Russia,

Germany and Italy, these venerable companies produce objects designed in contemporary styles by Salvador Dali and Philippe Starck, among others.

ART NOUVEAU AND THE 20C

At the end of the 19C, a movement to rehabilitate decorative arts and architecture, known as **Art Nouveau**, came to the fore. It is easily recognisable by its use of long, sinuous lines, often expressed in the shapes of vines and tendrils, flower stalks, butterfly wings and other curvaceous natural forms.

In France, the first works to appear were in Nancy, made by **Émile Gallé**; he produced glassware inspired by the patterns and forms of nature. His work was hailed at the Universal Exhibitions of 1884, 1889 and 1900 in Paris. Soon a group of artists working in various media (glass, wood, ceramic, engraving and sculpture) had gathered around him. Among them were **Daum**, **Majorelle**, **Vallin**, **Prouvé**, and together they formed the **École de Nancy.**

Between 1900 and 1910, the influence of the Nancy School became apparent in local architecture (about ten years behind decorative arts). Nancy is now, with Brussels, Vienna and Paris, one of the great centres of Art Nouveau architecture in Europe.

Musée de l'École de Nancy

© Ville de Nancy

The second half of the 20C saw some **architectural achievements** in the larger towns: the Tour de l'Europe in Mulhouse (1966); the Tour Altea in Nancy (1974); the Palais de l'Europe (1977). In Strasbourg the striking landmark **Palais des Droits de l'Homme** (European Court of Human Rights, 1995) by Richard Rogers, was followed by the **European Parliament building** (1997) which houses the largest debating chamber in Europe.

The most famous artist of the 20C to come from the region was **Jean (or Hans) Arp** (1887–1966) born in Strasbourg. A leader of the avant-garde, he produced sculptures, paintings and poetry. In Paris, he was acquainted with Modigliani, Picasso and Robert Delaunay He sought refuge in Zurich during the First World War, and while there became one of the founders of the Dada movement. An impressive collection of Arp's works and other modern and contemporary art works are assembled in the Musée d'Art Moderne et Contemporain in Strasbourg.

TRADITIONS AND FOLKLORE
ALSACE

Both the mountains and the plain are rich in local colour, and legends abound in Alsace. Of course, visitors today are not likely to see women wearing distinctive, bow-shaped black headdresses, unless there is a local heritage *fête* in progress. But the preservation of so much architectural patrimony – a miracle considering the strife and wars that long plagued the region – provides a setting that vividly evokes the past.

Some local traditions do persist, in particular those associated with saints' feast days. Each village celebrates the feast day of its patron saint, **la fête patronale**, also known as *messti* (Bas-Rhin), and *kilwe* or *kilbe* (Haut-Rhin) in local dialect. Folk dancing and traditional costumes enliven the festivities. Ribeauvillé has held its particularly popular fair in early September for centuries.

Many seasonal traditions would seem very familiar to a visitor from the United Kingdom or North America: brightly lit and sparkling trees, red and green ribbons, gingerbread men, and markets full of "stocking-stuffers" in December; carnival celebrated with doughnuts; Easter brings a rabbit who hides coloured eggs in the garden.

Legends often surround lakes, rivers, and the romantic ruins of castles. There are religious legends as well, often remembered in traditional ceremonies like the one held in Thann every 30 June, when three pines are set on fire. While the realm of legend sometimes

Alsacian dance during the wine festival in summer, Obernai

© Matthieu Colin/hemis.fr

Chapel of Mont Saint Odile

reflects aspects of reality and history, the advantage here is that good always conquers and evil is inevitably punished. The characters in these legends are knights and ladies, monks and beggars, saints and demons, gnomes and giants. The most famous legend in Alsace may be the story of **Mont Ste-Odile**.

The patron saint of Alsace (Odilia, Ottilia and other variations are found) was the daughter of Duke Adalric; she founded a convent on a mountain around the year 700 and was its first abbess.

From these historical facts, a legend has grown, which recounts the birth of a blind Odile, rejected by her father, and spirited away to safety by her mother. By this account, Odile, now a beautiful young woman, was baptised by St Erhard, her uncle, and miraculously recovered her sight. Her father decided to marry her off, despite the girl's religious vocation, and he pursued her through the forest as she ran from the fate he had devised for her. Suddenly, a rock opened up and enfolded her, protecting Odile from the duke. From that rock, a sacred spring came forth. Adalric got the message and built her a convent instead.

Many pilgrims came to visit the holy woman. It is said that, upon encountering a sick man dying of thirst, Odile struck the ground with her cane and brought forth a spring. The man drank and was cured. Many people came to pray at the site and wash their eyes with the curative water. Odile's intercession is still sought after by those with diseases of the eye.

LORRAINE

The traditional emblem of Lorraine is the **Croix de Lorraine**, a cross with two horizontal arms, the shorter one above the longer. It appeared on coins minted by the dukes of Lorraine, was made famous by General de Gaulle who took it for his personal standard, and is found on everything from biscuit tins to postage stamps. Its origins can be traced to the kingdom of Hungary, which used such a cross as its coat of arms. When the Árpád dynasty expired, a series of Angevin kings came to power, beginning with Robert of Anjou (1308–42). Ultimately, René II inherited the title from the dukes of Anjou and brought the emblem to his duchy of Lorraine. In 1477, the cross blazed on banners, rallying the people to the Battle of Nancy, and since that time on it has been known as the Lorraine Cross.

St Nicholas has also held a special place in the hearts of the people of Lorraine since the days of the Holy Roman Empire. With his bishop's mitre and backpack full of toys, he travels Lorraine on the night of 5–6 December. The patron saint of the region is celebrated in all the towns and villages with festive lights and parades. The beautiful Flamboyant church of St-Nicolas-de-Port was the site of many pilgrimages; the town was once one of the liveliest in Lorraine.

CHAMPAGNE-ARDENNE

In this region, as elsewhere in France, recent years have seen a renewed interest in ancestral traditions, including religious and pagan festivities and activities related to daily life in the countryside.

Carnival costume parades are coming back in style in many towns and villages where the custom had nearly died out. Around the textile centre of Sedan, costumes were commonly made from canvas sacks used to hold spools of yarn; five or six people would climb into one and march along side-by-side. Near Mézières, carnival-goers stick their heads through the rungs of a horizontal ladder draped with white cloth and pop out one or several burlesque faces at a time. Popular games are blindfold races, horseshoe throwing, and wheelbarrow races, with the loser buying the winner a round at the nearest café.

At nightfall, the crowd gathers round for the bonfire. A procession through the streets bears a sort of scarecrow who, from village to village, may be named Nicolas, Christophe, Joseph or Pansard, and may be dressed as a ragged beggar or a bridegroom. As the carnival figure burns and sparks fly up, dancing and singing mark the end of the festive day. In some places, the ashes from the fire are believed to have special powers, or bring good luck, particularly to young couples.

Although Mardi Gras is associated with the Christian rite, the carnival has well-documented pagan origins and is clearly associated with chasing out winter and preparing for spring.

A funny tradition still observed in villages is the May Day *charivari*. Young rascals band together on the eve of 1 May and spend the dark night going from house to house, where they quietly make off with anything that isn't nailed down or locked up: ladders, barrows, benches, rakes. The whole lot is then piled up on the main square, where everyone gathers the next morning, to laugh or complain according to temper, and to recover the goods.

LITERATURE

LITERATURE IN ALSACE-LORRAINE

In this border region, literary tradition has three expressions: French, German and dialect. German works represent the oldest, most prestigious tradition. The **Renaissance**, **Humanism** and the **Reform** marked the golden age of Alsatian literature. Gutenberg worked on developing his printing press in Strasbourg before getting it up and running in Mainz. The wonderful collection of the Humanist library in Sélestat is testimony to the regional attachment to the written word. The German author Goethe lived in Strasbourg in 1770–71, a memorable time because it marked the beginning

The Legend of the Lac du Ballon

Long ago, a green meadow lay like an emerald in the blue velvet folds of the Vosges forest, below the majestic Grand Ballon. The field belonged to a man who earned his living making charcoal, a *charbonnier*. A covetous bourgeois from the Guebwiller valley tried to buy the field, and when the collier refused, he bribed a local judge into forcing the forfeit of the land.

The proud new owner arrived with a fancy golden wagon to cut the fragrant hay, and he passed by the collier's simple dwelling with a smug, victorious grin. The wronged man shook his fist, and called on Providence to render the justice that the courts of law had denied him.

Suddenly, a menacing gloom came over the sky and a violent storm erupted in the high mountains, followed by a downpour so heavy it cut off all sight like a thick dark curtain. When the light returned, a round lake appeared in the place of the field, its deep waters covering the bourgeois, his wagon and horses.

The Last Word …
Can you identify the quotes below?

Here is a hint … half are from the pen of Voltaire, and the others are morals from the *Fables of La Fontaine*.

In this best of all possible worlds … all is for the best.
Better to suffer than to die: that is mankind's motto.
The secret of being a bore is to tell everything.

People who make no noise are dangerous.
Love truth, but pardon error.
It is a double pleasure to deceive the deceiver.

History is no more than a portrayal of crimes and misfortunes.
We heed no instincts but our own.
Thought depends on the stomach, but in spite of that, those who have the best stomachs are not the best thinkers.

A hungry stomach cannot hear.
I disapprove of what you say, but I will defend to the death your right to say it.
The opinion of the strongest is always the best.

Answers: The first is Voltaire, the second La Fontaine, the next one is Voltaire, and so on, in alternation.

of the so-called *Sturm und Drang* (Storm and Stress) movement. This style of literature exalted nature, feelings and human individualism, and was strongly influenced by the ideas of French author Jean-Jacques Rousseau, and by the works of Shakespeare, which had just been translated.

The **20C** was marked by the upheavals of war. German literature was still most prevalent, but by the end of the First World War, numerous works had been published in dialect, certainly in response to the need to express cultural identity in a region caught in the middle of a terrible power struggle. Between the wars, the French language got a foothold and today it is the language most commonly heard and used.

CHAMPAGNE: CRADLE OF FRENCH LITERATURE

In the **12C**, Champagne was home to many authors writing in the emerging French language. Bertrand de Bar-sur-Aube is reputed to have composed *Aimeri de Narbonne*, the best-known chapter of the ballad of William of Orange (later to inspire Victor Hugo). **Chrétien de Troyes** (c. 1135–c. 1183) wrote tales of chivalry based on the legends of Brittany, including the characters Lancelot and Perceval. The search for the Holy Grail and the Crusades inspired Geoffroi de Villehardouin (1150–1213), who wrote about his adventures in History of the Conquest of Constantinople. Another medieval bard, Jean, Sire de Joinville, described travelling to Egypt with St Louis (1309). The Count of Champagne, Thibaud IV, crowned king of Navarre in 1234, preferred to pen poetry, whereas his countryman Rutebeuf entertained with biting satires of the church, the university and tradesmen.

A major figure from the 17C was **Jean de la Fontaine**, celebrated for his *Fables*. Born into a bourgeois family in Château-Thierry, he married a local heiress in 1647, but separated from her 11 years later. An outstanding feature of his character was his life-long ability to attract wealthy patrons, thus freeing himself from the pedestrian worries of earning a living so he could devote his time to writing 12 books of fables and other works. The first collection of six books is based on the Aesopic tradition, whereas the second takes its inspiration from East Asian stories. His use of animal characters is a light-hearted ploy for expressing the everyday moral experience of humankind. His poetic

Voltaire

© HultonArchive/iStockphoto.com

technique has been called the exquisite quintessence of the preceding century of French literature. La Fontaine's *Fables* continue to form part of the culture of every French schoolchild, and his reputation has lost none of its glow.

The **18C** brought bold thinkers to the fore, and none more so than **Voltaire** (pseudonym of François-Marie Arouet). Upon his return to France after a two-year exile in England, Voltaire found refuge in Champagne in the château of Mme du Châtelet in Cirey-sur-Blaise. They lived a life both studious and passionate, translating Newton, conducting experiments in their laboratory, travelling and frequenting high society. She died in childbirth in 1749, ending their complex relationship of 15 years, and leaving her lover bereft. Voltaire's most famous work is *Candide* (1758), a satirical masterpiece on philosophical optimism.

The **19C** and **20C** produced two figures whose memory has been perpetuated by modern-day songwriters and film directors: **Paul Verlaine** and **Arthur Rimbaud**.

Verlaine was born in Metz in 1844, Rimbaud 10 years later in Charleville. The older poet was from a comfortable background, the well-educated son of an army officer. The younger was raised in poverty by his mother and yet distinguished himself as a gifted student. After graduating with honours from the Lycée Bonaparte, Verlaine became a clerk in an insurance company, then a civil servant. His early work was published in respectable literary reviews; he married and had a son. During the Franco-Prussian War (℗*see p79*), he was the press officer for the Paris insurgents of the *Commune*. Meanwhile, Rimbaud, a restless and despondent soul, lived on the streets of the capital in squalor, reading everything he could get his hands on – including the poetry of Baudelaire (considered immoral by the cultural establishment at the time) and works on the occult – and shaping his own poetic philosophy.

In 1871 the two met, moved to London and carried on a scandalous affair. While Verlaine vacillated between decadent thrills and anguished repentance, Rimbaud was seen as his friend's evil helmsman on their *Drunken Boat*. In 1873, a violent quarrel in Brussels ended with Rimbaud shot in the wrist and Verlaine in prison for 18 months. Rimbaud, both distraught and exhilarated, feverishly completed *A Season in Hell:... As for me, I am intact, and I don't care.*

By his 20th birthday, Rimbaud had given up writing and turned to gunrunning in Africa. In 1891, his right leg was amputated, and he died the same year. He has been cited as an inspiration by many, in particular the Beat poets, as well as musicians Jim Morrison, Bob Dylan and Patti Smith.

Verlaine, released from prison, became a devout Catholic and moved to England where he taught French. In 1877, he returned to France and began writing the series of poems to be published as *Sagesse* (Wisdom – or perhaps, simply 'wising up'). Further heartbreak (the deaths of a favourite student and the poet's mother) and a failure to reconcile with his wife drove Verlaine back to drink, but sympathetic friends encouraged him to continue writing and publishing, and supported him financially. His significant body of work marks a transition between the Romantic poets and the Symbolists.

Joan of Arc, heroine for all time

No discussion of the history of Lorraine, the Vosges or Champagne would be complete without some mention of Joan of Arc (Jeanne d'Arc), a country girl whose achievements were a decisive factor in awakening a national consciousness. The subject of books, films and plays, Joan attained sainthood in 1920. However, her canonisation did not put an end to speculation on the divine (or perhaps delusional) nature of the voices that guided her. She remains an enigma.

Born c. 1412 in Dorémy, on the border of the duchies of Bar and Lorraine (now in the Vosges *département*), Joan was the daughter of a tenant farmer of modest means and good reputation. According to the transcript of her trial, "at the age of 13, she received a voice from God, guiding her, and this voice came to her around noon, in the summer, in her father's garden." Joan believed that God spoke to her through the "voices" of Saint Michael, Saint Catherine and Saint Margaret.

The French crown was in dispute between the Valois king (the "Dauphin" Charles) and the Lancastrian English king Henry VI (allied with the duke of Burgundy). The villagers of Dorémy were under constant threat from the Burgundians, and had little love for Henry. Charles needed to reach Reims to be crowned in the cathedral and reign legitimately, but Reims was deep in enemy territory.

Joan, possessed of remarkable courage and drive, made the dangerous journey to Chinon to speak to the Dauphin. Charles, 25 years old at the time, had known only war and intrigue, and was unable to reconquer his kingdom or make a peace agreement with the Burgundians. In a legendary confrontation, Charles, unsure and receiving contradictory counsel, made Joan wait several days before allowing her to enter the castle. He then disguised himself as an ordinary member of the court. Joan was not fooled for an instant, knelt before him and said that she wanted to go to battle with the English. While Charles vacillated, Joan pressed on. She led attacks on Orléans, Beaugency and Patay, inspiring French troops and routing the English. Soon the mere sight of Joan's standard was enough to make loyalties waver; thus Joan brought the Dauphin to Reims. She also wrote to the Duke of Burgundy, urging him to make peace with the legitimate monarch.

In 1430, when the Duke of Burgundy laid siege to Compiègne, Joan entered the town under cover of night and twice repelled the enemy. Protecting her rear guard to the last, Joan was unhorsed and captured. Charles, deep in his endless negotiations with the Burgundians, did nothing to seek her release. The Duke accepted an offer of 10 000 francs from the University of Paris, controlled by English partisans, to turn the young prisoner over to be tried – not for offences against the Lancastrian monarchy, but for heresy. Indeed, Joan's manner of direct discourse with her God threatened the powerful church hierarchy; proving her a heretic could also bring discredit on Charles. For five months, she was imprisoned in the harshest conditions and her faith constantly called into question. Finally, her tormentors turned Joan over to the secular arm of justice, in order that she be condemned to death. On 30 May 1431, she was burned at the stake; witnesses to her death agreed that she died a faithful Christian.

Ruling as Charles VII, the new sovereign obtained a posthumous reversal of her sentence, perhaps more out of a perceived need to justify his coronation than a sense of justice. Despite his rather apathetic, indolent character, Charles VII made significant financial and military reforms which strengthened the French monarchy, and began to reunify the kingdom.

On 24 June 1920, the French parliament declared a national festival in honour of Joan, held on the second Sunday in May. She became, and remains, a symbol of the French spirit.

Nature

The easternmost portion of the area covered in this guide is the **Alsatian plain**. Barely 30km/18.6mi wide, it stretches, north to south, more than 170km/106mi. The border with Germany is traced by the Rhine, which forms an alluvial basin with the River Ill; a porous, friable blanket of marl and loam deposits, consisting predominantly of silt (known as *loess*). At the southern end, the pebbly soil of the **Sundgau** region links it to the Jura range.

Like a wall on the other edge of the narrow plain, the **Vosges** mountains rise abruptly, running parallel to the Rhine for the whole length of Alsace. This ancient range formed by folding movements of the earth 300 million years ago is made of crystalline rock (granites, porphyries) and ancient sedimentary rock, mostly sandstone. At the southern end, the mountain tops have distinctive, rounded shapes locally known as *ballons*. The glaciers left behind high mountain lakes. To the north, the lower altitude has resulted in a thicker sedimentary crust, and a forest cover. The western slope of the range is more gradual than the Alsatian side.

The geological history of the **Ardennes** uplands is a complex one, the result of intense folding, faulting, uplifts and denudations, with some of the older strata of rock thrust above the younger. The highest point of the plateau in France is the Croix de Scalle (502m), on the border with Belgium. The Meuse flows through deeply entrenched meanders between the tip of the French Ardennes, Givet and Charleville-Mézières. The rugged **Argonne** forest is drained by the River Aisne.

The region of **Champagne** is part of the Paris Basin, a vast bowl-like formation contained by the Ardennes and the Vosges (north and east) and the Morvan and Massif Armoricain (south and west). The landscape has been shaped by a series of concentric layers, one on top of the other in diminishing size, like a stack of saucers, with the oldest and smallest on top.

The **Lorraine** plateau marks the eastern rim of the basin.

LAND FORMATION
THE VOSGES AND ALSACE
Primary (Palaeozoic) Era
About 560 million years ago, France was covered in water. The earth's crust underwent a great upheaval and the so-called 'Hercynian folds' pushed up the bedrock of the Vosges and what is now the Black Forest, constituting a crystalline massif dominated by granite.

Secondary (Mesozoic) Era
This era began about 200 million years ago. The Vosges, planed down by erosion, were surrounded by the sea

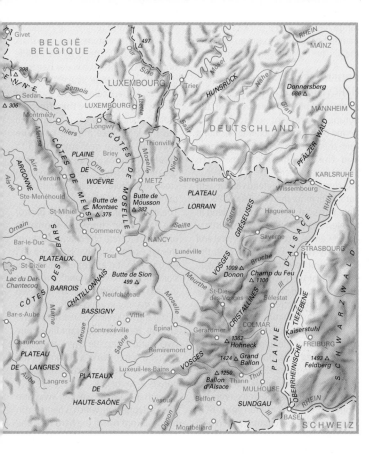

which filled the Paris Basin at different periods. At the end of the Secondary Era, the range was covered in water; sedimentary soils (sandstone, limestone, marl, clay and chalk) piled up on top of the primitive bedrock.

Tertiary Era

About 65 million years ago, a tremendous folding of the crust of the earth brought out the Alps. In reaction to this movement, the old Hercynian hills slowly lifted up. In the first phase, the Vosges and the Black Forest reached an altitude of nearly 3 000m. In the second phase, the central zone, unbalanced by the upheaval, collapsed inward. This sunken area was to become the Alsatian plain, separating the Vosges from the Black Forest, and explaining the symmetry of

the structure and relief found between the two areas.

Quaternary (Glacial) Era

The earth underwent a global cooling period some two million years ago. Glaciers covered the southern Vosges. Descending slowly, they widened the valleys and steepened the slopes, gouged the rock and left hollows that were later filled with water (Lac Noir, Lac Blanc). When the climate warmed, the accumulated earth and stones carried by the glaciers were finally deposited in formations known as moraines, some of which created natural dams and lakes (Lac de Gérardmer). Since the glaciers retreated, rainwater, rivers and streams have further eroded the Vosges. The old stone peaks have been laid bare in the south, whereas the northern end of the range has retained a thick sandstone mantle because it was preserved from the harshest glacier aggression.

ARDENNES: HERCYNIAN HISTORY

At the end of the Palaeozoic Era, the European continent was subject to a period of mountain-building, resulting from the collision between the African and the North American-North European continent.

The Hercynian belt extends in Western Europe for more than 3 000km/1 860mi from Portugal, Ireland and England in the west through Spain, France (Brittany, Massif Central, Vosges and Corsica) and Germany (Black Forest, Harz) to the Czech Republic in the Bohemian Massif. Analyses of the rocks and geological structures found in these zones indicate that they are the result of the seabed spreading, subduction of the oceanic crust and plate collision. The lateral compression of the upper layers of the earth pushed accumulated sediment upward, bringing ridges of hard, old rocks together like the jaws of a clamp. Thus, the Ardennes uplands emerged around 550 to 220 million years BCE. Spreading over the countries of France, Germany and Belgium, the region has been eroded over time until it now appears as a mostly flat plain. The River Meuse has marked a course through the very hard stone, revealed in the dramatic canyon-like walls of dark rock through which it winds. Near Givet, the river valleys widen as the water passes over bands of shale and limestone.

LORRAINE AND CHAMPAGNE

These two regions form the eastern part of the **Paris Basin**. At the end of the Primary Era, and into the early Tertiary Era, this vast depression was a sea.

A great variety of sedimentary deposits – sandstone, limestone, marl, clay, chalk – piled up 2 000m deep. By the middle of the Tertiary Era, the water began to drain from this wide 'saucer', whereas the rim, in particular to the east and southeast, rose under the effects of Alpine folding. Erosion worked to flatten out the land, creating the **Lorraine plateau**, where geology served to create a homogeneous landscape; greater diversity of soil composition created the more diversified landscapes of the **Pays des Côtes**.

The illustration of the eastern part of the Paris Basin shows the formation of cuestas (côtes). The characteristic of this type of escarpment is a steep cliff on one side and a gentler dip or back slope on the other. This landform occurs in areas of inclined strata and is caused by the manner in which different types of soil and rock react to weathering and erosion. Here, the resistant limestone layers surmount softer layers (clay, marl). Running water works a channel in the hard layer until it reaches the more porous zones below.

The softer areas are washed away and leave a depression, which is hemmed in by the abrupt rise of the hard rock (the front de côte or steep face); the softer surface slopes back at a gentle angle. This back slope, protected from wind, is characterised by loose, fertile soil whose chalky layers below the surface help the soil warm up quickly in the spring. These areas are ideal for cultivating vineyards. The Champagne region is made up of many small pays, areas with distinct climates and soils. **Champagne crayeuse** refers to the chalky soil which gave the region its name (etymological descendent of "calcareous plain"). This zone forms a circle with a circumference of about 80km/50mi, with Paris near the

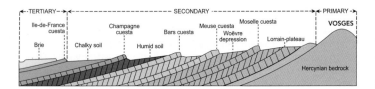

centre. The **Brie and Tardenois plateau** is crossed by rivers (the Marne, the two Morins and the Seine). Impenetrable marl holds in humidity, whereas siliceous limestone forms the upper layer.

The Barrois is another plateau, crossed by the valleys of the Saulx and the Ornain, home to the towns of Bar-le-Duc and Ligny-en-Barrois. It extends into the **Côte de Bars**, where the vineyards of the Aube *département* grow.

Between the Champagne and Bars cuestas lies the region known as **Champagne humide**, a verdant and well-watered area of woodlands, pastures and orchards. The creation of the lake-reservoirs in the **Der-Chantecoq** and **Orient** forests have further transformed the lay of the land, where the heavy, clay rich soil is more suited to grazing than cultivation.

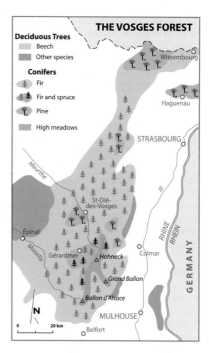

THE VOSGES FOREST

Deciduous Trees
Beech
Other species

Conifers
Fir
Fir and spruce
Pine
High meadows

Wissembourg
Haguenau
STRASBOURG
Meurthe
St-Dié-des-Vosges
Épinal
Moselle
Gérardmer Hohneck
Colmar
Grand Ballon
Ballon d'Alsace
MULHOUSE
Belfort
RHINE RHEIN
GERMANY
N
0   20 km

FORESTS AND WILDLIFE
ALSACE AND THE VOSGES

The Vosges mountains are particularly lovely thanks to the the forest cover, which changes subtly depending on altitude, orientation and the composition of the soil. The southern part of the range is known as *Vosges cristallines*, in reference to the granite content of the high mountains. The ballons are rounded, with moderate slopes on the western side. Facing the Alsatian plain, however, the rocky faces appear sharper and steeper.

The River Bruche marks the separation with the *Vosges gréseuses* – the "sandy" northern end. The range diminishes in altitude and the red sandstone so prevalent in the construction of castles and churches has also sculpted the landscape. The forest blanketing the whole hilly area is sometimes a harmonious mixture of species, and sometimes dominated by a single species, creating a variety of colours and distinctive woodland environments. Facing the region of **Lorraine**, the lower hills of the north are exposed to the wet western winds, and dominated by beech

trees. Firs grow at an altitude of 400m. In the higher southern peaks, Scotch pine grow above 700m. Beyond 1 000m, conifers yield to deciduous varieties, including beech, maple and mountain ash. On the highest ridge tops, there are no trees at all, just low brush and bilberry bushes.

On the warmer slope facing the **Alsatian plain**, firs begin to grow at 600m. Just above the vineyards, chestnut trees can be found; in the past their wood was used to stake out the grape vines. The warm, dry climate is congenial to spruce, but a large population of oak flourishes in the Harth forest.

Storks

No discussion of the wildlife in Alsace would be complete without the mention of storks. These stately, long-necked creatures are symbolic of the region, and believed to bring good luck.

Each spring, their return is awaited anxiously. After years of decline (due to hunting in their winter habitat in Africa, and accidents involving high-voltage electric lines), the population seems to be stabilising and the gracious birds are once again a common sight.

The migrating storks come to roost, typically atop chimneys, in the month of March. Storks are voiceless, or nearly so, but announce their presence by clattering their bills loudly. The male arrives first and begins work on a platform of twigs and vines. The circular nest is refurbished yearly, and may weigh up to 500kg for 2m in diameter. When the chosen mate has arrived, the couple produce three to six eggs in a season, which hatch after 36 days of incubation by both parents. Generously nourished with insects, larva, lizards, newts, mice, moles and snakes, baby storks grow quickly.

Vosges lakes

On each side of the crest of the Vosges, many lakes add to the pleasure of an excursion to the mountains. The largest is Gérardmer (115ha/284 acres), on the Lorraine side; one of the region's most popular winter resorts is located along its banks. The deepest lake is Lac Blanc (71m), on the Alsatian side.

The lakes were created by the glaciers that once covered the range, hundreds of centuries ago. Most are found at high altitudes, in bowl-like formations with steep waterfront terrain (Lac des Corbeaux, Lac Noir, Lac Blanc, etc.). Many are now used as reservoirs, useful when water is in short supply.

The lakes in the valleys were formed by glacier deposits, moraines, which retain or deviate waters. Gérardmer and Longemer are such lakes.

Bird sanctuaries and other animal reserves are found around many of the region's lakes and nature parks. There are numerous discovery trails and nature centres where visitors can learn more about the environment, the flora and fauna of the region.

ARDENNE

The Ardenne is the southwest margin of the larger Ardennes highlands and the adjacent lowlands in the Meuse and Aisne valleys. The thick, apparently impenetrable forest has been the scene of battles since the French Revolution. In addition to the sandstone, limestone and quartzite found in neighbouring regions, the Ardenne is famous for the blue slate quarried there. The oldest sections of the forest are majestic with hardwoods such as oak, beech and yellow birch; younger growth includes European white birch and willows.

The variety of soil quality has a strong influence on the height of trees: on the plateau a mature oak may yield only a dozen logs for the fire; an ash further south in the Signy-l'Abbaye area may climb more than 30m.

Game is abundant in the Ardennes forest, where hunting is popular. The region's emblematic animal is the wild

Storks in NaturOparC - Centre de réintroduction des cigognes et des loutres - in Hunawihr, Alsace

© René Mattes/hemis.fr

Montherme surrounded by River Meuse, Ardenne

© Christian Goupi/age fotostock

boar, sanglier. The wild population has returned from the brink of extinction thanks to better management. There is also a limited hunting season (two to six weeks, depending on the district) on the plains, for pheasant, partridge and hare. Each hunting permit is delivered with tags which the hunter must affix to the animals captured. Deer are now found only in animal parks; few escaped the devastation of the Second World War, however, the population has been restored thanks to the Belval animal reserve. Things have changed considerably since the days of Charlemagne: on 8 December 799, the Emperor and his party bagged two bison, two aurochs, 46 boar, 28 stags and a wolf, using spears, bows and arrows.

ARGONNE

The southernmost part of the French Ardenne is wooded and hilly, more temperate in every way than the highlands. The massif is a natural barrier between Champagne and Lorraine, about 65km/40mi long and 15km/9.3mi wide, rarely exceeding 200m in altitude. Beech groves are common on the slopes, and it is not unusual to see regal chestnuts atop the crests. Shrubs, berry bushes and reeds provide shelter for birds and other creatures. Some species have migrated to the area from other regions of France, including heather from Brittany; specialists may look out for a non-indigenous blue lily from England, a souvenir from soldiers of the First World War.

M. Janvier/MICHELIN

| *Beech* | *Spruce* | *Scotch pine* | *Fir* |

Place Stanislas, Nancy
© René Mattes/age fotostock

ARGONNE AND THE CÔTES DE MEUSE

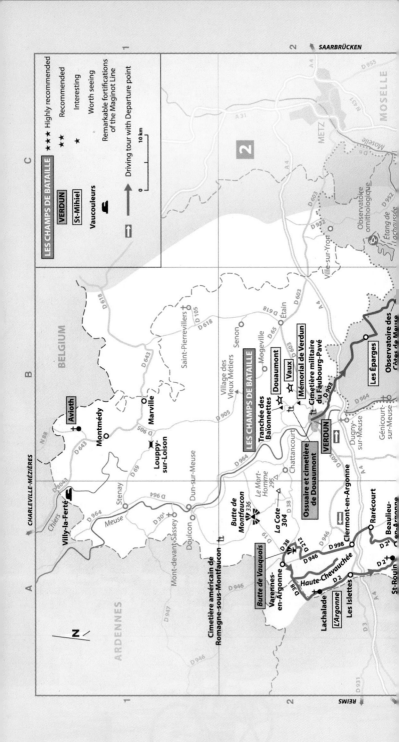

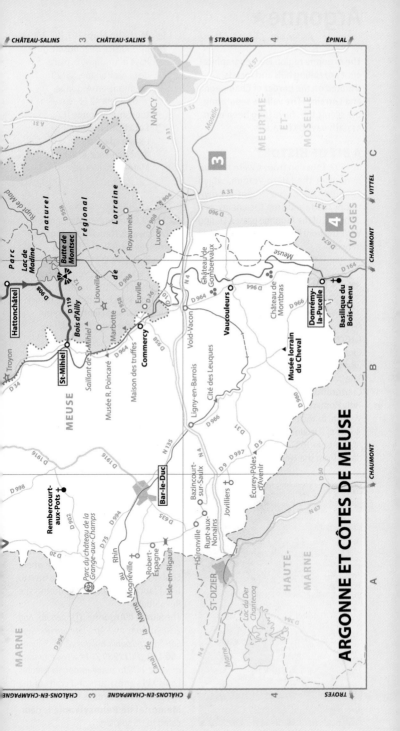

ARGONNE ET CÔTES DE MEUSE

NANCY

Moselle

A 33

A 31

A 31

MEURTHE-ET-MOSELLE

C

VITTEL

VOSGES

CHAUMONT

4

D 674

3

Parc naturel régional

Lorraine

de

Rupt de Mad

D 958

Lac de Madine

Butte de Montsec

D 904

Royaumeix

Lucey

D 908

D 611

Meuse

D 960

D 164

Hattonchâtel

D 906

Troyon

D 34

D 119

Bois d'Ailly

D 908

Liouville

Marbotte

D 958

Euville

D 901

D 36

St-Mihiel

Saillant de St-Mihiel

Musée R. Poincaré

D 964

Maison des truffes

Commercy

D 958

MEUSE

Void-Vacon

N 4

Château de Gombervaux

Château de Montbras

D 964

D 966

Vaucouleurs

Ligny-en-Barrois

Cité des Leuques

D 966

Musée lorrain du Cheval

D 960

Domrémy-la-Pucelle

Basilique du Bois-Chenu

CHAUMONT

Rembercourt-aux-Pots

D 998

D 902

D 1916

Parc du château de la Grange-aux-Champs

D 994

D 75

Bar-le-Duc

N 135

D 1916

Bazincourt-sur-Saulx

D 635

Haironville

Rupt-aux-Nonains

D 9

D 997

Jovilliers

Écurey-Pôles d'Avenir

D 5

N 4

D 50

CHAUMONT

au Rhin

Mognéville

Robert-Espagne

Lisle-en-Rigault

Canal de la Marne

MARNE

HAUTE-MARNE

ST-DIZIER

Lac du Der Chantecoq

Marne

N 4

D 384

D 994

MARNE

Argonne★

Ardennes, Marne, Meuse

The Argonne region is a geographical entity of rolling hills and forests situated on the border of Champagne and Lorraine. The valleys separating the scenic hills have long been used as pathways by invaders.

A BIT OF HISTORY

In 1792, Prussian troops were held up here after the fall of Verdun, which enabled Dumouriez to get his own troops ready and stop the enemy as it came out of the Argonne passes. During WWI, the front line actually split Argonne in two.

🚗 DRIVING TOUR

77km/48mi. Allow one day.

Clermont-en-Argonne

Clermont is picturesquely situated on a wooded hillside above the Aire valley. The former capital of the county of Clermontois belonged in turn to the Holy Roman Empire, to the bishopric of Verdun, to the county of Bar and to the duchy of Lorraine before becoming part of France in 1632. The **Église St-Didier** dates from the 16C.

- ♿ **Michelin Map:** 307: B/C 3/4.
- 🗊 Info: Office de tourisme du Pays d'Argonne, 6, place de la république, 55120 Clermont-en-Argonne. ✆03 29 88 42 22; www. tourisme-argonne.fr.
- ▶ **Location:** The Argonne region spans three *départements*: Ardennes, Marne and Meuse.

▶ Leave Clermont-en-Argonne on D 998 towards Neuvilly-en-Argonne. From Neuvilly, follow D 946. In Boureuilles, take D 212 on the right towards Vauquois. As you enter Vauquois, follow the surfaced path on the left, which leads to the hillock. Leave the car and climb along the footpath to the top of the hill.

Butte de Vauquois

No charge for visit of above-ground area. ●❧*Guided tour of underground installations: 1st Sun of the month 9.30–11am; 1 and 8 May, 9.30am–4.30pm; Jul–Aug Thu 2pm by arrangement.* ☞€5. ✆03 29 80 73 15. *www.butte-vauquois.fr.*
Between 1914 and 1918, there was fierce fighting on both sides over this hill.

▶ Return to D 38 which leads to Varennes-en-Argonne.

Varennes-en-Argonne

This small town, built on the banks of the River Aire, is famous as the place where Louis XVI was arrested when he tried to flee France with his family during the Revolution.
The **Musée d'Argonne** (🕐*open Jul–Aug 2.30–5.30pm; mid-Apr–late Jun and Sept Sat–Sun and public holidays 2.30–5.30pm.* ☞€4.50. ✆03 29 80 71 14; www.tourisme-argonne-1418.fr/musee-largonne) features Louis XVI's arrest, arts and crafts of the region and mementoes from WWI. The **Mémorial de Pennsylvanie** is dedicated to US soldiers.

Argonne countryside

© Stéphane Ouzounoff/Photononstop

L'ARGONNE

0 ——— 4 km

▶ Return to D 38 then turn left onto the Haute-Chevauchée road.

Haute-Chevauchée (Kaiser Tunnel)

◔ Closed for restoration. ℘03 29 87 40 12.

This is one of the main sites of WWI yet the road offers a pleasant walk to the **Kaisertunnel** and the Forestière military cemetery.

▶ Return to D 38 and continue to Four-de-Paris, then take D 2 to Lachalade.

Lachalade

The village is overlooked by the imposing silhouette of a former Cistercian abbey.

▶ Continue towards Les Islettes.

Les Islettes

This village was famous for its tileries, glassworks and earthenware factories.

▶ Beyond Futeau, D 2 goes through the Beaulieu forest.

Ermitage de St-Rouin

St Roding (or Rouin), a 7C Irish monk, settled in Argonne and founded a monastery which preceded the Beaulieu abbey.

▶ Continue along D 2 and turn left towards Beaulieu-en-Argonne.

Beaulieu-en-Argonne

Only a few walls of the Benedictine abbey remain apart from the huge 13C **winepress★**.

▶ From Beaulieu-en-Argonne take the forest road running alongside

the winepress building (on the left), continue straight on beyond the Trois Pins crossroads then turn right to Rarécourt.

Rarécourt

The **Musée de la Faïence** (◔ early Jun–Aug daily 10am–noon, 2–6.30pm. ⊛ €4. ℘07 87 77 29 82) is housed in a 17C–18C fortified building.

▶ From Rarécourt, return to Clermont-en-Argonne along D 998.

ADDRESSES

🛏 STAY

⊜⊜ **Hostellerie de l'Abbaye** – 7 Grande-Rue – 55250 Beaulieu-en-Argonne. ℘03 29 70 38 69. www.hotel-beaulieu-en-argonne.com. 8 rooms. Restaurant (⊜⊜). This establishment in the main street of the village houses the local café, a small number of well-maintained rooms and a simple restaurant. Lovely view of the Argonne and the surrounding mountain forests.

Rue des Ducs-de-Bar

© Hervé Hughes/hemis.fr

Bar-le-Duc★

Meuse

Partly built on top of a promontory, Bar-le-Duc is split into two: the Ville Haute or upper town, where the castle of the dukes of Bar once stood, and the Ville Basse or lower town, lying on both banks of the River Ornain, a tributary of the Marne. In the 10C, Bar was already the capital of a county whose influence rivalled that of the duchy of Lorraine, and in 1354 the counts of Bar became dukes. During WWI, Bar-le-Duc played an important role in the Battle of Verdun. Today the city is the administrative centre of the Meuse *département* and a commercial town where regular fairs and markets are held. Redcurrant jam is a famous speciality (Alfred Hitchcock claimed it was his favourite).

▪▪ WALKING TOUR

VILLE HAUTE★
Allow 30min
The former aristocratic district of Bar still boasts a stellar ensemble of 16C, 17C and 18C architecture.

Place St-Pierre
This triangular area in front of the west front of the Église St-Étienne, is lined with houses from different periods.

▶ **Population:** 16 783.
& **Michelin Map:** Michelin Local map 307: B-6.
🛈 **Tourist Office:** 7 r. Jeanne-d'Arc, 55000 Bar-le-Duc, ☎03 29 79 11 13. www.tourisme-barleduc.fr.
◖ **Location:** Bar-le-Duc is located half-way between Strasbourg and Paris, exit 30 (Verdun) on A 4, then N 35. The town is 40km/24.8mi to the south.

On the right as you face the church, **No. 25** is a fine medieval timber-framed house with corbelled upper floor, while **No. 21** has an Alsatian Renaissance façade. And **No. 29** is strictly Classical, with early-17C columns and windows.

Église St-Étienne
This former collegiate church of the late 14C contains several works of art including the famous **Transi★★** by Ligier Richier *(in the south transept)*, which depicts the Prince of Orange, René de Chalon, killed during the siege of St-Dizier in 1544 (the work was commissioned by his widow, Anne de Lorraine). A **Calvary** scene behind the high altar is also by Richier. In the north transept the **Statue of Notre-Dame-du-Guet** is revered locally – legend claims it shouted warnings during the siege of 1440.

Place de la Halle

You can glimpse the arcades of the former 13C covered market through the gateway of **No. 3**, which has a beautiful though damaged Baroque façade.

▷ Take rue Chavée and turn right.

Belvédère des Grangettes

This offers a view of the lower town.

▷ Return to rue Chavée, turn right onto rue de l'Armurier then left onto rue de l'Horloge.

Only the **clock tower** remains of the former ducal castle.

▷ Rue de l'Horloge on the left leads to avenue du Château; turn left.

Collège Gilles-de-Trèves

The university college was founded in 1571 by the dean of St-Maxe, Gilles de Trèves, who wished to stop young aristocrats from attending universities where the Reformation was gaining ground. Access is through a long porch with vaulting with a Latin inscription: "Let this house remain standing until ants have drunk the oceans dry and tortoises have gone all the way round the world".

▷ Continue along rue du Baile, passing Musée Barrois (see SIGHTS)

Rue des Ducs-de-Bar

This high street has several beautiful façades, including **No. 41**, with two 16C friezes decorated with military motifs, **No. 47** with gargoyles, and **No.**

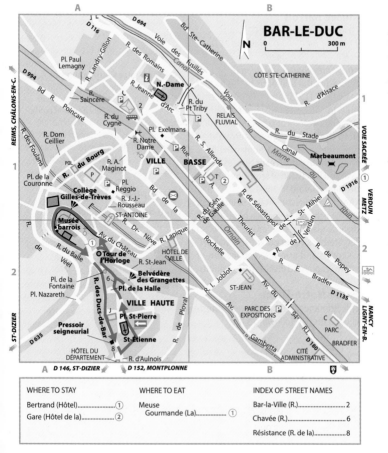

73 adorned with musical instruments. In a building at the end of the courtyard of **No. 75**, there is a 15C **winepress**.

VILLE BASSE
Château de Marbeaumont
This early-20C castle, once owned by bankers Varin-Bernier, was General Pétain's headquarters during WWI. The vast surrounding park has sports facilities and a campsite.

Rue du Bourg
The lower town was essentially a shopping district; from the 16C onwards, its high street became a highly-coveted address (richly decorated façades include **Nos. 26, 42, 46, 49** and **51**).

SIGHTS
Musée Barrois
🕐 Jul–Aug daily 2–6pm. 🕐 1 Jan, 1 May, 14 Jul, 15 Aug, 1 Nov and 25 Dec. ✆€3. ☎03 29 76 14 67. http://museebarrois.eklablog.fr. Housed in the buildings of the former tax office (1523) and the new castle built in 1567, the museum contains a rich archaeological collection ranging from the Bronze Age to Merovingian times with many Gallo-Roman exhibits. The **Chambre du Trésor** houses medieval and Renaissance sculptures (Pierre de Milan, Gérard Richier).
The museum also contains paintings of the French and Flemish Schools (Heindrick de Clerck, David Teniers Junior and Jan Steen), a collection of 16C and 17C weapons and armour, a collection of ethnography and local-history exhibits.

Église Notre-Dame
This Romanesque church was remodelled in the 17C following a fire.

EXCURSION
Rembercourt-aux-Pots
18km/11mi.

▶ Drive N out of Bar-le-Duc along D 116 towards Vavincourt.

The 15C village **church** has a magnificent **west front★** in a successful blend of Flamboyant and Renaissance styles. The towers were never completed.

ADDRESSES

🏠 STAY
🛏 **Hôtel Bertrand** – 19 rue de l'Étoile. ☎03 29 79 02 97. www.hotelrestaurant bertrand.com. 32 rooms. Don't be put off by the ancient aspect of this hotel – it has an annexe with reasonably priced rooms and is close to the town centre. A fully equiped balneotherapy room is available for guests.

🛏 **Hôtel de la Gare** – 2 pl. de la République. ☎03 29 79 01 45. www.barleduchotel.com. 25 rooms. Even though the minimalist decoration in reception is slightly cold, the simple comfort of the rooms meets the expectations of travellers.

🍴 EAT
🍽🍽 **La Meuse Gourmande** – 1 r. F.–de-Guise, Ville Haute. ☎03 29 79 28 40. www.meusegourmande.fr. Closed Sun Eve, Wed, Feb school holidays and public holidays. Located in a handsome 18C residence. Plushly decorated interior; the tables near the windows command a fine view of the lower town. Up-to-date cuisine and mouthwatering desserts.

SHOPPING
Ets Dutriez, À la Lorraine – 35 r. de l'Étoile. ☎03 29 79 06 81. www.groseille.com. Mon–Fri 9.30am–noon, 2–5pm, Sat 10am–noon, 2–7pm. The Maison Dutriez, which was founded in 1879, is the only establishment still producing redcurrant jam, deseeded with the help of a goose feather.

Woëvre Plain, the monument on Butte de Montsec in the background

Parc naturel régional de
Lorraine

*Meurthe-et-Moselle,
Meuse, Moselle*

Michelin Map: Michelin Local map 307: K to L-6.

Also See: Le Saulnois

The western section of the park straddles the *départements* of Meurthe-et-Moselle and Meuse, close to the towns of Nancy and Metz. This nature park offers visitors a wonderful natural environment, with numerous lakes that are home to thousands of migrating birds.

A BIT OF HISTORY

Created in 1974, the park surrounds the River Moselle. A protected area of pastoral countryside, the parkland spreads between the cities of Metz and Nancy and spans three departments.

SIGHTS
Nature trails

The western area of the park is crisscrossed with marked footpaths with explanatory panels: forest trail in the Forêt de la Reine, limestone-meadow trail in Génicourt-sur-Meuse, a vineyard trail in Lucey, and an educational hemp-growing trail around Toul.

Lac de Madine

Nonsard, on the northeast shore of the lake lies 25km/15mi W of Pont-à Mousson along D 958 to Flirey

(15km/9.3mi) then right onto D 904 to Pannes (7km/4.3mi) and left onto D 133 (3km/1.9mi).

This large lake (1 100ha) forms a vast outdoor leisure park offering many water sports (boating, swimming and sailing) and other activities (tennis, golf and riding) as well as the opportunity to relax in a pleasant country setting (catering, accommodation and camping). It is also possible to take a 20km/12.4mi walk, or bike ride, around the lake.

DRIVING TOUR

Côtes de Meuse★
From Verdun to St-Mihiel. 83km/52mi. Allow 2h30.

Leave Verdun by D 903 towards Metz and Nancy.

Soon after leaving Verdun, look to the right for a fine view of the Meuse valley and its wooded rolling countryside.

PRACTICAL INFORMATION

Maison du Parc – *r. du Quai, 54702 Pont-à-Mousson,* &03 83 81 67 67,. *www.pnr-lorraine.com.*

Nature walks – From Apr–Sept, the Parc naturel régional de Lorraine organises countryside outings. In additon to rental cottages listed with **gîtes de France**, some WWF-approved **Panda gîtes** are to be found in Lorraine. An information pack including guides to local wildlife, observation equipment (binoculars and compass) and maps are provided. Rental via individual owners, or through the **Loisirs-Accueil de Moselle** reservation service: &03 87 37 57 63.

Observatoire des Côtes de Meuse – *10 pl. de Verdun, 55210 Vieville-sous-les-Côtes.* &03 29 89 58 64. http:// *observatoiret83.weebly.com.* The Observatory is home to one of the most powerful telescopes in Europe (Newton telescope with 83cm diameter).

Golf de Madine – *55210 Nonsard.* &03 29 89 56 00. http://golfmadine.fr.

Lac de Madine – Madine Accueil *55210 Nonsard.* &03 29 89 32 50. www. *lacmadine.com.* Tourist facilities and accommodation mainly on the lake's northeast bank.

Madine 1 – *Camping de Nonsard 55210 Nonsard.* &03 29 89 56 76. Sailing harbour, restaurant, beach, bicycles for hire, and golf.

Madine 2 – *Camping d'Heudicourt 55210 Nonsard.* &03 29 89 36 08. Beach, playground and horse-riding centre.

Madine 2–3 – *55210 Nonsard.* Village of gîtes, sailing school, indoor tennis courts, bird park and communal hall (events organised in evenings).

▶ 7km/4.3mi beyond the intersection of D 903 and D 964, turn right onto DST 31, signposted Les Éparges, Hattonchâtel, then right again onto D 154.

Les Éparges

The outcrop overlooking the Woëvre Plain was the scene of fierce fighting during WWI.

Site des Éparges

🚶 Marked footpaths running through a dense forest (scarred by mines) lead from Le Trottoir national cemetery to the site of the fighting.

▶ Turn back and drive to D 908 via St-Rémy-la-Calonne and Combres-sous-les-Côtes. In St-Maurice-sous-les-Côtes, turn right onto D 101 then left onto the narrow DST 31 to Hattonchâtel.

Hattonchâtel★

This once fortified village, built on a promontory, owes its name to a 9C castle belonging to a bishop of Verdun named Hatton.

The neo-Romanesque town hall houses the **Musée Louise-Cottin** containing about 100 paintings by this artist (1907–74).

Situated at the end of a promontory, the former **castle**, dismantled in 1634 by order of Richelieu, was restored between 1924 and 1928. The view extends as far as Nancy.

▶ Follow D 908 S to Woinville then turn left onto D 119 to Montsec.

Butte de Montsec★★

The **monument★** at the top of an isolated hill (alt 275m) commemorates the American offensive of September 1918. From the memorial, the **view★★** embraces the Woëvre valley and Côtes de Meuse to the west and Lake Madine to the north.

▶ Turn round and drive back along D 119 to Woinville then on to St Mihiel.

St-Mihiel★ – 🕐*See ST-MIHIEL.*

Montmédy citadel

Montmédy

Meuse

There are two towns in one: Montmédy-Bas (lower town), on the banks of the River Chiers, and Montmédy-Haut (upper town), fortified during the Renaissance and remodelled by Vauban, which has retained its ramparts.

The town organises two lively festivals: the **Fête des Remparts** involving jugglers, clowns and tightrope walkers *(first Sunday in May)* and the **Fête des Pommes** centred on a busy market, exhibitions and tasting sessions *(first Sunday in October)*.

MONTMÉDY-HAUT

The upper town is perched on an isolated peak.

Citadelle★

A walk along the ramparts (⊙*Apr–Sept 10am–1pm, 1.30–6pm; Oct–Mar 10.30am–1pm, 1.30–5.30pm (except Sat–Sun in Jan–Dec).* ⊙*1 Jan, 24 Dec.* ⊛€5. ℘*03 29 80 15 90)* past glacis, curtain walls, bastions and underground passages, gives a good idea of the complexity and ingenious design of the citadel's defence system, modernised after 1870. From the top of the ramparts, the **view** extends over the lower town, the Chiers valley and numerous surrounding villages.

▶ **Population:** 2 339.
◔ **Michelin Map:** Michelin Local map 307: D-1.
🛈 **Tourist office:** 2 r. de l'Hôtel-de-Ville, 55600 Montmédy. ℘03 29 80 15 90. www.tourisme-montmedy.fr

Musées de la Fortification et Jules Bastien-Lepage

⊙*Open as for Citadelle.* ⊛€5. ℘*03 29 80 15 90.*

Situated at the entrance of the citadel, these museums are devoted respectively to the history of fortifications (models, historic documents, audio-visual presentation) and to the life and work of a native of the region, the painter Jules Bastien-Lepage (1848–84).

Église St-Martin

Dating from the mid-18C this church has retained its stalls and woodwork.

EXCURSIONS

Louppy-sur-Loison

14km/8.7mi S.

▷ Leave Montmédy by N 43 towards Longuyon then turn right in Iré-le-Sec.

The 17C **castle** (*Jul–Aug Tue–Sun 10am–6pm.* ⊛€6. ℘09 65 16 54 65; www.chateau-louppy.com) built by Simon

Basilique d'Avioth

de Pouilly, governor of Stenay (&see *Vallée de la MEUSE*), is still owned by his descendants.

Ruins of the original fortress can be seen near the church.

Marville

12km/7.5mi SE along N 43.

Founded in Gallo-Roman times under the name of Major villa, Marville has several 16C and 17C houses along the **Grand'Rue**.

In the **Église St-Nicolas** note the early-16C balustrade of the organ loft.

Cimetière de la chapelle St-Hilaire

The tarmacked path leading to the cemetery branches off N 43.

Situated at the top of the hill, the cemetery of the former Église St-Hilaire contains a walled ossuary said to house 40 000 skulls.

Avioth★★

8.5km/5.3mi N along D110.

Basilique d'Avioth★★

&☉*Jun–Sept Fri at 3pm.* ⊛€4. ℘*03 29 88 90 96. http://avioth.fr.*

This magnificent church, situated in the centre of the remote village of

Avioth, near the Belgian border, offers a striking contrast with its rural setting. Next to it stands an unusual monument, the Recevresse, intended to receive offerings from pilgrims.

Basilique Notre-Dame

The discovery of a statue of the Virgin Mary, believed to have been sculpted by angels, led to a pilgrimage during the early 12C and to the construction of the basilica from the second half of the 13C to the beginning of the 15C when the flamboyant gothic style prevailed.

Exterior – The **west doorway** arching is decorated with 70 figures, and Christ's Passion is depicted on the lintel. The **south doorway** is dedicated to the Virgin Mary and to Christ's childhood. Left of the south doorway stands **La Recevresse★**, a small yet elegant edifice in Flamboyant style decorated with fine tracery work.

Interior – The basilica includes a walkway (unusual in this region) and an ambulatory; radiating from it are shallow chapels fitted between the buttresses which happen to be inside the church according to a Champagne practice. Restoration work has brought to light 14C and 15C paintings and frescoes over the chancel screen and vaulting.

Worth noting in the chancel is the 14C high altar decorated with symbols of the four evangelists.

To the left of the altar, one can see the ancient statue of **Notre-Dame d'Avioth**, carved out of lime c 1110 and resting on a 15C stone throne. Note also the 14 polychrome statues placed high against the pillars of the east end .

The Gothic tabernacle on the right of the altar dates from the 15 C. The elegant pulpit dates from 1538 and is carved with Renaissance motifs.

St-Mihiel★

Meuse

Situated on the western edge of the Parc naturel régional de Lorraine, St-Mihiel has an important religious heritage as birthplace of the sculptor Ligier Richier. It is also a good base for river trips on the Meuse and exploring the WWI battlefields.

A BIT OF HISTORY

St-Mihiel's history was long intertwined with an important Benedictine abbey founded in 709 near the present town and relocated in 815 on the banks of the Meuse.

In 1301, St-Mihiel became the main town of the Barrois region east of the River Meuse. The city prospered both economically and culturally, notably in the 16C when renowned drapers and goldsmiths settled in St-Mihiel and the fame of **Ligier Richier** and his school of sculpture spread throughout eastern France. Born in St-Mihiel in 1500, Richier surrounded himself with talented sculptors and apprentices. In 1559 he was asked to decorate the town for the arrival of Duke Charles III and his wife. Fine examples of his considerable output can be seen in Bar-le-Duc, Hatton-châtel, Étain and Briey.

In September 1914, the German army launched a thrust in the area in order to skirt round the powerful stronghold of Verdun. They succeeded in establishing a bridgehead on the west bank of the Meuse, known as the St-Mihiel Bulge, which prevented supplies and reinforcements from reaching Verdun via the Meuse valley.

SIGHTS

Église St-Michel

The abbey church was almost entirely rebuilt in the 17C, except for its 12C square belfry and Romanesque porch. The first chapel on the south side contains a masterpiece by Ligier Richier: the **Fainting Virgin supported by St John★**. This walnut sculpture (1531) formed part of a calvary representing Christ (his head is now in the Louvre),

▶ **Population:** 4 370.

Michelin Map: Michelin Local map 307: E-5.

Tourist office: Rue du Palais du Justice, 55300 St-Mihiel. ℘03 29 89 06 47. www.coeurdelorraine-tourisme.fr.

▶ **Location:** S of Verdun at the junction of the D 901 and D 964.

Don't Miss: The Sepulchre by Ligier richier in the Eglise St-Etienne.

St Longin, Mary Magdalene and four angels. The baptismal chapel on the same side contains a funeral monument, carved in 1608 by Jean Richier, Ligier Richier's grandson.

Former Abbaye

Rue du Palais-de-Justice.
Jun–Sept Wed–Mon 2–6pm.
Apr–May and Oct, Sat–Sun 2–6pm.
Nov–Mar and public holidays. ≈€5 (combined library and museum ticket).
℘03 29 89 06 47.

The conventual buildings, next to the Église St-Michel, were rebuilt in the 17C and are almost intact. A large hall decorated with woodwork and ceilings in the Louis XIV style houses the **Bibliothèque bénédictine**, a rich collection including 74 manuscripts and 86 incunabula. In the south wing, the **Musée départemental d'Art sacré** contains many artefacts from the Meuse.

Maison du Roi

2 rue Notre-Dame.
This 14C Gothic house belonged in the 15C to King René of Anjou.

Église St-Étienne

The nave of this original hall-church was built between 1500 and 1545. Note the modern stained-glass windows and the Renaissance altarpiece in the apse. But the church is above all famous for the **Sepulchre★★** or Entombment sculpted by Ligier Richier from 1554 to 1564. Recently restored, 13 figures depict the preparations for Christ's Entombment: Salomé prepares the funeral bed, Joseph and Nicodemus hold the body of Christ, Mary Magdalene kisses Christ's feet. In the background, St John supports the Virgin Mary, an angel holds the instruments of the Passion, and two guards are throwing the dice for Christ's tunic.

The cliffs

Seven limestone cliffs, over 20m high, overlook the east bank of the river. In 1772, Mangeot, a native of St-Mihiel. carved a representation of the Holy Sepulchre in the first rock.

EXCURSIONS

Bois d'Ailly

7km/4.3mi SE along D 907 and a signposted forest road.

Heavy fighting took place here in September 1914: from the memorial a row of trenches leads to the Tranchée de la Soif (thirst trench) where a few soldiers held on for three days against the German Imperial Guard.

Vaucouleurs

Meuse

Along with the nearby village of Domrémy-la-Pucelle, the peaceful little town of Vaucouleurs is associated with the history of Joan of Arc. It has retained part of its 13C fortifications and offers visitors boat trips on the Marne-to-Rhine canal and walk through the forested Parc naturel régional de Lorraine.

A BIT OF HISTORY

In May 1428, a young shepherdess from Domrémy arrived in Vaucouleurs to see the governor and told him that God had sent her to save France. Robert de Baudricourt's first reaction was to send her back to her village but Joan of Arc persisted and after several months, urged by public enthusiasm, Baudricourt agreed to help. In February

Commercy

18km/11.2mi S along the River Meuse.

Commercy occupied a strategic position on the west bank of the River Meuse and the number of fortified houses and churches are a reminder of the constant threat of invasion the whole area lived under in the past. The town is famous for its madeleine cakes.

An imposing horseshoe esplanade precedes the **Château Stanislas** (👣 *guided tours Jul–Aug, 3pm.* ✆€4. *☎03 29 91 33 16; contact tourist office for details*). Designed in 1708 by Boffrand and d'Orbay for the Prince de Vaudémont, it was used as a hunting lodge before becoming the property of Stanislas Leszczynski, King Louis XV's father-in-law.

The former municipal baths, dating from the 1930s, have been turned into the **Musée de la Céramique et de l'Ivoire** (♿🕐*Jul–Aug Wed–Mon 2–6pm; May–Jun and Sept Sat, Sun and public holidays 2–6pm.* ✆€4.50. *☎03 29 92 04 77; www.commercy.fr*).

> ▶ **Population:** 2 069.
> 🖥 **Michelin Map:** Michelin Local map 307: E-7.
> ℹ **Tourist Office**: 15 rue Jeanne d'Arc, 55140 Vaucouleurs. *☎03 29 89 51 82. www.tourisme-vaucouleurs.fr.*
> ▶ **Location:** 21km SW of Toul by the D960.

1429, Joan left Vaucouleurs on her way to meet the king of France.

SIGHTS
Site du château

The ruins of the castle where Joan was received by Baudricourt in 1428.

The upper part of the Porte de France from where she left the town accompanied by a small escort remains, rebuilt in

Maison natale de Jeanne d'Arc

© Jean-Pierre De Mann/age fotostock

the 17C. The Chapelle castrale (⊙*open contact the Tourist Office*), consisting of three chapels, was built over a 13C crypt. In the central chapel is the statue before which Joan used to pray.

Église

The 18C church has frescoes on the vault and an elaborately carved church-wardens' pew and the pulpit (1717).

Musée Jeanne d'Arc

Hôtel de Ville. ⊙*Mar–Apr and Oct–Nov Mon–Fri 9.30am–noon, 2–6pm, Sat 10am–noon; May–Sept Mon–Sat 10am–noon, 2–6pm, Sun and public holidays 2–6pm; Dec–Feb Mon–Fri 9.30am–noon, 1.30–6pm.* ⊙*1 Jan, Easter Mon, 1 and 8 May, 1 and 11 Nov, 25 Dec.* ⊛€5. ℘*03 29 89 51 63.*
The highlight of this museum of local history and archaeology is the Christ de Septfonds, a magnificent oak crucifix from a nearby chapel where Joan of Arc went to pray for guidance.

EXCURSIONS

Domrémy-la-Pucelle★

19km/12mi S along D 964 then D 164.
This humble village is the birthplace of Joan of Arc (1412–31). An important pilgrimage takes place on the second Sunday in May, Joan of Arc's feast day, in Bois-Chenu Basilica (ও*see below*).
The **church** was remodelled in the 15C and extended in 1825. However, it

has retained a few objects that were familiar to Joan of Arc: a statue of St Margaret (14C) and the font over which she was christened.

Maison natale de Jeanne d'Arc★

ও⊙*Feb–Mar and Oct–Dec Wed–Mon 10am–1pm, 2–5pm; Apr–Sept daily 10am–1pm, 2–6.30pm.* ⊙*1 Jan, 25 Dec.* ⊛€3. ℘*03 29 06 95 86.*
The house where Joan of Arc was born is that of a comfortable peasant family; the walls are thick and there is the emblem of the family next to the arms of France over the door. Behind the house is a modern **interpretation centre★**.

Basilique du Bois-Chenu

1.5km/0.9mi from Domrémy by D 53 towards Coussey.
The late-19C basilica stands on the site where Joan heard the voices telling her about her mission. Start with the crypt (entrance on the left); statue of Notre-Dame-de-Bermont before which Joan prayed every Saturday.

Musée lorrain du Cheval

La Tour Ronde, Gondrecourt le Château, 20km/12.4mi S of Vaucouleurs by D 960 and D 966. ⊙*Jul–Aug Wed–Mon 2–6pm.* ⊛€3). ℘*03 29 46 43 85.*
🎫♿ This museum, housed in a 15C tower, offers a lively account of the role played by horses throughout history.

Verdun★★

Meuse

This ancient stronghold on a strategic position on the west bank of the Meuse has become the symbol in France of the violence of WWI.

A BIT OF HISTORY

Verdun started out as a Gaulish fortress, then became a Roman fort under the name of Virodunum Castrum. In 843, the treaty splitting the Carolingian Empire into three kingdoms was signed in the city which was ceded to the kingdom of Lorraine. In 1552, Verdun was seized by Henri II and became part of the French kingdom.

Occupied briefly by the Prussians in 1792, it was liberated following the French victory at Valmy in the Argonne. In 1870, the town was again besieged by the Prussians and was forced to capitulate. The occupation lasted three years. At the start of WWI, Verdun was, together with Toul, the most powerful stronghold in eastern France. The terrible Battle of Verdun took place all round the town between February 1916 and August 1917.

The Battle of Verdun

German troops had, since 1914, been trying in vain to skirt round Verdun and then to take it. Verdun nevertheless remained a formidable obstacle with its powerful citadel, its ring of forts and its gullied wooded plateaux. Yet this is where the German army, led by General von Falkenhayn, decided to strike a heavy blow in February 1916 in the hope of weakening the French army, lifting morale and thwarting the offen-

▶ **Population:** 19 144.
◔ **Michelin Map:** Michelin Local map 307: D-4.
🗎 **Tourist Office:** Place de la Nation, 55160 Verdun. ℘03 29 86 14 18. www.tourisme-verdun.com.
▶ **Location:** W of Metz by N3.
🔍 **Don't Miss:** The battle-fields and the Ossuaire de Douarmont.

sive which they suspected the Allies to be preparing (it actually came in July on the Somme). The Crown Prince, Emperor William II's own son, was entrusted with the operation.

German offensive
(February–August 1916)

The German offensive took the French high command by surprise. It began on 21 February, 13km/8mi north of Verdun, with the heaviest concentration of shelling ever experienced.

The resistance was stronger than expected but the Germans progressed slowly and the Fort de Douaumont soon fell, thus becoming a threat to the city. General Pétain, who was made commander in chief of the Verdun forces, began to organise the defence of the city. Reinforcements and supplies were brought in via the only available route, Bar-le-Duc to Verdun, nicknamed the **sacred way**.

The frontal attack was finally stopped on 26 February and, in March and April, German troops widened the front on both banks of the Meuse but failed to take several key positions. There followed a savage war of attrition: forts, ruined villages or woods were taken over and over again at a terrible cost in human lives. On 11 July, German troops finally received the order to remain on the defensive.

The Russian offensive and the Franco-British offensive on the Somme put an end to any hope the Germans may have had of taking the advantage at Verdun.

PRACTICAL INFORMATION

Museum and monument pass – The **Battlefields Pass** includes entrance to 5 sites: Mémorial de Verdun, Fort de Vaux, the Citadelle Souterraine, Fort de Douaumont and the Ossuary of Douaumont. €25 instead of €34.

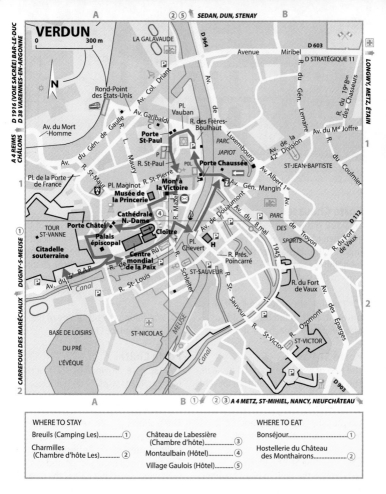

WHERE TO STAY		WHERE TO EAT
Breuils (Camping Les)..............①	Château de Labessière (Chambre d'hôte)...................③	Bonséjour....................................①
Charmilles (Chambre d'hôte Les)............②	Montaulbain (Hôtel)...............④	Hostellerie du Château des Monthairons...................②
	Village Gaulois (Hôtel)...........⑤	

French counter-offensive (October 1916–October 1917)

Three brilliant but costly offensives enabled French troops to take back all lost ground:

◆ **Bataille de Douaumont-Vaux** (24 October–2 November 1916) on the east bank.

◆ **Bataille de Louvemont-Bezonvaux** (15–18 December 1916), also on the east bank, which cleared the Vaux and Douaumont sectors once and for all.

◆ **Bataille de la Cote 304 et du Mort-Homme** (20–24 August 1917) on the west bank; German troops were forced

back to the positions they held on 22 February 1916 and tried in vain to counter-attack until October. The pressure on Verdun was released but it was only in September–October 1918, following the Franco-American offensive, that the front line was pushed back beyond its position of February 1916.

✏ WALKING TOUR

VILLE HAUTE★
Allow 1h30. Start from the tourist office. Walk across the bridge.

Palais épiscopal

Porte Chaussée
This 16C gateway used to guard the entrance of the town and served as a prison. It formed part of a thick wall surrounding the town and skirting the west bank of the River Meuse.

◐ Take rue des Frères-Boulhaut on the right, walk round the left side of place Vauban to reach rue St-Paul.

Porte St-Paul
The two drawbridges can still be seen. This was the only way in and out for vehicles before the ramparts disappeared in 1929. In front of the gate stands a bronze sculpture by Rodin (La Défense), offered to the town by the Netherlands.

◐ Follow rue St-Paul then rue St-Pierre on the right to place Maginot and turn left towards the cathedral past the Musée de la Princerie (&see below).

Cathédrale Notre-Dame★
Standing at the highest point of the town, the cathedral was built between 990 and 1024 in Rhenish style. The west chancel is typically Rhenish, the east chancel (1130–40) shows Burgundian influence.
After a fire in 1755 the Romanesque towers were replaced by two balustraded square Baroque towers. The nave was also transformed in Baroque style; the crypt was filled in and the Romanesque doorways concealed. The Romanesque part of the edifice was restored following the shelling of 1916.

Cloître★
The cloisters, on the south side of the cathedral, consist of three galleries: that on the east side has three 14C arched openings which once led to the chapter house; the other two galleries were built in Flamboyant style in 1509–17.

◐ Walk along the north side of the cathedral to place Châtel.

Porte Châtel
The 13C gate, crowned by 15C macchiolations, leads to place de la Roche.

Palais épiscopal★
The bishop's palace, set at the rear of a long semi-circular courtyard, was built in the 18C by Robert de Cotte. The municipal library is located in the west wing. The other part of the palace houses the Centre mondial de la Paix.

◐ Return along rue de Rû to place du Maréchal-Foch.

Hôtel de ville
This 1623 mansion is a fine example of Louis XIII style.

ADDITIONAL SIGHTS
Musée de la Princerie
16 rue de la Belle-Vierge.
◷*Apr–Oct Wed–Mon 9.30am–noon, 2–6pm.* ✆€3. ☏*03 29 86 10 62. www.musee-princerie-verdun.fr.*
The museum is housed in an elegant 16C house built by two rich canons. Note the 12C carved-ivory comb, medieval stat-

ues, glazed earthenware from Argonne and paintings by local artists.

Citadelle souterraine★

Avenue de la 5e R.A.P. ♿🕐*Feb and Dec 9.30am–noon, 1.30–5pm; Mar and Nov 9.30am–5.30pm; Apr–May and Sept–Oct daily 9am–6pm; Jun–Aug 9am–7pm.* 🕐*late Dec–Jan.* ✆€9. ☎03 29 84 84 42.

The citadel was built by Vauban on the site of the Abbaye de St-Vanne, of which only one 12C tower remains.

In 1916–17, the citadel was used as a rest area for troops during the Battle of Verdun. A self-guided vehicle takes visitors on a **round-trip★★** of the citadel where the soldiers' daily life during the Battle of Verdun is recreated through sound effects and reconstructed scenes.

Centre mondial de la Paix

In the bishop's palace. ♿🕐*Daily 10am–6pm.* ✆€5. ☎03 29 86 55 00. *www.cmpaix.eu.*

The exhibition of the World Peace Centre has seven sections: war, the earth and its frontiers, from war to peace, Europe, the United Nations for peace, human rights, and peace concepts.

Monument de la Victoire

🕐*Apr–Nov 2–5pm.* ✆*No charge.* ☎03 29 87 24 29.

Seventy-three steps lead to a terrace on which stands a high pyramid surmounted by the statue of a warrior wearing a helmet and leaning on his sword, as a symbol of Verdun's defence. The crypt beneath the monument bears the list of all the ex-servicemen who were awarded the medal of Verdun.

THE BATTLEFIELDS★★★

Almost a century on, the battlefields still bear the marks of the fierce fighting that took place from 21 February 1916 to 20 August 1917 in what is now known as the **Battle of Verdun**. In less than two years, this battle, which unfolded along a 200km/124mi front, involved several million soldiers and caused the death of 400 000 Frenchmen and almost as many Germans as well as several thousand American soldiers.

EAST BANK OF THE MEUSE

21km/13mi. About 3h. Michelin Local map 307: D-3.

This was the main sector of the battle, where the decisive turning point occurred.

▶ Drive E along avenue de la 42e-Division then avenue du Maréchal-Joffre and leave Verdun by N 3 towards Étain.

Cimetière militaire du Faubourg-Pavé

The cemetery contains the graves of 5 000 soldiers.

▶ Turn left past the cemetery onto D 112 towards Mogeville.

On the right, 6km/3.7mi farther on, stand the **Monument Maginot** and Souville Fort.

▶ Turn right on D 913 towards Verdun then left on D 913A towards the Fort de Vaux.

The land remains profoundly marked by the war. On the right, slightly off the road, is the **Monument des Fusillés de Tavannes**, a reminder of an episode of WWII.

Fort de Vaux

♿🕐*From 10am until: Feb–Mar and Oct–Nov 5pm; Apr and Sept 6pm; May–Jun 6.30pm; Jul–Aug 7pm; Dec 4.30pm.* 🕐*Jan.* ✆€4. ☎03 29 88 32 88.

Thirst drove the garrison to surrender on 7 June 1916 after two months' heroic resistance; the fort was reoccupied by the French five months later. From the top, there is a good view of the ossuary, cemetery and fort of Douaumont, the Côtes de la Meuse and Plaine de la Woëvre.

▶ Return to D 913 and turn right towards Fleury and Douaumont.

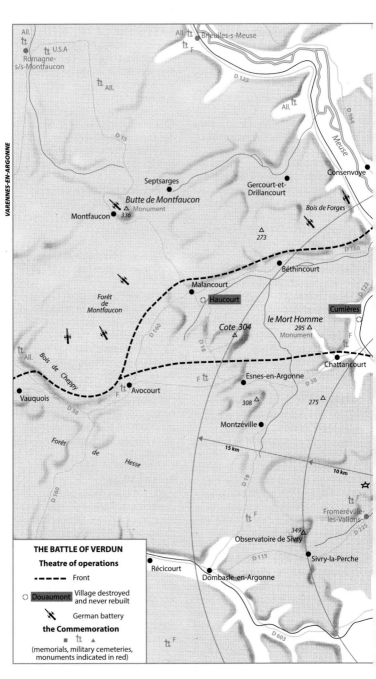

VARENNES-EN-ARGONNE

All.
Romagne-s/s-Montfaucon
U.S.A
All.
All.

Brieulles-s-Meuse
F

All.

Septsarges

Consenvoye

Gercourt-et-Drillancourt

Butte de Montfaucon
Monument
Montfaucon 336

Bois de Forges

273

Béthincourt

Malancourt
Haucourt

Forêt de Montfaucon

Cumières

Cote 304

le Mort Homme
295 Monument
F

308

Chattancourt

All.

Bois de Cheppy

F
Avocourt

F

Esnes-en-Argonne

275

Vauquois

Forêt de Hesse

308

Montzéville

15 km

10 km

Forêt de Hesse

Fromeréville-les-Vallons

349
Observatoire de Sivry

Sivry-la-Perche

THE BATTLE OF VERDUN

Theatre of operations

- - - - Front

◌ Douaumont — Village destroyed and never rebuilt

✳ German battery

the Commemoration

■ ⚰ ▲

(memorials, military cemeteries, monuments indicated in red)

Récicourt

Dombasle-en-Argonne

F

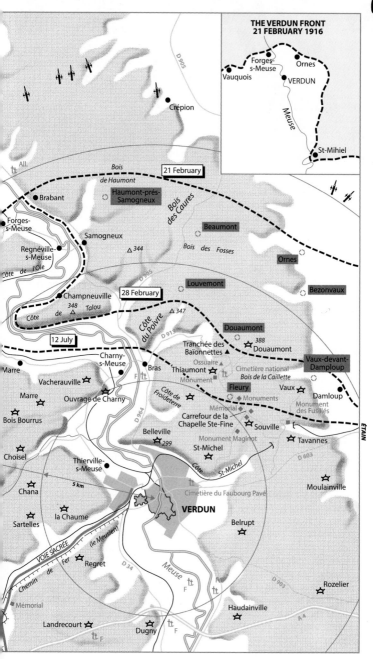

THE VERDUN FRONT
21 FEBRUARY 1916

Forges-s-Meuse
Ornes
Vauquois
VERDUN
St-Mihiel
Meuse

21 February
Bois de Haumont
Haumont-prés-Samogneux
Brabant
Bois des Caures
Forges-s-Meuse
Samogneux
Beaumont
Regnéville-s-Meuse
△ 344
Bois des Fosses
Ornes
Côte de l'Oie
Champneuville
Côte de 348 Talou △
Louvemont
Bezonvaux
28 February
△ 347
Douaumont
Côte du Poivre
Tranchée des Baïonnettes ▲
388 Douaumont
12 July
Charny-s-Meuse
Bras
Thiaumont
Vaux-devant-Damploup
Marre
Ossuaire
Cimetière national
Bois de la Caillette
Vacherauville
Monument
Fleury
Marre
Côte de Froideterre
Vaux
Ouvrage de Charny
Monuments
Damloup
Bois Bourrus
Mémorial
Monument des Fusillés
Carrefour de la Chapelle Ste-Fine
Choisel
Belleville
Souville
ÉTAIN
Thierville-s-Meuse
△ 299
Monument Maginot
St-Michel
Tavannes
Chana
Cimetière du Faubourg Pavé
Côte St-Michel
Moulainville
5 km
Sartelles
la Chaume
VERDUN
Belrupt
VOIE SACRÉE (le Meusien)
Regret
Meuse
Rozelier
Chemin de Fer
Mémorial
Haudainville
Landrecourt
Dugny

Ossuaire de Douaumont

© Bertrand Rieger/hemis.fr

At the Chapelle Ste-Fine crossroads, the Monument du Lion marks the most forward position reached by the Germans.

Mémorial de Verdun

🕐*Feb–Mar and Nov Mon–Fri 9.30am–5pm, Sat–Sun 9.30am–6pm; Sept–mid-Oct Mon–Fri 9.30am–6pm, Sat–Sun 9.30am–7pm; 1–21 Dec daily 9.30am–5pm.* ✆€11. 📞*03 29 88 19 16. www.memorialdeverdun.fr.*

Videos, maps and slide shows explain the various stages of the battle and a collection of uniforms, weapons, pieces of equipment and documents illustrate the fierce fighting which took place.

A little farther on, a stele marks the site of the former village of **Fleury-devant-Douaumont**, which was taken 16 times.

▷ Turn right onto D 913B.

Fort de Douaumont

🕐*Same hours as Fort de Vaux (above).* 🕐*Jan and 25–26 Dec.* ✆€4. 📞*03 29 84 41 91.*

The fort was built in 1855 on a high point (388m), hence its strategic importance. It was covered with a layer of concrete 1m thick over a layer of sand also 1m thick. Taken by surprise at the beginning of the German offensive, it was recaptured by the French at the end of October.

The tour takes visitors through galleries, casemates and arsenals. A chapel marks the site of the walled-up gallery

where 679 German soldiers, killed in the accidental explosion of an ammunition dump, were buried on 8 May 1916.

From the top of the fort, there is an view of the 1916 battlefield and the ossuary. Slightly farther on, to the right, a chapel stands on the site of the village church of **Douaumont** completely destroyed during the initial German attack.

▷ Return to D 913 and turn right.

Ossuaire de Douaumont

♿🕐*Usually from 9am (10am Sat–Sun), but closure times are variable; check website for current details.* ✆€6. 📞*03 29 84 54 81. www.verdun-douaumont.com.*

The ossuary, which was built to receive the unidentified remains of some 130 000 French and German soldiers killed during the battle, is the most important French monument of WWI.

At the centre of the monument stands the Tour des Morts (Tower of the Dead), 46m high, shaped like a military shell and carved with four crosses. At the top (204 steps), viewing tables enable visitors to spot the different sectors of the battlefield.

Tranchée des Baïonnettes

A massive door leads to the monument built over the trench where, on 10 June 1916, two companies of the 137 infantry regiment were buried. The tip of their rifles showing above ground was the only sign of their presence.

WEST BANK OF THE MEUSE
40km/25mi. About 2hr.
Michelin Local map 307: B/C-3
In September 1918, American troops led by General Pershing played a key role in this sector.

▶ Drive out of Verdun NW along D 38 to Chattancourt and turn right towards Le Mort Homme, the site of fierce fighting. All the German attacks of March 1916 were halted on this ridge. Return to Chattancourt, turn right onto D 38 and right onto D 18 after Esnes-en-Argonne; 2km/1.2mi on, a path on the right leads to the Cote 304.

La Cote 304
For nearly 14 months the Germans met here unflinching resistance.

Butte de Montfaucon
This is the highest point of the area (336m); the village which stood at the top was fortified and used by the Germans as an observation point.
A **monument** (🕐*May–Sept daily 9am–9pm; Oct–Apr Fri–Sun and school holidays 9am–5pm.* ✆*03 29 85 14 18)* commemorates the victory of the 1st US army during the offensive of September–November 1918. A monumental staircase leads to a column (57mhigh, 235 steps) surmounted by a Statue of Liberty. From the top, there is a good **view★** over the battlefield. The ruins of the village of Montfaucon can be seen near the monument; the village was totally destroyed and rebuilt 100m farther west.

Cimetière américain de Romagne-sous-Montfaucon
The American cemetary contains more than 14 000 graves in strict alignment amid shaded lawns and flower beds.

ADDRESSES

🛏STAY
🛏 **Camping Les Breuils** – *8 allée des Breuils.* ✆*03 29 86 15 31. www.camping-lesbreuils.com. Apr–Sept. Reservation*

advised. 162 places. Pleasant, quiet, well equipped campsite with swimming pool, paddling pool, snack bar and mobile home units for hire.

🛏 **Montaulbain** – *4 r. Vieille-Prison.* ✆*03 29 86 00 47. http://hoteldemontaulbain.fr. 10 rooms.* The rooms at this little hotel on a pedestrian street are rather cramped but very well kept. The cellars were the town prison in the 14C.

🛏🛏 **Chambre d'hôte Les Charmilles** – *12 Rue de la Gare, 55100 Charny-sur-Meuse.* ✆*03 29 86 93 49. www.les-charmilles.com. 3 rooms.* Once a café, this early 20C building is now a hotel offering pretty rooms with both old and new features.

🛏 **Village Gaulois** – *11 rue de Parge Marre par Charny, 55100 (12km/7.5m north of Verdun on the D964).* ✆*03 29 85 03 45. www.villagegaulois.com. 10 rooms.* Surrounded by greenery, this hotel offers a rustic ambience which is well worth the detour. Well appointed individually decorated rooms. Restaurant (🛏🛏).

🛏🛏🛏🛏 **Chambre d'hôte Château de Labessière** – *55320 Ancemont. (15km/9.3mi S of Verdun on D 34 (St-Mihiel road)).* ✆*03 29 85 70 21. www.chateau-labessiere.fr. Closed Dec 25, Jan 1.* 🍽 *4 rooms. Dinner 🛏🛏.* This 18C château miraculously survived unscathed through two world wars. Rooms are charming with old furniture, and stylish dining room. A pretty garden and swimming pool add to the pleasure.

🍴EAT
🛏🛏 **Bonsejour** – *33 route de Metz.* ✆*03 29 84 66 63. www.bonsejour-restaurant.fr.* Pizzas and Flammeküche cooked in a wood oven are the order of the day here although regional fare is also available. A traditional, warm and authentic ambience.

🛏🛏🛏 **Hostellerie du Château des Monthairons** – *26 Route de Verdun, 55320 Les Monthairons.* ✆*03 29 87 78 55. www. chateaudesmonthairons.fr. Closed Mon, Tue lunch.* A delightful Chatelaine family-run restaurant. Good quaitty modern dishes, regularly changing menus, and sensibly priced dishes. 22 **rooms** available (🛏🛏🛏🛏).

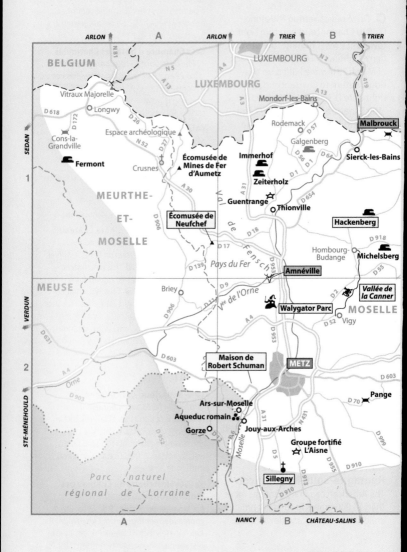

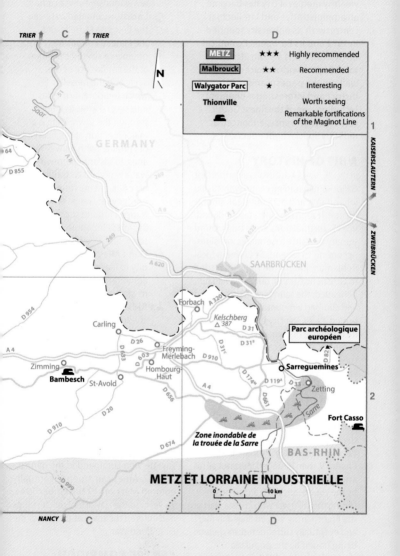

TRIER   C   TRIER

N

METZ	★★★	Highly recommended
Malbrouck	★★	Recommended
Walygator Parc	★	Interesting
Thionville		Worth seeing
		Remarkable fortifications of the Maginot Line

KAISERSLAUTERN

ZWEIBRÜCKEN

GERMANY

SAARBRÜCKEN

Saar

D 855

64

D 954

Carling

Forbach   A 320

Kelschberg
△ 387   D 31

D 31ᴮ

Parc archéologique
européen

A 4

Zimming   D 633   D 603   Freyming-
Merlebach

Bambesch   St-Avold   Hombourg-
Haut

D 26

D 910   D 31ᶜ

D 174ᴬ   D 119ᴬ   D 33

Sarreguemines

Zetting

D 656   A 4   D 661   Sarre

Fort Casso

D 20

D 910

Zone inondable de
la trouée de la Sarre

BAS-RHIN

D 674

D 999

METZ ET LORRAINE INDUSTRIELLE

0   10 km

NANCY   C   D

Metz★★★

Moselle

In the past, Metz played an important role as a religious centre and a military stronghold; the wealthy medieval city has become an administrative and intellectual centre, with its university founded in 1972 and its European Ecological Institute. Metz is also an attractive tourist centre with a choice of pleasant walks in the pedestrianised historic district and interesting monuments, including one of the finest Gothic cathedrals in France, enhanced at night by special light effects.

A BIT OF HISTORY

In the 2C, Metz was already an important Gallo-Roman trading centre with 40 000 inhabitants and a 25 000 seat amphitheatre. It soon became a bishopric and, in 275, fortifications were built round the city to ward off Germanic invasions. According to legend, **St Livier**, a local nobleman, fought the Huns then tried to christianise them, but Attila had him beheaded; the saint picked up his head and climbed a mountain where he was buried. Later, the city became a favourite residence of Emperor Charlemagne. In the 12C, Metz became a free city and the capital of a republic whose citizens were so wealthy that they often lent money to the dukes of Lorraine, the kings of France and even the Holy Roman emperors.

In 1552, the French king, Henri II, annexed the three bishoprics of Metz, Toul and Verdun. The Holy Roman Emperor, Charles V, then besieged Metz but all his attempts to take the city were thwarted by the young intrepid François de Guise. During the 1870 war with Prussia, part of the French army was encircled in Metz and eventually surrendered, its general being booed by the population.

On 19 November 1918, French troops entered the town after 47 years of German occupation.

In 1944, Metz was at the heart of heavy fighting once more as it lay on the path of the advancing American Third Army. It

▶ **Population:** 120 708.

✦ **Michelin Map:** Michelin Local map 307: I-4.

🅸 **Tourist Office:** 2 Pl. d'Armes. ✆03 87 39 00 00. www.tourisme-metz.com.

◖ **Location:** Situated between the Côtes de Moselle and the Plateau Lorrain, Metz occupies a strategic position at the confluence of the Seille and the Moselle, which temporarily divides into several arms as it flows through the town. Metz is a major junction at the heart of Lorraine (with railway lines, roads and motorways, waterways and air traffic), only 50km/31mi from the border with Germany. Metz-Nancy-Lorraine airport lies 25km/15.5mi south of the town.

⊛ **Don't Miss:** It would be a pity to leave town without admiring the cathedral and its stained-glass windows.

👫 **Kids:** Those travelling with children might want to save time for a trip to the Walibi-Lorraine theme park *(15min drive from Metz).*

was bitterly defended for two and a half months by the German forces stationed in the town; the surrounding forts were pounded by heavy allied artillery but the town was spared in memory of La Fayette who commanded the garrison in 1777. American troops eventually entered Metz on 19 November 1944, 26 years to the day after French troops had entered the town at the end of the First World War.

CENTRE POMPIDOU-METZ ★★★

1 parvis des Droits-de-l'Homme.
♿🕙*Daily except Tue: Apr–Oct 10am–6pm (Fri–Sun 10am–7pm); Nov–Mar 10am–6pm.* ✍*Ticket price based on*

PRACTICAL INFORMATION

Public transport: Espace-bus – *Pl. de la République.* *℘03 87 76 31 11.* The Metz bus service (Le Met') operates all over Metz and the vicinity.

Metz City Pass: the City Pass (€12.50) offers admissions to the Cour d'Or museum and the Centre Pompidou, plus an audio tour of Metz, while the **City Pass Plus** also serves as a day ticket for the transport system (€15).

Audio tours – Discover the town and its culture at your own pace by downloading the Metz Tour to your smartphone.

Metz Monument Tracker – With the Metz Monument Tracker® app, your smartphone or tablet will automatically show local monuments and their history.

Tours for disabled visitors – The tourist office has designed a number of accessible tours with accompanying adults for people with reduced mobility.

Tourist train – Apr to Oct daily.

Les Calèches de la Moselle – It is also possible to see the sights of the city from a horse-drawn calèche. Details from the tourist office, or call *℘07 71 73 68 28.*

---

the number of exhibition spaces open at the time of your visit. €7–€12 (free for under 26): annual passes are available and allow access to all exhibitions for a period of 1 year (€37). ℘03 87 15 39 39. www.centrepompidou-metz.fr.

The Centre Pompidou-Metz art centre is dedicated to modern and contemporary art presented in the form of temporary exhibitions, live performances, films and talks within its spaces. Workshops for children provide insight into artistic movements and highlight the potential for creativity.

CATHÉDRALE ST-ÉTIENNE★★★

&⃠ ⓘ*Mon–Sat 9am–12.30pm, 1.30–6pm, Sun and public holidays 1–6pm. ℘03 87 75 54 61. www.cathedrale-metz.fr.*

The entrance of the cathedral is on **place d'Armes**. From the square, there is a fine view of the south side of the cathedral. One is impressed by the harmonious proportions of the cathedral, built of yellow stone from Jaumont like several other edifices in Metz. The north and south sides are most remarkable. In order to appreciate the south side, it is better to stand on the pavement running along the town hall on the opposite side of the square.

The church is flanked by two symmetrical towers, the chapter tower on the north side and the **Tour de Mutte**

Centre Pompidou-Metz

on the south side; both built from the 13C onwards. The Tour de Mutte owes its name to the famous bell known as Dame Mutte, dating from 1605 and weighing 11t; the name is derived from the verb *ameuter* which originally meant "to call for a meeting." The bell used to ring for all major events and even today, it sounds the 12 strokes of midday and every quarter hour on election days.

▶ Enter through the Virgin's doorway, located to the left of the Tour de Mutte.

Inside the cathedral, the most striking feature is the height of the nave

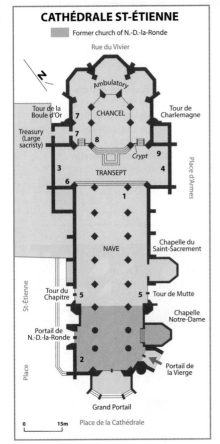

CATHÉDRALE ST-ÉTIENNE

Former church of N.-D.-la-Ronde

Rue du Vivier

N

Ambulatory

Tour de la Boule d'Or

CHANCEL

Tour de Charlemagne

Treasury (Large sacristy)

7

7

8

Crypt

9

3

TRANSEPT

4

Place d'Armes

6

1

St-Étienne

NAVE

Chapelle du Saint-Sacrement

Tour du Chapitre

5

5

Tour de Mutte

Chapelle Notre-Dame

Portail de N.-D.-la-Ronde

Place

2

Portail de la Vierge

Grand Portail

0   15m   Place de la Cathédrale

lon, Roger Bissière **5**, Marc Chagall **6** and **7**).

The west front is adorned with a magnificent 14C rose-window by Hermann from Munster, which unfortunately lost its base part when the large doorway was built in 1766. The openwork design of the edifice is even more apparent in the **transept** built in the late 15C and early 16C. The stained-glass window in the north part of the transept (**3**) is decorated with three roses; that in the south part of the transept (**4**) is by Valentin Bousch, an artist from Strasbourg.

The eastern wall of the south part of the transept has the oldest stained-glass windows (**9**) which illustrate six scenes from the Life of St Paul (13C). Note the starlike vaulting of the middle part of the transept.

The stained-glass window in the western wall of the north part of the transept, designed by Chagall in 1963, depicts scenes from the Garden of Eden (**6**).

In the ambulatory, two more stained-glass windows by Chagall can be seen above the sacristy door and the door leading to the Tour de la Boule d'Or on the left. Designed in 1960, they illustrate scenes from the Old Testament (Jacob's Dream, Abraham's Sacrifice, and Moses and David).

Crypt

Mon–Sat 9.30am–12.30pm, 1.30–6pm, Sun and public holidays 2–6pm. €4.

This was adapted in the 15C to preserve some elements from the 10C Romanesque crypt, the damaged tympanum of the 13C Virgin's doorway as well as various objects, carvings and reliquaries from the treasury. Note in particular a 16C **Entombment,** originally in the church of Xivry-Circourt, and, hanging from the vaulting, the famous Graoully, the legendary dragon slain by St Clement, which used to be carried in procession round the town until 1785. In the chancel, St Clement's

(41.77m), dating from the 13C and 14C. The impression of loftiness is enhanced by the fact that the aisles are rather low. This nave is, with that of Amiens Cathedral and after the chancel of Beauvais Cathedral, the highest of any church in France. Note the overhanging 16C choir organ (**1**) situated at the end of the nave, on the right-hand side.

Stained-Glass Windows★★★

These form a splendid ensemble covering more than 6 500m². They are the work of famous as well as unknown artists, completed or renewed through the centuries: 13C (**2**) and 14C (Hermann from Munster), 16C (Theobald from Lyxheim **3**, followed by Valentin Bousch **4**), 19C and 20C (Pierre Gaudin, Jacques Vil-

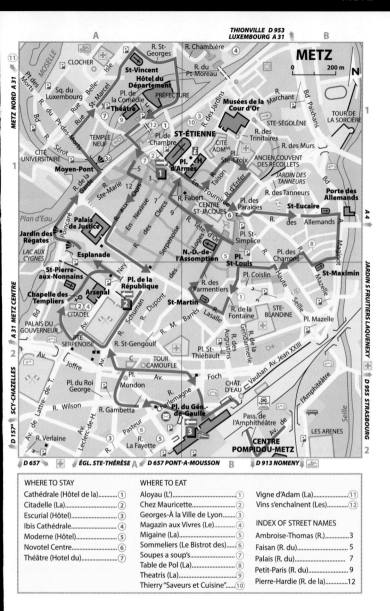

episcopal throne (**8**), carved out of a cipolin-marble column, dates back to Merovingian times.

Treasury
🕐 *Access as for Crypt.*
This is housed in the 18C sacristy. The most remarkable items include St Arnoult's gold ring (primitive Christian art), a 12C enamel reliquary, 12C and 13C ivory crosiers, Pope Pius VI's mule, and precious religious objects.

The Gueulard, a 15C carved-wood head, originally decorating the organ, used to open its mouth (hence its name) when the lowest note was sounded. During the storm in December 1999, a pinnacle weighing several tonnes was torn off, fell through the roof and lodged itself in the ceiling of the sacristy.

Grenier de Chèvremont

© Bruno Barbier/Photononstop

MUSÉE DE LA COUR D'OR★★

2 rue du Haut Poirier. ⏱*Daily except Tue 9am–12.30pm, 1.45–5pm.* ⏱*1 Jan, Good Friday, 1 May, 14 Jul, 1 and 11 Nov, 24–26 and 31 Dec.* ⬚€*5, no charge 1st Sun of month.* ℘*03 87 20 13 20. http://musee.metzmetropole.fr.*

The museum is housed in the buildings of the former Couvent des Petits Carmes (17C), the Grenier de Chèvremont (15C) and in several rooms that link or prolong this monumental ensemble. Elements of the antique baths are displayed in situ in the basement.

Section archéologique★★★

The exhibits, which were mostly found during excavations in Metz and the surrounding region, testify to the importance of the city, a major road junction in Gallo-Roman times and a thriving cultural centre during the Carolingian period.

Social life during the **Gallo-Roman period** is illustrated by remains of the large baths, the town wall and the drainage system as well as by everyday items (relating to meals, garments, jewellery and trade).

Various glass-cases are devoted to the methods of producing ironwork, bronzework, ceramics and glasswork.

Metz was the capital of Austrasia during the **Merovingian period** illustrated by graves, sarcophagi and tombstones bearing Christian emblems, jewels and objects of daily life (crockery), and damascened metal objects.

In the rooms devoted to **palaeo-Christian archaeology**, there is an important ensemble dating from the early Middle Ages, surrounding the chancel of St-Pierre-aux-Nonnains. This stone screen comprises 34 carved panels admirably decorated and extremely varied.

Architecture et cadre de vie

Exhibits in this section illustrate daily life, building techniques and decorative styles in the past, up to the Renaissance period.

Grenier de Chèvremont★

This well-preserved edifice, dating from 1457, was once used to store the tithe taken on cereal crops.

Beaux-Arts

Interesting paintings from the French School (Delacroix, Corot, Moreau), and the German, Flemish and Italian Schools. The School of Metz (1834–70) is mainly represented by its leading exponent, the painter, pastellist and stained-glass artist Laurent-Charles Maréchal.

The modern-art gallery contains works by artists including Bazaine, Alechinsky, Dufy, and Soulages.

WALKING TOURS

1 OLD TOWN

Place d'Armes

The square was designed in the 18C by Jacques François Blondel on the site of the former cloisters. The **town hall**, facing the south side of the cathedral has an elegant Louis XVI façade with two pediments.

▶ Follow rue En-Fournirue to the right of the town hall then turn left onto rue Taison. Turn right when you get to Place Ste-Croix.

The **Ancien couvent des Récollets** (former convent) now houses the European Ecological Institute. The 15C cloisters have been restored.

▶ Follow rue d'Enfer opposite and turn left onto rue En-Fournirue to place des Paraiges then continue along rue des Allemands.

Église St-Eucaire
The fine square belfry dates from the 12C and the west front from the 13C. The small 14C nave with its huge pillars looks out of proportion.

Porte des Allemands★
This massive fortress, which formed part of the town walls running along the Moselle and the dual-carriageway ring road south and east of Metz, straddles the River Seille. It gets its name from a 13C order of German hospitallers.
North of the Porte des Allemands, the fortified wall continues for another 1.5km/0.9mi, with numerous towers at regular intervals: Tour des Sorcières (Witches' Tower), Tour du Diable (Devil's Tower), Tour des Corporations (Guilds' Tower). A path follows the ramparts, first along the Seille then along the Moselle.

▶ Walk along boulevard Maginot and turn onto the fourth street on your right.

Église St-Maximin★
A fine carved head of Christ decorates the central pillar at the entrance.
The beautiful chancel is decorated with stained-glass windows by Jean Cocteau.

▶ Leaving St-Maxim, take a right at rue Mazelle and turn left.

Cross three squares in a row (Charrons, Pont-a-Seille and Quarteau).Turn left onto rue de la Fontaine and right onto rue Lasalle.

Église St-Martin-aux-Champs
A Gallo-Roman wall, once part of the town's fortifications, forms the base of the church; it is visible on both sides of the entrance.
The most attractive feature of this 13C church is its very low **narthex★** whose three sections, covered with pointed vaulting resting on four Romanesque pillars surrounded by colonnettes, open onto the lofty nave.

▶ Walk past the church and turn right onto rue des Parmentiers which runs onto rue de la Chèvre.

Église Notre-Dame-de-l'Assomption
This Jesuit church was erected in 1665 but the west front was completed in the 18C. The interior, decorated in the 19C, is lined with rich wood panelling. The Rococo confessionals come from the German city of Trier, as does the Baroque organ built by Jean Nollet.

▶ Continue along rue de la Chèvre then turn right onto rue de la Tête-d'Or.

Place St-Louis★
Situated in the heart of the old town, the rectangular place St-Louis is lined on one side with buttressed arcaded buildings dating from the 14C, 15C and 16C that once housed the money-changers' shops. At the end, on the corner of rue de la Tête-d'Or, note the three golden Roman heads protruding from the wall, which gave the street its name.

2 ESPLANADE★

This is a splendid walk laid out at the beginning of the 19C on the site of one of the citadel's moats: from the terrace, there is a fine view of Mount St-Quentin crowned by a fort and of one of the arms of the River Moselle.

Place de la République

This place has long been the location of military parades; at its centre is the statue of général Ney. Today, this square is the heart of historic Metz.

▶ Go down the stairs and cross boulevard Poincaré.

Jardin des Régates

This pretty turn-of-the-20C landscaped garden is located at the foot of the citadel.

▶ Walk along the Moselle and pass under the Moyen Pont. At the end of the quay, stairs allow you to cross the bridge.

Moyen Pont★

Pleasant **view★** of the arms of the River Moselle, the islands, the neo-Romanesque Protestant church (1901) and the two small bridges reflected in the water.

▶ Walk to place de la Comédie.

The 18C **theatre** overlooking place de la Comédie is the oldest in France; opposite stands the **Hôtel du Département**, also dating from the 18C.

▶ Walk round to the back of the Hôtel du Département and along rue du Pont Moreau then rue St-Georges and finally rue St-Vincent.

Église St-Vincent

The Gothic chancel of the church, flanked by two elegant steeples, is in striking contrast with the west front, rebuilt in the 18C and reminiscent of that of St-Gervais-St-Protais in Paris (outside only).

▶ Walk back to the Hôtel du Département and cross the river.

Palais de Justice

Built in the 18C, during the reign of Louis XVI, this edifice was intended to be the military governor's palace but the Revolution changed all that. In the courtyard, there are two interesting low-relief sculptures: one shows the Duc de Guise during the 1552 siege of the town, the other celebrates the 1783 peace treaty between England, France, the USA and Holland.

Église St-Pierre -aux-Nonnains★

&⃝Jul–Sept, daily except Mon, 2–6pm; rest of year Sat 1–6pm, Sun 2–6pm. ⃝Public holidays. ☏03 87 39 92 00.

Around 390, during the reign of Emperor Constantine, a **palæstra** or gymnasium was built on this site. When Attila plundered the town in 451, the edifice was partially destroyed, but the walls built of rubble stones reinforced at regular intervals by ties of red bricks were spared and used in the building of a chapel c 615.

Chapelle des Templiers

&⃝Jul–Sept, daily except Mon, 2–6pm, Sat–Sun, 1–6pm. ☏03 87 39 92 00.

This chapel, built at the beginning of the 13C by the Knights Templar established in Metz since 1133, marks the transition between the Romanesque and Gothic styles. Buildings of this type are rare and this chapel is, in fact, the only one of its kind in Lorraine.

Arsenal

&⃝Daily except Mon and public holidays 1–6pm. ☏03 87 39 92 00. www.arsenal-metz.fr.

The walls of the 19C arsenal were partially used to build this ultra-modern centre dedicated to music and dance. Its special shape and elaborate acoustics were inspired by the Musikverein in Vienna.

▶ Go down the large stairs to return to the Place de la République.

③ MODERN TOWN

After 1870, William II wanted to turn Metz into a prestigious German city. He entrusted his plan to Kröger, an architect from Berlin, who used pink and grey sandstone, granite and even basalt. The new district includes the wide **Avenue Foch**, the **chamber of commerce**, the imposing building of the **old station** (1878), and the **post office** designed by Kröger in neo-Romanesque style and constructed between 1908 and 1911.

Place du Général-de-Gaulle★

The **station** (1908) a huge neo-Romanesque edifice (300m long), profusely decorated (capitals, low-relief sculptures), is one of several buildings erected by the Germans at the beginning of the 20C to assert the power of the empire. The lamp posts in front of the station are designed by Philippe Stark.

SURROUNDS

Église Ste-Thérèse-de-l'Enfant-Jésus

Entrance along avenue Leclerc-de-Haute clocque.

Consecrated in 1954, this large church has an imposing nave and fine stained-glass windows by Nicolas Unsterteller.

EXCURSIONS

Scy-Chazelles

▷ 4km/2.5mi W along D 157A then turn right.

Robert Schuman's **house★** is located in the village, near the 12C fortified church where the "father of Europe" (1886–1963) is buried. This austere building, characteristic of Lorraine, conveys an impression of calm and serenity which this generous and modest man found conducive to meditation.

Vallée de la Canner

▷ Departure from Vigy, 15km/9mi NE along D 2 then D 52.

From Vigy to Hombourg *(12km/7.5mi),* a small tourist train, pulled by a real steam engine, follows the remote Canner valley through a densely forested part of the Lorraine plateau.

Château de Pange

▷ 10km/6mi E on D 999, D 70 and D 6.

Built between 1720 and 1756 on the site of an ancient fortress, along the banks of the Nied, a small tributary of the Moselle, the castle has retained its plain Classical façade.

Groupe fortifié de l'Aisne

▷ 14km/8.7mi S along D 913.

The former Wagner Fortress, built by the Germans between 1904 and 1910, formed part of the outer defences of Metz. Renamed Aisne after 1918, it was not, unlike Guentrange, incorporated into the Maginot Line (◐*see Ligne MAGINOT*); during the Second World War.

Sillegny

▷ 20km/12.5mi S along D 5.

This village in the Seille valley has a small 15C **church**, which looks unassuming but is entirely covered with **murals★** dating from 1540.

Gorze

▷ 18km/11mi SW along D 57, then right onto D 6B.

This village, which developed around a Benedictine abbey founded in the 8C, has retained a number of old Renaissance residences dating from the 17C and 18C. The **Maison de l'Histoire de la Terre de Gorze** (◐*daily except Mon: Apr–Jun and Oct 2–5pm; Jul–Sept 2–6pm.* ◈€3. ℘03 87 52 04 57. *www.musee-gorze.fr*) relates episodes of Gorze's prosperous past.

Aqueduc romain de Gorze à Metz

▷ 12km/7.5mi SW. Drive along N 3 to Moulins then continue along D 6 to Ars-sur-Moselle.

Seven arches of this 1C Roman aqueduct, which spanned the Moselle, are still standing alongside D 6, south of **Ars-sur-Moselle** (west bank). In **Jouy-aux-Arches** (east bank), another 16 arches, in a better state of preservation, span N 57.

ADDRESSES

🏠 STAY

🛏️🍽️ **Hotel Ibis Metz Centre Cathédrale** – 47 rue Chambière Quartier Pontiffroy. ℘03 87 31 01 73. www.accorhotels.com. 79 rooms. Ideal for exploring the city centre. Air conditioned rooms, Wi-Fi, and a restaurant overlooking the Moselle make for a convenient and pleasant stay.

🛏️🍽️ **Hôtel Moderne** – 1, r. Lafayette. ℘03 87 66 57 33. 43 rooms. In the centre of town offering comfort and good taste. The rooms are equipped with functional furniture but are nevertheless pleasant and those overlooking the street are soundproofed.

🛏️🍽️ **Escurial** – 18 r. Pasteur. ℘03 87 66 40 96. www.hotelmetzescurial.fr.. Closed Dec 29–Jan 1. 36 rooms. This hotel in the Imperial district provides modern and practical rooms, a breakfast area and large lounge with a warm and colourful atmosphere.

🛏️🍽️ **Hôtel de la Cathédrale** – 25 pl. Chambre. ℘03 87 75 00 02. www.hotel cathedrale-metz.fr. 20 rooms. A charming hotel situated in a lovely 17C house that was completely restored in 1997. The attractive rooms have cast iron or cane beds, old parquet flooring and furniture, some of which is oriental. Most rooms face the cathedral, just opposite.

🛏️🍽️🍽️ **Hôtel du Théâtre** – 3 r. du Pont-St-Marcel. ℘03 87 31 10 10. www.port-saint-marcel.com. 65 rooms. Restaurant 🛏️🍽️. An ideally located hotel in the historic town centre, providing freshly renovated rooms, more peaceful on the Moselle side. Fine regional furnishings in the reception area and regional wall paintings in the restaurant.

🛏️🍽️🍽️ **Novotel Centre** – place des Paraiges. ℘03 87 37 38 39. www.accorhotels.com. 120 rooms. Close to the cathedral, this contemporary hotel is directly accessible from a public car park. Rooms are spacious, very modern, and in spite of being in the centre of the city, surprisingly peaceful.

🛏️🍽️🍽️🍽️ **La Citadelle** – 5 ave. Ney. ℘03 87 17 17 17. www.citadelle-metz.com. A luxury hotel in the centre of the city, set in a former military building dating from the 16C. Michelin-starred **restaurant** (🛏️🍽️🍽️🍽️ see below) and **La Brasserie Christophe Dufossé** (🛏️🍽️🍽️).

🍽️ EAT

🍽️ **Chez Mauricette** – Marché couvert, Place de la Cathédrale. ℘03 87 36 37 69. www.chezmauricette.com. Closed Sun and Mon. This enticing market stall run by Mauricette and his team offers delicious food to go – French, Corsican, Swiss, German, Italian and Spanish – for those in a hurry to see the sites!

🍽️ **La Migaine** – 1–3 pl. St-Louis. ℘03 87 75 56 67. Closed Sun. You can eat at any time here, from morning to late afternoon. The tearoom in a pretty square surrounded by arcades serves copious breakfasts, meat pies, quiche Lorraine, cakes and tea – the choice is yours. Terrace in summer.

🍽️ **Soupes a soup's** – Marché Couvert, pl de la Cathédrale. ℘06 08 31 11 04. Situated in a splendid covered market constructed in 1785 the soup bar owned by a self-taught passionate cook, is a real success. Delicious soups of vegetables or fruit, hot or cold, traditional breads, kebabs and more can be sampled here.

🍽️ **Les Vins s'enchainement** – 8 r. Piques. ℘03 87 36 19 01. Closed Sat, Sun eve and Wed. In a small 18C pedestrianised street one can find this wine bar with its contemporary decor done by the clients. The owner, an informed sommelier, can suggest more than 30 cru served by the glass to accompany meats, cheeses, tartes, traditional cuisine and the famous house terrine.

🍽️🍽️ **L'Aloyau** – 3 pl. de-la-Fontaine. ℘03 87 37 33 72. www.laloyau.fr/aloyau. Closed Sun and Mon. Grandson and son of a butcher and one himself for 15 years before opening a restaurant. Well known for his beef, lamb and suckling pig dishes accompanied by delicious sauces, not to mention the sea food.

🍽️🍽️ **Georges – À La Ville de Lyon** – 9 r. Piques. ℘03 87 36 07 01. www.ala villedelyon.com. Closed Mon (except lunch on public holidays) and Sun eve. The restaurant rooms are split between outbuildings of the Cathedral – one room is set in a 14C Chapel – and the walls of a coaching house.

🍽️🍽️ **La Table de Pol** – 1/3, rue du Grand Wad. ℘03 87 62 13 72. www.latabledepol.fr. Closed Sun, Mon, and Wed eve. Enjoy the best of daily market produce in this cosy, chic restaurant in the Outre Seille area.

El Theatris – *2, place de la Comédie. ℰ03 87 56 02 02. www.eltheatris.fr. Closed Sun eve.* Brasserie dining; traditional cuisine using fresh, local produce. Beautiful terrace.

Thierry "Saveurs et Cuisine" – *5 r. Piques, "Maison de la fleur de Lys". ℰ03 87 74 01 23. www.restaurant-thierry.fr. Closed Wed and Sun.* Inventive cuisine enhanced by herbs and spices, an attractive brick and wood setting and a summer terrace all contribute to this stylish bistro's popularity.

Le Bistrot des Sommeliers – *10 r. Pasteur. ℰ03 87 63 40 20. www. lebistrotdessommeliers.fr. Closed Sat lunch, and Sun.* Colourful facade and decor on a wine theme in this bistro near the station.

A good selection of wines by the glass and dishes based on market produce on a blackboard.

La Vigne Adam – *50 r. Gén. de Gaulle F, 57050 Plappeville. ℰ03 87 30 36 68. http://lavignedadam.com. Closed Sun–Mon.* In the heart of the village, this old winegrower's house is now a trendy, modern wine bar/restaurant. Modern cuisine and a fine selection of wines.

Le Magasin aux Vivres – Hotel la Citadelle, *5 ave. Ney. ℰ03 87 17 17 17. Closed Sat lunch, Sun and Mon.* The best restaurant in Metz, and not by chance. This Michelin-starred eatery in the citadel is part of a beautiful contemporary hotel. Classic cuisine with a modern touch.

Amnéville ♯♯
Moselle

Lying at the heart of the Coulange Forest, covering 500ha, this former industrial town became an important spa following the discovery of ferruginous water at a temperature of 41°C; today it is a lively resort with good tourist facilities, including a splendid fitness centre, Thermapolis. Children will rejoice in the Walibi-Schtroumpf park nearby.

SIGHTS
Parc zoologique d'Amnéville★★
♿🕐*Apr–Sept 9.30am–7.30pm, Sun & holidays 8pm; Oct–Mar 10am to nightfall.* ✆€33 (children 3–11, €27). *ℰ03 87 70 25 60. www.zoo-amneville.com.*
About 600 animals representing almost 110 different species roam around in pens spread over a forested area covering 8ha. The zoo is committed to international programmes intended to protect endangered species. Educational shows, including the excellent Parrot's Jungle, add further interest to the visit. Located 300m from the zoo, the **Aquarium** (♿🕐*daily Feb–Jun and Sept*

▶ **Population:** 10 292.
♿ **Michelin Map:** Michelin Local map 307: H-3.
🛈 **Tourist Office:** Rue de l'Europe, 57360 Amnéville. ℰ03 87 70 10 40. www.amneville.com.
▶ **Location:** Amnéville is 5km/3mi from the A4 motorway (exit 35), along D 953 and is 15min from Metz by A 31, exit 37 (Mondelange).
👁 **Don't Miss:** The splendid fitness centre, Thermapolis *(see Addresses)* and of course the zoological park.
👫 **Kids:** Children will love the zoo, and will demand to visit the Walibi-Lorraine theme park. Older children might enjoy the motorbike and bicycle museum.

10am–6pm; Jul–Aug daily 9.30am–7pm; Oct–Jan Mon–Tue, Thu–Fri 1.10–dusk, Wed, Sat–Sun and school and public holidays 10am–dusk. 🚫*25 Dec 25, 1 Jan.* ✆€13.50 (child 3–11, €10.50). *ℰ03 87*

Parc zoologique d'Amnéville

© Parc zoologique d'Amnéville

70 36 61. www.aquarium-amneville.com)
offers species of fish and underwater
lifeforms from the Caribbean, Australian
rivers, African Lakes and the Amazon
valley. Several species of sharks share
a huge tank.

Parc d'Attraction Walygator★

3km/1.9mi S of Amnéville.
🕐*Jun–Aug 10.30am–6.30pm
(May–Jun and Sept Sat–Sun 10.30am–
5.30pm); rest of year check website for
details.* 🕐*Nov–Mar.* ⊛€25
(child 3–10, €21.50). 📞*03 87 30 70 07.
www.walygatorparc.com.*
Experience a pirate adventure with
Peter Pan, a "splashing" mission with
the "Splash Kids" or enjoy the circus and
a Western Show. There is also a choice
of shops and restaurants so visitors can
easily spend a whole day in the park.
Attractions include the **Odisséa**, a buoy
tossed about among rapids, and the
Waligator which splashes 12m down a
waterfall. For the more daring, there is
the **Comet Space** or the **Sismic Panic**.
But will you be brave enough to face the
Dark Tower, which will propel you 55m
upwards in two and a half seconds?

ADDRESSES

🏨 STAY

⊝⊝ **Hôtel Orion** – *Bois de Coulange, rue
de la Souorce, 57360 Amneville-les-Thermes.
2.5km/1.5mi S of Amnéville.* 📞*03 87 70 20
20. www.hotels-amneville.com. Closed 27
Dec–2 Jan and Sun Nov–Apr. 44 rooms.
Restaurant Le Gargantua* ⊝⊝. This spa
resort hotel offers simple, identical rooms
with rendered walls and cane furniture.
A modern building offering practical,
inexpensive accommodation.

🍴/ EAT

⊝⊝ **La Forêt** – *In the Bois de Coulange
leisure park. 2.5km/1.5mi S of Amnéville*
📞*03 87 70 34 34. www.restaurant-la
foret.com. Closed Sun evenings, and Mon–
Tue.* This popular Michelin 'L'Assiette' restaurant in the Bois de Coulange leisure
centre is surrounded by trees, and its
dining room and terrace are pleasantly
arranged with cane furniture and plants.
The cooking is good too.

SPORT AND RECREATION

Centre thermal St-Éloy – *Rue des
Thermes, 57360 Amnéville les Thermes .* 📞*03
87 70 19 09. www.cure-amneville.com. Open
Mar–mid-Dec.* The St-Éloy spring is rich
in salt, calcium and magnesium – and
naturally heated to 41.2°C. This modern

spa recommends its waters for treating rheumatic disorders, post-traumatic injuries and respiratory problems.

Thermapolis – *Av. de l'Europe ℘03 87 70 99 43. www.thermapolis.com. Open Mon–Wed 10am–10pm, Thu 9am–10pm, Fri–Sat 10am–midnight, Sun 9am–8pm.* This is the place to rediscover your vitality and sense of well-being. Bubbling pools, Turkish baths, hot marble surfaces. 2h (€14.90) or 3h (€19.20) admission, or membership available.

Amnéville-Aventures – *Centre thermal et touristique. Open Apr–May and Sept–mid-Oct Sat–Sun 1–7pm; Jun Wed 1–7pm, Sat–Sun 10am–8pm; Jul–Aug daily 10am–8pm; mid-Oct–early Nov daily 1–6pm. ℘03 87 73 45 60. www.amneville-aventures.com. ⊕⊛€23 (child 11–17, €20; 6–10, €16; 4–5, €11).* This is one of the largest multi-activity econature parks in Europe set in the heart of the spa and tourist centre of the region.

Sarreguemines
Moselle

This border town, situated at the confluence of the Sarre and the Blies, is often associated with the pottery manufacture that bears its name. Sarreguemines used to be the seat of a feudal domain guarding the borders of the duchy of Lorraine.

A BIT OF HISTORY
Pottery
The Sarreguemines manufacture, founded in 1790, developed in spite of financial difficulties and the annexation of Lorraine in 1870 thanks to the inspired management of the De Geiger family. Production reached its peak at the turn of the 20C; more than 3 000 workers produced majolica, porcelain, dinner sets and panels. Bought by the Lunéville-St-Clément group in 1979, the pottery now mainly produces floor tiles. In 1982, it was renamed Sarreguemines-Bâtiment.

SIGHTS
Musée de la Faïence de Sarreguemines
17 rue Poincaré. ⊙Daily Tue– Sun and Mon holidays 10am–noon, 2–6pm. ⊙1 Jan, 24-25 and 31 Dec. ⊕⊛€5, no charge 1st Sun of the month. ℘03 87 98 93 50. www.sarreguemines-museum.eu. Housed in the former residence of the manager of the earthenware manufacturer, the ceramics **collection★** retraces the history of Sarreguemines pottery

▶ **Population:** 22 108.
⚅ **Michelin Map:** Michelin Local map 307: N-4.
🄸 **Tourist Office:** 11 rue du Maire-Massing, 57203 Sarreguemines. ℘03 87 98 80 81. www.sarreguemines-tourisme.com.
▶ **Location:** 70km/43.5mi E of Metz, 91km/56.5mi NE of Nancy.

Winter garden, Musée de la Faïence de Sarreguemines

over the past 200 years. The **winter garden★★**, designed by Paul de Geiger in 1882, is particularly remarkable, with its monumental Renaissance-style majolica fountain offering a shimmering display of yellows, greens, ochres and browns.

Musée des Techniques faïencières
Moulin de la Blies, 125 av. de la Blies. ⚠️⏲️*Same hours as the Musée de la Faïence.* ✏️€5.

A living museum designed to explain the manufacture of earthenware. Authentic machinery and tools have been used in the reconstruction of a production unit on three levels; preparation, firing and decoration.

Circuit de la faïence de Sarreguemines
🚶 *3km/1.9mi. Get the leaflet from the Tourist office.*

A walking tour links the main sites connected with the manufacture of earthenware in Sarreguemines.

EXCURSION

Parc archéologique européen de Bliesbruck-Reinheim
9.5km/5.9mi E via Bliesbruck. ⏲️*Open mid-Mar–early-Nov daily 10am–6pm.* ✏️€5. 📞*03 87 35 02 20. www.archeo57.com.*

Stretching either side of the Franco-Germain border lies the remains of an antique settlement, apparently going back to the Neolithic period, which became an important city after the arrival of the Celts. Replicas (the originals are in Sarrebruck museum) of gold jewellery and a wine service found in the grave of the "Reinheim Princess" (c 400 BCE) are displayed in a reconstructed **tumulus** near the remains of a large villa. In Bliesbruck the **public baths★** are protected under a huge glass structure.

Sierck-les-Bains
Moselle

Sierck lies in a picturesque setting on the banks of the River Moselle. The old village climbs up the hill crowned by a fortress. The name alone recalls that Sierck was once a spa town with three springs, until the thermal establishment was replaced by the railway station.

SIGHTS
Château des Ducs de Lorraine★
⏲️*May–Sept Mon–Sat 10am–7pm, Sun and public holidays 10am–8pm; Mar–Apr and Oct–Nov Mon–Sat 10am–4pm, Sun and public holidays 10am–5pm.* ⏲️*Dec–Feb.* ✏️€5. 📞*03 82 83 67 97. www.chateau-sierck.com.*

The castle, built on a rocky promontory, still has most of its 11C defensive system. The nearby **Chapelle de Marienfloss**,

- ▶ **Population:** 1 705.
- ⚙️ **Michelin Map:** Michelin Local map 307: J-2.
- 🛈 **Tourist Office:** 3 place Jean de Morbach, 57400 Sierck-les-Bains. 📞03 82 83 74 14. www.otsierck.com.
- ▷ **Location:** Near to the Luxembourg and German borders, 17km/10.6mi NE of Thionville, Sierck is the starting point for boat trips on the Moselle.

all that remains of a once flourishing Carthusian monastery, has been restored and extended.

Château de Malbrouck★★
8km/5mi NE along N 153 then right along D 64. ⏲️*Apr–Jun and Sept–Oct Tue–Fri 10am–5pm, Sat–Sun and public*

holidays 10am–6pm; Jul–Aug Tue–Sun
10am–6pm. €5 (children under 16,
no charge). ℰ03 87 35 03 87.
www.chateau-malbrouck.com.
The 15C fortress of the lords of Sierck has
been restored by a clever modern restoration that doesn't attempt to imitate
the original. In 1705, during the War of
the Spanish Succession, John Churchill, Duke of Marlborough, used it as his
headquarters.

ADDRESSES

ⵏ/**EAT**

Auberge de la Klauss – 57480
Montenach. 3.5 km/2mi SE of Sierck on
D 956. ℰ03 82 83 72 38. www.auberge-
de-la-klauss.com. Closed Mon. There's a
cheerful rural atmosphere in this country
inn where regional cooking, good wines,
game in season and above all home-
made foie gras are a gourmet treat.

Thionville

Moselle

This old stronghold and iron town
is the nerve centre of the whole
industrial area which extends along
the west bank of the River Moselle.

A BIT OF HISTORY

The fortified town successively belonged
to the counts of Luxembourg, the dukes
of Burgundy, the Habsburgs and to the
Spanish before becoming French in 1659
by the Treaty of the Pyrenees.

SIGHTS
Tour aux Puces

Cour du Château. Tue–Sun 2–6pm.
€3.50 (no charge 1st Sun of the
month). 1 Jan, 1 Nov, 25–26 Dec.
ℰ03 82 82 25 52.
www.tourauxpuces.com.
This mighty 11C–12C keep, also known
as the Tour au Puits (Well Tower), is the
most important remnant of the feudal
castle of the counts of Luxembourg.
Inside, the **Musée du Pays thionvil-
lois** retraces the history of Thionville.

Beffroi

The 16C onion-domed belfry, situated
near the market square, houses four
bells including "Grosse Suzanne".

Château de la Grange★

Apr–Jun and Sept–Oct Sat–Sun and
public holidays; Jul–Aug daily. Guided
tours 2.30pm, 3.30pm, 4.30pm, 5.30pm.
€8.50. ℰ03 82 53 85 03.

> ▶ **Population:** 42 602.
> **Michelin Map:** Michelin
> Local map 307: h–I 2.
> **Tourist Office:** 31 place
> Anne Grommerch, 57100
> Thionville. ℰ03 82 53 33 18.
> www.thionvilletourisme.fr.
> **Location:** 30km/18.6mi
> north of Metz by the A31.

www.chateaudelagrange.com.
Designed in 1731 by Robert de Cotte, the
château was built over the foundations
of a fortress.

EXCURSIONS
Ecomusée des Mines de
Fer de Neufchef★

13km/8mi W. Tue–Sun 2–6pm.
25 Dec. €8. ℰ03 82 85 76 55.
www.musee-minesdefer-lorraine.com.
This hillside iron mine did not require
the drilling of a shaft, which means it
is now easily accessible to the public.

Ecomusée des Mines de
Fer d'Aumetz

22km/13.67mi NW. May–Sept daily
except Tue and Fri 2–6pm. €8.
ℰ03 82 85 76 55.
www.musee-minesdefer-lorraine.com.
The former Bassompierre iron mine provides a valuable insight into miners' life
in underground galleries.

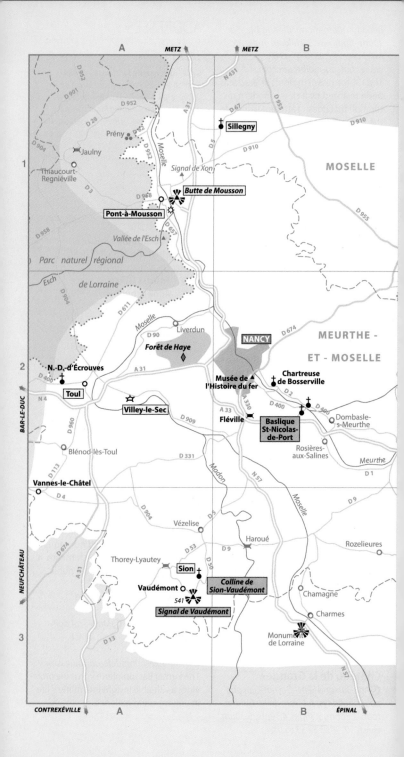

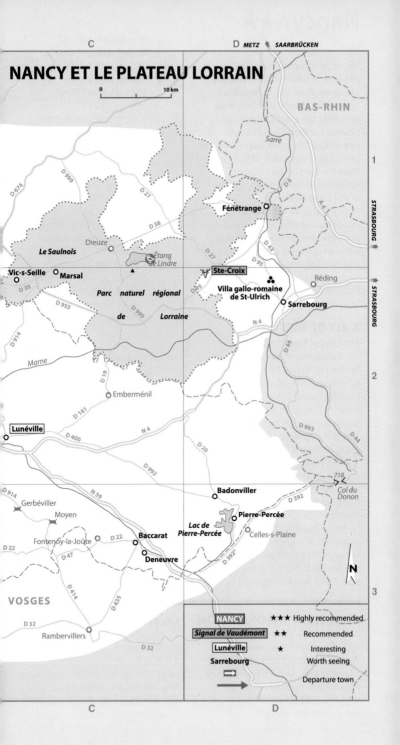

NANCY ET LE PLATEAU LORRAIN

0   10 km

METZ   SAARBRÜCKEN

BAS-RHIN

Sarre

STRASBOURG

1

Fénétrange

D 674
D 999
D 27
D 38
Dieuze
Le Saulnois
Étang de Lindre
Ste-Croix
Villa gallo-romaine de St-Ulrich
Réding
Vic-s-Seille   Marsal
Parc   naturel   régional
de   Lorraine
Sarrebourg
D 38
D 955
D 914
D 999
D 95
D 27
D 45
D 8
A 4
N 4
STRASBOURG

Marne
D 19
Emberménil
D 161
D 44
2
D 993
D 44

Lunéville
D 400
N 4
D 20
D 992

718
Col du Donon

Badonviller
D 392

D 914
Gerbéviller
N 59
Moyen
Pierre-Percée
Lac de Pierre-Percée
Celles-s-Plaine
D 392

D 22
Fontenoy-la-Joûte
D 22
Baccarat
D 47
Deneuvre

N

VOSGES
D 414
D 435
3
D 32
Rambervillers
D 32

NANCY	★★★	Highly recommended
Signal de Vaudémont	★★	Recommended
Lunéville	★	Interesting
Sarrebourg		Worth seeing
⇒		Departure town

C

D

153

Nancy★★★
Meurthe-et-Moselle

The former capital of the dukes of Lorraine offers visitors elegant 18C town planning, aristocratic architecture and beautiful vistas, including the most famous place Stanislas, a World Heritage site since 1983. The town has retained a remarkable ensemble of buildings from the turn of the 20C, fine examples of the decorative style of the École de Nancy.

Nancy is also an important intellectual centre with several scientific and technical institutes, a higher school of mining engineering, national centres of forestry research and study, and a cultural centre and theatre housed in a former tobacco manufacture.

▶ **Population:** 106 342.

Michelin Map: Michelin Local map 307: h-I 6.

Tourist Office: 14 pl. Stanislas, 54011 Nancy. ℘03 83 35 22 41. www.nancy-tourisme.fr.

Location: Nancy stands on the banks of the Meurthe, not far from the junction with the Moselle, and on the Marne Canal to the Rhine. It is 56km/34.8mi south of Metz.

Don't Miss: Place Stanislas or the Historic Museum of Lorraine.

Kids: La Pépinière zoo is good for younger children, while La Haye Leisure Park, outside Nancy, is ideal for older kids to let off steam.

A BIT OF HISTORY
Medieval beginnings

The foundation of Nancy occurred only in the 11C. Gérard d'Alsace, the first hereditary duke of Lorraine, chose to build his capital between two marshes; Nancy's only real advantage was its location in the middle of the Duke's land. At first the new capital consisted of the ducal castle and a few monasteries.

In 1228 Nancy was destroyed by fire and rebuilt almost immediately. In the 14C, what is now the old town was surrounded by a wall of which only the Porte de la Craffe has survived.

In 1476 Charles the Bold, Duke of Burgundy, occupied Lorraine as it was between Burgundy and Flanders (both belonging to him) but the following year, Duke **René II** returned to Nancy and stirred up a rebellion. Charles then lay siege in front of the town; he was killed at St-Nicolas-de-Port (*see ST-NICOLAS-DE-PORT*); his body was found in a frozen lake, half eaten by wolves.

Croix de Lorraine

The distinctive Croix de Lorraine, with two crosspieces, was a reminder of Duke René's illustrious ancestors, his grandfather good King René, Duke of Anjou and Count of Provence, and a more remote founder of the dynasty, the brother of Godefroy de Bouillon who led the first crusade and became king of Jerusalem. Used as a distinguishing mark by René II's troops on the battle-

PRACTICAL INFORMATION

Tourist train – Apr and Nov 11am–4pm; May–Sept 10am–6pm; Oct 11am–5pm. Tour of the historic town by miniature train. Departs from place de la Carrière on the hour except 1pm. €7 (child 6–14, €5). www.petit-train-nancy.fr.

City pass – This pass (€12) from the Tourist Office includes museums, public transport, guided tour, a 50% discount on cycle hire and 10% on products from the Tourisme shop. **Museum pass** (Le Museo Pass, €15) – available from any of the 7 museums to which it gives access.

Musée des Beaux-Arts, Place Stanislas

field of Nancy, the cross later became a patriotic symbol; (☞ *see Colline de SION-VAUDÉMONT*) in July 1940 it was adopted as the emblem of the Free French Forces.

The dukes and their city

As they became more powerful, the dukes of Lorraine set out to develop their capital city. A new palace was erected and, at the end of the 16C, Duke Charles III built a new town south of the old one. At the same time, Nancy became an important religious centre; in the space of 40 years, 13 monasteries were founded. However, the **Thirty Years War** stunted Nancy's economic growth as illustrated by **Jacques Callot**'s engravings entitled *Misfortunes of War*. When peace returned, Duke Leopold began the present cathedral designed by **Germain Boffrand** (1667–1754), who also built several mansions north of place Stanislas.

Stanislas the Magnificent

In the 18C, François III exchanged the duchy of Lorraine for the duchy of Tuscany. Louis XV, King of France, seized the opportunity and gave Lorraine to his father-in-law, **Stanislas Leszczynski**, the deposed king of Poland, on the understanding that the duchy would naturally become part of the kingdom of France after Stanislas' death. Stanislas was a peaceful man who devoted himself to his adopted land, embellished his new capital and made it into a symbol of 18C elegance with the magnificent square which bears his name in its cen-

tre. He encouraged artists of genius such as Jean Lamour, who made Nancy's superb wrought-iron railings.

Modern times

Between 1871 and 1918, Nancy welcomed refugees from the nearby regions occupied by the Germans and a modern town developed next to the three already existing ones – the old town, the dukes' town and Stanislas' town. The population of the new industrial town doubled in the space of 50 years.

In 1914 Nancy was barely saved from occupation but was bombed.

Occupied in 1940, Nancy was liberated in September 1944 by General Patton's army, with the help of the Résistance.

👣 WALKING TOURS

① LORRAINE'S CAPITAL CITY

Place Stanislas★★★

The collaboration between architect **Emmanuel Héré** and craftsman **Jean Lamour** resulted in a superb architectural ensemble (1751–60) characterised by the perfect harmony of its proportions, layout and detail. Place Stanislas forms a rectangle with canted corners, measuring 124m by 106m. Louis XV's statue in its centre was destroyed during the Revolution; in 1831 a statue of Stanislas replaced it and the square was renamed after him.

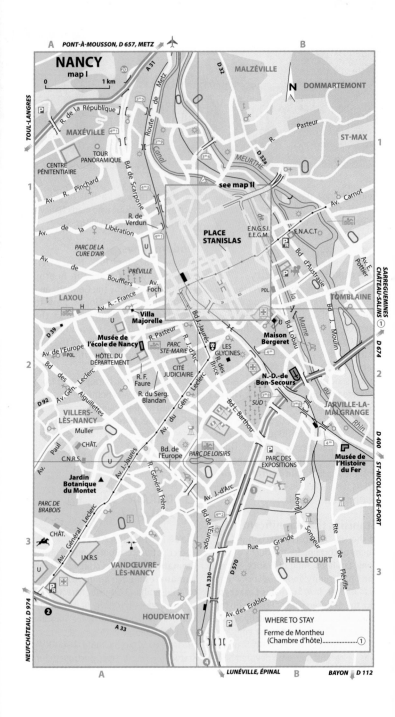

NANCY
map I

WHERE TO STAY

Ferme de Montheu
(Chambre d'hôte).....................①

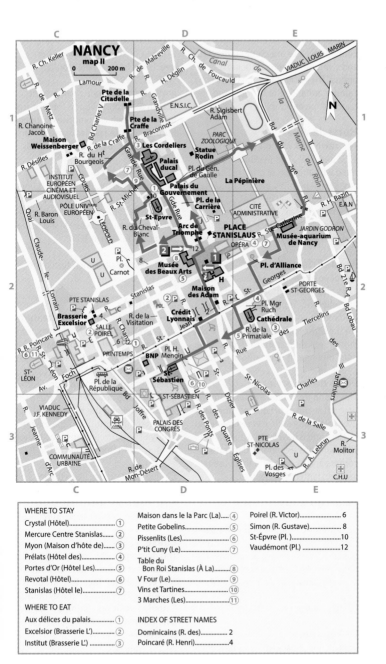

NANCY
map II

0   200 m

The square is surrounded by five tall **pavilions** and two one-storey pavilions; this emphasises the impression of space and harmony. The façades designed by Emmanuel Héré are elegant, graceful and symmetrical without being monotonous. The wrought-iron balconies by Lamour enhance the richness and elegance of the ensemble.

Hôtel de ville
The town hall was erected between 1752 and 1755. The pediment is decorated with the coat of arms of Stanislas Leszczynski: Polish eagle, Lithuanian knight, Leszczynski buffalo.
The interior rooms offer a splendid vista of place Stanislas, place de la Carrière and the Palais du Gouvernement.

Arc de Triomphe★
This deep triumphal arch, built between 1754 and 1756 to honour Louis XV, is modelled on Septimus Severus' arch in Rome.
On the right-hand park side, there is a monument dedicated to Héré, on the left a monument dedicated to Callot.

Place de la Carrière★
This elongated square dates from the time of the dukes of Lorraine; originally used for cavalry drills, it was remodelled by Héré and is now lined with beautiful 18C mansions. Fountains decorate the corners and at each end there are railings and lanterns by Lamour.

Palais du Gouverneur★
Facing the Arc de Triomphe across place du Général-de-Gaulle and place de la Carrière, this edifice is the former residence of the governors of Lorraine. The peristyle is linked to the other buildings in the square by an Ionic **colonnade★**.

▶ Turn right to enter the park.

La Pépinière
▲▲ This fine 23ha open space includes a terrace, an English garden, a rose garden and a zoo. Note the statue of the artist, Claude Gellée, known as Le Lorrain, by Rodin.

▶ Take the exit for rue Ste-Catherine.

Muséum-aquarium de Nancy
&⊙*Daily except Mon 9am–noon, 2–6pm.* ⊙*1 Jan, 1 May and 25 Dec.* ∞€5 *(free 1st Sun of the month).* ℘*03 83 32 99 97.* *www.museumaquariumdenancy.eu.*
▲▲ On the ground floor is the **tropical aquarium★** which comprises 70 ponds full of numerous species of fish; the first floor has over 10 000 stuffed animals.

Place d'Alliance
Designed by Héré, the square is lined with 18C mansions and adorned with a fountain by Cyfflé, commemorating the alliance signed by Louis XV and Maria-Theresa of Austria in 1756.

▶ Take rue Bailey, then turn right onto rue St-Georges.

Cathédrale
This imposing 18C edifice features superb railings inside the chapels, from Jean Lamour and François Jeanmaire. The graceful Virgin and Child in the apse was carved by Bagard in the 17C.
The sacristy houses the **treasury** (&●● *guided visits by arrangement.* ℘*03 83 35 26 03)* containing the ring, the chalice, the paten, the comb and the evangelistary of St Gauzelin, who was bishop of Toul during the first half of the 10C.

▶ Rue Montesquieu leads to rue Primatiale, which you follow to the right. Walk along the central market and continue until place Henri-Mengin.

Église St-Sébastien
This masterpiece by architect Jenesson was consecrated in 1732; it has a striking concave Baroque **façade★**. Inside, the three naves are surmounted by unusual flattened vaulting resting on massive Ionic columns. The chancel has retained some elegant woodwork. The side altars are the work of Vallin (École de Nancy).

▶ Retrace your steps and take a left onto rue St-Dizier, right onto rue

St-Georges and then left onto rue des Dominicains.

Maison des Adam

57 rue des Dominicains.
This is the elegant home of the Adam family, who were renowned sculptors in the 18C and decorated the house themselves.

▷ Return to Place Stanislas.

2 OLD TOWN AND NEW TOWN

The Old Town is the historic heart of the city, centred on place St-Epvre. When it extended outside its original gates, the New Town was born.

▷ Begin the walk at place Vaudémont and take Grande-Rue. Turn left onto rue Callot and continue to rue de la Monnaie.

The Hôtel de la Monnaie at No. 1 was built by Boffrand. This road leads to place de La-Fayette, a square adorned with a statue of Joan of Arc by Frémiet (a replica of the statue is in Paris).

▷ Turn right on rue de la Source.

The **Hôtel de Lillebonne** (*No. 12*), with its fine Renaissance stair case, houses the American library. Next door at no 10, note the unusual doorway of the Hôtel du Marquis de Ville, decorated with a bearded head.

▷ Take a right onto rue du Cheval-Blanc and then left onto rue de la Charité.

Basilique St-Epvre

Built in the 19C, in neo-Gothic style, this imposing church is dedicated to a 6C bishop of Toul. Its elegant west front is preceded by a monumental staircase (a gift from the emperor of Austria). The roof was blown off during the severe storm in December 1999.

▷ Take rue Mgr-Trouillet off place St-Epvre and continue on this road, which crosses rue St-Michel.

The Renaissance **Hôtel d'Haussonville** is at No. 9, with its outside galleries and Neptune fountain,

▷ Continue on the road which becomes rue des Loups.

The Hôtel des Loups (*No. 1*) again by Boffrand and the Renaissance doorway of Hôtel de Gellenoncourt (*No. 4*) are particularly worth noting.

▷ At the end of rue des Loups, turn right onto rue du Haut-Bourgeois.

Admire the Hôtel de Fontenoy (*No. 6*) designed by Boffrand at the beginning of the 18C and the **Hôtel Ferrari**★ (*No. 29*) also by Boffrand with emblazoned balcony, monumental staircase and a Neptune fountain in the courtyard.

▷ Turn left towards the gate.

Porte de la Craffe★

This gate, which formed part of the 14C fortifications, is decorated with the thistle of Nancy and the cross of Lorraine (19C). The gate was used as a prison until the Revolution. To the north stands the **Porte de la Citadelle** which used to secure the old town. This Renaissance gate is decorated with low-relief sculptures and trophies by Florent Drouin.

▷ Retrace your steps and then take the Grande-Rue.

Palais ducal★★

Dating from the second half of the 13C, the palace was in ruins when René II had it rebuilt after his victory over Charles the Bold of Burgundy.
In the 16C, Duke Antoine had the Porterie (gateway) completed together with the Galerie des Cerfs (Deer Gallery). In 1850 the palace was skilfully restored – the northern part was entirely rebuilt. The plain façade overlooking Grande-Rue enhances the elegant and rich

Art Nouveau Architecture in Nancy

Much of Nancy's architecture (commercial buildings, villas, houses) was influenced by the Art Nouveau movement. Interesting examples include:

Brasserie Excelsior (*70 rue Henri-Poincaré*), built in 1910 and decorated by Majorelle.

Chamber of commerce (*40 rue Henri-Poincaré*), designed by members of the École de Nancy in 1908, with wrought-iron work by Majorelle and stained glass by Gruber.

Maison Weissenburger
(*1 boulevard Charles V*), the architect's own 1904 house, with decorations and wrought-iron work by Majorelle.

House (*86 rue Stanislas*) built in 1906 by Eugène Vallin.

Building of the regional newspaper *L'Est Républicain* (*5 avenue Foch*), dating from 1912.

BNP bank (*9 rue Chanzy*), built in 1910, wrought-iron work by Majorelle.

Shop (*2 rue Bénit*), dating from 1900–01, the first metal-framed building to be erected; the stained glass is the work of Gruber.

Block of flats (*42–44 rue St-Dizier*) built in 1902 by Georges Biet and Eugène Vallin.

Crédit Lyonnais building (*7 bis rue St-Georges*) with stained glass by Gruber (1901).

Semi-detached houses (*92–92 bis quai Claude-le-Lorrain*) built by Émile André in 1903.

Villa Majorelle (*1 rue Louis-Majorelle, Not open to the public*). This house, originally named Villa Jika, was designed in 1899 by the Parisian architect Henri Sauvage (1873–1932) and built in 1901 for Louis Majorelle. Originally, it stood in a large park on the edge of town. It is possible to walk through the garden surrounding the villa.

House of the printer Jules Bergeret (*24 rue Lionnois*), built in 1903–04 and decorated with stained glass by Gruber and Janin.

A brochure entitled *"École de Nancy, itinéraire Art Nouveau"* suggests five itineraries which will help you discover the town's architectural heritage (*available from the tourist office; audio-guided tours are also available here*).

BELOW: 'Maison Huot'- 90-92bis quai Claude-le-Lorrain by Émile André

decoration of the **Porterie★★**. The former Ducal palace houses the Historical Museum of Lorraine.

ADDITIONAL SIGHTS
Musée de l'École de Nancy★★

🕐*Wed–Sun 10am–6pm.* ⌘*€6 (under 12, no charge), no charge 1st Sun of the month.* 🕐*1 Jan, 1 May, 1 Jul, 1 Nov and 25 Dec.* 📞*03 83 40 14 86.* *www.ecole-de-nancy.com.*

Housed in an opulent residence dating from the turn of the 20C, this museum offers a remarkable insight into the renewal movement in the field of decorative arts that took place in Nancy between 1885 and 1914 and became known as the **École de Nancy**. Taking inspiration in nature, this movement blossomed under **Émile Gallé**.

The museum contains exhibits characteristic of this movement: carved and inlaid furniture by Émile Gallé, Louis Majorelle, Eugène Vallin, Jacques Gruber and Émile André; book bindings, posters and drawings by Prouvé, Martin, Collin and Lurçat; glassware by Gallé, the Daum brothers and Muller; ceramics; and stained glass. Several furnished rooms, including a splendid **dining room** by Vallin (painted ceiling and leather wallcovering with delicate floral motifs by Prouvé) show the changing styles of middle-class interiors at the turn of the 20C.

On the first floor, there is an interesting bathroom decorated with ceramics by Chaplet, a businessman's office comprising leather-work with floral motifs, seats, a bookcase and a monumental filing cabinet.

Musée des Beaux-Arts★★

♿🕐*Daily except Tue 10am–6pm.* 🕐*1 Jan, 1 May, 14 Jul, 1 Nov, 25 Dec.* ⌘*€7 (child under 12, no charge; no charge 1st Sun of the month).* 📞*03 83 85 30 72. www.mban.nancy.fr.*

The impressively refurbished Museum of Fine Arts, housed in one of the pavilions on place Stanislas, contains rich collections of European art from the 14C to the present day which are not arranged chronologically – to their great advan-

Musée de l'École de Nancy

© Ville de Nancy

tage. For instance, the display of works illustrating the transition between the 18C and 19C takes us on a journey to the early 1940s then goes back to the Italian Renaissance and concludes in the 18C. The most remarkable paintings of the 17C French School include *Love taking its revenge* by Vouet, *Pastoral Landscape* by Claude Lorrain and *Charity* by Philippe de Champaigne.

The Modern Art collection, housed in the contemporary extension, is essentially represented by Manet, Monet, Henri Edmond Cross, Modigliani, Juan Gris, Georg Grosz, Picasso, and a few early-20C artists from Lorraine. Sculptures include works by Rodin, Duchamp-Villon, Lipchitz, and César.

Italian painting is well represented; also noteworthy are the landscapes and still-life paintings by Joos de Momper, Jan II Bruegel and Hemessen as well as The **Transfiguration** by Ruben.

18C painting, housed in the Emmanuel Héré pavilion, includes works by Jean-Baptiste Claudot, Desportes, François Boucher and Carle Van Loo.

The department of **graphic art** holds remarkable collections of prints by Jacques Callot (787 engravings) and 1 438 drawings by Grandville.

The Daum collection (300 pieces of glassware and crystal) is housed in what remains of the 15C–17C fortifications found while building the extension.

Musée Lorrain★★★

Housed in the former Palais Ducal; entrance: No. 64 Grande-Rue. ◑*Tue–Sun 10am–12.30pm, 2–6pm.* ◑*1 Jan, 1 May, 14 Jul, 1 Nov and 25 Dec.* ☞€6 *(under 12, no charge).* ✆*03 83 32 18 74. www.musee-lorrain.nancy.fr.*

The museum contains a wealth of exceptional documents illustrating the history of Lorraine, its artistic production and its folklore, displayed on three floors.

On the first floor, the Galerie des Cerfs, 55m long, contains mementoes of the House of Lorraine, as well as tapestries from the early 16C, paintings by Jacques Bellange, **Georges de La Tour** (*Woman with a Flea, Discovery of St Alexis' Body, Young Smoker, St Jerome reading*), Charles Mellin and Claude Deruet.

The pavilion at the bottom of the garden houses an **archaeological gallery** concerned with prehistory, the Celtic period, and Gallo-Roman and Frankish times.

▶ Walk across the garden.

The collections, displayed in the vaulted vestibule and gallery, illustrate the history of Lorraine from the Middle Ages to the 16C (sculptures).

A large area is devoted to Lorraine and Nancy during the lifetime of Stanislas: his creations including the square which bears his name, as well as to political, military and literary history from the Revolution to the Empire.

Église and Couvent des Cordeliers★

◑*Same hours as Musée Lorrain, and with a ticket from that museum.* ✆*03 83 32 18 74.*

The now-restored 15C Franciscan convent and adjacent church were erected on the initiative of Duke René II.

Église★

The church has only one nave as is usual for the church of a mendicant order. All the dukes are buried in the crypt. Most of the funeral monuments are the works of three great Renaissance artists, natives of Lorraine: Mansuy Gauvain, Ligier Richier and Florent Drouin.

A chapel on the left-hand side contains the **recumbent figure of Philippa of Gelderland★★**, René II's second wife, carved in fine limestone, one of the finest works of Ligier Richier. Against the south wall (near the high altar), note the funeral recess of **René II's funeral monument★**, carved by Mansuy Gauvain in 1509. The effigy of Cardinal de Vaudémont (d. 1587) is the work of Florent Drouin. The latter is also the author of a remarkable Last Supper, a low-relief sculpture after the famous painting by Leonardo da Vinci.

Chapelle ducale★

On the left of the chancel.

Built from 1607 onwards over the tomb of the dukes of Lorraine, the octagonal chapel was modelled on the Medici Chapel in Florence at the request of Charles III.

Couvent

The cloisters and some rooms of the former monastery are restored and now house a rich **Musée d'Arts et Traditions populaires** (Museum of Folk Art and Traditions).

Jardin botanique du Montet★

♿◑*Apr–Oct daily: garden 9.30am–6pm; greenhouses 9.30–11.45am, 1–5.45pm; Nov–Mar: garden Mon–Fri 9.30am–noon, 1–5pm, Sat–Sun 1–5pm; greenhouses Mon–Fri 9.30–11.45am, 1–4.45pm, Sat–Sun 1–4.45pm.* ◑*1 Jan, 1 May and 25 Dec and 1st Tue of the month (greenhouses).* ☞€5 *greenhouses (gardens: no charge).* ✆*03 83 41 47 47. www.jardinbotaniquedenancy.eu.*

The botanical gardens cover an area of 25ha including hot houses extending over 2 000m². The gardens contain some 15 thematic collections (Alpine, ornamental, medicinal plants, an arboretum etc) and 6 500 species grow in the hot houses: orchids, and insect-eating and succulent plants.

Église Notre-Dame-de-Bon-Secours★

Avenue de Strasbourg.

Built in 1738 for Stanislas by Emmanuel Héré, on the site of René II's chapel commemorating his victory over Charles the Bold (1476), this church is a well-known place of pilgrimage. Note the Baroque west front.

The richly decorated interior includes carved confessionals in Louis XV style, railings by Jean Lamour and a splendid Rocaille pulpit. The chancel contains **Stanislas' tomb★** and the monument carved by Vassé for the heart of Marie Leszczynska, Louis XV's wife, on the right-hand side and, on the left, the **mausoleum of Catherine Opalinsk★★**, Stanislas' wife.

EXCURSIONS

Musée de l'Histoire du fer

Daily except Tue 2–6pm (Sat–Sun and public holidays 10am–noon, 2–6pm. 1 Jan, Easter Sun, 1 Nov and 25 Dec. €5. 03 83 15 27 70. www.museehistoiredufer.fr.

Located in **Jarville-la-Malgrange** (*see plan I*) this museum is housed in a building that illustrates the role of metallic architecture in contemporary design. The museum reveals the evolution of iron-working from prehistoric times to the present, including techniques used to make weapons during the Gaulish period.

Leave Nancy SE on D 400.
In Laneuveville, immediately after the bridge on the Marne-Rhine canal, turn left onto D 126. The road veers to the right, offering a fine overall view of the Chartreuse de Bosserville before crossing the Meurthe. Turn left onto D 2; 1km/0.6mi farther on, an alleyway lined with plane trees leads to the Chartreuse de Bosserville.

Chartreuse de Bosserville

5km/3mi. Not open to the public.

Founded in 1666 by Duke Charles IV, this former Carthusian monastery is now occupied by a technical college. Bosserville was used as a military hospital from 1793 to 1813; hundreds of French and foreign soldiers died there, their bodies deposited in the former lakes of Bois Robin.

Leave Nancy S on the A 330 and continue to the Fléville exit (8km/5mi).

Château de Fléville

9km/5.6mi SE. guided tours (1h) at 2.30pm, 4pm, 5.30pm: Apr Sun; May–Jun and Sept–Oct Sat–Sun and public holidays; Jul–Aug, daily. Park and gardens are open without a guide. €9.50. 03 83 25 64 71. www.fleville.com.

The present edifice, erected in the 16C, replaced a 14C fortress of which only the square keep remains.

Once across the former moat, you are in the main courtyard. The tour of the interior includes the dukes of Lorraine's hall, Stanislas' bedroom, the 18C chapel, as well as several bedrooms.

Leave Nancy on D 400.
The information centre is near the entrance on the right.

Parc de loisirs de la forêt de Haye

9km/5.6mi W.

This leisure park (*www.parcdeloisirs-haye.com*) lies in the heart of the Haye forest, a vast area of rolling hills covering 9 000ha. The park was once used as hunting grounds by the dukes of Lorraine, but today includes several sports grounds, tennis courts, playgrounds, picnic areas, and marked itineraries for walking or running. It is also the starting point of long hikes, as well as riding and mountain-bike tours (*130km/81mi of paths and trails*) through the forest.

The **Musée de l'Automobile** (*Jul–Aug daily 2–6pm; rest of year Wed, Sat–Sun and public holidays 2–6pm. €5. 03 83 23 28 38; www.musee-automobile-lorraine.fr*) houses about 100 vehicles of different makes, dating from 1898 (such as the Aster of 1900) to 1989; note the collection GT saloon cars from the 1960s, radiator stoppers and advertising posters.

ADDRESSES

🏠 STAY

Weekends in Nancy – Hotel stays of two nights and more are rewarded by a welcome gift and reductions on visits to the town. Ask at the tourist office for a full list of hotels and conditions.

Hôtel Stanislas – *22 rue Ste Catherine. &09 50 71 80 23. www.hotel-lestanislas.fr. 17 rooms.* In the centre of Nancy adjacent to Place Stanislas and only 100m from the splendid Parc de la Pépinière, this small is ideally placed for exploring the old town.

Chambre d'hôte Ferme de Montheu – *54770 Dommartin-sous-Amance. 10 km/ 6.25mi NE of Nancy, Sarreguemines and Agincourt direction. &03 83 31 17 37. www. chambres-dhotes-ferme-du-montheu.com. 4 rooms.* This working farm in the middle of the country has lovely uninterrupted views, apart from a nearby high-tension power line. But that's soon forgotten in the peace of the simple rooms with their old furniture.

Hôtel Revotel – *41–43 avenue Raymond Poincarré. &03 83 28 02 13. 58 rooms.* Located in the town centre near to the station, metro, bus and shops/restaurants. Comfortable rooms in 2 categories; Superior or Standard.

Portes d'Or – *21 r. Stanislas. &03 83 35 42 34. www.hotel-lesportesdor.com. 20 rooms.* The main advantage of this hotel is its proximity to the Place Stanislas. The pastel-coloured rooms are not very large, but have modern furniture and are well equipped.

Hôtel Crystal – *5 r. Chanzy. &03 83 17 54 00. www.bwcrystal.com. Closed Dec 24–Jan 2. 58 rooms* This hotel near the station is a good place to stay in Nancy. Its modern, spacious rooms have been nicely arranged and decorated and feel welcoming. Cosy bar-lounge.

Mercure Centre Stanislas – *5 r. Carmes. &03 83 30 92 60. www. accorhotels.com. 80 rooms.* Ideally situated in the town centre shopping area, this hotel has complete, well-kept facilities. Rooms have furniture in the Art Nouveau style.

Maison d'hôte Myon – *7, rue Mably. &03 83 46 56 56. www.maison demyon.com. 5 rooms.* An entirely restored 18C hotel transformed into a *maison d'hôte* in the heart of Nancy near the Place Stanislas. The individual rooms are tastefully decorated and equipped with stylish furniture.

Des Prélats – *56 pl Mgr Ruch. &03 83 30 20 20. www.hoteldesprelats.com. 42 rooms.* This 17C building attached to the cathedral has been wonderfully restored with spacious, individually styled rooms and a pleasant veranda opening onto an inner courtyard.

🍴 EAT

Aux délices du Palais – *69 Grande Rue. &03 83 30 44 19. Closed Aug and 24–31 Dec.* Small restaurant cheerfully decorated. Excellent cuisine and menus regularly updated. Specialities include lasagne with salmon and spinach.

Les Pissenlits – *25 bis r. des Ponts. &03 83 37 43 97. www.les-pissenlits.com. Closed Sun and Mon.* There's always a crowd in this bistro near the market, and with good reason: the atmosphere is relaxed, the cuisine innovative and diverse.

V Four – *10 r. St-Michel. &03 83 32 49 48. www.levfour.fr. Closed Sun evening and Mon.* It may be small, but this Michenlin Bib Gourmand restaurant in the heart of the old city is popular among the locals, who enjoy its simple modern decor and its trendy cuisine. Terrace.

Excelsior Brasserie – *50, rue Henri-Poincaré. &03 83 35 24 57. www.brasserie-excelsior-nancy.fr.* A belle époque brasserie complete with beautiful *école de Nancy* windows and fittings and fixtures by all the leading artisans of the period. Typical brasserie cuisine in beautiful surroundings.

Brasserie de l'Institut – *2, rue Braconnot. &03 83 32 24 14.* One of Nancy's oldest cafés dating from 1903 designed by the architect Charbonnier and situated in the old town opposite the Porte de la Craffe.

Le P'tit Cuny – *99 Grande Rue. &03 83 32 85 94. http://restaurant-marchand.com.* Authentic Lorraine cuisine such as *choucroute, tête de veau* and veal pie are served in this rather cramped but welcoming small restaurant.

A La Table du Bon Roi Stanislas – *7 r. Gustave-Simon. ☏03 83 35 36 52. http://tablestan.free.fr. Closed Sun eve, Mon lunch, Wed lunch. Reservation advised.* Dedicated to King Stanislas who became Duke of Lorraine in the 18C and was said to be a good amateur cook. This historic restaurant has original recipes and sobre period decor not to be missed.

Vins et Tartines – *25 bis rue des ponts. ☏03 83 35 17 25. www.vins-et-tartines.com. Closed Sun–Mon.* As the name suggests, the concept of this restaurant is light meals with wine and bread. Hot/cold dishes, accompanied by salads and vegetables.

Les 3 Marchés – *8 rue St-Léon. ☏03 83 41 33 00. Reservation advised.* Small restaurant with excellent traditional cuisine. Decorated with large mirrors and corner library. Good wine selection.

Les Petits Gobelins – *18, rue de la Primatiale. ☏03 83 35 49 03. www.lespetitsgobelins.fr.* ocated in a pedestriansed area behind the cathedral, this Michelin L'Assiette restaurant enjoys a convivial atmosphere and serves creative cuisine. Reservations advised.

La Maison dans le Parc – *3 rue Ste-Catherine. ☏03 83 19 03 57. www.lamaisondansleparc.com. Closed Sun eve, Mon and Tue. Reservation essential.* This fine-dining Michelin-starred restaurant offers modern cuisine served with imagination and flair.

ON THE TOWN

L'Arq – *13 r. Héré. ☏06 66 96 43 23. Tue–Sun 6.30pm–4am, until 5am Fri and Sat.* This high-class bar with a refined décor has a good view of Place Stanislas. A wide choice of cocktails with atmospheric music. The place to go after 2am.

Nouveau Vertigo – *29 r. de la Visitation. ☏03 83 32 71 97. Tue–Thu 11am–2am, Fri 11am–4am, Sat 4pm–5am. Closed Mon–Sun.* The centre-piece of Nancy cultural life, this bar doubles up as a restaurant and venue for café-theatre evenings and concerts (jazz, Afro-jazz, rock and French music). It is often packed, and the drink flows freely, mainly beer and cocktails.

SHOWTIME

Get hold of a programme – The magazine *Spectacles à Nancy* will keep you informed (*www.spectacles-publications.com*).

Shows – The Opéra de Nancy et de Lorraine, Ballet de Nancy, Théâtre de la Manufacture, Centre dramatique national Nancy-Lorraine, Association de musique ancienne de Nancy, Ensemble Poirel, Orchestre symphonique et lyrique de Nancy, Association Lorraine de Musique de Chambre, Gradus Ad Musicam, La Psalette de Lorraine put on numerous concerts and shows each year in various venues around the city.

Opéra National de Lorraine – *1, rue sainte Catherine. ☏03 83 85 33 20. www.opera-national-lorraine.fr.* Check out the architecture of this magnificent theatre, open mainly during school holidays, but check website for details, which vary.

CCN Ballet de Lorraine – *3 r. Henri-Bazin. ☏03 83 85 69 00. www.ballet-de-lorraine.eu. 10am–1pm and 2–6pm.*

Nancyphonies – *www.nancyphonies.com.* From June to August, the streets resound to the sound of more than 30 classical music concerts.

Ensemble Poirel – *R. Victor-Poirel. ☏03 83 32 31 25. www.poirel.nancy.fr.* Stages an eclectic selection of theatre, opera, ballet, concerts and readings throughout the year, with shows by well-known and as well as lesser known names.

Théâtre de la Manufacture – *10 R. Baron-Louis. ☏03 83 37 42 42. www.theatre-manufacture.fr.* National drama centre of Nancy-Lorraine.

MJC Lillebonne – *14 r. du Cheval-Blanc. ☏03 83 36 82 82. www.mjclillebonne.org. Mon–Fri 8am–11pm, Sat 8.30am–6pm.* Wide choice of socio-educational and cultural concerts, theatre and dance.

Patrimoine en musique – Classical concerts in city churches.

Nancy-jazz-pulsations – *106 Grande Rue, 54 023 Nancy. ☏03 83 35 40 86. www.nancyjazzpulsations.com.* This October festival brings in jazz lovers for two weeks of concerts and musical entertainment.

Baccarat

Meurthe-et-Moselle

This small town lying on both sides of the River Meurthe is famous for its crystalworks founded in 1764.

A BIT OF HISTORY
Crystalworks

⌕ *Not open to the public.*

In 1764 King Louis XV allowed the bishop of Metz to revive an ancient glass-making tradition; in 1817 the glassworks were turned into crystalworks and since 1828, the works have been supplying kings, presidents and the international jetset, including Tsar Nicholas II, who commissioned a 3.85m tall candelabrum. There was a time of great prosperity at the beginning of the 19C and again in the 1950s. Glassworkers lived near the crystalworks because they had to run to the factory as soon as the bell rang signalling that the crystal had melted. Today, the high-tech crystalworks use a special furnace that fines down the melted mixture, and 38 highly qualified craftsmen have been nominated "best workers in France".

SIGHTS
Musée du Cristal Baccarat

🕐 *10am–12.30pm, 1.30–6pm. ☞€3.
℘03 83 76 61 37. www.baccarat.fr.*
Located in the mansion which once belonged to the crystalworks' founder, the museum displays antique and contemporary pieces: 19C opalines, agates, millefiori paperweights, plain, cut or carved glasses, and table sets ordered by sovereigns and heads of states. In the last room, the various techniques and tools used are illustrated. A shop on the premises sells items with a specific Baccarat mark.

Église St-Rémy

Built in 1957, the church has an unusual roof with large awnings. The steeple, a 55m pyramid, stands beside the church. The interior decoration, which consists in a huge low relief made up of concrete elements and **stained-glass panels★** in Baccarat crystal.

> ▶ **Population:** 4 519.
> 🞅 **Michelin Map:** Michelin Local map 307: L-8.
> 🯀 **Tourist Office:** 13, rue du Port. ℘03 83 75 13 37.
> 🞛 **Location:** Baccarat is half-way (60km/37.3mi) between Nancy and Gérardmer on N 59.

EXCURSIONS
Deneuvre

Excavations, carried near the village led to the discovery of a 2C Gallo-Roman sanctuary once dedicated to Hercules, now reconstructed in a museum.

Les Sources d'Hercule

♿🕐 *Mar–Apr and Oct Fri–Sun 2–5pm; May–Jun and Sept Fri–Sun 10am–12.30pm, 2–6pm; Jul–Aug daily 10am–12.30pm, 2–6pm. 🕐Nov–Feb. ☞€3.50. ℘03 83 75 22 82. www.museehercule.com.*
In the entrance hall there are explanations, maps, plans and models dealing with the discovery of the site. Three pools were at the disposal of those who wished to perform their ablutions; over centuries of use, the ex-voto offerings piled up around the springs.

Badonviller

17km/10.5mi NE via D 935 and D 992.
This industrial town, partly destroyed in August 1914, was, 30 years later, one of the first towns to be liberated by the French second armoured division. The scenic **road★** (D182A) leads to the tiny village of **Pierre-Percée**.

Lac de Pierre-Percée

Park near the barrage du Vieux-Pré and go to the viewpoint where an information panel explains the construction of the lake and its dam.
👫 To discover the province of the forester follow the botanical footpath from the Roche aux Corbeaux and stop at the bird observatory.

ADDRESSES

SPORT AND RECREATION

Fraispertuis City – *Jeanménil. 20km/14.5mi S of Baccarat on D 935, D 435 and D 32.* ℘*03 29 65 27 06. www.fraispertuis-city.fr. Open Apr–Sept, but see website for variable opening hours.* €*23 (under 1m40, €19).* Over twenty rides and attractions on a Far West theme can be enjoyed by children and adults alike. Restaurant facilities on site.

Painting Baccarat glassware

© Carlos Sánchez Pereyra/John Warburton-Lee/Photononstop

Lunéville
Meurthe-et-Moselle

Bedecked with wide streets, vast park and beautiful monuments, Lunéville sits between the River Meurthe and its tributary, the Vezouze.

A BIT OF HISTORY

At the beginning of the 18C, the duke of Lorraine, **Leopold**, often stayed in the town. Later on, Lunéville was the favourite residence of King Stanislas (*see NANCY*); writers and artists, among them Voltaire, Montesquieu, Saint-Lambert and Helvetius flocked to his court. Stanislas died in the castle in 1766.

CHÂTEAU DES LUMIÈRES DE LUNÉVILLE ★

Daily except Tue 10am–noon, 2–6pm. €*3* ℘*03 83 76 04 75. www.chateauluneville.meurthe-et-moselle.fr.*
This imposing castle surrounds a vast courtyard. A fire destroyed most of the castle's collections in 2003, and restoration went on for many years, with partial completion, sufficient to re-open, in 2010.

Parc des Bosquets★

May–Sept 6am–10pm; Oct–Apr 6am–7pm.
Laid out at the beginning of the 18C by Yves des Hours, the park was successively embellished by Leopold and Stanislas.

- **Population:** 20 054
- **Michelin Map:** Michelin Local map 307: J-7.
- **Tourist Office:** 2 Rue de la Tour Blanche, 54300 Lunéville. ℘03 83 74 06 55. www.tourisme-lunevillois. com.
- **Location:** Lunéville is located 30km/18.6mi E of Nancy.

ADDITIONAL SIGHT
Synagogue
Built in 1785, this edifice is a blend of Greek classical style and Baroque.

ADDRESSES

STAY

Hôtel des Pages – *5 quai des Petits-Bosquets.* ℘*03 83 74 11 42. www.logishotels.com. 34 rooms.* Close to the castle. Request a room that has been renovated in contemporary style. Bistro cooking at the Petit Comptoir restaurant.

EAT

Les Bosquets – *2 r. des Bosquets –* ℘*03 83 74 00 14. www.restaurantles-bosquets.fr. Closed Tue, Wed evening and Sun evening.* This small family restaurant is frequented by the locals and offers several fixed menus. The fixed-price lunch is particularly good value and the three simple dining rooms are often full.

Pont-à-Mousson★

Meurthe-et-Moselle

Pont-à Mousson developed from the 9C onwards around a bridge over the Moselle, beneath a knoll crowned with a fortress.
This strategic position accounts for the heavy shelling that the town was subjected to between 1914 and 1918 and in 1944. Pont-à-Mousson's industrial activity centres on a foundry of the St-Gobain group.The town is the headquarters of the **Parc naturel régional de Lorraine** and a convenient starting point of hikes and excursions.

▶ **Population:** 15 074.

Michelin Map: Michelin Local map 307: H-5.

Tourist Office: 52 pl. Duroc, 54700 Pont-à-Mousson. ℰ03 83 31 06 90. www.tourisme-pontamousson.fr.

Location: At a bridging point on the River Moselle; equidistant between Metz (31km/19.3mi) and Nancy (30km/18.6mi) by A31 motorway.

Don't Miss: The Ancienne Abbaye des Prémontrés and place Duroc.

SIGHTS
Ancienne abbaye des Prémontrés★

9 rue St-Martin. &🕐*Daily 10am–6pm.* 🕐*1 Jan and 25 Dec.* ℰ*03 83 81 10 32.* ⊗€*5. www.abbaye-premontres.com.*
The former Premonstratensian abbey is a rare example of 18C monastic architecture and is now a cultural centre. Around the cloisters are the warming-room, refectory, chapter house, sacristy, former chapel etc.
Three lovely **staircases★** lead to the conference rooms, bedrooms and library: the small spiral-shaped staircase, situated in a corner of the cloisters near the warming-room, is very elegant; on the other side of the chapel *(used as a concert hall)*, the oval Samson staircase is one of abbey's finest features; as for the great square staircase, located on the right of the sacristy, it is concealed by a beautiful wrought-iron handrail and matching banisters.

Ste-Marie-Majeure

The Baroque interior of the former abbey church has been preserved. Note the slightly curved piers supporting the vaulting.

Musée au Fil du Papier

13 rue Magot-de-Rogeville. &🕐*Daily except Tue 2–6pm.* 🕐*1 Jan, Easter Sun, 1 May, 14 Jul, 1 Nov and 25 Dec.* ⊗€*5.* ℰ*03 83 87 80 14.* *www.ville-pont-a-mousson.fr.*
The University of Lorraine, based in Pont-à-Mousson from 1572 to 1768, attracted printers, engravers and booksellers to the town. The museum shows their work and displays a remarkable collection of objects made of papier mâché.

Place Duroc★

The square is surrounded by 16C arcaded houses. In its centre is a monumental fountain dating from 1931, offered to the town by the American ambulance service. Several fine buildings include the 18C **Hôtel de Ville**, which has a monumental clock over the pediment, and the **Maison des Sept Péchés Capitaux**, adorned with caryatids representing the seven deadly sins and flanked by a Renaissance turret.

Église St-Laurent

The chancel and the transept date from the 15C and 16C. The central doorway and first two storeys of the tower date from the 18C, the rest of the west front being completed in 1895. Inside, note the polychrome triptych of a 16C altarpiece from Antwerp and a statue of Christ carrying his Cross by Ligier Richier; the chancel is decorated with fine 18C woodwork.

Église St-Martin

The church, located on the east bank of the Moselle, was built in the 14C and 15C and extended with side chapels in the 17C and 18C. The 15C west front is flanked by two dissimilar towers. Inside, note a Flamboyant Gothic funerary recess containing two medieval recumbent figures.

In the north aisle, is an Entombment comprising 13 characters by early-15C artists from Champagne and Germany; Ligier Richier was probably influenced by this work when he carved the St-Mihiel Entombment half a century later.

EXCURSIONS

Butte de Mousson★

7km/4.3mi by N57, then along D910 and D34 to Mousson, then 15min on foot.

A modern chapel stands at the top of the knoll alongside the ruins of the feudal castle of the counts of Bar.

ADDRESSES

⍻/EAT

Le Fourneau d'Alain – *64 pl. Duroc. ℰ03 8 3 82 95 09. www.lefourneau dalain.com. Closed Mon, Wed eve, Sun eve, .*

Appetising cooking by chef Alain Fornara in a pleasant dining room on the first floor of one of the fine arcaded houses on the main square. To complement your meal an excellent selection of wines and fine coffee blends are available.

St-Nicolas-de-Port★★

Meurthe-et-Moselle

The impressive Flamboyant basilica of St-Nicolas-de-Port dominates the centre of this small industrial town. It has been a popular place of pilgrimage since the 11C, when the city became the most prosperous economic centre in Lorraine and the venue of international fairs. In 1635, during the Thirty Years War, the town was ransacked by the expanding forces of the Swedish Empire, and only the church was spared.

SIGHTS

Basilique St-Nicolas★★

The splendid Flamboyant Gothic basilica was built as a shrine for one of St Nicholas' fingers, which had been brought here from Bari in Italy by knights from Lorraine and placed in a chapel dedicated to Our Lady. There followed a series of miracles and a church had to be built to accommodate the growing number of pilgrims, among them Joan

- ▶ **Population:** 7 677.
- ⚲ **Michelin Map:** Michelin Local map 307: I-7.
- ▮ **Tourist Office:** Place Camille-Croué-Friedmann, 54210 St-Nicolas-de-Port. ℰ03 83 48 58 75.
- ▶ **Location:** 12km/7.5mi SE of Nancy.

of Arc in 1429. The huge late 15C and early 16C church suffered fire and war damage and the roof was only repaired in 1735. After bomb damage in 1940, the church was again in need of extensive restoration. A bequest in 1980 provided the answer and, since 1983, the outside has resembled a building site.

Exterior

The west front features three doorways with Flamboyant Gothic gables. The central doorway bears a statue representing St Nicholas' miracle, believed to be the work of Claude Richier. On the north side, note six basket-handled recesses in which traders used to set up shop at pilgrimage time.

Interior

The interior stands out for its extremely tall nave (32m) and the tall pillars of the transept vaulting (28m high, the highest in France). The stained-glass windows of the apse, made by Nicole Droguet of Lyon in 1507 to 1510, are particularly remarkable; those of the aisle and chapels on the north side date from the same period and are the work of Valentin Bousch from Strasbourg. The Renaissance influence can already be seen in the decorative motifs.

The sanctuary that received St Nicholas' relic in the 11C was probably located where the **baptismal chapel** now stands. Several 16C painted wood panels illustrate scenes from his life. The **treasury** includes a silver gilt reliquary arm of St Nicholas (19C), the cardinal of Lorraine's ship (16C), a silver reliquary of the True Cross (15C) and Voltaire's ivory Crucifix.

Musée français de la Brasserie

62 r. Charles-Courtois.

🕐*Daily 2.30–6.30pm.* 🕐*1 Jan, 1 May, 24–25 and 31 Dec.* ☜€5.50. 🖉*03 83 46 95 52. www.passionbrasserie.com.*

The museum is housed in an old brewery which closed in 1986. The visit of the Art Deco brewing tower takes in the labora-tory, the malt loft, hops storeroom, the brewing room with its fine copper vats, the refrigerating equipment and the cold room with the fermentation vats.

Musée du Cinéma, de la Photographie et des Arts audiovisuels

10 rue Georges-Rémy.

&🕐*Wed–Sat 2–6pm, Sun 2.30–6.30pm.* 🕐*Public holidays except 15 Aug.* ☜€5 *(children €3.50).* 🖉*03 83 45 18 32. www.museecinemaphoto.com.*

👥 Magic lanterns and other forgotten equipment illustrate the evolution of moving pictures and animation from the early 19C to the birth of the cinema.

ADDRESSES

🍴 EAT

☞ **Auberge de la Mirabelle Chez Léon** – *6 rte de Nancy, 54210 Ferrières. 12km/7mi S of St-Nicolas-de-Port on D 115 and D 112.* 🖉*03 83 26 62 14. www. auberge-mirabelle.eu. Open daily for lunch only.* As its name suggests, Léon's farm specialises in mirabelle plums. In the old cowshed, which now serves as a restaurant.

Le Saulnois

Moselle

Situated to the southeast of Metz, the Saulnois is part of the **Natural Regional Park of Lorraine.** As the name of the region suggests, this is the 'Land of Salt' and even the village of Marsal and the town of Château-Salins echo this theme.

PARC ANIMALIER DE STE-CROIX★

12km/7.5mi NW of Sarrebourg or 63.6km/39.5mi east of Nancy.

🕐*Daily Apr–mid-Nov, 10am–6pm (Jul–Aug, 10am–7pm; early–mid-Nov*

🜂 **Michelin Map:** 307: K-6

🛈 **Tourist Office:** 🖉03 87 37 57 80. www.moselle-tourisme.com.

▶ **Location:** Marsal is 60km/37mi southeast of Metz on the D955; 33km/20.5mi northeast of Nancy on the N74.

10am–5.30pm). ☜€24.50 *(child 3–11, €16.50).* 🖉*03 87 03 92 05. www.parcsaintecroix.com.*

👥 This safari park shelters 1 200 animals from 80 different European species including wolf, lynx, fox, stork, deer, auroch and capercaillie.

MARSAL

Population: 261.
Situated on the western fringes of this part of the Parc naturel régional de Lorraine, an area once liable to flooding, this village has retained numerous Gallo-Roman ruins and a section of its defensive wall fortified by Vauban in the 17C, including an elegant gate, the Porte de France, which has been restored.

Maison du Sel

◉*Daily except Mon 9.30am–noon, 1.30–6pm.* ◉*24 Dec–7 Jan.* ⊛€4.
☎03 87 35 01 50.
Housed in the Porte de France, part of Vauban's fortifications, the salt museum relates the history of this precious commodity, gathered since Antiquity in the salt mines of the Seille valley.
🏃 A marked footpath leads to the nearby salt ponds.

Vic-sur-Seille

7km/4.3mi W of Marsal along D 38.
The administration of the diocese of Metz and the residence of the bishop were established here from the 13C to 17C. Visitors can still see the ruins of the bishop's castle. Vic was the birthplace of **Georges de La Tour** (1593–1652).
👥 The Base de loisirs de la Tuilière (leisure park), situated close to Vic-sur-Seille, offers fishing, swimming and other activities.

Sarrebourg

Moselle

This city of Roman origin belonged to the bishops of Metz during the Middle Ages and then to the duchy of Lorraine before becoming part of France in the late 17C. Today Sarrebourg is the starting point of fine excursions along the River Sarre in an area renowned for its crystal works.

- ▶ **Population:** 12 603.
- ⊙ **Michelin Map:** Michelin Local map 307: N-6.
- 🚩 **Tourist Office:** rue du Musée, 57400 Sarrebourg. ☎03 87 03 11 82. www.tourisme-sarrebourg.fr.
- ◉ **Location:** Sarrebourg is at the gateway to the Vosges, 73km/45mi NE of Strasbourg.

SIGHTS
Chapelle des Cordeliers

♿◉*Daily except Tue: Apr–Oct 10am–6pm (Sun 2–6pm); Nov–Mar 2–5pm.* ◉*1 Jan, 10–31 Jan, Easter, 1 May, 25–26 Dec.* ⊛€6. ☎03 87 03 14 64.
This deconsecrated Franciscan chapel houses the tourist office. Its west front is lit by a huge **stained-glass window★** by Marc Chagall illustrating *"peace"*. In the centre, vivid blues, reds and greens symbolise the Tree of Life in Genesis with Adam and Eve surrounded by the Serpent, Christ's cross, the Prophet Isaiah, the Lamb, the Candelabra, Suffering and Death illustrate mankind.

Musée du Pays de Sarrebourg

Rue de la Paix. ♿◉*Daily except Tue: Apr–Oct 10am–noon, 2–6pm (Sun and public holidays 2–6pm); Nov–Mar 2–6pm.* ◉*1 Jan, 10–31 Jan, Easter, 1 May, 25–26 Dec.* ⊛€6. ☎03 87 08 08 68.
The museum, housed in a modern space designed by the architect Bernard Desmoulin, contains regional archaeological finds, medieval sculpture (beautiful 15C Crucifix) and 18C ceramics and porcelain from nearby Niderviller.

Echoing the Chagall window of the Chapelle des Cordeliers, the entrance is dominated by a tapestry on the same theme of peace.

Cimetière national des Prisonniers

On the outskirts of town, on the right of rue de Verdun (D 27).
The cemetery contains some 13 000 WW1 graves . The monument facing the gate, 'Giant in chains', was sculpted by Stoll while he was a prisoner of war.

Colline de Sion-Vaudémont★

Meurthe-et-Moselle

The isolated horseshoe-shaped hill of Sion-Vaudémont is one of the most famous viewpoints in Lorraine. For 2 000 years, it has drawn pagan worshippers and, later, Christians. After the Franco-Prussian War of 1870, and after each of the two world wars, pilgrims came to pray on top of the hill. In 1973, a Peace monument was unveiled here.

SIGHTS

Basilique Notre-Dame de Sion★

The basilica dates mainly from the 18C, but the monumental 19C belfry sadly burnt down in 2003. In the apse (early 14C) is the statue of Notre-Dame-de-Sion, a 15C crowned Virgin Mary in gilt stone. There is a superb **panoramic view★** by the Calvary.

Signal de Vaudémont★★

2.5km/1.5mi S of Sion along D 53.
At the top of the Signal de Vaudémont (alt 541m) is the **Barrès Monument** (22m high) erected in 1928 in memory of writer and politician Maurice Barrès (1862–1923), a native of the area, who celebrated the hill, which he called the Colline inspirée in one of his novels. There is a superb **panorama★★** of the Lorraine plateau.

EXCURSIONS

St-Ulrich, Villa gallo-romaine

Guided tours by arrangement.
The 1C villa was the residence of a rich landowner. It was extended during the 2C to include more than 100 rooms, courtyards, galleries and even baths.

Fénétrange

15km/9mi N along D 43.
This small fortified town has several beautiful medieval houses, a fine largely 15C collegiate church and an elegant château.

- **Michelin Map:** Michelin Local map 307: H-8.
- **Tourist Office:** Rue Notre-Dame, 54330 Saxon-Sion. ℘03 83 25 14 85.
- **Location:** S of Nancy on the D50 near Vaudémont.

Vaudémont

The Tour Brunehaut, last remnant of Vaudémont castle, **original seat of the House of the dukes of Lorraine**, stand near the church. The village remains largely unspoiled by modernisation. Grand'Rue is lined with semi-detached houses or farms with a rounded-archway giving access to the barn. The houses, built of rubble stone with little ornamentation, have just one storey, with a loft under the roof and a cellar accessible from the street.

ADDRESSES

¶/EAT

⊖⊖ **Domaine de Sion** – *R. de la Cense-Rouge, 54330 Saxon-Sion.* ℘03 83 26 24 36. www.domainedesion.com. This fruit-grower has a distillery that can be visited. In the simple restaurant you can sample home-grown fruit and vegetables in various guises. Pick up a few things for an afternoon snack!

Toul★

Meurthe-et-Moselle

Situated on the banks of the River Moselle, the ancient bishopric of Toul occupies a strategic position at the intersection of several main roads and waterways.

A BIT OF HISTORY

The ancient city of Tullum, which was already a bishopric by the 4C, soon became so prosperous that it was granted its independence in 928 under the terms of the Mainz Charter.

In 1700, Vauban, Louis XIV's military engineer, built new ramparts round the city (the Porte de Metz is all that remains today).

The fortifications were improved at regular intervals so that on the eve of the First World War, Toul was considered one of the best-defended strongholds in Europe.

⚘ WALKING TOUR

There are Renaissance houses along rue du Général-Gengoult at Nos. 30, 28 and 26, and one 14C house at No. 8. The 17C is represented by Nos. 6 and 6 bis (former Pimodan mansion) and No. 4; No. 16 rue Michâtel has a fine Renaissance house decorated with gargoyles.

Cathédrale St-Étienne★★

♿ ⏰ *Apr–May 9am–6pm; Jun–Sept 9.30am–12.30pm, 1.30–6pm; Oct–May call tourist office for details: ☎03 83 64 90 60.*

The cathedral's magnificent **west front**★★, built 1460–96, is a superb example of Flamboyant Gothic; the statues were destroyed during the Revolution.

The interior shows the influence of the Champagne Gothic style, with high and low galleries over the main arcades and the aisles, extremely pointed arches, and the absence of triforium. Note, on the right, the fine Renaissance chapel with a coffered cupola.

▶ **Population:** 16 501.
⚭ **Michelin Map:** Michelin Local map 307: G-6.
ℹ **Tourist Office**: 1 Place Charles de Gaulle, 54200 Toul. ☎03 83 64 90 60. www.lepredenancy.fr.
▶ **Location:** Around 20km/12.4mi W of Nancy by A31.

Numerous old tombstones pave the floor of the cathedral, particularly in the transept. Before leaving, have a look at the elegant Louis XV-style gallery supporting the monumental organ (1963) placed beneath the great rose-window.

Cloître

Entered through a small doorway on place des Clercs, the 13C–14C cloisters are some of the largest in France. Note the beautiful capitals with foliage motifs and interesting gargoyles on the walls.

Ancien palais épiscopal

The former bishop's palace, built between 1735 and 1743, is now the town hall. The imposing **façade**★ is adorned with colossal-order pilasters.

Musée d'Art et d'Histoire★

25 rue Gouvion-St-Cyr.
⏰ *Daily except Tue 10am–12.30pm, 1.30–6pm.* ⏰ *1 Jan, Easter Sun and*

West front, Cathédrale St-Étienne

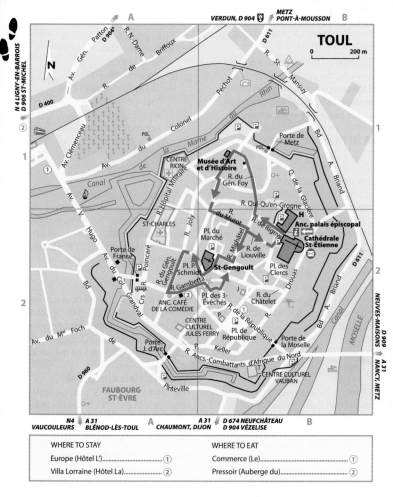

TOUL

0   200 m

WHERE TO STAY		WHERE TO EAT	
Europe (Hôtel L')	①	Commerce (Le)	①
Villa Lorraine (Hôtel La)	②	Pressoir (Auberge du)	②

Mon, 1 May, 14 Jul and 25 Dec. ⚏ no charge except during exhibitions.
☎03 83 64 13 38.

Housed in the old Maison-Dieu (alms-house), the municipal museum contains collections of painting, sculpture, Flemish tapestries, ceramics (Toul-Bellevue manufacture), religious art, antique and medieval archaeology, folk art. Boucher's *The Enjoyable Lesson* hangs in a Louis XVI-style salon.

The two world wars are illustrated by weapons, uniforms and mementoes. The 13C vaulted Gothic sick ward★, remodelled many times, was used both for worship and as hospital for all kinds of sick people.

Église St-Gengoult

Pl. Paul-Shmidt. ◷Jul–mid-Sept daily 10am–noon, 2–5.30pm.
☎03 83 64 90 60.

This former collegiate church, built in the 13C and 15C, is a fine example of Champagne Gothic architecture.

The west front has an elegant 15C doorway. Inside, note the change in style between the last two bays and the first two which have to support the weight of the towers.

The apsidal chapels open onto the chancel and the transept, typical of the Champagne school. The chapels are lit by fine 13C stained-glass windows.

Cloître St-Gengoult★★

These elegant 16C cloisters mix Flamboyant Gothic and Renaissance elements. The star vaulting has ornately worked keystones.

EXCURSIONS

Église Notre-Dame-d'Écrouves
4km/2.5mi W.

Built on a south-facing hillside overlooking Toul's industrial depression, the church, dedicated to Our Lady of the Nativity, has retained its 12C massive square belfry pierced with openings decorated with three colonettes.

Vannes-le-Châtel

18km S by D 960 then D 113.

This village has a long-standing glass-making tradition (Daum Crystalworks). It is, therefore, apt that a European research and training centre, the **Plate-forme verrière** (&.★●guided *tours Mon–Fri 8am–noon, 1–5pm. ✆03 83 25 49 40)* is based here. Its aim is to encourage craftsmen to create their own collection. There is an exhibition of contemporary glass and a demonstration of various techniques.

Villey-le-Sec★

7km/4.3mi E by N 4 then D 909; park outside village. ★●*Fort: Guided tours at 3pm: May–Sept Sun and public holidays (mid-Jul–mid-Aug daily except Mon).* ✆03 83 63 90 09. ✆€7. *www.villey-le-sec.com.*

This village, on top of a ridge overlooking the east bank of the Moselle, is a unique example in France of a village integrated within late 19C fortifications. Put up after the 1870 Franco-Prussian War, the north battery with its armour-plating, ditch, caponiers, observation cupolas, and cannon turret with three-storey shooting chamber is a forerunner of the later forts along the Maginot Line. A narrow-gauge railway carries visitors to the fort or redoute, which houses the ammunition stores and barracks, a museum and a memorial crypt.

ADDRESSES

⌖STAY

⊜⊜**La Villa Lorraine** – *15 r. Gambetta.* ✆*03 83 43 08 95. www.hotel-villa-lorraine. com. 20 rooms. Closed Sun Nov–Mar.* This small hotel in the heart of the fortified city has well soundproofed bedrooms with rustic furnishings and a pleasant breakfast room.

⊜⊜**Hôtel de l'Europe** – *373 ave. Victor Hugo.* ✆*03 83 43 00 10. www.hotel-europe54.com. 21 rooms.* A convenient hôtel when travelling by train. The ground floor still has a retro atmosphere.

⌘/EAT

⊜⊜**Auberge du Pressoir** – *7 Impasse. des Pachenottes, Lucey.* ✆*03 83 63 81 91. www.aubergedupressoir.com. Closed Sun and Wed eve, and Mon.* The old village station has become a restaurant with a simple renovated decor.

⊜⊜**Le Commerce** – *10 r. de la République.* ✆*03 83 43 00 41. Closed Sun eve, and Mon.* In the centre of Toul, discover a restaurant specialising in traditional cuisine and Lyonnaise dishes.

ON THE TOWN

Place des Trois-Évêchés – Most of the bars that are open in the evening are found in this central square. Sample the local speciality, *vin gris de Toul*, so named for its pink colour, which is obtained from the combination of gamay, pinot noir and a third grape variety from the Auxerre region.

TOURING WINE CELLARS

Vincent Laroppe – *253 r. de la République, 54200 Bruley.* ✆*03 83 43 11 04. www. laroppe.com. Mon–Sat 9am–noon, 2–6pm.* A lovely early 19C vaulted cellar with a wine-making museum. The owner makes an excellent red pinot noir as well as gris and Côtes de Toul. No charge for the tour and tasting.

Au Caveau "En Passant par la Lorraine" – *6 r. Victor-Hugo, 54200 Bruley.* ✆*09 83 89 24 40. Daily 10am–6pm.* This former boy's school is now a showcase for regional wines and produce.

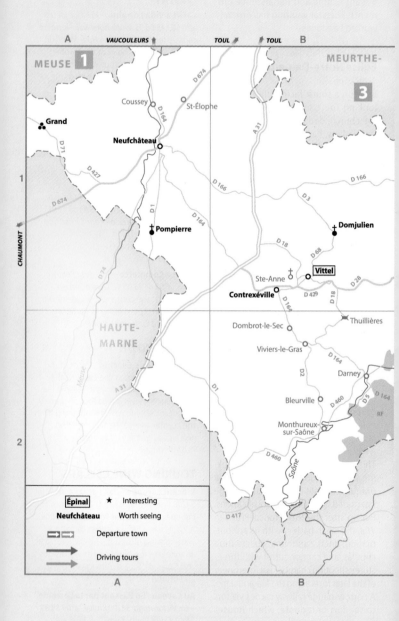

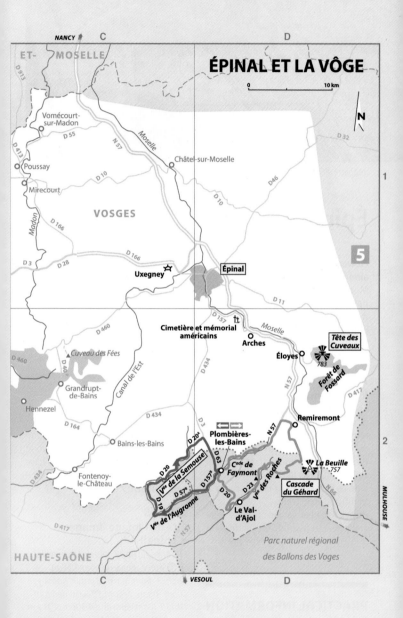

ÉPINAL ET LA VÔGE

0   10 km

N

Imagerie d'Épinal

Épinal★

Vosges

Flower-bedecked Épinal spreads along both banks of the River Moselle. Occupying a favourable position at an important crossroads, its historic prints and cotton industry once brought prosperity to the town. The splendid surrounding forested area covers 3 600ha.

A BIT OF HISTORY
Épinal prints
The enormous success of the Épinal prints lasted for almost two centuries. Most popular prints used to depict religious subjects until Jean Charles **Pellerin** began to illustrate secular subjects such as traditional songs, riddles, La Fontaine's fables and scenes of traditional French life.

Once it had been carved on wood (generally pear tree wood), the picture was printed on a Gutenberg type press.

PRACTICAL INFORMATION
Guided tours – The town of Épinal organises guided tours of the town (1h30 to 2h) in the summer. *Enquire at the tourist office.*

- ▶ **Population:** 34 048.
- & **Michelin Map:** Michelin Local map 314: G-3.
- ▤ **Tourist Office:** 6 Pl. St Goëry. ℘03 29 82 53 32. www.tourisme-epinal.com.
- ◗ **Location:** In the south of the Alsace Lorraine region, Épinal is 110km/68.4mi from Mulhouse and 71km/44.1mi from Nancy.

The different colours were hand-applied using stencil-plates; Pellerin is the only printing works of its kind still operating in Europe. The two world wars and new printing techniques have impacted but not destroyed this fascinating industry.

SIGHTS
Cité de l'Image (Imagerie d'Epinal)
Entrance via no 42 quai de Dogneville.
&.◷Mon 2–6pm, Tue–Sat 9.30am–noon, 2–6pm, Sun and public holidays 10am–noon, 2–6pm. ⟶Guided tour (1h) 10.30am, 3pm and 4.30pm. ◷1 Jan and 25 Dec. ⊛€11 (children under 18, €8). ℘03 29 34 21 87. www.imagerie-epinal.com.
The **Imagerie d'Épinal workshops** offer an insight into the techniques used

by the 200-hundred-year-old firm, with demonstrations of equipment.

Opposite, the **Musée de l'Image** (🕐 *Tue–Thu and Sat 9.30am–noon, 2–6pm, Fri 9.30am–6pm. Sun and public holidays 10am–noon, 2–6pm.* ⮕ *€6, under 18, €1.* ☎ *03 29 81 48 30; www.museedelimage.fr*) is devoted to old Épinal prints and temporary exhibitions.

Musée départemental d'Art ancien et contemporain★

1 pl. Lagarde ♿ 🕐 *Mon and Fri 9am–12.30pm, 2–5.30pm, Wed–Thu 9.30am–12.30pm, 2–5pm, Sat 10.30am–12.30pm, 2–6pm, Sun 2–6pm.* 🕐 *1 Jan, 1 May, 1 Nov and mid-Dec–eaarly Jan.* ⮕ *€5 (child 13–18, €3).* ☎ *03 29 82 20 33.*
http://museedepartemental.vosges.fr.

Located at the tip of an island in the River Moselle, the museum of ancient and contemporary art is built around the remains of the 17C Hôpital St-Lazare. It houses regional Gallo-Roman finds and also has a paintings department devoted mainly to the French School of the 17C and 18C and to the Northern School (Gellée, La Hyre, Vignon, **La Tour** and his *Job mocked by his Wife*, Brueghel, Van Goyen, Van Cleeve and, of course, **Rembrandt** and his *Mater Dolorosa*). The superb contemporary art section includes Minimal Art (Donald Judd), Arte Povera (Mario Merz) and Pop Art (Andy Warhol).

Job mocked by his Wife by Georges de La Tour, Musée départemental d'Art ancien et contemporain

© DEA/G DAGLI ORTI/age fotostock

Église Notre-Dame

Rebuilt between 1956 and 1958, the church has *cloisonné* enamel doors and a huge stained-glass window.

OLD TOWN★
Parc du Château★

🕐 *Apr–Sept 7.30am–7.30pm; rest of the year 8am–5.30pm.* ⮕ *No charge.* ☎ *03 29 82 53 32.*

This huge wooded park covers an area of 26ha. It occupies the sight of the former castle on top of the wooded sandstone hill; the medieval gardens have been laid out around the ruins.

Basilique St-Maurice

© Jean-Luc Bohin/age fotostock

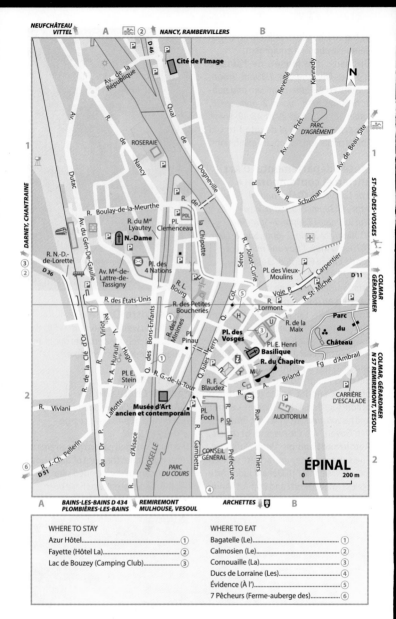

NEUFCHÂTEAU
VITTEL

NANCY, RAMBERVILLERS

Cité de l'Image

A   B

N

ÉPINAL

0   200 m

BAINS-LES-BAINS D 434   REMIREMONT
PLOMBIÈRES-LES-BAINS   MULHOUSE, VESOUL   ARCHETTES

WHERE TO STAY		WHERE TO EAT	
Azur Hôtel	①	Bagatelle (Le)	①
Fayette (Hôtel La)	②	Calmosien (Le)	②
Lac de Bouzey (Camping Club)	③	Cornouaille (La)	③
		Ducs de Lorraine (Les)	④
		Évidence (À l')	⑤
		7 Pêcheurs (Ferme-auberge des)	⑥

In the park there is a mini zoo, a play-ground and a plane to climb on – a perfect place for children to let off steam!

Basilique St-Maurice★

The basilica was consecrated in 1051 by Pope Léon IX. The west front has a belfry-porch characteristic of the Meuse region.

The 15C main doorway on the north side, known as the Portail des Bourgeois, is preceded by a deep porch, characteristic of the Champagne region.
The 13C nave has three storeys, arcades, triforium and high windows separated by moulded string-courses and is prolonged by a 14C chancel (choeur des chanoinesses).

▶ Walk to the right of the basilica.

Rue du chapitre
This street features a group of 17C and 18C houses built for the canonesses.

▶ Walk back past St-Maurice Basilica.

Place des Vosges

On this charming provincial former market square, note the 1604 so-called former bailiff's house – in fact built for a paper manufacturer.

▶ Walk to the river and turn left along quai Jules-Ferry towards place Foch.

EXCURSIONS
Fort d'Uxegney
6km/3.7mi NW by D 166 to Dompaire. Guided tours: May Sun, 3pm; Jun and Sept Sun 2pm and 4pm; Jul–Aug Mon–Sat 2pm and 4pm, Sun 2pm, 3pm and 4pm. €6. ℰ03 29 31 03 01. Uxegney, overlooking the Avière valley, was one of the last forts built near Épinal. Since it has never been damaged by war, the fort is still intact.

▶ The path leading to the cemetery (0.5km/0.3mi) starts on the right 1.8km/1.1mi beyond Donizé.

Cimetière et Mémorial américains
7km/4.3mi S along D 157.
The cemetery, which occupies a vast area (20ha) on top of a wooded plateau overlooking the River Moselle, contains the graves of 5 255 American soldiers killed during WWII. White-marble crosses and Jewish steles line up on impeccably trimmed lawns behind a chapel and a memorial.

ADDRESSES

🛏 STAY
Camping Lac de Bouzey – *19 rue Lac, 88390 Sanchey – 6km/3.7mi W of Épinal on D 460. ℰ03 29 82 49 41. www.*

lacdebouzey.com. Reservation advised. 160 pitches. Restaurant. This campsite beside Lake Bouzey includes an area for camper vans and mobile homes. The building beside the entrance houses the reception, an on-site shop and a bar-restaurant and nightclub.

Azur Hôtel – *54 quai des Bons-Enfants. ℰ09 70 35 69 63. www.azurhotelepinal.com. 20 rooms.* This 1950s hotel in the centre of town has modest-sized rooms that are simply furnished. Family atmosphere.

Best Western Plus La Fayette Hôtel and Spa – *3 rue Bazaine. ℰ03 29 81 15 15. www.epinalhotellafayette.com. 58 rooms.* Hotel complex on the doorstep of Épinal. Spacious functional rooms; ask for one of the new modern ones. Wellness centre, pool, sauna, jacuzzi. The **Restaurant le rochambeau** () serves unpretentious classic and regional cuisine.

🍽/EAT
La Cornouaille – *17 pl. des Vosges. ℰ03 29 34 27 76. Closed Tue eve, Sun and Mon.* This Breton restaurant is discreetly decorated with Brittany landscapes. The central kitchen is open so that you can watch your food being prepared, or you can choose to dine on the outside terrace.

Le Bagatelle – *12 r. des Petites-Boucheries. ℰ03 29 35 05 22. www. le-bagatelle.fr. Closed Sun.* On a little island between two branches of the River Moselle, this spruce restaurant is the best place for watching the canoeing/kayak competitions, as well as for enjoying inspired cooking.

L'Évidence – *24 r. Raymond-Poincaré. ℰ03 29 34 23 51. www. restaurant-alevidence-epinal.fr. Closed Mon (reservations required on Sun).* Family run restaurant with a colourful facade between the old town and the River Moselle. Slightly antiquated dining room. Traditional dishes.

Ferme-auberge des 7 Pêcheurs – *28–32 r. de la Division-Leclerc, 88220 Méloménil-Uzemain. 15km/9.3mi SW of Épinal on D 51 (via Chantraine). ℰ03 29 30 70 79. Closed Wed out of season.* The dining room here is an 18C forge, which feels solidly authentic with its old beams, exposed stone walls and open fireplace. There are bedrooms to let and a large, simply furnished holiday cottage for those who want to enjoy the peace and quiet of this old farm. A lovely area for walks.

⊜⊜🍴 **Le Calmosien** – *88390 Chaumousey – 10km/6.2mi W of Épinal on D 36 and D 460. ℘03 29 66 80 77. www. calmosien.com. Closed Jul 5–21, Sun evening and Mon.* In the village centre, this 1900s building is reminiscent of a school, with its white façade, brick-edged windows and steeply sloping roof. The old-fashioned decor and garden terrace are the setting for contemporary cooking, served either on fixed menus or à la carte.

⊜⊜🍴🍴 **Les Ducs de Lorraine** – *5 ave. de Provence. ℘03 29 29 56 00. www. restaurant-ducsdelorraine.com. Closed Sun.* A luxurious excuse to enjoy fine dining in this Michelin-starred restaurant. Very elegant, and serving modern cuisine. The dessert 'trolley' is very tempting.

TAKING A BREAK

Pâtisserie du Musée – *2 quai du Musée. ℘03 29 82 10 73. Tue–Fri 7.30am–7pm, Sat–Sun 7.30am–12.30pm, 2–7pm. Closed Mon.* This cake shop and tearoom must be one of the nicest in town, near the museum. Try the chocolate-praline charbonettes des Vosges.

SPORT AND RECREATION

Parks – Épinal boasts many parks: Parc entrances in rue d'Ambrail and rue St-Michel; Parc du plateau de la Justice, rue Henri-Sellier; Espace du Port, quai de Dogneville.

Neufchâteau

Vosges

Although there's no longer a castle, Neufchâteau owes its name to the former castle of the dukes of Lorraine destroyed together with the 18C fortifications. A prosperous medieval market town and the first free city of the duchy of Lorraine, it later became a busy industrial city specialising in furniture and food-processing. Its annual fair in mid-August is one of the oldest in the Vosges region.

SIGHTS
Hôtel de Ville
Place Jeanne-d'Arc.
The late-16C town hall has a fine Renaissance doorway. inside, there is a richly decorated **staircase★** dating from 1594 and 14C cellars with Gothic vaulting.

Église St-Nicolas
The church stands on the mound where the dukes of Lorraine's castle once stood

▸ **Population:** 6 927.
⚲ **Michelin Map:** Michelin Local map 314: C-2.
🛈 **Tourist Office:** 1 Place des Cordeliers, 88300 Neufchâteauf. ℘03 29 94 10 95. www.tourisme-ouest-vosges.fr.
The heart of town is the place Jeanne d'Arc, which is surrounded by old houses, mainly from the 17C–18C.
◗ **Location:** Mid-way between Nancy and Chaumont.
⚲ **Also See:** Domrémy-la-Pucelle (⚲see VAUCOULEURS: Excursions).

and, due to the sloping site, consists of two superposed churches.
The doorway and tower of the upper church are modern, but the nave dates from the 12C and 13C. The side chapels contain funeral monuments of wealthy

12C doorway, Église St-Martin, Pompierre

© Denis Bringard/hemis.fr

15C and 16C burghers; note the late-15C polychrome **stone group**★ representing the deposition of Christ.

Église St-Christophe

The church is mostly 13C, but parts date back to 1100. On the west front, arcading supported by slender colonnettes denotes a Burgundian influence. On the south side, the 16C christening-font chapel has remarkable vaulting with 12 keystone pendentives.

EXCURSIONS

Pompierre

12km/7.5mi S on D 74 then left on D 1.
The **Église St-Martin**, rebuilt in the 19C, has guarded its 12C Romanesque **doorway**★. Superbly carved recessed arches frame the three historiated bands of the tympanum depicting Biblical scenes.

Grand

22km/13.7mi W along D 53, then left onto D 3 to Midrevaux and by D 71E.
Grand is no ordinary village. To get there, you need to cross vast expanses of forest before coming to a small clearing in which there is a typical village, such as is often found in corners in the Champagne and Lorraine regions.
In Roman times, Grand, which was then called Andesina, was a water sanctuary dedicated to Apollo Grannus; the healing and oracular powers of this god attracted crowds of pilgrims including the emperors Caracalla in 213 and Constantine in 309.
A 1 760m long **rampart** surrounding a sacred area reserved for the deities was fortified with 22 round towers, three of which have been uncovered, and with gates every 80m. Excavations have revealed some 60 kinds of marble from all over the Empire, testament to the town's splendour.

Site archéologique gallo-romain de Grand

&. ⓘ*Mar and Oct–mid-Nov 2–5pm; Apr–Sep 10am–12.30pm, 1.30–6.30pm.* ⓘ*Mon except in Jul–Aug.* ◌€4. ✆03 29 06 77 37. www.culture.vosges.fr.

Amphitheatre

Built around the year 80 on a semi-oval plan, it could hold 17 000 spectators for gladiators fights. Abandoned at the end of the 4C, part of the walls and some arcades remain.

Mosaic★

Dating from the first half of the 3C, this is the biggest and one of the best-preserved Roman mosaics ever found in France; it used to pave the floor of an administrative basilica. In the centre are two characters thought to represent a pilgrim and a priest of Apollo Grannus.

Plombières-les-Bains✝✝

Vosges

A tranquil spa and holiday resort, Plombières has preserved the 19C charm of the days when it was frequented by Napoléon III.

A BIT OF HISTORY

The Romans built imposing baths in Plombières. Revived in the Middle Ages, the spa developed steadily. The dukes of Lorraine were regular visitors, Montaigne took the waters in 1580 and Voltaire spent several summers here. Louis XV's daughters stayed in Plombières for two consecutive seasons accompanied by a great many followers.

Napoleon's wife Josephine and her daughter Queen Hortense also spent some time here. In 1802, American engineer Robert Fulton gave a demonstration of the first steamship on the River Augronne, in front of the Empress. Napoleon III stayed several times and helped embellish the town. He met here with the Italian minister, Cavour, to agree on Nice and the Savoie being united with France.

VISIT

▶ The historic baths and thermal establishments lie along the lively high streets of rue Stanislas and rue Liétard.

Bain Stanislas

The former house of the Ladies of the Chapter of Remiremont. Built 1733–1736. A gallery carries the water to the Thermes Napoléon 600 m further on.

Étuve romaine

⏱Call for details. ℰ03 29 30 07 14. www.plombieres-les-bains.com.
The Roman steam room was discovered during excavations in 1856. In a nearby basement, the **Bain romain** can also be visited (*staircase on the square*).

▶ **Population:** 1 823.
♿ **Michelin Map:** Michelin Local map 314: G-5.
🛈 **Tourist Office:** Place Maurice-Janot, BP 1, 88370 Plombières-les-Bains. ℰ03 29 66 01 30. www.vosges meridionales.com.
▶ **Location:** In the picturesque Augronne valley, on the N 57 between Épinal and Vesoul.
🅿 **Parking:** Streets are very narrow, so use the free car parks on Promenades Mesdames, pl. Beaumarchais, parterre de l'ex-Hôtel du Parc, pl. Napoléon III.
🚫 **Don't Miss:** The Thermes Napoléon.

PRACTICAL INFORMATION

Guided tours – *Tours on foot or on the Petit Train leave from the Tourist office.*

Maison des Arcades

This fine 18C house (note the wrought-iron balconies) was built in 1762 for Stanislas Leszczynski whose coat of arms is carved on the façade. Under the arcade, the Crucifix spring was, for a long time, a public drinking fountain.

Bain national

Rebuilt in 1935, the baths have retained their First Empire (1800–14) façade. In the hall, the pump room is still in use.

Pavillon des Princes

This surprisingly modest pavilion was built during the Restoration (1814–30) for members of the royal family, and is now used for temporary exhibitions. It is here that Napoleon III secretly met Cavour in 1858.

Musée Louis-Français
⏱*Call for details.* ☎*03 29 30 06 74.*
The museum contains paintings by Louis Français, a native of Plombières, and his friends from the Barbizon School: Corot, Courbet, Diaz, Harpignies, Monticelli and Troyon.

Thermes Napoléon
These were erected by Napoleon III, whose statue adorns the entrance. The vast hall (55m long) is reminiscent of the Caracalla Baths in Rome.

Parc impérial
The park on the south of town was laid out by Baron Haussmann. It contains beautiful trees and some rare species.

Fontaine Stanislas
4 km/2.5mi SW of the town by D20.
In the middle of beechwoods, along a marked path, this small spring surges out of a rock covered in inscriptions from the 18C and early 19C.

🚗 DRIVING TOURS

Augronne and Semouse valleys★
33km/21mi round tour. Allow 1h.

▷ Leave Plombières along D 157 bis.

Vallée de l'Augronne
The road follows the river through pastureland and forested areas.

▷ In Aillevillers-et-Lyaumont, drive N along D 19 to la Chaudeau then turn right onto D 20 which follows the Semouse valley upstream.

Vallée de la Semouse★
This peaceful green valley with densely forested slopes is barely wide enough for the river, although there are a few narrow strips of pasture. Wireworks, rolling mills and sawmills once lined the banks, making use of its rapid flow (only one mill remains at Blanc Murger).

Thermes Napoléon

© Destination Plombières

▷ Turn right onto D 63 towards Plombières (fine views of the town).

Vallée des Roches
47km/29mi round tour. Allow 2h.

▷ Leave Plombières along N 57 towards Luxeuil.

The road soon climbs onto the plateau that marks the watershed between the Mediterranean and the North Sea, and then descends towards Remiremont.

Remiremont
⏱*See REMIREMONT below.*

▷ Drive S out of Remiremont along D 23. 3.5km/2.2mi further on, turn left onto D 57. Just after La Croisette d'Hérival, turn right onto a forest road through the Hérival forest. Shortly after passing a turning to Girmont and an inn on your left, you will reach the Cascade du Géhard.

Cascade de Géhard★
The waterfall is on the left below the level of the road. Foaming water cascades down into a series of potholes. The effect is particularly striking during the rainy season.

▷ Continue past the forest lodge on your left and the path to Hérival on your right and turn left along the

Combeauté valley, also known as the Vallée des Roches. In the village of Faymont, turn right near a sawmill and leave the car 50m farther on; continue on foot to the Cascade de Faymont.

Cascade de Faymont
The waterfall makes a remarkable setting amid coniferous trees and rocks.

Le Val-d'Ajol
Le Val-d'Ajol includes more than 60 hamlets scattered along the Combeauté and Combalotte valleys which have retained their traditional industrial activities (metalworks, weaving, sawmills).

▶ Turn right to return to Plombières.

ADDRESSES

🏨 STAY
🛏 **Hôtel de la Fontaine Stanislas** – *4km/2.5mi W of Plombières on D 20. ℘03 29 66 01 53. www.fontaine-stanislas.com.*

Closed 16 Oct–31 Mar. 13 rooms. Restaurant 🍴🍴. A good night's sleep is guaranteed in this hotel in a lovely setting overlooking the Plombières valley. The décor is slightly outdated, but nevertheless well kept. Veranda dining room.

🍴🍴 **Le Prestige Impérial** – *av. des Etats-Unis. ℘03 29 30 07 08. 80 rooms. Restaurant 🍴🍴.* This Second Empire hotel attached to the municipal spa has been decorated in a contemporary style. The restaurant, which has preserved its grandiose period, setting serves modern cuisine.

SPORT AND RECREATION
Spa – *av. des Etats-Unis. ℘03 29 30 07 00. Spa treatment centre: Mon–Sat 5.30am–noon; Calodae health and fitness centre: Mon, Tue, Wed, Sat 1.30–8pm, Fri 1.30–9pm, Sun 10am–8pm. Closed 1 Jan, 25 Dec.* Plombières waters are recommended for treating digestive ailments, nutritional problems, rheumatic disorders and post-traumatic osteo-articular therapy. Revitalising cures and weekend deals available for a "quick fix".

Remiremont
Vosges

The small town of Remiremont, situated in the deep and densely forested upper valley of the River Moselle, was once the seat of a famous abbey.

A BIT OF HISTORY
The Ladies of Remiremont
In 620, two disciples of St Columban, Amé and Romaric, founded two monasteries, one for men and one for women, on a summit overlooking the confluence of the Moselle and the Moselotte. The convent, which later moved down to the valley, became the Chapter of the Ladies of Remiremont under the direct control of the Pope and the Holy Roman Emperor. The canonesses were all aristocrats of ancient lineage. This chapter was, for centuries, one of the most important in the western world. The Revolution ended its prosperity.

▶ **Population:** 8 127.
🗺 **Michelin Map:** Michelin Local map 314: H-4.
ℹ **Tourist Office:** 4 bis, Place de l'Abbaye, 88200 Remiremont. ℘03 29 62 23 70. www.ot-remiremont.fr.
▶ **Location:** On the River Moselle on the N 57, S of Épinal.
👁 **Don't Miss:** The Promenade du Calvaire offers an overall view of the town and the Moselle valley to the north.

SIGHTS
Abbatiale St-Pierre
The former abbey church, topped by an onion-shaped belfry, is mostly Gothic but the west front and the belfry were rebuilt in the 18C. Note the beautiful 17C

marble ornamentation of the chancel and the 11C statue of Notre-Dame-du-Trésor in the chapel on the right. Beneath the chancel, there is an 11C **crypt**★ with rib vaulting.

Next door, the 18C former **abbatial palace** has a beautiful façade. A few of the 17C and 18C mansions inhabited by the canonesses still surround the church and the palace.

Rue Charles-de-Gaulle★

This picturesque arcaded street is a fine example of 18C town planning.

Musée municipal Charles-de-Bruyère

70 rue Charles-de-Gaulle. ◐*Daily except Tue: 2–6pm (Jan–Mar closed Sun; May–Sept 10am–noon, 2–6pm).* ◐*Oct, 1 Jan, 1 May, 1 Nov and 25 Dec.* ◛*€4 (ticket combined with the musée Charles-Friry) – no charge Sun.* ✆*03 29 62 59 14.*

The collections are devoted to local history and handicraft from Lorraine; precious manuscripts and tapestries from the former abbey are displayed together with Gothic sculpture from the Lorraine region, 18C ceramics and 17C northern paintings by followers of Rembrandt.

Maison-musée Charles-Friry

12 rue du Général-Humbert. ◐*Same hours as the museum above.* This former canonesses' mansion (18C and 19C) contains documents, statues and *objets d'art* connected with the Ladies from Remiremont and regional history. 17C–18C paintings include *Le Vielleur à la sacoche* (the Hurdy-gurdy Player) by Georges de La Tour.

The garden, which partly recreates the Grand Jardin of the abbey, is decorated with two ornamental fountains and a few other features from the abbey.

EXCURSIONS
La Beuille

11.6km/7.2mi S on the D 23 and D 57. After travelling 6km/3.7mi on the D 57 take the paved road on the left that leads to the car park of the cottage.

From the terrace the view overlooks the Moselle valley and Ballon d'Alsace.

Upper Moselle valley down-river from Remiremont★

27km/16.8mi. Allow 30min Leave Remiremont N along D 42, following the east bank of the Moselle.

Forêt de Fossard

The road runs between the river and the forest which bears traces of ancient religious settlements. It is crisscrossed by marked footpaths ideal for walking.

🚶 *3h. Start opposite the Gendarmerie in St-Étienne-lès-Remiremont.*

St-Mont offers a fine view as well as the ruins of the abbey (private property) founded by Amé and Romaric. A path leads to the mysterious Pont des Fées (Fairies' bridge).

Tête des Cuveaux★

🚶 *30min on foot there and back.* *Follow the road leading to the ridge line marked by a spruce forest and leave the car in the parking area (picnic area).* Turn right along the ridge to reach a viewing table, where there is a **panoramic view**★ of the Moselle valley, the Lorrain plateau and the Vosges.

Éloyes

This small town is a thriving centre for textile and food-processing industries.

Arches

Arches is known for its traditional paper industry; a paper mill was already operating here in 1469. The playwright **Beaumarchais**, author of *The Barber of Seville* and *The Marriage of Figaro*, bought the mill in 1779 in order to produce the necessary paper for the complete edition of Voltaire's works. As most of the great philosopher's writings had been banned in France, he printed what are now known as the Kehl editions in Kehl (across the Rhine from Strasbourg).

ADDRESSES

🛏 STAY

🛏 **Hôtel du Cheval de Bronze** –
59 r. Charles-de-Gaulle. 📞*09 70 35 68 33.
www.hotelchevalbronze.com.Closed Nov.
35 rooms.* The façade of this former
coaching inn in the town centre is
decorated with arches.

🍴 EAT

🍴🍴 **Le Clos Heurtebise** – *13 chemin des
Capucins, off r. Capit.-Flayelle.* 📞*03 29 62
08 04. www.leclosheurtebise.com. Closed
14–27 Jan, 5–14 May, Sun evening, Mon and
Wed.* In a former textile manufacturer's
residence in the upper part of the town,
this restaurant's terrace overlooks the
valley and the forest in fine weather. Fish
is a house speciality.

🍴🍴 **Le Chalet d'Etienne** – *34 r. des
Pêcheurs (opposite the shopping centre),
88200 St-Étienne-lès-Remiremont,
2km/1.2mi E of Remiremont on D 417,*
Gérardmer road. 📞*03 29 26 11 80. http://
lechaletdetienne.com.* A large white
modern building reminiscent of a chalet.
Much frequented by the locals, who
enjoy the good cooking. 7 Rooms (🍴🍴).

SHOPPING

Distillerie Lecomte-Blaise – *10 r. Gare
Nol, 88120 Le Syndicat. By the D 43 (La
Bresse direction) for 4km/2.5mi, turn right
towards Nol.* 📞*03 29 24 71 04. www.
lecomte-blaise.com. Mon–Sat 10am–noon,
2–6pm (9am Jul–Sept).* This traditional
distillery produces brandy made from
local fruit and wild berries. Tour of the
manufacturing premises, tasting and
produce for sale.

Moulin à huile – *68470 Storckensohn.*
📞*03 89 39 14 00. www.moulin-
storckensohn.com. Jul–Aug, Wed–Sun
2–5.30pm; Apr–Jun and Sept–Oct 1st and
3rd Sun of month. €3.50.* A restored 1732
mill with apple and walnut presses: watch
the pressing process before trying it
yourself, and making your own oil.

Vittel ⚑⚑

Vosges

This renowned spa resort, which
was highly fashionable during the
Belle Epoque, owes its fame to the
therapeutic qualities of its water
and its situation at the heart of a
picturesque wooded area.

SIGHTS
Parc★
This landscaped park has a bandstand
where concerts take place in summer.
Amid the greenery, discover the 1910
Grand Hôtel, the Casino and the new
Palais de Congrès (inaugurated 1970). It
is adjacent to vast sports grounds (horse
racing, polo, golf, tennis etc).

EXCURSIONS
Domjulien
8km/5mi NE along D 68.
The 15C–16C church (considerably
remodelled), contains some remarkable sculptures: an altarpiece (1541) of

▶ **Population:** 5 415.
🕐 **Michelin Map:** Michelin
   Local map 314: D-3.
🛈 **Tourist Office:** Place de la
   Marne, BP90 011, 88 801
   Vittel. 📞03 29 08 08 88.
   www.vitteltourisme.com.
◐ **Location:** 40km W of
   Épinal. The spa town is
   outside the town centre.

the Crucifixion and the 12 Apostles; an
early-16C Entombment; statues of St
George (16C) and St Julian and a fine
15C statue of the Virgin and Child play-
ing with an angel.

Contrexéville ⚑⚑
*4km/2.5mi SW (🕐 see INTRODUCTION:
Architecture and Art).*
Known since the 18C, this popular spa
town has five mineral springs used in the
treatment of kidney and liver dieases,
excess of cholesterol and obesity. In

Contrexéville thermal spring pavillion

© OT Contrexéville/Ville de Contrexéville

addition, the thermal establishment, built in 1912 in neo-Byzantine style, proposes slimming and fitness formulae.

ADDRESSES

🛏 STAY

🍽🛏 **Chambre d'hôtes Breton** – *74 r. des Récollets, 88140 Bulgnéville. 7.5km/4.6mi W of Contrexéville by D 164. ℘03 29 09 21 72. www.benoitbreton.fr. 🖨. 4 rooms.* This lovely mansion dating from 1720 is shown to its best advantage…hardly surprising as the owner is an antique dealer. The rooms are modern but attractively furnished with antiques. Pleasant garden.

🍽🛏🛏 **Hôtel d'Angleterre** – *162 r. de Charmey. ℘03 29 08 08 42. www.popinns. com. Closed Dec 20–Jan 1. 50 rooms. Restaurant 🍽🛏.* This grand early 20C hotel between the station and the thermal establishment has spacious comfortable rooms, a cosy bar and a shady garden. Traditional food served in the **restaurant**. Spa packages available.

🍴 EAT

🍽🛏 **César** – *125 av. Châtillon. ℘03 29 08 61 73. Closed Dec 23–Jan 16, Sun evening, Tue lunchtime and Mon* Flavoursome modern cooking is served in an elegantly restored dining room with an agreeable bar lounge by the entrance.

SHOPPING

Délices Lorraines – *184 r. de Verdun. ℘03 29 08 03 30.* A wide variety of regional specialities includes honey, Lorraine wines (côte de Toul), aperitifs

and liqueurs from the Vosges, wild fruit brandies and sweets (Vittel sweets, grès-rose des Vosges).

Écomusée vosgien de la brasserie – *48 r. de Mirecourt, 88270 Ville-sur-Illon. ℘03 29 36 58 05/03 29 36 53 18. www.musee-vosgien-brasserie.asso.fr. May–Jun and Sept–Oct Thu–Sun 3–6pm; Jul–Aug Tue–Sun 2.30–6pm.* Ville-sur-Illon is renowned for the purity of its water, and produced beer from 1627. In 1887, Jacques Lobstein, an Alsatian brewer, built a Bavarian-style industrial brewery here, in operation until 1975. It is now an eco-museum, and beers produced using traditional methods can be tasted or bought on the premises.

SPORT AND RECREATION

Golf Vittel Ermitage – *Avenue Gilbert Trigano, 88802 Viottel. ℘03 29 08 81 53. www.golf-vittel-ermitage.com.*

Thermes de Vittel – *Parc thermal. ℘03 29 08 76 54. www.thermes-vittel. com. Closed Jan.* The Vittel baths date from 1856. The sulphated calcic or magnesian water is used to treat liver and kidney ailments, post-traumatic injuries, nutritional problems and rheumatic disorders. Revitalising treatments.

Vittel Spa – *℘03 29 08 76 54. Apr–Oct.* The 11°C waters of the five natural mineral springs are prescribed for obesity, renal, urinary and biliary infections, and gout. Package for dieters.

ENTERTAINMENT

All year round there are concerts, folk events and musicals, horse shows, tennis tournaments and fireworks.

THE SOUTHERN VOSGES

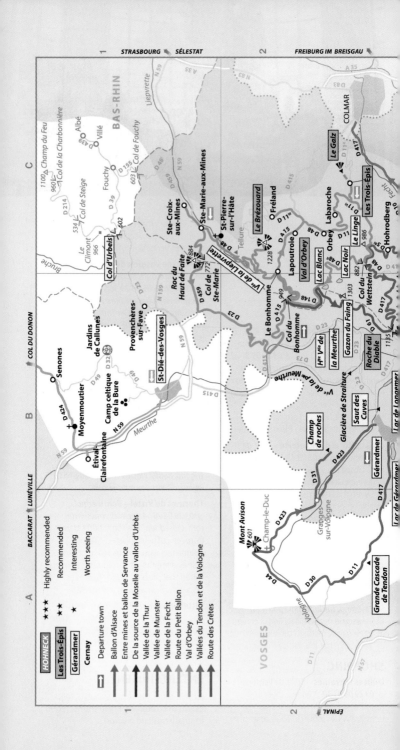

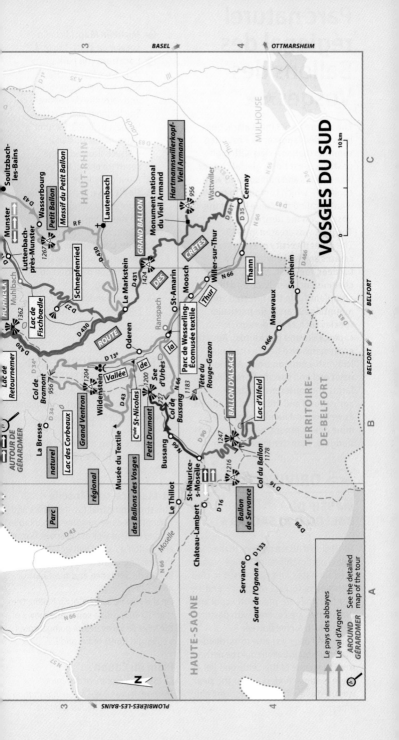

VOSGES DU SUD

0   10 km

Légende :

- Le pays des abbayes
- Le val d'Argent
- *AROUND GERARDMER*   See the detailed map of the tour

BASEL   *OTTMARSHEIM*

MULHOUSE

HAUT-RHIN

Soultzbach-les-Bains

Munster

Wasserbourg

Petit Ballon

Massif du Petit Ballon

Luttenbach-près-Munster

1267

Lautenbach

Monument national du Vieil Armand

Hartmannswillerkopf-Vieil Armand

956

Wattwiller

Cernay

GRAND BALLON

Schnepfenried

Le Markstein

1424

CRÊTES

DES

St-Amarin

Moosch

Willer-sur-Thur

Thann

Sentheim

HOHNECK

1362

Lac de Fischboedle

Muhlbach

Ranspach

Thur

N 66

ROUTE

Oderen

la

Parc de Wesserling-Écomusée textile

Masevaux

Lac de Retournemer

Col de Bramont

1204   956

Wildenstein

Vallée

de

See d'Urbes

1200

Tête du Rouge-Gazon

1183

BALLON D'ALSACE

Lac d'Alfeld

D 466

AUTOUR DE GÉRARDMER

La Bresse

Lac des Corbeaux

Grand Ventron

Musée du Textile

Petit Drumont

1202

Col de Bussang

Bussang

1247

1178

TERRITOIRE-DE-BELFORT

naturel

régional

des Ballons des Vosges

St-Maurice-s-Moselle

1216

Col du Ballon

BELFORT

BELFORT

Parc

Le Thillot

Moselle

Château-Lambert

Ballon de Servance

HAUTE-SAÔNE

Servance

Saut de l'Ognon

PLOMBIÈRES-LES-BAINS

N

191

Parc naturel régional des Ballons des Vosges★★

The nature park's main attraction is its varied landscapes – rounded summits (ballons) clad with high pastures, peat bogs, glacial cirques, lakes, rivers and hills covered with conifers – which combine to create what is called the "blue line of the Vosges", on the horizon.

The park was created in 1989. The great diversity of ecosystems creates an ideal environment for deer, roe-deer, wild boars, chamois and even lynx. Bird life is also plentiful in the forested and mountainous areas (in particular species such as the peregrine, capercaillie and blackbirds). Aquatic ecosystems also have a rich fauna (crayfish, common trout, Alpine newt etc) and specific flora. Villages, farms and museums illustrate agricultural and industrial traditions as well as local handicrafts: silver-mine development, weaving, wood-sledging, Munster-cheese making.

🚗 DRIVING TOURS

MASSIF DU BALLON D'ALSACE★★★

The Ballon d'Alsace belongs to the crystalline part of this range where granite predominates and the massif is clad with dense forests of spruce and fir trees; ravines are pleasantly cool and the heights are covered with pastures dotted with Alpine flowers.

The massif owes its name to its rounded shape, although ballon could be derived from the name of the Celtic god Bel as there is some evidence that the peak was used as a solar observatory in Celtic times.

- ⚙ **Michelin Map:** Michelin Local map 314: L-3 to M-4.
- ▷ **Location:** This park spans four *départements*: Haut-Rhin, Vosges, Haute-Saône and Territoire de Belfort. The Ballon d'Alsace is the highest peak (alt 1 250m) of the Massif du Ballon d'Alsace situated at the southern end of the Vosges mountain range.
- ⚛ **Don't Miss:** The panorama from the viewing platform on the Ballon d'Alsace (a 30min round-trip hike).
- 🧒 **Kids:** Children will find the fossils and minerals in the Maison de la Géologie fascinating.
- ⚛ Be prepared for misty conditions in this region.

① FROM ST-MAURICE-SUR-MOSELLE TO SENTHEIM

38km/23.6mi. Allow 2h. Add another 3 to 4 hours to take the walks mentioned as well as the geological itinerary.

The road leading to the Col du Ballon d'Alsace, built in the 18C, is the oldest in the area.

St-Maurice-sur-Moselle

This small industrial town (textiles and sawmills) is close to some remarkable beauty spots as well as the Rouge Gazon and Ballon d'Alsace winter resorts. It is the starting point of excursions to the Ballon de Servance and the Charbonniers valley.

On the way up to the Col du Ballon, the road (D 465) offers some fine views of the Moselle valley before going through a splendid forest of firs and beeches.

Plain du Canon

🚶 *15min on foot there and back.*
The path leaves D 465 by an information panel tied to a tree and runs down

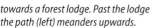

towards a forest lodge. Past the lodge the path (left) meanders upwards.

The place owes its name to a small gun once used by the local gamekeeper to create an echo.

There is a charming view of the wooded Presles valley over which tower the Ballon d'Alsace and Ballon de Servance, crowned by a fort.

Beyond **La Jumenterie**, whose name (*jument* means mare) is a reminder of a horse-breeding centre founded in 1619 by the dukes of Lorraine, there is a fine view of the Moselle valley and Ballon de Servance to the right.

The road reaches the high-pasture area. The **Monument aux Démineurs** by Rivière and Deschler is dedicated to bomb-disposal experts who died while performing their duty.

Col du Ballon

At the end of the parking area, there is a monument celebrating the racing cyclist René Pottier. There is a fine view of the summit of the Ballon d'Alsace, crowned with a statue of the Virgin Mary and, further right, of the Belfort depression

dotted with lakes and the northern part of the Jura mountains. A path leads to Joan of Arc's statue.

Ballon d'Alsace★★★

30min on foot there and back.
Preserve the environment! Walk along paths, don't cut through pastures or forests, and leave wild flowers and plants as you find them.

The path starts from D 465 in front of the Ferme-Restaurant du Ballon d'Alsace. It runs through pastures towards the statue of the Virgin Mary. Before Alsace became French once more, the statue stood exactly on the border. From the viewing platform, the **panorama**★★ extends north to Mt Donon, east across the plain of Alsace and the Black Forest and south as far as Mont Blanc.

The drive down to Lake Alfeld is very beautiful. Ahead is the Grand Ballon, the highest summit in the Vosges mountains (1 424m); later on there are fine views of the **Doller valley** and of the Jura and the Alps.

As the road comes out of the forest, the lake appears inside a glacial cirque.

Lake at the foot of the Grand Ballon

© Denis Bringard/hemis.fr

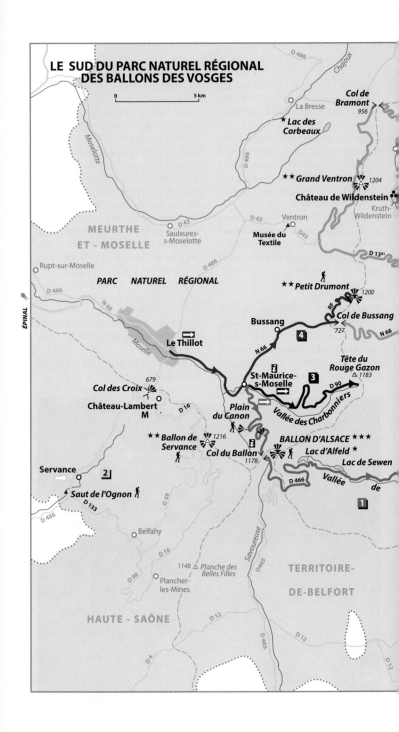

LE SUD DU PARC NATUREL RÉGIONAL
DES BALLONS DES VOSGES

0   5 km

D 486   Chajoux

Col de
Bramont
956

La Bresse

★ Lac des
Corbeaux

D 486

★★ Grand Ventron   1204

Château de Wildenstein   Kruth-
Wildenstein

MEURTHE   D 43   Ventron   Musée du
Textile
ET - MOSELLE   Saulxures-   D 43   D 13⁸¹
s-Moselotte

Moselotte

Rupt-sur-Moselle   D 486   ★★ Petit Drumont   1200

PARC   NATUREL   RÉGIONAL   RF   Col de Bussang

D 466   N 66   Bussang   727   N 66

Le Thillot   4

ÉPINAL   Moselle   N 66   Tête du
Rouge Gazon
△ 1183
St-Maurice-
s-Moselle   3

Col des Croix   679   D 90

Château-Lambert   D 16   Plain
M   du Canon   Vallée des Charbonniers

★★ Ballon de   1216   BALLON D'ALSACE ★★★
Servance   Col du Ballon   Lac d'Alfeld ★
1178   Lac de Sewen

Servance   2   Vallée
de
Saut de l'Ognon
D 133   1

G. 59   D 466

D 486   D 16

Belfahy   Savoureuse   TERRITOIRE-

D 98   1148 △ Planche des   D 465   DE-BELFORT
Belles Filles
Plancher-
les-Mines

HAUTE - SAÔNE   D 12   D 12

D 4   D 465   D 12

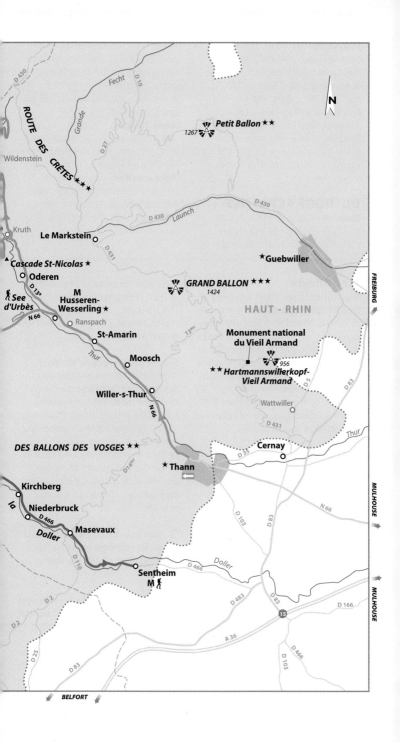

PRACTICAL INFORMATION

Maison du Parc – *Cour de l'Abbaye, 68140 Munster, &03 89 77 90 34. www.parc-ballons-vosges.fr. Feb–mid-Jun and mid-Sept–Christmas Tue–Fri and Sun 1.30–5.30pm; mid-Jun–mid-Sept Tue–Sun 10am–noon, 1.30–5.30pm. Closed Sun in Feb, Oct–Nov.* The park headquarters offers over 600sq m of permanent and temporary exhibitions devoted to the Vosges mountains.

OUTDOOR ACTIVITIES

Walking – One option is to follow waymarked discovery and historic trails. Some of these are detailed in a small brochure (on sale in the Maison du Parc). A calendar of winter and summer events is also published by the park, featuring outings (nature and heritage) organised by local associations, museum exhibitions and a diary of events.

Skiing, sledging – Some 20 resorts offer Alpine skiing, cross-country skiing, snow-shoeing and sledging. A few are equipped for night skiing.

Other activities – The park lends itself to the practice of paragliding, rock-climbing and mountain biking, bearing in mind, of course, that nature is vulnerable.

Lac d'Alfeld★

The artificial Lake Alfeld (covering an area of 10ha and reaching a depth of 22m) is one of the most attractive expanses of water in the Vosges region. It ensures that the River Doller has a regular flow, particularly when the thaw comes. The lake is framed by picturesque wooded heights.

The dam, built between 1884 and 1887, is 337m long and leans against a moraine left behind by ancient glaciers.

Lac de Sewen

Close to Lake Alfeld, this small lake is gradually filling up with peat. Alpine and Nordic plants grow on its shores.

▶ Farther downstream, D 466 follows the Doller which flows between high slopes covered with green pastures alternating with woods of fir and beech trees.

The valley is overlooked by the Romanesque church of **Kirchberg** perched on a moraine and, as you enter **Niederbruck**, on the left, by a monumental statue of the Virgin and Child by Antoine Bourdelle.

Sentheim
Maison de la Géologie

Mar–Oct,1st Sun of month; Jul–Sept every Sun. 1 Jan, 25 Dec. Museum: €3 *(children under 12, free). &06 47 29 16 20. www.geologie-alsace.fr.* The building, located opposite the church, houses a fine collection of fossils and minerals.

Sentier géologique de Wolfloch

Drive along D 466 towards Bussang, then turn right 300m after the church and follow the arrows to the starting point of the geological trail. Guided tours possible, at 2.30pm. Museum and sentier: €8 *(children under 12, free).* The itinerary extends over a distance of 5km/3mi and includes 12 geological sites. Allow 2h. It is advisable to obtain the brochure available at the Maison de la Géologie.

▶ Start from the presentation panel and walk to the right along the fields, following the markings illustrating a fossil.

The path goes across the great Vosges fault and gives an insight into the geology of the region from the Primary Era until today.

The fault separates the primary formations, uplifted when the Alps rose, from more recent sediments, often rich in fossils, which account for the presence of the sea 100 million years ago.

Ballon de Servance and the summit of the Ballon d'Alsace from the Charbonniers Valley

© Denis Bringard/hemis.fr

BALLON DE SERVANCE★★

2 ITINERARY STARTING FROM SERVANCE
20km/12.4mi. Allow 1h.

Situated a few miles west of the Ballon d'Alsace (crowned by a statue of the Virgin Mary), the Ballon de Servance (crowned by a military fort) reaches an altitude of 1 216m. The River Ognon begins here as a modest mountain stream.

Servance
The syenite quarries (producing a reddish stone used in the Paris opera pillars) are no longer in operation.
As you leave the village, a footpath starting on your right (*15min there and back*) leads to the **Saut de l'Ognon**, a picturesque waterfall gushing forth from a narrow gorge.

Col des Croix
Alt 679m.
Overlooked by the Château-Lambert Fort, this pass marks the watershed between the North Sea and the Mediterranean Sea.

Château-Lambert
Just 1km/0.6mi from the pass, this charming village has an interesting **Musée de la nature des Vosges saônoises – Espace Nature Culture** (◉ *mid-Apr–Sept daily 10am–1pm, 2–6pm; Oct–mid-Apr Wed–Fri and Sun 2–5.30pm.* ◉*Jan and Dec.* ℘*03 84 20 49 84*), with a farmer-miner's house, a mill, a smithy, a 17C press, and a former classroom.

▶ Return to the Col des Croix and turn left onto D 16; the road rises above the Ognon valley, offering fine views, before meandering through the forest.

Panorama du Ballon de Servance★★

▶ Leave the car at the beginning of the military road (no entry) for the Fort de Servance and take a marked path on the right which leads (15min on foot there and back) to the summit of the Ballon (alt 1 216m).

The panorama is magnificent: the Ognon valley, the glacial Plateau d'Esmoulières dotted with lakes and the Plateau de Langres to the west; Monts Faucilles to the north-west; the Moselle valley further to the right; the Vosges mountain range to the north-east (with their foothills stretching south and south-east) and to the east, the rounded summit of the Ballon d'Alsace.

197

VALLÉE DES CHARBONNIERS

③ ITINERARY FROM ST-MAURICE-SUR-MOSELLE
12km/7.4mi. Allow 30min.

St-Maurice-sur-Moselle
– *see* ①

▷ From St-Maurice-sur-Moselle, drive east along the road which follows the Charbonniers stream.

The inhabitants of this valley are believed to be the descendants of a Swedish and German colony hired by the dukes of Lorraine in the 18C for forestry work and coal mining. In the village of Les Charbonniers, turn left onto the Rouge Gazon road (winter sports): from the **Tête du Rouge Gazon**, there are good views of the Ballon de Servance.

TO THE SOURCE OF THE MOSELLE

④ ITINERARY FROM LE THILLOT
25km/15.5mi. Allow 1h30.

Le Thillot
Many tourists go through this busy industrial centre (textiles, tanning, industrial woodwork) on their way to the Vosges mountains. Guided tours of the nearby copper mines at **Les mines de cuivre des ducs de Lorraine** (◑*Apr–Sept 10am–7pm; rest of year consult website;* ◉€9; ✆*03 29 25 03 33; www.hautesmynes.com*) take visitors back to the 16C.

St-Maurice-sur-Moselle
– *see* ①

Bussang
Bussang is a summer and winter resort. The **Théâtre du Peuple** (folk theatre) founded in 1895, consists of a mobile stage using nature as its background and can seat 1 100 spectators. The actors, many of them local inhabitants, give performances of folk plays as well as plays by Shakespeare, Molière etc.

Petit Drumont★★

▷ 15min on foot there and back. Turn onto the forest road branching off D 89 just after the Col de Bussang. Leave the car near the inn and follow the path which rises through high pastures.

At the top of Petit Drumont (alt 1 200m), admire the **panorama★★** from the viewing table.

Col de Bussang
At the pass (alt 727m) a monument by Gilodi (1965) marks the source of the Moselle, which at this point is no more than a small stream.

⑤ Vallée de Munster★★
See MUNSTER.

⑥ Vallée de la Fecht
See MUNSTER.

⑦ Massif du Petit Ballon★
See MUNSTER.

VAL D'ARGENT

⑧ ROUND TOUR FROM STE-MARIE-AUX-MINES
65km/40mi. Allow 1h30.

The Vosges mountains are particularly rich in mineral resources, silver, copper and other metals, extracted since the Middle Ages. The mining industry had its heyday during the reign of Louis XIV; by the mid-19C, it was in decline. Great efforts have been made to restore the region's mining heritage and develop its touristic potential. Today, several protected, restructured mining sites are open to the public.

▷ Follow N 59 west out of Ste-Marie-aux-Mines through a green valley. The road then climbs sharply past a war cemetery on the right.

Col de Ste-Marie

From the pass (alt 772m), one of the highest in the Vosges mountains, look back towards the Cude valley and ahead to the Liepvrette valley, the Plaine d'Alsace and Haut-Kœnigsbourg Castle.

Roc du Haut de Faite

From the pass, 30min on foot there and back. Walk north along a path starting on the right of a gravestone. From the top, there is a fine **panorama** of the Vosges summits and the slopes on the Alsatian and Lorraine side.

▶ Return to N 59 and drive towards St-Dié. Turn left onto D 23, 2km/1.2mi beyond Gemaingoutte.

Circuit minier La Croix-aux-Mines

5.6km/3.5mi walk. Allow 2h45.
Start from the Chapelle du Chipal and follow the mining circuit panels marked with a black circle against a yellow background and bearing the emblem of the trail (crossed hammer and pickaxe). Miners extracted galena, a mineral ore of lead sulphide mixed with silver, from this Le Chipal site and others in the area.

▶ Continue along D 23 to Fraize and turn left onto N 415.

Col du Bonhomme

See Val d'ORBEY.

▶ On reaching the pass, turn left onto D 148.

Le Bonhomme

This pleasant resort was caught three times in heavy fighting during the two world wars. Mountain streams rush downwards to form the River Béhine.

Le Brézouard★★

45min on foot there and back.
You will be able to get fairly close to Mt Brézouard by car if you approach it via the **Col des Bagenelles** *(4km/2.5mi)* which offers a fine view of the Liepvrette valley.

Birthplace of Patchwork

Every year in September, an historic and artistic exhibition on patchwork and the Amish community takes place in Ste-Marie-aux-Mines. Founded in 1693 in Ste-Marie, the Amish movement emigrated to Pennsylvania in 1740. Amish women used to make up blankets with pieces of fabric and thus initiated the art of patchwork. Lessons in patchwork-making are available and there are lectures on the history of the Amish movement and the various techniques of patchwork-making in several venues throughout the valley.

▶ Leave the car in the parking area, near the Amis de la Nature refuge

Mt Brézouard and the surrounding area suffered complete upheaval during WWI.
From the summit, there is a sweeping **panorama★★**: the Champ du Feu and Climont to the north, with Mt Donon in the background; Strasbourg to the northeast, Mt Hohneck and Grand Ballon to the south. When the weather is clear, Mont Blanc can be seen in the distance.

▶ Return to Ste-Marie-aux-Mines along D 48.

The road winds its way through the forest then follows the Liepvrette valley.

Vallée de la Liepvrette★

Orchards take over from high pastures along this valley; the Liepvrette is a charming stream running between two roads on its way to Ste-Croix-aux-Mines.

Sentier patrimoine de Neuenberg

This heritage trail (from Échery short tour: 2h30, long tour: 4h) offers views of the mineworkers' tower, the tithe-

collector's house, flanked with a turret in characteristic Renaissance style, and a research gallery for the Enigma mine.

▶ Turn right in Échery

St-Pierre-sur-l'Hâte

Where there was once a Benedictine priory, an ecumenical church remains, known as the miners' church, built in the 15C–16C and restored in 1934.

Ste-Marie-aux-Mines

This small industrial town, located in the Liepvrette valley, owes its name to its former silver mines. Today, it is the meeting place of rock and fossil collectors who gather for the exhibition and exchange market organised every year during the last weekend in June. Ste-Marie has a famous weaving industry specialising in fine woollen cloth, both factory and homemade by craftsmen who have been passing their skills on from one generation to the next since the 18C. Twice a year, in spring and autumn, a fabric fair offers buyers from various countries a choice of fabrics woven in Ste-Marie.

Maison de Pays
ⓘ *Open Jun–Sept daily except Wed.* ℘*03 89 58 56 67.*
The building houses a rich collection of rocks, along with reconstructions of a workshops, tools and models where visitors can follow the different stages of mining and the manufacturing process of fabrics.
The **Mine St-Barthélemy** (*rue St-Louis.* ⓘ*Jul–Aug 11am, 1pm, 2pm, 3pm, 4pm, 5pm;* ⬤*€8 (child 5–16, €6).* ℘*03 89 58 62 11*) organises tours of the galleries hewn out of the rock by 16C miners and the **Mine d'argent St-Louis-Eisenthur** presents the various mining sites and techniques used in the 16C (*Guided tour by reservation at the tourist office. Wear walking shoes and warm clothes*).
An **historic trail** (🥾*2h30, booklet available at the tourist office*) enables visitors to discover miners' houses and mansions which show how flourishing the mining industry was in the 16C and early 17C.

▶ Leave Ste-Marie-aux-Mines by D 459 towards Ste-Croix.

Sentier minier et botanique de Ste-Croix-aux-Mines
A mining and botanic trail (🥾*3.8km/ 2.4mi; allow 2h30; on the left of the road as you leave the town, 100m before the panel marked "les halles").*
🥾 The trail winds through the Bois de St-Pierremont where several silver mines were located in the 16C. All along the way, panels provide information about the various species of trees.

ADDRESSES

🛏STAY

The park federation and the WWF have selected a few gîtes in splendid farmhouses and chalets, etc. They are an ideal means of getting back to grass roots (Maison du Parc – ⓒ*see p196.*

⊜ **Grand Hôtel du Sommet** – *On the summit of the Ballon d'Alsace , 90200 Lepuix-Gy.* ℘*03 84 29 30 60. www.hotel restaurantdusommet.com. Closed mid-Nov–mid-Dec, and Mon except school holidays. 25 rooms. Restaurant*⊜. Imagine waking up on a mountain top, surrounded by nothing but open air and fields of cows, with a view of the Belfort valley and, on a clear day, even the Swiss Alps. A good night's sleep is guaranteed in the simple but comfortable rooms.

⊜ ⊜ **Auberge Le Lodge de Monthury** – *Monthury, 70440 Servance – 4.5km/ 2.8mi N of Servance on D 263 road to Beulotte-St-Laurent.* ℘*03 84 63 82 26.* ✍. *Closed mid-Dec–mid-Jan. 5 rooms.* Immerse yourself in nature in this isolated 18C farm in the forests above the Ognon valley, facing the Ballon de Servance. Comfortable, simple rooms. The cooking uses local produce. Fishing in 7ha of private lakes.

SPORT AND RECREATION
Ecole de ski du Ballon d'Alsace – *ESF Chalet at La Gentiane, 70440 Servance.* ℘*03 84 29 06 65. www.esf.net.* During winter Ballon d'Alsace offers a huge range of snow sports. Although essentially a domain for cross-country skiing – 8 trails, 50km/30mi – it is proud of its 19 downhill ski slopes.

Route des Crêtes★

Haut-Rhin, Vosges

This strategic road was built during WWI at the request of the French High Command, in order to ensure adequate north-south communications between the various valleys along the front line of the Vosges. The magnificent (80km/49.7mi) itinerary enables motorists to admire the most characteristic landscapes of the Vosges mountains, its passes, its *ballons* (rounded summits), its lakes, its *chaumes* (high pastures where cattle graze in summer) and offers wide panoramas and extended views. Between the Hohneck and the Grand Ballon, the road is lined with *fermes-auberges* (farmhouses turned into inns during the season) where snacks and regional dishes are served from June to October. In winter the snowfields offer miles of cross-country tracks.

🚗 **DRIVING TOUR**

From Col du Bonhomme to Thann

83km/52mi. Allow half a day.

Col du Bonhomme

Alt 949m. The pass links the two neighbouring regions of Alsace and Lorraine (🕭 See Val d'ORBEY).
Beyond the pass, the road offers fine vistas of the Béhine valley to the left, with the Tête des Faux and Brézouard towering above. Farther on, the Col du Louchbach affords a beautiful view of the valley of the River Meurthe to the south.

▶ Turn right at Col du Calvaire.

Gazon du Faing★

🚶 *45min on foot there and back.*
As you reach the summit *(1303m)*, climb up to a large rock from where an

- 🕭 **Michelin Map:** Michelin Local map 315: G-8 to 10.
- ℹ **Tourist Office:** ✆03 89 75 50 35. www.hautes-vosges-alsace.fr.
- ▶ **Location:** This route starts 30km/18.6mi west of Colmar and heads south to Thann.
- 👁 **Don't Miss:** The stunning panoramas from Le Hohneck and the Grand Ballon.
- 👁 The Route des Crêtes is generally closed between the Hohneck and the Grand Ballon from mid-November to mid-March (ℹ *Enquire at the Tourist Office*).

extended panoramic **view** is to be had. In the foreground, the small Étang des Truites, changed into a reservoir by a dam, lies inside the Lenzwasen glacial cirque. Farther afield, one can see, from left to right, the Linge, the Schratzmaennele and the Barrenkopf heights; more to the right, beyond the Fecht valley and the town of Munster, a long ridge slopes down from the Petit Ballon; to the right of this summit, the silhouette of the Grand Ballon *(alt 1 424m)* rises in the distance; the twin summits of the Petit Hohneck *(alt 1 288m)* and Hohneck *(alt 1 362m)* can be seen farther to the right.

Lac Vert

🚶 A path starting near the 5km/3mi mark from the Col de la Schlucht leads to the Lac Vert, also known as the Lac de Soultzeren (coloured by lichens).

Col de la Schlucht

Alt 1 135m.
The pass links the upper valley of the River Meurthe (which takes its source 1km/0.6mi away from the pass) with that of the River Fecht.

▶ Alt 1 228m, 2km/1.2mi from the Col de la Schlucht towards Le Markstein, on the right of D 430.

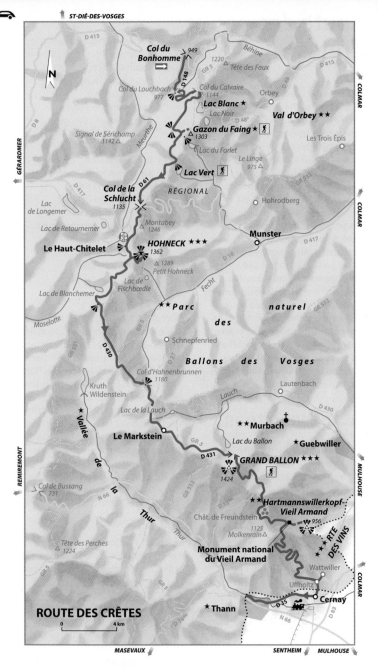

Jardin d'Altitude du Haut-Chitelet

♿🕐Jul–Aug 10am–6pm; Jun 10am–noon, 2–6pm; Sept 10am–noon, 2–5.30pm. ✍€5 (free 1st Sun of month). ☎03 83 41 47 47.

www.jardinbotaniquedenancy.eu.
These botanical gardens cover an area of 11ha; rockeries spreading over more than 1ha shelter 2 700 species of plants from the main mountain ranges of the

world. Farther on, the road offers a fine **view★** of the Valogne valley, Lake Longemer and Lake Retournemer. Note the village of Xonrupt and the suburbs of Gérardmer in the distance *(viewpoint)*.

Le Hohneck★★★

The steep access path starts from the Route des Crêtes, 4km/2.5mi S of the Col de la Schlucht; do not follow the private path which starts closer to the pass (3km/1.9mi) as it is in bad condition.
Beware of freezing winds near the summit.

This is one of the most famous and one of the highest summits in the Vosges mountains (alt 1 362m).

A splendid **panorama★★★** *(viewing table)* unfolds, encompassing the Vosges from Donon to the Grand Ballon, the Plaine d'Alsace and the Black Forest. In clear weather, the summits of the Alps are visible. The road runs through high pastures, known as **chaumes**. The Lac de Blanchemer can be seen on the right. Farther on there is a magnificent view of the Grande Vallée de la Fecht, followed by the lake and valley of the Lauch with the Plaine d'Alsace in the distance.

Le Markstein

This winter-sports resort is situated at the intersection of the Route des Crêtes and the upper Lauch valley.

As you drive along the cliff road, there are alternate views of the Thur valley and Ballon d'Alsace massif on one side and the Lauch valley and Petit Ballon on the other. The small **Lac du Ballon** lies inside a funnel-shaped basin.

Grand Ballon★★★

Leave the car by the hotel and follow the path on the left (30min on foot there and back).

There is a radar station at the summit. Grand Ballon, also known as Ballon de Guebwiller, is the highest summit (alt 1 424m) in the Vosges mountains. Just below the summit, the Monument des Diables Bleus was erected to commemorate various regiments of *chasseurs* (mountain troops).

From the top of Grand Ballon, the **panorama★★★** embraces the southern Vosges, the Black Forest and, when the weather is clear, the Jura mountains and the Alps.

Vieil-Armand★★

The name was given by the soldiers of WWI to the foothills of the Vosges (Hartmannswillerkopf) which slope steeply down to the Plaine d'Alsace. This strategic position was one of the most bloody battlefields along the Alsatian front (30 000 French and German soldiers killed). In 1915, attacks and counter attacks were repeatedly launched on its slopes.

The **Monument national du Vieil-Armand** was built over a crypt containing the remains of 12 000 unknown soldiers.

The **summit** can be reached on foot *(1h there and back)*. Walk through the cemetery situated behind the national monument, which contains 1 260 graves and several ossuaries. Follow the central alleyway and the path beyond it. Walk towards the summit of Vieil-Armand *(alt 956m)* surmounted by a 22m high luminous cross which marks the limit of the French front. Turn right towards the iron cross erected on a rocky promontory to commemorate the volunteers from Alsace-Lorraine.

A wide **panorama★★** can be had of the Plaine d'Alsace, the Vosges mountains, the Black Forest and the Alps.

Cernay

This small industrial town lies at the foot of Vieil-Armand, and still retains remains of its medieval fortifications, including the gateway of Thann, which displays the coat of arms of the village. A small museum here houses temporary exhibitions from time to time.

Drive W along D 35

Thann★ – *See THANN.*

Lac de Longemer

© Alexis Borg/Fotolia.com

Gérardmer★

Vosges

Gérardmer was destroyed by fire in November 1944, but the town has been completely rebuilt as a popular winter and summer resort. Every two years, there is a glorious daffodil festival in mid-April. The tourist office, created in 1865, is the oldest in France.

VISIT

LAKES

Lac de Gérardmer★

This is the largest lake in the Vosges region (2.2km/1.3mi long, 0.75km wide and 38m deep).

A walking or driving **tour**★ round the lake (6.5km/4mi) offers varied views of the lake framed by mountains. Several companies provide tours of the lake with commentaries from mid-April to end October. (*Ask at the tourist office for details.*)

Lac de Longemer★

5km.3mi E along D 417 and D 67A.
This lake (2km/1.2mi long, 550m wide and 30m deep) is surrounded by meadows.

Lac de Retournemer★

12km/7.5mi E along D 417 and D 67.
This small lake, fed by the waterfalls of the Vologne, is set inside a green basin.

▸ **Population:** 8 996.
◔ **Michelin Map:** Michelin Local map 314: J-4.
▯ **Tourist Office:** 4 Place des Déportés, 88400 Gérardmer. ℘03 29 27 27 27. www.gerardmer.net.
◖ **Location:** In the heart of the Parc Naturel Régional du Ballon des Vosges, Gérardmer is 80km/50mi from Mulhouse and 53km/33mi from Colmar.
◉ **Don't Miss:** The entire region is a treasure trove of beautiful countryside; the highlight is undoubtedly the panorama from Le Hohneck.

SKI RESORTS

Gérardmer-la Mauselaine✳

Free shuttle service in winter (weekends and school holidays) from Gérardmer to La Mauselaine. ℘03 29 60 04 05. www.gerardmer-ski.com/en.

The ski resort enjoys good snow cover which enhances the appeal of its 40km/25mi of ski runs (including the longest run in the Vosges massif: 4km/2.5mi) accessible to beginners as well as experienced skiers. The first Nordic ski area in the Vosges massif, the Domaine des Bas-Rupts is only 2.5km/1.5mi out of Gérardmer. Cross-country tracks totalling 100km/62mi run through the forest forming loops of various levels of difficulty located within the municipalities of Gérardmer, La Bresse and Xonrupt, accompanied by snowshoe trails.

La Bresse-Hohneck

The largest ski area in the Vosges region and includes 36 ski runs spread over three main areas, between Hohneck and La Bresse, around Lac de Retournemer and near the Col de la Schlucht.

🚗 DRIVING TOURS

VALLEYS OF THE MEURTHE AND PETITE MEURTHE★

1 ROUND TOUR NORTHEAST OF GÉRARDMER
55km/34mi. Allow 2h.

▷ Leave Gérardmer NE along D 417.

Saut des Cuves★

▷ Leave the car near the Saut des Cuves Hotel. Take the path starting upstream of the bridge and leading to the River Vologne spanned by two footbridges.

🏃 The mountain stream cascades down over granite in a succession of waterfalls; the largest is the Saut des Cuves.

▷ Turn left onto D 23 and drive for 2km/1.2mi then turn right.

Musée de la Faune Lorraine
♿🕐*Jul–Aug and Christmas holidays 10am–noon, 2–6pm (Sun 2–6pm); rest of year daily except Sat 2–6pm.*
🕐*25 Dec.* ✎*€6.50 (child 4–15, €4.50).*
📞*03 29 63 39 50.*
www.museefaunelorraine.com.
👥 This exhibition offers attractive dioramas and four aquariums illustrating aquatic life of the area.

▷ Continue driving and, 1km/0.6mi farther on, turn right onto D 23.

The road runs through the forest to the River Meurthe at Le Valtin. The slopes of the **upper valley of the Meurthe** are covered with pastures and forests.

▷ In Plainfaing, turn left onto N 415 then left again onto D 73.

On the way back to Gérardmer, the road follows the **valley of the Petite Meurthe**, which gradually narrows to go through the steep Straiture gorge.

Glacière de Straiture

▷ A small road branches off to the right; 0.7km/0.4mi beyond this intersection, a path to the south-east allows one to cross the river and reach the glacier.

🏃 A pile of rocks that holds traces of ice even at the height of summer.

▷ At the end of the gorge, the road crosses the Petite Meurthe, leads to the Col du Surceneux and back to Gérardmer.

2 LA BRESSE – HOHNECK – COL DE LA SCHLUCHT★★★

Round tour southeast of Gérardmer
54km/34mi. Allow 2h30.

▷ Leave Gérardmer S along D 486.

The road rises through the woods then runs down towards the valley of the River Bouchot to rise again towards the Col de Grosse Pierre.

La Bresse
Founded in 7C, this picturesque town has strong cheesemaking traditions and a textile industry. Ruined in 1944, La Bresse had to be entirely rebuilt.

▷ Via D 43, 1.5km/0.9mi from Ventron on the way to Col d'Oderen.

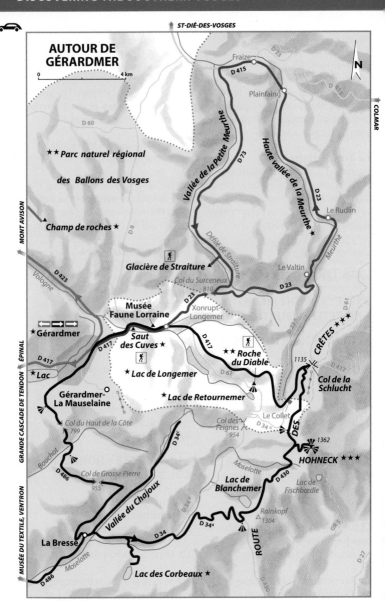

↑ ST-DIÉ-DES-VOSGES

AUTOUR DE GÉRARDMER

0   4 km

→ COLMAR

N

★★ *Parc naturel régional*
des Ballons des Vosges

★ *Champ de roches*

MONT AVISON

D 60

D 415

Fraize

Plainfaing

D 23

Vallée de la petite Meurthe

Haute vallée de la Meurthe ★

D 23

Le Rudlin

D 73

Le Valtin

Meurthe

D 23

D 61

Défilé de Straiture

Glacière de Straiture ▲

Col du Surceneux
810

Xonrupt-
Longemer

Musée Faune Lorraine

D 23

Saut des Cuves ★

★ *Gérardmer*

D 423

Vologne

D 417

D 417

D 417

D 67

★★ *Roche du Diable*

CRÊTES ★★★

1135

Col de la Schlucht

D 417

★ *Lac de Longemer*

★ *Lac de Retournemer*

★ *Lac*

ÉPINAL

Gérardmer-La Mauselaine

Col du Haut de la Côte
799

Bouchot

D 486

Col de Grosse Pierre
955

Vallée du Chajoux

D 34C

D 34C

D 34A

Col des Feignes
954

Le Collet

D 34

DES.

1362

HOHNECK ★★★

Moselotte

D 430

Lac de Fischbœdle

Lac de Blanchemer

Rainkpf
△ 1304

ROUTE

GRANDE CASCADE DE TENDON

La Bresse

D 486

Moselotte

D 34

D 34A

GR 5

D 27

MUSÉE DU TEXTILE, VENTRON

Lac des Corbeaux ★

Musée du textile

🕐 *Daily except Mon 10am–noon, 2–6pm. Self-guided visits are allowed with explanation and demonstration on machines.* 🕐 *Nov–mid-Dec, 1 Jan, 25 Dec.* ⊜ €4.50. ✆ 03 29 24 23 06. http://musee.ventron.fr.

Located in the heart of the Vosges mountains, this museum is devoted to the textile industry.

Vallée du Chajoux

D 34C runs north-east from La Bresse along a fish-abounding stream.

Lac des Corbeaux★

◆ A road, branching off to the right near the Hôtel du Lac, leads to this remote lake (23m deep).

The lake occupies the centre of a glacial cirque with densely forested slopes.
🚶 A footpath runs all the way round it (*30min on foot*).

▶ Return to D 34 and turn right along the Moselotte valley. Cross the river, ignoring D 34D on the left, and 2km/1.2mi farther on, after a bend to the right, leave the Col de Bramont road and follow the twisting D 34A, known as the Route des Américains.

As you reach the high pastures, the view extends to the right over the upper valley of the Thur, Wildenstein village and the Kruth-Wildenstein dam.

▶ Turn left onto the Route des Crêtes (D 430) which goes round the Rainkopf summit.

Down on the left in a wooded basin, you can see **Lac de Blanchemer**.
The road then reaches the chaumes (high pastures) of Hohneck.

Le Hohneck ★★★
♿*See Route des CRÊTES.*
Beyond the Hohneck heights, there are glimpses of Lake Longemer in the distance to the left and later on there are splendid **views★** of the Valogne valley, Lake Retournemer and Lake Longemer.

Col de la Schlucht
♿*See Route des CRÊTES.*

Roche du Diable★★
15min on foot there and back.Leave the car near the tunnel and follow a steep path leading to the viewpoint.
🚶 The **view★★** extends to the Valogne valley between Lake Retournemer and Lake Longemer.

Saut des Cuves★
♿*See* ① *above.*

③ VALLEYS OF THE TENDON AND THE VALOGNE

Round tour northwest of Gérardmer
61km/38mi. Allow 2h.
♿*See also map pp190-191.*

▶ Leave Gérardmer W along D 417. At the entrance of Le Tholy, turn right onto D 11 towards Épinal and drive for 5km/3mi. Turn left 200m before the Grande Cascade Hotel and follow the road down to the waterfall (800m).

Grande cascade de Tendon★
This double waterfall drops 32m in several steps through dense firs.

▶ Farther on, as you reach Faucompierre, turn right towards Bruyères along D 30 and D 44. In Bruyères, take the street to the left of the cemetery (towards Belmont), which leads to the foot of Mt Avison. Leave the car.

Tour-belvédère du mont Avison
🚶 *45min on foot there and back.*
This 15m high tower stands on the top (alt 601m) of one of the hills surrounding Bruyères. From the platform (82 steps, viewing table), the wide **panorama★** extends to the Tête des Cuveaux, Hohneck and Donon summits.

Champ de roches de Granges-sur-Vologne★

▶ In Granges-sur-Vologne, an industrial town with textile factories, turn left onto D 31 then right in Barbey-Seroux onto the forest road (second crossroads) which runs through the Vologne forest. 2.4km/1.5mi farther on, you come to another crossroads with a house standing nearby; turn left and leave the car 150m farther on.

🚶 This horizontal moraine, 500m long, cuts through the forest like a petrified river.

ADDRESSES

🏠 STAY

Chalet au Bord du Lac – *207, route d'Épinal, 88400 Gérardmer.* ℘*03 29 63 01 03. www.chaletauborddulac.fr. 22 rooms. Restaurant* 🍴🍴. This large chalet-restaurant overlooks the lake. It has simple, well-kept rooms, unpretentious cooking typical of the region – and a lovely view.

Hôtel Restaurant L'Aubergade – *Pl. des Déportés.* ℘*03 29 63 02 41. www.laubergade-gerardmer.fr. 18 rooms.* The façade and the plain but well-kept rooms of this family-run hotel are adorned with Tyrol-style frescos. Balconies on the first floor. Lovely little lounge with hearth. The restaurant (🍴🍴) and its warm rustic atmosphere are reminiscent of Austria. Traditional recipes and local foods.

Hôtel et Résidence Les Vallées – *31 r. P.-Claudel – 88520 La Bresse. 14km/8.75mi S of Gérardmer on D 486.* ℘*03 29 25 41 39. www.lesvallees-labresse.com. 54 rooms. Restaurant* 🍴. In this central hotel, you can relax in the pleasant modern rooms and enjoy the indoor swimming pool. Studio apartments to let.

🍴 EAT

Auberge de Liézey – *9 rte de Saucefaing, 88400 Liézey – 9.5km/6mi W of Gérardmer on D 417 and D 50.* ℘*03 29 63 09 51. www.aubergedeliezey.fr. Closed Mon and Tue except in school holidays.* In the snow or among the pine forests, depending on the season, this spacious chalet-farm, dating from 1799, offers hearty meals using produce from neighbouring farms. Horse-riding in summer. Seven simple, well-kept rooms.

Le Refuge – *88400 Gérardmer – 4km/2.5mi S of Gérardmer on D 486.* ℘*03 29 63 06 83.* To get away from it all head for this seductive restaurant decorated in the style of a mountain refuge, and with a warm and intimate setting. Wood fired kitchen, serving local produce.

ON THE TOWN

Cinéma-Casino du Lac – *3 av. de la Ville-de-Vichy.* ℘*03 29 60 05 05. www.joa-casino. com. Open daily 10am–2am (3am Fri–Sat).* This leisure centre includes fruit machines and gambling activities, a cinema-theatre and a seasonal restaurant with a lakeside terrace.

Brasserie les Rives du Lac – *1 av. de la Ville-de-Vichy.* ℘*03 29 63 04 29.* As you will quickly be able to tell, this is one of the nicest cafés in town, with the sound of water and the view of the blue lake and surrounding mountains.

SHOPPING

Craft market – *Pl. du Vieux-Gérardmé – Jul–Aug: Sat 8am–7pm.* This weekly market of local craftsmen and producers is one of the most popular in the region.

Le Jacquard Français – *35 r. Charles-de-Gaulle.* ℘*03 29 60 82 50. www.le-jacquard-francais.com.* Table linen, bath and beach towels.

Linvosges – *6 pl. de la Gare.* ℘*03 29 60 11 00. www.linvosges.com. Daily 9am–noon, 2–6pm. Closed Sun except school holidays.* This company, founded in 1922, continues the Vosges tradition of high-quality household linen, including bedding and table linen as well as products for the kitchen and bathroom.

La Saboterie des Lacs – *25 bd de la Jamagne.* ℘*03 29 60 09 06. https:// lasaboteriedeslacs.jimdo.com. Mon–Fri 10am–noon, 2–5pm.* This is a clog maker's workshop where you can watch clogs being manufactured from start to finish. You can also buy all types of clogs, from utility to decorative, made out of ash or maple wood.

Association des Artisans du Village de Liézey – *17 rte de Saucéfaing, 88400 Liézey – 7km/4.3mi NE of Gérardmer on D 50.* ℘*03 29 63 16 50. Apr–Nov: Sun 2.30–6.30pm, daily 2.30–6.30pm in school holidays.* More than 50 local craftsmen and producers exhibit their wares in this old farm.

EVENTS AND FESTIVALS

Fête des Jonquilles – for this colourful biannual daffodil festival *(mid-Apr)* more than 30 floats are covered with thousands of daffodils to celebrate the start of spring.

Fantastic'Arts – fantasy film festival held at the end of January. ℘*03 29 63 49 49. www.festival-gerardmer.com.*

View from Hohrodberg

Munster

Haut-Rhin

Irish monks arrived in the area in the 7C to complete the christianisation of Alsace and founded an abbey which gave its name to the village growing in its shadow (Munster comes from the Latin word for monastery). Today, the region lives on its traditional cheese industry and on the textile industry. Farther up the Fecht valley, to the south of Munster, is the rounded summit of the Petit Ballon, also known as Kahler Wasen, an area of high pastures where herds spend the summer and the famed Munster cheese is made.

VISIT

The Grand'Rue is a lively shopping street with attractive boutiques. The neo-Romaneque Protestant church was built in the 1920s.

The only remaining wing of the former abbots' palace, situated south of the market square, is now the headquarters of the **Parc naturel régional des Ballons des Vosges**. The **Maison du Parc** (*see Parc naturel régional des BALLONS DES VOSGES: Practical Information*) suggests various activities and presents a permanent exhibition illustrating the main features of the park.

▸ **Population:** 4 828.
Michelin Map: Michelin Local map 315: G-8.
Tourist Office: 1 r. du Couvent, 68140 Munster. 03 89 77 31 80. www.vallee-munster.eu.

🚗 DRIVING TOURS

5 VALLÉE DE MUNSTER★★

Round tour from Munster
55km/34mi. Allow 3h. Local map
See Parc naturel régional des BALLONS DES VOSGES

From Munster drive NW along D 417 then turn right onto D 5bis which winds its way up to Hohrodberg.

Hohrodberg
This summer resort spreads along sunny slopes that afford an extended **view★★** to the south-west of Munster, its valley and, from left to right, the summits rising in the background from the Petit Ballon to Hohneck.

The Vosges Summits

Donon 1009m
Champ du Feu 1100m
Ballon de Servance 1216m
Ballon d'Alsace 1250m
Petit Ballon or Kahler Wasen1 267m
Hohneck 1 362m
Grand Ballon or Ballon de Guebwiller
1 424m, *the highest summit*

🚶 During the climb, stop by the picnic area and walk along the road as far as the bend to admire the countryside. A brochure available from the tourist office suggests three marked footpaths: **Sentier de Rosskopf** (fauna and flora), **Sentier de Katzenstein** (landscapes and economic life) and **Sentier du Barrenkopf** (WWI).

Le Collet du Linge
On the right-hand side of the road lies a German military cemetery.

Le Linge
In 1915, following fierce fighting, French troops secured the western slopes of the Linge and Schratzmaennele. Walk to the right to reach the top of Linge, quite close, through what is left of the German sandstone trenches.

▶ Continue along D 11 which soon overlooks the Orbey valley.

Col du Wettstein
The cemetery contains the graves of 3 000 French soldiers.

▶ D 48 then runs down into the valley of the Petite Fecht and joins up with D 417 near Soultzeren.

The road winds up towards the Col de la Schlucht offering views first of the Fecht valley and then of the Petite Fecht valley. Hohneck can be seen to the south. The road leading to Lac Vert (♿ *see Route des CRÊTES*) branches off on the right just before a bend. The road runs

through the forest, finally overlooking the splendid glacial cirque, source of the Petite Fecht.

Col de la Schlucht
At the pass, D 417 joins up with the Route des Crêtes (♿ *see Route des CRÊTES*).

Jardin d'altitude du Haut-Chitelet –
♿ *See Route des CRÊTES*.

Le Hohneck★★★
♿ See *Route des CRÊTES*.

▶ Turn left onto the Route des Crêtes.

As you pass beneath a ski lift, you will glimpse of the Lac de la Lauch below, the Guebwiller valley and the Plaine d'Alsace in the distance.

▶ Turn back and follow D 27.

After a short climb, the road leaves the high pastures and offers a fine view on the left of the Hohneck massif.

Schnepfenried★
This popular winter sports resort is equipped with several ski lifts and has a beautiful **panorama★** of the Hohneck massif to the north with the Schiessrothried dam and lake lower down the slopes of the mountain.
🚶 From the summit of Schnepfenried (alt 1258m), just south of the resort, 1hr by foot there and back), there is a panoramic view★ from the Grand Ballon to Brézouard, the Fecht valley, and the Black Forest.

▶ In Metzeral, take D 10VI; turn right 1km/0.6mi farther on, cross the river and leave the car.

🚶 The footpath (3km/1.9mi, about 1hr) rises through the glacial valley of the Wormsa to reach Lac de Fischbœdle.

Lac de Fischbœdle★
Alt 790m.
This almost circular lake, barely 100m in diameter, is an artificial gem of the Vosges region, created c 1850.

Lac de Schiessrothried

1h on foot there and back along the winding path starting on the right as you reach Lake Fischbœdle. It is directly accessible by car from Muhlbach along D 310.

The lake, which covers 5ha, now a reservoir, lies at an altitude of 920m, at the foot of Hohneck.

Return to Metzeral and turn left onto D 10.

Luttenbach-près-Munster

Voltaire visited several times in 1754.

Return to Munster along the D 10 which follows the River Fecht.

6 VALLÉE DE LA FECHT

20km/12.4mi – local map.
see Parc naturel régional des BALLONS DES VOSGES

From Munster drive E along D 10.

Gunsbach

Albert Schweitzer spent part of his childhood here, returning regularly and had a house built after he won the Goethe prize in 1928; this is now a **museum** (*Tue–Sat 9–11.30am, 2–4.30pm. public holidays, Easter, 24 Dec–Jan. €5. 03 89 77 31 42. www. schweitzer.org*).

There is a water-themed **walking itinerary** (*4km/2.5mi, about 2hr 30min*) along the banks of the Flecht.

In Wihr-au-Val, cross the Fecht and D 417.

Soultzbach-les-Bains

The 17C **Chapelle Ste-Catherine** contains two interesting paintings (1738) by Franz-Georg Hermann, *Our Lady of Solace* and *St Nicholas of Tolentino*. The isolated parish **church** houses three gilt **altars**★★ (*guided tours Jul–mid-Sept, afternoons only. 03 89 71 11 16*).

Drive back to D 417 and turn right towards Colmar.

After the Fecht valley vineyards, the ruin of Plixbourg castle keep can be seen.

Turn left onto the D 10 to visit Turkheim and Colmar.

7 MASSIF DU PETIT BALLON★

40km/25mi. About 4h30 – local map see Parc naturel régional des BALLONS DES VOSGES

Drive out of Munster along D 417 towards Colmar then turn right 5km/3mi farther on and follow D 40.

Beyond Soultzbach, a road (D 43) on the right follows the Krebsbach valley.
In **Wasserbourg**, turn onto a forest road leading to an inn (Auberge Ried) where there is a fine view of Hohneck. The Kahler Wasen farm-restaurant stands on pastureland and the **view**★ extends down the Fecht valley and, beyond, across the Plaine d'Alsace.

Petit Ballon★★

Alt 1 267m.

1h15 on foot there and back from the Kahler Wasen farm-restaurant.

The **panorama** is superb: the Plaine d'Alsace and the Black Forest to the east; the Grand Ballon massif to the south; the valleys of the two Fecht rivers to the north and west.

Drive down via the Boenlesgrab pass and forest road.

The road offers a fine view of the Lauch valley. Beware of the two hairpin bends just before Lautenbach.

Lautenbach★

See GUEBWILLER: Guebwiller valley.

Follow D 430 on the right.

The road winds its way upwards then runs onto the next slope.

Le Markstein

See Route des CRÊTES.

ADDRESSES

⛨/ EAT

⊖⊜ **Restaurant des Cascades** – *6 chemin de Saegmatt, 68140 Stosswihr. 6km/3.75mi W of Munster on D 417 and minor road.* ℘*03 89 77 44 74. Closed Mon and Tue.* Tucked away by a stream on the route des Crêtes, this popular restaurant is renowned for its *flammekueches*.

⊖⊜ **Gilg** – *11 Grand'Rue.* ℘*03 89 77 37 56. www.patisserie-gilg.com. Open daily 7.30am–6.30pm, Sat 7am–6pm, Sun 7.30am–12.30pm. Closed 3rd week of Jan, two last weeks of Sept, 26 Dec, 1 Jan and Mon.* The present owner, grandson of Paul Gilg continues his ancestor's traditions in this pleasant tea-room.

SPORT AND RECREATION

Skiing – Munster's skiing domain is comprised of 4 regions: Schnefenried (downhill, cross-country), Gaschney (downhill), Tanet (downhill, cross-country) and Trois-Fours (cross-country).

Walking and Biking – The valley of Munster boasts some 350km/217.5mi of sign-posted walks and 250km/155mi of mountain-bike tracks.

Val d'Orbey★★

Haut-Rhin

The austere landscapes of Lac Noir and Lac Blanc contrast with the picturesque valleys of the River Béhine and the River Weiss. The circular tour also leads to Le Linge, one of the most dramatic battlefields of WWI. This is Welche country, a kind of French enclave (linguistically speaking) in Alsace. Welche is a Romance dialect, derived from vulgar Latin.

🚗 DRIVING TOUR

57km/35mi. Allow 4hr. Local maps ⓒ see Parc naturel régional des BALLONS DES VOSGES and p190–191.

Les Trois-Épis★★
This resort, which is a starting point for numerous hikes and interesting drives, gets its name from an apparition by the Virgin Mary in 1491, to a blacksmith. In her left hand she held a piece of ice as a symbol of a hardened heart and in her right hand she had three ears of corn (*épis de mais*) as a symbol of divine mercy and blessing.

- ⓒ **Michelin Map:** Michelin Local map 315: G-8.
- 🛈 **Tourist Office:** 48 r. Charles-de-Gaulle, 68370 Orbey. ℘03 89 78 22 78. www.kaysersberg.com.
- ◖ **Location:** Located at the northern end of the Route des Crêtes, W of Colmar, between Kayserberg, Munster and the Col du Bonhomme pass.

Le Galz★★
🚶 *1h on foot there and back.*
At the top a monument by Valentin Jæg commemorates the return of Alsace to France in 1918. The view extends as far as the Plaine d'Alsace, the Black Forest, the Sundgau and the Jura mountains.

Sentier de la forêt de St-Wendelin
🚶 *1h30 on foot from the car park on place des Antonins (brochure available from the tourist office). Follow the green squirrel markings.*
This forest trail explores the flora covering the Val d'Orbey slopes.

◖ From Les Trois-Épis drive W along D 11 for 3km/1.9mi then left onto D 11VI.

The road follows the ridge separating the Val d'Orbey and the Munster valley, offering fine views of both.

Val d'Orbey

Le Linge
See MUNSTER: Vallée de Munster.

▶ Turn right at Collet du Linge then, leaving the Glasborn path on your left, continue to the Col du Wettstein (war cemetery) and turn right again.

Lac Noir★
🅿 *Park by the lake.*
Lac Noir (*alt 954m*) sits inside a glacial cirque. A moraine reinforced by a dam retains the water on the east side; the lake is otherwise surrounded by high granite cliffs which contribute to the austerity of the landscape.

Lac Blanc★
The road skirts Lac Blanc (*alt 1 054m*, offering beautiful views of the glacial cirque that surrounds the lake (area: 29ha, depth: 72m). A strange rock, shaped like a fortress known as **Château Hans**, overlooks the lake.

▶ The road joins the Route des Crêtes at the Col du Calvaire. Turn right through the forest.

The road gives glimpses of the Béhine valley and the Tête des Faux, before reaching the Col du Bonhomme.

Col du Bonhomme
Alt 949m.
This pass links Alsace and Lorraine via the Col de Ste-Marie in the north and the Col de la Schlucht in the south (*see also Route des CRÊTES*). The road twists down from the pass into the Béhine valley offering fine views of the valley with the Brézouard summit in the distance and the Tête des Faux quite close by to the right, then passes beneath a rocky spur topped by the ruins of Gutenburg Castle.

Le Bonhomme
This is the beginning of Welche country. Streams rush down the slopes to form the River Béhine.

Lapoutroie
In this village a small **Musée des Eaux-de-Vie** (liqueurs and traditional distillery) is housed in an 18C coaching inn (&🕙*daily 9am–noon, 2–6pm. ✆No charge. ✆03 89 47 50 26. www.musee-eaux-de-vie.com*).

▶ Continue along N 415 towards Kaysersberg, past the intersection with D 48 (roundabout), then immediately left onto D 11IV leading to Fréland.

Fréland
The name means free land; miners from Ste-Marie-aux-Mines (*see Parc naturel régional des BALLONS DES VOSGES: Val d'Argent*) enjoyed various privileges such as the right to cut timber.

Maison du Pays Welche
2 rue de la Rochette. 🕙Apr–Oct Fri–Sun. ✆€4.50. ✆03 89 71 90 52. www.musee-pays-welche.alsace.
Local people have gathered objects illustrating the region's traditions and displayed them in an 18C presbytery.

Musées de la Vieille Forge, Musée de la Travérsée des siècles, Musée des Automates
𝄞03 89 47 58 30.
Here you can see an old water-powered smithy with its water-wheel and two adjacent museums, devoted to unusual tools and a collection of automatons.

▷ Return to N 415, at the roundabout take the D 48 towards Orbey.

Orbey
This village, made up of several hamlets, stretches along the verdant valley of the River Weiss. Beyond Orbey, the

D 11 climbs up a narrow valley past Tannach then, after a deep bend, continues to climb offering fine views of the Weiss valley overlooked by Grand Faudé. Further on it changes direction revealing the Walbach valley ahead with Le Galz and its monument beyond and the Plaine d'Alsace in the distance. Leaving **Labaroche** on your left, you will soon notice Grand Hohneck straight ahead and, nearby on your right, the conical summit of Petit Hohneck.

▷ Return to Les Trois-Épis, 3km/1.9mi beyond the intersection of D 11 and D 11VI.

St-Dié-des-Vosges★

Vosges

Situated in a fertile basin overlooked by pine-covered red-sandstone ridges, St-Dié owes its name to a monastery founded in the 7C by St Déodat. The town was partly destroyed by fire on four occasions, most recently in November 1944, towards the end of WWII. Textile and wood industries are the town's main economic activities.

▸ **Population:** 21 485.
✦ **Michelin Map:** Michelin Local map 314: J-3.
🛈 **Tourist Office:** 6 quai du Maréchal Leclerc, 88100 St-Dié-des-Vosges. *𝄞03 29 42 22 22.* www.tourisme-saint-die-des-vosges.fr.
▷ **Location:** St-Dié is 30km/ 18.6mi N of Gerardmer on the N 59.

A BIT OF HISTORY
The continent discovered by Christopher Columbus was first named America, in honour of the explorer Amerigo Vespucci, in a work entitled *Cosmographiæ Introductio*, published in St-Dié in 1507 by a team of scientists who called themselves the Gymnase Vosgien. In October, the town hosts an international event devoted to geography.

SIGHTS
Cathédrale St-Dié★
⏱Enquire at the tourist office for opening times. ⊶No charge.
The former collegiate church became a cathedral in 1777. Its imposing Classical west front dating from the early 18C is

flanked by two square towers. The vaulting and the east end have been rebuilt after being blown up in 1944.
Interior – In the Romanesque nave, strong piers alternate with weak ones, topped by carved **capitals★** having miraculously been spared by the explosion. There is a 14C Virgin and Child against the column situated on the right of the crossing. Some 13C windows in the second chapel on the north side illustrate episodes from the Life of St Déodat. In 1987, the cathedral acquired some fine abstract **stained-glass windows★** made by a team of 10 artists headed by Jean Bazaine.
Cloître gothique★ – The 15C and 16C canons' cloisters, linking the cathedral

Cloister, Cathédrale St-Dié

and the Église Notre-Dame-de-Galilée are remarkable, although they were never completed. Note the Flamboyant openings on the side of the courtyard, the ribbed vaulting and the 15C outdoor pulpit.

Église Notre-Dame-de-Galilée★

The church is typical of Romanesque architecture in southern Lorraine: a plain west front preceded by a belfry-porch with simple capitals. The originality of the nave lies in its groined vaulting, an unusual feature in such a large nave.

Musée Pierre-Noël – musée de la vie dans les Hautes-Vosges

13 Rue Saint-Charles. ⚓ 🕐 *May–Oct Tue–Sat 10am–noon, 2–6pm, Sun 2–6pm; Nov–Apr Tue–Sat 2–6pm (Wed 10am–noon, 2–6pm).* 🕐 *Mon and public holidays.* ⊛ *€5.* 📞 *03 29 51 60 35.*
The museum built on the site of the former bishop's palace includes an archaeological finds from La Bure, stuffed birds and sections devoted to the Vosges Forest, wood and textile crafts, agriculture and stock farming, ceramics and glassware. A room is devoted to Jules Ferry, a native of St-Dié. A Franco-German military exhibition has a display about pilot René Fonck, an ace of WWI, born near St-Dié. In addition, the museum houses the Goll collection of modern art.

Bibliothèque Victor Hugo

11 rue St-Charles. 🕐 *Tue 10am–6.30pm, Wed and Fri 10am–noon, 2–6.30pm, Thu 2–6.30pm, Sat 10am–noon, 2–6pm.* 🕐 *Public holidays.* 📞 *03 29 51 60 40.* *www.mediatheque.saint-die.eu.*
The library contains 230 000 works including 600 manuscripts and 140 incunabula (early printed books). Two treasures are the extremely rare *Cosmographiæ Introductio* and an illuminated gradual from the early 16C, with miniatures illustrating work in the mines during the Middle Ages.

Tour de la Liberté

🕐 *Apr–Oct 2–6pm; rest of year daily except Sun 2–6pm.* 🕐 *Mon and public holidays.* 📞 *03 29 45 45 04.*
The 36m Tower of Liberty, made of steel, canvas and cables, was erected in Paris for the Bicentenary of the Revolution in 1989 and moved to its present location a year later. It contains an unusual display of **jewellery** created by Heger de Lœwenfeld after paintings by Georges Braque, one of the initiators of Cubism. A spiral staircase leads up to a viewpoint, from where there is a stunning view of the town and the blue line of the Vosges mountains.

3C ore wash basin, Camp celtique de la Bure

© Denis Bringard/hemis.fr

EXCURSIONS

Camp celtique de la Bure

7.5km/4.6mi then 45min there and back on foot. Take N 59 and turn right 4km/2.5mi further on towards La Pêcherie then right onto the forest road to La Bure and left to La Crenée.

🚶 *Leave the car at the Col de la Crenée and take the path running along the ridge (starting behind a forest shelter) to the main entrance of the camp.*

This archaeological site has revealed traces of constant human occupation beginning roughly in 2000 BCE and ending in the 4C.

Occupying the western end (alt 582m) of a ridge known as the Crête de la Bure, the camp is elliptical and measures 340m by 110m diagonally. The outer wall consisted of an earth base (2.25m thick) and a wooden palisade interrupted by two gates and two posterns. The eastern approach of the camp was barred as early as the 1C BCE by a wall (murus gallicus, 7m thick) preceded by a ditch and from 300 onwards by a second Roman-type rampart. There were several pools in the camp (two of them dedicated to Gaulish goddesses) and important ironworks.

The archaeological finds are exhibited in the St-Dié Museum. From the camp, there are fine **views**★ *(viewing table)* of the Meurthe valley and St-Dié Basin.

Jardins de Callunes

In Ban-de-Sapt, 10km/6.2mi NE. Take D 49 from St-Die and then D 32 at St-Jean d'Ormont.

♿🕐*Apr Tue–Sun 10am–noon, 2–6pm; May daily 10am–noon, 2–6pm; Jun–Aug Tue–Fri 2–6pm, Sat–Sun 10am–noon, 2–6pm; Sept–Oct Thu–Sun 2–6pm.* ⊛€7.50. ℘03 29 58 94 94. *http://jardindecallunes.fr.*

These landscaped botanical gardens present 230 species of heather, as well as rhododendrons, azaleas, perennials and maple trees.

Provenchères sur-Fave

This town on the northern edge of the Parc Naturel Régional des Ballons de Vosges straddles de River Fave.

Col d'Urbeis★

The **observation tower**★ at Le Climont provides an exceptional panorama.

🚶 *1h30 on foot there and back. North of Climont, near the church, there is a sign pointing to the trail (steep climb).*

🚗 DRIVING TOUR

From St-Dié to the Donon pass

43km/27mi. Allow 2h30.

▷ Drive out of St-Dié along N 59.

Étival-Clairefontaine

This small town known for its paper mills lies on the banks of the Valdange, a tributary of the River Meurthe. The ruins of a paper mill dating from 1512 can still be seen on the riverside.

The **church**★ built in local Vosges sandstone has a transitional style (Romanesque to Gothic) nave and aisles (*Ask at the Tourist office in Senones about the possibility of guided visit.* ℘03 29 57 91 03. www.paysdesabbayes.com).

Moyenmoutier

The vast abbey **church** is one of the finest Baroque religious buildings in the Vosges (🚶 *Ask at the Tourist office in Senones about the possibility of guided visit. ℰ03 29 57 91 03. www.paysdesabbayes.com*).

Senones

This small town grew up near a Benedictine abbey. From 1751 to 1793, it was the capital of the principality of Salm, a sovereign state.

Senones has guarded a few princely residences and 18C mansions. The **former abbey** has a fine 18C stone staircase with wrought-iron banisters, which used to lead to the apartments where Voltaire stayed in 1754.

▶ From Senones, drive N along D 424 to La Petite-Raon (2km/1.2mi) then turn left onto D 49.

The forest road, which prolongs D 49, runs along the valley of the River Rabodeau. The **Col de Prayé** marked the old border between France and Germany. The road reaches the **Col du Donon** (*alt 727m 🔖 see Massif du DONON*).

ADDRESSES

🏨 STAY

😊😊 **Chambre d'hôte Le Bout du Chemin** – *6 rte d'Hadremont, 88580 Saulcy-sur-Meurthe. 4.5km/2.7mi S of St-Dié on N 415 towards Colmar. ℰ03 29 50 90 13. Closed Nov.🚭. 5 rooms. Reservation essential. Meals 😊.* The rooms in this B&B just outside St-Dié all have private terraces, ideal for looking at the wildlife that includes deer and squirrels. An attractive lounge has a fireplace and piano.

😊😊 **Hôtel Le Haut Fer** – *Rougiville, 88100 Taintrux. 6km/3.75 W of St-Dié on N 420 and minor road. ℰ03 29 55 03 48. Closed 1–10 Jan, Sun except Jul–Aug and public holidays. 16 rooms. Restaurant 😊.* This 1960s hotel is built outside the village on the site of a sawmill. The rooms are old-fashioned but well kept. There are a swimming pool, two tennis courts and a restaurant serving regional cuisine.

🍴 EAT

😊😊 **Voyageurs** – *22 r. d'Hellieule, 88100 Saint-Dié-des-Vosges. ℰ03 29 56 21 56. www.restaurant-des-voyageurs.fr. Closed Sun evening and Mon.* Some of the tables in this bright restaurant have a view of the extraordinary Tour de la Liberté. The decor is pastel-toned and contemporary. Traditional cooking and good choice of wines by the glass.

ON THE TOWN

Le FBI – *82 r. d'Alsace. ℰ03 29 55 09 81. Open Tue–Thu 6pm–3am, Fri–Sat 6pm–4am. Closed Mon.* This popular intimate bar is decorated with gleaming copperware, mahogany panelling and red velvet seats.

EVENTS AND FESTIVALS

Crayfish festival – *Mid-Jun in Etival-Clairefontaine.*

Relieving of the Guard of the Princes of Salm – *Some Sun mornings in Jul and Aug. ℰ03 29 57 91 03. www.paysdesabbayes.com.*

RECREATION

Pisciculture Ste-Odile – *27 r. Ste-Odile, 88480 Étival-Clairefontaine. 10km/6.25mi NE of St-Dié, towards St-Rémy on D 424. ℰ03 29 41 40 83. http://picard.thibault.free.fr. Open Tue–Sun 7am–8pm. Closed 2nd fortnight Jan.* A fish farm that raises trout, char, pike and other fish and which also creates all kinds of wonderful dishes with them. Rods can be hired for catching your own fish.

Papeteries de Clairefontaine – *19 r. de l'Abbaye, 88480 Étival-Clairefontaine. ℰ03 29 42 42 42. www.papiers-clairefontaine. com. Mon afternoon, Tue and Thu, Fri morning. Closed Jul 15–Sept, Wed and weekends.* Learn about paper-making on a guided tour at this papermill belonging to the famous stationers. The smell of exercise books will take you back to your school days.

Upper Thur valley viewed from the ruins of Wildenstein Castle

The Thur valley★

Haut-Rhin

⚲ **Michelin Map:** Michelin Local map 315: F-8 to H-10.
▷ **Location:** In the Vosges massif west of Mulhouse.

This large glaciated valley is a busy industrial area. While the upper Thur valley and the Urbès vale have remained rural with pasture- and forest-covered hillsides, the lower Thur valley is sprinkled with small towns that have a long-standing tradition in the textile industry.

🚗 DRIVING TOURS

INDUSTRIAL VALLEY

From Thann to Husseren-Wesserling
12km/7.5mi. About 30min.

Thann★ – ⚲*See THANN.*

▷ Drive NW out of Thann along N 66.

Willer-sur-Thur
The D 13BVI branches off to join the scenic Route des Crêtes, leading to the Grand Ballon (alt 1424m), the highest summit in the Vosges.

Moosch
A cemetery on the eastern slope contains the graves of almost 1 000 French soldiers killed in WWI.

St-Amarin
The **Musée Serret et de la vallée de St-Amarin** (🕐*May–Sept Wed–Mon 2-6pm.* ✆€3.50. ✆ *03 89 38 24 66; www.museeserret.fr)* covers local history through prints and paintings, headdresses, weapons, wrought-iron and emblems of brotherhoods.

Husseren-Wesserling★
The town is home to an important printed-fabric factory. The **Musée du Textile et des Costumes de Haute-Alsace** (👥🚻♿🕐*Check website for seasonal variations in opening hours both for the gardens and the museum.* 🕐*1 and 11 Nov, 25 and 31 Dec.* ✆€7– €9 (child 16–18, €3.50– €4.50). ✆*03 89 38 28 08. www.parc-wesserling.fr)* is housed in an old industrial building in the heart of a vast park. The museum deals with three main themes; from raw material to fabric, the history of the great industrial families, and the evolution of women's fashion.

UPPER VALLEY★

From Husseren-Wesserling to Grand Ventron★

46km/29mi. About 2h.

The upper Thur valley is dotted with granite knolls spared by glaciation. Three of these knolls overlook **Oderen**. From the southern approach to the village, there is a fine view of the escarpments of the Fellering woods. A fourth knoll, the forested Schlossberg, situated upstream, is crowned by the **ruins of Wildenstein castle**.

▷ In Kruth, turn left onto D 13B1.

Cascade St-Nicolas★

A succession of small waterfalls drop to the bottom of a lovely deep vale with densely forested slopes.

▷ Return to Kruth.

Between Kruth and Wildenstein, the road runs to the right of Schlossberg through a narrow passage where the Thur once flowed. Beyond Wildenstein, the road rises towards the Col de Bramont, offering a beautiful vista of the Thur valley then enters the forest.

Col de Bramont

Alt 956m.

The pass is situated on the main ridge of the Vosges.

▷ The access road branches off at the pass. Turn left onto the forest road (8km/5mi) via the Col de la Vierge on to the Chaume du Grand Ventron.

Grand Ventron★★

From the top (alt 1 204m), there is a vast **panorama★★** of the valley and the Vosges summits, including Hohneck, Grand Ballon and Ballon d'Alsace.

URBÈS VALE

11km/7mi. About 30min.

▷ The N 66 from Husseran-Wesserling starts along the Thur valley then enters the Urbès vale.

See d'Urbès

🅿 *Parking on the lake shore (signpost).*
The depression in which the lake (or see) is situated, was scooped out by the glacier that carved the Thur valley.
🚶 A marked path *(1h30)*, dotted with explanatory panels about local flora, fauna and traditional activities, explains this remarkable landscape. The road then rises gently towards the Col de Bussang, affording lovely views of the Thur valley and the surrounding heights.

Col de Bussang – 🚗 *See parc naturel régional des BALLONS DES VOSGES.*

From the pass, it is possible to drive down the upper Moselle valley (🚗 *see Remiremont*).

Lorraine's Iron and Steel Industry

The iron-ore deposits, located in the upper reaches of the Moselle, extend over a distance of 120km/75mi from the Haye forest to Luxemburg. In just over 100 years, three billion tonnes of minette, a type of ore with a relatively low iron content (about 33%) have been extracted; peak production was reached in 1962 with 62 million tons. There was a subsequent decline owing to competition from imported ore, richer in iron content, and to a drop in traditional outlets. The mines closed down one after the other; the closure of the Roncourt mine in August 1993 put an end to the mining activity in the area, with the exception of the Bure-Tressange site (4km/2.5mi east of Aumetz), which exports its ore to Luxemburg via an underground route.

Having diversified its production and invested heavily in new technology, the steel industry has now regained a certain competitiveness. Thus the Usinor-Sacilor group ranks third in the world. The area has also turned to other industries such as the car industry and nuclear energy.

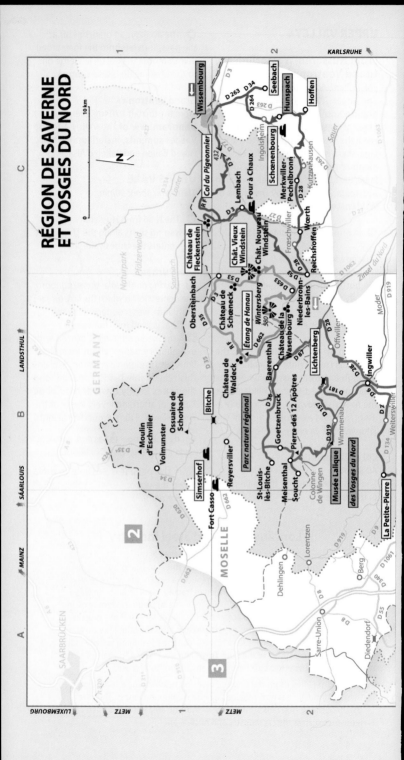

RÉGION DE SAVERNE
ET VOSGES DU NORD

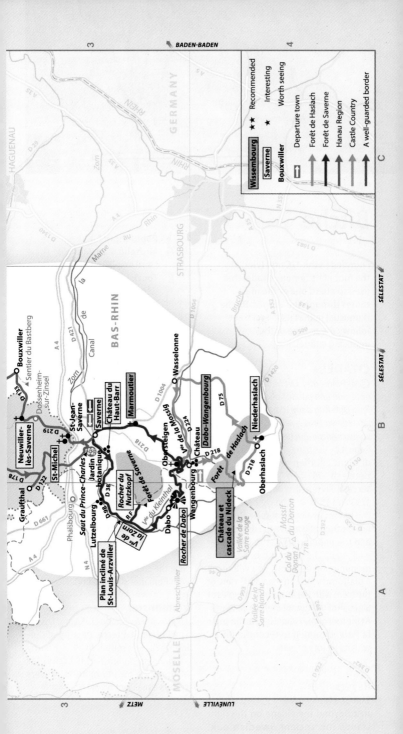

BADEN-BADEN

Wissembourg

Saverne

Bouxwiller

↑ Departure town

★★ Recommended

★ Interesting

★ Worth seeing

Forêt de Haslach

Forêt de Saverne

Hanau Region

Castle Country

A well-guarded border

GERMANY

HAGUENAU

BAS-RHIN

STRASBOURG

SÉLESTAT

SÉLESTAT

Bouxwiller
Sentier du Bastberg

Dossenheim-sur-Zinsel

Neuwiller-lès-Saverne

St-Michel

Grauffthal

St-Jean-Saverne

Saverne

Château du Haut-Barr

Marmoutier

Wasselonne

Jardin botanique

Saut du Prince-Charles

Rocher du Nutzkopf

Forêt de Saverne

Obersteigen

Vee de la Mossig

Château

Dabo-Wangenbourg

Niederhaslach

Lutzelbourg

Vee de la Zorn

Vee du Kleinthal

Wangenbourg

Forêt de Haslach

Plan incliné de St-Louis-Arzviller

Dabo

Rocher de Dabo

Château et cascade du Nideck

Oberhaslach

Abreschwiller

Vallée de la Sarre rouge

Massif du Donon

Col du Donon

Vallée de la Sarre blanche

MOSELLE

METZ

LUNÉVILLE

221

Citadel of Bitche

Bitche

Moselle

Founded in the 17C and lying at the foot of its famous citadel that used to guard one of the main routes through the Vosges, Bitche is unusual in that its main street follows the outline of the imposing citadel.

CITADEL★

🕐 *Mid-Mar–mid-Oct Mon–Sat 10am–6pm, Sun and public holidays 10am–7pm (Jul–Aug daily 10am–7pm).* ⚭€10. 📞 *03 87 96 18 82.*
www.citadelle-bitche.com.
Rebuilt by Vauban c. 1680, subsequently dismantled, then rebuilt once more between 1741 and 1754, the citadel successfully repelled Prussian attacks in 1793 and 1870–71. Today, there remain the impressive walls of red sandstone (visible from afar above the dense trees) and the underground structure. After walking up the ramp and beneath the monumental doorway, you will reach a platform which offers a 360° view of the town with the armoured steeples of Simershof (Maginot Line) to the west.
At the foot of the citadel is a **Jardin pour la Paix**, designed to reconcile Bitche with its history of wars.

EXCURSIONS
Reyersviller
5km/3mi W along N 62.
Just beyond the village on the right stands the ancient **Swedish oak**;

> ▶ **Population:** 5 440.
> 🎇 **Michelin Map:** Michelin Local map 307: P-4.
> 🄸 **Tourist Office:** 2 Avenue Général de Gaulle, 57230 Bitche. 📞03 87 06 16 16. www. tourisme-paysdebitche.fr.
> ◑ **Location:** Bitche, 21km/13mi from the German border and 80km/49.7mi from Strasbourg.

according to legend, the invading Swedes used it as a gallows during the Thirty Years War.

Simserhof★ –
ℹ *see Ligne MAGINOT.*

Ossuaire de Schorbach
6km/3.7mi NW along D 962 and D 162B to the left.
Near the church there is a small ossuary with Romanesque arcading.

Volmunster
11km/6.8mi NW along D 35A and D 34.
The **Église St-Pierre**, destroyed during WWII, was rebuilt in 1957. Nearby (*4km/2.5mi, signposted*) is **Eschviller Mill**, now a museum; an inn offers visitors a pleasant break.

Marmoutier ★

Bas-Rhin

Marmoutier's former abbey church is one of the most remarkable examples of Romanesque architecture in Alsace.

A BIT OF HISTORY

The abbey was founded in 590 by St Leobard, a disciple of St Columba (*see Luxeuil-les-Bains*).

In the 8C, it was named Maurmunster after one of its abbots, Maur. By the 14C, craftsmen and farmers lived in the shadow of the abbey and one of the oldest Jewish communities in Alsace was most probably invited by the abbots to deal with the abbey's trading activities. In 1792, during the Revolution, the abbey was abolished and the monks dispersed.

From **Sindelsberg** (*1.5km/0.9mi NW along the old Saverne road and a small surfaced road on the left*), there is a lovely bird's-eye view of Marmoutier.

Abbey church★★

May–Oct 9am–noon, 2–6pm (rest of year 4.30pm). ℘03 88 71 46 84.

The **west front★★** (*See Introduction: Art and Culture*) is the most interesting

▶ **Population:** 2 774.
◔ **Michelin Map:** Michelin Local map 315: I-4.
▯ **Tourist Office:** 50 rue du couvent, 67440 Marmoutier. ℘03 88 71 46 84. www.pointdorgue.eu.
▷ **Location:** Marmoutier is 6km/3.7mi south of Saverne on N4 and accessible off the A4-E25 Paris-Metz-Strasbourg motorway, Saverne exit.

part of the edifice. Built in local red sandstone, it consists of a heavy square belfry and two octagonal corner towers.

The porch has a central ribbed vault with a barrel vault on either side. The narthex, surmounted by several domes, is the only Romanesque part of the interior.

The transept houses some funeral monuments built in 1621 and the chancel contains beautiful carved wooden furniture: stalls in Louis XV style with charming angels and four canopies surmounted by foliage and branches. The organ, built by Silbermann in 1710, is one of the finest in the whole of Alsace.

Marmoutier with the abbey church

© CIP Point d'Orgue Tourisme et Culture/Office de Tourisme du Pays de Saverne

Neuwiller-lès-Saverne★

Bas-Rhin

Situated in the forested foothills of the northern Vosges mountains, this pleasant village has several fine balconied houses and two interesting churches.

SIGHTS
Église St-Pierre-et-St-Paul★

The former abbey church of one of the wealthiest abbeys in Alsace, the original church was remodelled in the 9C to receive the relics of the bishop of Metz, St Adelphus. The chancel, transept and first bay of the nave were built in the 12C. Two doorways on the north side face a vast square surrounded by canons' houses: on the right, a 13C doorway, framed by the statues of St Peter and St Paul, and on the left a 12C doorway with a fine tympanum depicting Christ giving his blessing.

Interior

🕐*Mar–mid-Nov, 8am–7pm.*
👁*Guided tours available of the crypt and the upper basilica (with tapestries of St-Adelphes). Contact the parish priest:* ✆*03 88 70 00 51.*
At the west end of the south aisle, the 13C tomb of St Adelphus rests on top of

- **Population:** 1 147.
- **Michelin Map:** Michelin Local map 315: I-4. Also see Parc naturel régional des VOSGES DU NORD.
- **Tourist Office:** 68 rue du Général-Goureau, 67340 Ingwiller. ✆03 88 89 23 45.
- **Location:** On the D 219, 13km/8.1mi north of Saverne.

eight tall columns. The south transept contains a 15C seated Virgin Mary★. The north transept houses a polychrome Holy Sepulchre dating from 1478. Above the group formed by the three Marys carrying perfume vases and surrounding Christ's body, a niche contains a 14C statue of the **Virgin Mary★**.
The **superposed chapels★** were built in the 11C on identical plans. The capitals of the lower chapel are plain whereas of the upper chapel, dedicated to St Sebastian, are carved with beautiful motifs. In addition, this chapel houses remarkable 15C **tapestries★★**, which depict St Adelphus' life and his miracles.

Église St-Adelphe

This church is characteristic of the transition between the Romanesque and Gothic styles (12C–13C).

Niederbronn-les-Bains⚜⚜

Bas-Rhin

Lying in the heart of a hilly area, this ancient spa town is a pleasant holiday resort and the ideal starting point for hikes and excursions in the Parc naturel régional des Vosges du Nord.

A BIT OF HISTORY
Founded by the Romans c 48 BCE and destroyed in the 5C, when barbarian

- **Population:** 4 423.
- **Michelin Map:** Michelin Local map 315: J-3. Also see Parc naturel régional des VOSGES DU NORD
- **Tourist Office:** 6 pl. de l'Hôtel-de-Ville. ✆03 88 80 89 70. www.niederbronn.com.
- **Location:** In the Northern Vosges Regional Park, 50km/31.1mi north of Strasbourg.

tribes swept across Western Europe, the town grew up around its mineral springs. It was restored in the 16C by Count Philip of Hanau; his work was continued in the 18C by the Dietrich family. In the second half of the 19C, the resort became popular and 3 000 people took the waters in 1869. The Dietrich metalworks prospered during the same period and today is the city's main employer.

VISIT

There are two springs:

✢ **Source Romaine** (Roman spring) which gushes forth in the town centre, in front of the municipal casino, recommended for various forms of rheumatism

✢ **Source Celtic** (Celtic spring) relatively low in mineral content, bottled since 1989

SIGHTS
Maison de l'Archéologie des Vosges du Nord

44 av. Foch. ♿⏱*Mar–Oct daily except Tue and Sat 2–5pm; Nov–Feb Sun 2–5pm.* ⏱*1 Jan, 25 Dec.* ✆*03 88 80 36 37.*
Modern display of local archaeological finds. One room is devoted to cast-iron stoves, which have been the speciality of Niederbronn for over 300 years.

Château de Wasenbourg

W of the town. 15min on foot there and back.
From the station, follow the alleyway lined with lime trees. Walk under the bypass and turn left onto the sentier promenade et découvertes (discovery trail), which leads to the ruins of the 13C castle. Nearby there are traces of a Roman temple.

ADDRESSES

🛏STAY

🍴🍴**Hôtel Cully** – *R. de la République.* ✆*03 88 09 01 42. Closed Feb 7–28, Dec 20–Jan 3. 40 rooms. Restaurant* 🍴🍴*.* In a busy street not far from the town centre, this hotel consists of two buildings separated by a lovely flower-decked terrace. The spacious, well-kept rooms in the main building are the best. Alsace and Italian cuisine served outdoors in summer.

🍴EAT

🍴🍴🍴**Anthon** – *40 rue Principale, 67510 Obersteinbach – 14km/8.75mi N of Niederbronn on D 653 and D 53.* ✆*03 88 09 55 01. www.restaurant-anthon.fr. Closed Tue–Wed and Jan.* This pretty red-painted house is a lovely place in a small picturesque village in the Vosges. The fine rotunda dining room has large French windows leading into the garden, where you can eat in summer. Two of the bedrooms have interesting Alsatian box-beds.

ON THE TOWN

Villa Le Parc (au Casino de Niederbronn) – *Pl. des Thermes.* ✆*03 88 80 84 84. www.lucienbarriere.com. Open daily Jul–Aug 1 times vary; rest of the year Tue–Sat. Closed in Feb and 24 Dec.* In summer the casino orchestra plays daily on the terrace of this restaurant where dinner with dancing also takes place. Enjoy the music while relaxing in the brasserie. Concerts every night in Jul–Aug. Colonial-style interior.

Ferme Charles-Dangler – *Lieu-dit Haul – 6km SE of Niederbronn in Haguenau direction on D 662, 67110 Gundershoffen.* ✆*03 88 72 85 73. Open daily 10am–noon, 2–8pm.* Accompanied treks (one to eight hours) for all levels on one of the farm's ten horses, to enjoy some of the 360km/225mi of waymarked paths around the town.

Établissement thermal – *Pl. des Thermes.* ✆*03 88 80 30 70. Feb–Dec daily 7am–5pm. Closed Sun.* The spa proposes balneotherapy and fitness cures.

La Petite-Pierre★

Bas-Rhin

A prosperous medieval town, later fortified by Vauban, Louis XIV's military engineer, La Petite-Pierre, also known as Lützelstein or Parva Petra, is a popular summer resort in the heart of the forested massif of the low Vosges and the starting point of more than 100km/62mi of marked footpaths.

▶ **Population:** 646.
🚌 **Michelin Map:** Michelin Local map 315: H-3.
🚩 **Tourist Office:** 2 rue du Château, 67290 La Petite-Pierre. ℰ03 88 70 42 30. www.ot-paysdelapetite pierre.com.
▶ **Location:** Situated in the Parc Naturel Régional des Vosges du Nord, 55km/34.2mi NW of Strasbourg.

OLD TOWN

▶ The old town is reached up a steep path; then follow rue du Château.

Église
The belfry and the nave were rebuilt in the 19C, but the Gothic chancel dates back to the 15C.

Maison des Païens
This Renaissance house in the gardens of the town hall was built in 1530 on the site of a Roman watchtower.

Chapelle St-Louis
Built in 1684 and once reserved for the garrison, the chapel now houses the unusual **Musée du Sceau alsacien** (Museum of Alsatian Heraldry) (🕑*Mar–Jun and Sept–Dec Sat–Sun and public holidays 10am–noon, 2–5pm; Jul–Aug daily except Mon 10am–noon, 2–6pm.*

🕑*Jan–Feb, 25 Dec. ℰ03 88 70 48 65; http://musee-sceau.com).* It illustrates the history of Alsace through reproductions of the seals that used to be the distinguishing marks of cities, important families, crafts or guilds, religious orders or chapters.

Château and Maison du Parc
Built in the 12C, the castle was remodelled several times, at the instigation of Georg Hans von Veldenz, the Count Palatine of the Rhine region. Today it houses the **Maison du parc** (🕑*Daily except Mon–Tue 10am–noon, 2–6pm. 🕑Jan, 24–25 and 31 Dec. ℰ03 88 01 49 59. www.parc-vosges-nord.fr).* Displayed in six thematic multimedia rooms, the exhibition helps you to discover the historic, cultural and technical heritage of the park.

▶ Follow rue des Remparts for views of the surrounding countryside.

Musée des Arts et Traditions populaires
♿🕑*Same hours as Musée du Sceau.* 🕑*Jan–Feb, 25 Dec. ℰ03 88 70 48 65. www.musee-sceau.com.*
The small museum of folk art and customs, housed in a 16C Magasin or warehouse, displays an interesting collection of cake tins, such as *springerle* (aniseed cake) and *lebkuche* (gingerbread).

▶ Continue along rue des Remparts back to rue du Château.

© Laure HERRMANN/ADT

Springerle

Château des Rohan

Saverne★

Bas-Rhin

The 16C peasant rebellion ended tragically in Saverne when the Duke of Lorraine besieged the town; he promised to spare the lives of the 20 000 peasants if they came out unarmed, but when they did, they were massacred to the last one by the duke's soldiers. Today, Saverne is a rather more peaceful town known for its annual rose festival and its marina.

A BIT OF HISTORY

From the 13C to the Revolution, Saverne belonged to the bishops of Strasbourg. These princes stayed in the castle and sometimes welcomed royal visitors (Louis XIV in 1681, Louis XV in 1744). Atfer being burnt down in 1779, it was rebuilt by **Louis de Rohan**, who lived there in lavish style.

SIGHTS

Château★

The elegant red-sandstone château of the house of Rohan was rebuilt in the Louis XVI style and stands in a beautiful park bordered by the Marne-Rhine canal. It served as barracks between 1870 and 1944. The south façade is visible from the square; to see the attractive north façade, you must walk through the gate and along the right side of the castle.

▶ **Population:** 11 883.
Michelin Map: Michelin Local map 315: I-4.
Tourist Office: 37 Grand'Rue, 67700 Saverne. ℘03 88 91 80 47. www.tourisme-saverne.fr.
Location: Situated on the Zorn river and the Marne-Rhine canal, 45 km/28mi northwest of Strasbourg.

The north **façade★★**, which is over 140m long is particularly impressive with fluted pilasters and a peristyle supported by eight Corinthian columns.

Musée

Jan–mid-Jun and mid-Sept–23 Dec Mon–Fri 2–6pm, Sat–Sun and public holidays 10am–noon, 2–6pm; mid-Jun–mid-Sept daily 10am–noon, 2–6pm. *Tue, 1 May, 1 Nov, 25 Dec.* €3.30. ℘03 88 71 63 95.

The museum contains archaeological finds from the Gallo-Roman period, collections devoted to the town's history: medieval sculpture, pieces from nearby castles (Haut-Barr, Geroldseck, Wangenbourg) and mementos of the House of Rohan, as well as the bequest of feminist politician Louise Weiss.

Roseraie

&,ⒸLate May–Aug daily 10am–7pm;
Sept 2–6pm. ⒸOct–late May. ☞€2.50.
📞03 88 71 83 33.
www.roseraie-saverne.fr.
550 varieties of rose grow in this splendid park on the bank of the River Zorn.

Half-timbered houses★

Two particularly fine timber-framed
houses (17C) stand on either side of the
town hall. Others can be seen at No.
96 Grand'Rue, on the corner of rue des
Églises and rue des Pères and on the
corner of rue des Pères and rue Poincaré.

Vieux château

The old castle, which was the former
residence of the bishops, is now an
administrative building. The stairtower
has a beautiful Renaissance doorway.

Église paroissiale

Rebuilt in the 14C and 15C, the parish
church has a 12C Romanesque belfry-
porch. In the nave are a pulpit (1495)
by Hans Hammer and a 16C high-relief
marble sculpture representing Mary and
John mourning Christ.
The chapel of the Holy Sacrament in the
north aisle is adorned with a 16C Pietà
and a wooden bas-relief, depicting the
Assumption. The 14C to 16C windows
illustrate the Adoration of the Magi and
scenes from the Passion. Gallo-Roman
and Frankish gravestones can be seen
in the garden adjacent to the church.

Ancien cloître des Récollets

The cloisters, built in 1303, have lovely
red-sandstone Gothic arcades and nine
murals (added in the 17C, restored) on
the right of the entrance.

EXCURSIONS

Jardin botanique du col de Saverne

ⒸDaily May–Aug, 10am–6pm; Apr
and Sept Sat–Sun and public holidays
2–6pm. 📞03 88 91 21 00.
www.jardin-botanique-saverne.org.
Situated at an altitude of 335m, this
botanical garden (2.3ha) includes an
arboretum, an Alpine garden, a small
bog and numerous species of fern and
orchid.

Saut du Prince Charles

Take forest track from botanical garden.
According to legend, a prince jumped
over the red-sandstone cliff with his
horse. There is a fine view of the foothills
of the Vosges and the Plaine d'Alsace.

St-Jean-Saverne

5km/3mi N.
The village church is all that remains of a
Benedictine abbey founded in the early
12C. It has an 18C belfry over an interesting Romanesque doorway. At the
entrance to the choir are Romanesque
capitals carved with foliage.
A road through the forest leads to the
Chapelle St-Michel (ⒸJun–Sept daily
1–6pm; rest of the year Sun 1–6pm.
ⒸDec–Feb), which dates from the same
period as the abbey. Follow a path on
the right of the chapel to the end of
the rocky spur from where the view★
extends over the hills of Alsace to the
Black Forest. The platform forms a circular hollow known as the École des Sorcières (witches' school). On the south
side of the chapel, 57 steps lead down
to a path on the left which leads to a
cave known as the Trou des Sorcières
(witches' hole).

Château du Haut-Barr

5km/3mi. From Saverne, follow D 102
which offers views of the Black Forest.
Turn onto D 171 winding through the
forest. Park the car near the entrance
of the castle. &,also see Parc naturel
régional des VOSGES DU NORD.
Solidly camped on three huge sandstone rocks overlooking the valley of
the River Zorn and the Plaine d'Alsace,
the 12C castle was completely remodelled by Bishop Manderscheidt of Strasbourg who, legend claims, founded the
Brotherhood of the Horn dedicated to
drinking Alsace wine out of the horn of
an aurochs!
A paved ramp leads from the main gate
to a second gateway. Past the chapel,

Saverne town

© Jürgen Wackenhut/imageBROKER/age fotostock

there is a terrace *(viewing table)*, from which the **view**★ extends towards Saverne, the Kochersberg hills and the Black Forest in the distance.

A metal staircase *(64 steps)*, fixed to the rock face, gives access to the first rock. Return to the restaurant and, immediately beyond it, go up 81 steps to reach the second rock linked by a footbridge, known as the Pont du Diable, to the third rock. This **view**★★ is even better as it offers a 360° panorama including the Vosges mountains, the Zorn valley (through which flows the canal linking the Marne and the Rhine), the Lorraine plateau and, in clear weather, the Strasbourg cathedral spire.

A reconstruction of **Claude Chappe's telegraph tower** stands on its original site; as a relay tower of the famous optical telegraph invented in 1794 by the engineer Chappe, it was used between Paris and Strasbourg from 1798 to 1852. The small **museum** includes an audio-visual presentation (🕐*mid-May–mid-Sept Tue–Sun 1–6pm; ℘03 88 52 98 99*).

ADDRESSES

🛏 STAY

🍽🛏 **Chez Jean** – *3 r. de la Gare.– ℘03 88 91 10 19. www.chez-jean.com. Closed 20 Dec–10 Jan. 40 rooms. Restaurant 🍽🛏 (Closed Sun eve, and Mon).* A good place to stay in Saverne. The cosy, welcoming rooms have been renovated and have wood panelling. There is a choice of cuisine, between the regional dishes in the wine bar and a more elaborate menu in the restaurant.

🍽 EAT

🍽🛏 **Le Caveau de l'Escale** – *10 quai du Canal. ℘03 88 91 12 23. www.escale-saverne.fr. Closed Sat lunchtime, Tue evening and Wed.* A discreet-looking restaurant near the canal, where you can hire boats. Meals are served in the vaulted cellar, with regional cooking and *flammekueches* in the evening. Friendly atmosphere.

🍽🛏 **Au Bain** – *7 r. du Mar.-Leclerc – 67700 Haegen. 6km/3.75mi S of Château du Haut-Barr on D 10 and D 102. ℘03 88 71 02 29. www.restaurant-au-bain.fr.* The younger generation of proprietors has transformed this old village bistro into a restaurant. It is simply decorated, with paper tablecloths and a classic menu, except on Sunday nights, when it's tarte flambée for everyone.

Parc naturel régional des Vosges du Nord ★★

Moselle, Bas-Rhin

The northern Vosges are relatively low yet often steep mountains which differ considerably from the rest of the massif. The sandstone cover has been torn open by deep valleys and shaped into horizontal plateaux or rolling hills generally less than 500m high. Erosion has carved the sandstone crust into isolated jagged rocks reminiscent of towers, mushrooms or arches. Numerous fortresses still stand on the densely forested heights.

THE REGIONAL PARK

Created in 1975, the regional park aims to safeguard the natural heritage and preserve the quality of life. Forests (beech, oak, pine, spruce) cover more than 60% of the area.

Walks, riding tours, bike tours and nature excursions enable visitors to discover local flora and fauna and get an insight into the lifestyle and economic activities of the region, with its charming Alsatian villages and their picturesque traditions, as well as crystalworks, technical and folk museums and, of course, old castles full of mystery. The Parc naturel régional des Vosges du Nord has been designated by UNESCO as one of the biosphere's world reserves.

🚗 DRIVING TOURS

1 HANAU REGION

Round-trip from Saverne
125km/78mi. Allow 4h30.

Saverne★
See SAVERNE.

- 🔆 **Michelin Map:** Michelin Local map 315: I to J-3.
- ▷ **Location:** The park extends from the north of the Lorraine plateau to the Plaine d'Alsace and from the German border to the A 4 Metz-Strasbourg motorway.

▷ Soon after leaving Saverne via Ottersthal, D 115 crosses the green Muhlbach vale then passes beneath the motorway.

St-Jean-Saverne
SAVERNE: St-Jean-Saverne.
Just beyond St-Jean-Saverne, the ruins of **Haut-Barr Castle★** (*see SAVERNE: Château du Haut-Barr*) can be seen on a wooded height, and soon after the ruins of Griffon Castle.

▷ Turn left to Neuwiller-les-Saverne via Dossenheim-sur-Zinsel.

Neuwiller-lès-Saverne★
See NEUWILLER-LÈS-SAVERNE.

Bouxwiller
This small town was, until 1791, the capital of the county of Hanau-Lichtenberg, extending across the Rhine and the picturesque streets are lined with German Renaissance houses. Part of the ramparts have been restored. The **Protestant church** (*Jul–Aug Fri 3–6pm, Sat 10am–noon, 3–6pm, Sun 11am–noon, 3–6pm. 03 88 70 71 15*) contains a fine **pulpit★** in sculpted stone and painted wood, an organ by Silbermann, and a seigneurial box pew with ornate stuccowork.

The **Musée du pays de Hanau** (*Jul–mid-Sept Wed–Fri 10am–12.30pm, 2–6pm, Sat–Sun 2–6pm; mid-Sept–Jun Wed–Sun 2–6pm. Jan, Easter Sun, 1 May, 24–26 and 31 Dec. €4.50. 03 88 70 99 15. www.museedupaysde-hanau.eu*) houses collections of painted furniture, glassware from Bouxwiller, and reconstructions of interiors.

THE PRACTICAL PARK

Maison du Parc – Château de la Petite-Pierre, 67290 La Petite-Pierre. ✆03 88 01 49 59. www.parc-vosges-nord.fr.

Entertainment – The park is the venue for exhibitions and shows year-round: music, theatre, literary festival. Christmas markets liven up the area throughout December, notably at Bouxwiller. A free information brochure about activities and events taking place is available from the Maison du Parc.

Courses – From April to October, the Maison du Parc organises nature-discovery outings lasting a whole day and monitored by professionals or voluntary helpers.

Discovery trails – Brochures/guides containing information about discovery trails, the cultural heritage, the region's history and traditional villages, are available from the Maison du Parc.

The former synagogue (1842) is now the **Musée judéo-alsacien** (&🕐*Early Mar–Oct Tue–Fri, Sun and public holidays 10am–1pm, 2–6pm.* ⚏€6. 🕐*Mon and Sat, and during Jewish festivals.* ✆*03 88 70 97 17; http://judaisme.sdv.fr*) which illustrates the history and culture of Alsace's Jewish community.
🚶 A 6km/3.7mi geological trail *(information from tourist office)*, extremely rich in fossils, leads to the summit of Bastberg. The summit is also accessible by car from Imbsheim (from Bouxwiller, follow D 6 then turn right just before Imbsheim).

▶ From Bouxwiller, drive to Ingwiller via Niedersoultzbach.

Ingwiller
🚶 This village offers a free guided tour of the **Sentier botanique et poétique du Seelberg** (*Seelberg botanic trail, 2h. For information, call* ✆*03 88 89 23 45*).

▶ Take D 28, through Offwiller to Zinswiller and turn left onto D 141 along the north bank of the Zinsel between Offwiller forest and Niederbronn forest. Arnsbourg Castle is on the right.

Baerenthal
This charming village is situated on the north bank of the River **Zinsel**. It is possible to go round the Baerenthal lake, a nature reserve with an exceptionally rich flora. An observation tower makes

Bouxwiller houses

© Christian FLEITH/ADT

it possible to watch birds, particularly migratory species in spring and autumn. Between Baerenthal and Mouterhouse, the road follows the valley once dotted with metalworks belonging to the De Dietrich family, now almost all gone.

▶ Continue along D 36 to Lemberg.

The narrow road winds along the Breitenbach stream. On the right is the Mouterhouse forest.

St-Louis-lès-Bitche

This is the headquarters of the **cristalleries de St-Louis**, former royal crystal works founded in 1767. It today produces a variety of ornaments and tablewares (⏰*shop: Mon–Sat 10am–noon, 1.30–5pm. ℘03 87 06 40 04*).

▶ Rejoin D 37 and turn right.

Goetzenbruck

Glass-making is the main activity here including an important factory producing glasses for spectacles.

Meisenthal

In the centre of the village, the old glassworks (closed 1970) house the **Maison du verre et du cristal** (&⏰*Apr–Oct Wed–Mon 2–6pm. ☞€6. ℘03 87 96 91 51; http://site-verrier-meisenthal.fr*) glass and crystal museum.

Cristalleries de St-Louis

© Cristalleries de St-Louis/Office de Tourisme du Pays de Bitche

Soucht

2km/1.2mi from Meisenthal.
A former workshop contains the **Musée du Sabotier**, where you can watch clogs being made (&⏰*Apr–Oct daily except Tue 2–6pm. ☞€3.50. ℘03 87 96 25 58; www.museedusabotier.fr*).

▶ Return to D 37.

From the Colonne de Wingen, there is a fine view of the Meisenthal valley.

Pierre des 12 apôtres

This ancient standing stone was only carved in the 18C following a vow. Under the cross, one can see the 12 Apostles. Lalique crystalworks are situated near **Wingen-sur-Moder**.

▶ Turn left in Wimmenau onto D157.

Château de Lichtenberg

Follow the Lichtenberg high street prolonged by D 257 to the path leading to the castle and leave the car. ⏰*Apr–Jun and Sept daily except Wed 10am–6pm; Jul–Aug daily 10am–6pm; Mar and Oct–early Nov daily except Wed 10am–5pm. ☞€4. ℘03 88 89 98 72. www.chateaudelichtenberg.com.*
The castle, which has a 13C keep, was restored following shelling in the 1870 Franco-Prussian War.

▶ Follow D 113 SW via Sparsbach.

La Petite-Pierre★ –

&*See La PETITE-PIERRE.*

Graufthal

This hamlet of the Zinsel valley has **troglodyte houses** dug into the redsandstone cliffs (70m high); they were inhabited until 1958 (⏰*Jul–Aug daily 2–6pm; mid-Mar–Jun and Sept–mid-Nov Sun and public holidays 10am–noon, 2–6pm. ☞€2. ℘03 88 70 19 59; www. maisonsdesrochers-graufthal.fr*).

▶ Return to Saverne.

② CASTLE COUNTRY

Round-trip from Niederbronn-les-Bains
54km/34mi. Allow 2h30.

The area on the borders of the German palatinate, of Lorraine and Alsace is dotted with ruined castles built during the 12C and early 13C by the powerful dukes of Alsace, the Hohenstaufens, or by landowners who contested their authority.

Niederbronn-les-Bains⧧⧧
See NIEDERBRONN-LES-BAINS.

▷ Leave Niederbronn towards Philippsbourg. Opposite the ruins of Wasenbourg castle, turn right off N 62 then left onto a forest road.

Le Wintersberg
This (*580m*) is the highest summit of the Vosges du Nord. From the watch tower (112 steps), there is a fine panorama of the lower Vosges.

▷ The 6.5km/4mi forest road rejoins N 62; turn right then right again onto D 87 just beyond Philippsbourg to Falkenstein castle.

Château de Falkenstein★
45min on foot there and back. Park at the crossroads and follow the second path on the left (marked with blue triangles) for 15min go up a few steps and turn left then right. Go through a doorway, turn left and walk around the peak on which the castle stands.
The castle, built in 1128, was struck by lightning and damaged by fire in 1564. Go through another door to find the vast cave known as the Salle des Gardes (guard-room). You will notice several natural caves, where the rockface has been carved by streaming water, as well as several man-made caves. After a footbridge and steps, you will reach the top of the castle, where there is a fine **panorama★**. According to legend, the ghost of a cooper haunts the cellars at midnight and with a mallet, strikes a number of times corresponding to the number of casks of wine that will be produced during the year.

▷ Rejoin N 62, turn right 3km/1.9mi after Philippsbourg to Hanau Lake.

Étang de Hanau★
The lake has facilities for watersports and there are two waymarked footpaths: the **Sentier botanique de la tourbière** and the **Promenade de l'arche naturelle de Erbsenfelsen**.

▷ Follow the forest road between the lake and Waldeck castle to join D 35 which leads to Obersteinbach past the ruins of Lutzelhardt castle.

Obersteinbach
Picturesque village with timber-framed houses on red-sandstone bases.
On the way out, D 53 is overlooked by several ruins which probably formed part of a line of defence guarding Haguenau's imperial castle at the end of the 12C (*see HAGUENAU*).

▷ Turn left in Wineckerthal.

Châteaux de Windstein
Car park at the end of the left branch of the road by restaurant-hotel Aux Châteaux.
The two Windstein castles, standing 500m apart, were destroyed in 1676 by French troops commanded by Baron de Montclar. On the top of knoll **Vieux Windstein★** (*45min on foot there and back*) dates from the late 12C and is partly troglodyte. On another mound **Nouveau Windstein** (*30min on foot there and back*) dates from 1340 and has some lovely Gothic arches.

▷ Return to Niederbronn along D 653.

③ A WELL-GUARDED BORDER

Round-trip from Wissembourg
42km/26mi. Allow half a day

Wissembourg★★
See WISSEMBOURG.

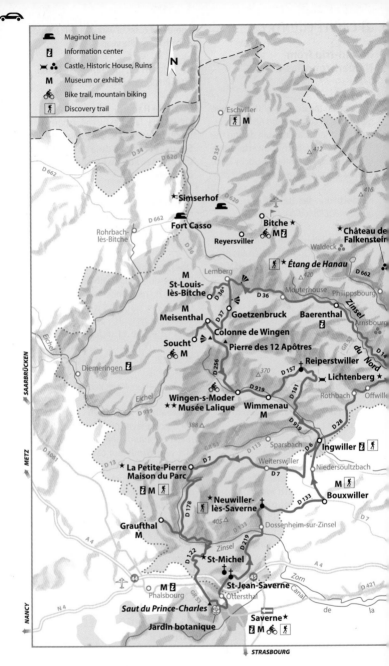

Col du Pigeonnier★ – Access on the left of the road coming from Climbach; 🚶 30min walk there and back. After about 15min you will see a superb **view★** of the Plaine d'Alsace.

Château de Fleckenstein★
🕐 Apr–Jun daily 10am–5.30pm; Jul–Aug daily 10am–6pm; rest of year, see website for details. ⚿€4.50. ℘03 88 94 28 52. www.fleckenstein.fr.

PARC NATUREL RÉGIONAL DES VOSGES DU NORD

The castle was part of the 12C defences of the northern border of the duchy of Alsace and was destroyed in 1680. The ruins occupy a remarkable position on a rock spur amid woods. Note the impres-sive square tower built against the main rock. Inside, stairs lead to several rooms hewn out of the rock, including the amazing Salle des chevaliers (Knights' Hall) with its central monolithic pillar, and then

Château de Fleckenstein

© Christian FLEITH/ADT

onto the platform (8m wide) where the seigneurial residence stood.

Lembach

This charming small town has some fine old houses, wash-houses, inns. Viewpoints around the village have explanatory panels on themes such as urbanism, geology and botany.

1km/0.6mi along the road to Woerth is the entrance of the **Ouvrage du Four à Chaux** (*see Ligne MAGINOT*).

▶ In Lembach, take the minor road along the Sauer to Reichshoffen.

The road goes through villages caught up in the 1870 Franco-Prussian War. Numerous roadside monuments commemorate the sacrifice of French and German soldiers killed in the fighting.

Reichshoffen

The village witnessed an heroic cavalry charge (6 August 1870), which ended in a massacre at nearby Morsbronnles-Bains.

Woerth

In the castle, the **Musée de la Bataille du 6 août 1870** contains uniforms, weapons, documents and pictures and a large diorama of the battle.

The **Sentier des Turcos** (starting just after the Alko France factory, on the

left, on the way out of Woerth towards Lembach) is a history trail (2km/1.2mi) explains the main stages of the battle.

Merkwiller-Pechelbronn

This was the main centre of the oil fields of northern Alsace. All extracting operations stopped in 1970 but the small **Musée français du Pétrole** (2.30–6pm: Apr–Jun and Sept–Oct Thu–Sun; Jul–Aug daily except Mon. €5. 03 88 80 91 08. www.musee-du-petrole. com) illustrates the main aspects of the industry.

Hoffen★

This traditional village nestles round its church and its strange town hall supported by three wooden pillars. A lime tree planted during the Revolution stands next to the old public well.

Hunspach★★

White timber-framed houses with canopied façades line the streets of this agricultural village (farmyards, orchards, fountains), regarded as one of the most beautiful in France.

Seebach★

This pretty flower-decked village has typical Alsatian canopied timber-framed houses surrounded by gardens.

ADDRESSES

🍴 STAY AND 🍽️ EAT

🍴 **Auberge des Mésanges** – *2 r. du Tiseur, 57960 Meisenthal.* *℘03 87 96 92 28. www.aubergedesmesanges.fr. 20 rooms. Restaurant🍴🍽️(closed from Sun eve to Tue lunch).* A good place to stay or eat after visiting the glass and crystal museum. The rooms are well equipped and impeccably kept. Simple, inexpensive meals, with *flammekueches* and pizzas starring at weekends.

🍴🍽️ **La Cour du Tonnelier** – *84 a Grand'rue, 67730 Bouxwiller.* *℘03 88 70 72 57. www.courdutonnelier.com. Closed Sun evening and Mon. 16 rooms. Restaurant🍴🍽️.* This pale pink house near the town centre conceals an impeccably run hotel. The rooms are decorated in warm colours, with lovely carpets and cherry wood furniture. The bathrooms are modern and functional. The small garden contains a swimming pool 🏊.

🍴🍽️ **Le Cheval Blanc** – *19 r. Principale, 67320 Graufthal.* *℘03 88 70 17 11. www. auchevalblanc.net. Closed Mon eve, Wed eve, and all day Tue.* This welcoming rustic inn remains faithful to regional cuisine. One dining room has a pretty faience stove.

🍴🍽️🍽️🍽️ **Auberge du Cheval Blanc** – *4 rte Wissembourg, 67510 Lembach.* *℘03 88 94 41 86. www.auchevalblanc.net. Closed all day Tue, Mon eve and Wed eve.* This old coaching inn offers a grand dining experience. Revisited Alsatian cuisine in this Michelin restaurant (🍴🍽️🍽️🍽️) with its fireplace and coffered ceiling, plus a simpler bistro🍴🍽️.

ON THE TOWN

Le Royal Palace – *20 r. Hochfelden, 67330 Kirrwiller, 4km/2.5 E of Bouxwiller.* *℘03 88 70 71 81. www.royal-palace.com. Times vary. Closed mid-Jul–Aug.* This glitzy cabaret is one of the biggest music halls in the country, pulling in the crowds from France and across the border.

Wangenbourg

Bas-Rhin

This charming summer resort is set amid meadows dotted with chalets and forests overlooked by the Schneeberg summit.
A tree-felling competition takes place on the Sunday following the 14 July celebrations.

VISIT
Castle ruins

The ruins are accessible on foot (15min there and back; leave the car in the parking area, 200m beyond the church; walk past a huge lime tree and follow a path which prolongs the main street).

The 13C and 14C castle belonged to Andlau abbey. The pentagonal keep and important sections of walls are still visible. A path, which partly runs along the castle moat, takes you round the huge sandstone outcrop crowned by the ruins.

▸ **Population:** 1 390.
⛊ **Michelin Map:** Michelin Local map 315: H-5.
🛈 **Tourist Office:** 32 avenue du Général de Gaulle, 67710 Wangenbourg-Engerthal. *℘03 88 87 33 50. www.suisse-alsace.fr.*
◖ **Location:** 40km/25mi west of Strasbourg by N4 and D224.

🚗 DRIVING TOURS

The picturesque **Dabo-Wangenbourg region**★★ lies on the border of Alsace and Lorraine.

FORÊT DE SAVERNE

78km/48.5mi round-trip N of Wangenbourg. Allow 3h30.

Obersteigen

This is a pleasant summer resort. The church marks the transition between the Romanesque and Gothic styles.

▶ Follow D 45 to Dabo.

The winding road enters a splendid forest and offers fine glimpses of the Rocher de Dabo, the fertile Kochersberg plateau and of the Plaine d'Alsace.

Rocher de Dabo★

Signposted Rocher St-Léon. ⓞ*Apr–Nov daily 10am–6pm.* ∞*€2.*
₰03 87 07 47 51. www.ot-dabo.fr.
This sandstone rock is crowned by two viewing tables and a chapel dedicated to St Léon (Leo IX). The **panorama★** from the top of the tower includes the main summits of the Vosges and the X-shaped village of Dabo.

Dabo

This summer resort lies in a very pleasant **setting★** in a forested area.

▶ Beyond Schaeferhof, bear left along D 45 and turn left again onto D 96 5km/3mi farther on.

On approaching Schaeferhof, one can see the hilltop village of Haselbourg.

Cristallerie de Vallerysthal

&ⓞ*Mon–Fri 10am–noon, 1–6pm, Sat–Sun and public holidays 10am–noon, 2–6pm.* ⓞ*1 Jan, 25 Dec.* ∞*No charge.*
₰03 87 25 62 04.
www.cristalleriedevallerysthal.fr.
In 1838, Baron Klinglin transferred the Plaine-de-Walsch glassworks here; the new works prospered employing up to 1 300 workers in 1914.

▶ Return to D 98C.

Rocher du Nutzkopf★

▶ Accessible by D 98D from Sparsbrod then a forest track on the left and finally a footpath signposted on the left (45min on foot there and back).

⚶ From the top (alt 515m) of this strange tabular rock, the **view★** extends to the Rocher de Dabo, the village of La Hoube and Grossthal valley.

▶ Return to D 98C then turn right onto D 98 which follows the Zorn valley.

Plan incliné de St-Louis-Arzviller★

&⚶*Guided tour with boat lift (30min):* ⓞ*Daily Apr–Jun and Sept–Oct 10am–5pm; Jul–Aug 10am–6pm.*
ⓞ*1 May.* ∞*€4.* *₰03 87 25 30 69.*
www.plan-incline.com.
It is best seen from D 98C. Inaugurated in 1969, this boat elevator is equipped with an inclined plane 108.65m long in order to clear the 44.55m drop. It replaced 17 locks which took a whole day to negotiate. Now, a 43m ferry truck going up sideways on rails transfers barges from one level to the other in 20min.

Vallée de la Zorn★

This pleasant wooded valley is the busiest route through the northern Vosges mountains. The ruins of the medieval **Château de Lutzelbourg** stand on a promontory; overlooking D 38–D 132.

Château du Haut-Barr★

&*See SAVERNE: Château du Haut-Barr.*

Saverne★ – &*See SAVERNE.*

Marmoutier★★ –
&*See MARMOUTIER.*

FORÊT DE HASLACH
44km/27mi round-trip S of Wangenbourg. Allow 2h30.

Beyond Wolfsthal, D 218 climbs up to the beautiful **Haslach forest**. A pleasant drive leads to the forest lodge then past a stele on the left, which commemorates the building of the road. Farther on (500m), the road starts winding down towards Oberhaslach.

Nideck waterfall

Château and Cascade du Nideck★★

Park in the car park below the forest lodge and follow signposted footpath (1h15 on foot there and back).

A 13C tower and 14C keep, standing in a romantic **setting★★**, are all that remains of two castles destroyed by fire in 1636. From the top of the tower and the keep, there are fine views.

◗ Walk to the right of the keep and follow a path on the left to the waterfall. Bear right beyond a wooden shelter and a small bridge to the viewpoint (very dangerous in spite of the railing).

From the belvedere, there is a splendid **view★★** of the glacial valley and the wooded chasm into which the waterfall drops from the top of a porphyry wall. To see the waterfall, continue past the viewpoint along a marked path *(30min there and back)*.

◗ Return to D 218.

Oberhaslach

This village is particularly lively on the Sunday following 7 November, when pilgrims come to pray to St Florent who, in the 7C, was believed to have the power to tame wild animals.

Église de Niederhaslach★

The village once had an abbey said to have been founded by St Florent in rather comic circumstances: for having cured his daughter, King Dagobert granted St Florent as much land as his donkey could delimit during the time the king spent washing and dressing; on the day in question, the king spent more time than he usually did and the donkey went galloping off, so that St Florent was given a considerable amount of land. The Gothic church, stands on the site of the former abbey. The doorway is framed by small statues and decorated with a tympanum illustrating the legend of St Florent curing King Dagobert's daughter. Note the beautiful 14C–15C stained-glass **windows★**.

◗ Follow D 75.

Wasselonne

An old tower is the only part left of the castle. The Wasselonne fair *(last Sun and Mon in August)* sees an impressive procession of floral floats.

◗ Drive W along D 224.

Vallée de la Mossig

Strange projecting sandstone rocks overlook the River Mossig. Strasbourg cathedral is built of sandstone from here.

Maison du Sel

Wissembourg★★

Bas-Rhin

Wissembourg grew up beside a prosperous Benedictine abbey; the city became a member of Decapolis (⌖*see MULHOUSE*) in 1354. Today, it still has a considerable part of its fortifications. The River Lauter splits into several arms here, giving character to the town, especially the Schlupf district known as the Little Venice of Wissembourg. The annual fair on Whit Monday offers visitors the opportunity to see many Alsatian costumes.

A BIT OF HISTORY

Stanislas Leszczynski, deposed king of Poland, having lost his fortune, settled in Wissembourg with his daughter Maria and a few loyal friends. In 1725, Duc d'Antin arrived from Paris and announced that King Louis XV wished to marry Maria. The royal couple was married by proxy in Strasbourg Cathedral; Louis XV was 15 years old, Maria 22.

SIGHTS
Hôtel de Ville
Place de la République.
Built of pink sandstone with pediment, small tower and clock (1741–52).

Église St-Pierre-et-St-Paul★
Rue du Châpitre.
This 13C largely Gothic church has an interesting 15C fresco, depicting St Christopher holding Jesus in his arms:

▸ **Population:** 8 034.
⚹ **Michelin Map:** Michelin Local map 315: L-2.
▤ **Tourist Office:** 11 place de la République, 67160 Wissembourg, ℘03 88 94 10 11, www.ot-wissembourg.fr.
◖ **Location:** On the German border, 33km north of Haguenau by D263.

PRACTICAL INFORMATION
Mini-train touristique – Tour with commentary in French, English or German (75min). Leaves from Place de la République. *Info from the Tourist Office. Tickets available from the driver.*

the largest painted character known in France (11m). The chancel is lit by 13C stained-glass windows, however, the oldest stained glass is the late 12C little rose of the Virgin and Child on the gable of the north transept. On the north side of the church, a gallery and two bays are all that remain of a splendid yet never completed **cloister**. A door leads to an 11C Romanesque chapel.

Ancien Hôpital
This was the residence of Stanislas Leszczinski from 1719 to 1725, when his daughter married Louis XV.

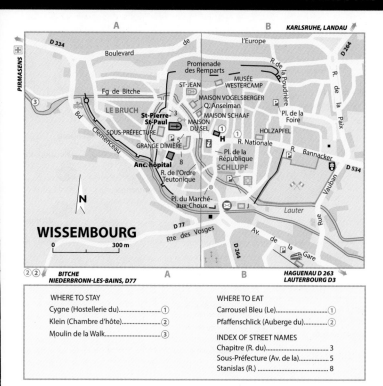

ADDRESSES

🛏 STAY

🛏 **Chambre d'hôte Klein** – *59 r. Principale, 67160 Cleebourg – 7km SW of Wissembourg via D 7.* ☎*03 88 94 50 95. www.chez.com/cleebourg.* ⌖. *4 rooms. Restaurant* 🍴🍴. This 18C Alsatian house is nestled in the heart of Cleebourg village. All the rooms are on the ground floor and are tastefully decorated with antique furniture.

🛏🍴 **Hostellerie du Cygne** – *3 r. Sel.* ☎*03 88 94 00 16. www.hostellerie-cygne.com. 16 rooms. Restaurant* 🍴🍴. Two adjoining houses, one dating from the late 14C.

🛏🍴 **Moulin de la Walk** – *2, r. de la Walk.* ☎*03 88 94 06 44. www.moulin-walk.com. 25 rooms. Restaurant* 🍴🍴🍴 *(closed Sun eve, all day Mon, and Fri lunch).* On the remains of an old water mill beside the Lauter, rooms here are functional and fresh. Run by three generations of the Schmidt family since 1949.

🍴 EAT

🍴 **Le Carrousel Bleu** – *17 r. Nationale.* ☎*03 88 54 33 10. www.le-carrousel-bleu.fr. Closed Wed eve, Sun eve and all day Mon.* This agreeable restaurant on the main street serves original recipes that transport you miles from the "Little Venice".

🍴🍴🍴 **Auberge du Pfaffenschlick** – *Col de Pfaffenschlick, 67510 Climbach, 12km/7.5mi SW of Wissembourg on D 3, Lembach direction, and the mountain road on D 51.* ☎*03 88 54 28 84. www.restaurant-du-pfaffenschlick.com. Closed Mon and Tue.* A restaurant in the middle of the forest, just opposite a cabin used as a canteen during the construction of the Maginot Line.

SHOPPING

Cave vinicole de Cleebourg – *Rte du Vin, 67160 Cleebourg.* ☎*03 88 94 50 33. www.cave-cleebourg.com. Mon–Fri 8am–noon, 1.30–6pm, Sat 8am–noon, 2–6pm, Sun and public holidays 10am–noon, 2–6pm. Closed 1 Jan, Easter, 25 Dec.* Free wine tasting and sales.

THE MAGINOT LINE

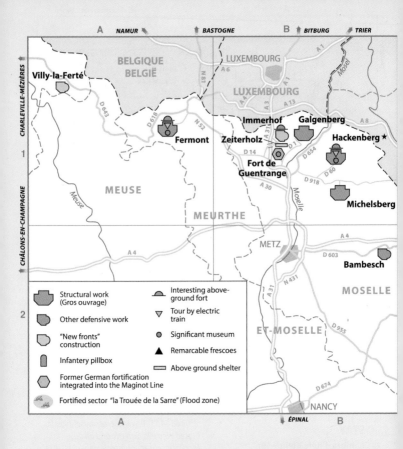

Between the two world wars French people put all their pride and trust in this mighty cement and steel north-eastern shield, created by war minister Paul Painlevé and named after his successor André Maginot (1877–1932). Built in the 1930s to deter invasion by Germany, the name is now synonymous with disaster even though it was impervious to most forms of attack, including aerial bombing and tank attacks. The Line has since become a metaphor for expensive investment that merely served to create a false sense of security.

A Bit of History

The lessons of WWI led France's politicians to design a new defensive perimeter, skirting the new 1919 borders. Modern warfare with tanks, aircraft and the use of gas ruled out a defence system based on isolated strongholds or forts and a network of open trenches. Instead, plans were drawn to divide the length of the border into fortified areas consisting of a continuous frontline, 20–60km/ 12–37mi long, and underground fortifications adapted to modern warfare.

The project was launched on 14 January 1930 as France's economy was gaining strength. Once completed, the Maginot Line consisted of mixed large works, infantry or artillery small works, shelters, strings of casemates and, behind a flood zone, simple pillboxes linked by barbed wire, minefields or anti-tank ditches and supporting one another by crossfire. Troops were meant to fill gaps in these fortified areas.

LIGNE MAGINOT

0 ————— 30 km

Interesting

Worth seeing

N

SAARLAND

DEUTSCHLAND

SAARBRÜCKEN

RHEINLAND-PFALZ

Simserhof ★

Fort Casso

Dambach-
Neunhoffen

Schœnenbourg ★

Zone
inondable

Four à Chaux

Hatten

Esch

BAS-RHIN

BADEN-
WÜRTTEMBERG

LUNÉVILLE

STRASBOURG   UFFHEIM, MARCKOLSHEIM

France's eastern wall

The number of works built in less than 10 years is amazing: 58 works along the north-east border, along with about 410 casemates and shelters for the infantry; 152 revolving turrets; 1 536 fixed cupolas with special armour-plating crowning the superstructures in reinforced concrete, the only parts of the fortifications that could be seen. Beneath, there were 100km/62mi of underground galleries. Yet from the very beginning, the project was cut back owing to lack of funds. From 1935 onwards, it was clear that the original purpose was being thwarted: several large works were replaced by pillboxes and casemates, artillery from WWI was substituted for ultra-modern technology, and there were too few anti-tank guns.

Large works were linked to an ammunition dump by electrified railway lines, today used to visit the galleries.

Defeat

By 1939, the Maginot Line, which did not extend along the northern border of France for political as well as economic reasons, was sadly under-equipped; moreover, it was not used as an offensive base during the Phoney War and was even deprived of part of its troops at the crucial moment when the German onslaught came in May–June 1940. It is hardly surprising that it did not fulfil the task assigned to it by its promoters.

Ligne Maginot★

During the cold war, some of the structures formed part of NATO's defence system. In 1965, the French army decided to stop maintaining the Maginot Line, leaving several of the works to be restored voluntarily by former soldiers.

For more information, contact Ligne Maginot de Cattenom et environs, 3 allée des Platanes Sentzich, 57570 Cattenom. ℘06 52 27 53 44; www.forticat.com.
Visits often last 2h. Wear warm clothing and walking shoes. Works not described in this guide include Ouvrage du Galgenberg and Abri du bois de Cattenom, both located near Cattenom.

The various works are described from the northwest to the southeast, from the Ardennes to the Rhine.

Petit ouvrage de Villy-la-Ferté

18km/11mi NW of Montmédy along N 43 and D 44.

Guided tours mid-Mar–mid-Nov Mon–Sat at 2pm and 4pm, Sun and public holidays 2pm, 3pm, 4pm. €6. ℘03 24 52 97 47 / 06 02 25 42 36. www.ouvragelaferte.fr.
This is one of the new front constructions built from 1935 onwards with zigzag entrances, revolving firing positions offering more protection, mixed-gun cupolas equipped and extremely precise anti-tank guns. Villy was meant to be the main western work of the Maginot Line, defending the Chiers Valley, but it was eventually reduced to a couple of infantry blocks flanked by two artillery casemates.
On 18 May 1940, the fort, no longer defended from the outside was encircled by German sappers; the more than 100 crew took refuge in the badly ventilated underground gallery and suffocated. Outside, close

● **Michelin Map:** Michelin Local map 307: A-1 to R-5, 315: G-1 to M-3.
● **Don't Miss:** Gros ouvrage du Simershof or the Fort de Guentrange.

to the field of anti-tank obstacles, a monument recalls this sacrifice. The overground constructions bear the mark of the attack: damaged cupolas, turret overturned by an explosion.

Gros ouvrage de Fermont

13km/8mi SW of Longwy along N 18 and D 172 to Ugny, then right onto D 17A and left onto D 174.

Guided tours: Jun and Sept Mon–Fri 3pm, Sat–Sun and public holidays 2pm, 3.30pm; Jul–Aug daily 2–4.30pm. €9. ℘03 82 39 35 34. www.ligne-maginot-fort-de-fermont.asso.fr.
This most western position on the Line consisted of two entrance blocks and seven combat blocks, including three equipped with artillery. In front, there is a monument dedicated to the troops. Ammunition elevators and small electric trains convey visitors to Block 4, an imposing artillery casemate covered with a concrete slab (3.5m thick, the maximum protection along the Maginot Line) and fitted with 75mm guns. The barracks have been left as they were in 1940, with kitchens, a bakery, a cold room, a sick bay, dormitories, NCOs' and officers' quarters, showers, soldiers' quarters etc. The tour of the overground installations includes revolving turrets, cupolas with periscopes and automatic rifles, cupolas equipped with grenade-launchers and casemates. Damage caused by 1940 fighting is clearly visible: submitted to heavy shelling, then attacked by assault troops from 21 June onwards, Fermont did not suffer defeat but was compelled to surrender six days later by the French high command.

Gros ouvrage de Fermont
© Yann Guichaoua/age fotostock

Fort de Guentrange

▶ 2km/1.2mi NW of Thionville.
Leave town along allée de la
Libération then turn right towards
Guentrange.

🎧Guided tours: May–Sept (2h) Sat–
Sun, 3pm, Wed 3pm. but check-in at the
tourist office. ⊜€3. ☎03 82 88 12 15.
www.fort-guentrange.com.
This former German stronghold, built
from 1899 to 1906 and occupied by
French troops in 1918, was integrated
into the Maginot Line in 1939-40 to
support the Thionville area. Some of
its technical advantages were adopted
throughout the Maginot Line: electrical machinery, telephone transmissions
etc. Besides the power station and its
still-functional eight diesel engines, the
most spectacular feature of the fort is
the 140m long barracks on four levels,
suitable for 1 100 men.

Abri du Zeiterholz

▶ 14km/8.7mi N of Thionville. Drive
towards Longwy then turn right onto
D 57. Go through Entrange and follow
the signposts from the chapel.

🎧Guided tours May–Sept,
guided tours Sun 2.30–5pm. ⊜€3.50.
☎03 82 34 54 51.

The Zeiterholz is the only shelter along
the Maginot Line that can be visited;
it was built of reinforced concrete on
two levels as an overground shelter,
quite different from cave shelters in
which men were accommodated in
underground areas. Its occupants were
entrusted with the defence of pillboxes
scattered between the larger works and
casemates.

▶ From the Zeiterholz shelter, go to
Hettange-Grande via Entrange-Cité
then turn left onto D 15 (signpost)
which leads to the Immerhof.

Petit ouvrage de l'Immerhof

🎧Guided tours only 2–5pm; limited
opening, and dates vary, check website
for details. ⊜€5. ☎03 82 53 09 61.
www.maginot-immerhof.fr.
Built between 1930 and 1935, this is one
of only two works along the Maginot
Line that were built overground owing
to the lie of the land and completely
covered with concrete.
Bedrooms, sick bay, washrooms etc are
in excellent condition because the fort
was, for a long time, used by NATO as
one of its headquarters.
Note the false cupolas intended to
deceive the enemy.

Gros ouvrage du Hackenberg★

◓ 20km/12.4mi E of Thionville. Leave the town by D 918. The route is signposted from Metzervisse.

&⌚•⚓*Guided tours only (2h30): mid-Nov–Mar Wed and Sat 2pm; Apr–mid-Nov Mon–Fri 2.30pm, Sat 9.30am, and then 2–5.30pm, Sun and public holidays 2–5.30pm.* ≋€10 (child 4–16, €5). ☏03 82 82 30 08. http://maginot-hackenberg.com.

The largest fort of the Maginot Line lies hidden in the heart of a forest covering 160ha, near the village of Veckring. It illustrates the definition of fan-shaped forts given by André Maginot, "forts split into several parts placed at strategic points." The fort could accommodate 1 200 men and its power station could supply a town of 10 000 inhabitants.

On 4 July 1940, the crew here was forced to surrender by order of the liaison officer of the French government, whose members had retreated to Bordeaux. Everything here is monumental: the massive blastproof door, the high-vaulted central station, miles of empty galleries and the huge power station all suggest an abandoned metropolis.

In order to understand the strategic importance of the fort, whose defence works overlooked both the Nied valley and the Moselle valley, drive up (or walk up if the weather is fine) to the fort chapel surrounded by ancient graves *(2.5km/1.5mi along the road starting from the end of the parking area; in front of the men's entrance, take the surfaced path on the left)*.

One can see the two observation towers emerging from the Sierck Forest. Behind the chapel, a path leads to a unique defence line (700m long) reinforced by five blockhouses.

Gros ouvrage du Michelsberg

◓ 2km/13.7mi E of Thionville along D 918 (access from the village of Dalstein). From Hackenberg, drive E along D 60, turn right onto D 60B then left onto D 118N to Dalstein.

•⚓*Guided tours (1h30): Apr–Sept, Sat 3pm, Sun and public holidays 2.30pm, 3pm, 5pm; Oct–Mar at 3pm, but check website for dates.* ◷1 Jan, 25 Dec. ≋€5. ☏07 50 66 39 19. www.maginot-michelsberg.fr.

The fort successfully withstood the attack launched against it on 22 June 1940 thanks to its own fire-power and crossfire from nearby forts. The crew only left Michelsberg on 4 July by order of the French high command and was granted military honours.

The medium-size fort includes an entrance block, two infantry and three artillery blocks. Artillery block no 6 has the famous turret fitted with a 135mm gun which smashed the German attack on 22 June 1940; the gun, still in good condition, weighs 19t and was the largest gun along the Line.

Petit ouvrage du Bambesch

◓ 9km/5.6mi W of St-Avold along N 3.

•⚓*Guided tours only (1h30) Apr–Sept, 2nd and 4th Sun of the month, 2pm, 2.30pm, 3.15pm and 4pm.* ≋€6. ☏06 76 76 61 62. www.lebambesch.com.

This is a good example of a work that was gradually modified owing to the shortage of funds: the number of blocks was reduced as was the artillery and the flanking support. The fort, limited to three infantry blocks, was attacked from the rear with heavy guns on 20 June 1940 and the cupolas were burst open. The crew, having heard of the tragedy of Villy-la-Ferté, chose to surrender.

The tour includes the barracks and combat blocks. The machine-gun turret is particularly narrow. Block No. 2 bears the marks of the 1940 German assault.

Zone inondable de la Trouée de la Sarre

This section, situated between two large fortified sectors of the Maginot Line, that of Metz and that of the Lauter, was not defended by fortified works but by a flood zone controlled by a system of diked reservoirs. When the Saarland became German once more in 1935, this system was reinforced by a network of pillboxes and anti-tank obstacles.

◐ Drive from St-Avold along N 56 to Barst (8km/5mi), turn right past the church then twice left onto rue de la Croix and the first path.

The path is lined with about a dozen pillboxes of the types built after 1935.

◐ Leave the path and take the next one on the right; park the car.

Some 50m underwater, the concreted railway carriage is the last anti-tank obstacle of the Trouée de la Sarre.

◐ Drive E out of Barst.

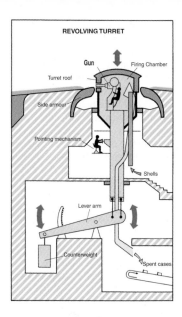

REVOLVING TURRET

Between Cappel and Puttelange-aux-Lacs, the road overlooks some reservoirs that were used to flood the area.

Gros ouvrage du Simserhof★

◐ 4km/2.5mi W of Bitche along D 35 then the military road starting opposite the former barracks of Légeret. Park the car and take the shuttle or walk to the site (10min).

&♿🚶*Guided tours only, daily except Mon (other than public holidays) mid-Mar–mid-Nov 10am–5pm (Jul–Aug, daily, 10am–6pm)..*❀€12. ℰ03 87 96 39 40. www.simserhof.fr.
The only parts visible from the outside are the south-facing entrance block, with its 7 tonne armoured door and its flankers, and the firing cupolas surmounting the combat blocks scattered over several miles so as to overlook the plain below (a few can be seen from D 35A, Hottwiller road, 1km/0.6mi from D 35).
The underground part of the work is in two sections, both on the same level and linked by a 5km/3mi gallery fitted with a 1.7km/1mi long railway line.

A documentary film retracing the history of the Maginot Line begins the tour, then a fully automatic vehicle takes visitors on a journey 30m below the surface, punctuated by moving accounts of what the troops defending the Maginot Line went through during the Phoney War, their heroic and mostly useless resistance to the German onslaught that followed and eventually led to defeat.

Fort Casso

◐ Rohrbach-lès-Bitche, 18km/11mi E of Sarreguemines along N 62. Turn left onto D 84 1km/0.6mi before Rohrbach.

🚶*Guided visits (2h): mid-Mar–mid-Jun and mid-Sept–mid-Nov daily 3pm; mid-Jun–Aug Mon–Fri 10am, 2pm, 4pm, Sat, Sun and public holidays 3pm, 4pm; 1–mid-Sept Mon–Sat 3pm, Sun and public holidays 3pm, 4pm; mid–end Nov Sat–Sun 3pm, Dec–mid-Mar Sun and 1st Sat of month, 3pm.*❀€6. ℰ03 87 02 70 41.
www.fortcasso-maginot.com.
There is a marked contrast between the Simserhof and this smaller front work, which features hammocks in the dormi-

tories, a mixed-weapon turret (the structure dates from WWI) and machine-gun turret in working order.

Attacked on 20 June 1940, Fort Casso was able to resist with the support of the guns of Simserhof and to avoid the fate of Villy-la-Ferté but the crew was eventually ordered to surrender.

Casemate de Dambach-Neunhoffen

Between Neunhoffen and Dambach, 20km/12.4mi E of Bitche along D 35, then right onto D 87 and D 853.

May 10, then 1st Sun of each month 2–6pm until Sept plus occasional openings Jul and Aug. *Guided tours possible (20min) by prior appointment.* 03 88 09 21 46.

This very basic model, consisting of a small concrete block on one level defended one of the 12 dikes of the flooding system of the Schwarzbach valley. It was not equipped with electricity; the ventilation system was operated by hand and foot pedal.

Ouvrage Four-à-Chaux

15km/9.3mi W of Wissembourg along D 3 then D 27 on the way out of Lembach.

(in French or German only) Jan–Mar and Nov–Dec Sat–Sun only 2.30pm; Apr and Oct daily 2pm and 4pm (French), 1.30pm and 3pm (German); May–Sept daily 10am, 2pm and 4pm (French), 10.30am, 1.30pm, 3.30pm (German); post Christmas holidays daily 2.30pm. €7. 03 88 94 48 62. www.lignemaginot.fr.

This medium-size artillery work (6 combat blocks, 2 entrances, crew: 580 men) has a unique inclined plane fitted with a rack, for the transport of small trucks between the fort and the entrance of the ammunition dump below. The museum includes a video room.

Fort de Schœnenbourg

12km/7.5mi S of Wissembourg along D 264. Follow the signposts.

Apr–early Nov Mon–Sat 2–6pm, Sun 9.30am–1pm, 2–4pm. €8. 03 88 80 96 19. www.lignemaginot.com.

This fort was one of the main components of the Haguenau fortified sector; its design took into consideration the experience gained at Verdun from 1916 to 1918; on completion in 1935, it was considered impenetrable.

On 20 June 1940, Schœnenbourg, having withstood the assault of a German division, was attacked by bombers and

Inside Fort de Schœnenbourg

© Christian FLEITH/ADT

Tunnel, Fort de Schœnenbourg

© Didier Zylberyng/hemis.fr

heavy mortars, the only fort to submit to such fire power. The fort managed to hold on until the armistice of 1 July.

Hatten

▶ 22km/13.7mi NE of Haguenau along D 263 then right onto D 28. Or, from Schœnenbourg (14km/8.7mi), drive to Soultz-sous-Forêts along D 264 then turn left onto D 28.

Abri de Hatten

&☉*Open Mar–mid-Jun and mid-Sept–mid-Nov Thu–Sun and public holidays 10am–6pm; mid-Jun–mid-Sept daily, 10am–6pm.* ⊜€7. ℘03 88 80 14 90. www.maginot-hatten.com.
The half-buried casemate provided shelter for the troops defending areas situated between fortified works of the Maginot Line. There is also an open-air display of vehicles including a T34 Russian tank, a US Sherman tank, some jeeps, and lorries.

Casemate d'infanterie Esch

☉*May–Sept Sun 10am–noon, 1.30–6pm.* ⊜€3. ℘03 88 80 96 19. www.lignemaginot.com.
This casemate was situated in the heart of the battle that took place in January 1945 between American and German tanks, devastating Hatten and the nearby villages.

▶ Marckolsheim, 15km/9.3mi SE of Sélestat along D 424. Leave Marckolsheim by D 10.

Mémorial musée de la Ligne Maginot du Rhin

&☉*Mid-Mar–mid-Jun and mid-Sept–mid-Nov Sun and public holidays 9am–noon, 2–6pm; mid-Jun–mid-Sept daily 9am–noon, 2–6pm.* ⊜€3. ℘03 88 92 56 98.
On the esplanade, note the Soviet gun, Sherman tank and machine-gun truck. Inside the eight compartments (beware of the metal steps) of the casemate, thaere are weapons and objects connected with the battle of 15–17 June 1940, when the casemate was bravely defended by 30 men.

ADDRESSES

⸙ EAT

⊜⊜ **La Tour des Saveurs** – *3 r. de la Gare, 57230 Bitche – 4km/2.5mi E of Simserhof on D 35.* ℘03 87 96 29 25. www.latourdessaveurs.com. *Closed every evening and all day Sun.* The Belle Époque-style dining rooms lend an undeniable charm to this restaurant, which is housed in a turreted building. Traditional cooking embellished with a regional flavour is the order of the day.

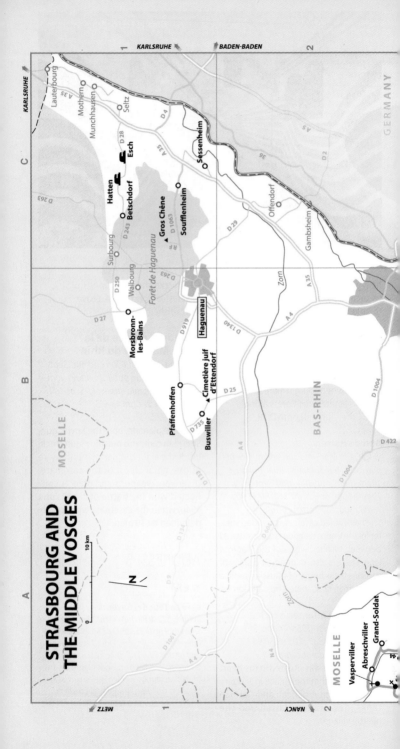

STRASBOURG AND THE MIDDLE VOSGES

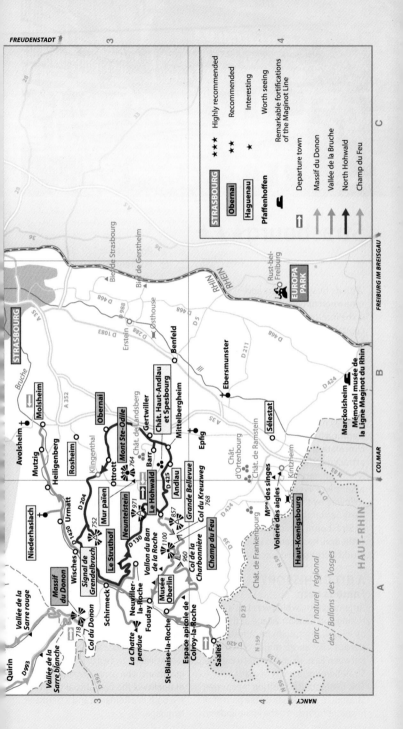

FREUDENSTADT

STRASBOURG

Bruche

Molsheim

Mutzig
Avolsheim
Heiligenberg
Rosheim
Niederhaslach
Urmatt
Signal de Grendelbruch
Wisches
Schirmeck
Le Struthof
Neuviller-la-Roche
Massif du Donon
Col du Donon
Vallée de la Sarre rouge
Quirin
Vallée de la Sarre blanche
La Chatte pendue
Fouday
Musée Oberlin
St-Blaise-la-Roche
Espace apicole de Colroy-la-Roche
Saâles

Klingenthal
Ottrott
Mur païen
Neuntelstein
Obernai
Mont Ste-Odile
Chât. de Landsberg
Gertwiller
Barr
Le Hohwald
Andlau
Grande Bellevue
Col du Kreuzweg
Chât. Haut-Andlau et Spesbourg
Mittelbergheim
Epfig

Vallon du Ban de la Roche
Col de la Charbonnière
Champ du Feu
Volerie des aigles
Mge des singes
Haut-Kœnigsbourg
Chât. d'Ortenbourg
Chât. de Ramstein
Kintzheim

Bief de Strasbourg
Bief de Gerstheim
RHIN
RHIN
Osthouse
Erstein
Benfeld
Ebersmunster
Sélestat
Marckolsheim
Mémorial musée de la Ligne Maginot du Rhin

Rust-bei-Freiburg
EUROPA PARK
FREIBURG IM BREISGAU

COLMAR

NANCY

Parc naturel régional des Ballons des Vosges

HAUT-RHIN

STRASBOURG / Obernai / Haguenau / Pfaffenhoffen

★★★	Highly recommended
★★	Recommended
★	Interesting
	Worth seeing
	Remarkable fortifications of the Maginot Line

Departure town

Massif du Donon
Vallée de la Bruche
North Hohwald
Champ du Feu

251

La Petite France

© René Mattes/hemis.fr

Strasbourg★★★

Bas-Rhin

With its busy river port and renowned university, Strasbourg is the intellectual and economic capital of Alsace. Built round its famous cathedral, Strasbourg is also a town rich in art treasures and one of the three "capitals" of Europe, for it is here that the European Parliament and the European Council are located. The city has proudly maintained its gastronomic tradition (foie gras, Alsatian wines, chocolate and liqueurs), which attract gourmets from all over the world. An important music festival takes place every year in June followed by the European Fair in early September. The historic centre of Strasbourg, which includes the cathedral, has been on UNESCO's World Heritage List since 1988.

- ▶ **Population:** 280 114.
- **Michelin Map:** Michelin Local map 315: K-5.
- **Tourist Office:** 17 place de la Cathédrale, 67000 Strasbourg. ℘03 88 52 28 28. www.otstrasbourg.fr.
- **Location:** Strasbourg is 156km/97mi east of Nancy on the A31 and A4, 165km/102mi east of Metz on the A4 and north of Mulhouse (116km/72mi) and Colmar 74km/46mi) on the A35.
- **Don't Miss:** Notre-Dame cathedral, and the picturesque Petite France district.
- **Kids:** Children (and adults) adore Strasbourg at Christmas time, and the challenge of climbing the cathedral spire.

A BIT OF HISTORY
Famous oath

Argentoratum, which was but a small fishing and hunting village at the time of Julius Caesar, soon became a prosperous city and a major crossroads between Eastern and Western Europe: Strateburgum, the city of roads.

This geographical position meant that Strasbourg found itself on the path of all invasions from across the Rhine and was destroyed, burnt down, ransacked and rebuilt many times throughout its history. In 842, it was chosen as a place of reconciliation by two of Charlemagne's grandsons, who swore an oath. This oath of fidelity is the first official text written both in a Romance and a Germanic language.

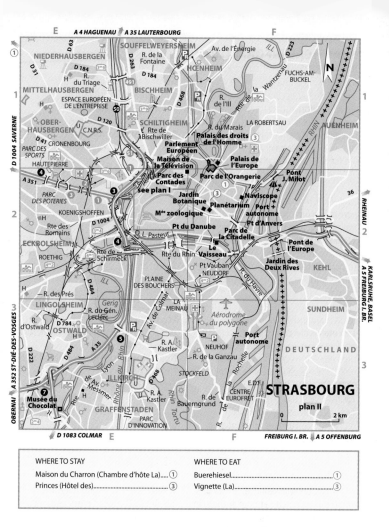

WHERE TO STAY	WHERE TO EAT
Maison du Charron (Chambre d'hôte La).....①	Buerehiesel...①
Princes (Hôtel des)..................................③	Vignette (La)..③

Gutenberg in Strasbourg

Born in Mainz in 1395, Gutenberg had to flee his native town for political reasons and came to settle in Strasbourg in 1434. He formed an association with three Alsatians to perfect a secret process which he had invented. But their association ended in a law suit in 1439 and this is how we know that the invention in question was the printing press. Gutenberg went back to Mainz in 1448 and, with his partner Johann Fust, he perfected the invention that deeply changed our society.

Rouget de Lisle's Marseillaise

On 24 April 1792, the mayor of Strasbourg, Frédéric de Dietrich, offered a farewell dinner to a group of volunteers from the Rhine army. The men talked about the necessity for the troops to have a song which would rouse their enthusiasm and the mayor asked one of the young officers named Rouget de Lisle, if he would write such a song.

The next morning, the young man brought him his Chant de guerre pour l'Armée du Rhin (War song for the Rhine Army). Shortly afterwards, volunteers from Marseille on their way north adopted the song which then became

PRACTICAL INFORMATION

PARK & RIDE: Several car parks on the outskirts of the city centre make it possible to park your car close to a tram station and to travel to the centre in just a few minutes with no need to worry about traffic conditions or parking. After paying the parking fee for the day, all occupants of the vehicle receive a ticket entitling them to a return journey by tram (*Mon–Sat 7am–8pm; outside these hours the car park is free, but payment is required to travel on the tram*).

TRAMWAYS: *03 88 77 70 70; www.cts-strasbourg.eu.* The public transporrt network includes 29 bus routes and 7 tram lines extending out from the city centre. In addition, 11 intercity buses link the city with the most beautiful Alsatian villages.

Tickets: There is a range of ticketing options from a single trip (€2) or 2 trips (€3.30), to 24h choices – see the CTS website (above) for details.

STRASBOURG PASS: Issued by the Tourist office, this pass allows free or half-price admission to 10 sights and monuments. *Valid for 3 days, it is on sale in the Tourist office information*

centres (place de la Cathédrale). *€21.50.*

Guided tours: The city organises guided tours (in English) for individuals by approved guides. *Enquire at the tourist office.*

Audio-guided tours – The itinerary, meant to last 1h30, enables visitors to discover the cathedral, the old town and the Petite France at their own speed. These audio tours are ideal for exploring at your own pace and at a time convenient to you. An accompanying leaflet is available to provide more detail *(deposit required). 24-hour hiring cost: €6. Apply at the Tourist office.*

Mini-train – *Apr to Oct.* Departure place du Château, next to the cathedral, every half-hour or every hour depending on time of year. *€5.20. 03 88 77 70 03. Guided tour of the old town (40min).*

Boat trips on the Ill – Guided trips (1h10) along the River Ill *(departure from the Palais Rohan pier)* taking in the Petite France, past Barrage Vauban, then the Faux Rempart moat as far as Palais de l'Europe. *03 88 84 13 13. www.batorama.com.*

---

known as the Marseillaise. It was designated the French national anthem in 1795. A plaque on the Banque de France building, at No 4 rue Broglie, recalls the memory of Rouget de Lisle.

1870–1918

On 27 September 1870, Strasbourg capitulated after being besieged and shelled by the Germans for 50 days. Under the terms of the Treaty of Frankfurt (10 May 1871), Strasbourg became a German city, which it remained until 11 November 1918.

European crossroads

Even before the end of the Second World War, major politicians (Winston Churchill, Robert Schuman, Konrad Adenauer, and Charles de Gaulle) agreed that Strasbourg should officially assume the role

it had played throughout its history and become a European crossroads. Reconciliation between former enemies would have its roots in a city that had become a symbol, Strasbourg, lying alongside a mighty river once dotted with defensive works and now acting as a link between countries at the heart of Europe.

The **European Council** was created on 5 May 1949; it now has 41 member states. The Council, which has a purely consultative role, sends recommendations to governments and establishes conventions that commit the states signing the agreements, with the object of harmonising legislation in various fields of common interest. The most famous is the European Convention for the Safeguard of Human Rights (1950). It shares its chamber with the European

Parliament, an important institution of the European Union; its members have been elected by universal suffrage since 1979; its role is consultative, financial and restraining.

Strasbourg shares with Brussels and Luxembourg the privilege of housing the main institutions of the European Union. Luxembourg houses the Court of Justice and the general secretariat of the **European Parliament**, whereas the Council, which has executive and legislative powers, and the Commission, which administers and controls, are both based in Brussels.

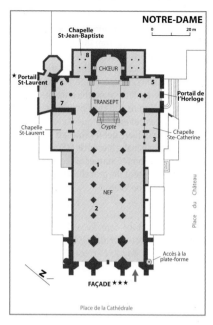

CATHÉDRALE NOTRE-DAME★★★

Notre-Dame is one of Europe's finest Gothic cathedrals and owes a great deal of its charm to the pink sandstone from the Vosges with which it was built.

Work began in 1015 on a Romanesque edifice on the site of a temple dedicated to Hercules. The cathedral architects were later influenced by Gothic art newly introduced in Alsace. In 1365, the towers were joined together up to the platform and then the north tower was raised. In 1439, Johann Hültz from Cologne added the spire which confers on the cathedral its amazing outline.

The Reformation whose main spokesman was Martin Bucer (1491–1551), settled in Strasbourg in 1523 (&see SÉLESTAT), was well received in Alsace. For many years, the old and the new religions fought for supremacy in the cathedral, Luther's proposals being posted on the main door. The Protestant faith finally triumphed and the cathedral only returned to Catholicism in 1681, during the reign of Louis XIV. In 1725, Louis XV married Marie Leszczynska in the cathedral. In 1770, Marie-Antoinette, arriving from Vienna to marry the future Louis XVI, was welcomed here by Louis de Rohan.

In August and September 1870, Prussian shells set fire to the roof and in 1944, allied bombing damaged several parts of the edifice, since restored.

Exterior
West front★★★

Erwin of Steinbach was the architect in charge of building to slightly above the Apostles' Gallery. The **central doorway**

Wise Virgins and the Foolish Virgins on the right doorway of the west front

is the most richly decorated. The tympanum is made of four historiated bands: the first three, dating from the 13C, are remarkably realistic; the fourth is modern. They depict scenes from the Old and New Testaments. The decoration of the **right doorway** illustrating the parable of the Wise Virgins and the Foolish Virgins, includes several famous statues (some of them have been replaced by copies, originals in the Musée de l'Œuvre Notre-Dame). The 14C statues of the **left doorway** represent the graceful Virtues striking down the Vices.

Spire★★★

330 steps. 👥♿ ⏱ *Apr–Sept daily 9.30am–8pm; Oct–Mar daily 10am–6pm.* 🕐 *1 Jan, 1 May, 25 Dec.* ✍€5 *(child 5–18, €2.50).* ✆ *03 88 43 60 32. www.oeuvre-notre-dame.org.*

The west-front platform is 66m high. The tower rises another 40m above the platform and is surmounted by Johann Hültz's graceful spire, whose tip is 142m above ground level.Octagonal at the base, it consists of six tiers of openwork turrets housing the stairs and is topped by a double cross.

From the platform there is a fine **view★** of the old town and the Rhine valley.

South side

The beautiful 13C **clock doorway**, the cathedral's oldest doorway, consists of two adjacent Romanesque doors separated by a statue of Solomon on a pedestal which recalls his famous Judgement. On the left of Solomon's statue, the Church, wearing a crown and looking strong and proud, holds the cross in one hand and the chalice in the other. On the right of the statue, the Synagogue, looking tired and sad, bends over in an effort to catch the fragments of her lance and the Tables of the Law which are dropping out of her hands. The band that covers her eyes is the symbol of error. The tympanum of the left-hand door depicts the **Death of the Virgin★★**. The outside dial of the astronomical clock can be seen above the doors.

North side

The late 15C **St Laurence doorway★** illustrates the martyrdom of St Laurence (restored 19C). On the left are the statues of the Virgin Mary, the three kings and a shepherd; on the right are five statues including St Laurence (originals in the Musée de l'Œuvre Notre-Dame).

Interior

The 12C, 13C and 14C **stained-glass windows★★★** are magnificent, even though they have suffered over the years.

Nave and south aisle

Work on the nave began in the 13C. The stained glass of the clerestory windows and that of the aisles date from the 13C and 14C. Note the 50 or so statuettes decorating the hexagonal **pulpit★★ (1)**, in true Flamboyant Gothic style, designed by Hans Hammer for the Reformation preacher Geiler of Kaysersberg.

The **organ★★** (**2**) has a magnificent polychrome organ case (14C and 15C) spanning the full width of a bay. The corbelled loft is carved with a representation of Samson with, on either side, a town herald and a pretzel seller. These articulated characters would sometimes come to life during sermons to entertain the congregation. St Catherine's chapelcontains an epitaph of the Death of Mary (**3**), dating from 1480, and 14C stained glass.

South transept

The **Angels** or **Last Judgement★★** pier (**4**), erected in the 13C, stands in the centre.

Astronomical Clock★ (5)

The cathedral's most popular feature was designed by mathematicians and built by Swiss clock-makers between 1550 and 1574, it stopped in 1780. Schwilgué, a native of Strasbourg, studied it for thirty years and then rebuilt it between 1838 to 1842.

The seven days of the week are represented by chariots led by gods, who appear through an opening beneath the dial: Diana on Mondays, then Mars, Mercury, Jupiter, Venus, Saturn and Apollo. A series of automata strikes twice every quarter hour. The hours are struck by Death. On the last stroke, the second angel of the Lion's Gallery reverses his hourglass.

The astronomical clock is half an hour behind normal time. The midday chiming occurs at 12.30pm. As soon as it happens, a great parade takes place in the recess at the top of the clock.

The Apostles pass in front of Christ and bow to him; Jesus blesses them as the cock, perched on the left-hand tower, flaps his wings and crows three times, a reminder of Peter's denial of Christ.

North transept

This contains splendid Flamboyant Gothic christening fonts (**6**). An unusual stone group represents Christ on the Mount of Olives (**7**). The 13C and 14C stained glass depicts emperors of the Holy Roman Empire.

Chapelle St-Jean-Baptiste

The 13C chapel, attributed to Erwin, contains the tomb of Bishop Conrad of Lichtenberg (**8**) who began the construction of the west front.

Tapestries★★

The cathedral owns 14 splendid 17C tapestries depicting scenes from the Life of the Virgin, designed by Philippe de Champaigne, Charles Poerson and Jacques Stella. They are hung in the nave on special occasions.

 WALKING TOURS

1 OLD TOWN★★★
Allow one day.

The old town nestles round the cathedral, on the island formed by the two branches of the River Ill.

Place de la Cathédrale★

The **Pharmacie du Cerf** on the corner of rue Mercière, which dates from 1268, was the oldest chemist's in France until it closed in 2000.

On the north side of the cathedral, the **Maison Kammerzell★** (1589), restored 1954 and now a restaurant, has splendid carved wood.

Place du Château

Here are the Musée de l'Œuvre Notre-Dame (*see MUSEUMS*) and the **Palais Rohan★**.

▶ Follow rue de Rohan then turn right onto rue des Cordiers.

Place du Marché-aux-Cochons-de-Lait★

A charming square lined with old houses including a 16C house with wooden galleries. The adjacent place de la Grande-Boucherie looks typically Alsatian.

▶ Turn left onto rue du Vieux-Marché-aux-Poissons.

The **Ancienne Douane** (former customs house) is on the right; it was rebuilt in 1965 for temporary exhibitions.

Pont du Corbeau

This is the former "execution" bridge from which those condemned for infanticides and parricides, tied up in sacks, were plunged into the water.

▶ A carriage entrance at No 1 quai des Bateliers leads to the Cour du Corbeau.

Cour du Corbeau★

Once a fashionable inn, which welcomed illustrious guests, such as Turenne, King Johann-Casimir of Poland, Frederick the Great and Emperor Joseph II, the picturesque courtyard dates from the 14C.

Quai St-Nicolas

The embankment is lined with some fine old houses; three are now the Musée Alsacien: *see MUSEUMS*). Louis Pasteur lived at No. 18.

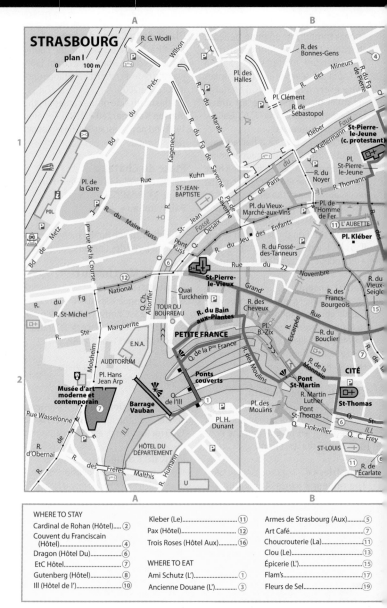

◗ Cross the Pont St-Nicolas and take quai St-Thomas.

Église St-Thomas

This five-naved church, rebuilt at the end of the 12C, became a Lutheran cathedral in 1529. It contains the 18C mausoleum of the **Maréchal de Saxe**★★ sculpted by Pigalle. The allegorical sculpture represents France weeping and holding the marshal's hand while trying to push Death aside. Strength, symbolised by Hercules, gives way to grief and Love can be seen crying as he puts out his torch. On the left, a lion (Holland), a leopard (England) and an eagle (Austria), are represented vanquished, next to crumpled flags.

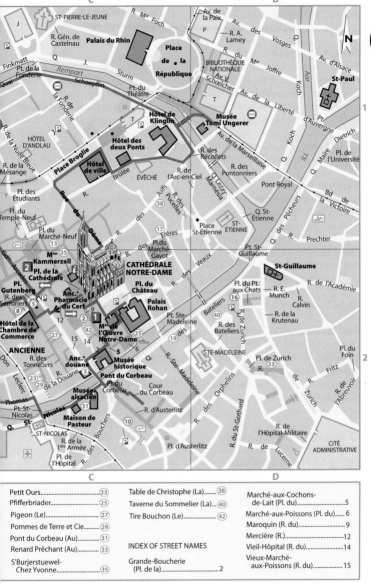

▶ Walk along rue de la Monnaie to the Pont St-Martin.

The bridge offers a fine **view**★ of the tanners' district. The river divides into four branches (watermills, dams and locks can still be seen).

▶ Walk along rue des Moulins then follow the edge of the island.

La Petite France★★

Once the fishermen's, tanners' and millers' district, this is today one of the most interesting and best-preserved areas of the old town. Quai de la Petite France runs alongside the canal, offering a romantic **view★** particularly at dusk of the old houses reflected in the water.

Ponts Couverts★

This is the name given to three successive bridges spanning the River Ill; each guarded by a massive square tower, remaining from the 14C fortifications. The bridges once had wooden roofs.

◗ Turn right just before the last tower and walk along quai de l'Ill.

Barrage Vauban

60 steps to Panoramic terrace.
◷*Daily 9am–7.30pm.* ◷*14–15 Jul.* ◉*No charge.*
There's a striking **view★★** of the Ponts Couverts, la Petite France and the cathedral from the terrace of the casemate bridge (part of Vauban's fortifications).

◗ Go back over the Ponts Couverts.

Rue du Bain-aux-Plantes★★

The street is lined with timber-framed corbelled houses dating from the Alsatian Renaissance (16C-17C). Note, the tanners' house (Gerwerstub, No 42), from 1572, and Nos. 31, 33, 27 and 25 (1651).

◗ Return to Grand'Rue.

Église St-Pierre-le-Vieux

This church consists of two adjacent churches: one Catholic and the other Protestant. The north transept of the Catholic church (rebuilt in 1866) contains 16C carved-wood panels by Veit Wagner, depicting scenes from the Life of St Peter and St Valerus. The **scenes★** from the Passion (late 15C-early 16C), at the end of the chancel, are believed to be by Henri Lutzelmann, a native of Strasbourg. The south transept contains **painted panels★** by members of the Schongauer School (15C).

◗ Return to the cathedral by Grand Rue, lined with 16C–17C houses.

2 OLD TOWN VIA PLACE BROGLIE

◗ Start in front of the cathedral, follow rue Mercière and turn right.

On **place Gutenberg** stand the Renaissance **Hôtel de la Chambre de Commerce** and Gutenberg's statue by David d'Angers. No. 52 rue du Vieux-Marché-aux-Poissons is the birthplace of Jean Arp (1887-1966), a sculptor, painter, poet and major protagonist of modern art.

◗ Take the busy rue des Grands-Arcades.

Place Kléber

On the north side is an 18C building called "l'Aubette" because the garrison came here at dawn (*aube*) to get their orders. In the centre is a statue of Strasbourg native **Jean-Baptiste Kléber** (1753–1800), a brilliant general of the Revolutionary period, who is buried beneath it. Reliefs depict his victories at Altenkirchen and Heliopolis.

Église St-Pierre-le-Jeune

www.saintpierrelejeune.org.
Three successive churches have stood on this site. All that remains of the first church is a tomb with five funeral recesses, believed to date from the end of the Roman occupation (4C); the lovely restored cloisters belonged to the church built in 1031. The present Protestant church (13C, restored 1900) contains a fine Gothic **rood screen** decorated with paintings from 1620.

◗ Walk along quai Schoepflin.

Place Broglie

This square was laid out in the 18C. On the south side is the **town hall★** built by Massol, former residence of the counts of Hanau-Lichtenberg. At the eastern end are the municipal theatre (1820) and the **Hôtel de Klinglin** (1736).

Rue du Dôme and adjacent streets

The old aristocratic district adjoining place Broglie has guarded several 18C mansions, particularly rue Brûlée: the **Hôtel des Deux-Ponts** (1754) at No. 13, the bishop's residence at No. 16, and at No. 9 the town hall's side entrance.

PALAIS DE ROHAN AND ITS MUSEUMS

On the 1st Sun of every month admission to all museums is free of charge.

Palais de Rohan★

The beautiful classical bishop's palace was built in 1704 for Cardinal Armand de Rohan-Soubise by royal architect Robert de Cotte.

Musée des Arts décoratifs★★

Daily except Tue 10am–6pm. 1 Jan, Good Friday, 1 May, 1 and 11 Nov, 25 Dec. €6.50. 03 68 98 51 60. www.musees.strasbourg.eu.

The Decorative Arts Museum is housed on the ground floor and in the stables wing and Hans-Hang pavilions.

The **Grands Appartements** rank among the finest 18C French interiors. The synod room, the king's bedroom, the assembly room, the cardinals' library, the morning room and the emperor's bedroom are particularly remarkable for their decoration, ceremonial furniture, tapestries and 18C paintings.

The museum, which is devoted to the **arts and crafts of Strasbourg and eastern France** from the end of the 17C to the mid-19C, containsone of the most important **ceramics collections★★** in France, including faience and porcelain from the Strasbourg and Haguenau manufacture, founded and run by the **Hannong** family from 1721 to 1781, and the Niderviller manufacture, founded in 1748 by the Baron of Beyerlé, the director of Strasbourg's royal mint.

Look for the "blue" period pieces, the transitional polychrome style, terrines shaped like animals or vegetables and above all magnificent crimson floral decorations which inspired many European manufactures after 1750.

Salon des Evêques, Musée des Arts décoratifs

© René Mattes/hemis.fr

Musée des Beaux-Arts★

2 place du Château. Same conditions as the Musée des Arts décoratifs. 03 68 98 51 60.

The Fine Art Museum is housed on the 1st and 2nd floors of the main building. **Italian painting** (primitive and Renaissance works) is very well represented by Filippino Lippi, Botticelli, Cima da Conegliano (*St Sebastian*) and Correggio (*Judith and the Servant*).

The **Spanish School** includes works by Zurbarán, Murillo, Goya and above all a *Mater Dolorosa* by El Greco.

The collection of paintings from the 15C–17C **Dutch School** is particularly rich: fine *Christ of Mercy* by Simon Marmion, *Engaged Couple* by Lucas of Leyden, several works by Rubens, *St John* (portrait of the artist) by Van Dyck, and *Going for a Walk* by Pieter de Hooch.

The French and Alsatian schools of the 17C–19C are illustrated by several works including *The Beautiful Woman from Strasbourg* by N de Largillière (1703).

The museum also has a fine collection of **still-life paintings**, among them the **Bunch of Flowers** by Velvet Brueghel.

Musée archéologique★★

2 place du Château. ⏱*Same conditions as the Musée des Arts décoratifs.* ☎*03 68 98 51 60.*

The archaeological collections concern the prehistory and early history of Alsace from 600 000 BCE to 800 CE. Numerous objects illustrate the Bronze-Age and Iron-Age civilisations: ceramics, weapons and tools, jewellery, ceremonial plates and dishes imported from Greece or Italy, and the Ohnenheim funeral chariot. The Roman section includes remarkable stone carvings and inscriptions, fine glassware and everyday objects. Among outstanding Merovingian items are the Baldenheim helmet and military decorations from Ittenheim.

ADDITIONAL MUSEUMS

Musée Alsacien★★

23–25 quai St-Nicolas. ⏱*Times and charges are the same as the Musée des Arts décoratifs.* ☎*03 68 98 51 60. www.musees-strasbourg.eu.*

This museum of popular art, located in a maze of quaint rooms in three 16C-17C houses, gives a good insight into the history, customs and traditions of Alsace.

Musée de l'Œuvre Notre-Dame★★

3 place du Château. ⏱*Times and charges are the same as the Musée des Arts décoratifs.* ☎*03 68 98 51 60. www.musees-strasbourg.eu.*

The **Œuvre Notre-Dame** is a unique institution founded to collect donations for the building, upkeep and renovation of the cathedral.

Medieval and Renaissance Alsatian art is displayed in the Maison de l'Œuvre (1347 and 1578-85), the Hôtellerie du Cerf (14C) and in a 17C house, surrounding four small courtyard. The Cour du Cerf is planted with vegetables and medicinal and ornamental plants to recreate the Paradisgärtlein depicted in medieval Alsatian paintings and prints.

The hall which contains pre-Romanesque sculpture leads to the Romanesque sculpture rooms and rooms displaying 12C and 13C stained glass, some

of it from the Romanesque cathedral; note the cloisters of Eschau (12C) and the **Christ's Head★★** from Wissembourg, the oldest representational stained glass known (c 1070). From there, the Cour de l'Œuvre, with a partly Flamboyant Gothic and partly Renaissance decor, leads to the hall of the builders' and stone masons' guild, whose woodwork and ceiling date from 1582. Next comes the main room of the Hôtellerie du Cerf where 13C works originally decorating the cathedral are exhibited.

The first floor houses an important collection of 15C–17C gold plate from Strasbourg. The second floor is devoted to the evolution of Alsatian art in the 15C, including **paintings★★** of the Alsatian School: Conrad Witz and Alsatian primitives, and Nicolas of Leyden.

A 1580 spiral staircase returns to the first floor **Renaissance wing**, where a room is devoted to Hans Baldung Grien (1484–1545), a pupil of Dürer, who was the main representative of the Renaissance in Strasbourg.

Musée d'Art Moderne et Contemporain★★

1 place Hans-Jean-Arp. ♿⏱*Times are the same as the Musée des Arts décoratifs, except Mon.* ☜€10. ☎*03 68 98 51 55. www.musees-strasbourg.eu.*

Standing on the bank of the River Ill, this modern building was designed by Adrien Fainsilber, the architect of the Cité des Sciences et de l'Industrie at La Villette in Paris.

Modern art from 1850 to 1950

Ground floor. The display covers the diverse artistic strands, which have left their stamp on the history of modern art, from the academic works of William Bouguereau to abstract works by Kandinsky, Poliakoff and Magneli. Renoir, Sisley and Monet illustrate Impressionism, and post-Impressionist and Nabis paintings Signac, Gauguin, Vuillard and Denis. Art at the turn of the last century is represented by a group of Symbolist works, notably Klimt's *Plenitude*.

Several rooms are devoted to **Jean Arp** and his wife Sophie Taeuber-Arp, who, in collaboration with Theo Van Doesburg, made a series of stained-glass panels recreating the constructivist interiors (1926–28) of l'Aubette on place Kléber. As a reaction against the WWI, the Dadaists signed derisory even absurd works (Janco, Schwitters). Following in their footsteps, the Surrealists Brauner, Ernst and Arp tried to introduce the world of dreams into their works.

Furniture by **Charles Spindler**, sculpture by François-Rupert Carabin, Ringel d'Illzach and Bugatti, and stained glass made in Strasbourg testify to the renewal of fine and decorative arts in Alsace around 1900.

Modern art from 1950 onwards

First floor. In the first room, works by Picasso, Richier, Pinot-Gallizio, Kudo and Baselitz reflect postwar uncertainty. The next room illustrates the Fluxus movement and Italian Arte povera, using so-called poor materials. The 60s and 70s are represented by the experiments of Buren, Parmentier, Toroni, Rutault, Morellet and Lavier, and the 80s and 90s by Grand, Balka, Boltanski, Ramette, Blaussyld and Pérez.

THE 19C GERMAN QUARTER

After 1870, the Germans erected a great number of monumental public buildings in neo-Gothic Renaissance style. They intended to transfer the town centre to the north-east, and include the orangery and the university. This district with its broad avenues is a rare example of Prussian architecture.

Place de la République

This vast square has a shady circular garden in the centre, with a war memorial by Drivier (1936). On the left is the Palais du Rhin, the former imperial palace (1883–88); on the right are the National Theatre, housed in the former Landtag Palace, and the National Library.

Parc des Contades

This park situated north of place de la République is named after the military governor of Alsace who had it laid out.

On the edge of the park, the **Synagogue de la Paix** was built in 1955 to replace the synagogue destroyed in 1940.

Maison de la Télévision FR3-Alsace

This was built in 1961; a monumental (30m x 6m) ceramic by Lurçat, symbolising the Creation, decorates the concave façade of the auditorium.

CAPITAL OF EUROPE
Palais de l'Europe★

Allée Spach, av de l'Europe.

&.▪... *The Palais de l'Europe is open to visitors Mon–Fri. It is closed at weekends and on French national holidays.*
To book a tour (English, French or German) contact the Service des visites, Directorate of Communications, Conseil de l'Europe, 67075 Strasbourg Cedex.
✆03 88 41 20 29. www.coe.int.

The palace houses the **European Council**, including the council of ministers, the parliamentary assembly and the international secretariat. The buildings, inaugurated in 1977 were designed by the French architect Henri Bernard. The palace contains 1 350 offices, meeting rooms, a library and the largest parliamentary amphitheatre in Europe.

Opposite, the **Parc de l'Orangerie★** was laid out by Le Nôtre in 1692 and remodelled in 1804 for Empress Josephine's stay, it includes a lake, a waterfall and a zoo where storks are a familiar sight, as they are on the chimney tops of buldings.

Palais des Droits de l'Homme

Nearby, on the banks of the River Ill, stands the futuristic new Palais des Droits de l'Homme, designed by Richard Rogers, which houses the European Court of Human Rights.

PORT AUTONOME AND THE RHINE

25km/16mi circuit. Allow 1h30.

Strasbourg is one of the most important ports along the River Rhine. Its impact on eastern France's economy equals that of a major maritime port because of the exceptionally good navigable conditions and the network of waterways, railway lines and roads linking the whole region with Western and Central Europe.

▶ From Pont d'Austerlitz, follow N 4. Shortly before the Pont Vauban, turn right onto rue du Havre, which runs parallel to the René-Graff dock.

Rue de la Rochelle, which prolongs it, leads to the southern, most modern part of the port, with its three main docks: Auguste-Detœuf (cereals), Gaston-Hælling and Adrien-Weirich (containers and heavy goods) and basin IV.

▶ Turn back along rue de la Rochelle and rue du Havre. Then turn right and cross the Pont Vauban. Avenue du Pont de l'Europe leads to the Rhine.

The river, which at this point is 250m wide, is spanned by the **Pont de l'Europe** (1960) linking Strasbourg with Kehl on the German side.

▶ Turn back and bear right to follow rue Coulaux, then rue du Port-du-Rhin.

From the **Pont d'Anvers**, the view embraces several docks.

▶ Drive over the bridge and turn right onto rue du Général-Picquart skirting the Bassin des Remparts.

▶ Take rue Boussingault then cross the Marne-Rhine canal and turn right along quai Jacoutot.

From the **Pont Jean-Millot**, at the entrance of the Albert-Auberger dock, the view takes in the Rhine.

ADDRESSES

🏨 STAY

Chambre d'hôte La Maison du Charron – 15 r. Principale, 67370 Pfettisheim – 13km/8mi NW of Strasbourg on D 31. ℘03 88 69 60 35. https://maisonducharron.com. 6 rooms. The owners of this 1858 property have done up the rooms individually by using different woods and patchwork. Small garden, stabling for horses and two holiday cottages.

Couvent du Franciscain – 18 r. du Fg-de-Pierre. ℘03 88 32 93 93. www.hotel-franciscain.com. 43 rooms. At the end of a cul-de-sac you will find these two joined buildings. We recommend the rooms in the new wing. The breakfast room is in the cellar. A good option 10min walking distance of the old city.

Hôtel Pax – 24–26, r. du Fg-National ℘03 88 32 14 54. www.paxhotel.com. 106 rooms. Restaurant (open Mon–Fri lunch). A family hotel in a busy street on the edge of the city's old district. Its plain rooms are well kept, and its restaurant serves regional dishes. You can eat in the vine-shaded courtyard in summer.

EtC Hôtel – 7 rue de la Chaine. ℘03 88 32 66 60. www.etc-hotel.com. 35 rooms. Situated in a peaceful area beside the Cathedral and la Petite France in the heart of the old city. Contemporary and friendly atmosphere.

Aux Trois Roses – 7 rue Zürich. ℘03 88 36 56 95. www.hotelroses-strasbourg.com. 33 rooms. Cosy duvets and pine furniture add to the welcoming feel of the quiet guestrooms in this elegant building on the banks of the Ill. Fitness area with sauna and jacuzzi.

Hôtel de l'Ill – 8 rue des Bateliers. ℘03 88 36 20 01. www.hotel-ill.fr. 27 rooms. Renovated hotel with family atmosphere. The rooms of differing sizes are impeccably clean, while the old-fashioned breakfast room has a cuckoo clock.

Le Kléber – 29 place Kléber. ℘03 88 32 09 53. www.hotel-kleber.com. 37 rooms. "Absolument framboise", "Myrtille sauvage" and "Fleur de lune" are just a few of the names of the rooms in this comfortable hotel. Contemporary, colourful decor with a sweet-and-savoury theme.

Des Princes – 33 rue Geiler. ℘03 88 61 55 19. www.hotel-princes.com. Closed Jul 25–Aug 25, Jan 2–10. 43 rooms. A welcoming hotel in a quiet residential neighbourhood. Guestrooms with classic furnishings and large bathrooms. Breakfast served to a backdrop of bucolic frescoes.

Hôtel Rohan – *17 r. Maroquin.*
*03 88 32 85 11. www.hotel-rohan.com. 37
rooms.* Named after the nearby palais de
Rohan, this little hotel is on a pedestrian
street near the cathedral. Its quiet,
pleasant rooms are furnished in Louis
XV, Louis XVI or rustic style; those on the
south side have air conditioning.

Hôtel du Dragon – *2 r. Écarlate.*
03 88 35 79 80. www.dragon.fr. 32 rooms.
A 17C residence with a resolutely
contemporary interior: shades of grey,
designer furniture, minimalist bedrooms
and art exhibitions.

Gutenberg – *31 rue des Serruriers.*
*03 88 32 17 15. www.hotel-gutenberg.
com. 42 rooms.* This building dating back
to 1745 is now a hotel with an eclectic
mix of spacious guestrooms. The bright
breakfast room is crowned by a glass
roof.

¶/ EAT

Flam's – *29 r. des Frères.* *03 88 36
36 90. www.flams.fr. Booking advisable
at weekends.* This half-timbered house
very close to the cathedral houses a
restaurant specialising in *flammekueches*.
The three dining rooms and two cellars
have been redecorated in lovely bright
colours. Note the superb 15C painted
ceiling.

Pfifferbriader – *14 pl. du Marché-
aux-Cochons-de-Lait.* *03 88 24 46 56.
www.winstublepfiff.com.* Feel at home
in this low-beamed dining room, with
windows decorated with wine-making
scenes. Tasty regional dishes including
käseknepfles, *choucroute* and *bäeckehoffe*
are served along with classic French
cuisine. Good choice of regional wines.

Le Pigeon – *23 r. des Tonneliers.*
*03 88 23 31 30. Closed 3 weeks in Jan and
3 weeks in Jun.* This typical winstub owes
its name to two pigeons sculpted on the
facade of one of the oldest houses in
Strasbourg. Traditional Alsatian cooking.

Art Café – *(at the Musée d'Art
Moderne et Contemporain) 1 pl. Hans-Jean-
Arp.* *03 88 22 18 88. Closed Mon, holidays
and museum closing times.* You may
not find a lovelier view of Strasbourg
than the one from the terrace of this
restaurant in the modern art museum.
The high design interior matches the
contemporary food. Brunch on Sunday
and holidays.

La Choucrouterie – *20 r. St-Louis.*
*03 88 36 52 87. http://restaurant
delachouc.com. Closed Aug, Sat lunch and
Sun lunch.* This 18C coaching inn was the
last place in Strasbourg to make pickled
cabbage. Feast and have fun in a slightly
chaotic setting, enlivened by music,
cabaret or theatre. Alsace cuisine served
with local white wine.

Petit Ours – *3 r. de l'Écurie
(quartier des Tonneliers).* *03 88 32 13 21.
Booking advisable.* Great little restaurant
decorated with Tuscany-inspired colours.
Light floods through the bay windows
of one room, and the cellar is also very
pleasant. Each dish (mostly fish) is
characterised by a particular herb or
spice.

Au Renard Prêchant – *34 r. de
Zürich.* *03 88 35 62 87. www.renard-
prechant.alsace. Closed lunchtime on Sat,
Sun and public holidays.* A 16C chapel in
a pedestrianised street, which takes its
name from the murals decorating its
walls telling the story of the preaching
fox. Rustic dining room, pretty terrace
in summer, and reasonable fixed-price
lunches.

L'Ami Schutz – *1 Ponts Couverts.*
*03 88 32 76 98. www.ami-schutz.com.
Closed Christmas Holidays.* Between the
Meanders of the Ill, typical cosy winstub
with wood panelling (the smaller
dining room has greater charm). Terrace
beneath the Lime trees.

Au Pont du Corbeau – *21 quai
St-Nicolas.* *03 88 35 60 68. Closed Jul
28–Aug 26, Feb half-term holidays, Sun
lunch and Sat except Dec.* A renowned
restaurant on the banks of the Ill,
next to the Alsatian Folk Art Museum.
Regionally-inspired Renaissance decor
and a menu that focuses on local
specialities.

La Vignette – *29 rue Mélanie at
La Robertsau.* *03 88 31 38 10. http://
lavignette-strasbourg-robertsau.com.* An
earthenware stove and old photos of
the neighbourhood adorn the dining
room of this café-restaurant. Appetising,
market inspired cuisine.

Ancienne Douane – *6 rue de la
Douane.* *03 88 15 78 78. www.ancienne
douane.fr.* This building, on the banks of
the River Ill, dating from 1358 has had a
variety of uses, but is now a charming
restaurant in the centre of the old city.

Tire Bouchon – *5 rue des tailleurs de pierre.* *03 88 22 16 32. www. letirebouchon.fr.* Charming restaurant located near the Cathedral in a typical narrow Alsatian street, with an extensive wine cellar and offering traditional cuisine.

Aux Armes de Strasbourg – *9 place Gutenberg.* *03 88 32 85 62. http:// auxarmesdestrasbourg.com.* An oasis of peace in the famous place Gutenberg in the old town. Enjoy Alsatian specialities on the terrace.

L'Épicerie – *6 rue de Vieux Seigle.* *03 88 32 52 41.* Nostalgic atmosphere with a 1960s ambiance. Renowned for its *tartines* and chocolate tart. Sandwiches always available or call in for breakfast.

S'Burjerstuewel – Chez Yvonne – *10 rue Sanglier.* *03 88 32 84 15. www.restaurant-chez-yvonne.net* This winstub is one of the city's institutions, evidenced by the photos and dedications of its famous guests. Regional cuisine with a modern twist.

Le Clou – *3 r. du Chaudron.* *03 88 32 11 67. www.le-clou.com. Closed Wed lunchtime, Sun and holidays.* This small wine bar in a little street near the cathedral is eternally popular, with its typical decor, friendly atmosphere and good Alsace cooking.

Fleur de Sel – *22 quai des Batelliers.* *03 88 36 01 54.* Opened in 2005 on the south bank of the Ill across the Pont Ste Madeleine. Traditional Alsatian and French cuisine and a large dessert menu.

La Table de Christophe – *28 rue des Juifs.* *03 88 24 63 27. www.tabledechristophe.com. Closed Mon evening and all day Sun.* A small neighbourhood restaurant with a rustic welcoming feel. The chef blends local and modern culinary influences, with a respect for the seasons.

Colbert – *127 Route de Mittelhausbergen.* *03 88 22 52 16. www.restaurant-colbert.com.* The young, talented chef serves imaginative modern dishes in a simple but elegant way; as a result the restaurant is often full. So, booking is essential.

L'Amuse Bouche – *3a rue Turenne.* *03 88 35 72 82. www. lamuse-bouche.fr.* Chic and yet casual, serving modern dishes prepared with imagination and skill. Away from the city centre, and close by the Parc des Contades, so ideal for a more relaxing and peaceful occasion.

Buerehiesel – *in the Parc de l'Orangerie.* *03 88 45 56 65. www. buerehiesel.fr. Closed Aug 2–Aug 24, Dec 30–Jan 21, Sun and Mon.* Famous chef Antine Westermann has handed over to his son Eric in the kitchens, but this remains one of Alsace's gastronomic temples. The setting is a stunning half-timbered farmhouse in the beauty of a large and popular park.

ON THE TOWN

Au Brasseur – *22 r. des Veaux.* *03 88 36 12 13. Daily 11.30am–1am. Closed 25 Dec, 1 Jan.* This micro-brasserie proposes a wide variety of beers brewed on the premises. Locals also come here to dine and for jazz, rock and blues concerts at weekends.

Bar à Champagne – *5 r. des Moulins.* *03 88 76 43 43. www.regent-hotels.com. 5pm–2am.* This is the hotel bar of the luxurious Regent Petite France, which was a mill for 800 years. No effort has been spared to ensure that you spend a relaxing evening here: the fine contemporary decor, the riverside terrace, discreet background jazz, a good choice of cocktails and the best champagnes.

Café de l'Opéra (in the opera house) – *Pl. Broglie.* *03 88 22 98 51. www. cafedelopera.fr. Mon–Sat 11am–1.30am, Sun 2–8pm.* The purple and gold decor in this theatre bar evokes the world of the stage. A classy setting for an intimate date over a glass of whisky or wine – or a hot chocolate with the family. Painting and photography exhibitions.

SHOWTIME

Demandez le programme! – To find out the programme of theatres, concerts, seminars, exhibitions and sporting events, get a copy of the monthy *Strasbourg actualités* or *Hebdoscope*, with weekly listings for arts and shows.

Andlau and its vineyards

Andlau ★

Bas-Rhin

This small flower-decked town, nestling in the green valley of the River Andlau, is in the heart of Riesling country, with three famous vintages produced nearby.

SIGHTS
Église St-Pierre-et-St-Paul★

The church is a fine example of 12C architecture (though the upper part of the steeple dates from the 17C) with an extraordinary **doorway★★**, adorned with the most outstanding Romanesque carvings in Alsace. Inside, the **chancel**, situated above the 11C **crypt★**, has impressive 15C stalls.

EXCURSION
Epfig

6km/3.7mi SE along D 253 and D 335. Drive through the village and follow D 603 towards Kogenheim.

▶ **Population:** 1 850.
◔ **Michelin Map:** Michelin Local map 315: I-6 – also see Route des VINS.
▮ **Tourist Office:** 5, rue du Général de Gaulle. ℘03 88 08 22 57. www.paysdebarr.fr.
▶ **Location:** Andlau lies at the foot of the Champ du Feu, along D 425 or 4km/2.4mi south of Barr along the Route des Vins.

Situated east of the village, above the Rhine valley, the **Chapelle Ste-Marguerite** was built in the 11C and 12C. According to legend, it was used by a congregation of nuns.

Haut-Andlau and Spesbourg castles★

9.5km/6mi to Hungerplatz forest lodge.
🚶 *1h30 on foot there and back from the lodge.*

WINE-TASTING

André Durrmann – *11 rue des Forgerons.* ℘*03 88 08 26 42. Visits by appointment. Closed 2nd fortnight Aug and Sun.* Instructive tours of the estate.
Marcel Schlosser – *Domaine du Vieux Pressoir, 5–7 rue des Forgerons.* ℘*03 88* 08 03 26. www.marcel-schlosser.fr. Visits by appointment. Tour of the cellars; wine tasting; sale of wine.
Gérard Wohleber – *14 rue du Mar.-Foch.* ℘*03 88 08 93 36. www.alsace-chalet.com. 8am–noon and 1–7pm.* In magnificent restored 1549 house.

Drive W along D 854 from Barr then continue on a surfaced path to the left which leads to Hungerplatz forest lodge. Leave the car there and follow the path running along the ridge to the ruins.

The ruined 14C **Château du Haut-Andlau★** was lived in until 1806.
The **Château de Spesbourg★** was destroyed in the 14C. There is a beautiful view to the south of vallée d'Andlau and l'Ungersberg.

Massif du
Donon★★
Moselle, Meurthe-et-Moselle, Vosges, Bas-Rhin

The Donon massif is recognisable from afar with its two-tier summit marking the boundary between Alsace and Lorraine. Numerous streams taking their source near the summit radiate across the splendid forests that cover the area. A road runs alongside each valley and there are cross-country skiing tracks and ski lifts.

A BIT OF HISTORY
Celts, Romans, Franks and all the Germanic tribes travelling west came through the Donon pass and there is evidence that an ancient god, probably Mercury, was worshipped here.

- **Michelin map:** Michelin Local map 315: G-5.
- **Tourist Office:** Office du tourisme du pays des lacs de Pierre-Percée – Base de loisirs Lac-de-la-Plaine 88110 Celles-sur-Plaine ℘03 29 41 19 25. www.paysdeslacs.com.
- **Location:** The Donon massif forms the southern part of the sandstone Vosges mountains, reaching their highest point at the Donon summit *(alt 1 009m)*.
- **Don't Miss:** The panoramic view from the summit of the Donon.
- **Kids:** The Lac de la Plaine recreation and sports centre is ideal for children.

🚗 DRIVING TOURS

SARRE ROUGE AND SARRE BLANCHE VALLEYS

Round tour from the Col du Donon
55km/34mi. Allow 2h.

Col du Donon
Alt 718m.

Donon
Alt 1 009m. About 1h30 on foot there and back. 🚶 *It is possible to leave the car at the Donon pass and follow the footpath starting on the right of Hôtel Velléda; alternatively, you can drive for 1.3km/0.8mi along the road*

branching off D 993 on the right, 1km/0.6mi from the pass.
P *Leave the car in the parking area (barrier) and walk the last 2km.*
There are two viewing tables on the summit. The **panorama★★** includes the Vosges mountain range, the Lorraine plateau, the Plaine d'Alsace and the Black Forest.
From the Col du Donon, the itinerary follows the **Vallée de la Sarre Rouge** or Vallée de St-Quirin then goes across the Lorraine plateau.

Continue straight on along D 145 and then D 44, ignoring the Cirey-sur-Vezouze road on your left. The itinerary enters the Lorraine region.

Grand Soldat
This hamlet is the birthplace of Alexandre Chatrian (1826–90), who collaborated with Emile Erckmann (1822-99) to write a series of novels inspired by Alsatian traditions and legends.

Abreschviller
A small **forest train** (&⌚*Apr–Oct, check website for details.* ⊜€*13 Return ticket (child 4–12,* ⊜€*9.50). ℘03 87 03 71 45; http://train-abreschviller.fr*), steam or diesel-powered, leads to Grand Soldat (*6km/3.7mi*).

▷ 3km/1.9mi farther on, turn left onto D 96F towards St-Quirin.

Vasperviller
On the foothills of the Donon, this village houses a remarkable little church designed in 1968 by the architect Litzenburger, the **Église Ste-Thérèse**.

St-Quirin
The 18C priory **church** is surmounted by two towers and a pinnacle crowned by onion-shaped domes. It houses a restored organ made in 1746 by Silbermann.

▷ Drive W out of St-Quirin along D 96 and, 2km/1.2mi farther on, turn left onto D 993.

The road follows the **Vallée de la Sarre Blanche** through lovely forests.
At the end of the tour, you are back in Alsace as you leave the Abreschviller road on your left to return to the Donon pass.

Europa Park★★★

In this theme park dedicated to Europe, more than 100 attractions and shows take visitors on a tour of twelve European countries: the character of each country, from the architecture to the vegetation and the gastronomy, is brought to life in great detail. In addition, the park, famous for its roller coasters (the most impressive being the Silver Star), offers a great deal of excitement to every member of the family.

Use the map given to you at the entrance to find your way among the various countries.
You might also like to get an overall view on board the panoramic EP-Express with main stations in Germany, England, Greece, Russia and Spain. The woodland and lake setting greatly enhances the appeal of the park. (⌚ Note that there may be long queues at the main attractions).

▷ **Location:** Europa-Park is located on the outskirts of Rust, between Freiburg and Strasbourg: *Straße 2, 77977 Rust-bei-Freiburg, Germany. ℘+49 7822 776 688. www.europapark.de.*

Germany
Your tour of Europe starts with the host country. Stroll along the German Alley lined with typical architecture from the different regions of Germany. Enjoy the rose garden of the medieval Balthasar Castle then take a look at a piece of the Berlin Wall.

France
For a breathtaking view of the Park and the Rhine valley as far as the Vosges and the Black Forest, take a glass lift up the Euro-Tower (75m). The Silver Star, Europe's highest (73m) and fastest roller coaster, offers guaranteed thrills,

Atlantica

© Europa-Park

as does Eurostat, a roller coaster speeding "through space" in the dark. Take a ten-minute break to enjoy the movie experience in 4D of Magic cinéma 4D, followed by a relaxing tour of the charming bistros and old-fashioned boutiques of the "quartier français".

Switzerland

The Swiss village with its old water mill and wooden chalets sets the scene. Take a thrilling bobsleigh ride down a metal run at 50km/hr then maybe a spinning plane ride or a Wild Mouse ride featuring a vertical lift and a hair-raising nose dive.

Greece

Welcome to Mykonos, one of the Greek islands. Enter Cassandra's Curse and discover the power of illusions then take up the challenge of the Poseidon water roller coaster for an unforgettable trip through Greek mythology or venture into the legendary world of the sunken city of Atlantis.

Russia

Discover a country full of contrasts from the traditional craftsmen's village to the Mir Space Station and test your nerves on the Euro-Mir ride with spinning gondolas hurtling towards the ground at a speed of 80kph.

PRACTICAL INFORMATION

Admission times and charges
subject to seasonal change – see website (*www.europapark.de*).

GETTING THERE

BY CAR – You can reach Europa-Park via the motorway A5 (exit 57b Rust). Follow the slip road 57b Rust and you will come directly to Europa-Park.

BY SHUTTLE – Express Drive provides personal direct shuttles from a variety of airports and major cities directly to Europa-Park *(See website: ℘+49 7223 9699-0)*.

VISITING TIP – Three information offices (ATM machines, lost property) located by the lake, at the main entrance (locker and buggy rental) and in Spain. Nestlé Schöller meeting points in every themed area.

WHERE TO STAY – There are several possibilities in Rust including the peaceful, comfortable Pension Kern *(Franz-Sales-Straße 30, 77977 Rust; ℘+49 7822 61278; http://pension kern.de. 7 rooms)*. For accommodation in Europa-Park see the next page.

Spain

Do not miss the spectacular stunts of the Duel of the Brothers featuring knights on horseback fighting it out in the arena or the Flamenco Show staged by the "Ballet Español".

The other countries also deserve a visit: plunge into a gigantic wave in Portugal, experience the famous Venice Carnival in Italy, race along the Silverstone track or book a seat at the Globe Theatre in England, get caught up in a pirates' attack on a Dutch colony in Holland, take a refreshing fjord-rafting ride in Scandinavia or float in a tree trunk down a fast flowing river in the Austrian Tyrol.

👥 Children's World

Lots of attractions to keep young children busy in beautiful scenery: boats, slides, roundabouts, a beach, climbing walls, a Viking ship, the Children's Lighthouse and more.

Further on, Adventure Land is an area of beautiful nature and exciting attractions for the whole family along the Fairy Tale Alley or through the jungle.

ADDRESSES

🛏 STAY

Accommodation inside the Park includes themed hotels, a guesthouse, a campsite and a tipi village. *Hotel and guesthouse reservation: ☎+49 7822 860 5679.*

Hotel Colosseo – This is one of the largest hotels in Germany; designed in the style of Ancient Rome, it features an opulent décor, 324 family rooms and 22 luxury suites, typical Italian restaurants, cafés and bars and a wellness area set within the walls of the Coliseum.

Hotel El Andaluz, Hotel Castillo Alcazar – Both hotels are steeped in Andalusian atmosphere: the first is designed in the style of a Spanish "finca" with terracotta floors and arcades, whereas the second suggests the grander style of a Spanish castle at the time of the Reconquista.

Circus Rolando – This guesthouse in the German area is convivial and more affordable (16 family and 7 double rooms, swimming pool and sauna).

Sucess Story

The Mack family, who has produced fairground vehicles since 1780 and roller coasters for the largest theme parks in the world since 1921, set up Europa-Park in 1975 as a showcase for its various ride models. The chosen location in the small border village of Rust was a surprise for many, but the grounds of Balthazar Castle (1442) offered 60 hectares of beautiful greenery. The European theme adopted in 1982 asserted the originality of the park. Since then, the park has consistently expanded and won many awards. Can we then speak of a model company? Maybe… Today the park sets itself apart from similar ventures by its concern for the environment (electric vehicles, solar panels).

Campsite – Idyllic location by a lake (200 pitches for camping cars and caravans; vast meadow for tents; playground, breakfast room and boutique; no prior reservation).

Tipi village – Wild West atmosphere; heated tipis, log cabins and covered wagons *(a total of 458 beds, bring sleeping bags and towels – breakfast in the Western Saloon – reservation: ☎+49 7822 860 5566.*

🍴 EAT

30 restaurants and fast food places reflect the diversity of European cuisine: French flavour at Marianne's, Scandinavian-style fish at the Fiskhuset, tapas at the Bodega or Greek specialities at the Mykonos.

Haguenau★

Bas-Rhin

Haguenau lies on the banks of the River Moder, on the edge of the vast Haguenau forest with its excellent footpaths and cycle tracks.

A BIT OF HISTORY

According to legend, **St Arbogast**, entrusted by the king of the Franks with the christianisation of northern Alsace, stayed in this forest, which was thereafter known as the **holy forest** until the end of the Middle Ages.

The town prospered in the shadow of the massive castle, a favourite residence of Frederick I Barbarossa (Redbeard) of the House of Hohenstaufen, who ruled the Holy Roman Empire from 1152 to 1190.

SIGHTS

Musée historique★

Mid-Sept–Jun Wed–Sun 2–5.30pm; Jul–mid-Sept Wed–Sun 10am–12.30pm, 1.30–6pm. 1 Jan, 25 Dec. €4. 03 88 90 29 39. www.ville-haguenau.fr.

The history museum is housed in an imposing early 20C edifice. It contains an important collection of Bronze and Iron-Age objects found in the region (Haguenau Forest, Seltz) along with a collection of Alsatian coins, medals, and written works printed in Haguenau during the 15C and 16C. On the first floor are the collections of ceramics, in particular those produced by the Hannong factory (See STRASBOURG).

Église St-Georges

This octagonal steeple of this 12C and 13C church houses the two oldest bells in France (1268).

Inside, note the superb **altarpiece★** representing the Last Judgement.

Église St-Nicolas

This Gothic church was founded by Emperor Frederick Barbarossa in 1189. The remarkable 18C **woodwork★** (*switch on the light to the left of the chancel*) decorating the pulpit, the organ loft and the choir stalls, was brought to

- ▶ **Population:** 35 014.
- **Michelin Map:** Michelin Local map 315: K-4.
- **Tourist Office:** 1 Place Joseph Thierry, 67500 Haguenau. 03 88 06 59 99. www.tourisme-haguenau-potiers.com. Guided tours of the town mid-Jun–mid-Sept: Wed at 10am.
- ▶ **Location:** Haguenau is located 25km/15.5mi north of Strasbourg on A 4 and easily in reach of many of the region's famous pottery villages (Betschdorf and Soufflenheim). It is 20km/12.4mi from the German border.
- **Kids:** Fantasialand in Morsbronn-les-Bains and Nautiland in Haguenau are theme parks popular with younger tourists.

St-Nicolas from the former Abbaye de Neubourg after the Revolution.

Musée alsacien

Mid-Sept–Jun Wed–Sun 2–5.30pm; Jul–mid-Sept Wed–Sun 10am–12.30pm, 1.30–5.30pm. 1 Jan, 25 Dec. €3 (children under 18, €1.50). 03 88 06 59 99. www.ville-haguenau.fr.

EXCURSIONS

Gros Chêne

6km/3.7mi E. Take the D 1063 and after 5km turn left onto the forest road.

This barely-standing ancient oak is the starting point of a botanic trail, a fitness itinerary and walks through the forest (*marked paths*). *Playground for children.*

Soufflenheim

14km/8.7mi E

This industrial town is famous for its **ceramic workshops** which produce typically Alsatian ceramics.

Betschdorf

16.5km/10mi NE on the D 263, then the D 243.

This lovely village is famous for its art pottery of grey sandstone with blue decoration. A **museum** (⊙*Apr–Sept Tue–Sat 10am–noon, 1–6pm, Sun 2–6pm.* ⊛€3.50. ℘*03 88 54 48 07. www.betschdorf.com*) housed in an old farmhouse displays an interesting collection of pottery from the Middle Ages.

Hatten

22km/13.7mi NE on the D 263 and the D 28.

The **Musée de l'Abri and Casemate d'infanterie Esch** are in the village; the **casemate** is situated on the left, 1km/0.6mi beyond Hatten on the way to Seltz (&*see Ligne MAGINOT*).

Morsbronn-les-Bains

11km/6.8mi N on the D 27.

The hot-water (41.5°C) springs of this small spa resort contain sodium chloride.

Sessenheim

21km/13mi E.

This charming village was immortalised by **Goethe** as the setting of his short-lived romance with the pastor's daughter **Friederike Brion**.

Inside the **Église protestante**, note the pastor's stall (Pfarrstuhl) where Goethe and Friederike used to sit side by side to listen to her father preaching. On the left of the church stands the **Auberge au Bœuf** (&*see below*), a typical Alsatian inn, displaying Goethe prints, letters and portraits. The **Mémorial Goethe**, next to the presbytery, was inaugurated in 1962.

ADDRESSES

⌂ STAY

⊖**Chambre d'hôte Krumeich** – *23 r. des Potiers, 67660 Betschdorf – 15km/9.3mi NE of Haguenau, Wissembourg direction on D 263 and D 243.* ℘*03 88 54 40 56.* ⌧. *3 rooms.* You can learn how to make salt-glazed stoneware from the owner of this house, and stay in one of the pretty rooms, furnished in old-fashioned style, and enjoy the garden.

⍩ EAT

⊖⊖**Au Bœuf** – *48 Grand'Rue, 67620 Soufflenheim – 15km/9.3mi E of Haguenau on N 63.* ℘*03 88 86 72 79.* Good beef features prominently on the menu, along with Alsatian dishes and *flammekueches*.

⊖⊖⊜**Le Jardin** – *16, rue de la Redoute, 67500 Haguenau.* ℘*03 88 93 29 39. Closed Tue–Wed.* Good contemporary cuisine without losing sight of the classical traditions expressed in fish soup, tuna carpaccio and chateaubriand, for example. Very interesting and decorated building.

⊖⊖⊜**Grains de Sel** – *113 Grand'Rue, 67500 Haguenau.* ℘*03 88 90 83 82.* Another restaurant that is part of the emerging trend to highlight its links with Nature, and its environmental credentials. That aside, the cuisine is modern, of high quality and matched by a good selection of wines.

⊖⊖⊜⊜**Auberge du Bœuf** – *1 rue de l'Eglise, 67770 Sessenheim.* ℘*03 88 86 97 14. www.auberge-au-boeuf.fr. Closed Mon and Tue.* It is easy to be seduced by this remarkable Michelin-starred eatery, with its little museum dedicated to Goethe (see above).

SPORT AND RECREATION

Thermes de Morsbronn-les-Bains – *12 rte d'Haguenau, 67360 Morsbronn-les-Bains.* ℘*03 88 09 83 93. www.valvital.fr. Closed Dec–Feb and Sun.* The thermal springs are recommended for treating rheumatic disorders and post-traumatic injuries. You can choose between the classic spa treatments and shorter pick-me-ups.

≗**Nautiland** – *8 r. des Dominicains.* ℘*03 88 90 56 56. www.nautiland.net. Mon–Fri noon–9pm, Sat–Sun and public holidays 9am–7pm. Closed 1 Jan, 24–25 and 31 Dec.* A water leisure centre offering cascades, springs, slides, sauna and Turkish bath.

SHOPPING

Markets – Weekly market Tue and Fri mornings in the Halle du Houblon. Organic market Fri afternoons, Rue du Rempart.

Château du Haut-Kœnigsbourg

Château du Haut-Kœnigsbourg★★

Bas-Rhin

First mentioned in 1147, the castlestands at an altitude of more than 700m, overlooking the Plaine d'Alsace.

A BIT OF HISTORY

In 1479 the castle became the property of the Habsburgs; in the 17C, it was destroyed by the Swedish artillery. In 1899 the ruined castle was offered to Kaiser William II who had it restored. The castle was returned to France in 1909.

VISIT

Allow about 1hr. ⏱*Jan–Feb and Nov–Dec 9.30am–noon, 1–4.30pm; Mar and Oct 9.30am–5pm; Apr–May and Sept 9.15am–5.15pm; Jun–Aug 9.15am–6pm.*

Michelin Map: Michelin Local map 315: I-7 – also see Route des VINS.

Location: The castle is about 21km/13mi north of Colmar. The road leading to it (2km/1.2mi) branches off D 159 at the intersection of the latter with D 1B1, near the Haut-Kœnigsbourg Hotel; 1km/0.6mi farther on, follow the one-way road on the right that goes round the castle (leave your car on the left).

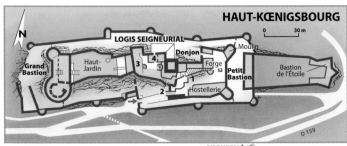

HAUT-KŒNIGSBOURG

1 Jan, 1 May, 25 Dec. ≋€9 (child 6–17, €5). ☏03 69 33 25 00. www.haut-koenigsbourg.fr.
Beyond the gate and the portcullis lies the lower courtyard surrounded by the buildings. A ramp leads to the lions' doorway (**1**) and to the moat separating the seigneurial residence from the rest of the castle. A fortified well (**2**), 62m deep, is located on the edge of the rocky promontory, near the residence. On the ground floor, there is a cellar (**3**) on the west side and kitchens (**4**).

Panorama★★
From the great bastion, panoramic views include; to the north, the ruins of Franckenbourg, Ramstein and Ortenbourg castles; to the east, across the Rhine, the heights of Kaiserstuhl with the Black Forest behind; to the south, Hohneck and, on the horizon, Grand Ballon and Route des Vins.can see the ruins of Œdenbourg or Petit-Kœnigsbourg.

ADDRESSES

🏨 STAY AND 🍴 EAT

⊜⊜ **Relais du Haut-Kœnigsbourg** – *Rte du Haut-Kœnigsbourg, 67600 Orschwiller. ☏03 88 82 46 56. Closed Sun evenings, Mon evenings and all day Tue from Oct to Apr. 26 rooms. Restaurant ⊜⊜.* This hotel-restaurant is worth a visit for its setting it commands superb views over the forest. The 1960s decor is in need of sprucing up, and only a few rooms have been redecorated; choose one of these if you are staying. Folk evenings.

Le Hohwald★★
Bas-Rhin

This prosperous and secluded resort is the starting point of a variety of drives through a picturesque region of forests, vineyards and charming villages. There are many traces of the area's ancient past, such as the pagan wall round Mont Ste-Odile, believed to have been built by the Celts.

🚗 DRIVING TOURS

1 NORTH HOHWALD★★

Round tour starting from Le Hohwald
91km/56.5mi. Allow one day.

▷ Leave Le Hohwald along D 425, which follows the wooded Andlau valley dotted with sawmills.

The ruins of Spesbourg and Haut-Andlau castles can be seen high up on the left (*see ANDLAU*).

▶ **Population:** 531.
⚲ **Michelin Map:** Michelin Local map 315: H-6.
🛈 **Tourist Office:** 15 Rue Principale, 67140 Le Hohwald. ☏03 88 08 33 92. www.lehohwald.fr.
⊛ **Don't Miss:** The walks and panoramic views in this region are breathtaking, notably from Mont Ste-Odile, Rocher de Neuenstein and the Champ du Feu.
👪 **Kids:** Les Naïades aquarium is home to 3 000 species of fish including sharks, piranhas and electric eels!

Andlau★ – *See ANDLAU.*

Between Andlau and Obernai, the road runs through vineyard-covered hills.

Mittelbergheim
Place de l'Hôtel-de-Ville is lined with lovely Renaissance houses with porches and window frames of typical sandstone

Mittelbergheim vineyards

© Christian FLEITH/ADT

from the Vosges region. Wine-growing here goes back to Roman times.

Barr – ⏱️*See Route des VINS.*

Beyond **Gertwiller**, famous for wine and glacé gingerbread, Landsberg castle can be seen in the Vosges foothills with, on the right, the convent of Ste-Odile.

Obernai★★ – ⏱️*See OBERNAI.*

Ottrott

Famous for its red wine and its two castles, the 12C Lutzelbourg castle and the larger 13C Rathsamhausen castle.

▶ Drive through the forest along D 204 as far as the Fischhütte inn and leave the car.

🚶*150m farther on, a path to the right leads (6km/3.7mi there and back) to the ruins of Guirbaden castle.*
Despite being ruined in the 17C, the 11C **Château fort de Guirbaden** has retained the outer shell of its seigneurial residence and its keep.

Signal de Grendelbruch★

🚶*15min on foot there and back.*
The wide **panorama★** encompasses the Plaine d'Alsace to the east and, to the

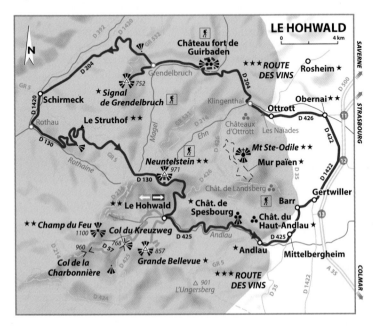

west, the Bruche valley and the Vosges mountain range with Donon in the foreground, crowned by a small temple. The road continues towards the Bruche valley (*see SCHIRMECK*).

Schirmeck – *See SCHIRMECK.*

▷ In Rothau, turn left onto D 130 which follows the Rothaine valley for 3km/1.9mi then veers suddenly left before reaching Le Struthof, which is now a memorial dedicated to victims of the WWII.

Le Struthof★★ – *See SCHIRMECK.*

▷ The road crosses a plateau, enters the forest and descends to La Rothlach. Leave the car 1.5km/0.9mi beyond La Rothlach and follow a path on the left leading to the Neuntelstein viewpoint.

Rocher de Neuntelstein★★
🚶 *30min on foot there and back.*
There is a splendid **view★★** of Mont Ste-Odile, Ungersberg, Haut-Kœnigsbourg and the Champ du Feu.

▷ Continue along D 130 and, at the intersection with D 426, turn right towards Le Hohwald. A left turn at that point would lead you to Mont Ste-Odile (*see Mont STE-ODILE*).

② CHAMP DU FEU★★

Itinerary southwest of Le Hohwald
11km/6.8mi. About 30min.

▷ Drive W out of Le Hohwald along D425.

Col du Kreuzweg
From the pass (alt 768m), the view extends over the valleys of the River Breitenbach and River Giessen.
The road (D 57) climbs towards the **Col de la Charbonnière**, offering superb views of the Villé valley and the Plaine d'Alsace and the Black Forest.

▷ On reaching the pass, turn right onto D 214 which goes round the Champ du Feu.

Champ du Feu★★
The vast **panorama★★** includes the Vosges mountains, the Plaine d'Alsace, the Black Forest and, the Swiss Alps.

▷ North of the tower, 1km/0.6mi to the left, D 414 leads to the Chalet Refuge and ski slopes of La Serva (winter only).

🚶 WALKING TOUR

Grande Bellevue★ (Viewpoint)
🚶 *1h30 on foot there and back.*
After a few minutes, you will get a clear view of Le Hohwald and the surrounding area.

▷ As you reach the former Belle-Vue inn (1km/0.6mi), take a path on the left and climb for 3km/1.9mi through the forest before reaching high pasture. From the summit, the view extends to Le Climont and Haut-Kœnigsbourg.

ADDRESSES

🛏️STAY

🍽🍽 **Chambre d'hôte Tilly's Inn** – *28 r. Principale. ☎03 88 08 30 17. 🗓. 3 rooms. By reservation only Restaurant 🍽🍽. The building has an appealing red façade decorated with naïve drawings. Two apartments.*

🍴/EAT

🍽🍽 **Ferme-auberge Lindenhof** –
11 rte du Kreuzweg – 2km/1mi W of Hohwald on D 425. ☎03 88 08 31 98. www.ferme-auberge-lindenhof.fr. Closed Dec 16–Jan 6, Wed evening from Oct 1–Jun 30 and Thu. 🗓 Booking advisable. Farm cooking (fromage blanc, Munster, gruyère as well as poultry and rabbit) is served on the large veranda of this ordinary-looking building, situated on the edge of the forest.

Paragliding over the Villé valley

SHOPPING

Lips – Musée du pain d'épices et de l'Art Populaire Alsacien – *Pl. de la Mairie, 67140 Gertwiller.* ℰ*03 88 08 93 52. www. paindepices-lips.com. Shop: Mon–Fri 8am–noon, 1.30–6pm, Sat 8am–noon, 2–6pm, Sun 10am–noon, 2–6pm. Museum: Feb–Nov Mon–Sat 9am–noon, 2–6pm, Sun 10am–noon, 2–6pm; Dec daily 9am–noon, 2–6pm.* A celebration of the historic gingerbread makers in the small winemaking village of Gertwiller, near Barr. Tasting. Daily tours in summer.

SPORT

École de parapente Grand Vol – *Ferme Niedermatten, 67220 Breitenbach – Villé direction on D 425.* ℰ*03 88 57 11 42. www. grandvol.com. Weekends from Apr–Nov.* Qualified instructors teach paragliding and monitor your progress. Special rates for beginners. Minimum age: 14.

Molsheim★

Bas-Rhin

This quiet old town lies in the Bruche valley, in the heart of a wine-growing area which produces the famous Bruderthal wine. The Messier-Bugatti factory, specialising in landing gear *(not open to the public)* is located out of town. Of its past as religious capital of Alsace, Molsheim has retained the imposing Jesuit church, which once belonged to the university transferred to Strasbourg, and part of the Carthusian monastery, the only one ever to be built in a town.

TOWN WALK
Église des Jésuites★
The church belonged to the famous Jesuit university founded in 1618 by Archduke Leopold of Austria. The Cardinal de Rohan transferred it to Strasbourg

> ▶ **Population:** 9 433.
>
> **Tourist Office:** 19 pl. de l'Hôtel-de-Ville. ℰ 03 88 38 11 61. www.ot-molsheim-mutzig.com.
>
> **Michelin Map:** Michelin Local map 315: I-5
>
> **Also See:** Route des VINS.

in 1702 in order to counteract the influence of the town's Protestant university. Although it was built between 1615 and 1617, the edifice was designed in the Gothic style.

▶ Follow rue Notre-Dame on the left of the building.

Tour des Forgerons
This 14C fortified gate, located in rue de Strasbourg, houses one of the oldest bells in Alsace, dating from 1412.

Rue de Strasbourg on the right leads to place de l'Hôtel-de-Ville.

La Metzig★

This graceful Renaissance building was built in 1525 by the butchers' guild whose meetings were held on the first floor, the ground floor being occupied by butchers' shops. On either side of the clock (1537), two angels strike the hours.

Take rue Jenner starting on the left of the square.

Note the two Renaissance canon's houses at Nos. 18 and 20, dating from 1628.

Follow rue des Étudiants on the right which runs past the Musée de la Chartreuse (*see description below*) then turn right onto rue de Saverne.

Maison ancienne

A beautiful timber-framed Alsatian house with wooden oriel (1607) can be seen along rue de Saverne.

Continue along rue de Saverne and rue des Serruriers across rue du Mar.-Foch. Turn left onto rue de la Boucherie then right onto rue St-Joseph. Rue du Mar.-Kellermann on the right leads back to the Église des Jésuites.

MUSEUM

Musée de la Chartreuse

May–mid-Jun and mid-Sept–mid-Oct 2–5pm; mid-Jun–mid-Sept 10am–noon, 2–6pm (Sat–Sun and public holidays 2–5pm). €4. *03 88 49 59 38. www.molsheim.fr.*

The priory of the former Carthusian monastery (1598–1792) houses a museum devoted to the history of Molsheim and its region, from prehistoric times to today. Objects discovered locally testify to the presence of man from the Palaeolithic period to Merovingian times.

In another building, the **Bugatti Foundation** displays mementos of the family and a few models of cars built here between the two world wars.

EXCURSIONS

Avolsheim

3.5km/2.2mi N.

This village has retained an old baptistery and, a famous church believed to be the oldest sanctuary in Alsace.

The **Chapelle St-Urlich** is a former baptistery containing fine 13C **frescoes** depicting the Trinity, the four evangelists and scenes from the Old Testament. The **Église St-Pierre** stands in rural surroundings, in the middle of a small cemetery. Although partly rebuilt in the 18C and 19C, the church, surmounted by an octagonal belfry, is a lovely example of Early Romanesque architecture (the edifice was consecrated in 1049). Original features include the base of the belfry-porch with the interesting narthex and doorway, the side doorways and, inside, the massive square piers supporting heavy rounded arches.

Mutzig

3.1km/2mi W on D 30

This small garrison town has a lovely fountain and a 13C gate. The **Fort de Mutzig** (1893) was the first "modern" fort built by the German empire, with concrete defences and electricity. The famous brewery closed in 1990 but the town still hosts a beer festival in September (*1st Sun*).

Near the river, the 17C **Château des Rohan** was converted into an arms factory after the Revolution. Today it houses a cultural centre and the **Musée régional des Armes** (*daily except Mon–Tue Jul–Sept 2–5.30pm, Sun 2–6pm. 03 88 38 31 98*) which displays firearms, swords, bayonets etc..

Obernai★★

Bas-Rhin

In the heart of wine-growing country, Obernai is a pleasant holiday resort. The picturesque old town, with its narrow streets, gabled houses, old shop signs and its well, is still partly surrounded by 12C ramparts.

 WALKING TOUR

Place du Marché★★

The golden hues of the surrounding buildings add to the charm of the picturesque market square; in its centre is a fountain with a statue of St Odile.

Ancienne Halle aux blés★

The old covered market at one end of the square dates from 1554.

Tour de la Chapelle★

This 13C belfry was the tower of a chapel now reduced to its chancel. The last storey, dating from the 16C, is Gothic; the spire, which soars 60m into the sky is flanked by four openwork bartizans.

Hôtel de ville★

(**H** *on the town plan*)
Despite being remodelled and extended in 1848, the town hall has kept some of its 14C–17C features. The oriel window and beautifully carved balcony on the façade date from 1604.

Puits aux six seaux

This elegant Renaissance well has a baldaquin with a weather cock on the top dated 1579. Six pails hang from the three pulleys.

Église St-Pierre-et-St-Paul

This imposing 19C neo-Gothic church houses a Holy Sepulchre altar (1504) and a reliquary containing the heart of the bishop of Angers, Charles Freppel, a native of Obernai, who died in 1891 and asked in his will that his heart be returned to the church of his native town once Alsace became French again.

▶ **Population:** 11 524.

🕭 **Michelin Map:** Michelin Local map 315: I-6.

🛈 **Tourist Office:** Place du Beffroi, 67213 Obernai. ✆03 88 95 64 13. www.tourisme-obernai.fr.

▶ **Location:** Obernai nestles beneath Mont Ste-Odile amid vineyards, 27km/16.8mi southwest of Strasbourg.

🕭 **Don't Miss:** The Hans em Schnokeloch folk festival in mid-July and the harvest festival on the 3rd Sunday of October.

🕭 **Also See:** Route des VINS.

His wish was fulfilled in 1921. The four 15C stained-glass windows are believed to be the work of Pierre d'Andlau or his pupil Thibault de Lyxheim.

Old houses★

There are many old houses in the streets around place du Marché, notably ruelle des Juifs, and towards place de l'Étoile. In rue des Pèlerins, note the three-storey stone house dating from the 13C.

Ramparts

The ramparts, built in the 12C, make a pleasant promenade. The best preserved part of the inside wall is the Maréchal-Foch section.

ADDRESSES

🏠 STAY

◓◓🗟 **Aux Chants des Oiseaux** – *Ottrot-le-Haut.* ✆03 88 95 80 81. *www.chantsdesoiseaux.com.* 16 rooms. Regional style house in the middle of the countryside. Pleasant colourful rooms. Wainscotted , timber-roofed breakfast room and poolside terrace. No restaurant.

◓◓🗟🗟 **À la Cour d'Alsace** – *3 r. Gail.* ✆03 88 95 07 00. www.cour-alsace.com. *49 rooms, 4 suites, 2 restaurants* ◓🗟🗟

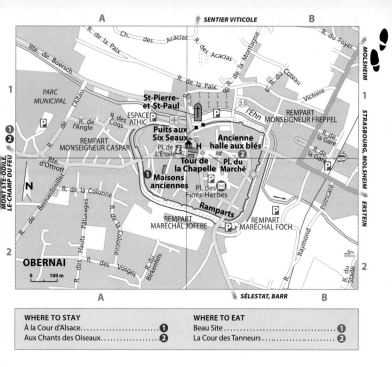

and ⊜⊜⊜⊜. Former property of the Barons of Gail with a central courtyard. Comfortable, variously dimensioned rooms in a soothing monochrome beige colour scheme. Stylish dining room and re-invented up-to-date cuisine. Regional dishes at the Caveau de Gail.

⍟ EAT

⊜⊜⊜ **Beau Site** – *Place de l'Eglise, Ottrot-le-Haut.* ℘*03 88 48 14 30. Closed Feb.* Large half-timbered house with an oriel window. This luxurious winstub, adorned with works by Spindler, focuses on regional delicacies.

⊜⊜⊜ **La Cour des Tanneurs** – *ruelle du Canal de l'Ehn.* ℘*03 88 95 15 70. Closed Tue and Wed.* Unpretentious, well cared for establishment. Informal atmosphere. Up-to-date, market fresh gourmet cuisine, accompanied by a fine Alsatian wine list.

ON THE TOWN

Bar Athic – *6 pl. de l'Étoile.* ℘*03 88 95 50 57. Jul–Aug daily 11am–3pm; rest of the year 3pm–3am. Closed Feb 21–Mar 16, Nov 22–Dec 2 and Dec 24 and 31.* This elegant cocktail bar, furnished with velvet armchairs and a piano for customers' use, also has a billiard room and another bar with a pewter counter.

SHOPPING

Cave d'Obernai-Divinal – *30 r. du Gén.-Leclerc.* ℘*03 88 50 44 56. www.cdhv.fr. Open Mon–Sat 10am–noon, 2–6pm. Closed public holidays.* Tasting and wine for sale. Guided tour by appointment.

Domaine Seilly – *18 Rue du Gal Gouraud.* ℘*03 88 95 55 80. www.seilly.com. Open Mon 9.30am–noon, Tue–Sat 9.30am–noon, 2–7pm.* Situated in an old draper's shop dating from 1628, this is now the shop of the wine-grower Seilly.

⊠ WALKING

Sentier viticole du Schenkenberg – *This 3.6km/2.2mi circuit (1h30 on foot) runs across 250ha of vineyards.* Park by the ADEIF Memorial. In summer, there is a weekly guided tour (Wed mornings) followed by a visit to a cellar. *Apply to the Tourist office.*

Pfaffenhoffen

Bas-Rhin

Once the main centre of the bailiwick of Hanau-Lichtenberg, the small industrial town of Pfaffenhoffen was fortified in the 15C to guard the south bank of the River Moder. In the 16C, it became one of the rallying points of rebellious peasants (&*see SAVERNE*). Today, the remaining fortifications enclose lovely timber-framed houses as well as an interesting museum of folk imagery, which testifies to one of the oldest artistic traditions in Alsace.

- ▶ **Population:** 2 825.
- &**Michelin Map:** Michelin Local map 315: j-3.
- **Tourist Office:** (Info Pt) &*03 88 07 80 05.*
- **Location:** 15km/9.3mi west of Haguenau, 37km/23mi northwest of Strasbourg.

PRACTICAL INFORMATION

Tourist train – *Tour with commentary (1h) leaves from the Tourist office.* &*03 29 66 01 30.*

SIGHTS

Musée de l'Imagerie populaire★

&*24 rue du Dr-Albert-Schweitzer.* *Wed–Sun: May–Sept 2–6pm; Oct–Apr 2–5pm.* *1–2 Jan, 1 May, 1 Nov, 24–25 and 31 Dec.* &*03 88 07 80 05.*

Housed in an old brewery, the museum illustrates the long-standing Alsatian tradition of popular pictures painted on request by itinerant or local painters. Whether painted on paper or vellum, behind glass or on objects, the rich collection includes religious pictures intended to encourage prayers, and protect houses, cattle and crops, and memento pictures illustrating important events in peoples' lives.

Other rooms house a collection of *Goettelbriefe* or christening wishes, one of the oldest traditions in Alsace, which lasted for nearly 400 years.

Old houses

There are many half-timbered houses dating from the 16C to 19C, particularly in rue du Docteur-Schweitzer and rue du Marché.

Synagogue

Dating from 1791, this is the oldest intact Alsatian synagogue. The imposing yet discreet building testifies to the importance of the Jewish community in the late 18C. Note the Kahlstub (communal room) and the room reserved for occasional guests.

Hôtel de ville

The façade is adorned with a medallion of Dr Schweitzer, who was made a freeman of the city.

The hall contains sculptures and Impressionist-style figurative paintings by Strasbourg artist Alfred Pauli (1898-1988).

EXCURSION

6km/3.7mi SW.

Cimetière juif d'Ettendorf

▶ From Pfaffenhoffen take the D 419A, then right along the D 25 to Ettendorf. At the end of the village, a small road parallel to the railway line leads to the cemetery (500m).

This is the oldest Jewish cemetery in Alsace; its stele spread over the hillside, blending into the landscape.

▶ Continue NW along D 735 to Buswiller (2km/1.2mi).

Buswiller

The village has some fine timber-framed houses. In the high street, note the carved gable of No. 17, painted in cobalt blue; the house, dated 1599, escaped destruction in the Thirty Years War.

Rosheim★

Bas-Rhin

Hiding amid the vineyards and ruined ramparts of the small wine-producing town of Rosheim are some of the oldest buildings in Alsace, including an interesting Romanesque church.

- **Population:** 5 075.
- **Michelin Map:** Michelin Local map 315: I-6 – also see Route des VINS.
- **Tourist office:** 94 rue du Général-de-Gaulle, 67560 Rosheim. ℘03 88 50 75 38. www.rosheim.com.
- **Location**: 27km/16.8mi W of Strasbourg.
- **Also See**: The Route des Vins.

TOWN WALK

Église St-Pierre-et-St-Paul★

Built in yellow sandstone in the 12C, although substantially restored in the 19C, the church has a massive 14C octagonal belfry over the transept crossing. Note the Lombardy banding decorating the west front and the walls, which is linked by arcading along the top of the nave and aisles. Lions devouring humans adorn the gable on the west front and are another Lombard feature.

Inside, strong piers alternate with weak piers surmounted by carved capitals (note in particular the ring of small heads, all different). The restored organ by Silbermann dates from 1733.

© Christian FLEITH/ADT
Église St-Pierre-et-St-Paul

Porte du Lion, Porte Basse and Porte de l'École

These gates are remnants of the town's fortifications.

Puits à chaîne and Zittglœckel

On Place de la Mairie, the town hall square, note the well dating from 1605 and the clock tower.

Maison romane

Amid numerous old houses on rue du Général-de-Gaulle, this house, situated between no 21 and no 23, is the oldest construction in Alsatian stone (second half of the 12C). It has two storeys pierced by small openings.

The building, restored in 2002, houses a museum devoted to Romanesque art.

ADDRESSES

EAT

⊖⊖ **Auberge du Cerf** – *120 r. du Gal-de-Gaulle. ℘03 88 50 40 14. Closed Jan 20–Feb 2, Sun evening and Mon.* This inn on the high street serves regional dishes in a family atmosphere.

⊖⊖⊖⊖ **Hostellerie du Rosenmeer** – *45 av. de la Gare, 2km N by D 35. ℘03 88 50 43 29. www.le-rosemeer.com. Closed Sun evening, all day Mon and Wed. 22 rooms.* Tasty inventive gourmet cuisine inspired by regional ingredients, served in a comfortable dining room.

WINE TASTING

Ten wine-makers open their cellars for tastings; ask at the Tourist office.

Mont Ste-Odile★★

Bas-Rhin

Mont Ste-Odile (alt. 764m) is one of the most popular sights in Alsace, drawing both pilgrims and tourists for the spectacular setting and views, with its pink cliffs rising out of the forest.

- **Michelin Map:** Michelin Local map 315: I-6
- **Location**: The mountain is southwest of Obernai.

A BIT OF HISTORY

In the 7C, the mountain was the site of the Hohenburg castle, summer residence of Duke Étichon. According to legend, he rejected his daughter Odile, who was born blind. Saved by her nurse, she miraculously recovered her sight on the day of her baptism and thereafter devoted her life to religion. Her father eventually made her a present of Hohenburg where she founded the convent.

SIGHTS
Convent

Pilgrims flock here all year round, in particular for the feast of St Odile. The porch gives access to the main courtyard. On the right is the **monastery church**, rebuilt in 1692. Inside, it has richly carved 18C confessionals; a door on the left leads to the 11C **Chapelle de la Croix★**. Four groined vaults are supported by a single Romanesque pillar with a carved capital. On the left, a low doorway decorated with Carolingian carvings leads to the small 12C **Chapelle Ste-Odile**, supposedly on the site of an earlier chapel where Odile died. An 8C sarcophagus contains the saints relics.

On the northeast corner of the terrace, the **Chapelle des Larmes** is on the site of the Merovingian cemetery (graves carved in the rock are visible outside). On the edge of the precipice is another chapel, the **Chapelle des Anges**. According to a local lore, if a young woman went round it nine times, she would be sure to find a husband.

Fontaine de Ste-Odile

The road leading down to St-Nabor *(D 33)* runs past the spring *(protected by a railing)* which is said to have gushed forth from the rock at St Odile's request. It is now a place of pilgrimage for people with eye complaints.

Mur païen

30min on foot there and back. Take the staircase on the left of the convent exit and follow the footpath at the bottom.
It would take four or five hours to walk round the remains of this mysterious wall running through forests and screes for more than 10km/6mi, but even seeing a part of it is an awe-inspiring experience: an average 1.7m thick and as much as 3m high in the best-preserved section. Some claim it dates from the 10C BCE, others it is a 1C BCE Germanic fort, others that it is Merovingian.

Schirmeck

Bas-Rhin

This lively small industrial town is the starting point for exploring the Bruche valley, with its forests and sawmills. A lovely west front and an octagonal tower are all that remains of the church (1754), while the Mémorial d'Alsace-Moselle gives an understanding of the region's more recent troubled history.

- **Population:** 2 430.
- **Michelin Map:** Michelin Local map 315: H-6.
- **Tourist office:** 114 Grand Rue, 67130 Schirmeck. ℘03 88 47 18 51.
- **Location:** On the N 420 which follows the Left Bank of the Bruche; 53 km/33 mi southwest of Strasbourg.

SIGHTS
Mémorial d'Alsace-Moselle★
&. ✵ ◷ Daily 9.30am–6pm ◷ 1 Jan,
1 May, 24–25 and 31 Dec. ☜€11.
℘ 03 88 47 45 50.
www.memorial-alsace-moselle.com.
Inaugurated in 2005 on a hill facing the former Struthof concentration camp, the memorial gathers souvenirs of the suffering endured by the people of Alsace and the Moselle from 1870 to the end of WWII. The area's annexation by Germany in 1940 is evoked, as are anti-semitism, the deportation and the concentration camp, the resistance and the postwar Franco-German reconciliation.

EXCURSION
Le Struthof
10km/6.2mi E. ◷ Daily: Mar–mid-Apr and mid-Oct–Christmas 9am–5pm; mid-Apr–mid-Oct 9am–6.30pm.
◷ Christmas–end Feb, 5 and 26 Apr, 1 May and 21 Jun. ☜€6 (child 10–17, €3).
℘ 03 88 47 44 67. www.struthof.fr.
During WWII the Nazis built the only concentration camp in France on this site. It is estimated nearly 22 000 deportees lost their lives here between 1941 and 1945.
The **Centre européen du résistant déporté** includes sections of the former concentration camp and is an interesting introduction to the site.
The **necropolis** above the camp contains the remains of 1 120 prisoners. In front stands the **memorial**; the base is the tomb of an unknown prisoner.

🚗 DRIVING TOUR

Vallée de la Bruche
70km/43.5mi

Saales
At the source of the River Bruche, Saales guards the pass (of the same name) in and out of the Vosges.

Saint-Blaise-la-Roche
This small town is an important crossroads. Here the Bruche is narrow and calm, surrounded by aspen and birch.

Mémorial d'Alsace-Moselle
© Christian FLEITH/ADT

▶ Turn right onto D 424. Follow the direction of Les Charasses.

Espace apicole de Colroy-la-Roche
◷ Jul–Aug daily 2–5pm except Tue and Sun. ◷ Sept–Jun. ☜€3 (children €2).
℘ 03 88 47 20 46. http://assoc-apiculteurs.valleedelabruche.fr.
The beekeeping centre to discover the lives of bees and harvest honey and wax. Its museum presents a beautiful collection of tools and bee hives.

▶ Go back on D 424, then take right to the direction of Ranrupt. Take a look at the Vosgienne farms of the hamlet of Fonrupt. At the Col de la Charbonnière take D 57 to the left.

Vallon du Ban de la Roche
The appearance of this still wild valley is softened by the presence of some pretty, isolated houses.

Waldersbach
The old Protestant presbytery of this charming village houses the **Musée Oberlin** (&. ◷ Oct–Mar daily except Tue 2–6pm. ◷ 1 Jan, Good Friday, Easter Sunday, 1 May, 24–25 and 31 Dec. ☜€5.
℘ 03 88 97 30 27. www.musee-oberlin.com), devoted to the philanthropist and amateur botanist Jean-Frédéric Oberlin (1740–1826), who created playschools and developed agriculture and crafts in the valley.

Fouday

Jean-Frédéric Oberlin is buried in the small cemetery adjacent to the Lutheran church, which has retained the groin-vaulted apse of the earlier Romanesque church.

▶ Take D1420 to the right. At Rothau, take the direction of Les Quelles. After 1km/0.62m, take a dirt road (towards the direction of Les Falle). On the right a signpost indicates the start of the marked trailroad. Parking is possible at the following curve.

Rocher de la Chatte pendue

🏃 *Allow 2h.* The trail climbs through the undergrowth to the summit of the plateau 900m, where there is a fine **view**★.

▶ Return to Rothau and take D 130. After 1 km/0.62m turn right towards Neuviller.

Neuviller-la-Roche

This charming mountain village is home to the **Musée des Arts et Traditions populaires** where furniture, tools and utensils depict the daily life of peasant workers of old (*Rue principale.* ☏*03 88 97 98 44.* ⏱*May and Sept, Sun 2–6pm, Jun–Aug Sat–Sun 2–6pm; rest of the year by appointment.* ⊚*€5*).

▶ Return to D 1420 and cross Schirmeck.

The road then passes through the small village of **Wisches**, which marks the boundary between the countries of French language and Alsatian dialect. At the exit of **Urmatt** there is a gigantic sawmill on the right.
A little detour is necessary to admire the **Église de Niederhaslach**★ (*see Wangenbourg*). The valley narrows between leafy slopes, with a view to the village of **Heiligenberg**, which can be seen on a promontory on the left bank.
Before reaching **Molsheim**★ (*see p278*), visit **Mutzig** and **Avolsheim** (*see Molsheim*).

Sélestat★

Bas-Rhin

This intimate historic city, lying on the west bank of the River Ill, has retained two fine churches and some interesting old houses. In the 15C and 16C, Sélestat was an important Humanist centre with one of the finest libraries in the world.

🚶 WALKING TOUR★

Allow 2h.

▶ From the tourist office, turn right onto rue du Vieux-Marché-aux-Vins. Cross place Gambetta and right on rue des Serruriers.

The **Ancienne Église des Récollets**, formerly part of a Franciscan monastery, is now a Protestant church.

▶ **Population:** 19 713.
⊙ **Michelin Map:**
Local map 315: I-7.
🛈 **Tourist Office:**
10, boulevard du Général Leclerc, 67607 Sélestat.
☏ 03 88 58 87 20.
www.selestat-haut-koenigsbourg.com.
▶ **Location:** Halfway between Colmar and Strasbourg.
◉ **Don't Miss:**
The Bibliothèque Humaniste.
👥 **Kids:** Eagles at the Volerie des Aigles and Barbary apes at Montagne des Singes.
⊙ **Also See:** Route des Vins.

▶ Turn left onto rue de Verdun.

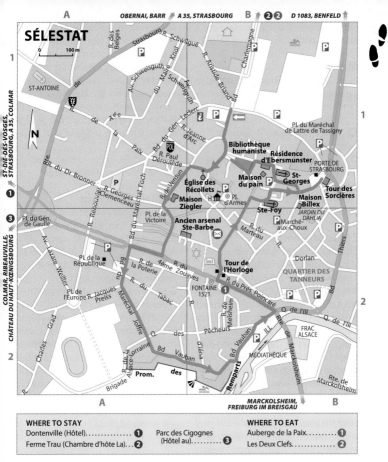

OBERNAI, BARR / A 35, STRASBOURG D 1083, BENFELD

SÉLESTAT

0   100 m

ST-DIE-DES-VOSGES, STRASBOURG, A 35, COLMAR

COLMAR, RIBEAUVILLE, CHÂTEAU DU HAUT-KŒNIGSBOURG

MARCKOLSHEIM, FREIBURG IM BREISGAU

WHERE TO STAY		WHERE TO EAT
Dontenville (Hôtel)............ ❶	Parc des Cigognes (Hôtel au).......... ❸	Auberge de la Paix.......... ❶
Ferme Trau (Chambre d'hôte La)... ❷		Les Deux Clefs.............. ❷

Maison de Stephan Ziegler

This 16C Renaissance house was built by one of the town's master builders.

◗ Continue to Place de la Victoire.

Arsenal Ste-Barbe

The 14C former arsenal has a fine façade with a double-flight staircase. The roof is crowned by two storks' nests.

◗ Continue on rue du 17-Novembre and turn right onto rue du 4e-Zouaves then left along boulevard du Maréchal-Joffre which leads to the ramparts.

Promenade des Remparts

There is a fine view from Vauban's fortifications.

◗ Walk along boulevard de Verdun then rue Poincaré.

Tour de l'Horloge

The clock tower dates from the 14C, the upper part was restored in 1614.

◗ Walk beneath the clock tower, then follow rue des Chevaliers straight ahead to place du Marché-Vert.

Église Ste-Foy★

This Romanesque church (12C), built of red sandstone and granite from the Vosges, was the church of a Benedictine priory. The capitals in the nave have beautiful floral motifs.

◗ Leave the church by the small door behind the pulpit and take the narrow lane on the right to place du Marché-aux-Choux.

Maison Billex

In 1681, the city of Strasbourg signed its surrender to Louis XIV in this fine Renaissance house.

▶ Walk to the Église St-Georges.

On the way, you will get a glimpse of the **Tour des Sorcières** on the right, part of the fortifications demolished by Louis XIV, and the Porte de Strasbourg, designed by Vauban in 1679.

Église St-Georges★

This imposing 13C to 15C Gothic church was considerably remodelled in the 19C. The nave is preceded by a wide narthex which spans the whole width of the west front and opens on the south side (place St-Georges) through an elegant doorway. The musician angels on the stained-glass of the west front date from the late 14C or early 15C; the rose-window (14C) above the south doorway of the narthex illustrates the Ten Commandments; three 15C stained-glass windows in the chancel depict scenes from the lives of St Catherine, St Agnes and St Helena; the modern stained-glass in the east end and the chancel is by Max Ingrand.

▶ Walk along rue de l'Église.

Résidence d'Ebersmunster

No. 8: Built in 1541, this was the town house of the Benedictine monks of Ebersmunster. The Renaissance doorway is decorated with Italian motifs.

▶ A few yards farther on, turn left onto the narrow rue de la Bibliothèque.

Bibliothèque humaniste★

🕐*Closed until 2018 for refurbishment.* 📞*03 88 58 07 20. www.bh-selestat.fr.*
Towards the middle of the 15C, Sélestat's Latin school flourished into a great Humanist school, which explains the extent of its splendid library now housed in the 19C grain exchange.

The library comprises two collections: the Latin library founded in 1452 and the private collection bequeathed by Beatus Rhenanus, a Humanist and close friend of Erasmus. Among the precious manuscripts are the Merovingian Lectionary (late 7C), the oldest work still in Alsace, and the *Cosmographiæ Introductio* printed in St-Dié in 1507 (🕐*see ST-DIÉ*).

▶ Turn the corner to rue du Sél.

La Maison du Pain

🕐*Feb–Nov daily except Mon: 9am–12.30pm, 2–6pm, Sun and public holidays 9–12.30pm, 2.30–6pm.* 🕐*Mid-Jan–early Feb, 1 Jan 25–26 Dec.* ⬥*€5 (child 14–18, €2.80).* 📞*03 88 58 45 90. http://maisondupain.org.*
👥 Learn all about Alsace's countless types of bread in this unusual bakery, with its tempting smell of baking bread. After an introductory room explaining the history of breadmaking and flour-milling, there is ancient bakery adorned with all the tools that were used in the pre-industrial age, and a modern bakery, where you can see frequent demonstrations of break-making, as well as a tasting room and shop.

EXCURSIONS

Volerie des Aigles

8.5km/5.3mi at Kintzheim by D 159, plus 30 min on foot there and back.
🕐*Apr–mid-Nov, check website for times.* 🕐*Mid-Nov–Mar.* ⬥*€9.50 (child 5–14, €6.50).* 📞*03 88 92 84 33. www.voleriedesaigles.com*
👥 The courtyard of the ruined castle is home to about 80 birds of prey. Some of them take part in spectacular **training demonstrations★** (except in bad weather).

Montagne des Singes

2km/mi further on by forest road and D 159, and footpath to the electrified fence.
🕐*Mar–Apr and Oct–Nov 10am–noon, 1–5pm; May–Jun and Sept 10am–noon, 1–6pm; Jul–Aug 10am–6pm.* 🕐*Dec–Mar.* ⬥*€9 (children 5–14, €5.50).*

03 88 92 11 05.
www.montagnedessinges.com.
300 Barbary apes, well adapted to the Alsatian climate, live in total liberty in a huge park (20ha) on top of a hill.

Benfeld
20km/12.4mi NE by N83.
The elegant 16C **town hall** has a lovely carved doorway and polygonal turret dating from 1617. The clock has three jacks striking the hours: Death, a Knight and Stubenhansel; a Traitor who in 1331 sold the city to its enemies for a purse of gold, which he holds in his hand.

Ebermunster
8km/5mi NE on D 1083.
A famous Benedictine abbey once stood in this peaceful village. Built c. 1725, the **abbey church★** can be seen from afar, surmounted by three onion-shaped steeples. The **interior★★** is considered to be the finest example of early-18C Alsatian Baroque art.

ADDRESSES

STAY
Chambre d'hôte La Ferme Trau – *53 rte Nationale, 67000 Ebersheim. *03 88 85 73 31. www.fermetrau.fr. 6 rooms.* A cereal farm near Sélestat with rooms available all year and evening meals available at weekends.

Hôtel Dontenville – *94 r. du Mar.-Foch, 67730 Châtenois. 5km/3mi W of Sélestat, St-Dié direction. *03 88 92 02 54. www.hotel-dontenville.fr. Closed Feb school holidays, Fri lunchtime and Tue. 13 rooms. Restaurant.* This 16C half-timbered hotel has retained the charm and simplicity of old Alsatian houses. The upper floor bedrooms are the best, with their exposed beams. Regional cuisine is served in the panelled dining room.

Hôtel au Parc des Cigognes – *Rte de Sélestat. *03 88 92 05 94. www.cigoland.fr. 44 rooms. Restaurant.* This regional style family farm has been transformed into a hotel and restaurant. The rooms are well equipped and traditional cuisine is on the menu.

EAT
Auberge de la Paix – *44 r. du Président Poincaré. *03 88 92 14 50. www.aubergedelapaix.net. Closed Mon eve, Sun eve and Wed.* The chef concocts traditional and contemporary regional dishes to satisfy the most discerning palate.

Les Deux Clefs – *23 r. du Gén.-Leclerc, 67600 Ebersmunster. 8km/5mi NE of Sélestat on N 83, Strasbourg direction, and D 210. *03 88 85 71 55. www.restaurantauxdeuxclefs.fr. Closed Sun eve, Mon and Thu Jan–Mar. Booking advisable at weekends.* This typical Alsatian building opposite Ebersmunster's lovely church used to house the monastery abattoir. Today the restaurant serves *matelote* (freshwater fish stew) and fried fish, along with other classic regional dishes.

SHOPPING
Local produce market – *Square Ehm, Sat morning.*

Patisserie Kamm – *15 r. des Clefs. *03 88 92 11 04. Tue–Sat 8am–7pm, Sun 8am–2pm, holidays 9am–noon. Closed 19 Jan–1 Feb.* In summer, the terrace of this patisserie is extremely popular, but all year round regulars come here for its mousses, original chocolates and homemade ice creams and sorbets. Light meals are served at lunchtime.

BICYCLE HIRE
Office du Tourisme – *Bd Leclerc. *03 88 58 87 20. May–Oct.* Sélestat has received an award for its 85km/53mi of cycle paths, and the tourist office can arrange the hire of new mountain bikes.

CALENDAR
Christmas Festivities – Sélestat, birthplace of the Christmas tree, puts on numerous events at Christmas. As well as the Christmas trees of the Christmas market, guided musical tours with story-tellers and costumed musicians, there are demonstrations of local specialities in the Maison du Pain and concerts in churches. *Enquire at the tourist office.*

Corso fleuri – On the second Saturday in August, floats decorated with 500 000 dahlias parade night and day in the town streets, accompanied by dancing and fireworks. *03 88 58 85 75.*

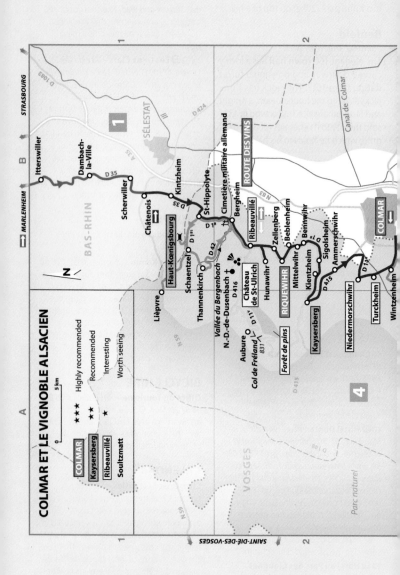

COLMAR ET LE VIGNOBLE ALSACIEN

★★★ Highly recommended
★★ Recommended
★ Interesting
Worth seeing

COLMAR
Kaysersberg
Ribeauvillé
Soultzmatt

0 ————— 5 km

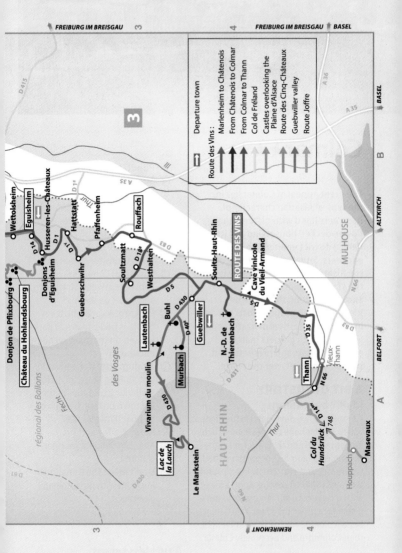

FREIBURG IM BREISGAU 3

FREIBURG IM BREISGAU • BASEL

Departure town

Route des Vins :

Marlenheim to Châtenois
From Châtenois to Colmar
From Colmar to Thann
Col de Fréland
Castles overlooking the Plaine d'Alsace
Route des Cinq-Châteaux
Guebwiller valley
Route Joffre

BASEL

A 36

MULHOUSE

ALTKIRCH

3

D 415

D 1ᵇ

Thur

A 35

III

D 8

Weitolsheim

Eguisheim

Husseren-les-Châteaux

Hattstatt

Pfaffenheim

Rouffach

D 1A

D 1

D 1

Guebschwihr

Donjons d'Eguisheim

Soultzmatt

Westhalten

D 18ᵉ

ROUTE DES VINS

Donjon de Pflixbourg

Château du Hohlandsbourg

Soultz-Haut-Rhin

Cave vinicole du Vieil-Armand

D 5

D 83

N 66

BELFORT

D 430

Buhl

Guebwiller

Lautenbach

N.-D. de Thierenbach

D 5ᵗ

D 35

des Vosges

Vivarium du moulin

Murbach

D 40ᵉ

D 431

Thann

Vieux-Thann

N 66

régional des Ballons

Fecht

D 430

Lac de la Lauch

Le Markstein

D 430

HAUT-RHIN

Thur

Col du Hundsrück 748

D 14ᵇⁱˢ

Houppach

Masevaux

D 61

REMIREMONT

3

4

Quai de la Poissonnerie, Petite Venise

Colmar★★★
Haut-Rhin

The great appeal of Colmar lies in the typical Alsatian character of its streets lined with picturesque flower-decked houses and its Little Venice district unaltered by time and wars. Situated in the heart of the Alsatian vineyards, Colmar is the starting point of numerous excursions along the Route des Vins. The town proudly hosts the international festival of gastronomy *(Festiga)*, which gathers many culinary talents and presents food products from all over the world.

A BIT OF HISTORY
Idyllic beginnings

A Frankish town developed in the Rhine valley, on the banks of the River Lauch, a tributary of the Ill. Emperor Charlemagne, and later his son, often visited. Labourers and craftsmen lived round the royal villa. In its centre stood a tower with a dovecote which is said to have given its name to the town: Villa Columbaria (*colombe* means dove in French), then Columbra and eventually Colmar.

An heroic mayor

Despite its peaceful doves, Colmar often had to fight for its freedom. In 1261 the son of a tanner, **Roesselmann**, bravely led the town militia against the bishop of Strasbourg's soldiers, paying for the city's freedom with his life.

▶ **Population:** 69 488.
⌚ **Michelin Map:** Michelin Local map 315: I-j 8 also see Route des VINS.
▤ **Tourist Office:** 4 r. des Unterlinden. ✆ 03 89 20 68 92. www.tourisme-colmar.com.
▶ **Location:** Colmar lies halfway between Strasbourg and Basle, on the A 35.
Ⓟ **Parking:** Most of the town centre is pedestrian; car parks located on the main avenues into town.
🕐 **Timing:** Start by heading for Unterlinden Museum, before embarking on a tour of the old town on foot, by train or by boat (Little Venice).
👥 **Kids:** The Toy and Train Museum delights younger children.
☺ **Don't Miss:** The Unterlinden Museum with its Issenheim altarpiece.

A ruthless tyrant

Two centuries later, Colmar temporarily came under the rule of the Duke of Burgundy, Charles le Téméraire, and his cruel bailiff, Pierre de Hagenbach. When the latter was at last defeated and condemned to death, the executioner of Colmar was chosen to carry out the sentence. The sword he used is still kept in the Musée d'Unterlinden.

Natives of Colmar

Colmar is the birthplace of several famous artists, including **Martin Schongauer** (1445–91) whose altarpieces and engravings were admired by Dürer and Venetian artists of the Renaissance, and **Auguste Bartholdi** (1834–1904), best remembered for the Statue of Liberty. Between 1870 and 1914, when Alsace was occupied by Germany, a talented artist, Jean-Jacques Waltz, better known as **Hansi**, stimulated the town's passive resistance to German influence and kept alive the traditional image of Alsace with his humorist drawings of grotesque-looking German soldiers and good-natured villagers in regional costume.

MUSÉE D'UNTERLINDEN★★★

🕐 Daily except Tue 10am–6pm (Thu 8pm). 🕐 1 Jan, 1 May, 1 Nov and 25–25 and 31 Dec. ⊗€13 (child 12–17, €8). ✆03 89 20 15 50.
www.musee-unterlinden.com.
This museum (opened in 1849 on place d'Unterlinden near the Logelbach canal) was formerly a 13C convent whose name means "Under the lime trees". For 500 years, its nuns were famous for their mysticism and austere way of life.

Ground floor

The 13C **cloisters★** are built of pink sandstone from the Vosges mountains. Note the larger arch half way down the western gallery, which stands over the old *lavabo*; the basin is still visible. In a corner is a Renaissance well.
The rooms surrounding the cloisters are devoted to **art** from the **Rhine valley**. There are rich collections of late-medieval and Renaissance painting and sculpture, as well as stained glass, ivories and tapestries. Primitive art from the Rhine region is repre-

PRACTICAL INFORMATION

Guided tours – Tours of the old town are organised from Feb–Sept (*French and German only*), as are 'Weird and Unusual Colmar' (French). You can also explore the Old Town in a horse-drawn carriage (✆03 89 41 52 43). For more information about all tours, enquire at the tourist office.
The magic of lights – The town's most beautiful buildings are lit up at night on Fri and Sat throughout the whole year and during major events.
Christmas Market – *late Nov–Dec.*
Tourist train – *departures every 30min Rue Kléber (near the Unterlinden Museum), 9am–6.30pm, €6.50 (2–12 year olds €3.50). ✆03 89 24 19 82. www.colmarentrain.fr.*
Boat trips – 👜 *See Little Venice.*

sented by Holbein the Elder, Cranach the Elder, Caspar Isenmann and Martin Schongauer (copper engravings). ⊗*It is advisable to visit rooms 1, 3 and 4 as a preliminary step to the discovery of the Retable d'Issenheim, which remains the prize exhibit.*

Retable d'Issenheim★★★ (Issenheim Altarpiece)

This is displayed in the chapel together with works by Martin Schongauer and members of his school (24-panel altarpiece depicting the **Passion★★**).

Issenheim Altarpiece, Musée d'Unterlinden

© Fabienne FESSLER/ADT

St Bernard (1090–1153)

Bernard de Fontaine (later known as Bernard de Clairvaux), a young aristocrat from the Bourgogne region, should have become a soldier to comply with his family's wishes. Yet, at the age of 21, he entered the Abbaye de Cîteaux together with his brothers and several uncles and cousins whom he had persuaded to follow him. He was only 25 when Étienne Harding, the abbot of Cîteaux, sent him away with the mission of founding Clairvaux. Being both a mystic and a fine administrator, Bernard soon embodied the Cistercian ideal: the strict observance of the rule of St Benedict (prayer and work) which had, according to him, been relaxed by the Benedictine Order.

Deprived of everything, the young abbot encountered immense difficulties: the harshness of the climate, diseases, physical hardship. For his monks and himself, he set the hardest tasks; "they ate boiled vegetables and drank water, slept on pallets, had no heating in winter and wore the same clothes day and night". Yet this new form of spirituality and Bernard's reputation attracted many enthusiasts and the success of the new abbey was immediate.

The young mystic wanted to reform the whole religious life of his time and he played a part in many of its concerns: the election of bishops, various councils, the papal schism, and the second crusade which he preached in Vezelay in 1146. Shocked by the failure of the crusade (1148) and by the rise of heretic beliefs, which he fought without success, he died in 1153 and was canonised in 1174.

The gallery of the former Dominican chapel (early-16C sculpture) makes a good viewpoint, enabling visitors to have an overall view of the different panels and fully appreciate the composition of the famous polyptych.

Painted by **Matthias Grünewald** at the beginning of the 16C for the high altar of the monastery at Issenheim, which was founded in 1298 and devoted to curing ergotism (also known as St Anthony's fire). The altarpiece was moved to Colmar in 1793. Very little is known about the artist's life, but he is admired for his expressionist style, his daring colours and light effects, and the poetry and humour that pervade his paintings.

Taken apart during the Revolution, the polyptych was only put together again in 1930. It is made up of a carved central part, two fixed panels, two pairs of opening panels and a lower part which also opens. In order to preserve this unique work of art, the different parts are displayed separately.

Several models with opening panels have been fixed to the chapel's walls, allowing visitors to see how the altarpiece opened out.

First floor

The collections here focus on regional history, Alsatian art, furniture, weapons, pewter, gold plate, wrought iron, 18C porcelain and earthenware (Strasbourg), including reconstructed interiors.

Basement

The Gallo-Roman room contains fragments of the 3C Bergheim mosaic. Farther on, the two barrel-vaulted naves of the former **cellar** of the convent (house the archaeological collections, from prehistory to the Merovingian period.

Two rooms are devoted to 20C paintings by Renoir, Rouault, Picasso, Vieira da Silva, Nicolas de Staël and Poliakoff.

 WALKING TOURS

1 OLD TOWN★★

Round tour starting from place d'Unterlinden

▷ Walk along rue des Clefs

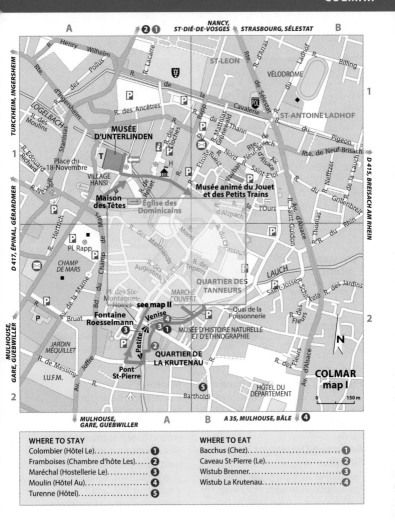

see map II

WHERE TO STAY

Colombier (Hôtel Le) **1**
Framboises (Chambre d'hôte Les) **2**
Maréchal (Hostellerie Le) **3**
Moulin (Hôtel Au) **4**
Turenne (Hôtel) **5**

WHERE TO EAT

Bacchus (Chez) **1**
Caveau St-Pierre (Le) **2**
Wistub Brenner **3**
Wistub La Krutenau **4**

The Hôtel de Ville is on the left; this 18C building belonged to the Abbaye de Pairis.

◗ When you reach place Jeanne-d'Arc, turn right onto Grand'Rue.

Temple protestant St-Matthieu
This former Franciscan church, now Protestant, is decorated with fine 14C and 15C **stained-glass windows**. At the top of the south aisle is the remarkable **Vitrail de la Crucifixion★** (15C), believed to be the work of Pierre d'Andlau.

◗ Turn left along the side of the church to reach place du 2-Février and look at the old hospital.

The roof of the 18C **Ancien Hôpital** features Alsatian dormer windows.

◗ Return to Grand'Rue and turn left

Admire along the way the Renaissance **Maison des Arcades★**, framed by two octagonal turrets and the **Schwendi Fountain**.
Walk past the **Maison du Pèlerin** (1571) to reach place de l'Ancienne-Douane.

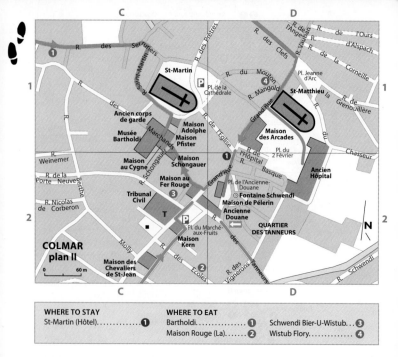

COLMAR plan II
0 — 60 m

WHERE TO STAY	WHERE TO EAT	
St-Martin (Hôtel)............❶	Bartholdi...............❶	Schwendi Bier-U-Wistub...❸
	Maison Rouge (La).......❷	Wistub Flory..............❹

Place de l'Ancienne-Douane

This picturesque square features timber-framed houses such as the **Maison au Fer Rouge**.

Ancienne Douane or "Koifhus"★

This former customs house is the most important civilian edifice in Colmar. The main building is from 1480; its ground floor was used as a warehouse to stock goods subject to municipal tax.

The great hall on the first floor, known as the Salle de la Décapole (the union formed by 10 Alsatian cities), was the meeting place for representatives of those cities. In the late 16C, a second building was added.

This is attractively decorated with a wooden gallery and flanked by a stair turret with canted corners; on the ground floor, three arches underline the opening and form a passage. Walk through to the other side and admire the fine outside staircase.

⬤ Take rue des Marchands opposite the customs house.

Maison Pfister★★

A hatter from Besançon had this lovely house built in 1537 and decorated with frescoes and medallions. The arcaded ground floor is surmounted by an elegant wooden gallery.

Next to the Maison Pfister, at no 9, stands a fine house (1609) adorned with a wooden gallery and a corner sculpted figure representing a merchant.

On the left of rue des Marchands, the 15C **Maison Schongauer**, also known as **Maison de la Viole**, belonged to the painter's family.

The small house opposite is known as the **Maison au Cygne**, where Schongauer reputedly lived from 1477 to 1490.

⬤ Walk through the arcades opposite the Musée Bartholdi (⬤see below), to place de la Cathédrale

On the square stand the oldest house in Colmar, **Maison Adolphe** (1350), and the **Ancien Corps de garde★** (1575). The town's magistrate was sworn in on this lovely Renaissance loggia; infamous sentences were also proclaimed here.

Opposite the former guardhouse stands the collegiate church of St-Martin, known as the cathedral.

Collégiale St-Martin★

This imposing edifice decorated with glazed tiles and red-sandstone projections was built in the 13C and 14C on the site of a Romanesque church.

The west doorway is flanked by two towers. The south tower is decorated with a sundial bearing the inscription *Memento Mori* (think of death). **St Nicholas' doorway**, which gives access to the south transept, is decorated with 13 small statues; the fourth one on the left represents the builder who signed in French, Maistre Humbert. Inside, note a 14C **Crucifixion★** in the axial chapel and a magnificent 18C organ loft by Silbermann.

▶ Leave place de la Cathédrale along rue des Serruriers

Église des Dominicains

🕐*Call for details.* ☞€1.50. 🕐*1 May, 25 Dec.* 🕾*03 89 41 27 20.*
Work began on the chancel in 1283, but the main part of the edifice was only completed in the 14C and 15C. Inside, altars and stalls date from the 18C, but the magnificent **stained-glass windows★** are contemporary with the construction of the church.

The famous 1473 painting by Martin Schongauer, the **Madonna of the Rose Bower★★**, can be seen at the entrance of the chancel; Virgin and Child form a charming picture against a golden background with rose bushes full of birds.

▶ Walk along rue des Boulangers then turn right onto rue des Têtes.

The fine Renaissance **Maison des Têtes★** (*No. 19*) owes its name to the numerous carved heads decorating the façade. The graceful gable is underlined by rows of scrolls; oriel windows complete the elaborate ornamentation.

▶ Return to place d'Unterlinden.

② PETITE VENISE★ (LITTLE VENICE)

Round tour starting from place de l'Ancienne-Douane

▶ From the square, follow rue des Tanneurs which runs along the canal

Quartiers des tanneurs

The tanners' district (renovated in 1974) is named for the inhabitants who used the river to tan and wash hides (a practise discontinued in the 19C). Timber-framed houses were narrow but high, creating lofts to dry the skins.

Cross the River Lauch to enter the **Krutenau district★**, once a fortified outlying area; this district's market gardeners once used flat-bottomed boats, similar to Venetian gondolas.

▶ Turn right along quai de la Poissonnerie

Cross the next bridge to the corner of rue des Écoles and rue du Vigneron, to see Batholdi's **Fontaine du Vigneron,** a celebration of Alsatian wines.

Continue along quai de la Poissonnerie then **rue de la Poissonnerie★** lined with picturesque fishermen's cottages. It runs into rue de Turenne, formerly rue de Krutenau, the old vegetable market.

▶ Take rue de la Herse then turn right onto a narrow street leading to the river.

Pleasant stroll along the bank to **Pont St-Pierre**. From the bridge, there is a lovely **view★** of Petite Venise.

Below the bridge, **boat trips** (*Promenade en Barques, 25min*) are available to explore the district further (🕐*late Feb–early Nov 10am–noon, 1.30–6.30pm; rest of year, call for details.* ☞€6 *(children under 10 no charge).* 🕾*03 89 41 01 94; www.barques-colmar.fr*).

▶ Turn right onto rue du Manège leading to place des Six-Montagnes-Noires.

Batholdi's **Fontaine Roesselmann**, stands on the square; it is dedicated to the town's hero (*see A Bit of History*). Walk towards the bridge on the right: the river, lined with willow trees, flows between two rows of old houses.

▶ Continue along rue St-Jean

On the left is the rather Venetian **Maison des Chevaliers de St-Jean** (1608). A little farther is the lovely place du Marché-aux-Fruits with its Renaissance style **Maison Kern**, the pink sandstone **Tribunal civil**★ and the Ancienne Douane.

▶ Return to place de l'Ancienne-Douane

SIGHTS
Musée Bartholdi
⊙Mar–Dec daily except Tue 10am–noon, 2–6pm. ⊙1 May, 1 Nov and 25 Dec. ⊛€6 (children under 18, no charge). ✆03 89 41 90 60. www.musee-bartholdi.fr.
The house in the heart of town where **Frédéric-Auguste Bartholdi** (1834–1904) was born is now a museum dedicated to the sculptor whose Statue of Liberty stands at the entrance of New York harbour. The second floor is entirely devoted to the statue's history.
The downstairs rooms have been turned into a museum of local history.
On the first floor, Bartholdi's private quarters, furnished exactly as they were when he lived here, celebrate the artist's life and works, while the last room displays a collection of Jewish art.
Bartholdi's works in Colmar:
◆ Statue of General Rapp, place Rapp
◆ Monument to Admiral Bruat, place du Champ-de-Mars
◆ Schwendi Fountain, place de l'Ancienne-Douane
◆ Wine-grower's Fountain, corner of rue des Écoles and rue du Vigneron.

Musée animé du Jouet et des Petits Trains (Toy Museum)
&⊙Jan–Nov daily except Tue 10am–5pm (Jul–Aug and Dec daily 10am–6pm). ⊙1 Jan, 1 May, 1 Nov and 25 Dec.

⊛€5 (child 8–18, €4). ✆03 89 41 93 10. www.museejouet.com.
👪 This collection, housed in a former cinema, includes railway engines (the Britannia, British model Pacific 213), trains on landscaped tracks across the entire second floor; Barbie© dolls; circus rides; large-size board games and automated figures – guaranteed to appeal to the child in us all.

ADDRESSES

🛏 STAY
⌸ **Chambre d'hôte Les Framboises** – 128 r. des Trois-Épis, 68230 Katzenthal. 5km/3mi NW of Colmar, Kaysersberg direction then D 10. ✆03 89 27 48 85. www.gites-amrein.fr. Closed Jan. 4 rooms. Leave Colmar behind and head for this village out in the vines. Accommodation in wood-panelled attic rooms.

⌸⌸ **Hôtel Au Moulin** – 500 Rte d'Herrlisheim, 68127 Ste-Croix-en-Plaine. 10km/6.2mi S of Colmar on A 35 and D 1. ✆03 89 49 31 20. http://aumoulin.pages perso-orange.fr. Closed mid-Dec–Mar. 17 rooms. 🅿. This old mill deep in the country is perfect for those seeking peace and quiet. A small museum of old local objects has been created in a neighbouring building.

⌸⌸ **Hôtel Turenne** – 10 rte de Bâle. ✆03 89 21 58 58. www.turenne.com. 83 rooms. On the edge of the old town, this hotel occupies a large, pleasing building with a pink and yellow façade.

⌸⌸⌸ **Hôtel Le Colombier** – 7 r. de Turenne, 68000 Colmar. 6km/3.5miles south of Colmar on D 14, then D 45. ✆03 89 23 96 00. www.hotel-le-colombier.fr. Closed Dec 24–Jan. 24 rooms. This lovely 15C house in old Colmar combines old stone and contemporary decor by retaining elements from its past, such as the superb Renaissance staircase. Contemporary furniture and modern paintings in the rooms.

⌸⌸⌸ **Hostellerie Le Maréchal** – 4 pl. Six Montagnes Noires. ✆03 89 41 60 32. www.hotel-le-marechal.com. 30 rooms. The rooms of these delightful Alsatian houses in Little Venice, most of which have a chocolate box charm, are furnished with brocades and antiques but also have 21C conveniences such as air conditioning and minibars.

🛇⊜🗑 **Hôtel St Martin** – *38 Grand'Rue. ℘03 89 24 11 51. www.hotel-saint-martin. com. Closed Dec 23–26, Jan 1–8. 40 rooms.* Three 14C and 17C houses in the old quarter, set around an inner courtyard with a turret and a Renaissance staircase. Cosy rooms with personal touches. Public car park nearby.

⌖/ EAT

🛇 **Winstub La Krutenau** – *1 r. de la Poissonnerie. ℘03 89 41 18 80. www. lakrutenau-colmar.com. Closed Jan–mid-Feb.* At this winstub beside the River Lauch you can go boating in Little Venice and eat a *flammekueche* on the flower-decked terrace beside the canal in summer.

🛇 **Schwendi Bier-U-Wistub** – *23–25 Grand'Rue. ℘03 89 23 66 26. Closed evenings on Christmas and New Year's Day.* A charming winstub with an ideal location in the heart of old Colmar. The principally wooden decor and the cooking, which is good quality and served in generous portions, are a tribute to Alsace. The terrace is a treat in summer.

🛇 **Le Caveau St-Pierre** – *24 r. de la Herse (Little Venice). ℘03 89 41 99 33. http://caveausaintpierre-colmar.fr. Booking advisable.* A pretty wooden footbridge across the Lauch leads to this 16C house, which offers a little slice of paradise with its rustic, local-style decor, cuisine, and a terrace stretching out over the water.

🛇⊜ **Chez Bacchus** – *2 Grand'Rue, 68230 Katzenthal. 5km/3mi NW of Colmar, Kaysersberg direction, then D 10. ℘03 89 27 32 25. Open Thu–Sat evening from Oct–mid-Jul 14, Sun and mid-Jul–Sept every evening except Tue. Booking advisable at weekends.* There's a friendly atmosphere in this wine bar dating from 1789 in a winemaking village. Massive exposed beams and helpings of Alsatian cuisine guaranteed to satisfy the healthiest of appetites. Automated puppets will entertain the children with a lively show.

🛇⊜ **Wistub Flory** – *1 rue Mangold. ℘03 89 41 78 80.* Decor heavy but don't let that deter you! Wide selection of regional dishes (ample portions) which can be enjoyed on the terrace when the weather is suitable.

🛇⊜🗑 **Bartholdi** – *2 rue des Boulangers. ℘03 89 41 07 74. www.restaurant-bartholdi.*

fr. Closed Sun eve and all day Mon. Lovers of Alsatian wines cannot fail to be delighted by the vast choice of local vintages offered by this spacious restaurant with the appearance of a Winstub.

🛇⊜🗑 **Wistub Brener** – *1 r. de Turenne. ℘03 89 41 42 33. www.wistub-brenner.fr. Closed Tue and Wed.* The terrace by the Lauch in Little Venice is very popular on fine days and the whole of Colmar meets here with obvious enjoyment.

🛇⊜🗑 **La Maison Rouge** – *9 rue des Écoles. ℘03 89 23 53 22. www.maison-rouge.net. Closed Sun and Mon.* The somewhat ordinary façade hides a delightful rustic interior with excellent regional and home-made cooking.

ENTERTAINMENT

La Manufacture – *6 rte d'Ingersheim. ℘03 89 24 31 78.* Contemporary theatre, as well as music and dance.

Folk nights – *Pl. de l'Ancienne Douane. May–Sept Tue at 8.30pm.*

Théâtre municipal – *Pl. du 18–Novembre. ℘03 89 20 29 01.* Classic plays, comedy and opera.

SHOPPING

Domaine viticole de la Ville de Colmar – *2 r. Stauffen. ℘03 89 79 11 87. www.domaineviticolecolmar.com. Mon–Fri 9.30am–12.30pm, 2–6pm, Sat 9am–noon, 2–5pm. Closed Sun, except the 3 Sun before Christmas.* Founded in 1895, this estate grows seven *cépages* and boasts a host of *grands crus* in addition to sparkling wines.

Caveau Robert-Karcher – *11 r. de l'Ours. ℘03 89 41 14 42. www.vins-karcher.com. Daily 8am–noon, 1.30–7pm. Closed Sun afternoon, 25–26 Dec.* The vineyards of this family business are northwest of Colmar, but the cellar, dating from 1602, is in a pedestrian street in the town centre. You can taste the whole range of Alsace wines and be shown around the cellar.

Fortwenger – *32 r. des Marchands, 68000 Colmar. ℘03 89 41 06 93. www. fortwenger.fr. Mon–Sat 9.30am–12.30pm, 1.30–6.30pm, Sun and public holidays 10am–12.30pm, 1.30–6pm. Closed 25–26 Dec and 1 Jan.* Charles Fortwenger founded his gingerbread factory in Gertwiller in 1768, but this Colmar shop sells a wide range of delicious chocolate, honey, icing sugar, aniseed and cinnamon treats. Also local souvenirs.

Eguisheim★
Haut-Rhin

This ancient village developed round an octagonal 13C castle. Surrounded by 300ha of vines and lying at the foot of three ruined towers, used as sundials by workers in the plain below, the village has hardly changed since the 16C. Two famous wines are produced locally. The wine-growers festival takes place during the fourth weekend in August. Visitors can follow the wine trail (*1h on foot; guided tours of cellars with wine-tasting included*).

VISIT
Grand'Rue
The doorways of the picturesque houses lining this street are adorned with coats of arms, with dates; also note the two Renaissance fountains.

Tour of the ramparts
The signposted itinerary follows the former watch path; the houses here offer a wealth of architectural features (balconies, oriels, and timber frames).

Church
Inside the modern church, to the right of the entrance, there is a chapel beneath the steeple. It contains the old doorway with its 12C tympanum illustrating Christ between St Peter and St Paul; the procession of Wise Virgins and Foolish Virgins forms the lintel. 19C Callinet organ.

🚗 DRIVING TOUR

Route des Cinq Châteaux★
20km/12.4mi round tour including five castles, plus about 1h45 on foot.

▶ Drive to Husseren (*see Routes des VIN*) along D 14. As you come out of the village, turn right onto the forest road, known as the Route des cinq Châteaux; 1km/0.6mi farther on, leave the car in the parking area and walk to Eguisheim's three castles (5min uphill).

▶ **Population:** 1 797.

🎡 **Michelin Map:** Michelin Local map 315: H-8 also see Route des VINS.

ℹ **Tourist Office:** 22A, Grand'Rue, 68420 Eguisheim. ✆ 03 89 23 40 33. www.ot-eguisheim.fr

▶ **Location:** Eguisheim is 7km/4.3mi from Colmar, 41km/25.5mi north of Mulhouse via N 83 or E 225-A 35 Colmar-Mulhouse road.

🕐 **Timing:** Allow at least half a day, and be aware that many events take place in the evenings in summertime.

Donjons d'Eguisheim
Three massive square keeps built of red Esandstone and known as Weckmund, Wahlenbourg and Dagsbourg stand at the top of the hill. They belonged to the powerful Eguisheim family (*see MULHOUSE*). Pope Léon IX was most probably born here (*see WANGENBOURG: Excursions*).

🚶 From here, the Château de Hohlandsbourg can be reached on foot (*1hr*).

▶ Alternatively, return to the car and drive on for about 6km/3.7mi

The road offers many fine viewpoints.

Château de Hohlandsbourg★
♿🕐*Apr–Jun Tue–Sun 10am–6pm; Jul–Aug daily 10am–7pm; Sept Tue–Sat 1–6pm (Sun 10am–6pm); Oct–mid-Nov Tue–Sat 1–5pm, Sun 10am–5pm.* 🎟*seasonal pricing: €7–€9 (child 6–17, €4.50–€6.50).* ✆03 89 30 10 20. www.chateau-hohlandsbourg.com. The imposing granite castle stands on the left; built c. 1279, it first belonged to the powerful House of Habsburg and was destroyed during the Thirty Years War. Restored in the 16C, it was adapted to the use of artillery.

Town square, Eguisheim

From the watch path, there is a magnificent **view**★★ of the Pflixbourg keep and Hohneck summit to the west.

Donjon de Pflixbourg

▶ A path, branching off to the left 2km/1.2mi further on, leads to the keep.

🏰 The fortress was of the representative of the Holy Roman Emperor.

▶ As you rejoin D 417, turn right towards Colmar. On leaving Wintzenheim (see Route des VINS: From Châtenois to Colmar), turn right onto N 83 then right again onto D 1bis to return to Eguisheim.

ADDRESSES

🏠STAY

🍽🍽 **Hostellerie du Château –**
2 r. du Château. ℰ03 89 23 72 00. www. hostellerieduchateau.com. 10 rooms and 1 suite. This old building on the village square has been completely renovated by the architect owner. Its stylish modern decor offers charming, light, pleasant rooms with old-fashioned bathrooms.

🍴EAT

🍽🍽 **La Grangelière** – *59 r. du Rempart-Sud. ℰ03 89 23 00 30. www.lagrangeliere.fr. Closed Sun evenings, and all day Wed and Thu from Nov–Apr.* This Alsatian house near the ramparts is slightly off the tourist trail. But you won't regret making the detour: the chef, who has worked in some major establishments, offers cooking that is both contemporary and very tempting.

🍽🍽🍽 **Le Caveau d'Eguisheim** –
3 pl. du Château-St-Léon, 68420 Eguisheim. ℰ03 89 41 08 89. Closed Mon and Tue. Only regional wines are on offer in this pretty local-style restaurant, situated in the village square. Fortunately they go very well with the chef's inventive cooking, which combines regional dishes and contemporary flavours, making eating here a pleasure.

SHOPPING

Charles Baur – *29 Grand'Rue. ℰ03 89 41 32 49. www.vinscharlesbaur.fr. Mon–Sat 9am–7pm, Sun 9am–noon (Sun afternoons by appointment). Closed Christmas.* Tour of the cellar, tasting and sale of Alsace wines.

Guebwiller★

Haut-Rhin

This small yet lively town, situated along the Route des Vins, has retained a wealth of architectural features.

A BIT OF HISTORY

Guebwiller developed from the 8C onwards under the control of the abbots; in 1275, the city was granted its own charter and allowed to build its own fortifications. Throughout the Middle Ages, vineyards were the main source of wealth; today the surrounding area produces four great wines, Kitterlé, Kessler, Saering and Spiegel.

TOWN WALK
Église Notre-Dame★

Built between 1760 and 1785 by the last prince-abbot of Murbach, the lofty **interior★★** of this church contains the striking high altar by Sporrer, representing the **Assumption★★** (1783).

▶ Walk along rue de la République

Place de la Liberté with its fountain (1536) is on the right.

Hôtel de ville★

Built in 1514 for a wealthy draper; note the 16C statue of the Virgin in a corner recess on the right.

▶ Continue to the Église St-Léger

Église St-Léger★

The **west front★★** of this church dates from the 12C and 13C.

▶ **Population:** 11 664.
▶ **Michelin Map:** Michelin Local map 315: H-9 also see Route des CRÊTES and Route des VINS.
▶ **Tourist Office:** 45 rue de la république, 68500 Guebwiller. ℰ03 89 76 10 63. www.tourisme-guebwiller.fr.
▶ **Location:** Guebwiller is located 25km from Colmar and Mulhouse on N 63.
▶ **Kids:** The Vivarium of Lautenbach provides a fascinating insight into the world of creepy-crawlies.

▶ Walk around the church.

The former bailiff's court of justice is located in a fine house dating from 1583 (No. 2 rue des Blés). Next comes a lovely **tithe cellar** and last is the former 16C **town hall.**

MUSEUM
Musée du Florival★

℗Thu–Fri 2–6pm, Sat–Sun and holidays 10am–noon, 2–6pm. ℗1 Jan, 1 May and 25 Dec. ℰ03 89 74 22 89.
The museum, housed in the former 18C residence of aristocratic canons from the chapter of Murbach abbey, focuses on the geology and history of the Florival valley, but it is most interesting for its display of the **works★** of **Théodore Deck**, such as a glazed tile veranda and vases coloured in a special blue named after the artist (1823–1891).

St Valentine's Day

These fortifications turned out to be very useful in 1445, on St Valentine's day, when the Armagnacs (opposed to the Burgundians and the English during the Hundred Years War) tried to take the town by surprise by crossing the frozen moat. A townswoman named Brigitte Schick gave the alarm; her shrieks were so loud that the attackers thought the whole population had been warned and they ran away, leaving their ladders behind. These are still kept in the Église St-Léger.

Théodore Deck (1823-91)

This native of Guebwiller was a potter and ceramist of genius. His research led him to discover in 1874 the lost formula of the turquoise blue characteristic of Persian ceramics; this blue was henceforth known as the *Bleu Deck*. Deck also found the secret of the famous Chinese celadon, reproduced oriental *cloisonné* and succeeded in decorating his ceramics with a gilt background. In his book, *Ceramics*, published in 1887, he disclosed his formulae and offered anyone interested in the subject the benefit of his experience. He was put in charge of the Manufacture nationale de Sèvres and spent the last years of his life perfecting his art and creating new types of porcelain. His funeral monument in Montparnasse cemetery in Paris, was carved by his friend Frédéric Auguste Bartholdi who sculpted the famous Statue of Liberty.

🚗 DRIVING TOUR

Guebwiller valley★★
From Guebwiller to Le Markstein. 30km/17mi. Allow 2h. Local map 🍂see Parc naturel régional des BALLONS DES VOSGES and p291.

The **Lauch valley** or Guebwiller valley is known as Florival (literally flower valley); walkers will appreciate the *zone de tranquillité* or car-free quiet area at the end of the valley, on either side of D 430.

▶ Drive out of Guebwiller along D 430 towards the Route des Crêtes and Le Markstein.

Lautenbach★
The village, which dates from the 8C, developed round a Benedictine abbey. Today, only the **church★** remains. The **vivarium** 👥 of the Moulin de Lautenback-Zell houses some fascinating insects. 🕐*Sept–Jun Tue–Sun 2–6pm; Jul–Aug daily 10am–6pm.* 🕐*3 weeks early Dec, 24–26 and 31 Dec, and 1 Jan.* 🎟*€8 (child 5–16, €4). ☎03 89 74 02 48. www.vivariumdumoulin.org.*

Just beyond Linthal, the Lauch valley becomes narrow and wild.

Lac de la Lauch★
A winding road leads to the calm waters of this artificial lake. Angling is allowed, but swimming is prohibited.

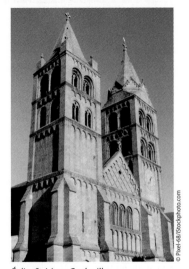
© Pixel-68/iStockphoto.com

Église St-Léger, Guebwiller

Le Markstein – 🍂*See Routes des Crêtes*

ADDRESSES

SHOPPING
Pâtisserie Christmann – *Pl. de l'Hôtel-de-Ville. ☎03 89 74 27 44. 7.30am–7pm.* Cakes, chocolates and delicious fruit tarts to be enjoyed in this tearoom.

Foire aux vins – This wine fair takes place every Ascension Thursday, offering the opportunity to taste and purchase sylvaner, pinot blanc, muscat d'Alsace, riesling, tokay d'Alsace, gewurztraminer, pinot noir, pinot rosé and crémant d'Alsace.

Kaysersberg

Kaysersberg★★
Haut-Rhin

Kaysersberg is a small city with a quaint medieval character, built on the banks of the Weiss, where the river runs into the Plaine d'Alsace. From the ruins of the medieval castle *(30min on foot there and back),* there is a lovely general view of the town and its famous vineyards.

▶ **Population:** 2 780.
Michelin Map: Michelin Local map 315: H-8 – also see Route des VINS.
Tourist Office: 39 rue du Gén.-de-Gaulle, 68240 Kayserberg. ℘03 89 78 22 78. www.kaysersberg.com.

A BIT OF HISTORY
In Roman times, it was already called *Caesaris Mons* (the emperor's mountain) because of its strategic position along one of the most important routes linking ancient Gaul and the Rhine valley.

TOWN WALK
This itinerary is centred on the high street, rue du Gén.-de-Gaulle.

Hôtel de ville★
Built in the Renaissance style characteristic of the Rhine region.

Église Ste-Croix★
Kaysersberg parish church stands beside a small square adorned with a 16C fountain, restored in the 18C and surmounted by a statue of Emperor Constantine.
The chancel contains, above the high altar, a wooden **altarpiece★★** in the shape of a triptych, a magnificent work by Jean Bongartz, the master from Colmar (1518).
The north aisle shelters a damaged 1514 Holy Sepulchre; note the group representing the holy women, by Jacques Wirt. According to an Alsatian tradition, a slit in Christ's chest is intended for the host during Holy Week.

Chapelle St-Michel
The two-storey chapel was built in 1463; the lower level is an ossuary and contains a stoup decorated with a skull.

Cemetery
A 16C wooden gallery provides a shelter for the unusual cross, known as the plague cross, dating from 1511.

▶ Go back to rue du Gén.-de-Gaulle, also known as Grand'Rue.

Old houses★

There are many old houses along rue de l'Église, rue de l'Ancien-Hôpital, rue de l'Ancienne-Gendarmerie and rue du Général-de-Gaulle (also called Grand-Rue). The **Renaissance well** dating from 1618, situated in the courtyard of No. 54 Grand-Rue, bears a humorous inscription.

▶ Continue towards the River Weiss.

Hostellerie du Pont

On the corner of rue des Forgerons, this elegant hostel has been restored; it was the former baths.

Pont fortifié★

The fortified bridge built in the 15C and 16C is in a charming setting.
The **Maison Brief★** is an elaborately carved 16C timber-framed house with covered gallery.

MUSEUMS
Musée Albert-Schweitzer

♿⏱*Mid-Mar–mid-Nov daily except Wed 9am–noon, 2–6pm; rest of year call for information.* ⏱*Jan–mid-Mar.* ✆*03 89 47 36 55.*
Standing next to Albert Schweitzer's birthplace in 1875, the museum retraces the life of the great humanist using documents, photos and personal mementoes and souvenirs.

Musée communal

⏱*Jul–Aug daily except Tue 10am–noon, 2–6pm.* ✆*03 89 78 22 78.*
Housed in a Renaissance dwelling with a square turret, the museum's exhibits include medieval religious art.

ADDRESSES

 STAY

🛏🍽 **Hôtel Les Remparts** – *4 rue de la Flieh.* ✆*03 89 47 12 12. www.lesremparts. info. Closed Feb. 40 rooms.* This hotel is situated in a quiet residential area not far from the market of the old town. Some of the rooms have terraces.

Albert Schweitzer

Born in Kaysersberg on 14 January 1875, Albert Schweitzer became a clergyman, a theologian, a famous organist, a musicologist, a writer and a missionary doctor. After WWI, he spent most of his life in West Africa where he founded a hospital, occasionally returning to Europe to give organ concerts. He was awarded the Nobel Peace Prize in 1952 and died in 1965 in Lambaréné (Gabon) where his work lives on. He had a house built in Gunsbach, where he spent his childhood during the time his father was the village pastor.

🛏🍽 **Hostellerie Schwendi** – *2 Place Schwendi, 68240 Kientzheim.* ✆*03 89 47 30 50. www.schwendi.fr. Closed 24 Dec–mid-Mar. 29 rooms. Restaurant* 🛏🍽. With its half-timbered façade, the hotel is located in the centre of a wine-making village. Charming and personalised rooms. Terrace near the fountain in nice weather. Sample the family estate wines, available in the dining room.

⟟⧫**EAT**

🛏🍽 **Le Couvent** – *1 r. Couvent.* ✆*03 89 78 23 29. Closed Thu out of season.* An unassuming restaurant that is worth seeking out. It has a good local reputation and is much frequented by winemakers. Alsace dishes and traditional cuisine.

SHOPPING

Caveau des Vignerons de Kientzeim-Kaysersberg – *20 r. du Gén.-de-Gaulle.* ✆*03 89 47 18 43. Easter–mid-Nov and Christmas holidays Wed–Mon 10am–7pm.* Alsace crémant (sparkling wine) and wines to taste and buy.

Pâtisserie Lœcken – *46 r. du Gén.-de-Gaulle.* ✆*03 89 47 34 35. Tue–Sun 8am–6.30pm (7pm in summer). Closed 25 Dec and 1 Jan.* Cake shop in a superb 16C wood-shingled house. The chocolates are home-made, while the teas come from all over the world. Alsace foie gras and coffee roasting.

Église de Murbach

© René Mattes/hemis.fr

Église de
Murbach ★★

Haut-Rhin

The village of Murbach nestles round the former abbey church of the famous Romanesque-style Murbach abbey.
Founded in 727 the abbey was already rich and famous in the 9C. "As proud as the Murbach hound" became a popular saying, referring to the black hound on the abbey's coat of arms.

VISIT

Allow 15min.
The 12C church has a richly-decorated flat wall on the **east end★★** which projects slightly. A gallery with 17 different colonnettes can be seen above two tiers of windows.

On leaving the abbey church, follow the Stations of the Cross to the Chapelle Notre-Dame-de-Lorette (1693) for enjoyable views of the surroundings.

 **Michelin Map:** Michelin Local map 315: G-9.

EXCURSION

Buhl

3km/1.9mi E along D 40.
The large neo-Romanesque **church** of this lively village (metalworks and plastics) houses a rare Alsatian painted triptych (7m wide) not inside a museum. The **Buhl altarpiece★★** was probably made c. 1500 by artists from the Schongauer School (&*see COLMAR: Musée d'Unterlinden*).

ADDRESSES

⑨/ EAT

◻◻ **Auberge de l'Abbaye** – *20 r. de Guebwiler, 68530 Murbach.* ✆*03 89 82 61 84. Closed Tue and Wed.* The menu is classic rather than regional, but *flammekueches* are served on Friday and Sunday evenings. Terrace and garden.

Ribeauvillé ★

Haut-Rhin

Ribeauvillé occupies a picturesque site at the foot of the Vosges mountains crowned with old castles. The small town is renowned for its Riesling and Gewürztraminer, Alsatian white wines, and is home to a wine festival in July.

▸ **Population:** 4 957.
🕭 **Michelin Map:** Michelin Local map 315: H-7 – also see Route des VINS.
🛈 **Tourist Office – Bureau d'accueil de Ribeauvillé:** 10 Grand'rue, 68150 Ribeauvillé. ✆03 89 73 23 23. www.ribeauville-riquewihr.com.

🐾 TOWN WALK

◗ Start at the tourist office housed in the former guardroom at no 1.

Grand'Rue ★★

This semi-pedestrianised street lined with half-timbered houses runs through the whole town. At the southern and eastern entrances, two old towers are crowned by storks' nests.

Pfifferhüs (Restaurant des Ménétriers).

No. 14. Note the two statues standing on a loggia above the door, which illustrate the Annunciation.

Halle au Blé

Place de la 1re-Armée.
The old covered corn exchange sits atop a secret passageway.

Fontaine Renaissance

The red-and-yellow-sandstone fountain (1536) is crowned by a heraldic lion.

Tour des Bouchers ★

This old belfry used to mark the separation between the upper and the middle town. The base dates from the 13C. Beautiful 17C timber-framed house at No. 78 Grand'Rue.

Place de la Sinne

This is a charming little square, lined with timber-framed houses, with a fountain (1860) in its centre.

Église St-Grégoire-le-Grand

The church dates from the 13C–15C. Note the tympanum of the west doorway and the fine ironwork on the door. In the south aisle, there is a 15C carved-wood Virgin and Child, gilt and painted, wearing the local headdress; the Baroque organ was made by Rinck.

◗ Return along Grand'Rue then take rue Klobb and rue des Juifs.

Maisons anciennes

16C and 17C houses can be seen on rue des Juifs, rue Klobb, rue Flesch and rue des Tanneurs (note the openings in the roof of No. 12 for drying skins).

Hôtel de ville

🐾*Guided tours: May–Sept Tue–Fri and Sun 10am, 11am and 2pm.* ◷*Public holidays.* ✆03 89 73 67 79.
The town hall houses a small **museum** with 17C gold plate and vermeil goblets that belonged to the local lords.

Pfifferdaj

The "day of the fifes" is one of the oldest festivals in Alsace. It takes place on the first Sunday in September. Travelling musicians used to gather in the town to pay homage to their suzerain. The statutes of their powerful corporation were recorded by Colmar's Council. Today, the Pfifferdaj or **Fête des Ménétriers** is a folk festival with a historic procession and free wine tasting at the Fontaine du Vin, place de l'Hôtel-de-Ville.

◐ Walk back along rue Flesch and rue des Tanneurs.

🐾WALKING TOUR

◐ Leave Ribeauvillé by the D 416. Leave the car in the parking area situated on the roadside, about 800m out of town.

🚶 *Walk up the Chemin des Stations (20min) or the Chemin Sarassin (40min).*

Notre-Dame-de-Dusenbach

The three chapels of this popular place of pilgrimage were destroyed on three occasions: by the English in 1365, by the Swedes in 1632 and by the Republicans in 1794. The **Virgin's Chapel**, a convent, a neo-Gothic church (1903) and a pilgrims' shelter (1913) were built over the ruins. The chapel stands on the edge of a promontory towering above the Dusenbach valley. Inside, above the altar, there is a 15C polychrome wood **Pietà**, said to perform miracles.

◐ Follow the Chemin Sarassin then the path leading to the castles.

Stop by the **Rocher Kahl**, at the halfway mark. From this granite scree, there is a fine bird's-eye view of the Strengbach valley and its forested slopes.

◐ At the intersection of forest lanes go straight on along the path signposted Ribeauvillé par les châteaux.

Château du Haut-Ribeaupierre

It is possible to walk through the ruins of this 12C castle (⊶ *the keep is closed to the public*).

◐ Retrace your steps (avoiding the direct path linking Haut-Ribeaupierre and St-Ulrich) back to the intersection and follow the marked path to St-Ulrich.

Château de St-Ulrich★

The stairs leading to the castle start from the foot of the keep, on the left.

The **castle** was not only a fortress, like most castles in the Vosges region, but also the luxury residence of the Comtes de Ribeaupierre. The stairs lead through the castle gate to a small courtyard. A door at the end of the courtyard gives access to the Romanesque Great Hall, lit by nine twinned rounded windows, which was once covered by a timber ceiling.

◐ Return to the small courtyard and go up the stairs to the chapel.

Retrace your steps to visit the oldest part of the castle including Romanesque living quarters, whose windows are decorated with fleurs-de-lys, another courtyard and the keep. The red-sandstone keep, built on a granite base, towers over the rest of the castle. From the top, the **panorama★★** extends over the Strengbach valley, the ruins of the **Château de Girsberg** (dating from the 12C and abandoned in the 17C), Ribeauvillé and the Plaine d'Alsace.

🚗 DRIVING TOUR

Col de Fréland

47km/29mi round tour. Allow 5h.

◐ Leave Ribeauvillé by the D 416, following the River Strengbach which flows through the beautiful Ribeauvillé forest. After 7km/4.3mi, turn left towards Aubure along a picturesque cliff road.

Aubure

The resort is situated on a sunny plateau and surrounded by pine and fir forests.

◐ Turn left onto D 11III. On the descent from the Col de Fréland, 1.5km/0.9mi from the pass, turn left onto a narrow road.

Château de St-Ulrich

The road runs through one of the finest **pine forests★** in France.

◯ After leaving the forest, drive on for 1km/0.6mi to return to D 11III.

There is a good view of the Weiss valley and part of the Val d'Orbey.

◯ Continue past Fréland and, 1.5km/ 0.9mi beyond the intersection with D 11IV to Orbey, turn left onto N 415.

Kaysersberg★★
See KAYSERSBERG.

◯ The road joins the Route des Vins back to Ribeauvillé (see Route des VINS).

Beblenheim
The village, which boasts a 15C Gothic fountain, lies close to Sonnenglantz (Sunshine), a famous hillside producing high-quality wines (Alsatian Tokay, Muscatel and Gewürztraminer).

Riquewihr★★★ – *See RIQUEWIHR.*

Hunawihr – *See Route des VINS.*

◯ Drive back to Ribeauvillé.

Castles overlooking the Plaine d'Alsace★★
46km/29mi round tour. Allow 2h.

◯ Leave Ribeauvillé W along D 1B.

Bergheim – *See Route des VINS.*

St-Hippolyte
An attractive village with flower-decked fountains and Gothic church.

◯ As you enter the village, turn left towards Haut-Kœnigsbourg then right 4km/2.5mi beyond St-Hippolyte and left 1km/0.6mi further on to take the one-way road round the castle.

Château du Haut-Kœnigsbourg★★
See Château du HAUT-KŒNIGSBOURG.

◯ Return to D 1B1 and turn right then right again onto D 481.

From Schaentzel to Lièpvre★
The picturesque forested road descends amid superb views of the Liepvrette valley and the ruined castles of the Vosges towering above it to the north.

◯ Return to D 1B1 and turn right onto D42.

Thannenkirch
This peaceful village lies amid dense forests. The road follows the **Bergenbach valley** down to the Plaine d'Alsace.

◯ At Bergheim, turn right towards Ribeauvillé.

Riquewihr★★★

Haut-Rhin

The attractive little town of Riquewihr was for several centuries the property of the Dukes of Wurtemberg. Spared by the many wars that ravaged the region, the town looks today just as it did in the 16C. It lies in the heart of a wine-growing area, and is especially lively during the grape harvest.

▶ **Population:** 1 201.

Michelin Map: Michelin Local map 315: H-8 – also see Route des VINS.

Tourist Office: 2 rue de la Première Armée, 68340 Riquewihr. ✆03 89 73 23 23. www.ribeauville-riquewihr.com

Location: Riquewihr lies 13km/8mi north of Colmar, just off the N63 within the Parc Régional des Ballons des Vosges.

Timing: Don't try to find a parking space in town; use one of the many outside car parks. Allow 2h to fully admire the town's old medieval houses.

✦ WALKING TOUR

▶ Go through the archway of the town hall and follow rue du Général-de-Gaulle straight ahead. On the left the Cour du Château leads to the Château.

Château des Ducs de Wurtemberg

Completed in 1540, the castle has kept its mullioned windows, its gable deco-rated with antlers and its stair turret. It houses the **Musée de la Communi-cation en Alsace** (✦*see Museums*). A small open-air museum of architectural remains and the 1790 Altar of Freedom can be seen in front of the east side.

▶ Continue along rue du Général-de-Gaulle.

No. 12, known as the **Maison Irion** (1606) has a corner oriel; opposite, there is a 16C well. Next door, the **Maison Jung-Selig** (1561) has a carved timber frame.

Maison Liebrich★ (Cour des cigognes)

A well dating from 1603 and a huge winepress from 1817 stand in the pic-turesque courtyard of this 16C house, surrounded by balustraded wooden galleries (added in the 17C).
Opposite stands the **Maison Behrel** adorned with a lovely oriel (1514) sur-mounted by openwork added in 1709.

▶ Take the first turn on the right and follow rue Kilian.

Maison Brauer

This house, at the end of the street, has a fine doorway dating from 1618.

▶ Continue along rue des Trois-Églises.

Place des Trois-Églises

The square is framed by two former churches, St-Érard and Notre-Dame, converted into dwellings, and a 19C Protestant church.

▶ Return to rue du Général-de-Gaulle.

Maison Preiss-Zimmer★

The house that belonged to the wine-growers' guild stands in the last but one of a succession of picturesque court-yards. Further on, on the right, stands the former **tithe court** of the lords of Ribeaupierre.
On place de la Sinn, which marks the end of rue du Général-de-Gaulle, is the pretty 1580 **Fontaine Sinnbrunnen**.

Street of Riquewihr

Rue et cour des Juifs

Narrow rue des Juifs leads to the picturesque Cour des Juifs, the old ghetto, from which a narrow passageway and wooden stairs lead to the ramparts and the **Musée de la Tour des Voleurs** (*see Museums*).

Dolder★

Built in 1291, this gate was reinforced during the 15C and 16C.

▷ Go through the gate to the Obertor.

Obertor (upper gate)

Note the portcullis and the place where the former drawbridge was fixed. On the left, you can see a section of the ramparts and a defence tower.

▷ Return through Dolder and along rue du Général-de-Gaulle then turn right onto rue du Cerf.

Maison Kiener★

No. 2. The house built in 1574 has a pediment with an inscription and a bas-relief depicting Death getting hold of the founder of the house. Opposite, the **Auberge du Cerf** dates from 1566.

▷ Continue along rue du Cerf then turn left onto rue Latérale.

Rue Latérale

Lovely houses on this street include the **Maison du marchand Tobie Berger** at No. 6, which has a 16C oriel and a Renaissance doorway in the courtyard.

▷ Turn right onto rue de la 1re-Armée.

Maison du Bouton d'Or

No. 16. The house goes back to 1566. An alleyway, just round the corner, leads to another tithe court known as the Cour de Strasbourg dating from 1597.

▷ Retrace your steps then continue past the Maison du Bouton d'Or along rue Dinzheim to rue de la Couronne.

Maison Dissler★

No. 6. With its scrolled gables and loggia, this stone house (1610) is an interesting example of Renaissance style.

▷ Continue along rue de la Couronne back to rue du Général-de-Gaulle.

MUSEUMS
Maison Hansi

&🕐*Mon noon–6.30pm, Tue–Sun and public holidays 10am–6.30pm.* 🕐*1 Jan, mid-end Jan, 25 Dec.* ⊗€*5.* ℘*03 89 41 44 20. www.hansi.fr.*

This museum contains watercolours, prints and decorated ceramics by the

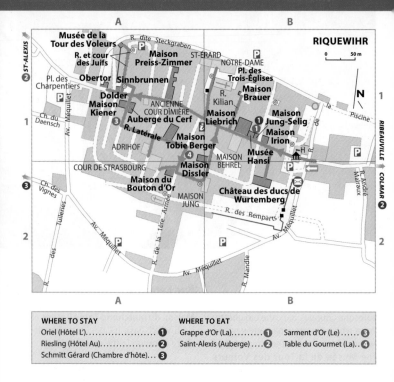

WHERE TO STAY

Oriel (Hôtel L')......................... ❶

Riesling (Hôtel Au).................. ❷

Schmitt Gérard (Chambre d'hôte)... ❸

WHERE TO EAT

Grappe d'Or (La).......... ❶

Saint-Alexis (Auberge) .... ❷

Sarment d'Or (Le) ...... ❸

Table du Gourmet (La).. ❹

Colmar artist and cartoonist, JJ Waltz, known as Hansi (🕭 *see COLMAR),* whose brother was a chemist in Riquewihr.

Musée de la Tour des Voleurs (Museum of Thieves)

🕔*Apr–Oct daily 10.30am–1pm, 2–6pm.* 🕔*Nov to Easter.* ⌾€7 *(combined ticket with Musée du Dolder).* 📞*03 89 86 00 92.* The tour includes the torture chamber, the dungeon, guardroom and the caretaker's lodgings of this former prison.

Musée du Dolder

Access by staircase to left of the Porte du Dolder.
🕔*Apr–Oct Sat–Sun and public holidays 2–6pm; mid-Jul–late Aug daily 2–6pm.* 🕔*Nov to Easter.* ⌾€7 *(combined ticket with Tour des Voleurs).* 📞*03 89 58 44 08.* The museum houses mementoes, prints, weapons, tools and furniture, associated with local history.

ADDRESSES

🛏 STAY

🍽 **Chambre d'hôte Schmitt Gérard** – *17 rue des Vignes.* 📞*07 71 10 23 66. www. chambres-schmitt.fr. Closed Jan–Mar.* 🖨. A house with a garden at the top of the village, on the edge of a vineyard. Impeccably clean panelled rooms under the roof.

🍽🍽 **Hôtel au Riesling** – *5 rte des Vins, 68340 Zellenberg.* 📞*03 89 47 85 85. www. au-riesling.com. 36 rooms.* 🅿. In the heart of the vineyards this hotel proudly carries the name of the famous wine. The rooms of this long building are partly modernised and rather sedate. The rustic style restaurant offers a pretty view of the vines. Traditional menu.

🍽🍽🍽 **Hôtel L'Oriel** – *3 r. des Écuries-Seigneuriales.* 📞*03 89 49 03 13. www. hotel-oriel.com. 22 rooms.* This 16C hotel is easily recognised by its wrought-iron sign. The sloping walls, maze of staircases, exposed beams and bedrooms with Alsatian furniture create a romantic atmosphere. Also three more modern rooms in the annexe.

⍭/EAT

◔◔ **Auberge St-Alexis** – 68240 St-Alexis 6km W of Riquewihr on minor road and forest track. ℘03 89 73 90 38. www.saintalexis.fr. Closed Fri. It's definitely worth venturing into the forest to this old 17C hermitage. You will be rewarded with simple authentic dishes, such as vegetable soup, *choucroute* and fruit tarts, made from local farm produce.

◔◔◔ **Le Sarment d'Or** – 4 r. du Cerf. ℘03 89 86 02 86. http://riquewihr-sarment-dor.fr. Closed Sun evening, Tue lunch and Mon. Pale wood panelling, a pretty fireplace and huge beams create a lovely warm atmosphere in this restaurant in one of Riquewihr's fine 17C houses. The cooking is traditional with some modern touches. Plush, comfortable rooms.

◔◔◔ **Le Grappe d'Or** – 1 r. des Ecuries Seigneuriales. ℘03 89 47 89 52. www.restaurant-grappedor.com. Closed Wed Feb–Mar, and Thu. This welcoming house from 1554 has two dining rooms with well-worn walls, one adorned with rustic tools and the other with a pretty earthernware stove. Locally sourced menu.with a pretty earthernware stove. Locally sourced menu.

◔◔◔◔ **La Table du Gourmet** – 5 Rue de la 1ère Armée. ℘03 89 49 09 09. www.jlbrendel.com. Closed Wed except mid-Apr–mid-Nov; Thu lunch, and all day Tue. This restaurant has character, not least its chef, Jean-Luc Brendin, who devizes outstanding dishes, often organic, and using ingredients from his own garden.

Rouffach★

Haut-Rhin

Set at the foot of vine-covered hills, Rouffach is a prosperous agricultural centre, which has preserved many traces of its medieval past.

SIGHTS
Église Notre-Dame-de-l'Assomption

This church is mostly 12C–13C although the transept is older (11C–12C). The north and south towers were added in the 19C; the latter was never completed owing to the Franco-Prussian War of 1870.

Inside, strong piers alternate with weak ones as is the custom in 12C architecture from the Rhine region. Note the octagonal christening font (1492) in the south transept. An elegant staircase, leaning against the piers of the crossing, is all that remains of the 14C rood screen. On the left of the high altar, there is a lovely 15C tabernacle. A Virgin and Child under a canopy, carved c 1500, adjoins a pillar on the north side of the nave.

▸ **Population:** 4 835.
 Michelin Map: Michelin Local map 315: H-9 – also see Route des VINS.
 Tourist office: Place de la République, 68250 Rouffach. ℘03 89 78 53 15. www.ot-rouffach.com
 Location: 15 km/9.3mi south of Colmar and 28km/17.4mi north of Mulhouse.

12C Heroes

In 1106, Emperor Henry V kidnapped a young girl and settled her in Rouffach castle. In defense of the young girl, the village women took up arms. Their husbands followed and together they attacked the castle. Panic-stricken, Henry V fled from Rouffac leaving behind his crown, his sceptre and his imperial cloak, which were placed as offerings on the Virgin's altar.

Tour des Sorcières

The machicolated tower covered with a four-sided roof crowned by a stork's nest dates from the 13C and 15C and was used as a prison until the 18C.

Old houses

On place de la République are the old grain market (late 15C–early 16C), the Gothic Maison de l'Œuvre Notre-Dame and the former town hall, which has a fine twin-gabled Renaissance façade.

EXCURSION
Pfaffenheim

3km/1.9mi N along N 83.

This ancient wine-growing village has a church with a 13C apse, adorned with floral friezes. The notches visible on the lower part of the apse were perhaps made by wine-growers sharpening their pruning knives.

ADDRESSES

⊗ STAY

⊜⊜ **Hôtel Relais du Vignoble** – *33, rue des Forgerons, 68420 Gueberschwihr. 6km/3.75mi N of Rouffach. ℘03 89 49 22 22. www.relaisduvignoble.com. Closed 26 Jan –6 Mar. 30 rooms.* A hotel run by a family of wine-growers. The large modern building faces the plain, with spacious, rather fussily decorated rooms on the second floor.

⊗ EAT

⊜⊜⊜ **Auberge au Vieux Pressoir** – *68250 Westhalten. 6km/3.75mi SW of Rouffach on N 83 and minor road. ℘03 89 49 60 04. www.bollenberg.com. Closed Sun evening.* A large wine-maker's house sitting in vineyards, with typical Alsatian decor and a collection of old weapons.

Soultz-Haut-Rhin

Haut-Rhin

This ancient town grew up around a vein of rock salt that still exists. Many old houses dating from the 16C to 18C, are adorned with oriels, stair turrets, porches bearing the construction date and inner courtyards which can be glimpsed through open doors.

▶ **Population:** 7 332.
◔ **Michelin Map:** Michelin Local map 315: H-9.
▯ **Tourist Office:** 14 place de la République, 68360 Soultz-Haut-Rhin. ℘03 89 76 83 60.
◖ **Location:** The town merges into neighbouring Guebwiller in a huge commercial zone, but the old town is well-preserved.

SIGHTS
Old houses

Apart from the tourist office dating from 1575, there are several fine old houses in the historic centre: Maison Litty (1622) at No. 15 rue des Sœurs; Maison Vigneronne (1656) at No. 5 rue du Temple; Maison Horn (1588) at No. 42 rue de Lattre-de-Tassigny; Maison Hubschwerlin (16C) with its lovely courtyard, at No. 6 rue des Ouvriers. In rue Jean-Jaurès is the family mansion (1605) of the Heeckeren d'Anthès, a powerful Alsatian industrial dynasty; one of its members, Georges-Charles de Heeckeren, killed the Russian writer Pushkin in a dual near St-Petersburg in 1837.

Église St-Maurice

The church, which shows great unity of style, was built between 1270 and 1489. The tympanum of the south doorway bears a 14C representation of St Maurice on horseback.

Inside, there is a fine early-17C pulpit, an organ by Silbermann (1750), a late-15C polychrome relief sculpture of St George slaying the dragon, and a mural of St Christopher.

Promenade de la citadelle

This walk, on the west side of town, follows a section of the ramparts, including the Tour des Sorcières (witches' tower).

La Nef des jouets

&⊙*Mid-Mar–Dec Wed–Mon 2–5pm.* ⊙*Jan–mid-Mar, 1 May, 24–25 and 31 Dec.* ⊛€5 (child 6–16, €2). ℘03 89 74 30 92.

▲▲ This eclectic toy collection gathered by two enthusiasts is displayed in the 12C former headquarters of the Order of the Knights of the Hospital of St John.

Château- Musée du Bucheneck

⊙*May–Oct Wed–Mon 2–5pm.* ⊛€5 (child 6–16, €1.50). ℘03 89 76 02 22.

The local history museum is housed in an 11C fortress, seat of the episcopal bailiff from 1289 to the Revolution.

ADDRESSES

♈/EAT

⊜⊜ **Metzgerstuwa** – *69 r. du Mar.-de-Lattre-de-Tassigny.* ℘03 89 74 89 77. www. metzgerstuwa.fr. *Closed Sun, except public holidays.* The chef, also a butcher, makes everything himself: regional dishes, bread, *charcuterie, terrine, pieds farcis* and so on.

Thann★

Haut-Rhin

This small southern town is renowned for having the most richly decorated Gothic church in the Alsace. The steep, south-facing vineyards and volcanic soils of the Rangen mountain produce one of the most reputed of all the Alsace wine appellations, celebrated since the 16C.

A BIT OF HISTORY
From legend to history

The founding of Thann is steeped in legend. When Bishop Thiébaut of Gubbio in Umbria died in 1160, he bequeathed his episcopal ring to his most trusted servant who took it, together with the bishop's thumb, hid it inside his staff and arrived in Alsace the following year. One night, he went to sleep in a fir forest after having driven his staff into the ground. In the morning, he was unable to lift it out of the ground. At the same time, three bright lights appeared above three fir trees; the lord of the nearby castle of Engelbourg saw the lights and arriving promptly, deciding to build a chapel on the very site where the miracle had occurred. The chapel soon became a popular place of pilgrim-

▸ **Population:** 8 099.
⚫ **Michelin Map:** Michelin Local map 315: G-10 .
🅱 **Tourist Office:** 7 rue de la 1ère Armée, 68800. ℘03 89 37 96 20. www.hautes-vosges-alsace.fr.
▶ **Location:** 21km/13mi E of Mulhouse on the N66.
⚫ **Also See:** The Thur valley and the Route des Vins.

age and the town of Thann, meaning fire tree, grew up around it. Each June, three fir trees are burnt in front of the church in commemoration.

SIGHTS
Collégiale St-Thiébaut★★

The Gothic architecture of the collegiate church (14C–early 16C) shows a continuous progression towards the Flamboyant Gothic style. The west front has a remarkable 15m high **doorway**★★ with an elegant tympanum; on the north side there is a Flamboyant Gothic doorway with fine 15C statues.

Inside, a polychrome wood statue of the wine-growers' Virgin, carved c 1510, is bonded to the central buttress pier of the pentagonal chapel (access from

Thann vineyards in autumn
© Katja Kreder/imageBROKER/age fotostock

the south aisle). At the end of the aisle, in St-Thiébaut's chapel, a polychrome wood statue of the saint dating from 1520 stands on the altar. The chancel is adorned with 15C statues of the 12 Apostles. However, the outstanding feature is the 15C oak **stalls★★**, which express all the fantasy of the Middle Ages in a profusion of carved foliage, gnomes and comic characters. The chancel is flooded with light pouring in through eight superb 15C **stained-glass windows★**.

L'œil de la Sorcière

1h on foot there and back.
Engelbourg Castle, built by the counts of Ferrette, became the property of the king of France who, 10 years later, gave it to Cardinal Mazarin. In 1673, Louis XIV ordered its destruction. The lower part of the keep remains intact – its centre appears to be looking over the plain, hence its nickname, the "witch's eye."

Musée des Amis de Thann

Jul–Aug daily except Mon 2–6pm. Jun and Sept Fri–Sun 2–6pm. ℘03 89 37 27 57. www.les-amis-de-thann.com. Housed in the 1519 corn exchange, the museum illustrates the town's history including the vineyards, the castle, the church and cult of St Theobald, furniture and popular art, the world wars, and the beginnings of the textile industry.

DRIVING TOUR

Route Joffre
18km/11mi from Thann to Masevaux.

▶ Drive NW along N 66 to Bitscgwiller and turn left onto D 14BIV.

This road was built by the army during WWI to establish vital communications between the valleys of the Doller and the Thur. The road affords a magnificent **view★** of the Thur valley overlooked to the North by the Grand Ballon.

Col du Hundsrück
Alt 748m.
View of the Sundgau area and the Jura mountains to the south and the Plaine d'Alsace to the east.

▶ The road goes through the hamlet of Houppach.

Masevaux
This small commercial town, originally developed around an abbey, has some lovely squares surrounded by 16C and 17C houses.

ADDRESSES

STAY AND EAT

Le Moschenross – *42 r. du Gén. de Gaulle. ℘03 89 37 00 86. www. moschenross.fr. Closed Jul 1–20. 22 rooms.* Dominated by the Rangon vineyard, this hotel-restaurant serves traditional cooking in a spacious dining room.

Hostellerie Alsacienne – *16 R. du Mar.-Foch, 68290 Masevaux. ℘03 89 82 45 25. www.hostellerie-alsacienne. com. Closed Sun eve and Mon. 8 rooms.* Situated in a pedestrian street, this rustic inn serves appetising local dishes. Comfortable rooms. The menu is simple but there is enough choice, and the interior is carved wooden panelling.

Route des Vins★★★

The well-signposted 180km/112mi itinerary, known as the Route des Vins (Wine Road), winds its way along the foothills of the Vosges from Marlenheim to Thann, the northern and southern gateways to Alsace where there are information centres about Alsatian vineyards and wines. The numerous flower-decked villages along the route, nestling round their church and town hall, are one of the most charming aspects of the Alsace region, no doubt enhanced by convivial wine-tasting opportunities.

ALSATIAN VINEYARDS

Wine-growing in Alsace goes back to the 3C; since then, the region has been concerned with looking after its vineyards to the exclusion of any other form of agriculture.

The landscape is characterised by terrace cultivation, with high stakes and low walls climbing the foothills of the Vosges. In the region entitled to the *appellation contrôlée* (label of origin), seven types of vines are grown: Riesling, Gewürztraminer, Sylvaner, Pinot Blanc, Tokay Pinot Gris, Muscat d'Alsace and Pinot Noir. These in turn give their name to the wines made from their grapes.

🚗 DRIVING TOURS

1 MARLENHEIM TO CHÂTENOIS
68km/42mi. Allow 4h.

Marlenheim
Renowned wine-growing centre *(information available about Alsatian wines).*

Wangen
Wangen is a typical wine-growing village with twisting lanes lined with old houses and arched gates. Until 1830 the villagers had to pay St Stephen's abbey

---

Michelin Map: Michelin Local map 315: I/G-5/10.

Tourist Office:
Dambach-la-Ville – Place du Marché, 67140 Dambach-la-Ville. ☎03 88 92 41 05. www.dambach-la-ville.fr.
Turckheim Corps de Garde, 68230 Turckheim. ☎03 89 27 38 44. www.turckheim.com.

PRACTICAL INFORMATION
Maison des Vins d'Alsace, – *12 av. de la Foire-aux-Vins, 68012 Colmar. ☎03 89 20 16 20; www.vinsalsace.com.*

---

in Strasbourg an annual tax calculated in litres of wine. The Fête de la Fontaine (Fountain Festival) is a reminder of this ancient custom: on the Sunday following 3 July, wine flows freely from Wangen's fountain.

Westhoffen
Wine-growing village with 16C and 17C houses and a Renaissance fountain.

Molsheim★ – *See MOLSHEIM.*

Rosheim★ – *See ROSHEIM.*

▷ Beyond Rosheim, the road runs through hills offering numerous viewpoints across the Plaine d'Alsace, with castles perched on promontories (Ottrott, Ortenbourg, Ramstein and Landsberg).

Boersch
This typical Alsatian village still has three ancient gateways and a picturesque **square★** lined with old houses, the most remarkable being the town hall dating from the 16C. A Renaissance well marks the entrance of the square. Leave Boersch via the Porte du Haut (upper gate). Stop at the **Marquetry workshop**

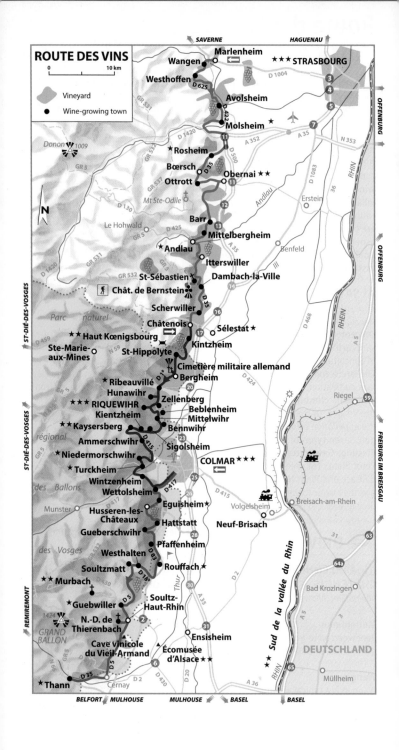

ROUTE DES VINS

0   10 km

Vineyard

● Wine-growing town

SAVERNE
HAGUENAU
★★★ STRASBOURG

Marlenheim
Wangen
Westhoffen
D 625
Avolsheim
Molsheim
A 352
A 35
N 353
OFFENBURG
Donon 1009
GR 5
★ Rosheim
Bœrsch
Ottrott
Obernai ★★
Mt Ste-Odile
Barr
Mittelbergheim
★ Andlau
Itterswiller
St-Sébastien
Dambach-la-Ville
Chât. de Bernstein
Scherwiller
Châtenois
Sélestat ★
Kintzheim
Haut Kœnigsbourg ★★
Ste-Marie-
aux-Mines
St-Hippolyte
Cimetière militaire allemand
Bergheim
★ Ribeauvillé
Hunawihr
Zellenberg
★★★ RIQUEWIHR
Beblenheim
Kientzheim
Mittelwihr
★★ Kaysersberg
Bennwihr
Ammerschwihr
Sigolsheim
★ Niedermorschwihr
COLMAR ★★★
★ Turckheim
Wintzenheim
Wettolsheim
Munster
Husseren-les-
Châteaux
Eguisheim ★
Hattstatt
Gueberschwihr
Neuf-Brisach
Pfaffenheim
Westhalten
Rouffach ★
Soultzmatt
★★ Murbach
★ Guebwiller
Soultz-
Haut-Rhin
N.-D. de
Thierenbach
GRAND
BALLON 1424
Cave vinicole
du Vieil-Armand
Ensisheim
Écomusée
d'Alsace ★★
★ Thann
Cernay
BELFORT MULHOUSE
MULHOUSE
BASEL
BASEL
DEUTSCHLAND
Müllheim
Bad Krozingen
Breisach-am-Rhein
Volgelsheim
Riegel
FREIBURG IM BREISGAU
Sud de la vallée du Rhin
RHIN
OFFENBURG
Erstein
Benfeld
ST-DIÉ-DES-VOSGES
Parc   naturel
régional
des Ballons
des Vosges
REMIREMONT

Chapelle St-Sébastien, Dambach-la-Ville

(🕐*Mon–Sat by arrangement.* 📞*03 88 95 80 17. www.spindler.tm.fr*) to see an exhibition of its work.

Ottrott
🔵*See Le HOHWALD: Driving Tour* 1.

Obernai★★ – 🔵*See OBERNAI.*

Barr
Barr is an industrial town (famous tanneries) as well as a wine-growing centre producing quality wines: Sylvaner, Riesling and above all Gewürztraminer. The annual wine fair is held in the town hall, a fine 17C building decorated with a loggia and a carved balcony; go into the courtyard to admire the rear part. An 18C mansion, known as the **Folie Marco** (🕐*10am–noon, 2–6pm: May–Sept daily except Tue.* 📞*03 88 08 94 72*) houses 17C–19C furniture, porcelain, pewter and mementoes of local history.

Mittelbergheim
🔵*See Le HOHWALD.*

Andlau★ – 🔵*See ANDLAU.*

Itterswiller
The flower-decked houses line the high street of this charming wine-growing village climbing up the hillside. Note the partly Gothic tower of the church which contains a 13C or 14C mural.

🚶 A footpath leads visitors on a tour of the vineyards *(about 1h, viewpoint).*

Dambach-la-Ville
This renowned wine-growing centre (Frankstein vintages) lies in a picturesque setting overlooked by woods. The town centre with its timber-framed houses was once surrounded by ramparts, of which three town gates remain. A wine fair takes place on 14 and 15 August. 🚶 400m beyond the Porte Haute (upper gate) turn left for the path to the **Chapelle St-Sébastien**, which has a late-17C Baroque altar. The path continues *(2h on foot there and back)* to the ruined **Château de Bernstein** (12C–13C), built on a granite ridge. There is a fine view of the Plaine d'Alsace.

Scherwiller
Lying at the foot of Ortenbourg and Ramstein castles, this village has retained its guardhouse, fine 18C timber-framed houses and old wash house along the River Aubach. Art, handicraft and Riesling fair during the third weekend in August.

Châtenois
Note the unusual Romanesque belfry, with a spire and four timber bartizans, and the picturesque 15C gatehouse known as the Tour des Sorcières (witches' tower) crowned by a stork's nest.

Church and vineyards of Hunawihr

© FreeProd/age fotostock

② FROM CHÂTENOIS TO COLMAR

54km/34mi. Allow 5h.

As far south as Ribeauvillé, the road is overlooked by numerous castles: Haut-Kœnigsbourg, the ruins of Kintzheim, Frankenbourg, St-Ulrich, Girsberg and Haut-Ribeaupierre.

Kintzheim
🕭*See SÉLESTAT: Volerie des Aigles.*

St-Hippolyte – 🕭*See RIBEAUVILLÉ.*

Bergheim
The Porte Haute, a 14C fortified gate, leads into this wine-growing village shaded by an old lime tree believed to date back to 1300. The northern section of the medieval wall, which protected Bergheim from the Burgundians in 1470, is still standing with three of its original round towers. The village has many old houses and a picturesque market square. The red-sandstone **church** has some 14C features; the rest dates from the 18C.

Cimetière militaire allemand
1.2km/0.7mi N of Bergheim along a road branching off D 1B on the left.
Built on a hillside, the cemetery contains the graves of German soldiers killed during WWII. Fine **view★** from the cross at the top.

Ribeauvillé★ – 🕭*See RIBEAUVILLÉ.*

Beyond Ribeauvillé, the road rises half way up the hillsides offering a wider panorama of the Plaine d'Alsace. The heart of the Alsatian wine-growing centre is situated here, between Ribeauvillé and Colmar. Charming villages and famous wine-growing centres are scattered across the rolling hills lying on the edge of the Vosges.

Hunawihr
The square belfry of the church is as massive as a keep. The church is surrounded by a 14C wall which had only one entrance defended by a tower. The six bastions flanking the wall can still be seen. From the church, there is a good view of the three castles of Ribeauvillé and the Plaine d'Alsace.

The church is used for Catholic and Protestant church services. The chapel on the left of the chancel contains 15C-16C frescoes depicting the Life of St Nicholas, the miracles he accomplished and the canonisation of St Huna.

👥 A centre devoted to the return of storks **Centre de réintroduction des cigognes et des loutres** (♿🕓*daily late Mar–early-Nov, check website for variable hours.* ✆€10 (child 13–18, €9; 5–12, €7). *℘03 89 73 72 62. www.cigogne-loutre. com*) has been trying to encourage storks to remain in Alsace throughout the winter and to nest at the centre or in nearby villages. More than 200 storks are fed and looked after here. Every afternoon, there is a show involving various animals that are particularly clever at fishing: cormorants, penguins, sea-lions and otters. In 1991, a centre for the safeguard and reproduction of otters was created.

👤👤 The **Jardin des Papillons exotiques vivants** (♿ 🕐 *Apr–Sept 10am–6pm; Oct 10am–5pm.* ⊛ €8 *(child 5–14, €5.50). ☎03 89 73 33 33. www.jardins despapillons.fr)* includes more than 150 species of exotic butterflies, flying about freely inside a hothouse full of luxuriant vegetation.

A short distance from Hunawihr stands the small village of **Zellenberg**, at the top of a hill, overlooking Riqhewihr and the vineyards. A **historic trail** *(40min, booklet available from the town hall or the tourist offices of Ribeauvillé and Riquewihr)* indicates the most interesting old buildings.

Riquewihr★★★ – *⌖See RIQUEWIHR.*

Beblenheim – *⌖See RIBEAUVILLÉ.*

Mittelwihr
At the southern end of the village is the Mur des Fleurs Martyres, a wall which, throughout the German occupation was decked with blue, white and red flowers as a token of Alsatian loyalty.

The hillsides all around enjoy a microclimate which causes almond trees to flower and yield fruit. The reputation of the Riesling and Gewürztraminer made in this area is steadily growing.

Bennwihr
This is another famous wine-growing village, with a monumental fountain in its centre. The modern **church** is brightly lit by a colourful stained-glass window stretching right across the south side. Note the soft tones of the stained glass decorating the chapel on the left.

Sigolsheim
This is supposed to be the place where, in 833, the sons of Louis the Meek, Charlemagne's son, met before capturing their father to have him imprisoned.

The Église St-Pierre-et-St-Paul dates from the 12C. The Romanesque doorway is adorned with a tympanum carved in a style similar to those of Kaysersberg and Andlau.

▶ Follow rue de la 1re-Armée (the main street) beyond the Couvent des Capucins to the national necropolis.

Nécropole nationale de Sigolsheim
The necropolis, standing up 124 steps on top of a hill and surrounded by vines, contains the graves of 1 684 French soldiers killed in 1944. From the central platform, there is a splendid **panorama★**.

Kientzheim
This wine-growing village has several interesting medieval buildings, fortifications, squares, wells and sundials.

The **Porte Basse** is a fortified gate surmounted by a grinning head which was placed there as a warning to attackers that they did not stand a chance to get past this mighty tower. The medieval **castle** is the headquarters of St Stephen's Brotherhood, the official body controlling the quality of Alsatian wines. Housed in an outbuilding, the **Musée du Vignoble et des Vins d'Alsace** (🕐*10.30am–12.30pm, 3–6pm: Jun–Oct daily; May Sat–Sun.* ⊛ €5, child under 10, €2; ☎03 89 48 21 36; www.musee-du-vignoble-alsace.fr)* is devoted to all aspects of wine-making from vineyard to wine. Inside the church, next to a 14C statue of the Virgin Mary, are the **tombstones★** of Lazarus von Schwendi (d 1583), who brought Tokay vines back from Hungary, and of his son (*⌖see KAYSERSBERG*).

The **Chapelle Sts-Felix-et-Régule** contains naïve 'paintings on canvas and wood, dating from 1667 to 1865.

Kaysersberg★★ –
⌖See KAYSERSBERG.

Ammerschwihr
Situated at the foot of vine-covered hills, Ammerschwihr was destroyed by fire following the bombings of December

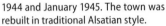

1944 and January 1945. The town was rebuilt in traditional Alsatian style.

All that remains from its past are the Gothic **Église St-Martin**, the Renaissance former town hall, two fortified towers, and the **Porte Haute**, on the western edge of the town. The gate's square tower, crowned by a stork's nest, is decorated with the arms of the town and a painted sundial.

Niedermorschwihr★

This lovely village set among vineyards has a modern church with a 13C spiral belfry. The high street is lined with old houses with oriels and balconies.

Turckheim★

This ancient fortified town is the last place in Alsace where a night watchman (May–Oct every evening at 10pm) walks through the streets carrying his lamp and horn; he stops and sings at every street corner.

Admire the three fortified gateways, **Place de Turenne** with its 16C and 17 houses and the ornate **Hôtel des Deux-Clefs** on Grand'Rue.

Wintzenheim

This famous wine-growing centre (Hengst vintage) is a pleasant city, fortified in 1275. The old manor of the Knights of St John is now the town hall.

Colmar★★★ – *See COLMAR.*

③ FROM COLMAR TO THANN
59km/37mi. Allow 3h.

Colmar★★★ – *See COLMAR.*

▷ Drive out of Colmar along D 417.

Wettolsheim

This village claims the honour of being the birthplace of Alsatian vine-growing, which was introduced here during the Roman occupation. A wine festival takes place during the last weekend in July.

Eguisheim★
See EGUISHEIM.

Husseren-les-Châteaux

This is the highest point of the Alsatian vineyards (alt 380m) and starting point of a tour of the five castles of Eguisheim (*see EGUISHEIM: Route des Cinq Châteaux*) above the village.

Hattstatt

This once-fortified village has an early-11C church with a 15C chancel containing a stone altar and 15C baptistery. Note the fine Renaissance calvary on the left of the nave. The 16C town hall stands next to fine old houses.

Gueberschwihr

A magnificent three-storey Romanesque belfry (all that remains of an early-12C church) overlooks this peaceful hillside village. Note the Merovingian sarcophagi nearby.

Pfaffenheim
See ROUFFACH: Excursion.

Rouffach★
See ROUFFACH.

Shortly beyond Rouffach, Grand Ballon (*see Route des CRÊTES*) comes into view.

Westhalten

Picturesque village with two fountains and several old houses.

Soultzmatt

Charming city on the banks of the Ohmbach. The local Sylvaner, Riesling and Gewürztraminer are highly rated as are the mineral springs. There is a wine festival in early August. The **Château de Wagenbourg** stands nearby.

Guebwiller★ – *See GUEBWILLER.*

Soultz-Haut-Rhin
See SOULTZ-HAUT-RHIN.

▷ Turn right onto D 51.

Basilique Notre-Dame de Thierenbach

The onion-shaped belfry can be seen from afar. The basilica was built in 1723 in the Austrian Baroque style by the architect Peter Thumb. An important pilgrimage, going back to the 8C and dedicated to Notre-Dame-de-l'Espérance takes place in the church. The basilica contains two Pietà: the miracle-working Virgin Mary dating from 1350 and the Mater Dolorosa dating from 1510.

☛ Return to Soultz-Haut-Rhin and follow D 5 towards Cernay.

Cave vinicole du Vieil-Armand

This cooperative, on the outskirts of Soultz, groups 130 wine-growers and organses tastings. Two great wines are produced: Rangen, the most southern of Alsatian wines and Ollwiller, grown just beneath Vieil Armand. In the basement, a museum contains equipment used in the old days in vineyards and cellars.

☛ Continue along D 5 then turn right onto D 35.

Thann★ – *See THANN.*

ADDRESSES

🏠 STAY

🛏️🛏️ **Hôtel Le Vignoble** – *1 rue de l'Eglise, 67650 Dambach-la-Ville.* ℘*03 88 92 43 75. www.hotel-vignoble-alsace.fr. Closed Jan and Sun out of season. 7 rooms.* The bells of the nearby church remain silent throughout the night, so nothing will stop your enjoyment of the stylish little rooms in this converted Alsace barn built in 1765.

🛏️🛏️ **Domaine Bouxhof** – *R. du Bouxhof, 68630 Mittelwihr.* ℘*03 89 47 93 67. Closed Jan. 3 rooms.* The owners will show you around the listed cellars of this lovely 17C house set among vines. Breakfast in the 15C chapel is a must.

🛏️🛏️ **Hôtel Berceau du Vigneron** – *Pl. de Turenne, 68230 Turckheim.* ℘*03 89 27 23 55. 16 rooms.* This traditional hotel in lovely place de Turenne has slightly old-fashioned but spacious and well-kept rooms. The breakfast room is typically Alsatian, with its wooden chairs and red-checked napkins.

🛏️🛏️ **Château d'Andlau** – *113 rue de la Vallée, 67140 Barr.* ℘*03 88 08 96 78. www.hotelchateauandlau.fr. 22 rooms. Restaurant* 🍽️🍽️🍽️. In a serene bucolic setting, this hotel proposes rustic bedrooms, traditional cooking and excellent wines.

🍽️ EAT

🍽️ **Le Ferme du Sonnenberg** – *67520 Nordheim, 3km/1.8mi N of Marlenheim on D 220.* ℘*03 88 04 12 84. www.ferme cabri.com. Closed Mon–Tue.* Goats are raised on this farm, and that is their priority. They have a samll café serving their own produce; so goats' cheese and kid are on the menu, as well as charcuterie and other regional dishes.

🍽️🍽️ **À la Truite** – *17 r. du 25 Jan, 68970 Illhaeusern.* ℘*03 89 71 83 51. www. restaurant-alatruite.com. Closed Tue evening and all day Wed.* This 1950s waterfront restaurant has a colourful dining room and summer terrace by the river. Simple, no-frills cooking.

SPORT AND RECREATION

Canoës du Ried – *68970 Illhauesern.* ℘*03 88 82 65 46 / 06 08 91 85 56. www.canoes-du-ried.com.* With its vast network of rivers, the Ried area is ideal for discovering by canoe. Canoes can be hired for between 2h and 3 days, with or without accompaniment.

CALENDAR

Advice – Grapes are harvested between late Sept and mid-Oct, during which time access to the wine paths is often restricted. Enquire on site.

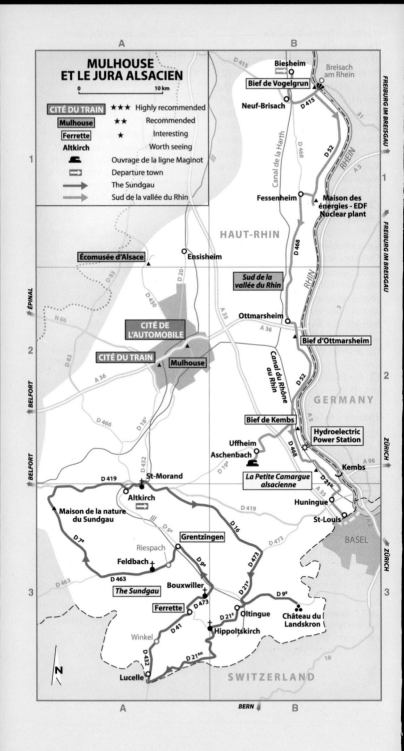

MULHOUSE ET LE JURA ALSACIEN

0   10 km

CITÉ DU TRAIN	★★★	Highly recommended
Mulhouse	★★	Recommended
Ferrette	★	Interesting
Altkirch		Worth seeing

Ouvrage de la ligne Maginot
Departure town
The Sundgau
Sud de la vallée du Rhin

Biesheim
Bief de Vogelgrun
Breisach am Rhein
Neuf-Brisach
FREIBURG IM BREISGAU

Canal de la Harth
Fessenheim
Maison des énergies - EDF Nuclear plant

HAUT-RHIN
FREIBURG IM BREISGAU

Écomusée d'Alsace
Ensisheim
RHIN

Sud de la vallée du Rhin
ÉPINAL

Ottmarsheim
Bief d'Ottmarsheim

CITÉ DE L'AUTOMOBILE
CITÉ DU TRAIN
Mulhouse
BELFORT

Canal du Rhône au Rhin
GERMANY

Bief de Kembs
Hydroelectric Power Station

Uffheim
Aschenbach
Kembs

BELFORT

St-Morand
La Petite Camargue alsacienne

Altkirch
Huningue
St-Louis

Maison de la nature du Sundgau
Grentzingen
BASEL

Riespach
Feldbach
Bouxwiller

The Sundgau
Ferrette
Oltingue
Château du Landskron

Winkel
Hippoltskirch

N
Lucelle
SWITZERLAND

BERN

324

Mulhouse★★

Haut-Rhin

Situated in the northern foothills of the Sungdau area, Mulhouse has several attractive features including its rich past as an independent republic, its strong industrial tradition and its prestigious museums. Since 1975 this modern and dynamic town has been the seat of the Université de Haute-Alsace, which specialises in high technology.

A BIT OF HISTORY
A passion for independence
From the 12C onwards, Mulhouse strove to liberate itself from its feudal bonds and in 1308 it acquired the status of an imperial city, thus becoming a virtually independent republic, acknowledging the Holy Roman Emperor as its sole suzerain. Encouraged by the latter, Mulhouse formed, with nine other imperial cities, a league of defence against the power of the nobility, known as **Decapolis**.

In 1515, under threat from the Habsburgs' territories which completely surrounded it, Mulhouse left Decapolis and entered into an alliance with the **Swiss cantons,** an inspired decision that placed the town under the protection of the kingdom of France: the intervention of Henri IV in favour of his allies and the cession to France of the Habsburgs' possessions in Alsace under the treaty of Westphalia (1648) enabled the Republic to retain its independence. Even the revocation of the Edict of Nantes in 1685 did not really threaten this bastion of Calvinism, which remained the only Alsatian territory not under French control after the Sun King had annexed Strasbourg in 1681.

Calvinist citadel
In 1524 the Republic's government adopted the principles of the Reformation and a little later on adhered to Calvinism. As a consequence, theatrical performances were banned, inns had to close at 10pm and the citizens' clothing had to be discreet in style and colour. However, the new religion also spurred

▶ **Population:** 113 766.

🎔 **Michelin Map:** Michelin Local map 315: h-I 10.

ℹ **Tourist Office:** 1 av. Robert-Schuman, 68100 Mulhouse. ℘03 89 35 48 48. www.tourisme-mulhouse.com

◑ **Location:** Mulhouse is on the A 35 to Strasbourg (100km/62mi north) and Basles (32km/20mi south) and on the A 36 which crosses through the town from east to west before heading out to Belfort and Montbéliard-Sochaux *(both less than 50km/31mi away).*

☺ **Don't Miss:** From the top of the Tour de l'Europe *(revolving restaurant),* there is a great view of the town and the surrounding area.

👪 **Kids:** Mulhouse has several Industrial museums (automobiles, trains, electricity, etc.).

PRACTICAL INFORMATION
Guided tours – The tourist office organises tours of the town *(1h30, in French and German).* Jul–Aug on *Saturdays.* ⊛€5.

industrial development and prompted original social and cultural initiatives.

Union with France
In 1792 the new French Republic imposed a commercial blockade on Mulhouse and the town opted for union with France. During the union festivities, which took place in 1798 on place de la Réunion, the flag of the city was rolled inside a case bearing the colours of the French flag and the following inscription was written on the case: *La République de Mulhouse repose dans le sein de la République française* (the Republic of

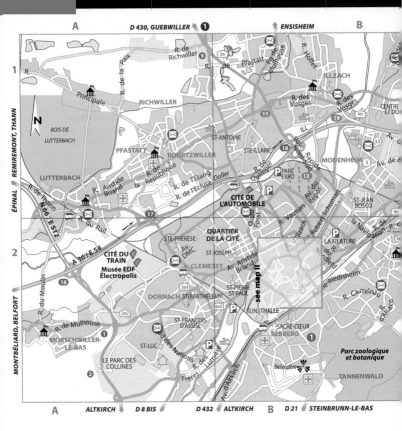

Mulhouse rests in the bosom of the French Republic).

Together with the rest of Alsace, Mulhouse was German from 1870 to 1918 and from 1940 to 1944.

It took the French first armoured-car division two months to completely liberate the town.

A Famous Resident

Born in Mulhouse in 1859, **Alfred Dreyfus**, a captain in the intelligence service, was wrongly accused and convicted in 1894 of having passed on military secrets to the Germans. He spent years imprisoned in Cayenne before his case was reviewed following pressure from the press, particularly from the famous open letter by Émile Zola entitled *J'accuse* which earned its author one year's imprisonment and a heavy fine.

INDUSTRIAL MUSEUMS

♣♣ Cité de l'Automobile: Collection Schlumpf★★★

Entrance along avenue de Colmar. ♿ ⏰ *Jan Mon–Fri 1–5pm, Sat–Sun 10am–5pm; Feb–Mar and early Nov–mid-Jan daily 10am–5pm; Apr–early Nov daily 10am–6pm.* ⏰ *25 Dec.* ✎ *€13 (child 7–12, €10.50).* ✆ *03 89 33 23 23.* http://citedelautomobile.com.

This fabulous collection of 500 vintage cars (not all of them on permanent display) was set up with passionate enthusiasm over a period of 30 years by the Schlumpf brothers, who owned a wool-spinning mill in the Thur valley upstream of Thann.

Many of these cars can be regarded as authentic works of art such is the refinement of their bodywork, the smoothness of their aerodynamic lines, the finish of their wheels and hubs, and the design of their radiator grill.

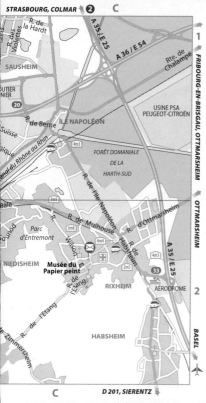

STRASBOURG, COLMAR · ② C

1

SAUSHEIM

OUTIER
NIER
20

R. des
Violettes
R. de
la Hardt

A 36 / E 25

A 36 / E 54

Rte. de
Chalampé

USINE PSA
PEUGEOT-CITROËN

ÎLE NAPOLÉON

R. de Berne

Suisse

R. de l'Île Napoléon

FORÊT DOMANIALE
DE LA
HARTH-SUD

4m3

Canal du Rhône au Rhin

Bâle

3m3

R. de Mulhouse

Parc
d'Entremont

3m8

unod

Wilson

3m4

R. de
l'Étang

RIEDISHEIM

Musée du
Papier peint

R. d'Ottmarsheim

R. de Habsheim

2m5

RIXHEIM

AÉRODROME

33

4m3

A 35 / E 25

2

HABSHEIM

Zimmersheim

FRIBOURG-EN-BRISGAU, OTTMARSHEIM

OTTMARSHEIM

BASEL

C

D 201, SIERENTZ

MULHOUSE
map I

0 ——— 750 m

WHERE TO STAY
Arc en Ciel (Relais) . . . . . . ①
Au Cheval Blanc . . . . ②

WHERE TO EAT
L'Esterel . . . . ①

Cité de l'Automobile : Collection Schlumpf

© C. Recoura/Cité de l'Automobile : Collection Schlumpf

👥 Cité du Train: Musée français du Chemin de fer★★★

Situated in the western part of the town, near Lutterbach. ⏱*Daily: Apr–Oct 10am–6pm; Nov–Mar 10am–5pm.*

🎫€12 (child 7–17, €9.50). 🔒25 Dec. 📞03 89 42 83 33. *www.citedutrain.com.* The French Railways (SNCF) collection, splendidly displayed, illustrates the evolution of railways from their origin

Cité du Train: Musée français du Chemin de Fer

until today. The main hall includes footbridges offering a view inside carriages, pits making it possible to walk beneath engines, and driver's cabins.

The panorama of steam engines that spans more than 100 years includes famous engines such as the Saint-Pierre, built of teak, which ran between Paris and Rouen from 1844 onwards, the very fast Crampton (1852) which already reached speeds of around 120kph/75mph and the 232 U1 (1949), the last operating steam engine.

The museum also boasts the drawing-room carriage of Napoleon III's aides-de-camp (1856) decorated by Viollet-le-Duc, and the French President's carriage (1925) decorated by Lalique and fitted with a solid-silver washbasin. In striking contrast, the bottom of the range includes one of the fourth-class carriages of the Alsace-Lorraine line.

♣♣ Musée EDF Electropolis★

Situated in the western part of the town, Électropolis shares a vast parking area with the Musée du Chemin de Fer.
&.◐*Daily except Mon: Apr–Oct 10am–6pm; 1st week in Jan, mid-Feb–Mar, Nov–Dec 10am–5pm.* ◐*1 Jan, early Jan–mid-Feb, Good Friday, 1 May, 1 adn 11 Nov and 25–26 Dec.* ⇔€8 *(child 6–18, €4). ℘03 89 32 48 50. www.edf.fr.*

A large masonry cube and an elliptical gallery surrounding it are the unusual setting of the exhibition showing the different stages of the production of electricity and its various uses.

Musée de l'Impression sur étoffes★

&.◐*Daily except Mon 10am– noon, 2–6pm (open Mon in Dec 2–6pm).* ◐*1 Jan, 1 May and 25 Dec.* ⇔€10 *(child 12–18, €5). ℘03 89 46 83 00. www.musee-impression.com.*

The Museum of Printed Fabric is housed in a former industrial building, which once belonged to the Société Industrielle de Mulhouse.

The Museum of Printed Fabric (created in 1857) illustrates the birth and development of the industry from 1746 onwards: engraving and printing techniques are explained, and impressive machines used throughout the ages are employed for regular demonstrations. There are displays of original 18C shawls with oriental motifs.

This museum and its lovely shop are a must for anyone interested in fashion, interior design and the decorative arts.

Musée du Papier peint★

In Rixheim, 6km/3.7mi E towards Basle; &*see town map.* ◐*10am–noon, 2–6pm: May–Oct daily; Nov–Apr daily except Tue.* ◐*1 Jan, Good Friday, 1 May and 25 Dec.* ⇔€8.50. *℘03 89 64 24 56. www.museepapierpeint.org.*

The Wallpaper Museum is housed in the right wing of the former headquarters of an order of Teutonic knights where, c 1797, Jean Zuber set up a wallpaper factory, which brought fame to his family. The superb **collection**★★ of panoramic wallpaper was exported throughout the world (mainly to North America) during the 19C.

WALKING TOURS

PLACE DE LA RÉUNION— HISTORIC CENTRE OF MULHOUSE

Ancien hôtel de ville★★

Erected in 1552 by an architect from Basle in a kind of Renaissance style characteristic of the Rhine region and decorated on the outside by artists from the Constance area, this edifice is unique in France. The shields bearing the arms of the Swiss cantons.

On the right side of the building, you can see a grinning stone mask similar to the Klapperstein or gossips' stone weighing 12–13kg, which was tied to the neck of slanderers condemned to go round the town riding backwards on a donkey. This punishment was used for the last time in 1781.

On the left side of the square, note the Poêle des Tailleurs, once used by the tailors' guild and, a bit farther along rue Henriette, the 16C Poêle des Vignerons, used by the wine-growers' guild.

Temple St-Étienne

🕓*Daily except Tue May–Sept, 1–6.30pm.* 🕓*Public holidays.* ᴓ*No charge.* 🕾*03 89 46 58 25.*
This neo-Gothic building has retained several 14C **stained-glass windows**★ from the previous church demolished in 1858, said to be the finest in all Alsace.

▷ Walk diagonally across the square.

On the corner of rue des Boulangers stands the oldest **pharmacy** in Mulhouse (1649).

▷ Leave place de la Réunion and follow rue des Bouchers; turn right onto rue des Bons-Enfants then take the first turning on the left, rue des Franciscains.

On your left you will see the mansion built by the Feer family (1765-70). Halfway along the street are the manufactures of printed calico, the most famous

Ancien hôtel de ville

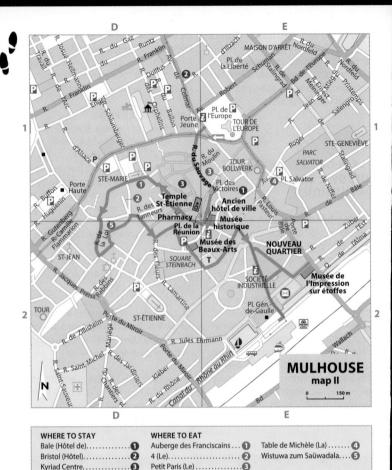

MULHOUSE
map II

0   150 m

WHERE TO STAY	WHERE TO EAT	
Bale (Hôtel de)............❶	Auberge des Franciscains ... ❶	Table de Michèle (La) ....❹
Bristol (Hôtel)..............❷	4 (Le)......................❷	Wistuwa zum Saüwadala....❺
Kyriad Centre..............❸	Petit Paris (Le) ....❸	

being the Cour des Chaînes inaugurated in 1763 in a 16C building.

◗ Continue along rue de la Loi.

Note to your right and on the corner of rue Ste-Claire, a manufacturing complex dating from the 18C.

◗ Take passage des Augustins then the first street on the right followed by rue Henriette on the left; go through passage Teutonique on the right and turn left onto rue Guillaume-Tell where the Musée des Beaux-Arts is situated. The street leads back to place de la Réunion.

THE INDUSTRIAL TOWN
The Nouveau Quartier
SE of the historic centre, beyond place de la République.
A new residential complex intended for young industrialists was built from 1827 onwards on the edge of the old town centre. Known as the **Nouveau Quartier**, it consists of arcaded buildings modelled on those of rue de Rivoli in Paris, surrounding a central triangular garden, the square de la Bourse.

Working-class garden-cities
On both sides of the Ill diversion canal.
Social urban planning launched by the Société Industrielle was a novelty in

Europe. From 1855 onwards, the Cité de Mulhouse and the Nouvelle Cité were built on both sides of the Ill diversion canal. Each family had lodgings with a separate entrance and a small garden. A leasing system enabled workers to become property owners.

The availability of public services was remarkable for the time. The Quartier de la Cité, which has been preserved around the Église St-Joseph, is worth a visit.

ADDITIONAL SIGHTS
Musée historique★★
Place de la Réunion. ◷*Daily except Tue and public holidays 1–6.30pm (Jul–Aug 10am–noon, 1–6.30pm).* ✆*No charge.* ✆*03 89 33 78 17. www.musees-mul-house.fr/musee-historique.*

Housed in the former town hall, the rich and varied collections of this museum illustrate the history of the town and daily life in the region over the past 6 000 years. The collection includes reconstructed rooms, the original Klapperstein and the **silver-gilt cup** offered by the town to the representative of the French government in 1798 when Mulhouse was united with France.

👥 The former **corn loft** (access from the second floor across a footbridge built in the 18C) contains a collection of toys: dolls' houses, outfits, crockery and games. The folk-art gallery houses reconstructions of regional interiors (kitchen and bedroom from the Sungdau area), pottery, woodcarvings etc. Note the monumental mechanical piano dating from the beginning of the 20C and the 18C sledge.

Musée des Beaux-Arts
Just off place de la Réunion. ◷*Daily except Tue and public holidays 1–6.30pm.* ✆*No charge.* ✆*03 89 33 78 11. www.musees-mulhouse.fr/musee-des-beaux-arts.*

The Fine Arts Museum contains works by Brueghel the Younger, Teniers, Ruysdael, Boucher and other 17C and 18C painters; 19C landscapes and mythological scenes.

👥 Parc zoologique et botanique★★
S of the town centre, on the edge of the Rebberg district. ◷*Dec–Feb 10am–4pm; Mar and Oct–Nov 9am–5pm; Apr and Sept 9am–6pm; May–Aug 9am–7pm.* ✆*€15.50 ((Nov–20 Mar) and children €9.50).* ✆*03 69 77 65 65. www.zoo-mulhouse.com.*

This zoological and botanical garden, covering an area of 25ha and sheltering more than 1 000 animals, aims at preserving, breeding and studying rare and endangered species by collaborating with other zoos and various agencies. Interesting animals include gibbons, lemurs, deer, wolves, panthers, sea lions and penguins.

ADDRESSES

🛏 STAY

🍴 **Hôtel de Bâle** – *19 passage Central.* ✆*03 89 46 19 87. www.hoteldebale.fr. 32 rooms.* A small hotel in the pedestrianised area of the town centre. The rooms benefit from comfortable beds and are well furnished. The breakfast room is furnished in regional style.

🍴 **Au Cheval Blanc** – *27 rue Principal, 68390 Baldersheim.* ✆*03 89 45 45 44. www.hotel-cheval-blanc.com. 82 rooms.* Alsatian style hotel passed down from father to son for over a century. Comfortable, good quality rooms with rustic furnishing. Inn-type dining room, reached via the village café. Restaurant with wide choice of regional dishes and game in season.

🍴 **Relais Arc En Ciel** – *2 Rue du Périgord, 68270 Wittenheim. Situated just to the north of Mulhouse. Leave the D430 at junction 8 in the direction of Wittenheim and take the rue du Périgord on the left.* ✆*03 89 52 42 22. 39 rooms.* ♿🅿. In a quiet location 5km/3m from Mulhouse. Well equipped rooms and swimming pool. The restaurant *(open Mon–Fri)* serves traditional French cuisine.

🍴 **Kyriad Centre** – *15 rue Lambert.* ✆*03 89 66 44 77. www.hotel-mulhouse.com. 70 rooms.* Smart practical bedrooms in contemporary style; rooms are more spacious and comfortable in the business category. Breakfast on the terrace during the summer. Located in a pedestrianised area.

⊜⊜⊜ **Hôtel Bristol** – 18 av. de Colmar. ℘03 89 42 12 31. www.hotelbristol.com. ♿. 95 rooms. This early 20C hotel near the old town has a spacious hall and lounge decorated with Art Deco-inspired furniture. The many rooms are large, well equipped and air-conditioned. Some bathrooms have corner baths. A good place to stay in Mulhouse. Restaurant (⊜⊜⊜).

¶/EAT

⊜ **Auberge des Franciscains** – 46 r. des Franciscains. ℘03 89 45 32 77. www.auberge-des-franciscains.com. Closed all day Tue, and Sun evenings. Exposed timber beams, handsome copper pots and pans above the bar and shelves adorned with old beer mugs: a warm welcome awaits visitors to this beer tavern. Wide choice of local dishes: baeckehofe, choucroute, cassolette au munster, etc.

⊜⊜ **Wistuwa zum Saüwadala** – 13 r. de l'Arsenal. ℘03 89 45 18 19. Closed Mon lunchtime, and all day Sun. You can't miss this restaurant with its typical façade in the centre of old Mulhouse. Beer mugs hang from the ceiling, the tablecloths are gingham, and the cuisine is genuine Alsace. Several menus, including one for children.

⊜⊜ **Le Petit Paris** – 12 rue de Moselle, 68100 Mulhouse. ℘03 89 61 17 85. www.lepetitparis.pro. Closed all day Sun. Located in a pedestriansed part of the city not far from the Place de la Réunion. Menus are regularly changed to reflect the produce of the season. Well worth locating.

⊜⊜ **Le 4** – 5 Rue Bonbonnière, 68100 Mulhouse. ℘03 89 44 94 11. www.restaurantle4.com. Closed all day Mon and Sun eve. In the centre of Mulhouse, the young couple who run this small restaurant are inventive with their use of spices. As a result, the cuisine if surprising and refreshing.

⊜⊜ **La Table de Michèle** – 16 r. Metz. ℘03 89 45 37 82. www.latabledemichele.fr. Closed Sat lunch, all day Sun and Mon. The chef Michèle Brouet concocts classic and seasonal dishes; all inspired with authenticity and a delicacy. Dining room has rugged wood decor and soft lighting.

⊜⊜⊜ **L'Esterel** – 83 av. de la 1ere Division Blindée. ℘03 89 44 23 24. www.esterel-weber.fr. Closed Sun eve, Wed eve and all day Mon. Near the zoo, a small rustic restaurant with a veranda extension; the shaded terrace is extremely popular in fine weather. Traditional menu with a southern slant.

ON THE TOWN

Charlie's Bar – 26 r. de Sinne. ℘03 89 66 12 22. www.hotelduparc-mulhouse.com. Daily 10am–1.30am (Fri–Sat 3am) Closed Jan 1 and May 1. The Hotel du Parc's piano bar is a classy spot, much frequented by businessmen and the Mulhouse bourgeoisie. In this lovely setting you can hear music worthy of the best jazz clubs: nightly piano concerts (from 7pm), with duets on weekends (from 10pm). The cocktails are irresistible!

SHOPPING & BROWSING

Au Moulin Poulaillon – 176 r. de Belfort, 68200 Muhouse. ℘03 89 42 24 04. www.poulaillon.fr. Mon–Fri 6am–8pm (Sat 7pm). Closed holidays. In addition to thirty different sorts of bread, this bakery run by an enthusiastic young woman has a tea-room well worth a look: old wooden floorboards, beams, restored mill and oven.

Alsaticarta – 31 av. Clemenceau. ℘03 89 46 13 57. Daily except Sun 2–6.30pm, Sat 9am–noon, 2–6pm. Items of regional interest, books, paintings, and postcards.

Christmas market – Mid-Nov to end Dec.

SPORT AND RECREATION

Mulhouse has five municipal swimming pools, four of which are equipped for disabled persons.

Piscine Pierre-et-Marie-Curie – 7 r. Pierre-et-Marie-Curie. ℘03 89 32 69 00. Former municipal baths with indoor pools (mid Sept–end May), sauna and Turkish baths, or relaxation baths and Roman baths, in a stunning marble and glass decor dating from the last century.

Stade nautique – 53 bd Charles-Stœssel. ℘03 69 77 66 66. Outdoor site in a shaded 7-hectare area. Includes slides.

Blacksmith's workshop, Écomusée d'Alsace

Écomusée d'Alsace★★

Haut-Rhin

Some 50 traditional old houses scattered over an area of almost 25ha give an insight into housing in the different rural areas of Alsace. The wish to preserve the regional heritage was at the origin of this open-air museum: old houses from the 15C to 19C, doomed to be demolished, were located all over Alsace, then carefully taken apart and rebuilt in the new village. The museum, inaugurated in 1980 and continually expanding, has now turned to the region's industrial heritage with the renovation of the various buildings of the potash mine Rodolphe (1911–1930) adjacent to the museum.

VISIT

Mid-Mar–early Nov daily 10am–6pm; late Nov–early Jan Tue–Sun 10.30am–6.30pm. €15 (child 4–14, €10). ℘03 89 74 44 74. www.ecomusee.alsace.

Visitors can walk through the museum's vast area and take as much or as little time as they wish, although half a day seems to be the minimum; activities centred on Alsatian life are organised in the evening, particularly in summer.

Some 70 **timber-framed Alsatian houses** with their courtyards and gardens, grouped according to their original area, Sungdau, Ried, Kochersberg, or Bas-Rhin, illustrate the evolution of

- **Michelin Map:** Michelin Local map 315: H-9
- **Location:** The Écomusée d'Alsace is 9km/5.6mi southwest of Ensisheim along A 35 in the heart of the Alsatian countryside in Ungersheim.
- **Timing:** Allow at least half a day and be aware that most of the events take place in the evenings in summertime.
- **Kids:** The entire complex will appeal to children of all ages.

PRACTICAL INFORMATION

PURCHASES – You may purchase souvenirs, crafts and local delicacies on site; there are also telephone booths, letter boxes, a hotel, bakery, and restaurants.

EVENTS – Wide range of activities depending on the season (boat trips, funfair, theme days, International Festival of the Home and guided tour of the potash mines by train).

building techniques and give an insight into social life in traditional Alsatian villages. These fine buildings have one thing in common, the *stube* or living room, the focus of family and social life (meals, Sunday receptions, evening gatherings, sometimes even serving as

333

master bedroom). But, most important, it contained an imposing earthenware stove! You will see several such stoves during your tour of the museum.

Other buildings house exhibitions or shows on such themes as the Alsatian headdress, fishing, and recurring feasts. Several workshops are operating: a blacksmith's, a potter's with an impressive wood oven, a cartwright's, a distillery, and an oil-mill.

Natural environment

Ancient plant species can be seen growing in their recreated natural environment and there are demonstrations of traditional farming methods. There are beehives, an apple orchard, as well as cowsheds and stables sheltering domestic animals. Storks return regularly to nest on the weathered roofs.

Merry-go-rounds

A section of the museum is devoted to funfairs; note in particular the **Eden-Palladium** merry-go-round, the last of the great Belle Epoque merry-go-rounds in France (1909).

ADDRESSES

🏠 STAY

🛏🛏🛏 **Hôtel Les Loges de l'Écomusée** – *At the Écomusée.* ℘*03 69 58 50 25. www.hotellesloges.fr. Closed 3 Jan–20 Feb. 30 rooms.* This attractive hotel consists of small, locally inspired buildings. It has been designed as a village, and offers simple, modern rooms with mezzanines, split-level and studio apartments.

🍴 EAT

🍴🍴 **La Taverne** – *At the Écomusée.* ℘*03 69 58 50 25. Open 7.30–9pm.* The decor is that of an old Alsatian inn, with beams and roof timbers, while the hearty cooking includes pork, sauerkraut and other typical regional dishes. A nice way of discovering more about the traditions mentioned in the museum, with a good atmosphere as well.

Ensisheim

Haut-Rhin

Excavations have revealed that the site was inhabited as far back as the fifth millennium BCE, but the name of Ensisheim was mentioned for the first time in 765. The city became the capital of the Habsburgs' territories in Alsace and remained the capital of western Austria until 1648. The town has fine Gothic and Renaissance mansions.

VISIT
Palais de la Régence

This fine Gothic edifice erected in 1535 was decorated in Renaissance style.Note the ground floor vaulting of the arcade decorated with emblems bearing the coats of arms of Alsatian towns.

Musée de la Régence

🕐*Closed until the end of 2018 for renovation, and improvement of the*

▶ **Population:** 7 497.
🚗 **Michelin Map:** Michelin Local map 315: I-9 – also see Route des VINS.
▷ **Location:** Ensisheim (just 9km/5.6mi from the Écomusée d'Alsace) is also a mere 27km/16.8mi from Colmar.

access. Check the village website for details. ℘*03 89 83 32 10. www.ensisheim.net.*
In the first room of the museum is a meteorite which fell on Ensisheim on 7 November 1492.

Hôtel de la Couronne

Turenne, Louis XIV's great general, stayed here in 1675 before his victory at the battle of Turckheim, which led to the Peace of Nijmegen and the final union of France and Alsace.

The Sundgau★
Haut-Rhin

The southernmost area of Alsace in the foothills of the Jura has been deeply carved by the tributaries of the upper Ill; the resulting hills and limestone cliffs are crowned by forests and the valleys are dotted with numerous lakes – full of carp, a local gastronomic speciality – pastures and rich crops. Flower-decked farmhouses often have timber-framed walls in an ochre colour or clad with wooden planks. Altkirch is the only town of any importance, but many prosperous villages are scattered along the rivers or across sunny hillsides.

- **Michelin Map:** Michelin Local map 315: H/I-11.
- **Tourist Office**: 7 r. de Bâle, 68210 Dannemarie. ℘03 89 07 24 24. www.sudalsace-largue.fr.
- **Location**: Bordered by the Swiss frontier and the Mulhouse–Basle and Mulhouse–Belfort motorway.

INDUSTRIAL MUSEUMS

👥 Musée du Sapeur Pompier

Housed under the same roof, the Fire Brigade Museum, devoted to the history of this dangerous and prestigious profession, displays some 20 hand pumps, the oldest dating from 1740, steam-powered fire engines, others dating from the early 20C, uniforms, weapons and a big collection of helmets.

🚗 DRIVING TOUR

Round Tour from Altkirch
117km/73mi. Allow half a day.

Altkirch

The old town is perched on a hilltop overlooking the Ill valley. The first settlement was established in the valley, round the old church (alt kirch), then Altkirch was rebuilt on the hilltop at the end of the 12C. In the heart of the Sundgau region and the ideal base for fishing and horse-riding enthusiasts.

▶ Drive E out of Altkirch on the D 419 along the south bank of the River Ill.

St-Morand

This village is a place of pilgrimage. The **church** contains the beautiful 12C sarcophagus of saint, Morand, who converted the Sungdau to Christianity, and was reputed to cure headaches.

The road continues along the Thalbach valley before reaching the plateau. It then runs down towards the Rhine offering views of the Jura mountains, the Basle depression and the Black Forest.

▶ As you enter Ranspach-le-Bas, turn off D 419 to the right. On leaving Ranspach-le-Haut, turn left towards Folgensbourg, where you turn S onto D 473 then left onto D 21bis to St-Blaise. Then take D 9bis to Leymen.

Château du Landskron

🔼 *30min on foot there and back.*

This castle, believed to date from the 11C, is in ruins. Reinforced by Vauban in the 17C, it was besieged and destroyed in 1814. From its privileged position on a height overlooking the border, the view embraces the small town of Leymen below and, farther north, the forested Sundgau and Basle region.

▶ Return to St-Blaise and continue along the upper Ill valley.

Oltingue

In the centre of this pretty village, the **Maison du Sundgau (Musée Paysan)** (ⓞ*Mar–mid-Jun and Oct–Nov Sun 2–5pm; mid-Jun–Sept Tue, Thu, Sat–Sun 3–6pm.* ⓞ*Jan–Feb.* ⬤€2.50. ℘*03 89 40 79 24; http://musee.paysan.free.fr*) highlights regional architectural styles and displays furniture, crockery and kitchen utensils illustrating rural life in the past, including kugelhopf tins appropriately shaped for different feast days.

Hippoltskirch

The **chapel** (⏰*Mar–Oct Sun 11am–5pm, other days by appointment.* ✆*03 89 40 44 46*) has an unusual painted coffered ceiling and a painted-wood balustrade along the gallery. Naive ex-voto paintings on the walls are dedicated to a miracle-working statue of the Virgin, on the left of the nave.

▶ Leave Kiffis on your left and follow the international road (D 21BIII) which skirts the Swiss border (and briefly crosses it beyond Moulin-Neuf) along the bottom of a wooded coomb.

Lucelle

This lakeside village at the southern tip of Alsace, once stood next to a wealthy Cistercian abbey.

▶ Drive N along D 432.

Ferrette★

The former capital of the Sundgau area was, from the 10C onwards, the residence of independent counts whose authority extended over much of Alsace. This region became the property of the House of Austria in the 14C and was ceded to France in 1648 by the Treaty of Westphalia. The prince of Monaco is still entitled to be called Count of Ferrette. The small town, lying in a picturesque **site★**, is overlooked by the ruins of two castles built on an impressive rocky spur rising to an altitude of 612m.

The **Musée du Sapeur-pompier d'Alsace** (⏰*Apr–Oct daily except Mon, other than public holiday Mons, 10am–6pm;* ✆*03 89 68 68 18; www.musee-sapeur-pompier.fr*) houses a collection of fire engines dating from 1648 to 1969, including wheel engines, ladders, sidecars, hand, steam and motor pumps and fireproof suits from the 19C.

▶ Drive to Bouxwiller along D 473.

Bouxwiller

This pretty village adorned with fountains is built on a hillside. The **Église St-Jacques** contains a lovely 18C gilt-wood pulpit, from the Luppach Monastery, and an elaborate Baroque altarpiece.

▶ D 9 bis follows the upper Ill valley to Grentzingen.

Grentzingen★

The characteristic timber-framed houses of this flower-decked village are lined up at right angles to the road. A few still have their original ochre colour.

▶ Turn left in Grentzingen and continue through the village or Riespach.

Feldbach

The restored 12C Romanesque **church** has two parts, one for the nuns and one for the congregation.

▶ Continue on the D 463 and then turn right onto D 7B towards Altenach to visit the **Maison de la nature du Sundgau** 👥 (✆*03 89 08 07 50; www.maison-nature-sundgau.org*).

▶ Return to Altkirch by the D 419.

ADDRESSES

🛏 STAY

🍽🍽 **Chambre d'hôte Moulin de Huttingue** – *68480 Oltingue. 1.5km/1mi S of Oltingue on D 21B.* ✆*03 89 40 72 91. Closed Jan–Feb.* 🍴*. 2 rooms.* Beside the Ill, which is only a stream here, this former flour mill has combined part of its original interior, such as the lovely wooden pillars, with a modern décor. Pretty garden and terrace in summer. Holiday cottage.

Vallée du
Rhin★★
Haut-Rhin, Bas-Rhin

Michelin Map: Michelin Local map 315 : N 3 to j 11.

Marking the border between France and Germany, the River Rhine is flanked on the French side by the foothills of the Vosges, along which runs the Route des Vins, and on the German side by the dense Black Forest. From time immemorial men have attempted to harness its fast impetuous flow and its fearsome spates by building dikes, cutting its arms off and gradually forcing it to follow an artificial course. In spite of this, the "Vater Rhein" is still there, ready to welcome you along part of its journey to the North Sea.

A BIT OF HISTORY

With a total length of 1 298km/807mi, including 190km/118mi along the Franco-German border, the Rhine is the seventh longest river in Europe. The spates of the Rhine were fearsome; this is the reason why no town, not even Strasbourg, settled on its banks. When the water level rose catastrophes were frequent and many an Alsatian village was destroyed by flooding.

In the 8C and 9C, boatmen from Strasbourg sailed downriver to the North Sea in order to sell wine to the English, the Danes and the Swedes.

At the end of the Middle Ages, these boatmen controlled the Rhine between Basle and Mainz and theirs was the most powerful guild in Strasbourg. Some 5 000 wagoners, with 20 000 horses at their disposal, carried inland goods unloaded in Strasbourg.

Harnessing of the Rhine

Water transport was at its height under Napoleon I and in 1826, the first steamships, operating regular sailings along the Rhine, called at Strasbourg. Unfortunately, dikes built along the Rhine during the 19C to control the river flow caused the river bed to become deeper by 6–7cm per year. This, in turn, uncovered rock lying at the bottom of the river and rendered navigation impossible when the water level was low. Water transport consequently declined. In order to bring boats and barges back to the Alsatian section of the Rhine, the French decided in 1920 to divert part of the river between Basle and Strasbourg to a low-gradient canal. Begun in 1928 and completed in the 1960s, the Grand Canal d'Alsace also offers the possibility of tapping the river's considerable potential of hydroelectric power.

🚗 DRIVING TOUR

Sud de la Vallée du Rhin★★

Biesheim

This small town has two specialist museums, the **Musée Gallo-Romain** (€2.50; 03 89 72 01 58) and the **Musée de l'Instrumentation Optique** (€3; 03 89 72 01 59).

THE PRACTICAL RHINE

Locks and dams on the Rhine have information panels relating the history of the Rhine, explaining how power stations work and describing the role of locks and dams. Visits of hydroelectric power stations are restricted by the Vigipirate security plan.

Dams at Kembs, Rhinau and Strasbourg can be used by cyclists and pedestrians to cross between France and Germany.

Boat trips – Themed cruises starting from Huningue, Rheinfelden, Augst or Basel last half a day or a day. Various sections of the Rhine are explored.

Neuf-Brisach

This octagonal stronghold built by Vauban, Louis XIV's military engineer and architect has retained its austere 17C character in spite of the damage incurred during the 1870 siege and WWII. The area within the 2.4km/1.5mi long walls is divided by a network of streets intersecting at right angles. In the centre stands the Église St-Louis and the vast place d'Armes (parade ground) with a well in each of its four corners. It is possible to walk along the ditch from the Porte de Belfort (southwest) to the Porte de Colmar (northwest). This pleasant stroll (about 30min) reveals the main elements of the fortifications: bartizaned bastions, ravelins etc.

The **Porte de Belfort**, no longer used as a gate, houses the **Musée Vauban** (&.⏰May–Sept daily except Mon 10am–noon, 2–5pm. ⌨€2.50. ☎03 89 72 03 93; www.neuf-brisach.fr), created in 1957, containing a relief map of the stronghold with a *son et lumière* show.

Vogelgrün

The border-bridge over the Rhine offers a **view★** of the river, the hydroelectric power station and Vieux-Brisach (Breisach) across the border.

Bief de Vogelgrün★

The power station is similar to those at Ottmarsheim and Fessenheim. Downstream from Vogelgrün are four more reaches; each one comprises a dam on the river, a feeder canal supplying water to the power station and navigation locks and another canal returning the diverted flow to the Rhine.

The power station is decorated with a huge fresco (1 500m²) by Daniel Dyminski from Mulhouse, entitled *Nix from Vogelgrün*, and a large bronze allegorical sculpture by Raymond Couvègnes, entitled *Electricity*.

Fessenheim

Situated less than 1km/0.6mi from the Fessenheim lock, bief de Fessenheim is the first French **nuclear power station** to have used a high-water-pressure reactor.

Bief d'Ottmarsheim★

&. *See OTTMARSHEIM.*

Canal du Rhône au Rhine

The expanded canal between Niffer and Mulhouse was completed in 1995 and today constitutes the first stretch of the Rhône–Rhine canal.

Uffheim

Casemate de l'Aschenbach (&.*see Ligne Maginot*)

Bief de Kembs★

Situated downriver from the dam, the reach includes the canal and a recently modernised double lock.

Hydroelectric power station★

Built between 1928 and 1932. Today, it produces 938 million kWh every year.

Barrage de Kembs

9km/5.6mi S of Kembs.
The dam was the only one built along the first four reaches; it diverts the major part of the river flow towards the Grand Canal d'Alsace. The hydroelectric power station uses the remaining flow.

Petite Camargue alsacienne★

9km S of Kembs along D 468. Park near the stadium in St-Louis-la-Chaussée.
The oldest nature reserve in the region, created in the mid-19C.

River Traffic

Rhine barges are between 60m and 125m long, and between 8m and 13m wide. Among these, there are many self-propelled barges with a capacity of 3 000t for carrying gas. Navigable between Basle and Rotterdam, the Rhine carries more than 10 000 boats every year and these in turn transport 190 million tonnes of freight. Strasbourg is France's second largest river port after Paris.

🚶 Three marked footpaths, one leading all the way around the large marsh *(3km/1.9mi)*, offer the opportunity to observe the flora and fauna of local copses, ponds, marshland and heaths.

Huningue

Huningue is the only stronghold that they dared to build at the Rhine. Old Huningue had been situated at the south of the town today, but its inhabitants were moved in the 17C when the fortress of Vauban was constructed, only few traces of which remains today. In the old bâtiment de l'Intendance, the **Musée Historique** (*rue des Boulangers.* 🕐*1st and 3rd Sun of the month 2.30–5.30pm.* 🕐*Aug.* 𝄐*03 89 89 33 94*) shows a scale model of the fortress, the town's historical documents, particularly of the last three wars and some faïence ceramics and regional costumes.

St-Louis

At the gateway to France, the town was founded by Louis XIV in 1684. Today a town of culture, in 2004 the **Musée d'Art contemporain** (♿🕐*Wed–Sun 1–6pm.* 𝄐*03 89 69 10 77. http://fondationfernet-branca.org*) was opened at the site of the old Fernet-Branca distilleries. The building, still topped by the eagle-emblem of the brand, has been elegantly restored and each year exhibits works of a contemporary artist.

OTTMARSHEIM
Just off the A 36, 18km/11mi E of Mulhouse.
This village, situated on the edge of the vast Harth forest, acquired fame through its church, a unique example of Carolingian architecture in Alsace. Nowadays, Ottmarsheim is also known for its hydroelectric power station, the second of eight such power stations along the Grand Canal d'Alsace.

Église★
The church, consecrated by Pope Leo IX c. 1040, is a rare example of Carolingian architecture. With its unusual octagonal floor plan, topped by a cupola, it is a reduced-scale replica of the Palatine

Octagonal church, Ottmarsheim
© SelenaRus/iStockphoto.com

chapel in Aachen cathedral. All the measurements are divisible by three, the figure symbolising the Holy Trinity. The upper part of the belfry is 15C as is the rectangular chapel on the southeast side, whereas the Gothic chapel left of the apse was built in 1582. The church was badly damaged by a fire in 1991 but some 15C murals depicting St Peter's Life and Christ in Glory presiding over the Last Judgement have been skilfully restored.

Centrale hydroélectrique★
🕐*The power station is open subject to Vigipirate security plan; call for details* 𝄐*06 77 11 62 18. www.edf.com.*
The hydroelectric power station, the reach and the locks (1948–1952), form the second section of the Grand Canal d'Alsace, which was the first stage of the harnessing-of-the-Rhine project between Basle and Lauterbourg.
Locks – of equal length (185m) but different widths (23m and 12m). They are closed by angled gates upstream and by lifting gates downstream. The whole operation takes less than half an hour: 11min in the small lock and 18min in the large lock. The control room overlooks the two locks.
Power station – The engine room is vast and light. The four units have a total output of 156 million watts and produce an average of 980 million kWh every year.

*Harvesting in Hautvillers vineyards,
the village of Cumières in the background*
© Richard Soberka/hemis.fr

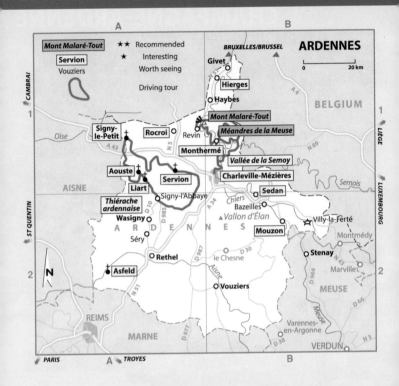

In Rimbaud's footsteps

A native of Charleville, **Arthur Rimbaud** (1854–91) was a brilliant student at the local college and one of his most famous poems, *Le Bateau ivre* (The Drunken Boat) dates from his student days. Unhappy at home, where his authoritarian mother ruled the household, he became a rebel and repeatedly ran away to Charleroi and Paris where he met Verlaine. He followed the older poet to Belgium and London and, in 1873, he wrote another of his famous poems, *Une Saison en Enfer* (A Season in Hell). He later abandoned literature to travel to the Red Sea and the Far East. Repatriated for health reasons at the age of 37, he died in hospital in Marseille and was buried in the old cemetery of his home town.

Arthur Rimbauld drawn by Paul Verlaine

Rimbaud's childhood home from 1865 to 1879 (7 quai Rimbaud) and his college, now the local library (4 place de l'Agriculture) can be seen near the museum; his birthplace (12 rue Bérégovoy) is situated south of place Ducale; his grave is near the entrance of the old cemetery (avenue Charles-Boutet). A bust of Rimbaud was erected on square de la Gare in 1901.

© S. Sauvignier/MICHELIN

Arcades at Place Ducale

Charleville-Mézières★

The commercial city of **Charleville** stretches along the north bank of the river overlooked by Mount Olympus, whereas **Mézières**, an administrative and military centre, nestles inside a meander of the Meuse. The towns were united in 1969.

A BIT OF HISTORY

A Gallo-Roman city destroyed in the 5C by Barbarian invaders stood on the site of Montcy-St-Pierre; the market town of **Arches** developed on the site of Charleville in 9C, acquiring a royal palace while Mézières, founded around the year 1000, was just a village; in the 13C, both towns belonged to the Count of Rethel and Nevers.

In 1565, Louis de Gonzague of the House of the dukes of Mantua, acquired the duchy of Nevers and the earldom of Rethel. **Charles de Gonzague** (1580-1637) succeeded his father and in 1606, turned Arches into the main city of a principality named for himself. By 1627 the building of the town was completed, under the supervision of architect Clément Métezeau.

In 1590, a citadel was built; the Prussian advance was stopped here for 45 days in 1815. During the First World War, Mézières was the headquarters of the German forces.

▶ **Population:** 50 789.
♿ **Michelin Map:** Michelin Local map 306: K-4 Local map see Méandres de la Meuse.
🚹 **Tourist Office** – 4 Pl. Ducale, 08102 Charleville-Mézières. ✆03 24 55 69 90. www. charleville-tourisme.com.
▶ **Location:** Charleville-Mézières is located right in the north of Champagne, 87km/54mi from Reims on the N 19 and A 34.
👁 **Don't Miss:** Place Ducale is one of the finest Louis XIII-style squares in France.
👪 **Kids:** The clock embedded in the wall of the Institute of Puppetry is the scene of puppet shows every day *(see Horloge du Grand Marionnettiste).*

CHARLEVILLE
Place Ducale★★

Designed by **Clément Métezeau** (1581-1652), the square is characteristic of the Louis XIII architectural style and shows many similarities with Place des Vosges in Paris, which is attributed to Louis Métezeau, Clément's brother.

The square (126m long and 90m wide) is lined with **arcades** surmounted by pink brick and ochre-coloured stone **pavilions** topped by slate-covered pitched roofs, forming a harmonious and colourful ensemble.

A public passageway crosses the museum courtyard, linking place Ducale and place Winston-Churchill.

Horloge du Grand Marionnettiste

Place Winston-Churchill.
Incorporated into the façade of the Institut international de la Marionnette, this 10m high brass automaton is by Jacques Monestier; its head and eyes are moved by clockwork on the hour between 10am and 9pm. A short puppet show depicts an episode of the legend of the Four Aymon Brothers, the 12 scenes being enacted every Saturday at 9.15pm. A World Puppet Festival, where new puppet masters practice their craft, takes place every three years.

Vieux Moulin

The former ducal mill looks more like a monumental gate with its imposing Henri IV-Louis XIII façade; it was designed to match the Porte de France in the south. It houses the **Musée Rimbaud** (&*see opposite*).

MÉZIÈRES
Basilique Notre-Dame-d'Espérance

Although it was remodelled over several centuries, this basilica is essentially in Flamboyant-Gothic style, except for the belfry-porch erected in the 17C. The interior is grandiose; light pours in through beautiful abstract **stained-glass windows★**, made between 1955 and 1979 by René Dürrbach.

In the 19C, the basilica was dedicated to the black Notre-Dame-d'Espérance; the statue stands on top of an altar situated to the right of the chancel.

Ramparts

Part of the medieval ramparts remain: Tour du Roy, Tour de l'École, Tour Milart, Porte Neuve, and Porte de Bourgogne.

Préfecture

House in the former Royal Engineers School (17C–18C).

SIGHTS
Musée de l'Ardenne★

31 place Ducale. &*Tue–Sun 10am–noon, 2–6pm.* *1 Jan, 1 May and 25 Dec.* *03 24 32 44 60.*
This modern museum contains a large **archaeology** department illustrating the first human settlements in the Ardennes, while the first-floor rooms display **weapons** made in the royal weapon manufacture, documents about the founding of Charleville (17C relief maps) and 3 000 **coins** and **medals**.
The **pharmacy** (1756) was originally in the former Hôtel-Dieu hospital and was still in use until just 25 years ago.
The top floor houses collections devoted to **folk art and traditions**.

Musée Rimbaud

Quai Rimbaud. &*10am–noon, 2–6pm, daily except Mon.* *03 24 32 44 65.*
Housed inside the old mill, the museum, recently renovated, is entirely devoted to the life and work of Rimbaud.
A footbridge, behind the museum, gives access to Mount Olympus.

EXCURSIONS
Parc animalier de St-Laurent

Route de St-Laurent.
6km/3.7mi E along D 979.
Apr–Sept Mon–Wed and Fri 2–6pm, Sat–Sun and public holidays 1.30–7pm; Oct–Mar daily 1.30–5.30pm. *Thu and 1 Jan.* *No charge.* *03 24 57 39 84.*
Stroll through this zoological park covering 38ha, which extends beyond the city to the outskirts of Aiglemont and Saint-Laurent.

Forêt d'Élan★

8.5km/5.3mi S.

Drive out of Mézières along D 764 to Flize and continue S along D 33 to Élan.

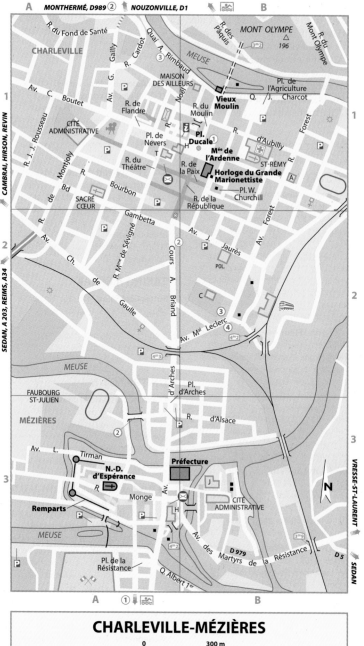

CHARLEVILLE-MÉZIÈRES

0   300 m

WHERE TO STAY

Fleuritel (Hôtel)..①
Lac des Vieilles-Forges (Camping départemental).....②
Paris (Hôtel de)..③
Pélican (Hôtel Le)...④

WHERE TO EAT

Armorini..①
Côte à l'Os (La)...②
Val Fleuri (Le)...③

Close to the River Meuse, the Vallon d'Élan, with its steep pasture-covered slopes, looks like a mountain valley. The 17C Gothic **abbey church** forms a harmonious architectural ensemble with the **abbey manor** flanked with elegant turrets. The **Forêt d'Élan**, covering 872ha, has beautiful oaks and beaches.

ADDRESSES

⌂ STAY

⊖ **Camping départemental Lac des Vieilles-Forges** – 08500 Les Mazures - ℘04 42 16 89 90. Reservation advisable. 300 pitches. Open Apr–mid-Sept. Separated from the lake by a road and a small clump of trees, this campsite offers clearly defined and well-kept pitches. Visitors appreciate the one-night booking facility either for a pitch or a cottage for 6 people. Children enjoy the leisure and activity area by the lakeside.

⊖⊖ **Hôtel Fleuritel** – 1 boulevard Jean Delautre. ℘03 24 37 41 11. www.hotel-fleuritel.com. 35 rooms. Restaurant⊖. This establishment, housed in a contemporary building, looks like a chain hotel. It has 35 very comfortable rooms accessible via a gallery. The restaurant, open from Monday evening to Friday lunch, offers a buffet-style breakfast, a stopover evening meal and a menu written on a board. Adequate and inexpensive.

⊖⊖ **Hôtel de Paris** – 24 av. Georges, Corneau. ℘03 24 33 34 38. www.hotelde paris08.fr. 27 rooms. This early 20C hotel is situated on a busy avenue near the station. The light, simple rooms are well soundproofed. Pleasant, helpful staff.

⊖⊖ **Hôtel Le Pélican** – 42 av. du Mar.-Leclerc. ℘03 24 56 42 73. www.hotel-pelican-charleville.com. 20 rooms. 🅿. This redbrick building has been renovated both outside and inside. Some rooms are personalised and double-glazing considerably reduces the din coming from the avenue. Pleasant breakfast area.

⸮/ EAT

⊖ **La Côte à l'Os** – 11 cours Aristide-Briand. ℘03 24 59 20 16. www.restaurant-charleville-lacotealos.fr. Closed Sun evening. You can be sure of a warm welcome in

this town-centre restaurant, situated in an avenue lined with horse chestnut trees. With a pleasant terrace, a traditional winstub-style "La Taverne", and a traditional regional menu.

⊖⊖ **Amorini** – 46 pl. Ducale. ℘03 24 37 48 80. Closed Sun and Mon. This local trattoria offers a typical Italian setting with murals representing cherubs. Dishes and wines from across the Alps are served in the dining room or sold over the grocery counter.

⊖⊖ **Le Val Fleuri** – 25 quai Arthur-Rimbaud. 200m from the Rimbaud Museum. ℘03 24 59 94 11. Closed Sat lunch and Sun Evening. Located on the first floor of a house overlooking the River Meuse, this restaurant, boasting a pale-colour décor, is run by a friendly couple. Specialities from the Ardennes.

TAKING A BREAK

Sutter Côté Salon – Passage République. ℘03 24 58 33 62. One of this tearoom's delicious specialities are Carolos, meringues made with praline and macaroons. Lunchtime brings simple meals, including mixed salads and snacks.

ON THE TOWN

La Petite Brasserie Ardennaise – 25 quai Arthur-Rimbaud. ℘03 24 37 53 53. Since 1997 this micro-brewery has offered a wide selection of beers. Seven varieties of beer are brewed on-site, including Oubliette, which you are not likely to forget, despite its name.

Le Mawhot – Quai Charcot. ℘03 24 33 54 35. Summer: open daily 4pm–1am. Winter: closed Oct, Mon and Tue. The Mawhot is a legendary reptile from the Ardennes region. The chatty barman, pays homage to this beast by telling wonderful tales of the legendary Aymon brothers and their black steed Bayard. Drink in the stories as well as a home-made brew.

PUPPETRY

Institut International de la Marionnette. 7 pl. Winston-Churchill. ℘03 24 33 72 50. www.marionnette.com. Run by the pupils of the National College of Puppetry, the institute's theatre offers a high-quality programme for kids and adults.

Givet

This border town, guarded by the Charlemont fortress, is made for wandering. From the bridge over the River Meuse, there is a fine overall view of the old town, the Tour Victoire and the Fort de Charlemont.

A BIT OF HISTORY

Givet Notre-Dame, on the east bank, is a former industrial district. The west bank's **Givet St-Hilaire** is the old town nestling round a church. It was described by Victor Hugo in derisive terms: "the architect took a priest's or a barrister's hat, on this hat he placed an upturned salad bowl, on the base of the salad bowl he stood a sugar basin, on the sugar basin a bottle, on the bottle a sun partly inserted into the neck and finally on the sun he fixed a cock on a spit".

SIGHTS

Givet was fortified by Charles V of Spain in 1555; the town retains three of its old gates with drawbridges, Porte Charbonnière, Port de Rancennes and **Porte de France** (to the south).

Centre européen des métiers d'art

&. Tue–Sat 10am–noon, 2.30–6pm, Sun and Mon 2.30–6pm. 1 Jan, 25 Dec. No charge. 03 24 42 73 36. www.cema-givet.com.
Located in a former 17C toll-house, you can watch craftsmen at work and buy local products in the vaulted cellar.

Fort de Charlemont★

Access to the citadel is by shuttle departing from the tourist office (Rue du Château, 08320 Vireux-Wallerand. 03 24 42 92 42; www.valdardenne-tourisme.com) Fri–Sun only at 10.30am, 11am, 3pm, 3.30pm. €7.
This small citadel was fortified by Emperor Charles V and named after him, then was redesigned by Vauban. Since 1962, the fort has been used as a commando training centre.

> **Population:** 6 779.
> **Michelin Map:** Michelin Local map 306: K/L-2.
> **Location:** In the northernmost tip of Champagne, Givet is closer to Brussels (109km/68mi) than to Reims (133km/83mi).
> **Kids:** Children will appreciate the chance to let off steam at the water sports centre of Givet.

EXCURSIONS

VALLÉE DE LA MEUSE – SOUTH OF GIVET

23km/14.3mi

Leave Givet by N 51 which runs along black-marble quarries.

Hierges★

The village sits below the ruins of a castle *(illuminated at night)* built between the 11C and 15C, once the seat of a barony.

Along N 51 cross the river 2km/1.2mi beyond Fépin.

Haybes

This resort offers several walks, in particular to the viewpoint at **La Platale** *(2km/1.2mi from Haybes along the scenic Morhon road: picnic area)*, which affords a close-up view of Fumay, and to the viewpoint of **Roc de Fépin** *(8km/5mi E along D 7; access signposted)*.

ADDRESSES

STAY AND EAT

Val St-Hilaire – 7 quai des Fours. 03 24 42 38 50. www.hotel-val-st-hilaire. com. 20 rooms. This large building on the Meuse quayside has comfortable contemporary. Pleasant terrace in an inner courtyard in the summer.

Méandres de la
Meuse★★

The River Meuse takes its source in the foothills of the Plateau de Langres, not far from Bourbonne-les-Bains, at an altitude of only 409m; it flows into the North Sea 950km/590mi farther on, forming with the Rhine a common delta along the coast of The Netherlands where it is known as the Maas.

GEOGRAPHICAL NOTES

The course of this peaceful river often changes, flowing along the bottom of the ridge known as the Hauts de Meuse, then crossing a large alluvial plain (beyond Dun-sur-Meuse), and meandering through the Ardennes.

The section from Charleville-Mézières to Givet is the most picturesque part of the river: the Meuse has dug its deep and sinuous course through hard schist, which is sometimes barren and sometimes forested (hunting for wild boar and roe-deer is a favourite pastime in the area. The railway line linking Charleville and Givet follows the river, which is linked to the Aisne by the Canal des Ardennes dug in the mid-19C.

River traffic is reduced to barges not exceeding 300t because the river bed not deep enough in places, whereas downriver from Givet, the river has been adapted to allow barges of up to 1 350 tonnes through.

🚗 DRIVING TOURS

1 THE FOUR AYMON BROTHERS

Round tour from Charleville-Mézières
57km/35mi. Allow 4h.

▷ Leave Charleville along D 1 which soon follows the Meuse.

Michelin Map: Michelin Local map 306: K-3/4.

Nouzonville
This industrial centre (metalworks and mechanical industries), situated at the confluence of the Meuse and the Goutelle, follows a long-standing nail-making tradition introduced in the 15C by people from Liège running away from the duke of Burgundy, Charles the Bold.

▷ Continue along D 1 to Braux.

Braux
The former collegiate **church** has retained its Romanesque apse, chancel and transept but the nave and the aisles date from the 17C and 18C.

Note the rich 17C marble altars with low-relief sculptures and above all the fine 12C christening font, carved out of blue stone from Givet and decorated with grotesques.

▷ Cross the River Meuse.

From the bridge, there is an interesting vista on the left of the **Rocher des Quatre Fils Aymon★** (alt 260m), whose outline formed by four sharp points suggests the legend of the Four Aymon Brothers escaping from Charlemagne's men on their famous horse Bayard.

Levrézy (Bogny-sur-Meuse)
A former factory houses the **Musée de la Métallurgie** which illustrates the making of nuts and bolts with tools and machines still in working order (forge, and planing and milling machines). (🕐10am–noon, 2–6pm: May–Sept daily; Oct–Apr daily except Sun–Mon. 🕐mid-Dec–Feb. ✺€6. ✆03 24 35 06 71. www.musee-metallurgie-ardennes.fr).

🚶 The **Sentier Nature et Patrimoine du Pierroy** (the Pierroy Nature and Heritage Trail) leads past typical geological features (conglomerate and schist) and the remains of quartzite quarries, offering fine views of the Meuse valley.

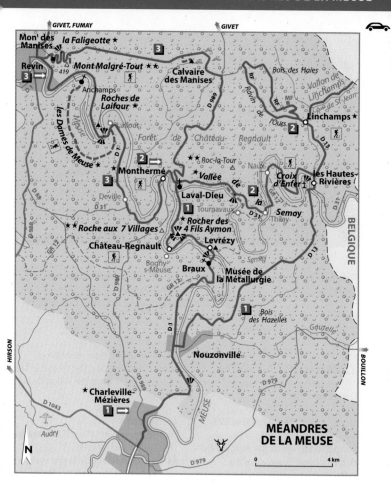

Château-Regnault (Bogny-sur-Meuse)

Once the main centre of a principality, Château-Regnault had its castle razed to the ground by Louis XIV. The **Centre d'exposition des Minéraux et Fossiles des Ardennes** displays rocks from the Ardennes region together with fossils from various parts of the world (🕐*2–6pm: Jun–Aug daily except Mon; Sept Sat–Sun and public holidays. ◎€3, children under 12, no charge. 📞03 24 32 05 02. http://museegeologieardenne. monsite-orange.fr).*

In order to reach the **Monument des Quatre Fils Aymon**, drive up rue Léon-Bosquet then rue du Château to the parking area.

🚶 A footpath (300m) leads to an artificial ledge on the site of the former Château Regnault (12C) of which nothing remains. Steps lead up to the monument: from there, the **view** extends over the meanders of the Meuse, the factories lining its course, workers' housing estates and private mansions.

◐ Continue along D 1 which runs beneath the railway line before crossing the Semoy that flows into the Meuse at Laval-Dieu.

Laval-Dieu
ᗕ*See MONTHERMÉ.*

◐ Turn right onto D 31 to Thilay.

© Gérard Labriet/Photononstop
Revin by the Meuse

The road follows the Semoy valley (&*see Vallée de la SEMOY*).

◗ Return to Charleville along D 13 which runs through the Bois de Hazelles.

2 VALLÉE DE LA SEMOY★

27km/17mi from Monthermé to Linchamps – 1h30.

Monthermé – &*see MONTHERMÉ*

From the Meuse to the Belgian border, the River Semoy (called Semois in Belgium) meanders across pastures between steep slopes covered with forests of oak, fir and birch trees and inhabited by roe-deer and wild boar. The green secluded valley is a paradise for anglers fishing for trout and for anyone who needs to break up a family vacation with a little solitude.

🚶 The **Sentier du Fer, du Schiste et de la Forêt** (*75km/47mi*) runs the whole length of the Semoy valley, offering ramblers the choice of seven round tours; a topographical guide is available from the tourist office in Monthermé.

◗ Leave Monthermé along D 31.

Les Hautes-Rivières

This is the largest village along the French section of the River Semoy. It extends over 2km/1.2mi to Sorendal.

◗ Drive S towards Nouzonville, climbing 1.5km/0.9mi to the beginning of the path leading to the Croix d'Enfer.

Croix d'Enfer

🚶 *30min on foot there and back.*
View★ of the valley, the village of Les Hautes-Rivières and the Vallon de Linchamps.

Linchamps★

N of Hautes-Rivières along D 13. The area is beautiful and remote.
🚶 The isolated village is the starting point of walks through the **Ravin de l'Ours** and **Bois des Haies**, across a hilly area reaching altitudes in excess of *500m*.

3 MONT MALGRÉ TOUT

Round tour from Revin

40km/25mi. Allow 2h30, including 1h15 on foot.

Revin

Revin occupies an exceptional position within two deep meanders of the Meuse. There are a few 16C timber-framed houses along quai Edgar-Quinet; note in particular the **Musée du Vieux Revin, Maison espagnole** on the corner of rue Victor-Hugo, which has been turned into a museum holding a annual exhibition about traditions and customs of the Ardennes (🕐*Jun–Aug daily 10am–noon, 2–6pm; Apr and Oct Wed–Sat 1.30–5.30pm; May and Sept Wed–Sun 2–6pm. ✆No charge. ℘03 24 40 19 59; www.ville-revin.fr).*

A building situated on the edge of the **Parc municipal Rocheteau** houses a **Galerie d'art contemporain** (Galerie d'art Maurice Rocheteau) including works by Georges Cesari (1923–82) (♿🕐*Apr–Sept daily 10am–8pm; Oct–Mar daily except Sat–Sun and public holidays 2–5pm. ✆No charge. ℘03 24 40 10 72).*

▶ On the outskirts of Revin, the winding Route des Hauts-Buttés branches off D 1 and rises 300m in a series of hairpin bends to the Monument des Manises standing on the roadside.

Monument des Manises

The monument is dedicated to the 106 members of the Maquis des Manises resistance group, killed by the Germans in June 1944. Take in the remarkable bird's-eye **view** of Revin and the surrounding area.

Point de vue de la Faligeotte★

The viewing-platform of La Faligeotte also offers an interesting **view** of Revin and the meanders of the Meuse.

▶ The road reaches the edge of the plateau.

Mont Malgré Tout★★

▶ Park the car 400m from a signpost bearing the inscription "Point de vue à 100m." The footpath begins here (1h on foot there and back).

Four Brothers and Their Legendary Steed

The deep and impenetrable Ardennes forest is the favourite haunt of wild animals, pagan spirits and fantastic creatures. Among the many legends that flourish in the thick woods, the most famous is undoubtedly the legend of *The Four Aymon Brothers,* sometimes called *The Renaud de Montauban Tale,* which relates the feats of four brave knights astride their mighty horse, **Bayard**.

© S. Sauvignier/MICHELIN

Aymon was the Duke of Dordogne and an ardent supporter of Charlemagne. In a complicated dispute, the duke's brother killed a son of Charlemagne, and was then killed himself by supporters of the king. Aymon's four sons, handsome and valiant (as legend must have it), could not suffer their uncle's murder and finally had to flee; their mother provided them with the family treasury to help them on their way. They established themselves in the thick forest of the Ardennes in a castle, Montfort, built into the rocky cliff above the Meuse.

This epic can be compared to the *Chanson de Roland,* the earliest masterpiece of the French *chansons de gestes* (songs of deeds), which formed the core of the Charlemagne legends. Numerous episodes were gradually added to the simple story which, in the 13C, became a poem intended to be read. The 15C prose version is a precursor of the novel form.

Precious manuscripts, incunabula (books handwritten before 1501) and old editions of this work are kept with the archives of the *département,* and many place names recall the brothers' heroic exploits.

🚶 The steep path leads to a television relay. From there it is possible to walk through a thicket of birch and oak trees and reach a higher viewpoint (*alt 400m*) offering a wide **view** of Revin, the meanders of the Meuse, the Dames de Meuse across the river to the south and the Vallée de Misère to the west.

▶ Drive 6km/3.7mi along Route des Hauts-Buttés to the signpost marked Calvaire des Manises, and park the car.

Calvaire des Manises
🚶 *15min on foot.*
A path leads to the clearing where the members of the Resistance were massacred: Here you'll find calvary, monuments and common grave.

▶ Continue along the same road to the intersection with D 989 and turn right. The road runs through the Château-Regnault Forest.

Monthermé
🚶 *See MONTHERMÉ.*
The road (D 1) crosses back to the west bank, running close to the hill topped by the **Roche aux Sept Villages** (🚶 see *MONTHERMÉ*).

▶ Continue along D 1 which goes through Deville before reaching Laifour.

From the bridge, there is an impressive **view**★★ of the Roches de Laifour and Dames de Meuse.

Roches de Laifour★
(⊶*Not accessible to cars*)
This promontory rises 270m above the river bed; its schist slopes dropping steeply towards the river are a striking feature of this wild landscape.

Dames de Meuse★
(⊶*Not accessible to cars*)
According to legend, this steep ridge owes its name to three unfaithful wives who were turned to stone by God's wrath. Legend or no, this ridge

is breathtaking. The line forms a black gullied mass whose curve follows the course of the Meuse; it reaches an altitude of 393m at its highest point and rises 250m above the river bed.

▶ Leave the car at the entrance to Laifour village.

🚶 A **path** branches off D 1 south of Laifour, climbs to the Dames de Meuse refuge and reaches the edge of the ridge (*2h on foot there and back*); the walk affords a fine **view**★★ of the valley and the village. From there, another path follows the top of the ridge and leads to **Anchamps** (*about 2h30 on foot*).

▶ Drive along D 1 which crosses the Meuse and offers impressive views of the Dames de Meuse before reaching Revin.

ADDRESSES

🏨 STAY AND 🍴 EAT

⊜⊜ **Le Moulin Labotte** – *52 r. Edmond-Dromard, 08170 Haybes.* ☎*03 24 41 13 44. Closed Sun evening and Mon.* From your table you can admire the fine restored machinery of this old water mill, which stands on the edge of a river surrounded by woods. Local game features prominently. A few rooms are available.

MINI CRUISES

Head to one of the boarding points at Charleville, Monthermé and Revin to enjoy an informative and entertaining boat trip on the Meuse. (*1h30 –2h30*). ☎*03 24 33 77 70.*

FESTIVAL

Story-tellers relate local legends during the **Festival des Trois Vallées** in July. *Enquire at Bogny-sur-Meuse tourist office,* ☎*03 24 33 94 78.*

Roc de la Tour

Monthermé★

Situated just beyond the confluence of the Semoy and the Meuse, this is the ideal starting point for exploring the Ardennes region on foot or by bike. And, getting out of the car is the ideal way to see this region.

VISIT
Vielle ville

A long street lined with old houses runs through the old town and leads to the fortified **Église St-Léger★** (12–16C), built of fine stone from the Meuse region. Inside note the Romanesque christening font and the wealth of 16C painted decoration (○*Jul–Aug Tue, Thu and Sat 3–6pm.* ☎03 24 54 46 73).

Laval-Dieu

This industrial suburb of Monthermé grew round an **abbey of Premonstratensians** established here in the 12C. The former **abbey church** still stands on a peaceful wooded site.

EXCURSIONS
Roche à Sept Heures★

2km/1.2mi along D 989 to Hargnies then left at the top of the hill onto the tarmac path.

From this rocky spur, there is a elevated **view★** of Monthermé and the meander of the Meuse with Laval-Dieu upstream and, farther away, Château-Regnault and the Rocher des Quatre Fils Aymon.

▶ **Population:** 2 495.
Ⓖ **Michelin Map:** Michelin Local map 306: K-3. (Ⓖ*see also below*).
ℹ **Tourist office** Pl. Jean-Baptiste Clément, 08800 Monthermé. ☎03 24 54 46 73. www.meuse-semoy-tourisme.com.

Roche aux Sept Villages★★

3km/1.9mi S. Follow the Charleville road (D 989).

As the road rises, the **view★★** slowly extends over the valley. Steps climb this rocky peak rising above the forest. From the top there is a view of the meandering River Meuse lined with seven villages from Braux in the south to Deville in the north. Next to Château-Regnault stands the jagged Rocher des Quatre Fils Aymon.

▶ The road continues to climb beyond the Roche aux Sept Villages; at the top, a path leads to the viewpoint of the Roche de Roma.

Roche de Roma★

Alt 333m. **View★** of the Meuse between Monthermé and Deville.

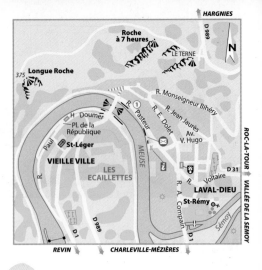

ᨑᨑWALKING TOURS

Longue Roche★

The tarmac path continues beyond the Roche à Sept Heures for a farther 400m to a parking area. From there, you can walk to the viewpoint (30min there and back).

🚶 This is another rocky spur (alt 375m) overlooking the Meuse. A path running along the ridge (12km/7.5mi) offers bird's-eye views of the valley. The **panorama★★** is wilder and sharper than that of the Roche à Sept Heures.

Roc de la Tour★★

3.5km/2.2mi E then 20min on foot there and back. The forest road (Route forestière de la Lyre) branches off D 31 on the left as you leave Laval-Dieu; it rises through the wooded vale of a stream (the Lyre). Parking 3km/1.9mi farther on; leave the car and follow the footpath.

🚶 This ruin-like quartzite spur surrounded by birches stands in a dramatic setting overlooking the Semoy and affords a panoramic **view★★** of the wooded heights of the Ardennes massif. Helpful paths for climbers have been marked out on rocks by the Club alpin français.

🚶 From Roc-la-Tour, there are various possibilities of walks (35km/22mi) through the Semoy and Meuse valleys

(information panels located in the parking area). Choose one that fits your ability level and enjoy the great outdoors.

ADDRESSES

🏠 STAY AND 🍴EAT

🛏🍽 **Le Franco-Belge** – *2 r. Pasteur, 08800 Monthermé.* 🕿*03 24 53 01 20.* 🅿. *15 rooms. Restaurant*🍽. If you have worked up an appetite rock-climbing, you can refuel at this unpretentious family inn, which serves simple dishes, to be enjoyed in the old-fashioned interior or, better still, on the terrace, in the shade of the trellis. Game is often on the menu. Spotless rooms.

SPORT AND RECREATION

MOUNTAIN-BIKING

Monthermé is the starting point of four marked mountain-bike itineraries of varying length (*from 15 to 50km/9 to 31mi*) and difficulty; a brochure is available from the tourist office.

Mouzon★

This small town, lying on an island formed by the River Meuse and the Canal de l'Est, has transformed from a Gaulish trading centre (Mosomagos) to a Roman military post. It later became a favourite residence of the archbishops of Reims. Mouzon was besieged by the Holy Roman Emperor Charles V in the 16C, and by Turenne and troops from Luxemburg in the 17C. The last factory to produce industrial felt is based here.

🐾 TOWN WALK

🚶 A marked itinerary, starting from the Porte de France site in the south, follows the town's fortifications (brochure available from the tourist office).

Porte de Bourgogne

This fortified gate, dating from the 12C to the 17C is all that remains of the town's fortifications.

SIGHTS
Abbatiale Notre-Dame★

&.ⒸApr–Oct 9.30am–7pm, Sun and public holidays 2–7pm; rest of year 9.30am–5pm. 🖉03 24 26 56 11.
The 13C nave and 12C **chancel** rest on massive round piers, as in Laon Cathedral on which Mouzon is modelled. The 18C organ and carved-wood organ case (1725 are the only remaining examples of the work of Christophe Moucherel in northern France.

Musée du Feutre

Rue Jean Claude Stoltz. ⒸApr–Oct 10am–noon, 2–6pm.⊛€4 (children €1.50) – free 1st Sun of month. 🖉03 24 26 19 91.
👥Founded in 1987, the Felt Museum, housed in one of the abbey's former farmhouses, is devoted to the **history** and manufacture of felt (one of the world's oldest textiles).

▶ **Population:** 2 279.
🏛 **Michelin Map:** Michelin Local map 306: M-5.

EXCURSIONS
Site gallo-romain du Flavier

4km/2.5mi SE on D 964 to Stenay.
The remains of a Gallo-Roman sanctuary, discovered on this site in 1966, include the foundations of three small temples dating from 50 BCE to 350 CE.

Pavillon d'accueil du territoire du sanglier

▷ 12km/7.5mi along D 19 to Carignan then follow D 981 and turn right towards Mogues.

Wild boars have been popular in the region from the Gallo-Roman period until today: the Sedan football club even chose a wild boar as their mascot. The exhibition offers visitors an interactive journey in the footsteps of this symbolic animal living in the Ardennes forests.

Stenay

36km/22mi drive S of Mouzon.

▷ Leave Mouzon SE along the scenic D 964 towards Stenay.

This former stronghold, situated on the east bank of the river and the canal, lies in the heart of beer country.
The vast **Musée Européen de la Bière** (European Beer Museum) (ⒸMar–Nov 10am–12.30pm, 1.30–6pm. ⊛€5, no charge for children under 18. 🖉03 29 80 68 78. www.museedelabiere.com) is housed in the former supply stores of the 16C citadel turned into a malt factory in the 19C. The uninitiated discover how brewers make beer from spring water, barley turned into malt, and hops. The 16C residence of the former governor of the citadel, situated on the edge of town, houses the **Musée du pays de Stenay**, which contains collections of archaeology as well as arts and crafts.

Rethel

The town has been almost entirely rebuilt after destruction in the two World Wars. French poet, **Paul Verlaine,** spent several quiet years in the town in the 1870s teaching literature, history, geography and English.

Église St-Nicolas

This unusual Gothic edifice consists of two churches built side by side. The left-hand church (12C–13C) was used by monks from a Benedictine monastery. The right-hand church (15C–16C) was the parish church. Features include an aisle lit by Flamboyant Gothic windows and a richly decorated doorway.

EXCURSIONS

Asfeld

22km/13.7mi SW along D 18 then D 926. This village on the south bank of the River Aisne has an unusual Baroque church, **Église St-Didier★** built in brick in the shape of a viol, which was designed in 1683 by the Dominican priest, François Romain, who built the Pont-Royal in Paris. Consisting entirely of curves, it has a central rotunda flanked by four semi-oval cupolas and a brick colonnade round the outside.

Boudin Blanc

The gastronomic speciality of Rethel is a white sausage made from fresh pork meat without any preservatives. It carries the *Ardennes de France* seal as a guarantee of quality. The original recipe is said to have been invented by a chef of Cardinal Mazarin to whom the Comté of Rethel once belonged. Today *boudin blanc*, which is celebrated in Rethel in an annual fair on the last weekend in April, comes in different sizes and can be prepared in various ways: in a pastry case, barbecued or as a tasty stuffing for *crêpes* (pancakes).

- ▶ **Population:** 8 136.
- **Michelin Map:** Michelin Local map 306: I-5.
- **Tourist office:** 3 quai d'Orfeuil, 08300 Rethel. ℘03 24 38 54 56.
- **Location:** Rethel lies on the banks of the River Aisne and the Canal des Ardennes halfway between Reims and Charleville-Mézières.

Wasigny

16km/10mi N along D 10.

The road goes through **Séry** where a 1.7km/1mi **botanic trail** allows nature lovers to discover the local flora; orchids as well as other flowers, plants and bushes characteristic of sheep pasture. A 16C–17C **manor house** guards the entrance to the village. A fine 15C covered market stands in the village centre.

ADDRESSES

🍴 STAY AND EAT

⊖⊖ **Le Moderne** – *2 pl. Victor Hugo. ℘03 24 38 44 54. www.hotel-lemoderne.fr. 20 rooms. Restaurant (⊖⊖).* Many of the rooms have been pleasantly renovated, living up to the establishment's name.

SHOPPING

Charcuterie Yves Duhem – *9 r. Colbert. ℘03 24 38 46 19. Tue–Sat 8.30am–12.30pm, 2.30–7pm; Sun 9am–noon.* Since 1798, this shop has been making boudin blanc and other high-quality pork meat specialities.

FESTIVAL

The **Festival de viole de gambe** is held every two years *(next in June 2010)* in Asfeld: concerts, exhibition of stringed instruments. ℘03 24 72 96 99.

Rocroi★

Sitting in the middle of a star-shaped citadelle, the small 16C town of Rocroi was the site of one of the most famous battles of the Thirty Years War. Rocroi, whose name means King's Rock, changed its name to Roc Libre (free rock) during the Revolution.

SIGHTS
La Citadelle

Built by Henri II in 1555 to counter the threat of Charlemont fort in Givet, occupied by the Spaniards, the stronghold was further fortified in 1675 by Vauban, who was appointed *Commissaire général des fortifications* in 1678. Starting from the Porte de France to the southwest, follow the tourist trail running east, which gives an idea of the complexity of the defence system.

Musée de la Bataille de Rocroi

Pl. du Luxembourg. Mid–Apr–late Sept Mon–Wed 2–5.30pm, Thu–Sat 2–6pm, Sun 10am–noon, 2–6pm. €4. 03 24 54 58 65.
Housed in the former guardhouse, the museum presents a film illustrating the manoeuvres which led the future Grand Condé to victory over the Spanish army at the battle of Rocroi (1643).

▶ **Population:** 2 426.
Michelin Map: Michelin Local map 306: J-3.
Tourist office: Place d'Armes, 08230 Rocroi. 03 24 54 20 06. www.otrocroi.com.
▶ **Location:** On the Ardennes plateau 6km/3.7mi from the Belgian frontier, 28km/17.4mi NW of Charleville-Mézières.

Circuit de la Bataille

A waymarked footpath *(13.5km/8.5mi)* leads from the museum to the site of Rocroi battle through moorland dotted with a wide variety of interesting plants, including wild orchids and gentians.

ADDRESSES

⏚ EAT

Le Vauban – *2 pl. d'Armes.* 03 24 54 18 69. *Closed Wed, holidays and evenings except at weekends.* This venerable building and its lovely terrace are situated on the huge parade ground.

Sedan★

This frontier town sits beneath the largest fortress in Europe. South of the town, a 13ha artificial lake welcomes bathers and sailors. In addition to textiles, industrial activities include metalworks, chemicals and foodstuffs.

A BIT OF HISTORY

Sedan is mentioned for the first time in 997 as belonging to Mouzon abbey. In 1594, it became the property of the La Tour d'Auvergne family.
Henri de La Tour d'Auvergne, Viscount of **Turenne** and Marshal of France

▶ **Population:** 18 672.
Michelin Map: Michelin Local map 306: L-4.
Tourist office: 35 r. du Ménil, 08200 Sedan. 03 24 27 73 73. www.tourisme-sedan.fr.
▶ **Location:** Near the Belgian frontier, 23km/14.3mi SE of Charleville-Mézières by A203.
Kids: The huge fortress is a must.

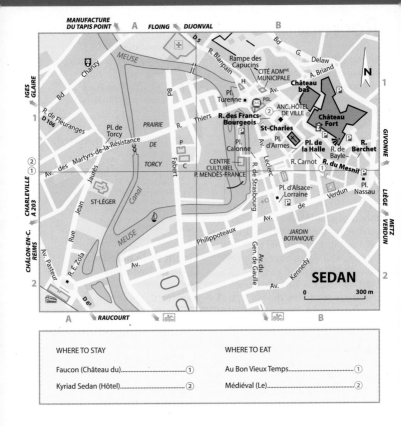

(1611–75) is famed for his faithful service to Louis XIII and Louis XIV during the Thirty Years War.

SIGHTS
Château Fort★★
👥 *Place du Château.*
🕐*Jul–Aug daily 10am–6pm; rest of the year 10am–5pm.* €8.50 (children €5). 📞03 24 29 98 80.
www.chateau-fort-sedan.fr.
This fortress covering an area of 35 000sq m on seven levels is the largest in Europe. It was built on a rocky spur on the site of a monastery. Work began in 1424; the **twin towers** and the **ramparts** date from that period. The latter (30m high), surrounded by ditches, were completed by bastions in the 16C. The **Château bas** was built in the 17C outside the walls (probably by Salomon de la Brosse who designed the Luxembourg Palace in Paris). Between 1642 and 1962,

the stronghold was army property. The town then acquired it and undertook its restoration.

Historium
The tour of the castle (*audio-guides, explanatory panels*) includes reconstructed scenes with wax figures illustrating the lifestyle of princes, soldiers and servants in the past.

Musée du Château Fort
The twin towers house archaeological finds, ethnographic exhibits and documents relating to the town's history. One room is devoted to the Franco-Prussian War of 1870 and the First World War.

Manufacture du Tapis Point de Sedan
13 bd. Gambetta.
In this traditional carpet factory, weavers can be seen working on looms dating

Sedan at the Height of the Cloth Industry

The heart of old Sedan, where many private mansions testify to the cloth industry's prosperity, is being carefully restored. **Dijonval** (*Av. du Général-Margueritte*) was a royal cloth manufacturer founded in 1646 and functioning until 1958. Its imposing 18C façade extends either side of a pedimented central pavilion. Henri de la Tour d'Auvergne had **Église St-Charles** built for the Calvinist faith in 1593, after the Revocation of the Edict of Nantes it became a Catholic church and a vast rotunda-shaped chancel was added in 1688.

The 18C mansion at **No. 33 place de la Halle** likely was both a private house and warehouse. The main building has wings like the Dijonval. Built as a private mansion in 1629, the Hôtel de Lambermont at **No. 1 rue du Mesnil** became a royal manufacture in 1726. Opposite stands another draper's house dating from 1747. The former dyer's workshop at **No. 3 rue Berchet** was acquired in 1823 by the owner of the royal manufacture. The 18C building with fine wrought-iron work at **No. 1 rue des Francs-Bourgeois** was probably a draper's workshop.

from 1878. The motif is drawn on paper and transcribed onto cardboard. It takes five weavers three months to make a carpet 6 sq m.

EXCURSION

Bazeilles

3km/1.8mi SE along N 43.

Bitter fighting took place here in 1870. The **Maison de la dernière cartouche**, where a group of French soldiers resisted to their last round, is now a museum containing French and German items gathered on the battlefield (○*daily except Mon and Tue: Apr–Sept 1.30–6pm; Oct–Mar 1.30–5pm.* ○*15 Dec–5 Jan.* €*3.* ℰ*03 24 27 15 86. www.maisondeladernierecartouche.com*). Nearby, an ossuary contains the remains of some 3 000 French and German soldiers.

ADDRESSES

🛏 STAY

⊜ **Hôtel Kyriad Sedan** – *89 av. de la Marne, 08200 Sedan.* ℰ*03 24 29 44 44. 38 rooms. Restaurant*⊜ *(Mon–Fri evenings only).* Close to the town centre and part of a small chain of inexpensive hotels. The rooms are fitted with functional, contemporary furniture. Each room has a full en suite bathroom. Buffet-style breakfast, simple restaurant relying on traditional cuisine.

⊜⊜⊜⊜ **Château du Faucon** – *Rte de Vrigne-aux-Bois, 08350 Donchery. 4km west of Sedan along A 203.* ℰ*03 24 41 87 83. www.domaine-chateaufaucon.com. 31 rooms. Restaurant*⊜⊜. This vast and beautiful estate of 28ha offers different kinds of accommodation (large stylish bedrooms in the 17C castle or dorms in the converted outbuildings), a restaurant and many leisure activities.

⏱/ EAT

⊜⊜ **Au Bon Vieux Temps** – *3 pl. de la Halle.* ℰ*03 24 29 03 70. www.restaurant-aubonvieuxtemps.com. Closed Sun evening, Wed evening, and all day Mon.* Lovely naïve-style frescoes (views of Sedan and the Ardennes) hang on the walls of this comfortable restaurant close to the castle. Traditional menu.

⊜⊜ **Le Médiéval** – *51 r. de l'Horloge, 08200 Sedan.* ℰ*03 24 29 16 95. Closed Sat lunch, Sun evening and all day Mon.* Located in the old district, at the foot of the castle, this small restaurant will delight you with its classical and regional cuisine.

Thiérache Ardennaise★

This area of forest and meadows southwest of Charleville-Mezières is good walking country and noted for its unusual fortified churches and farms, reflecting a history of constant invasion.

A BIT OF HISTORY

Churches were fortified during the late 16C and throughout the 17C in an effort to protect villages from the successive wars and hordes of plundering mercenaries that constantly invaded the region.

Tall square keeps, round towers and bartizans were added to medieval churches, which were intended to shelter villagers in case of need; extra accommodations were added above the nave, explaining the presence of ceilings in most churches.

DRIVING TOUR

Round Tour from Signy-l'Abbaye
116km/72mi. Allow one day.

Signy-l'Abbaye

This Vaux valley village grew up near a famous Cistercian abbey founded in 1135 and destroyed in 1793.

The parish church was built in 1900 on the site of the former sanctuary. The **Salle Guillaume-de-Saint-Thierry** (*Jul–mid-Sept Sat–Sun and public holidays 3–7pm. No charge. 03 24 52 87 26*), named after St Bernard's biographer, houses an **exhibition** devoted to the former abbey and its grounds.

Forêt de Signy

Signy Forest, which extends over 3 535ha, is made of two massifs separated by the Vaux valley: the small forest (oak, beech) to the southeast and the damper large forest (oak, ash, maple) to the northwest.

> **Michelin Map:** Michelin Local map 306: E/F/G-3/4.
> **Tourist Office:** Maison de la Thiérache, place de la Mairie, 08290 Liart. 03 24 54 48 33.

Make a detour to the northeast, via the forest road, to admire the 18C covered market in **Saint-Jean-aux-Bois**.

▷ Drive to Liart, NW of Signy by D 27.

The road passes the **Fontaine Rouge** (100m on right), a ferrous spring marking the start of a 4km/2.5mi footpath, then goes through the oak forest and reaches the path (parking area) leading down to the Gros Frêne.

A stump and a slice of trunk are all that remain of this imposing ash tree, fallen in 1989 (45min there and back).

Two other marked footpaths, 5km/3mi and 6km/3.7mi long, start from the parking area.

Liart

The medieval west front of the **Église Notre-Dame-de-Liart★** was flanked in the 17C by a massive rectangular keep reinforced by brattices, crenels and loopholes whereas the east end was fortified by an octagonal tower with stairs leading to an attic above the chancel.

▷ Continue along D 27.

Aouste

The **Église St-Rémi★** was built in the 17C on the ruins of a 15C church. The machicolated main doorway is reinforced by three brattices and a turret. The square tower, pierced with loopholes and strengthened by buttresses, was reached via a spiral staircase. This church had a bread oven in the nave and a well to feed the villagers in times of siege.

▷ Turn left onto D 36 to La Férée then right onto D 236. In Blanchefosse,

Fortified church, Signy-le-Petit

turn right onto D 10 to Mont-St-Jean, then right again onto D 977 to Rumigny.

Rumigny

As you enter the village admire the Renaissance **Château de la Cour des Prés** (1546) (🕐*mid-Jul–Aug daily except Sat 2–6pm.* ☎*03 24 35 52 66*), which was fortified at the request of François I. Two halls on the ground floor have impressive fireplaces and drawing rooms with 18C panelling. Upstairs, the bedrooms open onto the gallery decorated with family portraits. The castle is also a hotel (👍*see Addresses*).

▶ Continue along D 27.

Hannapes

Although it was not fortified, the **Église St-Jean-Baptiste** provided shelter to the villagers in case of invasion.

▶ Turn right onto D 31. Turn left onto D 10 to Fligny.

Fligny

Above the chancel of the **Église St-Étienne**, there is a room intended as a shelter, flanked with a round tower.

▶ Continue along D 10.

Signy-le-Petit

The imposing 17C **church★**, fortified by brick-built corner towers, stands in the centre of a large square. The 18C château was remodelled in the 19C.

👪 The Étang de la Motte has a sand beach and supervised bathing in summer, as well as bike hire, a swimming pool and table tennis.

▶ Drive towards Rocroi and Charleville then turn right onto D 34 to Tarzy.

Tarzy

A tower with canted corners pierced with loopholes was built to the left of the belfry of the hilltop **church**.

Antheny

Despite being destroyed by fire several times, the village still has a few 16C and 17C fortified houses.

The **Église St-Remy**, standing in the middle of the cemetery, features a buttressed square tower. The upper windows were blocked up in the 15C–16C for defence.

▶ Continue along D 34 via Champlin and Estrebay.

Prez

An attic above the chancel in this church was used for defence purposes. A round tower pierced with loopholes was added in the 16C. 18C stucco panels depicting Christ's life surround the chancel.

▶ Continue along D 34 past Le Malpas, then left onto D32 towards La Cerleau , then right on D36 towards Flaignes.

Flaignes-Havys

Clovis made a present of Flaignes to St Remi when he was baptised in Reims. The **Église St-Laurent**, fortified in the 16C–17C, has an unusually imposing chancel flanked by a round tower. In Havys, the **Église St-Gery** has a round tower pierced all round with loopholes used not only as look-outs but also to light the spiral staircase.

▶ Continue along D 20 to Cernion then turn left to l'Échelle.

The Hôtel Beury, a former 18C coaching inn, is home to the **Centre d'art et de littérature** which boasts contemporary art exhibitions, a **literary café**, artists' residences and a sculpture garden.

▶ Drive SE to Rouvroy-sur-Audry and cross D 978 to reach Servion.

Servion

The **Église St-Étienne★** has a remarkable fortified porch with slate-roofed turrets. Now deconsecrated, it is used for exhibitions.

▶ Continue along D 9. After Rémilly-les-Pothées, turn right onto D 39 towards Fagnon.

Ancienne Abbaye de Sept Fontaines

The former abbey, dating from the 17C, owes its name to the seven springs.

▶ Take the D 34 to Évigny.

Évigny

Two **traditional houses** (*guided 1h tour by appointment, mid-Jun–Aug Sun 2.30–6.30pm. ℘03 24 58 21 41*) illustrate life in the past. The first shows a reconstruction of a peasant home. The second has a **bakery** where you can buy traditionally baked loaves.

▶ Turn back along D 34 then take D 3 left to Launois-sur-Vence.

Launois-sur-Vence

A 17C **posting inn** made communications between Amsterdam and Marseille easier. The buildings surrounding a vast courtyard include the postmaster's house, the timber-framed coach house, the stables, sheep pen and vaulted cider cellar. It is now occupied by the tourist office and a **cultural centre**.

ADDRESSES

🏠 STAY AND 🍴 EAT

Ferme-auberge de Gironval – *Gironval, 08460 Thin-le-Moutier. 10km/ 6.2mi NE of Signy-l'Abbaye on D 2. ℘03 24 54 74 40. Closed 16–30 Aug. Booking necessary. 5 rooms.* 😊😊. This inn housed in a former flour mill draws many regulars. The dining room with stone and wood decor offers a pretty view of the mill wheel. The cooking, using local farm produce, is a treat.

Auberge de l'Abbaye – *2 pl. Aristide-Briand, 08460 Signy-l'Abbaye. ℘03 24 52 81 27. www.auberge-de-labbaye.com. 7 rooms. Restaurant (😊😊) – Closed Wed lunch.* This old stone posting inn set in a picturesque village has a pleasant country feel. The cooking is simple and regional. Small, well-kept bedrooms and a welcoming atmosphere.

Chambre d'hôte La Cour des Prés – *6 Place Nicolas Lacaille, 08290 Rumigny. ℘03 24 35 52 66. Closed Nov–Mar and Tue Jul–Aug. 2 rooms.* A lovely welcome awaits you in this fortified house, built in 1546 by the provost of Rumigny. Enjoy a dinner-concert in summer.

Vouziers

Once a simple medieval village, Vouziers became in the 12C the rallying point of pilgrims with sick children seeking a cure from St Maurille, a 4C archbishop of Reims. Vouziers later developed into an important trading centre following the creation of an annual fair.

VISIT
Église St-Maurille

The west front has an interesting Renaissance triple **doorway**★, the first part of a new church whose construction was interrupted by the Wars of Religion. For over 200 years, the doorway stood isolated. In 1764, it was joined to the existing edifice by means of two additional bays. The statues of the four evangelists are placed in recesses separating the three portals. The tympanum of the left door represents a skeleton, whereas the right one shows the risen Christ.

EXCURSIONS
Forêt de Croix-aux-Bois

The **Bois de Ham footpath** (5.5km/3.5mi) winds through the forest, planted with chestnuts, beeches and oaks, to the Étang de la Demoiselle; along the way, panels provide information on the forest biotope.

Canal des Ardennes

The canal, dug during the reign of Louis-Philippe (1830–48), links the River Meuse to the River Aisne and to the waterways of the Seine basin. There are 27 locks between Semuy and Le Chesne, over a distance of just 9km/5.6mi; perhaps the most interesting is in Montgon. Northeast of Le Chesne, the canal follows the fertile valley of the River Bar.

Lac de Bairon

Set in hilly surroundings, this lake (4km/2.5mi wide)is used as a reservoir of the Canal des Ardennes. It is divided into two by a causeway.
The lake offers various activities including fishing, canoeing and walking and a bird sanctuary.

▶ **Population:** 4 216.
 Michelin Map: Michelin Local map 306: K-6.
Tourist Office: 10 pl. Carnot, 08400 Vouziers. ℰ03 24 71 97 57. www.argonne-ardennaise.fr.
▶ **Location:** 22km/13.7mi E of Rethel by D946 on a branch of the Ardennes Canal.

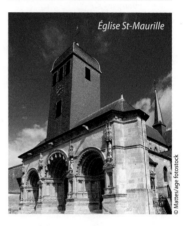
Église St-Maurille

© Mattes/age fotostock

Parc Argonne Découverte (Nocturnia) (Olizy)

11km by D946. Open Feb–early Nov from 10am, but check website for seasonal closing times. ℰ03 24 71 07 38. www.parc-argonne-decouverte.fr.
Opened in 2006, this centre is devoted to nocturnal species: birds of prey, bats and insects. In a dark room, an informative interactive route recreates the night-time environment.

ADDRESSES

🏠 STAY AND ⑂ EAT

⊜⊜ **Chambre d'hôte Auberge du Pied des Monts** – 6 rue de la Fontaine, 08400 Grivy-Loisy. 7km/4.3mi NW of Vouziers on D 946 and D 21. ℰ03 74 11 64 40. 5 rooms. Restaurant ⊜⊜ – Closed Wed and Sun eve. An inn in the centre of a quiet, green, rural village. The rooms, four of which are huge with mezzanines, are in the converted stables of an old farm.

MARNE

0 —— 20 km

REIMS ★★★ Highly recommended
Châlons-en-Champagne ★★ Recommended
Cramant ★ Interesting
Vertus Other sight described in this guide

Driving tour

AISNE

ARDENNES

Soissons

Aisne

Massif de St-Thierry

Fismes

REIMS

Romanesque churches in the Ardre valley

Rilly-la-Montagne

St-Lié D 26

PARC NATUREL RÉGIONAL DE LA MONTAGNE DE REIMS

Braux-Ste-Cohière

Hautvilliers

Faux de Verszy

Valmy

Chatillon-s-Marne

Dormans

M A R N E

Marne

Ste-Menehould

CHÂTEAU-THIERRY

N 3

Épernay

Cramant

N.D. de l'Épine

Aisne

ROUTES DU CHAMPAGNE

Orbais-l'Abbaye

Côte des Blancs

Châlons-en-Champagne

MEUSE

Fromentière

Montmirail

Baye

Montmort-Lucy

Étoges

Vertus

St-Armand-s-Fion

Vallée du Petit Morin

Villevenard

Mont Aimé

Ponthion

Marais de St-Gond

Allemant

Vitry-le-François

SEINE-ET-MARNE

Forêt de Tranconne

Sézanne

Musée du Pays du Der

St-Dizier

A U B E

Aube

Lac du Der-Chantecoq

HAUTE-

Wassy

Villenauxe-la-Grande

Montier-en-Der

MARNE

Nogent-s-Seine

TROYES

Portrait of Jean de La Fontaine (c.1684) by Hyacinthe Rigaud

© Mairie de Château-Thierry

La Fontaine

Born in Château-Thierry in 1621, La Fontaine was more inclined towards walking than studying. However, he thought he had a religious vocation and entered a seminary, soon discovering that he had made a mistake. He then became a lawyer, returned to his home town and got married, but Fontaine remained a daydreamer and neglected both his work and his wife. Then he heard an officer recite a poem and had a revelation: he had to become a poet himself.

At the age of 36, he became official poet to Fouquet (the Superintendent of Finances under Louis XIV) and received a regular income from him. After Fouquet's arrest and subsequent imprisonment, La Fontaine settled in Paris where he always seemed able to attract rich patrons and where he was widely acclaimed until his death in 1695. Today his *Fables* (&see Art and Culture: Literature) are universally known and loved.

Fête Jean de La Fontaine is held in Château-Thierry on the weekend closest to 24th June. ℘*03 23 83 10 14.*

Châlons-en-Champagne★★

Formerly known as Châlons-sur-Marne, the town resumed its original name of Châlons-en-Champagne in 1998. A number of 17C and 18C mansions give the city a certain bourgeois character, which contrasts nicely with the charm of its restored timber-framed houses and its old bridges spanning the Mau and the Nau canals. The tree-lined banks of the Marne form an attractive sight in the western part of the town.

▶ **Population:** 46 134.
◔ **Michelin Map:** Michelin Local map 306: I-9.
🛈 **Tourist Office** – 3 Quai des Arts, 51000 Châlons-en-Champagne. ☎03 26 65 17 89. www.chalons-tourisme.com.
◔ **Location:** At the heart of the Champagne-growing region, between Épernay and Vitry-le-François.
◔ **Don't Miss:** St-Étienne Cathedral in town and farther afield, the Basilique Notre-Dame-de-l'Épine.

A BIT OF HISTORY

Catalaunum (Châlons-en-Champagne) was an active Gallo-Roman city; in June 451, the Roman army under General Aetius defeated the Huns led by their powerful chief **Attila**.
The exact location of the battle is uncertain, but it was in the fields around the city of Catalaunum, giving it the name of **Champs Catalauniques**, which later became a symbol of deliverance from the Barbarian threat.
A site known as the Camp d'Attila, lying 15km/9.3mi northeast of Châlons, is said to be the place where the Huns camped on the eve of the battle.

WALKING TOURS

QUARTIER DE LA PRÉFECTURE

▶ Start from place Foch overlooked by the town hall and the north side of the Église St-Alpin.

Hôtel de ville

The town hall was designed in 1771 by Nicolas Durand; the main hall is Doric.

Bibliothèque Georges Pompidou

◔*Tue, Thu and Fri 1–6pm, Wed and Sat 10am–6pm.* ◔*Sun, Mon and public holidays.* ☎*03 26 26 94 26.*
The library is housed in a beautiful 17C residence, once the home of the gov-

ernors of the city. It was raised by one storey in the 19C. It holds some precious manuscripts and books that are not on display, such as the **Roman de la Rose**, a famous 13C allegory in medieval French, and Queen Marie-Antoinette's book of prayers bearing her farewell to her children, written on the day of her execution.
Walk through the **Henri-Vendel passageway**. Note the former doorway of Église St-Loup closing the courtyard.

▶ Return to rue d'Orfeuil and continue along rue de Chastillon

On the corner of rue des Croix-des-Teinturiers stands a fine Art Nouveau house built in 1907.

Rue de Chastillon

The street was once lined with workshops. Even numbers were occupied by well-off people whereas odd numbers were lived in by manual workers.

▶ Turn left onto rue de Jessaint which crosses the Mau. Return to rue Carnot

Préfecture

The 1759 Préfecture occupies the former residence of the royal treasurers of the Champagne region; the design by Legendre and Durand already points to

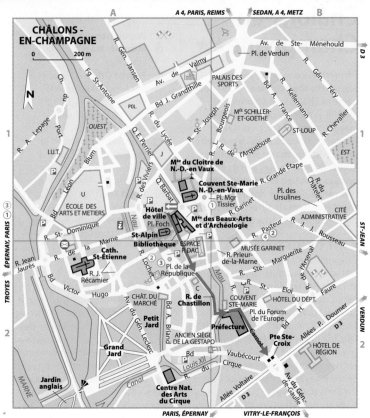

CHÂLONS-EN-CHAMPAGNE

0   200 m

A 4, PARIS, REIMS   *SEDAN, A 4, METZ*

TROYES   *ÉPERNAY, PARIS*

ST-JEAN   *VERDUN*

PARIS, ÉPERNAY   *VITRY-LE-FRANÇOIS*

WHERE TO STAY	WHERE TO EAT
Grosse Haie (Chambre d' Hôte La).................①	Carillon Gourmand (Au)..①
Pasteur (Hôtel)..②	Chaudron Savoyard (Le).......................................②
Pot d'Étain (Hôtel Le)..③	Moissons (l'Auberge des)......................................③
	Petit Pasteur (Le)..④

Louis XVI's sober style. **Marie-Antoinette**, who stopped in on her way to marry the heir to the French throne, returned after her arrest in Varennes (⌖*see ARGONNE: Varennes-en-Argonne*). Behind the Préfecture, in a circus modelled in 1887 on the Cirque d'Hiver in Paris, the **Centre National des Arts du Cirque** trains all-round circus artists.

Porte Ste-Croix

This triumphal gateway, erected in 1770 to welcome **Marie-Antoinette** en route to her marriage, was known as the Porte Dauphine; it was never completed (only one side has decorativeh carvings).

LE JARD

Part of the bishop's estates, this former meadow probably is where St Bernard preached in 1147 (visit his mat in the nearby Treasury); Pope Eugene III consecrated the church the same year. The 18C park is crossed by avenue du Maréchal-Leclerc; it has three sections:

♦ the **Petit Jard**, a landscaped garden in the Napoleon III style, with a flower clock, laid on the site of the former ramparts.

♦ the **Grand Jard**, with its views from the footbridge linking it to the Jardin Anglais across the canal.

- the **Jardin anglais**, an 1817 English-style garden alongside the Marne.

SIGHTS
Cathédrale St-Étienne★★
The cathedral is the seat of the Bishop of Châlons and was consecrated in 1147 by Pope Eugene III. Two royal marriages took place here during the reign of Louis XIV.

Exterior
The north side is in Gothic style, though the transept is flanked by a partly-Romanesque tower, part of a previous cathedral destroyed by fire in 1230.

Interior
The edifice is nearly 100m long and looks quite imposing in spite of its relatively short chancel. Daylight pours into the 27m high nave. The Gothic west front and the two bays closest to it were erected in 1628.
The cathedral has wonderful **stained-glass windows★**, which reveal the evolution of stained-glass making between the 12C and 16C. In the chancel stands an imposing 17C high altar with a baldaquin, believed to be the work of Jules Hardouin-Mansart. The windows above the high altar, dating from the 13C, depict Christ in glory, the Crucifixion and the Holy Mother.

Treasury
The lower part of the Romanesque tower adjacent to the north transept houses the treasury, including 12C stained-glass panels (representing the Crucifixion and the discovery of St Stephen's relics).

Église Notre-Dame-en-Vaux★
This former collegiate church is in the Romanesque style from the beginning of the 12C, but the vaulting, the chancel and the east end date from a century alter, fine examples of the Early Gothic style (go to the far side of place Monseigneur-Tissier in order to get a good overall view). There is a peal of 56 bells.

▶ Enter the church through the south doorway

The **interior★★** has harmonious simple proportions; the nave features a marked contrast between the pillars topped by Romanesque capitals, supporting vast galleries, and pointed Gothic vaulting. The nave is lit by a set of **stained-glass windows★**. The finest, from the 16C, are on the north side.

▶ Walk up the north aisle starting from the west doorway.

Second bay: the *Legend of St James* (1525) by the master glass-maker from Picardie, Mathieu Bléville, illustrates a battle which took place in 1212 between Christians and Moors (the pilgrims' route to Santiago de Compostela went through Châlons); **Third bay**: the *Dormition* and *Coronation of the Blessed Virgin*, red and gold symbolising her glory; dated 1526; **Fourth and fifth bays**: *Legends of St Anne and Mary*; *Christ's childhood*; **Sixth bay**: The *Compassion of the Virgin Mary*, against a blue background dotted with silver stars, with a *Deposition*, a *Pietà* and *Mary Magdalene* (1526).

▶ Walk round the church to rue Nicolas-Durand where the entrance of the Musée du cloître de Notre-Dame-en-Vaux is situated.

If you intend to visit the city museums, ask about the Museum Pass, valid for 15 days for the 3 municipal museums. €4.

Musée du cloître de Notre-Dame-en-Vaux★
Rue Nicolas-Durand. Daily except Tue 10am–noon, 2–6pm. €3.50 (no charge 1st Sun of month) – ticket gives access to other museums. 1 Jan, 1 May, 1 and 11 Nov, 25 Dec. 03 26 69 99 61.
The cloister museum contains remarkable sculptures from Romanesque cloisters, discovered in 1960. Built in the 12C next to Notre-Dame-en-Vaux, they were demolished in 1759 by the canons who replaced them with their own quarters. A vast room contains reconstructions and several valuable exhibits such as

16C Entombment, Basilique Notre-Dame de l'Épine

carved or ringed columns and 55 **statue columns★★**: the finest depict prophets, famous biblical characters or saints and characters from the Middle Ages. Some of the rarest examples of medieval architecture and decorative arts open to the public can be found here.

Musée des Beaux-Arts et d'Archéologie

Place Godart. &. ⏱Mon and Wed–Fri 2–6pm, Sat–Sun 10am–noon, 2–6pm. ⏱1 Jan, 1 May, 1 and 11 Nov, 25 Dec. €3.50 (no charge 1st Sun of month) – ticket gives access to other museums. ✆03 26 69 38 53.

The town museum includes two floors of collections: **Ground floor:** collection of Hindu deities (16C–17C), 13C recumbent figure of Blanche de Navarre, Countess of Champagne, 15C Head of Christ from the rood screen of Notre-Dame-en-Vaux, three polychrome wooden altarpieces, and a Head of St John the Baptist by Rodin. **First floor:** fine arts gallery and local archaeological finds from the Palaeolithic period to the 17C. Don't miss the Gallic period, ornithological and furniture collections.

Église St-Alpin

Partly surrounded by houses, the church, built between the 12C and 16C, is a mixture of Flamboyant Gothic and Renaissance styles. In the south aisle chapels, there are **Renaissance windows★** with magnificent grisaille stained glass.

Église St-Jean

Access via rue Jean-Jacques-Rousseau.

The raised area in front of the church allows access to the 14C west section. A small 15C chapel, known as the **Cross-bowmen's Chapel**, sits off the south aisle (19C stained-glass windows).

EXCURSIONS

Basilique Notre-Dame de l'Épine★★

8km/5mi E along N 3.

Modelled on Reims cathedral in the early 15C, this basilica has been an important place of pilgrimage since the Middle Ages, when shepherds discovered a statue of the Virgin Mary in a burning thorn bush.

Exterior

The south spire (55m high) is ringed by a crown made up of fleurs-de-lis; the north spire, demolished in 1798 to make room for a telegraph installation, was rebuilt in 1868. Walk along the south side of the church to observe the numerous realistic **gargoyles★**.

Interior

The basilica is a pinnacle of Gothic architecture. The chancel is closed off by an elegant **rood screen** from the late 15C (note the 14C statue of the Virgin Mary under the right-hand arcade) and by a stone screen which is Gothic on the right side and Renaissance on the left. Walking round the chancel (starting from the north side) you will see a Gothic **tabernacle-reliquary** with Renaissance ornamentation. Farther on, a chapel houses a fine 16C **Entombment**.

ADDRESSES

🛏 STAY

🛌 **Hotel Pasteur** – *46 r. Pasteur, 51000 Châlons-en-Champagne. ℘03 26 68 10 00. Closed 26 Dec–3 Jan. Booking advisable. 28 rooms.* 🅿️. *Meals*🍽🍽. A slightly antiquated bourgeois atmosphere pervades this establishment located close to the town centre. A 17C staircase leads to the spacious, comfortable rooms with high ceilings. Pleasant inner courtyard.

🛌 **La Grosse Haie** – *Chemin de St-Pierr. 51510 Matougues. 12km/7.5mi W of Châlons on D 3, Épernay direction. ℘03 26 70 97 12.* 🍴. *3 rooms. Evening meal* 🍽🍽. Little matter that this farm-inn is close to the road: the orchard, vegetable and botanical gardens, children's activities and farm produce ensure you have an enjoyable stay.

🛌🛌 **Hôtel Le Pot d'Étain** – *18 pl. de la République, 51000 Châlons-en-Champagne. ℘03 26 68 09 09. www.hoteldupotdetain. com. 30 rooms.* The hotel is located on a lively, town-centre square. The rooms are soundproofed, with sober decor, rustic or modern furniture and good quality beds. The owner, formerly a baker, makes it a point of honour to serve an impeccable breakfast.

🍴 EAT

🍽🍽 **Le Chaudron Savoyard** – *9 r. des Poissoniers, 51000 Châlons-en-Champagne. ℘03 26 68 00 32. Closed Sun and 1–15 Jul.* Don't go by the Champagne-style façade of the building; here the cooking is devoted to the Savoy region. It can either be enjoyed in the ground-floor dining room with its exposed beams, or in the first-floor dining room, where the atmosphere is more reminiscent of the mountains.

🍽🍽🍽 **Auberge des Moissons** – *8 rte Nationale, 51510 Matougues. 12km/7.5mi W of Châlons on the Épernay road (D 3). ℘03 26 70 99 17. www.auberge-des-moissons. com. Open every evening from Monday to Saturday, Saturday lunch, and Sunday only for lunch. Booking essential.* Those who enjoy good, local food will appreciate the home-raised chicken, duck, rabbit and turkey. After a hearty meal, don't miss the small farm museum, or a visit to the stables, the garden and the farmyard.

🍽🍽 **Le Petit Pasteur** – *42 r. Pasteur, 51000 Châlons-en-Champagne. ℘03 26 68 24 78. www.restaurant-lepetitpasteur.com. Closed Sun evening, Sat lunch and all day Mon.* Pleasant restaurant comprising a contemporary-style dining room and, during the high season, an attractive flower-decked terrace. Traditional fare.

🍽🍽🍽 **Au Carillon Gourmand** – *15 bis pl. Mgr-Tissier, 51000 Châlons-en-Champagne. ℘03 26 64 45 07. www. carillongourmand.com. Closed Sun evening, Wed evening, and all day Mon.* Situated close to the collegiate church of Notre-Dame-en-Vaux, this restaurant boasts a convivial dining room extended by an open veranda on the street side. Traditional dishes and daily suggestions prepared according to availability.

ENTERTAINMENT

Philippe Génin – *27 pl. de la République. ℘03 26 21 46 63. Tue–Sat 8am–7.30pm; Sun 8am–1pm, 3–7pm.* This tearoom serving pastries, ice cream, chocolate and light lunches is the ideal place for a snack. Be sure to sample the home-made chocolate, plus the delicious Châlonnais cake, which goes marvellously with a glass of local champagne. Terrace in summer.

Brasserie de La Bourse – *32 pl. de la République, 51000 Châlons-en-Champagne. ℘03 26 70 96 27. http://cafe. restaurant-labourse.com. 9.30am–2am.* Mahogany panelling, red or black velvet covered seats, gleaming copperware and numerous mirrors make this one of the most chic and pleasant places in town. Seen-and-be-seen on the huge terrace on the busiest square in Châlons-en-Champagne.

GUIDED TOURS AND BOAT TRIPS

Promenades sur l'eau – *3 quai des Arts. ℘03 26 65 17 89. Jun–Sept tour daily from 2.30pm (some Fri evenings).* Boat tours on the Mau and the Nau give a surprising new perspective to many of Châlon's sights.

Châlons-en-Champagne on foot – The Office de Tourisme also organises walking tours of Châlons in summertime. *Call for details.*

Routes du
Champagne★★★

The Champagne vineyards, known since ancient times, produce a world-famous type of wine. The reputation of the so-called "Devil's Wine" grew considerably from the 10C onwards, as a consequence of the fairs which took place during the 12C and 13C; by the time the Renaissance came, it had spread beyond the borders of France. Yet, up to the 17C, Champagne was a predominantly red wine with a slight tendency to sparkle. According to tradition, modern Champagne was "invented" by Dom Pérignon, a monk from the Benedictine abbey of Hautvillers, who mixed various local wines. Success was almost immediate: kings, princes and European aristocrats elected Champagne as their favourite drink for festive occasions. The great Champagne firms were set up in Reims and Épernay from the 18C onwards: Ruinart in 1729, Fourneaux (which later became Taittinger) in 1734, Moët in 1743, Clicquot in 1772, Mumm in 1827. Since then, Reims and Épernay have consistently prospered as tourists continue to enjoy winding their way through the Champagne vineyards.

🚗 DRIVING TOURS

1 CHAMPAGNE KINGDOM★★

Round tour starting from Montchenot
See Parc naturel régional de la MONTAGNE de REIMS.

2 CÔTE DES BLANCS★★

From Épernay to Mont-Aimé
28km/17.4mi. Allow 2h.

Stretching between Épernay and Vertus, the Côte des Blancs or Côte Blanche,

- 🧭 **Michelin Map:** Michelin Local map 306.
- ▶ **Location:** The Champagne Route is signposted by an official logo and most of the drives leave from Reims, Épernay or Château-Thierry.
- 👁 **Don't Miss:** The Champagne cellars of Reims (*see REIMS Addresses*).
- 🕐 **Timing:** To do full justice to this magnificent region, allow at least 2 full days. Start with a day in Reims before setting out on a choice of 4 different itineraries.

owes its name to its white-grape vineyards consisting almost exclusively of **Chardonnay** vines. The refined grapes grown here are used to produce vintage and blanc de blancs (made only from white grapes) Champagne.

The majority of the great Champagne firms own vineyards in this area; some of these are even equipped with heating systems to protect the vines from frost in winter.

Like the Montagne de Reims, the Côte des Blancs is a bank sloping down from the edge of the Île-de-France cuesta, facing due east and almost entirely covered with vines. In front of this limestone cuesta stand outliers such as Mont Saran (239m) and Mont Aimé (240m).

The twisting lanes of the villages dotted along the slopes are lined with winegrowers' houses complete with characteristic high doorways.

The road described below runs half way up the slopes, offering views of the vineyards and the vast plain of Châlons.

Épernay★ *See ÉPERNAY.*

▶ Leave Épernay SW along D 951

Côte des Blancs vineyards near Cramant

Château de Pierry

&♿🕐*Mon–Sat 9.30am–noon, and Wed and Fri 2.30–5pm.* 👓€8. ℘*03 26 54 02 87. www.chateau-de-pierry.fr.*

The town hall now occupies the house where Jacques Cazotte lived; the author of *Le Diable amoureux* (the Devil in Love) was guillotined in 1792.

A tour of the 18C Château de Pierry includes reception rooms, private apartments, a wine-press and cellars dating from 1750 as well as a small museum.

A booklet to take home, and a glass of champagne are offered at the end of the visit (€12).

▶ In Pierry, turn left onto D 10.

This road offers views of Épernay and the Marne valley on the left.

Cuis

The Romanesque **Église St-Niçaise** stands on a platform overlooking the village. From D 10, there are scenic vistas of the Montagne de Reims.

Note the huge bottle (over 8m tall) marking the village of Cramant.

▶ Continue along the D 10 which affords views of the Montagne de Reims.

Cramant★

This village is on the heart of an area producing the famous Cramant wine made from white Chardonnay vines,

and therefore sometimes called Blanc de Cramant. At the village entrance stands a giant Champagne bottle more than 8.6m tall and measuring nearly 8m round the base created in 1974.

Avize

Also famous for its wine, Avize runs a school for future Champagne wine-growers. The 12C church has a 15C chancel and transept. A walk above the little town to the west offers views of the whole area.

▶ Continue along D 10.

Oger

Producing a *premier cru de la Côte des Blancs*, one of the area's top quality wines, Oger has a pretty church dating from the 12C–13C with a high square tower and flat east end.

Musée des Traditions, de l'Amour et du Champagne

🕐*Mar–Nov 9am–noon, 2–6pm (Sun and public holidays 10am–noon, 2–5.30pm).* 🕐*25 Dec.* 👓€7. ℘*03 26 57 50 89.*

This charming museum examines wedding traditions between 1880 and 1920, including bouquets made of paper, leather, gilt-metal and shell flowers. Champagne is of course part of the tradition and there is a display of old labels and a tour of the 18C cellars with their collection of old tools (tasting).

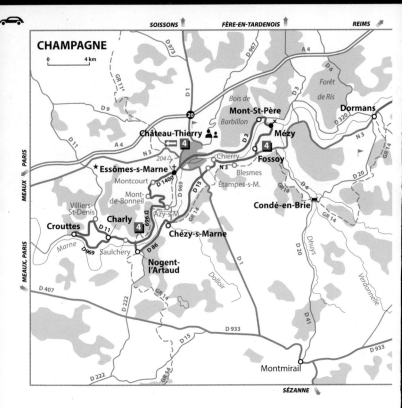

CHAMPAGNE

A dining room is available for prix fixe meals for groups; champagne tastings are included in the price.

*Musée de la Vigne et du Vin,
Le Mesnil-sur-Oger*

© ADT Marne

Le Mesnil-sur-Oger

This wine-growing village is strangely spread out but features a grotto dedicated to the Virgin.

Musée de la Vigne et du Vin★

🐚 *Guided tours (2h, including a taste of 3 champagnes) Mon–Fri 10am and 3pm; Sun and holidays 10.30am.* ⏱ *1 Jan, Easter, 25 Dec.* 📞 *03 26 57 50 15. www.champagne-launois.fr.*

This museum displays wine-presses and tools that illustrate wine-growing's history; the traditional production techniques of corks, bottles, and barrels are also featured.

▷ A small road winds its way across the vineyards to Vertus.

Vertus

This charming town surrounded by vineyards once had several springs and was the property of the counts of Champagne who lived in a castle now

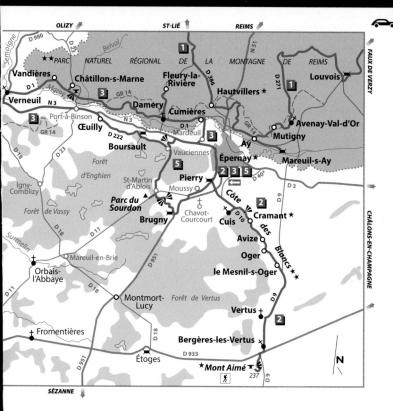

demolished except for the Porte Baudet. During the Middle Ages, Vertus was enclosed by a defensive wall.

Église St-Martin was built on piles in the late 11C and early 12C. Damaged by fire in 1167, partly destroyed during the Hundred Years War and remodelled several times, it was finally restored after a 1940 fire. The pointed vaulting over the transept and east end dates from the 15C. Note the delicately carved 16C *Pietà* in the south transept and the 16C stone statue of St John the Baptist near the christening fonts. Stairs lead from the north transept to three 11C crypts; note the capitals of the central crypt, beautifully carved with foliage motifs. On the way down to **Bergères-lès-Vertus** with its small Romanesque country church, the road affords pleasant views of the surrounding area.

▶ South of Bergères-lès-Vertus, turn right onto the road leading to Mont Aimé.

Mont-Aimé★

Inhabited since prehistoric times, this isolated hill (237m high) was fortified successively by the Gauls, the Romans and the counts of Champagne who built a feudal castle; its ruins are today scattered among the greenery.

On 10 September 1815, the Russian army held a great parade here; they were stationed in this area during the occupation of France by several European countries following the fall of Napoleon.

In one of the corners of the old fortifications, a viewpoint (viewing table) offers an extended **view** of the Côte des Blancs to the north and of the plain of Châlons to the east.

VALLÉE DE LA MARNE★

The round tours starting from Épernay and Château-Thierry offer an opportunity of discovering wine-growing villages climbing the vine-covered hillsides on both banks of the River Marne. During the First World War, the fate of

France and of the Allies was sealed on these banks during two decisive battles, which took place in 1914 and 1918 (↻see *Château-Thierry: EXCURSIONS*).

③ ROUND TOUR WEST OF ÉPERNAY
Allow 4h. 63km/39mi.

▷ Leave Épernay along N 3, turn right towards Mardeuil then cross the Marne and follow the north bank of the river to Cumières.

Cumières
Lying at the foot of vineyards shaped like an amphitheatre, this village nestles on the banks of the River Marne, with fishing boats gently swinging along the quays. There are **boat trips** (*Cruises on the Marne: Reservations at Croisière et Champagne, 12 r. de la Coopérative, 51480 Cumières. ℘03 26 54 49 51. www. champagne-et-croisiere.com*) through vineyard country. Locks are negotiated along the way.

▷ Continue W on D 1.

Damery
Damery offers fine walks along the banks of the River Marne; the 12C–13C **church** once belonged to the Benedictine abbey of St-Médard de Soissons; it contains a *Virgin with Child* by Watteau (18C). Note the carved capitals of the pillars supporting the belfry: they represent an interesting bestiary against a background of intertwined stems.

▷ Turn right towards Fleury-la-Rivière.

Fleury-la-Rivière
The walls of the **Coopérative vinicole** (wine-growers' cooperative society) (⛓○9am–12.30pm, 2–5pm, Sat 9am–12.30pm, 2–6pm, Sun and holidays by request. ○25 Dec, 1 Jan, 1 May; ℘03 26 58 42 53) are decorated with a huge **fresco** by Greg Gawra, which depicts the history of the Champagne region, work in the vineyards and the cellars.

The **Cave aux Coquillages** takes the form of an underground trail (200m) that reveals the story of the tropical sea that once covered the land (℘03 26 58 36 43; www.geologie-oenologie.fr).

▷ D 324 runs through villages and across vineyards and fields. In Cuchery, turn left to Châtillon-sur-Marne.

Châtillon-sur-Marne
Camped on a vine-covered hill overlooking the Marne, this ancient fortified town was the fief of Eudes de Châtillon who became Pope under the name of Urbain II (1088–99) and launched the first crusade.

▷ Leave the car in the car park and follow rue de l'Église then turn right onto rue Berthe-Symonet.

Statue d'Urbain II
Eighty blocks of granite were brought all the way from Brittany in carts pulled by oxen in order to build this 33m high statue. It was erected in 1887 on the mound once crowned by the castle keep.

▷ Drive W along D 1 to Vandières

Vandières
The 18C castle stands in the middle of a park, at the top of the village. The 11C church has a beautiful porch. There are fine views of the valley framed by hills to the south.

▷ Continue along D 1.

Verneuil
This small, carefully-restored 12C–13C **church** stands beside the Sémoigne, a tributary of the Marne.

▷ Continue to Vincelles then Dormans.

Dormans
The park of this peaceful flower-decked riverside town is the setting of the **castle** (housing both the tourist office and temporary exhibitions) and of the **Mémorial**

Vineyards of Châtillon-sur-Marne with the Statue d'Urbain II

des Batailles de la Marne, a memorial chapel dedicated to the battles of the Marne, consisting of two storeys and a crypt surmounted by a chapel.

On the lower level, note the marble sundial to the right of the crypt, and the viewing table illustrating the course of events during the second battle of the Marne to the left. The upper level features the chapel and an ossuary containing the remains of 1 500 unknown soldiers. From the memorial it is possible to reach the mill across the park.

Moulin d'en Haut

○ *Apr–May and Sept 2–6pm; Jun–Aug 2.30–6.30pm.* ○ *Mon.* ☎ *03 26 58 85 46.*

This former communal mill houses an interesting collection of over 3 000 **rural tools** for working in the vineyards, in the fields and in the woods.

Church

This Gothic church features a square tower above the crossing, with paired bays on each of the four gables; the north transept is flanked by a turret surmounted by an octagonal pinnacle. The most interesting part of the church is the flat east end dating from the 13C, with High Gothic windows.

▷ Follow N 3 to Port-à-Binson.

The road affords a view of Châtillon overlooked by the statue of Pope Urbain II.

▷ Drive to Œuilly along N 3.

Œuilly

This old fortified hillside village has a three-part **eco-museum** (*guided tours Apr–Oct daily except Tue 10.30am–noon, 2–4.30pm (Sun and public holidays 2–4.30pm); Nov–Mar daily except Mon–Tue 10.30am–noon, 2–4pm.* ○ *Christmas holidays, 1 May.* ☞€7, children under 17, €4. ☎ *03 26 57 10 30).*

The **Maison champenoise**, dating from 1642, illustrates the life of a wine-grower and his family at the end of the 19C; the **Musée de la Goutte** (a famous wine brandy) houses the former village still and an exhibition on the traditional techniques used by coopers; the **École communale 1900** (village school) retains its desks, stove and blackboard.

▷ Follow D 222 to Boursault.

Château de Boursault

Built in 1848 in neo-Renaissance style for the famous Veuve Clicquot, this vast castle was the venue of magnificent receptions given by Madame Clicquot and later by her great-granddaughter, the Duchess of Uzès.

▷ Continue to Vauciennes and follow D 22 towards the River Marne, then N 3 to Épernay.

The road offers fine **views**★ of the Marne valley, the village of Damery and the Montagne de Reims.

© stocknshares/iStockphoto.com

Château de Boursault

④ ROUND TOUR FROM CHÂTEAU-THIERRY

60km/37mi. Allow 4h.

The Aisne vineyards that follow the River Marne between Crouttes and Trélou (near Dormans) belong to the Champagne wine-growing region.The *pinot meunier* vines thrive on the Marne Valley soil and grow on half the area covered by the Champagne vineyards.

▷ Leave Château-Thierry SW along D 969 which follows the meanders of the river.

Essômes-sur-Marne

The **Église St-Ferréol**★ was founded as an Augustinian abbey church in 1090 by Hugues de Pierrefonds. The **interior**★ shows Lancet-Gothic architecture. Note the elegant triforium with its narrow twin openings, the Renaissance choir stalls and, in the south transept, the 16C chapel closed off by a colonnade.

▷ Make a detour via Montcourt then turn left onto D 1400.

The road runs through vineyards, offering, between Mont-de-Bonneil and Azy, an interesting **panorama** of a meander of the Marne with the wooded Brie region in the background.

▷ Rejoin D 969 in Azy and continue past Saulchery to Charly.

Charly-sur Marne

This is the most important wine-growing centre of the Aisne département.

▷ Follow D 11 to Villiers-Saint-Denis and turn left onto D 842 to Crouttes.

The road offers a wide **view** of the deep meander of the Marne to the south.

Crouttes-sur-Marne

This wine-growing village owes its name to its cellars dug out of the rock. Leave the car near the town hall and walk up to the church picturesquely perched above the village.

▷ Return to Charly along D 969 and cross the river; turn left onto D 86 to Nogent-l'Artaud.

Nogent-l'Artaud

Very little remains of the former 13C abbey of the Poor Clares Order.
Between Nogent and Chézy, the road (*D 86*) overlooks the Marne and offers fine views of the slopes planted with vines.

Chézy-sur-Marne

There are fine walks along the banks of the Dolloir, a tributary of the Marne.

▶ Follow D 15. The road runs under D 1 to Étampes-sur-Marne and joins N 3 in Chierry.

Between Chierry and Blesmes, the road offers a fine **panorama** of the valley. Turn left onto a minor road 1.5km/0.9mi beyond Blesmes.

Fossoy

The Déhu cellars, run by the seventh generation of a wine-growing family, welcome tourists along this Route du Champagne. Former stables have been turned into a small museum.

Musée de la Vigne et du Vin (Le Varocien)

🐛Guided tours by appointment.
🕐Sat–Sun and holidays.
📞03 23 71 90 47.
The tours include explanations about the vines and tools used in the area by wine-growers. Note the refractometer dating from 1863, used for measuring alcoholic concentration.

▶ Continue along the minor road to Mézy.

Église de Mézy

The triforium of this 13C Gothic church conceals a circular gallery.

▶ Cross the River Marne and turn left onto D 3 which runs along the north bank.

Mont-St-Père

Paintings by Léon Lhermitte (1844–1925), a native of this village, were inspired by rural life and landscapes (Harvesters' Payday can be seen in the Musée d'Orsay in Paris).

▶ On its way to Château-Thierry, the road (D 3) skirts the Bois de Barbillon.

⑤ COTEAUX SUD D'ÉPERNAY★

Round tour south of Épernay

🕐See ÉPERNAY: Driving Tour.

ADDRESSES

🛏 STAY

🍽 Chambre d'hôte Ferme du Grand Clos – R. Jonquery, 51170 Ville-en-Tardenois – 17km/10.6mi SW of Reims on D 980. 📞03 51 42 99 15. 🛏. 4 rooms. In this old farmhouse, built out of local stone, the spacious rooms have been completely refurbished and include their own lounge area. A warm welcome and very reasonable prices make this a good place to stay on the champagne route.

🍽🍽 Chambre d'hôte Les Botterets – 7 r. du Fort, 51190 Oger – 13km/8 mi S of Épernay on D 10. 📞03 26 57 94 78. 🛏. 6 rooms. Renovated bed and breakfast rooms in two traditional village houses. The rather ordinary decor is compensated for by the genuinely friendly welcome and the typical atmosphere of a wine-producing village.

🍴 EAT

🍽🍽 Auberge de la Chaussée – 5 Avenue de Paris, 51480 Vauciennes. 6km/3.75mi W of Épernay on N 3. 📞03 26 58 40 66. www.aubergedelachaussee.fr. Closed Fri and Sun evening. Fans of traditional dishes such as calf's head will love this inn, which is easily accessible by the N 3. Unpretentious setting with black and white chequered floor. Simple, clean rooms.

🍽🍽 Au Bateau Lavoir – 3 r. Port-au-Bois, 51480 Damery. 5km/3mi W of Épernay on D 22 then N 13. 📞03 26 58 40 88. www.le-bateau-lavoir.fr. Closed Mon. This pretty, flower-decked little building enjoys a prime location on the banks of the Marne. The dining room is modern and bright thanks to its large bay windows. Traditional cooking.

🍽🍽 Le Caveau – R. de la Coopérative, 51480 Cumières. 5km/3mi NW of Épernay on D 301. 📞03 26 54 83 23. www.lecaveau-cumieres.com. Closed Sun evening, Tue evening, and all day Mon. Cross a small room decorated on a wine theme, then go down the long hallway leading to this superb restaurant in a cellar dug out of the chalk. Carefully set tables. Regional specialities.

CHAMPAGNE TASTING

In addition to the major wine cellars in Reims and Épernay, here we have selected a few of the many others recommended for their winemaking premises:

Breton Fils – *12 r. Courte-Pilate, 51270 Congy. 15km/9.3mi S of Épernay on N 951 and D 943. ☎03 26 59 31 03. www.champagne-breton-fils.com. Daily 9am–noon, 2–5.30pm. Closed 3rd Sun in May, Christmas Day and 1 Jan.* This vineyard owner and grower will let you visit his cellars, which are typical of the Champagne region.

Champagne Milan – *6 rte d'Avize, 51190 Oger. 15km/9.3mi S of Épernay. ☎03 26 57 50 09. www.champagne-milan.com. Call for details of visiting and tasting arrangements.* The convivial visit to the cellars and manufacturing premises culminates with a champagne tasting.

Corbon – *541 av. Jean-Jaurès, 51190 Avize. 10km/6.2mi S of Épernay. ☎09 66 42 34 93. www.champagne-corbon. fr. By appointment only. Closed late Dec to late Jan.* This family-run champagne producer's organises tastings of two champagnes with a commentary. Among the interesting options are the process of *dégorgement à la volée*, when the cork is taken out and the sediment removed, and blending.

Dehu Père & Fils – *3 r. St-Georges, 02650 Fossoy. 9km/5.6mi SE of Château-Thierry on N 3. ☎03 23 71 90 47. www.champagne-dehu.com. Mon–Sat by appointment only.* After visiting the museum, which exhibits a collection of tools used in the cultivation of vines and winemaking, you will be invited to a champagne tasting.

F.P. Arnoult Coopérative vinicole – *rte de Damery, 51480 Fleury-la-Rivière. ☎03 26 58 42 53. Mon–Fri 8.30am– 12.30pm, 2–5.15pm, Sat 9am–12.30pm and 2–6pm, Sun by appointment. Closed Mon afternoon and Wed.* The walls of this cooperative cellar are decorated with a superb 550sq m.fresco, depicting the region's history. The tasting room, where home-made products are sold, boasts a magnificent view over the vineyard and the Marne valley.

Launois Père & Fils – *2 av. Eugène-Guillaume, 51190 Le Mesnil-sur-Oger. 11km/6.8mi S of Épernay on D 40. ☎03 26 57 50 15. www.champagne-launois.fr. Mon–Fri 8am–noon, 2–6pm, Sat–Sun 10am–1pm, 3–5pm. Museum: by appointment Mon–Fri 10am and 3pm, Sat–Sun 10.30am. Closed Christmas Day, 1 Jan and Easter.* Founded in 1872, this owner-grower's establishment includes its own wine museum, and the visit includes a wine tasting.

Champagne Drappier – *Rue des Vignes, 10200 Urville. ☎03 25 27 40 15. www. champagne-drappier.com. Mon–Sat 8am–noon, 2–6pm; closed Sun and public holidays. Tasting and sales without appointment at the Domaine in Urville only.* Although the vines in Urville were originally planted by the Romans 2 000 years ago, it was the founder of Clairvaux abbey, Saint Bernard, who had the cellars at Drappier built in 1152. Seven centuries later, in 1808, around this magnificently preserved legacy from medieval times, the family domaine was created, and is today headed by Michel Drappier.

Champagne Didier Sebille – *12 rue Saint-Mange, 51300 Bassu. ☎03 26 73 95 94. www.champagne-sebille.com.* The Sébille champagne production is one of 12 000 vineyards in Champagne, and here the work is invariably done by the family, *en famille*, working together both at the time of the harvest and throughout the year as the care of the vines dictates.

Champagne G Tribaut – *88 rue d'Eguisheim, 51160 Hautvillers. ☎03 26 59 40 57. http://champagne.g.tribaut.com. Open daily for tastings and sales, but not visits to the cellars: 9am–noon, 2–6pm. Closed Sun Jan–Feb.* Hautvillers is one of the most famous villages in the Champagne region, made so by Dom Perignon who was based at the nearby abbey. They own 12ha of vines in the Premier Cru village and grow all three grape varieties. The vineyard and the champagnes are tended by five members of the family who have also opened a small museum of viticultural tools in the heart of Hautvillers.

Château-Thierry

Château-Thierry is mainly renowned as the birthplace of the French poet and world-famous fable-writer, **Jean de la Fontaine**.

VISIT

▷ Start from place de l'Hôtel-de-Ville and walk up rue du Château to Porte St-Pierre.

Porte St-Pierre
This is the only one of the four town gates still standing.

Château
Go in through **Porte St-Jean**; note the embossed decoration, characteristic of the late-14C. The former garrison (now razed) offers fine **views** of the town, the Marne valley and the monument on top of Cote 204 (*see Excursions*).

On the **Tour de Bouillon** there is a map engraved on stone showing the layout of the ancient castle, of particular interest to arhcaeologists.

🔶♿ In the upper courtyard the **Spectacles des Rapaces** puts on flying displays (*Sat–Sun and Wed 3pm and 5pm. €9 (child 5–13, €6). 03 23 83 51 14. www.aigles-chateau-thierry.com*).

▷ Walk back along Grande Rue.

▶ **Population:** 14 634.
🔶 **Michelin Map:** Michelin Local map 306: C-8.
ℹ **Tourist office**: 2 Place des États Unis, 02400 Château-Thierry. 03 23 83 51 14. www.lesportesdela champagne.com.

▷ **Location:** Château-Thierry is located on the A 4 between Paris and Reims.

🕐 **Timing:** Start by touring the town on foot before heading farther afield.

🔶 **Kids:** La Fontaine's birthplace is generally a hit with younger children, while teenagers might find a tour of the battle sites and war cemeteries interesting.

SIGHTS
Maison Jean de La Fontaine
🕐*Apr–Oct Tue–Fri 9.30am–noon, 2–5.30pm, Sat–Sun 9.30am–6pm; Nov–Mar Tue–Sat 9.30am–noon, 2–5.30pm.* 🕐*1 Jan, 1 May, 1 Nov and 25 Dec.* €4 *(guided visits €7). 03 23 69 05 60. www.musee-jean-de-la-fontaine.fr.* This mansion, built in 1559, houses since 1876 a **museum** devoted to La Fontaine. 🔶 It contains magnificent editions of

Château de Château-Thierry

the *Fables* and *Tales*, including those illustrated by Oudry in 1755 and Gustave Doré in 1868, along with objects decorated with scenes from the *Fables*.

Caves de champagne Pannier

23 r. Roger-Catillon, W of town. &
🕐*Tour by request, daily except Sun and holidays 9am–12.30pm, 2–6pm.* ✆*03 23 69 51 33. www.champagnepannier.com.*
An audio-visual presentation combined with a tour of the cellars located in 13C stone quarries enables visitors to follow the process of Champagne-making.

EXCURSIONS
Condé-en-Brie

16 km/10mi E along N3.
This small town has kept an interesting covered market with Doric columns and a castle (🕐*Apr–Oct daily except Mon 2.30–5.30pm.* ✆*03 23 82 42 25. www. chateaudeconde.com).*

THE BATTLE OF THE MARNE

16km/10mi NW. Allow 2h.

▶ Drive west out of Château-Thierry along N 3 and turn left at the top of the hill along the avenue leading to Cote 204.

Monument de la Cote 204

Cote 204 was held by the Germans in June 1918. It took both a French and an American division more than five weeks to dislodge them. Enjoy the fine **view** of Château-Thierry, and the Marne valley.

▶ Return to N 3 and, at the crossroads, continue straight on along D 9 to Belleau.

Bois-Belleau

These woods were taken by the Marines in June 1918. The vast **American cemetery** contains 2 280 graves. An American aircraft carrier was named USS Bois Belleau in commemoration; the ship was sold to France in 1953. The **German cemetery** is 500m farther on.

Maison Jean de La Fontaine

© Marie de Château-Thierry

▶ Return to the crossroads and turn right onto a narrow road marked Belleau wood.

The Marines **monument** is inside the woods, the scene of fierce fighting.

VALLÉE DE LA MARNE

This Route du Champagne meanders through woods and across vineyards along the hillsides overlooking the River Marne (✆*see Routes du CHAMPAGNE: Driving Tour* ③).

ADDRESSES

🛏 STAY

🛏 **Chambre d'hôte La Grange du Moulin** – *15 r. du Moulin, 02810 Bussiares. 13km/8mi W of Château-Thierry on N 3 and D 9.* ✆*03 23 70 92 60.* 🔄*. 4 rooms. Evening meal* 🍽🍽*.* This ancient ivy-covered building houses beautifully refurbished and comfortable rooms and a pleasant dining room with exposed beams and old-fashioned furniture. The small garden is very popular in summer.

🛏 **Chambre d'hôte M. et Mme Leclère** – *1 r. de Launay, 02330 Connigis. 12km/7.5mi E of Château-Thierry on N 3 and D 4.* ✆*03 23 71 90 51. www.chambres-hotes-champagne-leclere.com. 5 rooms. Evening meal* 🍽🍽*.* The champagne producers/ owners welcome visitors in their 16C home, surrounded by vineyards.

Lac du **Der**★★

Created in 1974, this artificial lake, the largest in France (4 800ha, 1.5 times the area of the Lac d'Annecy), was intended to regulate the flow of the River Marne; a feeder canal, 12km/7.5mi long, diverts two-thirds of the flow when the river is in spate and another canal supplies the Paris region. This low-lying area was chosen for the lake because of the waterproof qualities of its clay soil. Part of the Der forest (meaning oak in Celtic) disappeared beneath the surface of the lake together with the three villages of Chantecoq, Champaubert-aux-Bois and Nuisement.

🚗 DRIVING TOUR

83km/52mi. Allow 3h.

▶ Start from Giffaumont where the Maison du Lac (tourist office of Lake Der-Chantecoq) is located. A cycle track runs right round the lake.

Giffaumont-Champaubert

👫 The **watersports centre** offers activities for children, roller-skating and mountain-biking tracks. There are **beaches** on Champaubert and Larzi-court peninsulas as well as at Nuisement and Cornée du Der.

A **marina**, which can accommodate up to 500 boats, is the place to buy your daily, monthly or annual **fishing permit** Opposite (*access on foot along the dike*), Champaubert Church stands alone jutting out into the lake.

Grange aux abeilles

🕐*Noon–2.30pm, 6.30–9pm: Easter–Aug daily except Tue; Sept–Nov Wed–Sun; rest of year Thu–Sun.* 🕐*Dec–mid-Feb.* 👓*No charge.* 📞*03 26 72 61 97. www.restaurant-lagrangeauxabeilles.com.*
An exhibition, an audio-visual show and glass beehives showcases the work of bees and bee-keepers.

▶ Follow D 13, then D 12 towards Montier-en-Der.

🕐 **Michelin Map:**
Local map 306: K/L-11.

🛈 **Tourist office:** 51290 Lac-du-Der-Chantecoq. 📞03 26 72 62 80.

◐ **Location: Lac du** Der is located roughly halfway between Châlons-en-Champagne and Bar-sur-Aube. It is a 40km/25.5mi drive from the Parc Naturel Régional de la Forêt d'Orient.

👫 **Kids:** Giffaumont watersports centre will give children ample opportunity to work off surplus energy, after which you can take them to the nature museum and/or to the Regional Der Museum (*see below*).

Ferme de Berzillières

🕐*Jul–Aug afternoons; May–Jun and Sept Sat–Sun and public holiday after-noons.* 📞*03 25 04 22 52.*
This restored farmhouse contains a museum of agricultural tools.

▶ Go back along D 12 and, 500m farther on, turn left towards Troyes then right towards Châtillon-sur-Broué.

Châtillon-sur-Broué

This village is characteristic of the Der area, with its square **church** steeple and its timber-and-cob houses.

▶ Continue towards the lake.

Opposite the harbour, a path (🅿*at the entrance*) leads to the Maison de l'Oiseau et du Poisson.

Maison de l'Oiseau et du Poisson

Between Giffaumont and Arrigny.
♿🕐*Jul–Aug and Oct–Nov 10am–6.30pm; rest of the year daily except Sat, 1.30–6pm.* 🕐*Christmas–Jan.*
👓*€6 (children under 16, €3.50).*
📞*03 26 74 00 00.*

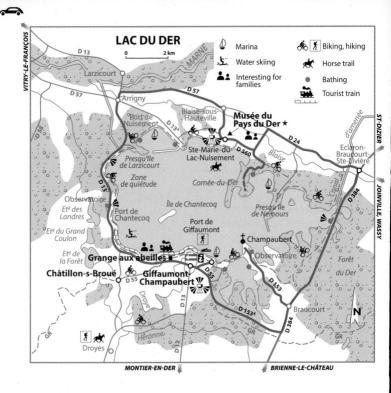

LAC DU DER

0   2 km

Marina

Water skiing

Interesting for families

Biking, hiking

Horse trail

Bathing

Tourist train

VITRY-LE-FRANÇOIS

D 13

Larzicourt

D 57

D 57

Arrigny

Port de Nuisement

Blaise-sous-Hauteville

Musée du Pays du Der ★

D 134

Presqu'île de Larzicourt

Ste-Marie-du-Lac-Nuisement

D 560

D 24

Eclaron-Braucourt-Ste-Livière

Zone de quiétude

Cornée-du-Der

Blaise

ST-DIZIER

d'amance

Observatoire

Et⁹ des Landres

Port de Chantecoq

Île de Chantecoq

Presqu'île de Nemours

D 384

JOINVILLE, WASSY

Et⁹ du Grand Coulon

Port de Giffaumont

Champaubert

Observatoire

Forêt du Der

Et⁹ de la Forêt

Grange aux abeilles

Châtillon-s-Broué

D 55

Giffaumont-Champaubert

D 13

D 134

Braucourt

D 153

D 384

Droye

D 12

Héronne

GR

Droyes

GR

GR

N

MONTIER-EN-DER

BRIENNE-LE-CHÂTEAU

This nature museum is housed in the very characteristic timber-framed Ferme des Grands Parts.
Several **aquariums** present the main local species of fish. The **panoramic tower** offers superb views.

Nature-discovery trails lasting half a day or a day are organised around various themes: the lake's bird population, aquatic life, ponds around the lake, the forest, and interpreting landscapes.

Cranes' Migratory Habits

Every year in autumn, cranes leave Scandinavia and travel to the milder climates of Spain and Africa. They fly over Champagne in successive waves, usually by night, and give out an impressive loud cry. Some of these cranes remain in the region throughout the winter and show a particular liking for meadows situated near a lake. They fly back north in the spring. Thousands of them stop by the Ferme aux Grues, near the Lac du Der-Chantecoq, where grain is purposely spread over a large area to attract them. This large grey bird, with its long neck and long legs, has a wing span of 2m and weighs 4–7kg. It feeds on grain, grass and young shoots as well as insects, molluscs and worms.

R. Corbel/ MICHELIN

Birdwatching: Two **roads** run along dikes; several peaceful areas have been set aside as bird sanctuaries (Chantecocq, Champaubert, Étangs d'Outines and d'Arrigny) and there are **nature trails** and **observatories** nearby.

◐ Continue along D 13. Drive E out of Arrigny and follow D 57 to Blaise-sous-Hauteville; turn right onto D 60.

Musée du Pays du Der★

&♿⏱Mar–Jun and Sept–Nov 9.30am–6pm; Jul–Aug 9.30am–7pm. ⏱Dec–Feb. ⊜€6 (child10–14, €4). ☎03 26 41 01 02. www.villagemuseeduder.com.
👥 This stop is both a village and a museum (**Village-musée**), made of several timber-framed buildings saved from flooding when the lake was created, illustrating regional **crafts and traditions**, the school-town hall housing the **Maison de la Nature**, the **smithy's house**, a dovecote, etc.

Château d'eau panoramique

In Ste-Marie-du-Lac-Nuisement as in Giffaumont-Champaubert, the water towers stand 20m high and afford views of the lake. Road D 560 leads to the Cornée du Der, a wooded peninsula jutting out into the lake.

◐ Return to D 24 and turn right to Éclaron, then right again onto D 384.

The road offers a fine view of the lake before entering the Der forest.
In Braucourt, it is possible to turn right onto D 153 leading to **Champaubert Church** at the tip of the peninsula of the same name.

◐ Turn right 1.5km/0.9mi beyond Braucourt onto D 153A. Continue along D 55 to return to Giffaumont-Champaubert.

ADDRESSES

🛏 STAY

⊜ Chambre d'hôte Au Brochet du Lac –
15 Grande-Rue, 51290 St-Remy-en-Bouzemont. 6km/3.75mi W of Arrigny on D 57 and D 58. ☎03 26 72 51 06. www.au-brochet-du-lac.com. 5 rooms . 🅿. Evening meal ⊜. This lovely timber-framed house offers rooms with country furniture and a big common room. This is perfect place from which to explore the lake and surroundings. Mountain bikes and canoes for hire.

⊜⊜ Le Cheval Blanc – *21 r. du Lac, 51290 Giffaumont-Champaubert. ☎03 26 72 62 65. www.lecheval-blanc.net. 14 rooms. Restaurant ⊜⊜ – closed Tue lunch, Sun evening and Mon.* Simple, bright rooms in this peaceful lakeside resort. Varied, attractive menus. Summer terrace.

SPORT AND RECREATION

Boat trips – *station nautique de Giffaumont (La Paloma): mid-Mar–mid-Sept 2.30pm, 4pm and 5pm. ☎06 16 45 30 98, and mid-Apr–Aug on L'Eider (port de Nuisement at Arrigny) ☎03 26 72 14 81. www.lembarcader.fr.* Tours on the lake.

Water sports – There are two marinas, one in Nemours, the other in Nuisement, a water sports centre in Giffaumont, six beaches with lifeguards, a zone for motorboats and water-skiing, and fishing banks and routes.

Tours – 225km/140mi of waymarked footpaths in circuits of 5 to 15km (3 to 9.4mi). 4 cycling circuits to explore. 250km/155mi of waymarked mountain biking paths around the lake.

Train du Der – *R. du Port. ☎ 06 16 72 35 04. www.lacduder.com.* Guided tours (1hr) about the dam and Lac du Der.

Train aux oiseaux – Tours with observations about the birdlife of the lake with members of the LPO Champagne-Ardenne (Oct–Nov). *Book at the tourist office.*

Nature observation – Contact the Maison du Lac in Giffaumont for information. All year round the lake sees a wealth of wildlife, particularly from autumn to spring with the arrival of the great migratory birds. More than 270 species have been observed, which makes the lake the third richest migratory stopover area in France.

Épernay★

Épernay is, with Reims, the main wine-growing centre of the Champagne region and the meeting point of three major wine-growing areas: the Montagne de Reims, the Côte des Blancs and the Marne valley. There are many opulent 19C buildings, particularly around the avenue de Champagne where you will see the great names of the famous sparkling wine such as Moët et Chandon and Mercier.

SIGHTS

Take a break in the **Jardin de l'Hôtel de ville**, designed in the 19C by the Bülher brothers, landscape gardeners who also designed the Parc de la Tête d'Or in Lyon.

🚗 DRIVING TOUR

Round trip south of Epernay★
28km/17.4mi. Allow 1h. Local map.

👜*see Routes du CHAMPAGNE* ⑤

The Épernay hills form the edge of the Île-de-France ridge.

▶ Leave Épernay along D 51.

The road follows the Cubry valley with vineyards on both sides of the river.

Château de Pierry
👜*See Routes du CHAMPAGNE.*
As you come to Moussy, look left towards the church of Chavot (13C), on a peak.

▶ Turn right 1km/0.6mi beyond Vaudancourt onto D 951.

Château de Brugny
The castle overlooks the Cubry valley. Built in the 16C, remodelled in the 18C, the square stone keep and round brick bartizans, are particularly attractive.

▶ In Brugny, take D 36 leading to St-Martin-d'Ablois.

▶ **Population:** 24 101.
⚲ **Michelin Map:** Michelin Local map 306: f-8.
🛈 **Tourist Office:** 7 av. de Champagne. ℘03 26 53 33 00. www.ot-epernay.fr.
▶ **Location:** Épernay is halfway between Reims and Châlons-en-Champagne and 145km/90mi from Paris on A 4.
👁 **Don't Miss:** Épernay's prestigious Champagne cellars (👜*see Addresses*).

There are interesting **views★** of the glacial Sourdon cirque, with the church of Chavot on the right, Moussy in the centre and Épernay forest on the left.

▶ Turn left onto D 11 towards Mareuil-en-Brie.

Parc du Sourdon
🕐*Apr–Oct 9am–7pm.* ✏*No charge.*
The Sourdon takes its source under a pile of rocks then flows through the park.

▶ Drive back to D 22 and turn left. The road runs through Épernay forest (private property) and the village of Vauciennes then reaches N 3. Turn right towards Épernay.

ADDRESSES

🍽 STAY

🍴 **Les Berceaux** – *13 r. des Berceaux. ℘03 26 55 28 84. www.lesberceaux.com. 28 rooms. Restaurant* 🍴. A warm welcome and high-quality service in this century-old hotel. The façade is pleasing and the modern rooms are soundproof. Indulge your taste buds with the restaurant's, refined cuisine, or snack in the wine bar.

🍴 **Chambre d'hôte Manoir de Montflambert** – *51160 Mutigny. 7km/4mi NE of Épernay on D 201. ℘03 26 52 33 21. www.manoirdemontflambert.fr. 4 rooms*

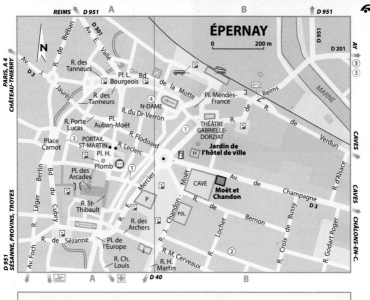

WHERE TO STAY		WHERE TO EAT	
Berceaux (Les)............................ ①		Cave à Champagne (La).......................... ①	
Clos Raymi (Hôtel)..................... ②		Cépages (Les).. ②	
Manoir de Montflambert		Saint-Vincent (Auberge)......................... ③	
(Chambre d'hôte)................... ③		Table de Kobus (La)................................. ④	

and 1 suite. This old hunting lodge dates from the 17C. Overlooking the Marne plain and the vineyards, it stands proudly on the edge of the forest. The prices in this peaceful bed and breakfast are justified by the open fireplaces, the lovely wood panelling and the imposing staircase leading to the bedrooms.

Hôtel Clos Raymi – *3 r. Joseph-de-Venoge.* $\mathcal{P}$*03 26 51 00 58. www.closraymi -hotel.com. 7 rooms.* This lovely redbrick mansion belonged to the Chandon family. Refined personalised rooms. Pleasant breakfast room opening on to the garden.

♈/EAT

La Cave à Champagne – *16 r. Gambetta.* $\mathcal{P}$*03 26 55 50 70. www.la-cave -a-champagne.com. Closed Tue in Jul–Aug and Wed.* In this district abounding in restaurants, La Cave à Champagne has an undeniable advantage over its competitors: a regional wine list… at reasonable prices! This is the ideal

opportunity to have a champagne dinner in the small dining room decorated with a collection of bottles of this precious beverage.

Les Cépages – *16 r. de la Fauvette.* $\mathcal{P}$*03 26 55 16 93. Closed Wed and Sun evenings, and all day Thu.* The name refers to grape varieties. With an excellent choice of champagnes, the menu is both contemporary and well prepared.

La Table de Kobus – *3 r. du Dr-Rousseau.* $\mathcal{P}$*03 26 51 53 53. www. la-table-kobus.fr. Closed Sun evening, Thu evening and all day Mon.* The attractive, contemporary yet unpretentious dishes are served in a large, high-ceilinged room, decorated in bistro style. This modern restaurant is popular with groups – you are welcome to bring your own wine, at no extra charge.

Auberge Saint-Vincent – *1 r. St-Vincent, 51150 Ambonnay. 20km E of Épernay on D 201, D 1 and D 37.* $\mathcal{P}$*03 26 57 01 98. www.aubergesaintvincent.fr. Closed Sun evenings, and all day Mon.* A

Mercier celler

© ADT Marne

De Castellane – *57 rue de Verdun.*
🚃*Guided tours (Mid-Mar–23 Dec;*
10–11am, 2–5pm) start at €14, and include
free access to the tower, the museums and a
glass of De Castellane Brut. 📞*03 26 51 19 11*
(visitor information). www.castellane.com.
The 6km/3½mi long cellars, the tower
and the museum can be visited. A climb
of 237 steps leads to the top of the
tower, which is 60m high, which affords
a view of Épernay and its vineyards. The
museum is devoted to the evolution of
the Champagne-making process.

pretty, regional-style inn with a happy
combination of traditional and modern
decor. Traditional cuisine.

CHAMPAGNE CELLARS
IN ÉPERNAY

The main Champagne firms line both
sides of the avenue de Champagne (*east*
of the town centre), above the limestone
cliff riddled with miles of galleries which
remain at a temperature of 9–12°C. Most
organise tours.

Moët et Chandon – *20 avenue de*
Champagne. Apr–Sept daily 10am–5pm.
📞*03 26 51 20 20. www.moet.com.*
Moët et Chandon was the first
Champagne firm; its story is linked to that
of Hautvillers Abbey (🍷*see MONTAGNE*
DE REIMS: Hautvillers) which it owns, and
to Dom Pérignon whom it honoured by
naming its prestigious champagne after
him. The founder of the firm, Claude
Moët, began producing champagne in
1743; in 1962, the firm became a limited
company (the Moët-Hennessy-Louis
Vuitton group). During the very thorough
tour visitors can observe the complete
champagne process, including *remuage*
(moving the bottles) and *dégorgement*
(releasing the deposit).

Mercier – *73 avenue de Champagne;*
(parking opposite the main building).
Closed until June 2018, for renovation work,
but online ticketing systems are available
from April 2018. 4 tours are available,
ranging in price (2017) from €16 to €25 per
person. 📞*03 26 51 22 22.*
www.champagnemercier.fr.
In 1858, Eugène Mercier merged several
Champagne firms under his own name
and had 18km/11.2mi of galleries dug.
Mercier is the second Champagne
producer after Moët et Chandon and
it belongs to the same group. Visitors
descend in a panoramic lift for a cellar
tour in a small automatic train.

ON THE TOWN

La Marmite Swing – *160 av. Foch.*
📞*03 26 54 17 72. Bar and restaurant:*
Tue–Thu 11am–midnight, Fri 11am–1.30am,
Sat 5pm–3am. Cabaret and nightclub:
Fri, Sat and day before public holidays
midnight–5am. Closed Aug.
A brightly coloured bistro with hanging
tables and swing chairs and a concert
room (jazz, blues, rock, world music) that
turns into a nightclub after midnight.
Rum and Afro-West Indian evenings are
a speciality.

SHOPPING

Dallet – *26 r. du Gén.-Leclerc.* 📞*03 26 55*
31 08. www.chocolat-vincentdallet.fr.
Tue–Sun 7.30am–7.45pm.
Something different for a sweet tooth:
chocolates flavoured with aromatic herbs
from the garden! The house speciality *le*
pavé d'Epernay is prepared using
marzipan and marc de champagne.

Beaumont des Crayères – *64 r. de*
la Liberté, 51530 Mardeuil. 📞*03 26 55 29*
40. www.champagne-beaumont.com.
Taste and buy champagnes from this
international maker, in business since
1955.

Chocolat Thibaut – *ZA de Pierry.*
Pôle d'activités St-Julien, 51530 Pierry.
2km/1.2mi S of Épernay on D 11. 📞*03*
26 51 58 04. www.chocolaterie-thibaut.
com. Mon–Sat 9am–noon, 2–7pm, except
Mon morning and public holidays. Guided
tours 9–11.30am and 2–6.30pm. No visits
during the fortnight before Christmas,
Easter, last week of Jan and public holidays.
This chocolate craftsman will make his
specialities while you watch. You can
taste and buy the produce in
the shop next door.

Fismes

Fismes was a traditional stop for the kings of France en route to being crowned in Reims. Albert Uderzo, cartoonist for the team who created Asterix, is from Fismes.

SIGHTS
Musée
🕐 Tue–Sat 9.30am–12.30pm, 2–5pm.
🕐 21 Dec–4 Jan. 🚫 No charge.
📞 03 26 48 81 28.

A small museum, housed at the tourist office, contains fossils found in the area and 19C porcelain.

Église Ste-Macre
The 11C church was over an ancient oratory to house the remains of the saint.

🚗 DRIVING TOUR

Romanesque Churches in the Ardre valley
Round tour of 52km/32mi.

The Romanesque churches in this area are shaped like a basilica.

▶ Leave Fismes S along D 386 towards Épernay.

The road follows the River Ardre, a favourite haunt of anglers. Quarries once provided stone for Reims.

Crugny
Modified several times, the nave of the **Église St-Pierre** dates primarily from the 11C.

Savigny-sur-Ardres
It was from Savigny that General de Gaulle (who was only a colonel at the time) broadcast his first appeal to the French people on 28 May 1940 (plaque on the house opposite the church).

▶ Beyond Faverolles and Tramery, the road runs beneath the A4 motorway.

▶ **Population:** 5 523.
🔵 **Michelin Map:** Michelin Local map 306: E-7.
ℹ **Tourist Office:** 28 r. René-Letilly. 📞 03 26 48 81 28. www.fismes-tourisme.fr.
▶ **Location:** Fismes is on the N 31 between Soissons and Reims.

Poilly
11C and 12C **church** dedicated to St Rémy.

▶ Turn right onto D 980 to Verneuil.

Ville-en-Tardenois
The 12C **church** is surmounted by an elegant tower and saddleback roof.

▶ Turn right onto D 23 to Lhéry.

Lhéry
The late 12C **church** marks the transition from the Romanesque to the Gothic.

Lagery
The village square has a 18C covered market and a picturesque wash house.

▶ Drive W along D 27 towards Coulonges-Cohan at the intersection with D 25 and turn left.

Arcis-le-Ponsart
A picturesque fortified wall encloses this 12C **church** and a ruined 17C castle.

▶ Continue N along D 25 to Courville.

Courville
In medieval times, the archbishop of Reims had a castle here.

▶ Turn left onto D 386.

St-Gilles
The present church is all that remains of the former priory.

▶ D 386 leads back to Fismes.

Parc naturel régional de la **Montagne de Reims**★★

The Montagne de Reims is a picturesque massif covered with vineyards and woods and offering a wide choice of scenic drives. Created in 1976, the nature park extends over an area of 50 000ha between the towns of Reims, Épernay and Châlons-en-Champagne and includes 68 villages and hamlets. The largely-deciduous forest covers more than a third of the park's area; part of it is a biological reserve.

GEOGRAPHICAL NOTES
Forest and vines

The Montagne de Reims is a section of the Ile-de-France cuesta jutting out between the Vesle and the Marne towards the plain of Champagne. The Grande Montagne (high mountain) extends east of N 51 whereas the Petite Montagne (small mountain) spreads to the west of N 51. The highest point of the massif (287m) is located south of Vezy but, apart from Mont Sinaï (*alt 283m*) and Mont Joli (*alt 274m*), there are no distinct summits.

Wild boars and roe-deer roam freely here. The north, east and south slopes are covered with 7 000ha of vineyards producing some of the best Champagnes.

VISIT

🚶 There are numerous possibilities for exploring the park: footpaths starting from Villers-Allerand, Rilly-la-Montagne, Villers-Marmery, Trépail, Courtagnon and Damery; walks along the canal picnic areas, and viewpoints in Ville-Dommange, Hautvillers, Dizy, Verzy and Châtillon-sur-Marne.

In addition to the sights listed in the itinerary, **Olizy** has a small **Musée de l'Escargot de Champagne** (snail museum) and offers a farm tour.

🦴 **Michelin Map:** Local map 306: F-7/8 to G-7/8.
ℹ️ **Tourist information:** Maison du Parc, 51480 Pourcy. ☎03 26 59 44 44. www.parc-montagne dereims.fr. 🕐Mon–Fri 1.30–5.30pm (Fri 4.30pm).

The Maison du Parc in **Pourcy** organises numerous cultural and outdoor activities every year. There are other information centres about the park in **Hautvillers** and **Châtillon-sur-Marne**.

🚗 DRIVING TOUR

Champagne Kingdom
100km/62mi. Allow one day.

▶ Drive out of Reims along N 51 to Montchenot then turn left onto D 26 towards Villers-Allerand.

The road follows the northern ridge of the Montagne de Reims.

Rilly-la-Montagne

The **Ferme des Bermonts** houses a collection of agricultural tools illustrating daily life in Champagne at the turn of the 20C. From Rilly there are fine walking possibilities on the slopes of **Mont Joli** through which goes the railway tunnel (3.5km/2.2mi long) of the Paris-Reims line.

Mailly-Champagne

🚶 1km/0.6mi beyond Mailly-Champagne, there is an interesting **Carrière géologique** (geological quarry) showing a cross section of the Tertiary formations of the eastern Paris Basin.

The geological trail (*Free access to the trail, allow 2h30; purchase a Guide from the Maison du Parc if you're planning on visiting the site alone.* 👣*Guided tours organised by the Regional Park authorities.* ☎03 26 59 44 44) takes visitors 70 million years back in time.

Faux de Verzy in winter

From the road *(D 26)*, one can spot to the right, a contemporary **sculpture** by Bernard Pages celebrating the Earth.

Verzenay

This wine-growing village is overlooked by a **windmill** to the west and a 1909 **lighthouse**, now a wine museum.

Musée de la Vigne★

&. ⓒTue–Fri 10am–5pm, Sat–Sun and public holidays 10am–5.30pm. ⓒJan. ⊛€8 (museum and lighthouse €9) ℘03 26 07 87 87.
www.lepharedeverzenay.com.
A wooden footbridge leads to the restored lighthouse towering above a modern wooden building.

Verzy

This village developed under the protection of the Benedictine abbey of St-Basle, founded in the 7C and destroyed in 1792.

Faux de Verzy★

▷ In Verzy, take D 34 towards Louvois. On reaching the plateau, turn left onto the Route des Faux. From the parking area, follow the path over a distance of about 1km/0.6mi.

🐾 *Guided tours organised by the Regional Park authorities. Enquire at the Maison du Parc.*

🚶 The Faux (from the Latin *fagus* meaning beech) are twisted and stunted beech trees. This is the result of a genetic phenomenon, probably reinforced by natural layering. The site features footpaths, a playground and a picnic area.

Observatoire du Mont Sinaï

▷ Parking area on the other side of D 34. Walk along the forest road and, 200m farther on, turn right onto a very wide path (30min there and back).

🚶 A vaulted chamber on the edge of the ridge marks the observation post from which General Gouraud studied the positions and the terrain during the battle of Champagne in 1918. There is a view towards Reims and the Champagne hills.

▷ Return to D 34 towards Louvois.

Château de Louvois

Erected by Mansart for Louis XIV's minister, the **castle** (⟳ *not open to the public*) became the property of Louis XV's daughters; the park was designed by Le Nôtre but little remains today. From the gate, one can see the present castle (a pavilion partly rebuilt in the 19C).

▷ Drive N along D 9 to Neuville-en-Chaillois then turn left onto D 71, which goes through the forest.

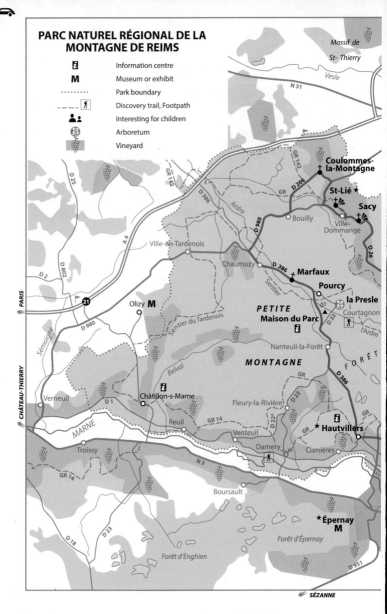

PARC NATUREL RÉGIONAL DE LA MONTAGNE DE REIMS

- **?** Information centre
- **M** Museum or exhibit
- ·········· Park boundary
- – · – · – 🚶 Discovery trail, Footpath
- 👥 Interesting for children
- 🌳 Arboretum
- Vineyard

Germaine

👥 A small museum, the **Maison du bûcheron** is devoted to all the aspects of forestry (marking, clearing, cutting, felling, carrying).

⊳ Follow D 271 to Avenay-Val-d'Or.

Avenay-Val-d'Or

The **Église St-Trésain** from the 13C and 16C, has a 16C organ in the south transept. 🚶 A discovery trail starting from the station *(brochure available from the Maison du Parc)*, enables visitors to discover a rural community.

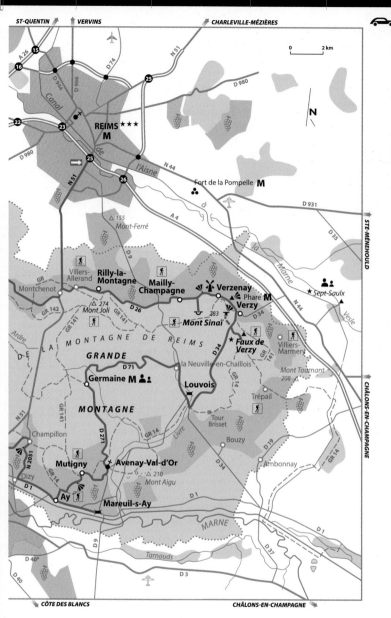

> Follow D 201 opposite the station and immediately after the railway line, take the small road that climbs through the vineyards to Mutigny.

Mutigny

Stand near the church for a **view** of Ay and the Côte des Blancs on the right, and Châlons and the plain straight ahead.

The **Sentier du Vigneron** (*guided visits by arrangement mid-Mar–mid-Oct. 06 84 98 50 54. http://sentierduvigneron.com*), which starts from the village, offers ramblers a 2km/1.3mi round tour lined with explanatory panels.

On the way down to Ay, there are glimpses of Épernay and the Côte des Blancs.

Ancienne abbaye Saint-Pierre, Hautvillers

Ay

This ancient city, well liked by several French kings including Good King Henri (IV), hosts the annual **Henri IV Festival** in early July.

Institut International des vins de Champagne

Located in a 19C mansion, the institute is devoted to research concerning Champagne, its history, artistic representations, brand image, and undertakes the training of students with the cooperation of Reims university. *See Addresses*.

▶ In Ay, turn left onto D 1 to Mareuil-sur-Ay.

Mareuil-sur-Ay

The castle was erected in the 18C and the estate was bought in 1830 by the duke of Montebello who created his own make of Champagne.

▶ Return to Ay and continue to Dizy then turn onto N 2051 to Champillon.

Between Dizy and Champillon, the road rises through endless vineyards. There is a good **view★** of the vineyards, the Marne valley and Épernay from a terrace on the side of the road.

Hautvillers★

According to tradition, **Dom Pérignon** (1638–1715), who was in charge of the cellars of the Benedictine abbey, was the first to blend various wines to produce a vintage and initiated the use of corks. Dom Pérignon is buried in **St-Sindulphe abbey church:** his black-marble tombstone is located to the left of the high altar over which hangs a vast chandelier (1950) made up of four wheels from winepresses.

Ancienne abbaye Saint-Pierre

Founded in 650 by St Nivard, a nephew of King Dagobert, the abbey followed Saint-Maur's rule (similar to Benedictine). The most beautiful manuscripts of the **École de Reims** were produced here. Today it is owned by Moët et Chandon.

Look through the railing into the park for a glimpse of the **Pavillon des Dames de France**, used by Louis XV's daughters when on pilgrimage.

Jardin botanique de la Presle

Carrefour de la Presle. ○*Mon–Fri 2–6pm, Sat 9am–noon, 2–6pm.* ○*Public holidays and some Sun afternoons, enquire).* ○€5. ℘03 26 59 43 39.

This garden features lovely spiraeas, willows and roses, including the Rose de la Marne.

▶ Continue northwards along D 386.

Pourcy

The **Maison du Parc**, designed by Hervé Bagot, houses the offices of the nature park as well as an information centre.

Verger conservatoire

Access from the Maison du Parc. This conservatory is designed to safeguard some 25 endangered fruit tree species.

Marfaux

The **church** here boasts fine capitals.

◔ Beyond Chaumuzy, turn right onto D 980 then, as you reach Bouilly, turn left onto D 206.

Coulommes-la-Montagne

There is a fine Romanesque **church**.

◔ Turn right to rejoin D 980 via Pargny-les-Reims; 1.5km/0.9mi farther on, turn left towards St-Lié.

Chapelle St-Lié★

This chapel, dating from the 12C, 13C and 16C, stands on a mound near Ville-Dommange that was probably a holy grove in Gallo-Roman times. There is an extended **view★** of Ville-Dommange, the ridge, Reims and its cathedral and the plain as far as the St-Thierry massif.

Sacy

The Église St-Rémi has an 11C east end and a 12C square belfry. From the cemetery there is a fine view of Reims.

◔ Continue on the D 26 and return to Reims via the D 51.

ADDRESSES

⌂ STAY

⊜⊜ Chambre d'hôte Delong – *24 r. des Tilleuls, 51390 St-Euphraise-et-Clairizet. 16km/10mi SW of Reims on D 980 and D 206. ✆03 26 49 74 90. 4 rooms.* This former cowshed in a vineyard has been renovated to provide rooms with lovely stone walls, exposed timberwork and pleasant bathrooms. You can visit the cellars and press-house and taste the champagne produced on the estate.

⊜⊜ La Famille Guy Charbaut – *12 r. du Pont, 51160 Mareuil-sur-Aÿ. ✆03 26 52 60 59. www.champagne-guy-charbaut.com. 6 rooms. Evening meal ⊜⊜⊜.* As father and son wine growers since 1930, the Charbaut family accommodate you in their 1837 home and show you the cellars dug out of the chalk. Spacious rooms. Meals served in a magnificent storeroom.

ⵜ⁄ EAT

⊜⊜⊜ Le Cheval Blanc – *3 Place Edouard Mignot, 51400 Sept-Saulx. ✆03 26 03 51 91. www.restaurantchevalblanc.fr. Closed Mon and Tue.* This peaceful former coaching inn (*26 rooms. ⊜⊜*) is well off the beaten track. The spruce, flowery courtyard has been converted into a terrace. A branch of the River Vesle winds through the attractive park, where you can play tennis, volleyball and golf, or simply stroll around in fine weather.

CHAMPAGNE CELLARS

Institut International des Vins de Champagne – *Villa Bissinger. 15 r. Jeanson, 51160 Aÿ. ✆03 26 55 78 78. www.villabissinger.com. Open Apr–Oct, 1st Sat of the month, 2.30pm, tasting and commentary of 4 champagnes. ⊛€25 per person.* The institute also organises several courses for beginners throughout the year, lasting from a 2 hours (minimum 2 people: €75 per person) to a full day (minimum 4 people: €250 per person). ⊘ *The 'per person' price reduces if there are more people in the group.*

Serge Pierlot – *10 r. St-Vincent, 51150 Ambonnay. 6.5km/4mi SE of Louvois on D 34 and D 19. ✆03 26 57 01 11. Open Mon–Fri 9am–noon, 2.30–6.30pm, Sat 9am–noon, 2.30–6pm, Sun 9am–noon. Closed early-end Jan, end Aug–early Sept.* In his shop at the end of an alley, Serge Pierlot exhibits an 18C winepress and other vine-growing and winemaking implements used by his ancestors.

Soutiran-Pelletier – *12 r. St-Vincent, 51150 Ambonnay. 6.5km/4mi SE of Louvois on D 34 and D 19. ✆03 26 57 07 87. www.soutiran.com. Tasting Mon–Sat 8am–noon, 2–6pm, visit by appointment only. Closed Sat from end Dec–Easter.* In this typical village, the Soutiran Pelletier establishment will take you to see its presses, vats and cellars, as well as giving explanations of the techniques used in winemaking.

Montmirail

The low, roughcast houses of this once fortified town cling to the slopes of a promontory overlooking the rural valley of the Petit Morin. Paul de Gondi, who later became the famous **Cardinal de Retz**, was born in Montmirail castle in 1613. After the death of Cardinal Richelieu and Louis XIII, this dangerous schemer used his ecclesiastical influence to destabilise the regency of Anne of Austria during Louis XIV's childhood.

▶ **Population:** 3 768.
◉ **Michelin Map:** Michelin Local map 306: D-9.
▯ **Tourist information:**
4 pl. Rémy-Petit,
51210 Montmirail.
𝄞 03 26 81 40 05.
www.tourisme-montmirail-brie-champenoise.fr.

CHÂTEAU

Guided tours Jul–Sept Mon–Thu 2.30pm and 3.30pm. €6.
𝄞 03 26 81 40 05.
The 17C brick-and-stone castle was acquired in 1678 by one of Louis XIV's ministers, the **Marquis de Louvois**; his great-granddaughter married the Duc de La Rochefoucauld whose descendants still own the castle.

EXCURSIONS

Colonne commémorative de la bataille de Montmirail

4km/2.5mi NW along D 933.
A column surmounted by a gilt eagle (1867) commemorates one of the last battles won by **Napoleon** in 1814.
A century later, in September 1914, the German army commanded by Von Bülow was attacked here by French troops who managed to stop the German advance.

Jardins de Vieils-Maisons

12km/7.5mi W along D 933. ◷*Jun–late Sept daily except Wed–Thu 2–6pm.*
€6. 𝄞 03 23 82 62 53.
www.jardins-vielsmaisons.net.
The park has more than 2 000 different plant species. An 1840 garden features rhododendrons, old roses and hydrangea round-out the collection.

Verdelot

15km/9.3mi W along D 31.
The imposing **church**, dating from the 15C–16C, stands on the hillside. Note the intricate vaulting and the height of the aisles almost level with the chancel vaulting. On either side of the chancel, there are small statues of St Crépin and St Crépinien, patron saints of cobblers, to whom the church is dedicated. A seated Virgin Mary in carved walnut, forming part of a 19C altarpiece, is reminiscent of 12C or 13C representations of the Virgin carved in the Auvergne and Languedoc regions.

VALLÉ DU PETIT MORIN

24km/15mi. Allow 1h.

▶ Leave Montmirail along D 43 heading southeast.

This 90km/56mi long tributary of the Marne, which takes its source east of Montmirail (◉*see Marais de ST-GOND*), flows through meadows, marshy at times, dotted with groves of poplars.

Abbaye du Reclus

A holy hermit called Hugues-le-Reclus, retired to this remote vale (c. 1123) and gave it his (fitting) name. In 1142, St Bernard founded a Cistercian abbey.

▶ Beyond Talus-St-Prix, turn left onto D 951 towards Baye.

Baye

St Alpin, a native of Baye who became bishop of Châlons, was buried in the 13C church. Baye is the birthplace of Marion de Lorme (1611–50) who, like Ninon de Lenclos, was famous for her numerous love affairs; her legend inspired Victor Hugo to write a play.

Orbais-l'Abbaye

This pretty village has one the finest Gothic churches in Champagne, remnant of an important Benedictine abbey founded in the 7C. The village is a starting point for excursions through the Surmelin valley and Vassy forest.

▶ **Population:** 598.
‡ **Michelin Map:** Michelin Local map 306: E-9.
▶ **Location:** Orbais is situated on the D 11 between Epernay and Montmirail.

SIGHTS
Church★

The building of the church (end of the 12C and 13C) was probably supervised by Jean d'Orbais, one of the master builders of Reims cathedral. It incorporates the chancel and transept of the former abbey church as well as two bays from the original nave. Note the unusual flying buttresses of the transept and the apse which meet on the same abutment; the slender spire dates from the 14C. Inside, the **chancel★**, with its ambulatory and radiating chapels, is considered to be the prototype of that of Reims cathedral. The entrance to the transept is furnished with early-16C choir stalls carved with Biblical scenes and amusing figures on the misericords.

🚗 DRIVING TOUR

Churches and Castles

▶ From Orbais, take the D 242 to Fromentières (6km/3.7mi).

Église de Fromentières

Behind the high altar, the church contains a monumental early 16C Flemish **altarpiece★★**, which was bought by the vicar in 1715 for a modest sum. The signature, a severed hand, is the emblem of Antwerp. The paintings on the side panels depict episodes from the New Testament; the central panel comprises three tiers of delicately carved scenes, illustrating Christ's Life and Passion.

▶ Drive along D 933 to Étoges (11km/6.8mi).

Étoges

This wine-growing village is close to the Côte des Blancs. There is a fine view of the elegant 17C **château**, now a hotel, from the bridge across the moat.
The 12C **church**, remodelled in the 15C and 16C, has a Gothic rose window and a Renaissance doorway; it contains several 16C recumbent tomb figures.

▶ Drive 8km/5mi along D 18.

Château de Montmort-Lucy

⚓ Not open to the public.
The brick and stone château occupies a commanding position above the Surmelin valley. It was here that General von Bülow ordered the retreat from the Marne in 1914 (‡ see MONTMIRAIL). Begun in the 12C but rebuilt in the late 16C, still has a rather feudal appearance with its 14m deep moat. The lower part of the castle is reached by a ramp designed for horses, similar to that in the château at Amboise.

ADDRESSES

🛏 STAY

⊖⊖⊜ **Le Château d'Étoges –** 4 r. de Richebourg, 51270 Étoges. ℘03 26 59 30 08. www.chateau-etoges.com. Closed mid-Jan–mid-Feb. 28 rooms. Restaurant ⊖⊖⊜. For an evening of refinement, why not stay at this 17C château with its ceremonial reception rooms, grand dining room and old-fashioned bedrooms, which is set in spacious grounds just outside the village? Louis XIV loved the grounds, so it is likely you will as well.

Provins★★

Seine-et-marne

Whichever way one approaches the medieval town of Provins, the outline of the Tour César and the dome of the Église St-Quiriace can be seen from afar. The lower town lies on the banks of the Voulzie and the Durteint, beneath the promontory on which stand the romantic ruins celebrated by Balzac and painted by Turner. The formidable ramparts are the backdrop for medieval festivals and displays in summer. The town, which boasts no fewer than 58 historic monuments, is on UNESCO's World Heritage list. Clay from the Provins Basin, extracted from open quarries since time immemorial, supplies potters as well as brick and tile manufacturers with a complete range of raw materials.

A BIT OF HISTORY

The lower town developed from the 11C on around a Benedictine priory built on the spot where the relics of St Ayoul (or Aygulf) had been miraculously found. Under the leadership of Henri I (1152–81), Count of Champagne, known as the Liberal, Provins became a prosperous trading town and one of the two capital cities of the Champagne region.

The Provins fairs

The two fairs, held in Provins from May to June and from September to October, were, with those of Troyes, the most important of the Champagne fairs. There were three stages to each fair: first of all there was the display during which traders showed their merchandise, comparing prices and quality; next came the sale during which goods changed hands; the payment of the goods came last and, for this operation, sellers and buyers needed the help of money changers, notaries and fair keepers. The latter were initially police officers responsible for the prevention of theft and fraud, but by the 13C they had acquired real judicial power.

▶ **Population:** 12 353.
◔ **Michelin Map:** Michelin Local map 312: I-4.
▯ **Tourist office:** Chemin de Villecran, 77160 Provins. ℘01 64 60 26 26. www.provins.net.
◖ **Location**: 80km/50mi SE of Paris by the A4 motorway.
◑ **Don't miss**: The rampart walk and the Tour de César.
♟♙ **Kids**: The medieval jousting and falconry displays: La Bataille des Remparts, Les Aigles des Remparts and La Légende des Chevaliers (◔see Addresses).

PRACTICAL INFORMATION

Pass Provins – *Valid 1 yr. €12 (children €8.50).* Gives one entry to the Tour César, Souterrains, Grange-aux-Dîmes and the museum, plus discounts on three historic spectacles, the rosary and the tourist train.

Guided tours of the town – The town organises 2hr tours by approved guides. *Apr–early Nov Sat–Sun and public holidays, depart tourist ofice at 11am. €8.* ℘01 64 60 26 26. www.provins.net.

During the fair, the city looked like a huge market hall full of a colourful crowd of people from northern regions as well as from the Mediterranean. Transactions were made in local currency, hence the growing importance of Italian bankers who could calculate complex exchange rates; by the end of the 13C, they had taken control of the fairs and money changing took precedence over the sale of goods.

The first annual fair, which was the most important, took place on the hilltop, near the castle, the second near the Église St-Ayoul.

Ramparts of Provins

Medieval town

Two separate towns developed simultaneously: the Châtel or upper town and the Val or lower town. They were later included within the same fortifications. In the 13C the city already had a population of more than 10 000 inhabitants. Apart from numerous merchants, there were weavers, fullers, dyers, cloth-makers, shearers, without forgetting money changers, guards entrusted with police duties, and other judicial representatives of the counts of Champagne. Numerous inns, shops and a thriving Jewish community added to the town's cosmopolitan atmosphere.

The counts of Champagne stayed in Provins for long periods and were surrounded by a lively court. Thibaud IV (1201–53), known as the Chansonnier, encouraged the arts and wrote songs that rate among the best 13C literature. In the 14C, the town's activities declined and the fairs were supplanted by those of Paris and Lyon.

The Hundred Years War confirmed the end of economic prosperity for Provins.

Roses

According to tradition it was **Thibaud IV the Troubadour** who brought roses back from Syria and grew them successfully in Provins. Edmund Lancaster (1245–96), brother of the King of England, married Blanche of Artois and was for a while suzerain of Provins, at which time he introduced the red rose into his coat of arms.

WALKING TOUR

UPPER TOWN★★

Allow 2h. It is advisable to park in the car park near Porte St-Jean. This is also the location of the tourist office and the departure point for the small tourist train.

Porte St-Jean

St John's Gateway was built in the 13C. This stocky construction is flanked by two towers that are partially hidden by the buttresses that were added in the 14C to support the drawbridge.

▶ Follow allée des Remparts which overlooks the old moat.

Remparts★★

The town walls were built in the 12C and 13C along an existing line of defence. They constitute a very fine example of medieval military architecture. A house straddling the curtain wall was the home of the Provins executioners. The last one to live here was Charles-Henri Sanson who executed Louis XVI. The most interesting part of the ramparts runs between Porte St-Jean and Porte de Jouy. The Tour aux Engins, on the corner, links the two curtain walls; it derives its name from a barn nearby in which engines of war were housed. In summer, shows are organised within the ramparts: **Les Aigles des remparts**; **A l'assaut des remparts** and **La Légende des Chevaliers** (♿ *see Addresses*).

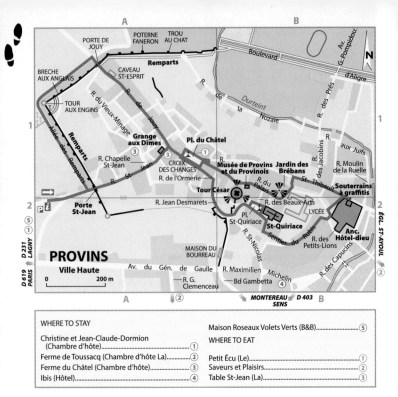

▶ Beyond the 12C Porte de Jouy, take rue de Jouy which is lined by picturesque low houses with long tiled roofs or an overhanging upper storey.

Place du Châtel

This vast rectangular square is bordered by attractive old houses: the 15C Maison des Quatre Pignons (southwest corner), the 13C Maison des Petits-Plaids (northwest corner), and the Hôtel de la Coquille to the north.

The remains of Église St-Thibault (12C) stand on the northeast corner. In the centre, next to an old well stands the Croix des Changes, where the edicts of the Counts of Champagne were posted.

Walk past the **Musée de Provins et du Provinois**, housed in the "Maison Romane" (Romanesque house).

Jardin des Brébans

From the public garden, there is a striking view of the nearby Église St-Quiriace and, next to it, of the Lycée (high school) built on the site of the former palace of the counts of Champagne.

▶ Follow rue St-Thibaud.

Ancien Hôtel-Dieu

This former hospital was originally a palace founded in the 11C by Count Thibaud I for the countesses of Blois and Champagne. Remodelled several times, the building has retained its 13C Gothic doorway, a Romanesque doorway supported by two colonnettes and a 12C vestibule surmounted by groined vaulting. Note the carved-stone Renaissance **altarpiece** depicting the Virgin and Child implored by a kneeling donor.

▶ Follow the Sentier du Rubis and turn right to reach the collegiate church.

Collégiale St-Quiriace

The church was begun in the 11C. The transept and nave date from the 13C, the dome from the 17C. In front of the church a Cross stands on the site of the old bell-tower which collapsed in 1689. The **chancel★** and square ambulatory are the oldest parts (second half of the 12C). Note early-Gothic features such as the rounded arcading of the blind triforium.

The south bay of the chancel was covered in 1238 by an octopartite vault (formed by assembling four diagonal arches), characteristic of the region.

Tour César★★

🕐 *Jan–Mar and Nov–Dec 2–5pm; Apr–early Nov daily 10am–6pm.* 🕐 *1 Jan, 25 Dec.* ⊜€5. 🕿*01 64 60 26 26.*

This superb 12C keep, 44m high and flanked by four turrets, is the emblem of the town. It was once part of the walls of the upper town. The pyramidal roof was built in the 16C.

The revetment wall which encloses the base of the keep was added by the English during the Hundred Years War, in order to house the artillery.

The guardroom on the first floor is octagonal and 11m high; it is topped by vaulting formed of four arcades of pointed arches ending in a dome and pierced by an orifice through which the soldiers on the floor above were passed supplies. The gallery encircling the keep at the height of the turrets was originally roofed over. The **view★** extends over the town and the countryside.

A very narrow stairway leads to the top level. Under the fine 16C wooden roof, the bells of St-Quiriace have hung here since the church lost its bell-tower.

▶ Return to Porte St-Jean via place du Châtel then rue St-Jean on the left.

SIGHTS
Grange aux Dîmes★

Rue St-Jean. 🕐 *Jan–Mar and Nov–Dec Sat–Sun and public holidays 2–5pm; Apr–early Sept daily 10am–7pm; early Sept–early Nov Mon–Fri 2–6pm, Sat–Sun and public holidays 10am–6pm.*

Tour César

© S. Sauvignier/MICHELIN

🕐 *1 Jan, 25 Dec.* ⊜€4.50. 🕿*01 64 60 26 26. www.provins.net.*

This massive 13C building belonged to the canons of St-Quiriace, who hired out the space to merchants during the fairs. Later the barn became a store for the tithes (dîmes) levied on the harvests of the peasants. The ground floor consists of a vast hall.

Musée de Provins et du Provinois

7 rue du Palais. 🕐 *Jan and Nov–mid-Dec Sat–Sun and public holidays noon–5.30pm; Feb–mid-Jun and mid-Sept–early Nov noon–5.30pm; mid-Jun–mid-Sept daily 11am–6.30pm.* 🕐 *18 Dec–5 Jan.* ⊜€4. 🕿*01 64 01 40 19.*

The museum is housed in one of the oldest buildings in the town, "The Romanesque House". The cellar containing capitals and Merovingian sarcophagi displayed around an 11C pier.

On the ground floor are displayed **the sculpture and ceramic collections★**. Stone and polychrome carved-wood statues, most of them from demolished churches, are valuable examples of medieval and Renaissance art in the Provins region. The collection of ceramics illustrates the great quantity and diversity of the local production since prehistoric times: Neolithic pottery, Gallo-Roman tiles, fragments of sigillate bowls and goblets, funeral vases, floor tiles with inlaid decoration, and finials. Iron-Age and Bronze-Age jewellery, Meroving-ian iron buckles and sarcophagi are also exhibited.

Église St-Ayoul

In 1048 Thibaud I, Count of Troyes and Meaux (and Count Thibaud III of Blois), grand protector of the abbeys, installed the monks from Montier-la-Celle in the St-Ayoul district in the Lower Town.

The three doorways project far beyond the line of the gable on the west front. Missing parts of the **central doorway★** were replaced with new pieces made by the sculptor Georges Jeanclos, who was responsible for the bronze **statues★** with antique patina which harmonise well with the medieval reliefs.

Note the beautiful woodwork by Pierre Blasset (1610–63): the high altar and altarpiece as well as panelling and carved coffers in the aisles. In the north aisle are three 16C **statues★★**: a grace-ful if rather affected Virgin Mary and two musician angels with wonderfully draped clothes.

Tour Notre-Dame-du-Val

This belfry, standing within the ruins of the former Porte Bailly, is all that remains of the collegiate church founded in the 13C by Countess Marie de Champagne and rebuilt in the 15C–16C.

Église Ste-Croix

According to local legend, the church gets its name from a fragment of the True Cross brought back by Thibaud IV from the seventh crusade. A second aisle in Flamboyant style was added in the 16C. The Romanesque belfry, topped by a modern spire, towers above the crossing. Note the Burgundy-style modillioned cornice round the east end.

Underground galleries (Souterrains)

Entrance in rue St-Thibault, left of the Ancien Hôtel-Dieu.

Guided tours only (in English from Apr–early Nov Sat–Sun and public holidays at 2.30pm; all other tours are in French): check website for the many varied times and tours. ①1 Jan, 25 Dec. €4.50. ☎01 64 60 26 26. *www.provins.net.*

Provins has a substantial network of underground passages, some marked with ancient graffiti. The section that is open to the public, entered through a vaulted chamber in the old hospice, runs through a layer of tufa which lies parallel to the base of the spur on which the Upper Town stands.

EXCURSION

St-Loup-de-Naud★

9km/5.6mi SW.

This once fortified village is built on a rocky spur. The early 11C **church★** belonged to a Benedictine priory.

Under the 12C **doorway★★**, reminis-cent of the royal doorway of Chartres cathedral: the tympanum is decorated with a Christ in Glory surrounded by the emblems of the Evangelists, the apostles framed by arcading adorn the lintel, statue-columns line the embra-sures and various characters decorate the recessed arches of the archivolt. The St-Loup sculptures mark a transition in architectural style that eventually led to Gothic realism. Inside: the early Roman-esque style of the chancel switches to early Gothic in the nave which includes two 12C bays with ribbed vaulting next to the porch, followed by two older bays, one with barrel vaulting, the other with groined vaulting.

ADDRESSES

🏠 STAY

🛏 **Chambre d'hôte Christine et Jean Claude-Dormion** – *2 r. des Glycines, 77650 Lizines. 15km/9.4mi SW of Provins on N 19 and D 209. ☎01 60 67 32 56. http://dormion. cpur.fr. 5 rooms and 2 gîtes .* This farm dating back three centuries and still in operation offers wonderful rustic rooms, each with basic kitchen facilities. Lovely breakfast room with large bay window. The garden and orchard are very inviting.

🛏 **La Ferme de Toussacq** – *In the hamlet of Toussacq, alongside the Seine. 77480 Grisy-sur-Seine. 20km/12.5mi S of*

Provins on N 19, Nogent-sur-Seine road on D 78 and D 411. ☎ *01 64 01 82 90.* 🖃. *5 rooms.* This hamlet is in a rural setting on the banks of the Seine. The simple rooms are located in what were formerly the outhouses of the château. In the restaurant, traditional recipes made with produce from the farm; vegetarian dishes sometimes available.

⊜⊜ **Chambre d'hôte Ferme du Chatel** – *5 r. de la Chapelle-St-Jean.* ☎ *06 73 79 36 68. www.fermeduchatelprovins.com. 5 rooms.* The main attraction of this farmhouse, built from the 12C to the 18C, is its location in the heart of the medieval city. The rooms are quiet, well maintained and have exposed timberwork. Huge garden with fruit trees.

⊜⊜ **Hôtel Ibis** – *77 Ave du Gén.-de-Gaulle.* ☎ *01 60 67 66 67. www.accorhotels. com. 49 rooms. Restaurant⊜.* In a calm district, with a medieval architectural style and contemporary styled rooms. Neo-rustic restaurant.

⊜⊜ **La Maison Roseaux Volets Verts (B&B)** – *3 & 5 Rue Maximilien-Michelin.* ☎ *01 64 08 92 95. 5 rooms.* At the foot of the medieval city, these two 19C houses provide modern comforts and historic charm. Rooms are lovingly decorated, some overlooking the pretty gardens.

⌘/ EAT

⊜⊜ **Le Petit Écu** – *9 pl. du Châtel (upper town).* ☎ *01 64 08 95 00. www.lepetitecu. com.* In the lovely Place du Châtel in the heart of old Provins, this pretty half-timbered restaurant offers an original rustic buffet menu at weekends during the season. On weekdays the menu is more traditional.

⊜⊜ **Saveurs et Plaisirs** – *6 Pl. St-Ayoul.* ☎ *01 60 58 41 70. Closed Mon evening and all day Sun.* A contemporary restaurant with a dedicated, self-taught chef, with a choice between traditional or "creative" menus, heavy on fish dishes.

⊜⊜ **La Table de St-Jean** – *3 r. St-Jean.* ☎ *01 64 08 96 77. Closed Sun evenings in winter, Tue evenings and Wed.* In the upper town, opposite the tithe barn, this restaurant is in a half-timbered house that is possibly 11C. You can enjoy your meal in the rustic dining room or on the terrace in a pretty flower-decked courtyard.

SHOWTIME

Les Aigles des Remparts – 🛉🛉 *Théâtre des Remparts, Porte de Jouy.* ☎ *01 60 58 80 32. www.vollibre.fr. Apr–early Nov. €12 (child 4–12, €8).* This show of equestrian falconry includes birds of prey in free flight, cavaliers and wolves. Don't miss a visit to the breeding cages, accompanied by the falconers.

La Bataille des Remparts – ☎ *01 64 60 26 26. www.provins.net. Opening times and ticket sales at the tourist office. €8 (child 4–12, €5.50).* Near the porte St-Jean and in the moat you can watch an impeccably produced medieval show. You will discover how the old war machines and arms were used.

La Légende des Chevaliers – ☎ *01 64 60 26 26. www.provins.net. Opening times and ticket sales at the tourist office. €12 (child 4–12,€8).* Within the defensive ditches, go back to the 13C and watch knights battle it out in lance and sword combats, as well as hand-to-hand fighting, with weapons of the time including axes and iron balls on chains.

SHOPPING

La Chèvrerie – *1 r. de Jouy (upper town).* ☎ *01 64 01 04 62. Open Fri–Sun and public holidays 11am–7pm.* The Favreau brothers never tire of talking about their beloved goats' cheeses, made in their goat farm (which can also be visited). Substantial snacks also available.

Gaufillier – *2 av. Victor-Garnier.* ☎ *01 64 00 03 71. Open Tue–Sat 8am–12.30pm, 2.30–7.15pm; Sun 8am–12.30pm.* This chocolate maker-baker-confectioner has been wowing his customers for more than ten years with rose-flavoured treats: jam, ice cream, caramels, fruit jellies, nougats, tea, lemonade.

La Ronde des Abeilles – *3 r. des Beaux-Arts (upper town).* ☎ *01 60 67 65 97. Open Wed–Mon 2–7pm.* The speciality of this pretty sweetshop is Provins rose-flavoured honey, but it also sells other products originating in the beehive (royal jelly, pollen and wax) as well as numerous treats such as fruit and vegetables cooked or preserved in honey, gingerbread and mead.

Reims★★★

Reims is famous for its magnificent cathedral, where French kings were traditionally crowned. Despite heavy damage in World War I, the city also has a wealth of other architectural masterpieces, including the UNESCO World Heritage listed Basilique St-Remi and Palais du Tau. Reims is also, together with Épernay, the capital of Champagne and most cellars are open to the public.

A BIT OF HISTORY
Ancient times

Reims' origins date back to pre-Roman times when it was the fortified capital of a Gaulish tribe, the Remes. After the Roman conquest, it became a thriving administrative and commercial city with many public buildings. The **Porte de Mars** and the **Cryptoportique** are the only two remaining buildings. In the 3C, the town's strategic position increased its military importance as the Romans desperately tried to stop invading hordes from the east. At the same time, Reims became a Christian city and the first cathedral was built.

Clovis' christening

Then came the conversion of **Clovis**, king of the Franks, who was baptised by the bishop of Reims, **Remi** (440–533), on Christmas Day shortly before the year 500. The whole population rejoiced and led a procession from the former imperial palace to the baptistery situated near the cathedral. According to legend, a dove brought a phial containing holy oil used by Remi to anoint Clovis. This phial was carefully preserved and used for the coronation of every king of France from the 11C to 1825, the most famous of whom was Charles VII in 1429, at the height of the Hundred Years War, in the presence of Joan of Arc.

Medieval Reims

From the end of the 5C and through whole medieval period, Reims was an important religious, political and artistic centre (**École de Reims**). The powerful

- ▶ **Population:** 186 505.
- **Michelin Map:** Michelin Local map 306: G-7.
- **Tourist Office**: 6 rue Rockefeller, 51100 Reims. ℘03 26 77 45 00. www.reims-tourisme.com.
- **Location:** Reims is 112km/ 69.6mi NE of Provins and 143km/89mi from Paris on the A 26 motorway.
- **Don't Miss:** The magnificent Cathedral Notre-Dame and the interior of the Basilica of St Rémi.
- **Timing:** Allow at least one day to see the city's main sights.
- **Kids:** Motor enthusiasts love the Musée de l'Automobile, while the Parc nature des Sept-Saulx has activities for all ages.
- **Also See:** Many of the leading Champagne houses are located in Reims, see Routes du Champagne.

PRACTICAL INFORMATION

City Pass Reims – *provides admission to numerous museums, the Planetarium and the Palais de Tau. €22 (24h); €32 (48h), and €42 valid for 72hr. Enquire at tourist office. www.reimscitypass.com.*
Guided tours – Reims, City of Art, organises tours by approved guides. *Enquire at tourist office.*

archbishops of Reims played the role of arbiters between kings and princes who came to stay at the Abbaye de St-Remi. One of the archbishops, **Gerbert,** became Pope in 999.

During the 11C, 12C and 13C, the town expanded and acquired some splendid edifices such as the abbey church of St-Remi and the cathedral. **Guillaume aux Blanches Mains,** who was archbishop from 1176 to 1202, contributed to the prosperity of the town by granting it a charter and, by the beginning of the 13C, Reims had doubled in size.

Modern times

Badly damaged during the First World War when 80% of the town's buildings were destroyed, Reims was spared during the Second World War. The capitulation of the German forces on 7 May 1945 was signed in Reims where General Eisenhower had his headquarters.

Today the textile industry, which brought prosperity to the town as early as the 12C, has practically disappeared. However, the production of Champagne remains one of the town's main activities. The city's artistic tradition is also maintained by the famous stained-glass workshops which once employed the talents of Villon, Chagall, Braque and Da Silva.

© Richard Soberka/hemis.fr

West front, Cathédrale Notre-Dame

CATHÉDRALE NOTRE-DAME★★★

Its homogenous architectural style and superb sculptures make Cathédrale Notre-Dame one of the finest cathedrals in Christendom.

In 1210, Archbishop Aubry de Humbert decided to build a Gothic cathedral (the third to be erected on this site) modelled on those being built at the time in Paris (1163), Soissons (1180) and Chartres

(1194). The edifice was designed by Jean d'Orbais and five successive architects followed the original plans, which explains the extraordinary homogeneity of the cathedral. Their names were inscribed on the original paving stones which unfortunately disappeared in the 18C. Jean d'Orbais built the chancel, Jean le Loup the nave and the west front which Gaucher de Reims decorated with statues and three portals, Bernard

Jean-Baptiste de la Salle and Schooling for the Poor

Small schools intended for children of poor families began to open in Reims from 1674 onwards, at the instigation of Canon Roland. His work was continued by Jean-Baptiste de la Salle.

Born in Reims in 1651, Jean-Baptiste de la Salle belonged to a rich aristocratic family who intended him to pursue a brilliant career within the Church. However, the young canon decided instead to devote his energies and his wealth to educating the poor. He began by founding the Communauté des Sœurs du Saint Enfant Jésus, which spread throughout the countryside. The nuns ran schools and catechism classes but they also taught adults. A few years later, Jean-Baptiste de la Salle founded the Communauté des Frères des Écoles Chrétiennes, which expanded considerably.

In 1695, he published a work entitled *The Running of Schools,* in which he explained his theories about teaching: he was in favour of collective teaching and wanted French to replace Latin. However, his ideas, which were revolutionary at the time, only triumphed long after his death (Rouen 1719).

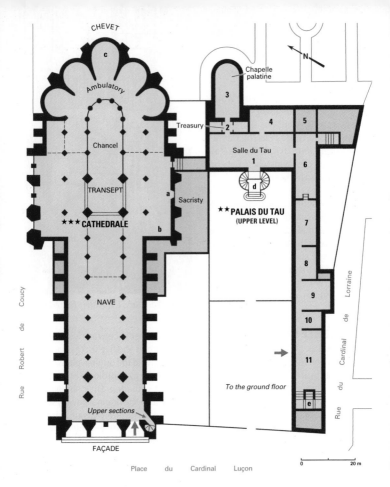

de Soissons designed the rose-window and the gables and finished the nave vaulting. By 1285, the interior had been completed. The towers were erected in the 15C; others were planned but a severe fire, which damaged the roof structure in 1481, halted the project. The cathedral was regrettably altered in the 18C (suppression of the rood screen, some stained glass and the labyrinth), but it was not damaged during the Revolution. Unfortunately, a long restoration programme had just been completed when, in September 1914, heavy shelling set fire to the timber roof structure causing the bells and the lead of the stained glass to melt and the stone to split. More shell damage occurred throughout the First World War and a new restoration

programme was launched. The damaged timber vault was replaced by a concrete roof structure. The cathedral was finally reconsecrated in 1937.

Exterior

More than 2 300 statues decorate the exterior. Some of them, which were badly damaged by war and bad weather have been replaced by copies., The original are now exhibited in the Palais du Tau.

West front

Best seen in the setting sun, the west front of Reims cathedral is reminiscent of Notre-Dame in Paris, but here the vertical lines are emphasised by the pointed gables and pinnacles, the slender colonnettes and the tall statues decorating the kings' gallery.

The **three doorways**, lined up with the three naves, are surmounted by elaborately carved gables contrasting with the openwork tympanums. The 13C statues adorning the doorways are from four workshops employed successively.

Central doorway (the Virgin's portal)

This is composed of several elements starting with, against the upright post, the smiling Virgin Mary; on the right, the Visitation and the Annunciation; on the left, Jesus at the Temple; on the gable, the Coronation of the Virgin. Above the rose-window is the scene depicting David slaying Goliath; the **kings' gallery** includes 56 statues (4.5m high); in the centre, Clovis' christening.

North side

On the north side of the cathedral the **flying buttresses** are surmounted by recesses, each containing a large angel with open wings, among them the famous "smiling angel".

North transept

The façade has three **doorways** decorated with statues which are older than those of the west front. The right doorway comes from the Romanesque cathedral: the tympanum is adorned with the Virgin in glory framed by foliage. The upright post of the middle portal is decorated with a statue of Pope Calixtus. The embrasures of the left doorway have six fine statues representing the Apostles and the **tympanum** is carved with scenes of the Last Judgement.

East end

From cours Anatole-France, there is a fine **view**★ of the east end of the cathedral with its radiating chapels surmounted by arcaded galleries and its superposed flying buttresses.

Interior

Inside, the cathedral is well lit and its proportions are remarkable (138m long and 38m high); the impression of loftiness is enhanced by the narrowness of the nave in relation to its length and by the succession of very pointed transverse arches. The three-storey elevations of the **nave** consist of the main **arcading** supported by round piers, a blind **triforium** (level with the roofing of the aisles) and tall **clerestory windows**, divided into lancets by mullions. **Capitals** are decorated with floral motifs. The chancel has only two bays but the space used for services extends into the nave as there was always a large number of canons and a lot of space was needed for coronations. The chancel used to be closed off by a rood screen on which the royal throne was placed. **Pillars** get gradually narrower and closer together, thus increasing the impression of height. The **radiating chapels** are linked by a passage typical of the region's architectural style.

The inside of the **west front**★★ was the work of Gaucher from Reims. The large rose-window (12min diameter) is located above the triforium arcading backed by stained-glass windows of similar shape. A smaller rose decorates the doorway.

On either side, a number of recesses contain statues. Floral motifs, similar to those of the nave capitals, complete the decoration. The very well preserved **inside of the central doorway** has scenes of the life of the Virgin and the life of John the Baptist.

Stained glass★★

The 13C stained-glass windows suffered considerable damage: some were replaced by clear glass in the 18C, others were destroyed during the First World War. Those of the **apse** are still intact: in the centre is the donor with suffragan bishops on either side. The great 13C **rose-window**, dedicated to the Virgin Mary, looks best in the setting sun. Jacques Simon, a member of the family of stained-glass makers who have been restoring the cathedral for generations, has reconstructed some of the missing windows, notably the wine-growers' window (**a**). His daughter Brigitte Simon-Marcq made a series of abstract win-

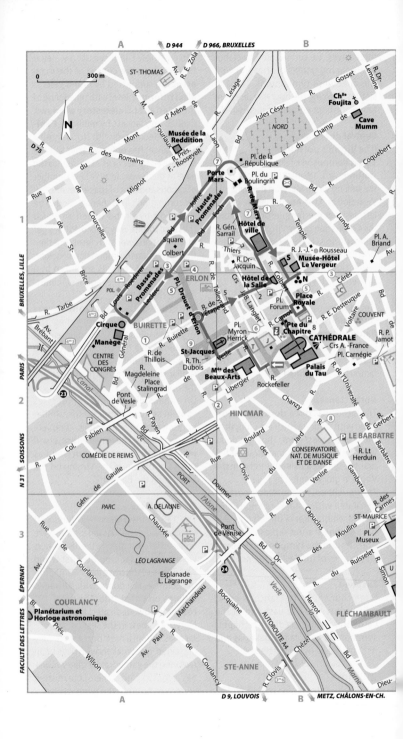

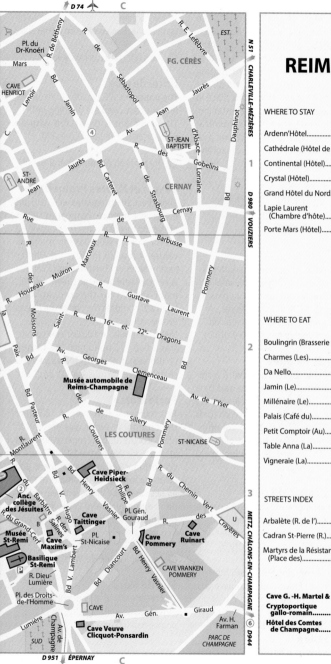

REIMS

WHERE TO STAY

Ardenn'Hôtel............................①
Cathédrale (Hôtel de la).........②
Continental (Hôtel)................③
Crystal (Hôtel)........................④
Grand Hôtel du Nord.............⑤
Lapie Laurent
 (Chambre d'hôte)...............⑥
Porte Mars (Hôtel)..................⑦

WHERE TO EAT

Boulingrin (Brasserie du)......①
Charmes (Les)........................②
Da Nello.................................③
Jamin (Le)..............................④
Millénaire (Le).......................⑤
Palais (Café du)......................⑥
Petit Comptoir (Au)...............⑦
Table Anna (La)......................⑧
Vigneraie (La)........................⑨

STREETS INDEX

Arbalète (R. de l')............................2
Cadran St-Pierre (R.)........................5
Martyrs de la Résistance
 (Place des)...................................8

Cave G. -H. Martel & Cie........B
Cryptoportique
 gallo-romain.....................N
Hôtel des Comtes
 de Champagne..................S

dows including one entitled the River Jordan to the right of the christening font (**b**) in the south transept.

In 1974, **Marc Chagall** decorated the apsidal chapel (**c**) with luminous blue-dominated stained-glass made in the Simon workshop: in the centre, Abraham's Sacrifice and the Crucifixion; on the left, a Tree of Jesse and on the right, great events which took place in the cathedral such as Clovis' christening. The cathedral has a 15C **astronomical clock**. Each hour struck starts two processions: the Adoration of the Magi and the Flight into Egypt.

❧ WALKING TOUR

TOWN CENTRE
Allow 2h.

▶ From the square in front of the cathedral, walk along rue Rockefeller and turn right onto rue Chanzy, passing the Musée des Beaux-Arts (♿*see Sights). Turn left on pedestrian rue de Vesle. Turn right onto rue Max-Dormoy.*

Église St-Jacques
The 13C–14C Gothic nave with a traditional triforium is prolonged by a Flamboyant Gothic chancel (early 16C) framed by two Renaissance chapels (mid-16C) with Corinthian columns. The modern abstract stained-glass was designed by Vieira da Silva (side chapels) and Sima (chancel).

Place Drouet-d'Erlon
Named after one of Napoleon's generals, this lively pedestrian-friendly space lined with cafés, restaurants, hotels and cinemas is the heart of the city.

▶ At the Fontaine Subé, turn right onto rue de l'Étape and continue as far as rue de l'Arbalète.

Hôtel Saint-Jean-Baptiste de la Salle★
This Renaissance house, built in 1545–56, is the birthplace of **Jean-Baptiste de la Salle** (♿*see above*). The harmoni-ous façade, adorned with Doric pilasters on the ground floor and Ionic ones on the first floor, is flanked by a pavilion whose carriage entrance is decorated by statues of Adam and Eve on either side.

▶ Turn left onto rue du Dr-Jacquin.

Hôtel de ville
The imposing 17C façade survived the fire that destroyed the building in 1917. The pediment is decorated with an equestrian bas-relief of Louis XIII.

▶ Turn left on rue du Général-Sarail.

Basses et Hautes Promenades
These vast, shady squares were laid out in the 18C to replace the moat and glacis of the old fortifications. They provide a useful parking area close to the town centre. A fun fair invades the Hautes Promenades at Christmas and Easter.

A remarkable wrought-iron railing, made in 1774 for the coronation of Louis XVI, stands at the end of the Basses Promenades.

Nearby on boulevard du Général-Leclerc, stand two 19C buildings, the **Cirque** (1 100 seats) and the **Manège** (600 seats) where various events are held.

Porte Mars★
This triumphal arch (height: 13.5m) of the Corinthian order was erected in honour of the Roman Emperor Augustus after the 3C. During the Middle Ages, it was incorporated into the ramparts and used as a town gate. It consists of three arches decorated inside with bas-reliefs depicting Jupiter and Leda, as well as the founders of Rome, Romulus and Remus.

▶ Walk along rue de Mars.

Rue de Mars
The façade of No. 6 is decorated with mosaic panels illustrating the Champagne-making process.

Palais du Tau and the cathedral

Hôtel des Comtes de Champagne

This Gothic mansion belongs to the Taittinger Champagne house.

▷ The street leads to place du Forum.

Cryptoportique gallo-romain

This large half-buried Gallo-Roman monument, dating from the 3C, stands on the site of the ancient city's forum. The lower level was used as a grain store and the upper level for promenades.

▷ Take rue Colbert to place Royale.

Place Royale★

This arcaded square with balustraded roofs, designed by Legendre in 1760, is characteristic of the Louis XVI style. The Hôtel des Fermes, on the south side, houses administrative offices. The statue of Louis XV by Pigalle, which used to stand in the centre of the square, was destroyed during the Revolution and the holy coronation phial was smashed on the pedestal; another statue by Cartellier replaced the original during the Restoration (1814–30).

▷ Turn right along rue Carnot.

Porte du Chapitre

This 16C gate, flanked by two corbelled turrets, formed the main entrance to the chapter house.

▷ Go through the gateway to return to the cathedral.

SIGHTS
PALAIS DU TAU★★

2 place du Cardinal-Luçon. &⏱*Jan–Apr and Sept–Dec daily 9.30am–12.30pm, 2–5.30pm; May–Aug daily except Mon 9.30am–6.30pm.* ⏱*1 Jan, 1 May, 1 and 11 Nov, 25 Dec.* ⌷€*8.* ℘*03 26 47 81 79. www.palais-du-tau.fr.*
The archbishops' palace owes its strange name to its T shape, resembling ancient episcopal croziers; it contains the cathedral treasury and some of the original statues.

The building was remodelled in 1670 by Robert de Cotte. Severely damaged in September 1914, at the same time as the cathedral, it was restored over a considerable number of years.

The vaulted Gothic **lower room** to the left of the entrance contains an exhibition showing the evolution of the cathedral site and of the canons' district, which has disappeared. From here, stone fragments of the rood screen can be seen in the lower chapel.

On the first floor, the **Galerie du couronnement de la Vierge (1)** contains some of the 17 wool-and-silk tapestries offered by Archbishop Robert de Lenoncourt to the Cathedral in 1530, together with large 13C statues of kings from the north and south transepts.

The **Salle du roi de Juda (2)** contains a huge 14C statue of Judah from the kings' gallery), tapestries and the upper part of an angel with spread wings.

The **Salon carré (3)** is adorned with 17C tapestries from Reims, depicting scenes from Christ's childhood, . The two large statues of the Magdalene and St Peter came from the west front.

Note, in the **Salle du Cantique des Cantiques (4)**, four precious 17C hand-embroidered hangings.

The **Salle des petites sculptures (5)** houses masks and gargoyles, as well as the statues of Abraham and Aaron from the south doorway.

The **Salle du Goliath (6)** contains monumental statues of St Paul, St James, Goliath (5.4m) wearing a coat of mail, as well as allegorical representations of the Synagogue (blindfolded) and the Church, damaged by shelling. Fragments of the rood-screen, demolished in 1744, can also be seen.

The **Salle du Tau (7)** was used for the festivities that followed coronations. Lined with cloth bearing fleurs-de-lys,

the symbol of French royalty, and decorated with two huge 15C Arras tapestries illustrating the story of Clovis, it is has an elegant vaulted ceiling, shaped like a ship's hull.

The **Salle Charles X (8)** is devoted to the coronation of 1825. It contains the royal cloak as well as garments used by heralds and a painting of *Charles X in regal dress* by Gérard.

The **treasury (9)** is exhibited in two rooms: the left one houses royal gift, such as Charlemagne's 9C talisman, which contains a piece of the True Cross, the coronation chalice, the reliquary of the Holy Thorn, carved out of crystal, the 15C reliquary of the Resurrection and the reliquary of St Ursula, a delicate cornelian vase decorated with enamelled statuettes dating from 1505.

The right-hand room contains ornaments used for the coronation of Charles X: the reliquary of the Holy Phial, a large offering vase and two gold and silver hosts, the necklace of the Order of the Holy Spirit worn by Louis-Philippe and a copy of Louis XV's crown.

The 13C doorway of the **palatine chapel (10)** is surmounted by the Adoration of the Magi. On the altar are the cross and six gilded candelabra made for the wedding of Napoleon and Marie-Louise.

BASILIQUE ST-REMI★★

Remi was buried in 533 in a small chapel dedicated to St Christopher. Shortly afterwards, a basilica was constructed. In the 8C, the Abbaye de St-Remi was founded here by a group of Benedictine monks. Work on the present basilica began c 1007 and was consecrated by Pope Leo IX in 1049. The chancel was built over the grave of St Remi.

The building was remodelled in the late 12C and the Gothic basilica we see today dates from that period. A few minor changes occurred in the 16C and 17C. Used as a barn during the Revolution, the church was restored in the 19C and again after the First World War. Many archbishops of Reims and the first kings of France were buried inside; the Holy Phial was kept in the church.

Statue of Eve, Salle du Goliath, Palais du Tau

© Godong/UIG/age fotostock

Nave, Basilique St-Remi

© isogood/iStockphoto.com

Interior★★★

The basilica is very narrow (26m) in relation to its length (122m) and dimly lit, which makes it look even longer. The 11C nave consists of 11 bays with rounded main arches resting on piers whose capitals are decorated with animals and foliage. Note the crown of light symbolising the life of St Remi, a copy of the original destroyed during the Revolution.

The four-storey Gothic **chancel** is closed off by a 17C Renaissance screen and lit by 12C stained-glass windows depicting the Crucifixion, the Apostles, Prophets and archbishops of Reims.

Behind the altar, St Remi's grave, rebuilt in 1847, has retained its 17C statues and representing **St Remi**, Clovis and the 12 peers who took part in the coronation. Colonnades surrounding the chancel separate the ambulatory from the **radiating chapels** whose entrance is marked by two isolated columns. The polychrome motifs decorating the capitals are the original ones and the statues date from the 13C and 18C.

The 45 stone slabs, inlaid with lead (biblical scenes), which can be seen in the first bay of the north aisle, come from the former Abbaye St-Nicaise.

The south transept houses an Entombment dating from 1530 and the altarpiece of the Three Christenings (1610) showing Christ between Constantine and Clovis.

Musée-abbaye St-Remi★★

53 rue Simon. Mon–Fri 2–6.30pm, weekends 2–7pm. 1 Jan, 1 May, 14 Jul, 1 and 11 Nov, 25 Dec. €5, no charge 1st Sun of the month. 03 26 35 36 90.

The former royal abbey comprises a group of well-restored 17C and 18C buildings and some remnants of the medieval abbey.

Ground floor

The main courtyard leads to a building with an imposing Louis XVI-style façade. The cloisters, designed by Jean Bonhomme, date from 1709; they adjoin the basilica whose flying buttresses overlap into one of the galleries.

The **chapter house** has some magnificent Romanesque capitals. The former 17C refectory and kitchen contain the **Gallo-Roman collections** illustrating the ancient city of Durocortorum which later became Reims. Note the fine mosaics, the large relief map (1:2 000) and **Jovin's tomb★**, a splendid 3C and 4C Roman sarcophagus.

First floor

A superb staircase (1778) leads to the gallery where the **St-Remi tapestries★★** are exhibited; commissioned by Archbishop Robert de Lenoncourt for the basilica, they were made between 1523 and 1531. Each one consists of several scenes depicting various episodes of St Remi's life and the miracles he accomplished.

On the left of the staircase, four rooms (10–13 and 25) are devoted to the **history of the site** on which the abbey was built: 12C stone and bronze sculptures, and 17C enamel work from the Limoges area illustrating the lives of St Timothy, Apollinarius and Maurus.

Follow the **regional archaeological trail** (rooms 20–27) from the **Palaeolithic** and **Neolithic** periods (tools and funeral objects) via the **Protohistoric** period (Bronze Age to the Roman conquest, including objects discovered in chariot graves and Gaulish necropolises) and up to **Gallo-Roman times** (handicraft, agriculture, clothing, jewellery, medicine, games, household items).

The **Merovingian** period is represented by jewellery, pottery, glassware and weapons found in nearby necropolises. The exhibits displayed in the flying-buttress gallery were seized during the Revolution: St Gibrien's crozier, and the 14C Virgin's triptych, carved out of ivory.

The next gallery shows the evolution of **medieval sculpture** from the 11C to the 16C; note the delicately carved tympanum and the carved-wood console representing Samson and the Lion.

The **Gothic room** contains fragments of destroyed lay and religious buildings: carvings from the Église St-Nicaise, and the reconstructed façade of the 13C Maison des Musiciens (House of Musicians), formerly on rue de Mars.

A large room contains uniforms, military gear, weapons and documents illustrating the main events of the city's **military history**, note the glass cabinets devoted to the Champagne regiments, the famous battles of the Revolutionary period, and the military parade which took place on the occasion of Charles X's coronation in 1825.

ADDITIONAL SIGHTS
Musée des Beaux-Arts★
8 rue Chanzy. ⏱*Daily except Tue 10am–noon, 2–6pm.* ⏱*1 Jan, 1 May, 14 Jul, 1 and 11 Nov, 25 Dec.* ✆€5. ✆*03 26 35 36 00. www.reims.fr.*

The art museum, housed in the 18C former Abbaye St-Denis, covers the period from the Renaissance to the present.

Ground floor
The highlight is 13 portraits (16C) of German princes by **Cranach the Elder** and **Cranach the Younger;** these are extremely realistic drawings enhanced by gouache and oil paint. Admire also 27 landscapes by **Corot** (1796–1875) and the portrait of a seated Italian youth, painted by Corot during his stay in Rome in 1826. The Flemish, Dutch and French schools are also represented. There are also ceramics from the principal French and foreign manufacturers and some sculptures by Reims artist, René de Saint-Marceaux (1845–1915).

First floor
The first room contains some strange 15C and 16C grisaille paintings heightened by colours, which include four series of picturesque scenes (the *Apostles*, *Christ's Vengeance* and *Christ's Passion*). They may have been used as sets for mystery plays or lined along the way from St-Remi Basilica to the cathedral on coronation days.

The following rooms are devoted to French painting from the 17C on.

Musée-hôtel le Vergeur★
36 place du Forum. ⏱*Daily except Mon 2–6pm, but check website for dates affected by exhibitions.* ⏱*1 Jan, 1 May, 14 Jul, 1 Nov, 25 Dec.* ✆€5. ✆*03 26 47 20 75. www.museelevergeur.com.*

This 13C–16C mansion, which belonged to **Nicolas Le Vergeur**, a wealthy grain merchant, has a picturesque gabled façade with a timber-framed upper part over a stone base. A Renaissance wing, overlooking the garden, has an interesting frieze carved with battle scenes. The 13C great hall and the floor above it contain paintings, engravings and plans concerning the history of Reims and the splendour of coronation ceremonies.

The living quarters, decorated with panelling and antique furniture, recall the life of Baron **Hugues Krafft**, a patron of the arts who lived in the mansion until his death in 1935 and bequeathed it together with its contents to the Friends of Old Reims. One of the drawing rooms contains an exceptional collection of **engravings by Dürer★** including the Apocalypse and the Great Passion.

Ancien collège des Jésuites

1 place Museux. ○*Daily 2–6pm.* ⊗*No charge.* ✆*03 26 85 51 50. www.ville-reims.com.*

In 1606, the Jesuits were allowed by King Henri IV to found a college in Reims; they then erected the chapel (1617–78). Clinging to one of the walls and still giving grapes is a 300-year-old vine, brought back from Palestine by the Jesuits. The college prospered until the Jesuits were expelled from France in 1762; it was then turned into a general hospital.

The tour includes the **refectory**, decorated with 17C woodwork and paintings by Jean Helart depicting the Life of St Ignatius Loyola and St Francis-Xavier. Note the magnificent table top carved out of a single piece of oak; a branch of the same tree was used for the table of the public prosecutor's office upstairs.

A Renaissance staircase leads to the **library★**, elaborately adorned with Baroque woodwork and a coffered ceiling supported by garlands, scrolls and cherubs. It was the setting chosen by Patrice Chéreau for his film *La Reine Margot* with Isabelle Adjani and Daniel Auteuil. Note the small reading cubicles and the table with hoof-shaped feet. The tour of the underground galleries (refreshing in summer) includes a 17C cellar, a 12C gallery and a Gallo-Roman gallery. One wing of the former college houses the Planetarium, the other is a temporary exhibition space for the **Fonds régional d'art contemporain**.

Planétarium et Horloge astronomique

49 av. du Général-de-Gaulle. &○*Planetarium: Wed, Sat–Sun afternoons; check website for variable details. Some programmes are more adapted for children than others. Children under 5 are admitted only to programmes appropriate to their age*

group. ○*1 Jan, 1 May, 14 Jul, 1 and 11 Nov, 25 Dec.* ⊗€6, *no charge 1st Sun of the month.* ✆*03 26 35 34 70.*

A wing of the former Jesuit college houses a planetarium and an astronomical clock made between 1930 and 1952 by Jean Legros, a native of Reims.

Chapelle Foujita★

33 rue du Champ-de-Mars. &○*May–Oct daily except Tue 10am–noon, 2–6pm.* ○*1 Jan, 1 May, 14 Jul, 1 and 11 Nov, 25 Dec.* ⊗€5, *no charge 1st Sun of the month.* ✆*03 26 40 06 96.*

Designed and decorated by **Léonard Foujita** (1886–1968) and donated by the Champagne firm Mumm, the chapel was inaugurated in 1966. Stained glass and frescoes depicting Biblical scenes celebrate the mystical inspiration felt by the Japanese painter in the Basilique St-Remi.

Foujita, who belonged to the early-20C school of art known as the École de Paris, converted to Christianity and was baptised in Reims Cathedral.

Musée de la Reddition

12 rue Franklin-Roosevelt. &○*Daily except Tue 10am–noon, 2–6pm.* ○*1 Jan, 1 May, 14 Jul, 1 and 11 Nov, 25 Dec.* ⊗€4, *no charge 1st Sun of the month.* ✆*03 26 47 84 19. www.reims-tourisme.com.*

General Eisenhower established his headquarters in this technical college towards the end of the Second World War and this is where the German capitulation act was signed on 7 May 1945. The Salle de la Signature (Signing Room) has remained as it was at the time.

Musée automobile de Reims-Champagne

≛≛ *84 avenue Georges-Clemenceau.* &○*Daily except Tue: Mar–Oct 10am–noon, 2–6pm; rest of the year Wed–Mon 10am–noon, 2–5pm.* ○*25 Dec–1 Jan.* ⊗€9 *(children under 10, €4).* ✆*03 26 82 83 84. www.musee-automobile-reims-champagne.com.*

Created in 1985, this car museum houses a collection of 100 vintage cars and prototypes in excellent condition including famous makes such as Delahaye, Salmson, Porsche, Jaguar, a Sizaire-Berwick limousine dating from 1919 and a Messier coupé from 1929. Models, pedal cars, posters, early-20C advertisements and enamelled plates are also displayed.

EXCURSIONS

Fort de la Pompelle

9km/5.6mi SE by N 44 towards Chalons-en-Champagne. 👍🕐*Daily except Mon: Apr–Sept 10am–6pm; Oct–Mar 10am–5pm.* 🕐*Mid-Dec–mid-Jan.* 🎟€5. 📞*03 26 49 11 85.*

The fort sits on top of a 120m-high hill. It was built between 1880 and 1883 for the defence of Reims. At the beginning of the First World War, it was under constant German attack but its resistance contributed to the victory of the Battle of the Marne.

A path leads from the lower car park to the fort, which has remained in the state it was in at the end of the war. Guns are displayed in front of the fort and trenches and casemates are visible on the south side. The **museum** houses mementoes of the war: medals, uniforms, weapons and a collection of 560 **German helmets★**.

Grinyland – Parc nature de Sept-Saulx★

22km/13.7mi SE by N 44 towards Châlons-en-Champagne. 👍🕐*Check website for seasonal opening hours and charges.* 📞*03 26 03 24 91. www.grinyland.com.*

👪 This nature park, situated in the east of the Parc naturel regional de la Montagne de Reims, has a water theme. Visitors can cross a **peat bog** via a succession of wooden footpaths winding their way just above the water. These unusual paths are lined with willows and reeds as well as explanatory panels and games. The park is dotted with thematic islets, including bamboo island, flower island and duck island.

Canoes are available for a trip along the canals (1km/0.6mi); picnic areas equipped with tables and play areas are also at the disposal of visitors (open-air dancing at weekends in summer).

🚗 DRIVING TOUR

Massif de St-Thierry
50km/31mi round tour. Allow 1h30.

▶ Leave Reims along avenue de Laon, N 44 and take the first left (D 26) after La Neuvillette.

The road climbs up the Massif de St-Thierry, a section of the Île-de-France cuesta jutting into the plain of Champagne. The area has a wealth of Romanesque porch churches.

St-Thierry

This village overlooking the plain of Reims has a 12C church with a porch characteristic of Champagne Romanesque architecture. In the 18C Archbishop Talleyrand, uncle of the famous 19C minister, built a château on the site of a 6C abbey. It was demolished on the eve of the Revolution. Only five Romanesque pillars of the chapter house, remain.

▶ Continue to Trigny along D 26 via Chenay with fine views of Reims.

Trigny

This picturesque village was the starting point of the route taken by kings on their way to be crowned in Reims. A viewpoint offers a fine panorama.

▶ In Trigny, turn right onto D 530 leading to Hermonville.

Hermonville

An imposing arcaded porch extends across the west front of the **church** (late 12C). The doorway recess shelters an 18C statue of the Virgin Mary. The Early Gothic interior offers a striking contrast with the 18C baldaquined altar.

▶ Detour via D 530 N to Cauroy-lès-Hermonville.

Cauroy-lès-Hermonville

The early 12C **church** is worth seeing for its wood-panelled Romanesque nave and Champagne-style porch, said to be the oldest in the region.

▶ Return to Hermonville and drive W along D 30 across the highest point of the Massif de St-Thierry. In Bouvancourt, turn left onto D 375.

Just before reaching Pévy, enjoy the charming bird's-eye **view** of the village nestling in the valley.

Pévy

This village has an interesting **church** whose Romanesque nave contrasts with the Gothic chancel. The interior contains a Romanesque font and a 15C stone altarpiece.

▶ Follow D 75 down to the River Vesle and cross over at Jonchery; N 31 leads back to Reims.

ADDRESSES

🏨 STAY

🛏 **Ardenn'Hôtel** – *6 r. Caqué.* ℘*03 26 47 42 38. www.ardennhotel.fr. 14 rooms.* This hotel with an attractive brick façade has many points in its favour. You will certainly be won over by its location in a quiet little town-centre street, the unfailing cleanliness of the tastefully decorated rooms and the smiling service.

🛏 **Chambre d'hôte Lapie Laurent** – *1 r. Jeanne-d'Arc, 51360 Val-de-Vesle. 21km/12.5mi SE of Reims on N 44 and left on D 326.* ℘*03 26 03 92 88. Closed 15 Dec–15 Jan.* 🍴*. 5 rooms.* Five lovely pastel-toned rooms are available on this farm in the heart of a village. The attractive decor mixes old and modern styles and there's an immaculate downstairs breakfast room.

🛏🛏 **Grand Hôtel du Nord** – *75 pl. Drouet-d'Erlon.* ℘*03 26 47 39 03. www. hotel-nord-reims.com. Closed Christmas holidays. 50 rooms.* Mostly refurbished rooms in a 1920s building set on Reims' pedestrian main square. Many restaurants, and much going on nearby.

🛏🛏 **Hôtel de la Cathédrale** – *20 r. Libergier.* ℘*03 26 47 28 46. www.hotel-cathedrale-reims.fr. 17 rooms.* This smart but welcoming hotel stands in one of the streets that lead to the cathedral. The small rooms have comfortable beds and are bright and cheerful, while the breakfast room is decorated with old engravings.

🛏🛏 **Hôtel Crystal** – *86 pl. Drouet-d'Erlon.* ℘*03 26 88 44 44. www.hotel-crystal.fr. 69 rooms.* An astonishing haven of greenery right in the centre of town is an attractive feature of this 1920s house. The bedrooms all have excellent bedding. Breakfast is served in a delightful flowered courtyard-garden in summer.

🛏🛏🛏 **Hôtel Continental** – *93 pl. Drouet-d'Erlon.* ℘*03 26 40 39 35. www. grandhotelcontinental.com. Closed 21 Dec–7 Jan. 61 rooms.* The attractive façade of this central hotel adorns the city's liveliest square. The rooms, in varying styles, are reached by a splendid staircase (if you're after calm avoid the rooms overlooking bd du Général-Leclerc). Elegant Belle Epoque sitting rooms.

🛏🛏🛏 **Hôtel Porte Mars** – *2 pl. de la République.* ℘*03 26 40 28 35. www.hotel-portemars.com. 24 rooms.* It's a pleasure to drink tea near the fire in the cosy sitting room, or enjoy a drink in the sophisticated bar. A delicious breakfast is also served in the attractive glass-roofed dining room decorated with photographs and old mirrors. Each of the comfortable, well-sound-proofed rooms have a personal touch

🍴 EAT

🍽🍽 **Brasserie du Boulingrin** – *31 r. de Mars.* ℘*03 26 40 96 22. www.boulingrin. fr. Closed Sun.* This Art Deco restaurant dating from 1925 is an institution in Reims. The owner is much in evidence, overseeing operations and ensuring a convivial mood. The menu is inventive and the prices reasonable.

🍽🍽 **La Table Anna** – *6 r. Gambetta.* ℘*03 26 89 12 12. www.annas-latableamoureuse. com. Closed Wed eve, Sun eve and all day Mon.* Champagne takes pride of place in the window of this establishment next door to the music conservatory. Some of the paintings adorning the walls are the work of the owner, an artist at heart. Traditional dishes are renewed with the seasons.

🍽🍽 **La Vigneraie** – *14 r. de Thillois.* ℘*03 26 88 67 27. www.vigneraie.com. Closed Sun eve, all day Mon, and Wed lunch.* La Vigneraie, situated just off pl. Drouet-d'Erlon, boasts a fantastic collection of carafes. Tasty classical menu and fine wine list. Excellent value-for-money.

⊜⊜🍽 **Le Jamin** – *18 bd. Jamin. ℘03 26 07 37 30. www.lejamin.com. Closed all day Mon, Sun eve, Wed eve.* In this little local bistro, perfectly mastered traditional cooking is served in a rustic dining room. Look for the good-value daily specials on the blackboard.

⊜⊜🍽 **Café du Palais** – *14 pl. Myron-Herrick. ℘03 26 47 52 54. www. cafedupalais.fr. Closed all day Sun and all day Mon.* This lively café near the cathedral was founded in 1930, and still has its original glass roof. Popular with locals for its generous salads, daily dishes and home-made patisseries. You can also enjoy a reasonably priced glass of champagne.

⊜⊜🍽 **Les Charmes** – *11 r. Brûlart. ℘03 26 85 37 63. www.restaurant lescharmes.com. Closed Sun eve, Wed eve and all day Mon.* Close to the famous champagne cellars and St-Remi basilica, this convivial family restaurant is decorated with paintings on wood. Good selection of whiskies.

⊜⊜🍽 **Au Petit Comptoir** – *17 r. de Mars. ℘03 26 40 58 58. www.au-petit-comptoir.fr. Closed Sun and 24–31 Dec–2 Jan.* This trendy restaurant behind the town hall has a striking modern interior to match the updated dishes of Patrice Maillot.

⊜⊜🍽 **Da Nello** – *39 r. Cérès. ℘03 26 47 33 25.* A Mediterranean welcome awaits you at this Italian restaurant where the tables all have a view of the kitchen and the pizza oven is right in the centre of the room. Fresh pasta, grills and daily specials according to what the market has to offer… all served with an authentic Italian accent.

⊜⊜🍽 **Le Millénaire** – *4 r. Bertin. ℘03 26 08 26 62. www.lemillenaire.com. Closed Sun.* A spacious dining room near place Royale is hung with modern paintings. Appetising modern cooking.

CHAMPAGNE CELLARS IN REIMS

The famous **Champagne firms★★** are gathered in the Champ de Mars district and along the limestone slopes of St-Nicaise hill, full of galleries known as crayères, often dating from the Gallo-Roman period. The depth and extent of the galleries (totalling 250km/155mi) makes them ideal Champagne cellars.

Pommery – *5 place du Gén.-Gouraud. Open Easter to mid-Nov guided tour (1h) 9.30am–7pm, Sat and Sun 10am–7pm; mid-Nov to Easter 9.30am–6pm, Sat and Sun 10am–6pm. Closed Christmas school holidays. ℘03 26 61 62 56. www.pommery. com.* This firm, founded in 1836 by Narcisse Gréno and Louis Alexandre Pommery, was expanded by the Pommery's widow who inaugurated Brut Champagne and built the present buildings in 1878. She also linked the Gallo-Roman crayères by building 18km/11mi of galleries, and acquired many vineyards so that Pommery now owns 300ha of the finest Champagne vines. The tour enables visitors to discover the different stages of Champagne-making through galleries decorated with 19C sculptures, and to see a 75 000l tun by Émile Gallé, from 1904.

Taittinger – *9 place St-Niçaise. Guided tour (1h): Apr–mid-Nov daily 9.30am–5.30pm; Nov–Apr 9.30am–1pm, 1.45–5.30pm. Closed 1 Jan, 25 Dec. ℘03 26 85 84 33. www.taittinger.com.* In 1734, the Fourneaux family of wine merchants launched into the production of sparkling wine made according to Dom Pérignon's methods. In 1932, Pierre Taittinger took over the management of the firm which was then named after him. Today, the Taittinger vineyards extend over 250ha and the firm owns 6 grape-harvesting centres on the Montagne de Reims, the Château de la Marquetterie in Pierry, the Hôtel des Comtes de Champagne in Reims (⟳*see REIMS*) and superb cellars. Visitors can enjoy a detailed tour of the cellars among 15 million bottles maturing in the cool Gallo-Roman galleries and in the crypts of the former 13C Abbaye St-Nicaise, destroyed during the Revolution.

Veuve Clicquot – *1 place des Droits-de-l'Homme. Guided tour and tasting (1h30) – see website for indivdual tours at varying prices, which start at €25 per person. ℘03 26 89 53 90. www.veuve-clicquot.fr.* This firm, founded in 1772 by Philippe Clicquot, was considerably expanded by his son's widow (whose maiden name was Ponsardin). In 1816, she introduced *remuage* into the process of Champagne-making. Today, Veuve Clicquot-Ponsardin, which owns 265ha

Mosaics showing Champagne making, rue de Mars

of vines and exports three quarters of its production, is one of the best-known Champagne firms outside France.

Ruinart – *4 rue des Crayères. Guided tour (1hr 30min) daily by request to the "visites et réceptions" department. Prices depend on the programme.* ℘*03 26 77 51 21. www.ruinart.com.* Founded in 1729, this Champagne firm prospered during the Restoration period (1814–30) and again after 1949, having gone through years of decline during the two world wars. Today Ruinart belongs to the Moët-Hennessy group. Its three levels of Gallo-Roman galleries are particularly interesting.

Piper-Heidsieck – *51 boulevard Henri-Vasnier. Open 9.30–12.30pm, 2–6pm. Closed Jan–Feb and 25 Dec.* ℘*03 26 84 43 44. www.piper-heidsieck.com.* Take a gondola car to tour these cellars, which extend 16km/10mi underground. The various stages of Champagne-making are explained by an audio-visual film presented by the firm, founded in 1785.

Mumm – *34 rue du Champ-de-Mars. Times vary throughout the year, and charges depend on the tour chosen – see website for details.* ℘*03 26 49 59 70. www.mumm.com.* After its creation in 1827, this firm prospered throughout the 19C in Europe and in America; today, it owns 218ha of vines and its cellars (open to the public) extend over a total distance of 25km/16mi. Three different tours are offered, with varying degrees of information on the champagne-making process.

Maxim's – *17 rue des Créneaux. Guided tour (1h) 10am–7pm. Closed 1 Jan, 25 Dec.*

℘*03 26 82 70 67.* Tour of the galleries dug between the 4C and 15C: a visit to the cellars is followed by a film and ends, like every good event, with a Champagne tasting. The museum houses a collection of machinery and tools used during the different stages of wine-growing.

SHOPPING

Deleans – *20 r. Cérès.* ℘*03 26 47 56 35.* Cocoa-based specialities have been made here in the old-fashioned way since 1874. Try the Néluskos (chocolate-coated cherries in cognac) and petits bouchons de champagne.

Fossier – *25 cours Jean-Baptiste Langlet.* ℘*03 26 47 59 84. Mon 2–7pm, Tue–Sat 9am–7pm.* Founded in 1756, the biscuit and chocolate maker Fossier creates the ultimate in Reims confectionary (biscuits roses and croquignoles). Pay a visit to the shop and factory and learn how to "piouler" (stir) your glass of champagne correctly.

La Petite Friande – *15 cours Jean-Baptiste Langlet.* ℘*03 26 47 50 44. Summer: Tue–Sat: 10am–noon, 2–7pm; winter: Mon–Sat 10am–noon, 2–7pm.* For more than 170 years, the establishment has prided itself on being the specialist in authentic bouchons de champagne, made with *marc de champagne.* Another of its delicious creations are *bulles à la vieille fine de la Marne.*

CALENDAR

Flâneries musicales d'été – *Jul and Aug.* More than 150 free concerts all over the town, including shows by major classical musicians in some of the town's most prestigious venues.

Marais de St-Gond

This marshland, situated below the Île-de-France cuesta and covering more than 3 000ha, owes its name to a 7C coenobite. In September 1914, the area and the surrounding heights were the scene of fierce fighting between Von Bülow's second German army and **General Foch's** 9th French army. Foch eventually succeeded in driving the Germans back to the River Marne.

🚗 DRIVING TOUR

Round tour starting from Mondement

36km/22mi. Allow 1h30.

This drive goes through lonely expanses of marshland, which has been partly drained and turned into pastures or arable land. The south-facing slopes of the limestone hills around the marsh produce a fine white wine.

Mondement

Mondement hill (alt 223m) was at the heart of the fighting in September 1914.

🧭 **Michelin Map:** Local map 306: F-9/10.

🚶 **Walking:** A botanic trail starting from Reuves allows you to discover the diversity of marshland fauna and flora.

The German troops eventually withdrew after suffering heavy losses. The monument commemorates these events.

Allemant

This tiny village clinging to the hillside has a surprisingly large Flamboyant Gothic **church** with a double transept and a high tower over the crossing.

▶ Follow D 39 to Le Mesnil then D 45.

Coizard

Charming Romanesque village church.

▶ Drive east along D 43.

Villevenard

Wine-growing village. The tastefully-restored 12C church has a Romanesque nave and a fine octagonal tower.

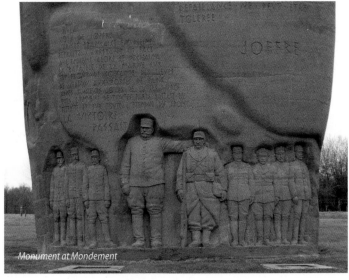
Monument at Mondement

© ADT Marne - Coll.ADT Marne

Ste-Menehould

Ste-Menehould is famous for its speciality of pigs' trotters and as the town where Louis XVI stopped to dine when attempting to flee Paris during the French Revolution in June 1791. A young boy recognised the monarch and the king was arrested at Varennes (& see ARGONNE).

SIGHTS
Place du Général-Leclerc
Split into two by the main road (N 3), the square is lined by fine pink-brick buildings, including the **town hall** (1730), designed by Philippe de la Force who rebuilt the city after the fire of 1719.

Butte du Château
The upper town has a villagey feel with its low timber-framed, flower-decked houses. The 13C–15C **Église Notre Dame** sits in a cemetery.

Musée d'Art et d'Histoire
Pl. du Général-Leclerc. Oct–May Tue–Fri 2–6pm, Wed 10am–noon, 2–6pm, Sat 10am–5pm, Sun 2–6pm; Jun–Sept Tue 2–6pm, Wed–Sun 10am–12.30pm, 2–6pm. Dec–Jan, 1 May and 11 Nov. €5. 03 26 60 62 97.
Housed in an 18C mansion, the museum contains various regional collections.

EXCURSION
Château de Braux-Ste-Cohière★
5.5km/3.4mi W by N3 and D384.
Not open to the public.
The buildings were erected in the 16C and 17C by Philippe de Thomassin, governor of Châlons for the Household Cavalry. In 1792, General Dumouriez made his headquarters here to prepare for the Battle of Valmy against the Prussians. Today, the vast moated château is used for cultural events by the **Association culturelle Champagne-Argonne**. In the courtyard, the dovecote houses the **Musée régional d'Orientation** (geology, local history, popular art).

▶ **Population:** 4 461.
Michelin Map: Michelin Local map 306: L-8.
Tourist Office: 15 place du Général-Leclerc, 51800 Ste-Menehould. 03 26 60 85 83. www.argonne.fr.
Location: Located near the A4 motorway, the town consists of a lower Ville Basse and the upper Ville Haute on the Butte du Château.

© ADT Marne

Musée d'Art et d'Histoire

ADDRESSES

⏁/EAT
Aux Berges de la Biesme – *La Vignette. 8km/5mi E of Ste-Menehould on N 3 towards Verdun. 03 26 60 09 22. http://auxbergesdelabiesme.free.fr. Closed Mon evening and all day Wed.* This white house with a flowered façade is conveniently located on the N 3. Carefully prepared traditional dishes are served in a pleasant dining room, with panelled walls, parquet floors and a small fireplace.

Sézanne

Peacefully settled on a hillside riddled with underground galleries and cellars, the lively agricultural and industrial town of Sézanne was host to frequent trade fairs from medieval times forwards.

SIGHT
Église St-Denis
Place de la République.
This Flamboyant Gothic church is flanked by a massive Renaissance tower; inside see the fine star vaulting.

🚗 DRIVING TOUR

Forêt de Traconne
54km/34mi round tour. Allow 2h.

🚶 The dense Traconne forest, covering almost 3 000ha, mainly consists of hornbeam thickets beneath tall oak trees. It is crisscrossed by numerous footpaths including a discovery trail.

◯ Drive W out of Sézanne along D 239. In Launat, turn left towards Le Meix-St-Époing and, 500m farther on, right towards Bricot-la-Ville.

Bricot-la-Ville
This tiny village hidden in the heart of the forest has a charming little church, a lily-covered pond, and a manor house, which was home to Benedictine nuns.

◯ Continue along the Grand Morin Valley to Châtillon-sur-Morin (fortified church), then turn left onto D 86 which joins D 48. In Essarts-le-Vicomte, turn left onto D 49.

L'Étoile
On the edge of this grass-covered roundabout, which has a column topped by an 18C iron cross in its centre, stands a twisted stunted birch from the Bois des Faux de Verzy (🕭*see Parc naturel régional de la Montagne de REIMS*).

▶ **Population:** 5 248.
🕭 **Michelin Map:** Local map 306: E-10.
🚩 **Tourist Office:** Pl. de la République, 51120 Sézanne. ✆03 26 80 54 13. www.sezanne-tourisme.fr.
◯ **Location:** 45km/28mi S of Épernay by D 951, from where there is a picturesque view of the town. A ring of broad avenues, which replaced the fortifications, surrounds the old town.

◯ Follow D 49 to Barbonne-Fayel then turn right onto D 50.

Fontaine-Denis-Nuisy
A 13C fresco of the Last Judgement in the north transept of the **church**, depicts damned souls roasting in a vast cauldron.

◯ Drive along D 350 towards St-Quentin-le-Verger. In St-Quentin-le-Verger, turn left onto D 351 then right onto the Villeneuve-St-Vistre road, D 373, back to Sézanne.

ADDRESSES

🏠STAY AND 🍴 EAT

🍽 **Hôtel de la Croix d'Or** – *53 r. Notre-Dame. ✆03 26 80 61 10. Closed Sun evenings and Wed. 10 rooms. Restaurant🍽🍴.* Situated on the town's main shopping street. The ivy-clad façade, rustic furniture, traditional cooking and comfortable modernised rooms have a charming provincial feel.

Collégiale Notre-Dame de l'Assomption

Vitry-le-François

Vitry-le-François is the capital of the Perthois area, a fertile plain extending from the River Marne to the Trois-Fontaines forest. The town occupies a strategic position on the east bank of the Marne, at the intersection of the Marne-Rhine and Marne-Saône canals.

A BIT OF HISTORY

King François built Vitry, gave it his name, and commissioned an engineer from Bologna to designed the grid plan, the fortifications and a citadel. In 1940, the city was 90 percent destroyed by bombs. After the war, it was rebuilt.

SIGHTS
Collégiale Notre-Dame de l'Assomption

The 17C–18C church is an interesting example of the Classical style with a harmonious west front flanked by twinned towers adorned with scrolls and surmounted by flame vases. Inside, the imposing nave and transept are prolonged by a late-19C apse.

Porte du Pont

Fine triumphal arch (1748) erected in honour of Louis XIV. Taken down in 1938, it was only re-erected in 1984.

EXCURSIONS
St-Amand-sur-Fion★

10km/6mi N along N 44 then D 260.
Lying on the banks of the River Fion, the village has numerous timber-framed

▸ **Population:** 13 603.
 Michelin Map: Michelin Local map 306: J-10.
 Tourist Office: 8 esplanade de Strasbourg, 51300 Vitry-le-François. ℘03 26 74 45 30. www.tourisme-vitry-francois.com.
▸ **Location:** 29km NW of St-Dizier by N4.

houses, five mills and a few washhouses. The **church★** is a successful mixture of Romanesque and Gothic styles. The beautiful arcaded porch dates from the 15C.

Ponthion

10km/6mi NE along D 982 then D 14.
In 754, a meeting in this village between Pope Stephen II and Pepin the Short, the first Carolingian king, led to the creation of the Papal States. See the medieval church with a lovely 12C porch.

ADDRESSES

⅋/EAT

⊜⊜ **La Cloche** – *34 r. Aristide-Briand. ℘03 26 74 03 84. Closed Sun evening Oct–May and Sat lunch.* Two lovely oldfashioned buildings are separated by an inner courtyard, which serves as a terrace in summer. Tasty food made from fresh produce.

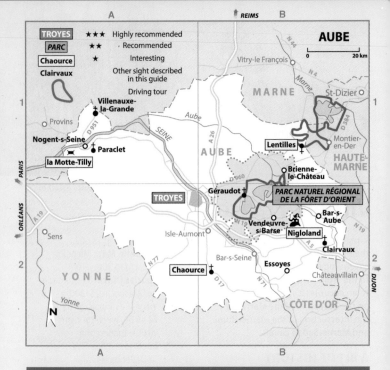

Renoir's atelier, Essoyes

© Patrick Escudero/hemis.fr

Renoir

The artist **Pierre-Auguste Renoir** (1841–1919) was born in Limoges, but went to Paris as a young man, where his talents developed under the Impressionists. In later years, Renoir was a frequent visitor to the Champagne region where his wife Aline was from (*see Troyes: ESSOYES*) and which he represented in many of his paintings. In 1919, after having received many honours and having exhibited in the major museums of the world, his work was officially accepted by the Louvre.

Bar-sur-Aube

In medieval times, an important fair took place in Bar-sur-Aube. Today, the town thrives on the Champagne trade.

❧ WALKING TOUR

▶ Start from place de l'Hôtel-de-Ville.

Hôtel de ville
The town hall is housed in the former Ursuline convent (1634).

Rue d'Aube
The post office (**Nos. 16 and 18**) is a fine 18C mansion with beautiful wrought-iron balconies. **No. 15** is another 18C house. **No. 33** dates from the end of the 16C, whereas **No. 44** boasts a Renaissance rounded arch over the door.

▶ Turn left onto rue Jeanne-de-Navarre.

Église St-Maclou
☞ *Not open to the public.*
11C former chapel for the counts of Bar.

▶ Walk round the right side of the church.

A small circular window in the east end made it possible for the Blessed Sacrament to be visible even at night.

▶ Continue along rue Mailly.

Note the elaborate doorway of the *sous-préfecture*, a former salt storehouse.

▶ Continue along rue Armand then rue Nationale, the town's lively shopping street.

At **No. 14**, the deconsecrated **Chapelle St-Jean**, dating from the 11C and 12C, once belonged to the Order of St John.

▶ Follow rue St-Jean then turn left onto rue du Général-Vouillemont.

- ▶ **Population:** 5 302.
- ⚲ **Michelin Map:** Michelin Local map 313: I-4.
- ℹ **Tourist office:** Bd du 14-Juillet, 10200 Bar-sur-Aube. ℘03 25 27 24 25. www.tourisme-cotedesbar.com.
- ◉ **Location:** Bar-sur-Aube is located on the N 19, a starting point to drive the Champagne Route.
- ◈ **Don't Miss:** A tour of the Champagne cellars.
- ♟ **Kids:** Children will love Nigloland.

Cellier aux Moines
Near the east end of the church, this former town house of the Clairvaux monks (now a restaurant) has a 13C cellar, used by local wine-growers as their headquarters during the 1912 rebellion, when the Bar region won the right to continue calling its wine Champagne.

Église St-Pierre★
The west front and south side of this 12C church are lined with a covered gallery (making it look like a *halle* or covered market, hence its name Halloy).

Médiathèque
13 rue St-Pierre.
The library is housed in the early-17C Hôtel de Brienne.

Turn left onto rue Thiers, which has retained some timber-framed houses.

▶ Cross rue Nationale again and follow the narrow rue de la Paume and rue du Poids to return to the town hall.

EXCURSIONS
Chapelle Ste-Germaine
4km/2.5mi.

▶ Leave Bar-sur-Aube by D 4, SW of the town, 3km/1.9mi further on, turn left in a bend onto a steep path and continue on foot.

Côte des Bars vineyards

The path leads to a pilgrimage chapel dedicated to Germaine, a virgin martyred by the Vandals in 407. Walk past the chapel and around the house to the viewing table which offers **glimpses** of Bar-sur-Aube, the valley, Colombey-les-Deux-Églises and its cross of Lorraine, and the Dhuits and Clairvaux forests.

🚶 Walkers might prefer to walk all the way to the chapel: past the bridge on the River Aube, take rue Pierre-Brossolette then continue straight on alongside the *lycée* (secondary school) and follow the path climbing through the woods (*30min*) up to the chapel.

Arsonval

6km/3.7mi NW along N 19.

The **Musée Rostislas-Loukine** (*R. Nationale.* ☞*guided tours by arrangement.* ☞*no charge.* ☎*03 25 27 92 54*), housed in a former primary school, celebrates **Rostislas Loukine** (1904–88), a Belgian of Russian origin who spent time in the region (also has temporary exhibitions).

👥 Nigloland★

9km/5.6mi NW by N 19 to Dolancourt.
&⏱*Early-Jul–3rd week of Aug 10am–7pm; rest of year hours vary; check website for details.* ☞€*32 (children under 12 €29, less than 1m tall no charge).* ☎*03 25 27 94 52. www.nigloland.fr.*
This leisure park offers attractions such as trips in a vintage car dating from 1900 and along an enchanting river. Do not miss the cinema show on the 180° screen or the presentation of the Niglo Company (electronic automata) staged in the theatre of the Canadian Village, one of four themed villages.

In addition there are no fewer than 39 individual attractions and shows that will provide entertainment for everyone.

Soulaines-Dhuys

18km/11.2mi N along D 384.
With its timber-framed buildings (*colombages*) this is a charming village, through which flows the River Laines, which produces a resurgence. On the edge of limestone country, the area is wooded and dotted with ponds. It is also sparsely populated, but has a wealth of walking trails, monuments and calm and agreeable places to visit.

Bayel

7.5km/4.7mi SE along D 396.

Écomusée du Cristal (Crystalworks)

&⏱*Mon–Sat 9am–12.30pm, 2–5.30pm.* ⏱*1 May, 1 and 11 Nov, 24 Dec–4 Jan.* ☞€*8.* ☎*03 25 92 42 68.*
Bayel is famous for its prestigious crystalworks founded in 1666 by the Venetian glass-blower Jean-Baptiste Mazzolay, although crystal has been produced in Bayel since around 1300. So prestigious was the quallity of the glass that King Louis XIV gave it the label Royal Manufacturer of Crystal in Bayel under letters patent. The factory later became the Royal Crystal of Champagne.

The **Écomusée du Cristal** is housed in three small workers' cottages (*entrance through the tourist office*).

The plain 12C **church** contains a 16C polychrome stone **Pietà★** likely created by the Master of Chaource, who worked also in Troyes (&*see TROYES*).

Brienne-le-Chateau

The town is now a major supplier of cabbage for sauerkraut; one quarter of all the cabbages of France are grown here. There is even a festival celebrating *la choucroute au champagne* (sauerkraut cooked in Champagne) that takes place on the third Sunday in September.

A BIT OF HISTORY
Napoleon Bonaparte in Brienne

Napoleon Bonaparte attended military school here, and returned briefly to Brienne in 1814, at the end of the Napoleonic Wars, when he attacked a coalition of Prussian and Russian troops. During his exile on the island of St Helena, he recalled his youthful years in Brienne and left the town a considerable sum of money.

SIGHTS
Musée Napoléon

34 rue de l'École-Militaire.
The museum is currently closed for renovation, and expected to re-open during 2018; check the website for details. ℘03 25 92 82 41. www.musee-napoleon-brienne.fr.
Housed in his former military school, the museum contains mementoes of Napoleon and relates the various episodes of the French campaign of 1814.
The chapel houses an exhibit of the **Treasuries** of nearby churches: sculptures, paintings, and gold plate.

Hôtel de ville

The money bequeathed by Napoleon was partly used to build a town hall (1859). Note the building's pediment: Napoleon surmounted by an eagle.

Église St-Pierre-et-St-Paul

The nave dates from the 14C and the chancel, surrounded by an ambulatory, from the 16C.

▶ **Population:** 3 039.
⌚ **Michelin Map:** Michelin Local map 313: H-3.
ℹ **Tourist office:** 34 r. de l'Ecole Militaire. ℘03 25 92 82 41. www.ot-brienne-le-chateau.com.
◐ **Location:** Brienne lies across a flat area, close to the River Aube, within the Parc naturel régional de la Forêt d'Orient.

Covered market

A market takes place regularly beneath the fine 16C timberwork and tiled roof.

EXCURSIONS
Brienne-la-Vieille

1km/0.6mi S along D 443.
This port used to be the main timber supplier of the capital by the log-floating method. Rough timber would come by cart from the nearby forests of Orient, Temple and Clairvaux. The logs would then be tied into floats which would be guided down the River Aube, then the Seine until they reached Paris. The 12C **church** boasts 15C statues.

Écomusée de la Forêt d'Orient

See Parc naturel régional de la Forêt d'Orient.

Rosnay-l'Hôpital

9km/5.6mi N along D 396.
The **Église Notre-Dame**, dating from the 12C and 16C, stands on a once-fortified mound, on the banks of the River Voire. Walk along the left side of the church to reach the stairs leading to the vast **crypt**, erected in the 12C but rebuilt in the 16C at the same time as the church above it.

Abbaye de
Clairvaux

In June 1115, St Bernard settled with 11 monks in the remote Val d'Absinthe, to found one of the four major houses of the new Cistercian Order. Simplicity and voluntary deprivation led to a plain and austere architectural style.
St Bernard strove to fight against the opulence of many abbey churches. The Abbaye de Clairvaux soon acquired considerable influence. The abbey workshop produced more than 1 400 illuminated manuscripts, many preserved in Troyes' library. Post-Revolution, the abbey became a prison in 1808.

VISIT

Guided tours only (1h15) at fixed times Feb–Dec: check website for details of variable guided tour times. Jan. €8.50 (under 18, no charge; 18–25 €5). ℘03 25 27 52 55. www.abbayedeclairvaux.com.

- **Michelin Map:** Michelin Local map 313: I-5.
- **Location:** The Abbey is 16km/10mi south of Bar-sur-Aube on the D 396.

Enter through the Porte du Midi. Immediately to the left is the former Hostellerie des Dames and, Petit Clairvaux; opposite stand the austere monastic buildings of Haut Clairvaux.

Bâtiment des convers★
The lay brothers' 12C building is all that remains of Clairvaux II.

Clairvaux as a prison
The socialist and revolutionary Louis-Auguste Blanqui (1872), Philippe d'Orléans (1890), many Resistance members (1940–44), several ministers of the Vichy government (after the Liberation of France) and insubordinate generals during the Algerian War of Independence were all held in Clairvaux.

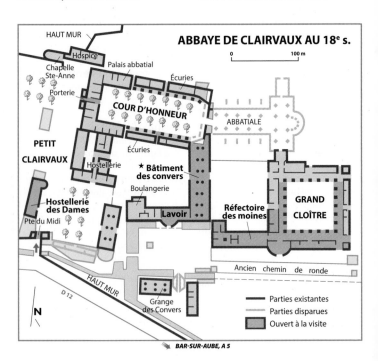

ABBAYE DE CLAIRVAUX AU 18e s.

HAUT MUR
Hospice
Chapelle Ste-Anne
Palais abbatial
Écuries
Porterie
COUR D'HONNEUR
ABBATIALE
PETIT CLAIRVAUX
Écuries
Hostellerie
★ Bâtiment des convers
Boulangerie
GRAND CLOÎTRE
Hostellerie des Dames
Pte du Midi
Lavoir
Réfectoire des moines
Ancien chemin de ronde
HAUT MUR
D 12
Grange des Convers
N

— Parties existantes
— Parties disparues
■ Ouvert à la visite

BAR-SUR-AUBE, A 5

Parc naturel régional de la Forêt d'Orient

Parc naturel régional de la Forêt d'Orient★★

Created in 1970 round the artificial Lac d'Orient, the nature park extends over 70 000ha and comprises vast forests and three large artificial lakes. It lies on the border of two contrasting areas known as *Champagne crayeuse and Champagne humide*.

The park both helps preserve the natural environment as well as cultural and architectural heritage while offering a wide choice of outdoor activities, including walking, boat trips, water sports, fishing, swimming and diving.

- ⚭ **Michelin Map:** Michelin Local map 313: F-3 to H-4.
- ▶ **Location:** In the south of the Champagne region, the Forêt d'Orient can be reached from Troyes east on N 19 or D 960 or from Bar-sur-Aube west on N 19.
- 👥 **Kids:** At Mesnil-St-Père are an animal reserve (especially interesting at dusk) and a bird sanctuary – don't forget your binoculars! The automata museum at Lusigny might also be an alternative on wet days.

A BIT OF HISTORY
Forêt d'Orient
Once part of the vast Der forest stretching from the Pays d'Othe in the southwest to St-Dizier in the northeast, the Forêt d'Orient today covers 10 000ha of wetlands dotted with lakes. It is named for the knights who once owned the area (⚭ *See the educational trail running through the forest*).

🚶 Two long-distance and several short-distance footpaths run through the forest, popular with walkers and cyclists

PRACTICAL INFORMATION
Maison du Parc – *10220 Piney, ✆03 25 43 81 90. www.pnr-foret-orient.fr.*

alike: itineraries totalling 140km/87mi are detailed in a topographical guide available from the Maison du Parc.

Lakes
The park includes three lakes that used to regulate the flow of the River Seine and the River Aube.

427

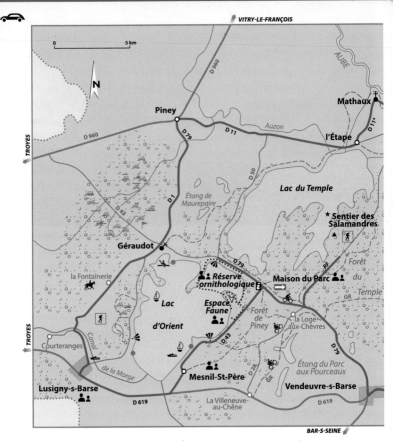

Lac d'Orient

The oldest (1966) and largest of the lakes, Lac d'Orient covers 2 500ha and offers many leisure activities such as sailing and scuba diving. There are two marinas and three sand beaches in Géraudot, Lusigny-sur-Barse and Mesnil-St-Père. A scenic road runs round the lake.

Lac du Temple

Created in 1991 and covering an area of 1 830ha, this lake is enjoyed by anglers and canoeists.

Lac du Temple and Lac Amance are linked by a canal 1.6km/1mi long.

Lac Amance

The smallest lake with an area of only 490ha/1 211 acres, is reserved for motorised water sports (☾ see Port Dienville below).

Angling is allowed everywhere except in the southern creek of the Lac du Temple and the northeast creek of the Lac d'Orient, a bird sanctuary.

🚘 DRIVING TOUR

Tour of the Lakes

64km/40mi. Allow half a day.

▶ Start from the Maison du Parc.

Maison du Parc

The Maison du Parc (see panel above) is on the road that runs around the two lakes, equidistant from Géraudot and Mesnil-St-Père, at the intersection of the D 79 and D 43. ⏱ *Jul–Aug 10am–6pm; Apr–Jun and Sept–Oct 10am–12.30pm, 1.30–5.30pm; rest of year 1–5pm.* ⏱ *mid-Dec–1 Jan.*

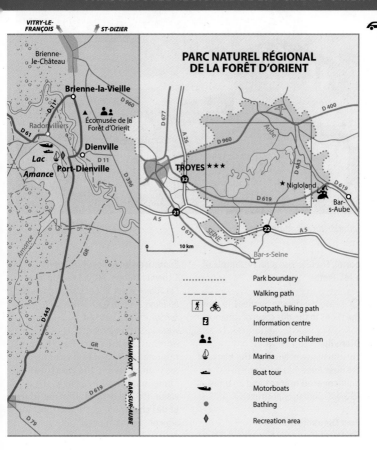

PARC NATUREL RÉGIONAL
DE LA FORÊT D'ORIENT

· · · · · · · · · · ·	Park boundary
– – – – –	Walking path
🚶 🚴	Footpath, biking path
ℹ	Information centre
👨‍👦👧	Interesting for children
⛵	Marina
🚤	Boat tour
🛥	Motorboats
●	Bathing
◈	Recreation area

This traditional timber-framed house was taken apart and rebuilt in the Forêt de Piney. It is both an information centre about the park and an exhibition area.

▶ Drive along D 79 for 4km/2.5mi towards Vendeuvre-sur-Barse then turn left onto the Route forestière du Temple (closed at some periods of the year).

This road running through the Forêt du Temple features informative panels about the species of trees.

🚶 A forest trail (2.5km/1.5mi), the **Sentier des Salamandres**, starting opposite Lusigny beach, introduces visitors to a dozen characteristic species. In Lusigny, you can enjoy a **boat trip** (⬇See Addresses).

Nature lovers know:

🌿 *not to pick flowers, fruit or plants, or gather fossils;*

🌿 *to take all rubbish and empty cans out of the protected zone;*

🌿 *to leave pets, particularly dogs, at home because they might frighten wild animals;*

🌿 *to stay on the paths, because hillside shortcuts cause erosion.*

▶ Make a U-turn and return to the D79 in the direction of Vendeuvre-sur-Barse.

Vendeuvre-sur-Barse
Église Saint-Pierre-et-Saint-Paul – This 16C edifice boasts an interesting Renaissance sculpture on the North

Église St-Quentin, Mathaux

portal. There is also a nice example of a 16C Pietà.

▶ Leave Vendeuvre by the N 19 then the D 443 in the direction of Amance.

Dienville
This small town, lying on the banks of the River Aube, has an impressive stone-built **covered market** and an unusual 16C–18C pentagonal **church**.

Port Dienville
◷*Mar and Oct daily except Wed–Thu 10am–noon, 2–5pm; Apr–Jun and Sept Mon–Fri 10am–noon, 2–5pm, Sat–Sun and public holidays 9.30am–12.30pm, 1.30–6pm; Jul–Aug Mon–Fri 10am–1pm, 2–6pm, Sat–Sun and public holidays 9.30am–6.30pm.* ◷*Nov–Feb.* ℘*03 25 92 27 69.*
www.lacs-champagne.fr.
On the outskirts of the town, this leisure and water-sports centre on the edge of Lake Amance attracts speedboat and motorboat racing enthusiasts (*boats for hire on Lake Amance*).

▶ Continue northwards to Brienne-la-Vieille (D 443).

Brienne-la-Vieille
♿*See BRIENNE-LE-CHÂTEAU: Excursions.*

▶ Return to Radonvilliers along D 11B then turn right onto D 61 towards Mathaux.

Écomusée de la Forêt d'Orient
1 chemin Milbert. ♿◷*Mar–Nov Tue–Sat 10am–noon, 2–6pm, Sun and public holidays 2–6pm.* ◷*Oct–Feb.* ⌒*€5–€7.50.* ℘*03 25 92 95 84.*
www.lacs-champagne.fr.
Administered by the Parc naturel régional de la Forêt d'Orient, this museum includes the **Boutique** (a former smithy which has been left as it was in 1903) and the **Maison des jours et des champs** (collection of tools and agricultural machinery).

▶ Return to Radonvilliers along D 11B then turn right onto D 61 towards Mathaux.

Mathaux
The lovely 18C timber-framed **church** has a wood-shingled square tower.

▶ Drive along D 11A to L'Étape, then bear right towards Piney (D 11).

Shortly after **L'Étape**, you will see the canal feeding water from the Lac du Temple back to the River Aube. There are wide **views** of the lake.

▶ Continue to Piney.

Piney
Note fine 17C wooden **covered market**.

▶ Leave Piney by D 79 then follow D 1 to Géraudot.

Géraudot

The nave of the **church** (*follow the directions on the signpost on the church door to pick up the key*) dates from the 12C and with a chancel and stained glass windows from the 16C.

◗ Continue along D 1 and 1km/0.6mi farther on turn right towards Courteranges.

Ferme du Rasle

◷*Mid-May–Sept by arrangement.* ℘*03 25 41 26 53.*
Medieval life is recreated in this ancient farmhouse which, in the 12C, belonged to Larrivour Cistercian abbey.

◗ Follow D 1 to Lusigny-sur-Barse.

Lusigny-sur-Barse

At the entrance of the village stands a 1986 wood and steel **sculpture** (25m in diameter spanning the Barse canal) by Klaus Rinke.

Nature trail

🚶 Opposite Lusigny beach.

◗ Drive along N 19 then turn left to Mesnil-St-Père.

Mesnil-St-Père

This village, with its timber-and-brick houses, is the largest **water sports centre** on the shores of Lac d'Orient.
Boat trips on the lake are organised aboard panoramic motorboats.

👥 Sentier du Lapin Blanc

This fun route, which explores the village, its flora and fauna, was especially designed for small children to enjoy. ℘*03 25 43 38 88.*

◗ Follow D 43 back to the Maison du Parc.

Espace Faune de la Forêt d'Orient

◷*Late Mar–late Sept daily exept Fri 2–8pm; Oct daily except Fri 2–6pm.* ◉€5 (child 3–12, €3). ℘*03 25 43 38 88.* 👥 Located on a peninsula (89ha), this **wildlife observation area** is a chance to discover the local fauna. Two observation points offer good views of wild boars, deer and roe-deer roaming around freely. The former eat acorns, rodents and insects; they are active day and night, which makes it easier to see them. Deer and roe-deer on the other hand are plant eaters and are mainly active at night, which means waiting patiently to catch a glimpse of them.

◗ Go past the Maison du Parc and turn left onto D 79 towards Géraudot.

Réserve ornithologique

👥 The north-east bank of Lake Orient, is a **bird sanctuary** for waterfowl with an **observation point**.

ADDRESSES

🛏 STAY AND 🍴 EAT

◎ **Chambre d'hôte** – *Aux Colombages Champenois, 33 r. du Haut, 10270 Laubressel. 7km/4.3mi NW of Lusigny-sur-Barse on N 19 and D 186. ℘03 25 80 27 37.* ⊡. *5 rooms.* Two lovely local-style half-timbered guest houses offering comfortable rooms with exposed beams and local farm produce at the dinner table.

◎ **La Bergeotte** – *6 r. de Dienville, 10220 Brevonnes. ℘03 25 46 31 44.* ⊡. *2 rooms. Evening meal* ◎⊜. A warm welcome awaits you on this little farm, which was entirely rebuilt in 1940. Kitchen facilities available.

◎⊜ **Hotel Relais Paris Bale** – *6 rue du r Relais du Poste, Le Menilot, 10270 Montiéramey. ℘03 25 41 20 72. www.la-mangeoire.fr. 5 rooms. Restaurant* (**La Mangeoire** ◎⊜). An interesting combination of timber-framed hotel and restaurant in an area that is ideal for walking, or having dinner on a boat.

◎⊜⊜ **Au Vieux Pressoir** – *5 r. du 28-août-1944, 10140 Mesnil-St-Père. ℘03 25 41 27 16. Closed Sun evenings Oct–Mar and Mon lunchtime.* Sample regional meals in this half-timbered house on the outskirts of a village on the edge of the Forêt d'Orient. Rooms available (**Auberge du Lac** ◎⊜⊜).

Nogent-sur-Seine

Aube

This small town lying on both banks of the Seine and on an island linked to the river bank by a watermill, is overlooked by mills, silos and the cooling towers of the nuclear power station.

SIGHTS

Old town

The old town has several timber-framed houses including the **Pavillon Henri IV** and the **Maison de la Turque**, mentioned by Flaubert in his novel *L'Éducation sentimentale*.

Église St-Laurent

Built in the 16C, the church is a pleasant blend of Flamboyant Gothic and Renaissance styles. An imposing tower on the left of the main doorway is decorated in the Renaissance style and surmounted by a lantern which supports the statue of St Laurence holding the grid on which he was roasted alive. The Renaissance aisles have large windows and the buttresses are adorned with carved capitals and gargoyles. Note the pediment on the south doorway.

Musée Paul-Dubois-Alfred-Boucher

Rue Alfred-Boucher. ◯*Wed–Sun 2–6pm.* ◯*Dec–Jan, 1 and 8 May.* ⊜€*4.* ℘*03 25 39 71 79.*

The **archaeological** collection features Gallo-Roman pottery found in Villeneuve-au-Châtelot, and coins. On the first floor, there are **paintings** (17C–19C), **sculptures** and plaster casts by regional artists including the two sculptors after whom the museum is named. Note in particular a landscape of Nogent painted in 1764 by Joseph Vernet, entitled *Le Livon*.

The painting was lost until discovered in London in 1996. It forms a pair with another painting now in the Fine Arts Museum in Berlin.

▶ **Population:** 6 096.
⚙ **Michelin Map:** Michelin Local map 313: B-3.
🛈 **Tourist Office**: 5 Rue Saint Epoing, 10400 Nogent-sur-Seine. ℘03 25 39 42 07 www.tourisme-nogentais.fr.
▶ **Location:** On the Seine, 19km/11.8mi SE of Provins.

EXCURSIONS

Jardin botanique de Marnay-sur-Seine

10km/6mi W along N 19 then left on D 68. ♿◯*May–mid-Oct Tue–Fri 10am–6pm, Sat–Sun and public holidays 3–7pm; rest of year the garden is closed at weekends, but remains open during the week except on Mon.* ⊜€*5.* ℘*03 25 21 94 18.* www.jardin-botanique.org.

Created in 1999, these botanical gardens house 3 000 species of plants, including many endangered ones. Stroll down the gardens along the Evolution path or among medicinal plants and herbs.

Château de la Motte-Tilly★

6km/3.7mi SW along D 951. ◯*Jan–mid-May and mid-Sept–Dec 10am–noon, 2–5pm; mid-May–mid-Sept daily except Mon 10am–noon, 2–6pm.* ⊜€*6.* ◯*1 Jan, 25 Dec.* ℘*03 25 39 99 67.* www.chateau-la-motte-tilly.fr.

Built in 1754 on a natural terrace overlooking the Seine, this château for Abbé de Terray (1715–78), one of Louis XV's finance ministers. Simple yet elegant, its main features are the unusually high roofs and the arcades linking the main building to the pavilions.

The château was opened to the public following the bequest of the Marquise de Maillé (1895–1972), an archaeologist and art historian. The family furniture was restored and is on display.

The ground-floor **reception rooms★★** are beautifully furnished and decorated with painted panelling. Two rooms on

Château de la Motte-Tilly

the first floor recall the benefactress: her green bedroom and the Empire-style bedroom of her father.

Dangerous Liaisons by Milos Forman was filmed in the château in 1989.

After visiting the interior, admire the **park** with its beautiful ornamental lake and canal.

Ancienne abbaye du Paraclet

6km/3.7mi SE along N 19 and D 442.
♿☕ *Guided tour late Jul–Aug; call for details.* ⊘ *Not open to the public rest of the year.* ☎ *01 42 27 88 24.*

Little remains of this abbey associated with celebrated medieval lovers **Abélard** (1079–1142) and **Héloïse** (1101–1164). A theologian and philosopher, Abélard retired to here after the Church had condemned his teaching in 1121. He built a modest oratory and was joined by students who camped round the oratory. Héloïse became the abbess of Le Paraclet in 1129. There is nothing left of the abbey except a cellar located beneath the farm buildings. Behind the chapel, an obelisk marks the site of the crypt where the couple was buried. Transferred in the 15C to the main church of Le Paraclet, their remains were taken away during the Revolution and now rest together in a grave in the Père-Lachaise cemetery in Paris.

Villenauxe-la-Grande

15km/9.3mi N along D 951.
This small town sits amid the rolling hills of the Île-de-France cuesta. The 13C **Eglise St-Pierre-et-St-Paul** has a striking Gothic chancel and 13C **ambulatory★**, lit by twin windows with five-foiled oculi. The **modern stained glass windows★**, inaugurated in 2005, are the work of artist David Tremlett and glassmakers Benoît and Stéphanie Marq (Ateliers Simon-Marq, Reims).

ADDRESSES

🛏 STAY

🛏 **Chambre d'hôte Rondeau Robert** – *12 r. Chêne, 10400 La Motte-Tilly. 6km/3.75mi SW of Nogent-sur-Seine on D 951 towards Fontainebleau.* ☎ *03 25 39 83 85.* ⊟. *5 rooms.* Time passes peacefully on this property located in a tiny village in the Seine valley.

🍴 EAT

🍴🍴 **Le Beau Rivage** – *R. Villiers aux-Choux.* ☎ *03 25 39 84 22. www.hotel-beaurivage-nogentsurseine.com. Closed Sun even and all day Mon.* Near the Château de La Motte-Tilly, the white-washed façade of this modern house hides a terrace on the banks of the Seine.

Troyes★★★

The former capital of Champagne became a prosperous commercial city through its annual fairs as well as its artistic centre with a wealth of churches, museums and mansions. The town has now expanded outside the ring of boulevards surrounding the centre (shaped like a Champagne cork). Troyes is France's main hosiery centre in a tradition going back to the 16C, though it is now equally famed for its factory outlets.

A BIT OF HISTORY
The counts of Champagne
In the 10C, Troyes came under the authority of the counts of Champagne. One of them, **Henri I 'the Liberal'** founded 13 churches and 13 hospitals. His grandson, **Thibaud II**, a knight-poet, founded the Champagne fairs and brought fame and fortune to the town. When the last heiress of the counts of Champagne, Jeanne, married the king of France, Philippe le Bel, in 1284, her dowry included the Champagne region.

The shameful Treaty of Troyes
During the strife between Burgundians and Armagnacs at the height of the Hundred Years War, **Isabeau of Bavaria**, wife of mad French king, Charles VI, signed the shameful Treaty of Troyes disowning the dauphin (heir to the French throne) and sealing the marriage of Catherine of France with Henry V of England who was proclaimed regent pending his accession to the French

- ▶ **Population:** 61 220.
- ⚬ **Michelin Map:** Michelin Local map 313: E-4.
- ▤ **Tourist Office:** 16, rue Aristide Briand, 10014 Troyes. ✆03 25 82 62 70. www.tourisme-troyes.com.
- ▶ **Location:** Troyes lies on the A5, 179km/111mi from Paris and 125km/77mi from Reims.
- ⚬ **Don't Miss:** Troyes' Gothic churches and cathedral and the Fauve paintings in the Musée d'Art Moderne.

throne. Burgundian and English troops then occupied Troyes, which was liberated by Joan of Arc in 1429.

Major artistic centre
The city's artistic activities have multiplied since the Renaissance. The school of sculpture was famous throughout Champagne and even in neighbouring Burgundy. Sculptors such as **Jean Gailde** and **Jacques Julyot** created a wealth of charming works. Stained-glass makers, such as **Jehan Soudain** and **Linard Gontier**, were also well established and, from the 14C to 17C, their workshops produced all the fine stained glass decorating the town's churches. The artistic tradition continued into the 17C with painter **Pierre Mignard** and sculptor **François Girardon**, both natives of Troyes.

PRACTICAL INFORMATION
Guided tours – Troyes, City of Art and History, organises tours by authorised guides of the town. *Early Jul–mid-Sept at 2.30pm, €5.50.*
The rest of the year audioguides can be reserved and themed tours are organised from Oct to Jun. *Enquire at the tourist office or on www.tourisme-troyes.com.*

Pass'Troyes – *Enquire at the tourist office.* The tourist pass €12 valid one year, includes a guided visit or audio guide, free museum entrance, reductions in the factory shops and a champagne tasting.
Tourist circuit – The city has created several well signposted tours of the city's most noteworthy sites. *Brochure from the tourist office.*

Capital of hosiery

Troyes' tradition of hosiery dates back to the early 16C, with a handful of manufacturers of hand-knitted bonnets and stockings. In 1745, the Trinity Hospital (Hôtel de Mauroy) introduced special looms so that poor children in its care could learn to make stockings. By 1774, the hosiers' guild counted no fewer than 40 members. The industry further developed in the 19C and today counts 150 firms employing 10 000 people.

 WALKING TOUR

HISTORIC CENTRE★★

Allow 4h.

Medieval Troyes consisted of two separate districts: the Cité, the aristocratic and ecclesiastical centre surrounding the cathedral, and the Bourg of the commercial burghers where the Champagne fairs took place. In 1524, a fire swept through the town. The prosperous inhabitants took this opportunity to build the more opulent houses that are still visible today.

The timber-framed houses had pointed gables, cob walls and corbelled upper floors. More opulent houses had walls of limestone rubble and brick in the traditional Champagne style. The most elegant mansions were built of stone, an expensive material in the region due to the absence of hard-stone quarries.

▶ Start from place Alexandre-Israël.

Place Alexandre-Israël

The square is overlooked by the Louis XIII façade of the **town hall**. Note the motto over the porch, dating from the 1789 Revolution: Liberty, Equality, Fraternity or Death.

Rue Champeaux

This unusually wide 16C street was the district's main thoroughfare. On the corner of rue Paillot-de-Montabert stands the **Maison du Boulanger** which houses the Thibaud-de-Champagne cultural centre; opposite, you can see the **Tourelle de l'Orfèvre** which owes its name to its first owner, a goldsmith.

▶ Walk beside the church then take rue Mignard back to rue Champeaux.

Across the street is the 1526 **Hôtel Juvénal-des-Ursins.** The white-stone façade has a pedimented doorway and a charming Renaissance oratory.

Ruelle des Chats★

A medieval atmosphere pervades this narrow lane lined with houses whose gables are so close that a cat can jump from the one to the other. The bollards marking the entrance of the alleyway were to prevent carriage wheels from hitting the walls of the houses. The street was closed by a portcullis at night.

▶ The road widens into rue des Chats.

On the left, a passageway leads to the **Cour du Mortier d'or**, a fine courtyard built with various ancient elements.

▶ Turn left onto rue Charbonnet.

Hôtel de Marizy

Erected in 1531, this beautiful stone mansion has a Renaissance corner turret, decorated with figures and emblems.

▶ Turn left onto rue des Quinze-Vingts then right onto rue de la Monnaie.

Rue de la Monnaie

The street is lined with fine timber-framed houses. At **No. 34** stands the 16C Hôtel de l'Élection, clad with shingles, and at **Nos. 32–36** the stone early-16C Hôtel de la Croix d'Or, former residence of one of the town's mayors.

▶ Continue along rue de la Monnaie. Turn left onto rue Colbert and left onto rue de la Bonne terie. At place Jean Jaurès, turn right onto rue de Turenne.

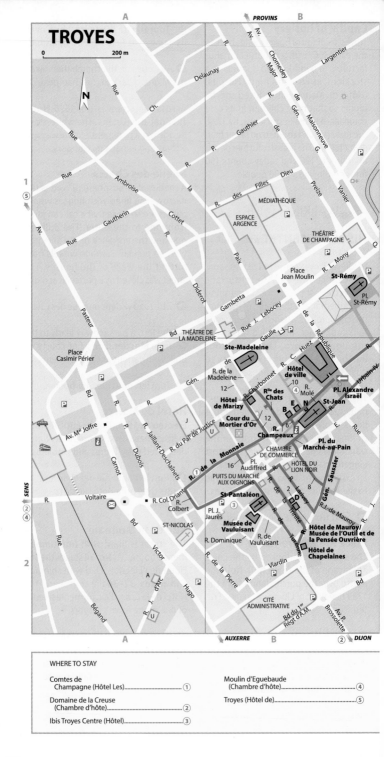

TROYES

0 _____ 200 m

N

PROVINS

AUXERRE

SENS

DIJON

WHERE TO STAY

Comtes de Champagne (Hôtel Les) .... ①	Moulin d'Eguebaude (Chambre d'hôte) .... ④
Domaine de la Creuse (Chambre d'hôte) .... ②	Troyes (Hôtel de) .... ⑤
Ibis Troyes Centre (Hôtel) .... ③	

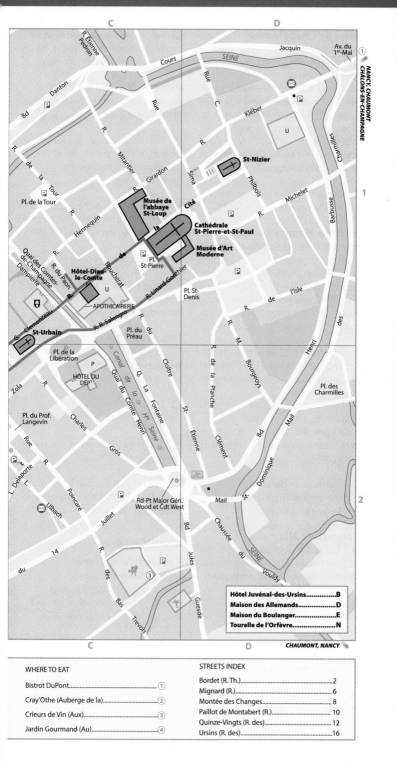

NANCY, CHAUMONT
CHÂLONS-EN-CHAMPAGNE

Hôtel Juvénal-des-Ursins	B
Maison des Allemands	D
Maison du Boulanger	E
Tourelle de l'Orfèvre	N

CHAUMONT, NANCY

WHERE TO EAT

Bistrot DuPont .... ①

Cray'Othe (Auberge de la) .... ②

Crieurs de Vin (Aux) .... ③

Jardin Gourmand (Au) .... ④

Hôtel de Chapelaines
55 rue Turenne.
The house on the corner of rue de Vau-luisant is a good example of Champagne bond (brick and limestone rubble), with a Renaissance façade dating from 1524 to 1536. It has been recently restores, so you can see features such as the corbelled upper part rests on consoles includes carved heads. On the corner is a fine *Virgin of the Apocalypse*.

◖ Follow rue du Général-Saussier, then turn left onto rue de la Trinité.

Hôtel de Mauroy★★
7 rue de la Trinité. ♿*See also Musée de l'Outil et de la Pensée ouvrière.*
This mansion was built by rich mer-chants in 1550. The street façade has a chequered bond typical of Champagne, whereas on the courtyard side (visible as part of the museum), the building fea-tures a polygonal turret surrounded by timberframing, bricks, chequered slate-cladding and string-courses. Don't miss the Corinthian columns supporting the wooden gallery.
The building later became the Hôpital de la Trinité, a home for poor children. In 1745 special looms were brought in, marking the start of machine-made hosiery in Troyes.

◖ Next door, on the corner of rue de la Trinité and rue Thérèse-Bordet, is the Maison des Allemands.

Maison des Allemands
Built in the 16C and decorated in the 18C, this timber-framed house used to welcome German merchants in town.

◖ Turn right onto rue Thérèse-Bordet, then right again onto rue Larivey leading to rue Général-Saussier.

Rue du Général-Saussier
The street is lined with fine old houses; **No. 26**: Hôtel des Angoiselles with a pinnacled tower; **No. 11**: 18C mansion where Napoleon stayed; **No. 3**: fine stone-and-brick 17C house.

◖ Retrace your steps, turn right on rue de la Montée-des-Changes, which leads to place du Marché-au-Pain.

Place du Marché-au-Pain
There's a good view of the clock tower of the Église St-Jean.

◖ Rue Urbain IV leads to place de la Libération. Cross the canal and follow rue Roger-Salengro, then rue Linard-Gonthier.

No. 22 is the Hôtel du Petit Louvre, the former bishop's residence (14C), turned into a coaching inn in 1821.

◖ Turn left towards place St-Pierre.

The **Musée d'Art Moderne** housed in the former bishop's palace and the **cathedral** are on the right.

Rue de la Cité
This street follows the old Roman road from Lyon to Boulogne, which inter-sected the road from Paris to Troyes.

◖ Take a few steps along rue du Paon, with its timber-framed houses.

Across rue de la Cité is the 18C **Hôtel-Dieu**, now part of Reims University.

◖ Cross the canal again and pass north of St-Urbain Basilica to return to place Alexandre-Israël.

CHURCHES
Cathédrale St-Pierre-et-St-Paul★★
♿ ◷*Mon–Sat 9.30am–12.30pm, 2–5pm, Sun and public holidays 2–5pm.* ◷*1 Jan, 1 May, 1 and 11 Nov, 25 Dec.* ℘*03 25 76 98 18.* *www.cathedraledetroyes.com.*
The cathedral, built between the 13C and 17C, has remarkable proportions, exceptionally rich decoration and a beautiful nave. Martin Chambiges, who built the transept of Beauvais cathedral and also worked on Sens cathedral, con-tributed to the ornate **west front** (early

Vault of the nave, Cathédrale St-Pierre-et-St-Paul

16C) adorned with a splendid Flamboyant Gothic rose-window.

The three doorways have richly carved gables. The sculptures were destroyed during the Revolution. The cathedral was intended to have two towers, but only the north tower was completed in the 17C (height: 66m). A plaque on the base of the tower reminds visitors that Joan of Arc stayed in Troyes on 10 July 1429.

On the north side, admire the **north-transept** doorway (13C) which has a huge rose-window.

Interior

This vast sanctuary conveys an impression of power and lightness, lit by fine **stained-glass windows★★**.

Those of the **chancel** and **ambulatory** go back to the 13C. Note the warmth and intensity of the colours; they mainly depict isolated characters and scenes from the Life of the Virgin. The windows of the nave, dating from the early 16C, are completely different: they are more like paintings on glass with red as the dominant colour. The most remarkable are, on the north side, the *Story of the True Cross*, the *Legend of St Sebastian*, the *Story of Job* and that of *Toby*; on the south side, the *Story of Daniel* and *Joseph*, the *Parable of the Prodigal Son* and a magnificent *Tree of Jesse*.

The **rose-window of the west front** by Martin Chambiges, was completed in 1546 and decorated with stained glass by Jehan Soudain. The fourth chapel along the north aisle is lit by famous stained glass made in 1625 by Linard Gontier, known as the **mystical wine-press:** Christ is seen lying beneath the winepress with blood pouring out of the wound in his side into a chalice. Out of his chest grows a vine whose branches support the 12 Apostles.

Treasury★

The cathedral treasury, exhibited in a 13C vaulted room, includes an 11C ivory box, four 11C cloisonné enamels representing the four Evangelists, a 9C manuscript psalter, two missal covers inlaid with precious gems, the 12C reliquary of St Bernard, late-12C regional enamels, an embroidered 14C cope and gold plate from the 16C to 19C.

Basilique St-Urbain★

This is a perfect example of Gothic architecture from the Champagne region. It was built 1262–86, by order of Pope Urban IV, a native of Troyes, on the site of his father's workshop.

Exterior

The **west front** is 19C but the doorway beneath the porch goes back to the 13C; the tympanum is decorated with the Last Judgement. However it is the east end that is most remarkable with its graceful flying buttresses, elegant windows, delicate pinnacles, the gargoyles and profusion of decoration.

Rood screen, Église Sainte-Madelaine

Interior

The chancel is almost entirely composed of stained-glass windows, rarely seen in Early Gothic architecture. The medallions of the low windows, the clerestory windows and high chancel windows, and the medallions of the Chapelle St-Joseph on the left of the chancel are all decorated with **13C stained-glass**. The chapel on the right of the chancel contains the statue of the smiling **Virgin with the Grapes**★.

Église Ste-Madeleine★

ⓘMay–Sept Tue–Sat 10am–12.30pm, 2–7pm, Sun and public holidays 2–5pm; rest of year 9.30am–12.30pm, 2–6pm, Sun 2–5pm. ⓘ1 Jan, 1 May. ✆03 25 73 82 90.

The nave contains a remarkable stone rood **screen**★★, carved in Flamboyant style in 1508–17 by Jean Gailde, a local sculptor and architect. It consists of three pointed arches underlined by delicate festoons and is decorated with a profusion of foliage and carved figures in Renaissance dress. On the top is a balustrade with fleur-de-lys motifs; on the chancel side, a staircase, lined with grotesques, leads to the gallery.

The east end is decorated with brightly coloured Renaissance **stained glass**★. In the south aisle, against a pillar of the nave, is a **statue** of **Martha**★, by the Master of Chaource, one of the main exponents of 16C sculpture in Troyes. In the north aisle, note the wooden statue of saint Robert de Molesmes (early 15C), founder of the Cistercian Order.

As you come out of the church, note the Flamboyant doorway of the former charnel house (1525) decorated with a salamander, emblem of King François I.

Église St-Pantaléon★

ⓘMay–Sept Tue–Sat 10am–12.30pm, 2–7pm, Sun and public holidays 2pm–5pm; rest of year 9.30am–12.30pm, 2–5pm, Sun 2–5pm. ⓘMon and public holidays. ✆03 25 82 62 70.

This 16C church contains an important collection of **statues**★ brought here from churches and convents that were destroyed during the Revolution. Note, against the first pillar on the right, the statue of St James by **Dominique Florentin**, which is believed to be a self portrait and, opposite, the pulpit, a Gothic *Mater Dolorosa*; the pillars of the chancel are adorned with *Charity and Faith* also by Dominique Florentin, which reveal an Italian influence.

Église St-Jean

ⓘEnquire at tourist office for opening times.

Catherine de France (daughter of Charles VI and Isabeau of Bavaria) and Henry V of England celebrated their mariage here in 1420. Above the altar are two paintings by Mignard. The tabernacle was made in 1692 after drawings by Girardon.

Église St-Remy

🕐*Enquire at tourist office for opening times.*

The restored 14C and 16C church has a delicate spiral steeple. The interior is adorned with 16C grisaille panels and bas-relief medallions and a bronze crucifix by Girardon, who was a parishioner.

Église St-Nizier

🕐*Jul–Aug by appointment at the tourist office.*

This 16C church roofed in brightly coloured glazed tiles can be seen from afar. It contains a beautiful *Entombment*, a 16C *Pietà* and a 16C *Christ Mocked* by artists from the Troyes School.

MUSEUMS

Musée d'Art moderne★★

Place St-Pierre. ♿🕐*Apr–Oct Tue–Sun 10am–1pm, 2–6pm; Nov–Mar 5pm.* 🕐*Public holidays.* ✆€5.50. ☎*03 25 76 26 80.* *www.musees-troyes.com.*

In 1976, industrialists Pierre and Denise Levy, donated their rich collection of late 19C and early 20C art and African and Oceanic art to the State. It is now housed in the former bishop's palace.

Fauvism★★ is particularly well represented. The fauves (wild beasts) were so-named for their pure, brilliant colours applied straight from the tube. The Levy collection includes works by Derain (*Hyde Park, Big Ben*), Vlaminck (*Landscape in Chatou*), Braque (*Landscape at l'Estaque*) and Van Dongen.

The first few rooms contain paintings by Courbet, Degas, Seurat (*The Anglers*, a study which he used for his painting *The Grande Jatte*), Vallotton and Vuillard.

More recent works include those by Robert Delaunay before his abstract period, by de la Fresnaye, Modigliani, and numerous post-fauvist paintings by **Derain**.

The collection of **African art**, which influenced many early 20C artists, includes statues, reliquary figures and headdresses in the form of antelopes.

Maison de l'Outil et de la Pensée ouvrière★★

7 rue de la Trinité. 🕐*Daily 10am–6pm.* 🕐*Tue during Oct–Mar, 1 Jan, 25 Dec.* ✆€7. ☎*03 25 73 28 26.* *http://mopo3.com.*

This museum is housed in the Hôtel de Mauroy restored by the **Compagnons du Devoir**. Visitors can admire a great number of 18C tools. A large room contains some of the impressive "master pieces" made by master craftsmen.

Musée de Vauluisant★

4 rue de Vauluisant. 🕐*Apr–Oct Wed–Sun 10am–1pm, 2–6pm; Nov–Mar 5pm.* 🕐*Public holidays.* ✆€3, no charge 1st Sun of the month (except during exhibitions).* ☎*03 25 73 05 85.*

This Renaissance mansion contains two museums. The **Musée d'Art troyen★** presents regional art from the Middle Ages to the 17C, including a Christ on the Cross sculpture believed to be by the Master of Chaource, as well as paintings and stained glass work. The **Musée de la Bonneterie** covers the history of hosiery manufacture, seen in looms and a reconstruction of a 19C workshop.

Musées Saint-Loup

1 rue Chrétien-de-Troyes. 🕐*Apr–Oct Wed–Mon 10am–1pm, 2–6pm; Nov–Mar 5pm.* 🕐*Public holidays.* ✆€5; no charge 1st Sun of the month (except during exhibitions).* ☎*03 25 76 21 68.*

The abbey, dating from the 17C and 18C and extended later, now house three museums. The **Musée d'Histoire naturelle** (Natural History Museum) has a collection of mammals and birds. Skeletons, rocks and meteorites are exhibited in the cloisters.

The **Musée d'Archéologie★** features regional archaeological finds displayed in the abbey cellars. Highlights are the Apollo from Vaupoisson, a Gallo-Roman bronze statue, and the Pouan treasury, weapons and jewellery found in a 5C Merovingian grave.

On the first floor, the painting gallery of the **Musée des Beaux-Arts** covers the major schools from the 15C to the

19C. The 17C is well represented with paintings by Rubens, Van Dyck, Philippe de Champaigne, Le Brun and Mignard.

EXCURSIONS
Chaource★
29km/18mi S.

This village, which has given its name to a famous creamy cheese, has a 19C cast iron covered market and some 15C timber-framed houses.

Église St-Jean-Baptiste★
🕒*Apr–Oct daily 8.30am–7pm. Nov–May 9am–6pm.*

The semi-underground chapel, left of the 13C chancel, contains a magnificent polychrome stone **Entombment★★** carved in 1515 by the Master of Chaource; the facial expression of the Holy Women is extremely moving. Another chapel houses a 16C **gilt-wood crib★** in the shape of a polyptych.

Museums
The **Musée du Fromage** (🕒*Not currently open for visits by individuals; check website or call for latest details: ℰ03 25 40 10 67; https://museedufromage.jimdo.com*) has a collection of objects and tools connected with cheese-making from copper cauldrons to small huts once used by Pyrenean shepherds in summertime. The film shown is mainly devoted to Chaource, a cheeses with an Appellation d'Origine Contrôlée (AOC) label.
The **Musée des Voitures à Pedales** (*Place de l'Église. ℰ06 10 04 69 66*) displays a collection of more than 200 pedal cars from the late 19C to today. 👫 Kids will also enjoy the collection of wooden cars and toys.

Essoyes
58km/36mi SE.

Nestling on the banks of the Ource river, this peaceful little village is famous for its connection to Renoir, and indeed the artist and his wife are buried in the cemetery here. "Chemins de Renoir" are marked around the village so that visitors can follow in the artist's footsteps.

ADDRESSES

🛏 STAY
🍽 **Les Comtes de Champagne** – *54–56 r. de la Monnaie. ℰ03 25 73 11 70. http://troyes.brit-hotel.fr. 46 rooms.* It is said that the counts of Champagne used to mint coins in the four 12C houses which make up this hotel. Rooms with kitchenettes are ideal for families. The huge fireplace in the breakfast room testifies to the age of the premises.

🍽🍽 **Hôtel de Troyes** – *168 av. du Gén.-de-Gaulle. ℰ03 25 71 23 45. www.hoteldetroyes.com. 23 rooms.* Rooms are spread over two buildings either side of a bright plant-filled veranda. Modish colour schemes are combined with modern furniture.

🍽🍽 **Hôtel Ibis Troyes Centre** – *R. Camille-Claudel. ℰ03 25 75 99 99. www.accorhotels.com. 77 rooms.* Benefiting from the latest Ibis standards as far as comfort is concerned: air-conditioned rooms, new-look bathrooms, pleasant breakfast room.

🍽🍽 **Chambre d'hôte Moulin d'Eguebaude** – *36 Rue Pierre Brossolette, 10190 Estissac. ℰ03 25 40 42 18. https://moulineguebaude.jimdo.com. Closed 1 Jan and 25 Dec. 🍴. 8 rooms.* Located on a vast fish-farming estate, this typical wheat mill from the Champagne region (1789) offers fresh, simple rooms. Those in the annex are even more pleasant. Shop selling local produce.

🍽🍽🍽 **Chambre d'hôte Domaine de la Creuse** – *10800 Moussey. ℰ03 25 41 74 01. www.domainedelacreuse.com. 3 rooms.* This traditional 18C Champagne house is built around a lovely central courtyard laid out as a garden. Vast and attractive rooms at garden level.

🍴 EAT
🍽🍽 **Aux Crieurs de Vin** – *4–6 pl. Jean-Jaurès. ℰ03 25 40 01 01. www.auxcrieursdevin.fr. Closed Sun and Mon.* Wine connoisseurs will appreciate this establishment, which is part wine and spirits shop, part atmospheric pre-1940s style bistro. The cuisine is a pleasure too, with fresh market-inspired cooking and regional dishes.

😋😋 **Au Jardin Gourmand** – *31 r. Paillot de Montabert. ☏03 25 73 36 13. Closed Mon lunch and Sun.* Andouillette reigns at this restaurant in old Troyes with its oak-panelled dining room and peaceful courtyard terrace.

😋😋 **Bistrot DuPont** – *5 pl. Charles-de-Gaulle, 10150 Pont-Ste-Marie. 3km/1.8mi NE of Troyes on N 77. ☏03 25 80 90 99. www.bistrotdupont.com. Closed all day Mon, Thu evening and Sun evening.* Flowers and smiles from the staff provide a fine welcome. In a simple but carefully planned setting, the cheerful dishes suit the style of the bistro.

😋😋 **Auberge de la Cray'Othe** – *31 Grande-Rue, 10190 Messon. 12km/7.5mi W of Troyes on N 60 and left on D 83. ☏03 25 70 31 12. Open Thu–Sun. Booking necessary.* This beautiful farm houses a pleasant restaurant decorated with paintings of the village and surrounding area.

SHOPPING

Specialities – Above all Troyes is renowned for its *andouillettes* (chitterling sausages) – grilled, unaccompanied or drizzled with olive oil flavoured with browned *fines herbes* and garlic. Try them with *mustard au vin de champagne* or Meaux mustard, accompanied by mashed potatoes, kidney beans or fried onion rings.
Other specialities include Chaource cheese, cider or *champagne choucroute*, *rosé des Riceys*, and *cacibel* (aperitif made with cider, blackcurrant and honey).

Halle de l'Hôtel-de-ville – *Tue–Thu 7.30am–12.45pm, 3.30–7pm, Fri–Sat 9.30am–7pm, Sun 9am–12.30pm.* Among the stalls inside the covered market, visit **La Boucherie Moderne** for *andouillettes* made by Gilbert Lemelle, the largest French manufacturer of these chitterling sausages, the **Charcuterie Audry Chantal**, for homemade Troyes *andouillettes*, and **Jean-Pierre Ozérée** for his fine selection of cheeses, including Chaource, Mussy and Langres.

Market – As well as the Halles, there's another daily market in the Place St-Remy halls, especially on Saturdays. There is another in the Chartreux area on Wed and on Sun morning. A farmers' market is held every third Wed of the month on Boulevard Jules-Guesde.

Patrick Maury – *28 r. du Gén.-de-Gaulle. ☏03 25 73 06 84. www.andouillette-maury.fr. Mon–Sat 8am–12.45pm, 2–7.30pm.* Opposite the market is this tiny boutique prized for its *andouillette de Troyes*, black pudding and other home-made *charcuterie*.

Factory Outlets – Troyes is well known for its factory outlets on the outskirts of town (St-Julien-les-Villas and Pont-Ste-Marie sites), offering discount prices on numerous fashion labels.

Marques Avenue – *114 bd de Dijon. ☏03 25 82 80 80. www.marquesavenue.com. Mon–Fri 10am–7pm, Sat from 9.30am.* With 80 boutiques, Marques Avenue is the biggest centre for *fins de séries* (end-of-line) discount fashion stores in Europe. Here you will find all the big brand names, both French and foreign.

Mc Arthur Glen – *Voie des Bois, 10150 Pont-Ste-Marie. ☏03 25 70 47 10. www.mcarthurglen.com. Mon–Fri 10am–7pm, Sat 10am–8pm. Closed 1 May.* Opened in 1995, the village includes 80 end-of-line shops along an outside covered gallery.

Marques City – *Pont Ste-Marie. ☏09 71 27 02 66. www.marquescity.fr. Mon 2–7pm, Tue–Fri 10am–7pm, Sat 9.30am–7pm.* 30 shops of clothes, sportswear and shoes are known for their good price reductions all year round.

ON THE TOWN

La Cocktailerie – *56 r. Jaillant-Deschainets. ☏03 25 73 77 04. Tue–Sat 5pm–3am.* The clientele of this smart bar ranges from businessmen to dating couples. A hundred or so cocktails are on offer, around 45 whiskies and many prestigious champagnes.

Le Bougnat des Pouilles – *29 r. Paillot-de-Montabert. ☏03 25 73 59 85. Daily 6pm–3am.* The high-quality vintages in this wine bar are sought out by the proprietor himself. The walls are often hung with exhibitions of painting and photography. The atmosphere is laidback and the music a blend of jazz, blues and world music. Concerts twice a month.

Le Tricasse – *16 r. Paillot-de-Montabert. ☏03 25 73 14 80. Mon–Sat 3pm–3am.* Troyes's most famous nightspot offers a mix of music, from jazz to salsa to house (DJ Saturday night). Rum, champagne, cocktails and wines are specialities.

A   B

Vitry-le-François

St-Dizier

Langres ★★ Recommended
Joinville ★ Interesting
Grand   Other sight described in this guide
       Driving tour

MARNE

Lac du Der-Chantecoq

MEUSE

Wassy

Montier-en-Der

Joinville

Domrémy-la-Pucelle

Brienne-le-Château

Vallée de la Blaise

Blécourt

Grand

AUBE

Cirey-sur-Blaise

HAUTE-

Neufchâteau

Bar-s-Aube

Argentolles

Vignory

VOSGES

TROYES

Vendeuvre-s-Barse

Colombey-les-Deux-Églises

Vittel

MARNE

Contrexéville

Chaumont

Abbaye de Morimond

Châteauvillain

Tuffiere de Rolampont

Faverolles

Rolampont

Plateau de Langres

Arc-en-Barrois

Lac de Chames

L. de la Mouche

Lac de la Liez

Langres

Land of the Four Lakes

Cascade d'Étuts

Sts-Geosmes

Fayl-Billot

CÔTE-D'OR

Auberive

Baissey

Lac de la Vingeanne

HAUTE-MARNE

Gorges de la Vingeanne

HAUTE-SAÔNE

N

0   20 km

A   DIJON   B

© Philippe Lemoine/Tourisme Haute-Marne

Mémorial Charles-de-Gaulle, Colombey-les-Deux-Églises

Charles de Gaulle in Colombey-les-Deux-Églises

Silence fills my house. From the corner room where I spend most of the day, I embrace the horizon towards the setting sun. No house can be seen over a distance of 15 kilometres. Beyond the plain and the woods, I can see the long curves sloping down towards the Aube valley and the heights rising on the other side. From a high point in the garden, I behold the wild forested depths. I watch the night enveloping the landscape and then, looking at the stars, I clearly realise the insignificance of things.

Charles de Gaulle, *Mémoires de guerre*

Chaumont

Chaumont-en-Bassigny has retained its medieval character. It boasts a collection of old and contemporary posters and several annual events.

🐾WALKING TOUR

OLD TOWN

▶ Start from square Philippe-Lebon.

🐾 The town organises guided tours of the town with an audio-guide system *(enquire at the tourist office)*.
From the square there is a **view** of the keep, the ramparts and the towers of the Basilique St-Jean.

▶ Walk down rue de la Tour-Chartron on the right which runs along the former ramparts.

Look out for the **Tour d'Arse**, a hexagonal 13C tower below.

▶ Walk up rue Monseigneur-Desprez to place St-Jean.

Note the mansion dating from 1723.

▶ Follow rue du Palais leading to place du Palais and walk up the steps to the esplanade surrounding the keep (view of the Suize valley). The former tanners' district lies below.

Donjon
🔒 *Not open to the public.*
The remaining vesitage of the castle owned by the Counts of Champagne, this 11C–12C tower was used as a prison in the 19C; its walls are almost 3m thick at the base.

▶ Follow rue Hautefeuille on the left.

Rue Guyard and **rue Gouthière** feature historic mansions and towers.

▶ Continue along rue Hautefeuille then take rue Decrès.

▶ **Population:** 23 926.
🗺 **Michelin Map:** Michelin Local map 313: K-5.
ℹ **Tourist office:** 7 av. du Gén. de-Gaulle. ✆03 25 03 80 80. www.tourisme-chaumont-champagne.com.
▶ **Location:** Chaumont occupies the edge of a steep plateau separating the River Suize and the River Marne. It is 100km/62mi SE of Troyes.
👁 **Don't Miss:** The summer festivals (🔒*see Addresses*).

Note, at No. 17, the Louis XIV doorway.

Basilique St-Jean-Baptiste★
The west front, surmounted by two towers, dates from the 13C. (Later parts are from the 16C).
In the chapel at the west end of the nave, on the left-hand side, there is a highly realistic **Entombment★★** (1471). The basilica also contains paintings and sculptures from the School of Jean-Baptiste Bouchardon.

▶ Turn left onto rue Girardon.

Two mansions with splendid doorways stand on a small square: Hôtel de Grand on the left is in Louis XIII style and Hôtel de Beine on the right (Louis XIV style).

▶ Walk along rue Damrémont then to scenic rue Bouchardon. Rue St-Jean leads to place de la Concorde overlooked by the town hall.Then return to square Philippe-Lebon via rue Laloy, rue Toupot-de-Beveaux and rue de Verdun.

SIGHTS
Musée d'Art et d'Histoire
Pl. du Palais. 🕐*May–mid-Sept daily except Tue 2.30–6.30pm; rest of year daily except Tue 2–6pm.* 🕐*1 Jan, 1 May and 25 Dec.* ∞€2 *(under 18, no charge).*

Ticket gives access also to Musée de la Crèche. 𝒫*03 25 03 86 80.*

Housed in the vaulted rooms of the former palace of the counts of Champagne, the museum displays **archaeological collections, paintings and sculptures** from the 16C to the 20C (works by Paul de Vos, Nicolas Poussin, François Alexandre Pernot).

Musée de la Crèche

Rue des Frères-Mistarlet. ◷*May–mid-Sept daily except Tue 2.30–6.30pm; rest of year daily except Tue 2–6pm.* ⊛€2 *(under 18, no charge). Combined ticket with Musée d'Art et d'Histoire.* 𝒫*03 25 03 86 80.*

This museum exhibits a collection of **crèches★** (nativity scenes with figurines) from the 17C to the 20C.

Les Silos, Maison du livre et de l'affiche

&◷*Jul–Aug Tue–Fri 2–6.30pm, Sat 9am–1pm; Sept–Jun Tue and Thu–Fri 2–7pm, Wed and Sat 10am–6pm.* ◷*Sun, Mon and public holidays.* ⊛*No charge.* 𝒫*03 25 03 86 86.*

The former grain silos are now a cultural centre housing a library, reference room and a poster museum.

EXCURSIONS

Viaduct★

1km/0.6mi west.

🚶 Approaching Chaumont from the west along D 65, one immediately spots the magnificent 654m long **viaduct★**, towering 52m above the valley.

🚗 DRIVING TOUR

Plateau de Langres

94km/58mi from Chaumont to Langres. Allow half a day.

The watershed between the Paris Basin, the Rhine valley and the Rhône valley is situated on this plateau and the Seine, the Aube, the Marne and the Meuse all have their source in the area.

◐ Leave Chaumont along D 65 and follow it to Châteauvillain.

Châteauvillain

Parts of the town's fortifications (14C to 16C) still survive. The west front of the **Église Notre-Dame de l'Assomption** is thought to have been designed by architect Soufflot (the Paris Panthéon).

◐ Continue along D 65 then turn left onto D6 towards Arc-en-Barrois.

Arc-en-Barrois

Nestling at the bottom of a valley and surrounded by forests, this town is a lovely place to stay.

◐ Follow D 159 towards Aubepierre-sur-Aube and turn left onto the D 20.

Cascade d'Etufs★

Leave the car in the parking area.

One of the finest waterfalls in the Haute-Marne. Several successive waterfalls in a lovely shaded site.

◐ Continue on the D 20 to Auberive.

Auberive

A Cistercian abbey founded in 1133 (⊶*not open to the public*).

◐ On the way out of Auberive, take the Acquenove forest road.

Source de l'Aube

A pastoral setting with picnic facilities.

◐ Follow D 293 to Baissey.

Moulin de Baissey

◷*May–Sept Sat–Sun and public holidays, 2.3–5.30pm.* ⊛€2.50. 𝒫*03 25 88 41 64.*

Tour this functioning medieval mill to see paddle wheel, millstones, gears.

◐ Drive to Sts-Geosmes along D 141 then N 74.

Sts-Geosmes

The 13C **church**, dedicated to three saints martyred on this site, is built over a 10C crypt with three naves.

◐ N 74 leads to Langres.

ADDRESSES

🛏 STAY

🍽🍽 **Hôtel L'Étoile d'Or** – *2km from Chaumont along the road to Langres. ☏03 25 03 02 23. www.logishotels.com. 11 rooms. Restaurant 🍽🍽*. Noise from the nearby N 19 is reduced by the efficient double-glazing. The rooms, which sometimes feature wood-panelling or sloping ceilings, are fairly comfortable.

The exposed stone walls, fireplace and Louis XVI chairs give the restaurant style. Traditional cuisine.

🍽🍽 **Grand Hôtel Terminus-Reine** – *Pl. du Gén.-de-Gaulle. ☏03 25 03 66 66. www.relais-sud-champagne.com. 54 rooms. Restaurant🍽🍽*. The rooms of this hotel opposite the station are bright and welcoming. The restaurant serves pizzas plus traditional cuisine.

⚌⚌ **Auberge de la Fontaine** – *Pl. de la Fontaine, 52210 Villiers-sur-Suize. 21km from Chaumont along N 19 and D 154. ℘03 25 31 22 22. www.aubergedelafontaine.fr. 7 rooms. Restaurant⚌⚌.* This inn houses the village bar and a pleasant rustic-style restaurant offering local cuisine. A recent wing, located 50m away, houses the rooms and the local grocer's. Garden. Barouche rides available.

⚌⚌ **Hôtel le Grand Val** – *Rte de Langres, 52000 Chamarandes. ℘03 25 03 90 35. Closed Sun evening from Nov to Easter. 53 rooms. Restaurant⚌⚌.* This imposing hotel dating from the 1960s is slightly set back from the main road. Sixties atmosphere in the restaurant.

⚑ EAT

⚌⚌ **Le Parc** – *1 pl. Moreau, 52210 Arcen-Barrois – 16km S of Chaumont along D 65 then D 10. ℘03 25 02 53 07. www.relais-sud-champagne.com. Closed Sun evening, Mon from Apr–mid-Jun, Tue lunch from mid-Jun–mid-Sept, Tue and Wed from mid-Sept–Feb.* This former coaching inn, believed to date back to the 17C, now houses a brightly decorated dining room extended in summer by a flower-decked terrace. Classical cuisine, quiet, functional rooms.

⚌⚌⚌ **Au Rendez-vous des Amis** – *4 pl. des Tilleuls, 52000 Chamarandes – 3.5 km from Chaumont. ℘03 25 32 20 20 www.au-rendezvous-des-amis.com. Closed Sat lunch.* This convivial inn offers a well-prepared traditional cuisine served in an updated rustic setting or, in summer, on the terrace facing the church. Pleasant rooms.

CALENDAR

Festival International de l'Affiche – *May–Jun in various locations around town. Information: ℘03 25 03 86 80. www.ville-chaumont.fr.*

"Grand Pardon de peine et de coulpe", has been celebrated since the 15C to ward off plague, famine and war. Whenever midsummer's day falls on a Sunday, processions in the streets, floral decorations and theatre performances help continue the tradition.

Plaisirs de la Chasse et de la Nature fair – *last Sat–Sun of Aug, at Chateauvillain.* Equipment, displays and fireworks.

Colombey-les-Deux-Églises

Colombey rose to fame through its most illustrious citizen, **Charles de Gaulle**, who had his home at La Boisserie from 1934 until his death in 1970. He is buried in the village cemetery, near the church. In his *Memoirs*, De Gaulle lovingly described this Champagne region: "steeped in sadness and melancholy… former mountains drastically eroded and resigned… quiet, modest villages whose soul and location has not changed for thousands of years…".

La Boisserie

⚒⚒ Daily Apr–Sept 10am–1pm, 2–6.30pm; Oct–Mar daily except Tue 10am–12.30pm and 2–5.30pm (lae Nov–mid-Dec daily except Tue 10am–

▶ **Population:** 692.
⚒ **Michelin Map:** Michelin Local map 313: J-4.
🛈 **Tourist office:** Place de l'Église, 52330 Colombey-les-Deux Eglises. ℘03 25 03 80 80. www.tourisme-chaumont-champagne.com.
▶ **Location:** On the edge of the Champagne region and on the borders of Burgundy and Lorraine, Colombey has, since time immemorial, been a stopover on the road from Paris to Basle.
👁 **Don't Miss:** Look out for eight informative panels dotted around the village, bearing quotes from General de Gaulle.

noon, 2–4.30pm). ⊙Mid-Dec–Jan.
⊚€5.50 (children under 18, €4) –
€16.50 ticket combined with visit to the
memorial. ℘03 25 01 52 52.

During WWII, La Boisserie was severely
damaged by the Germans. General
de Gaulle only returned with his family in May 1946 after repairs. It has not
changed since that time and the public is
encouraged to visit this home, where the
great, yet flawed, French leader spent
so much time thinking and writing.
German Chancellor Konrad Adenauer
was the only politician ever to be
invited to La Boisserie. In order to secure
Franco-German reconciliation, De Gaulle
invited him to his home in September
1958 during the German Chancellor's
state visit to France.

The public are allowed into the downstairs drawing room, full of mementos,
books, family portraits and photographs
of contemporary personalities, into
the vast library and the adjacent study
where General de Gaulle spent many
hours, and the dining room.

Mémorial Charles-de-Gaulle★

⊙May–Sept daily 9.30am–7pm; Oct–
Apr Wed–Mon,10am–5.30pm. ⊙24–25
and 31 Dec and Jan. ⊚€13.50 (children
under 12, €8) – €16.50 ticket combined
with visit to La Boisserie. ℘03 25 01 50
50. www.memorial-charlesdegaulle.fr.

Inaugurated on 18 June 1972, the
memorial overlooks the village and
surrounding forests (including the Clairvaux Forest where St Bernard founded
his famous abbey in the 12C) from a
great height of 397m.

EXCURSION
Argentolles

4km/2.5mi NW along D 104.

This village on the "Route touristique du
Champagne" itinerary (⊙see Planning
Your Trip) offers visitors an **exhibition
on vines and wine** (⊙Apr–Nov Sat–Sun
and holidays. ℘03 25 02 58 05). Housed
in a former wash house, the exhibition
includes a video presentation, wine-
grower's tools, Champagne production
process etc.

Joinville

This small town nestles between the
River Marne, dotted with mills, and a
hill crowned by a ruined castle once
owned by the dukes of Guise.

A BIT OF HISTORY

One of the most prominent lords of this
barony was the famous 13C chronicler,
Jean de Joinville (1224–1317), a loyal
companion of King Louis IX, known as
St Louis, whom he followed to Egypt in
1248 to take part in the seventh crusade.
A 3m high statue of Joinville was erected
in 1861 in rue Aristide-Briand.

SIGHTS
Château du Grand Jardin★

⚿⊙Apr–mid-May and mid-Nov–early
Nov Sat–Sun and public holidays 2–6pm;
mid-May–mid-Sept daily except Tue

▶ **Population:** 3 541.
⚲ **Michelin Map:** Michelin
Local map 313: K-3.
Tourist Office: Pl. Saunoise,
52300 Joinville. ℘03 25
94 17 90. www.tourisme-
joinville.com.
▶ **Location:** Joinville lies off
the N 67 which skirts the
town, 32km/20mi south of
St Dizier and 45km/28mi
north of Chaumont.

11am–7pm. ⊙22 May. ⊚€4 (no charge
1st Sun of month). ℘03 25 94 17 54.

This 16C castle is named for its large
well-maintained garden. Exhibitions,
performances and concerts are organised in the castle throughout the year.

Château du Grand Jardin

Auditoire

Guided tours at 3pm: May–Sept Sun only; Jul–Aug Sat–Sun and public holidays. €5. 03 25 94 37 64. www.auditoire-joinville.fr.

This seigneurial tribunal, erected in the 16C, also served as a prison.

Chapelle Ste-Anne

The chapel (1504) stands in the centre of the cemetery; light pours in through lovely stained-glass windows by artists from the Troyes School. Note the 15C **Christ in bonds** in polychrome wood.

EXCURSIONS

Blécourt

9km/5.6mi S along N 67 to Rupt then right onto D 117.

This 12C Gothic **church** contains a 13C *Virgin and Child* (Champagne School).

ADDRESSES

STAY AND EAT

 Hotel de la Poste – *Pl. de la Grève.* 03 25 94 12 63. *Closed Sun evenings.* This family-run establishment in the town centre offers traditional cooking and 11 small, functional rooms for a simple stay.

 Le Soleil d'Or – *9 r. des Capucins.* 03 25 94 15 66. *26 rooms. Restaurant.* You will be utterly charmed by this late-17C house with a traditional decor of stone and exposed beams, artfully combined with contemporary materials, especially glass. Comfortable rooms.

 Camping La Forge de Ste-Marie – *52230 Thonnance-les-Moulins. 13km/8mi E of Joinville on D 427.* 03 25 94 42 00. *www.laforgedesaintemarie.com. Open May–mid-Sept. Booking advisable.* Located in the countryside near a forest and a lake, the buildings of this former 18C forge have been turned into holiday accommodation. The forge contains a heated indoor pool with a terrace. Shady camping areas. Indoor tennis court, golf course, fishing and kids' club.

 Chambre d'hôte Le Moulin aux Écrevisses – *Rte de Nancy, 52300 Thonnance-lès-Joinville. 5km/3mi E of Joinville on D 60.* 03 25 94 13 76. *www. ecrevisses.fr. 4 rooms. Restaurant.* This former mill by a small river on the edge of a forest is the ideal place to relax and enjoy yourself, thanks to its garden, fishing lake and the numerous walks possible in the region. The rooms are plain but comfortable. This is also the site of the only crayfish-farming in Europe – so prepare your palate!

Langres★★

A promontory of the Langres plateau forms the remarkable setting of this ancient city, one of the three capitals of Burgundy under the Gauls.

A BIT OF HISTORY
Gallo-Roman city

The Lingons, a Gaulish tribe who gave their name to Langres, became Caesar's allies. The town prospered under Roman occupation. However, when Nero died in 70 CE, one of their chiefs, by the name of **Sabinus**, tried to usurp the supreme power but failed and, according to legend, found temporary refuge in a cave close to the source of the Marne.

St Didier

According to legend, St Didier, who was the third bishop of Langres was made a martyr for having defended the town. After he was beheaded, he picked up his head, left on horseback and died on the spot where a chapel was later built.

Royal stronghold

During the Middle Ages, the bishops of Langres became dukes and peers of the realm, and often advisors to the king. When Champagne was united with France in 1284, Langres became a royal fortress. Langres is the birthplace of **Denis Diderot**, the 18C philosopher, **Jeanne Mance,** the

▶ **Population:** 8 413.
🖑 **Michelin Map:** Michelin Local map 313: L-m 6.
ℹ **Tourist Office:** Square Olivier Lahalle, 52201 Langres. ☎03 25 87 67 67, www.tourisme-langres.com.
◐ **Location:** Langres is one of the gateways of Burgundy and a tourist stop-off on the north–south European route (A5, A31).

missionary who founded Canada's first hospital in Montreal in the mid 17C, and painter **Claude Gillot** (1674–1722), one of Watteau's masters.

🐾 WALKING TOUR

ALONG THE RAMPARTS★★
4km/2.5mi. About 1h30.

The ramparts evolved from the Hundred Years War to the 19C and offer a magnificent panorama, including: to the east the Marne valley, the Lac de la Liez and the Vosges mountains when the weather is clear; to the north the Colline des Fourches crowned by a chapel; to the west the slopes of the Bonnelle valley and farther afield the Plateau de Langres and its wooded slopes.

Denis Diderot (1713–84)

The son of a cutler, Denis Diderot was a brilliant pupil of the local Jesuit college and he seemed destined for a religious career, but he went on to study in Paris instead and only came back to Langres five times during his life. However, he spoke about his native town in his *letters* to Sophie Volland and in his *Journey to Langres*.

Interested in many subjects, he wrote numerous works, including essays such as *Letters about the blind for the attention of those who can see,* for which he was imprisoned in Vincennes, novels *(The Nun),* satires *(Jacques the Fatalist),* and philosophical dialogues *(Rameau's Nephew).* He was also an art critic *(Salons).* Yet his name is first and foremost linked with that of the *Encyclopaedia,* a monumental work which he undertook to write with D'Alembert in 1747 and to which he devoted 25 years of his life. Completed in 1772, the 35-volume *Encyclopaedia* represents the sum total of scientific knowledge and philosophical ideas during the Age of Enlightenment.

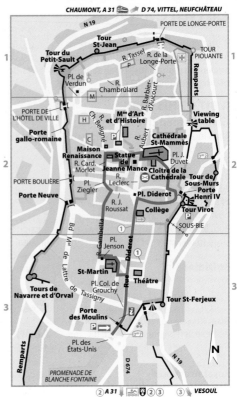

LANGRES

0   200 m

WHERE TO STAY

Cheval Blanc (Hôtel le)..........①

Japiot (Chambre d'hôte)......②

Orangerie
(Chambre d'hôte L')............③

WHERE TO EAT

Délices-Pâtisserie Henry
(Aux)....................................①

Trois Provinces
(Auberge des).......................②

Voiliers (Auberge des)...........③

Start from Place des États-Unis south of the old town.

Porte des Moulins

This is the monumental entrance (1647) to the city; its style is characteristic of Louis XIII's military architecture.

Tour St-Ferjeux

This tower, built around 1469–72, was specially adapted for artillery warfare. A polished-steel sculpture by the Dutch artist Eugene Van Lamsweerde, *Air*, dedicated to the philosopher Gaston Bachelard, stands on the tower.

Tour Virot

This semicircular tower was used to defend the Sous-Murs district, an area below the walls of the city.

Porte Henri IV

This gate (1604) has retained traces of its defence system.

Viewing table

From this point, the view includes the Sous-Murs district below, surrounded by its own wall, and the ramparts on either side; the Lac de la Liez and the Vosges mountains can be seen in the distance.

Tour St-Jean

This former gun tower was fitted as a military dovecote in 1883.

Tour du Petit-Sault

This elongated gun tower (c. 1517–21) contains two vaulted rooms linked by a large staircase. From the terrace (*viewing table*), there is a view of the Bonnelle valley and of the Plateau de Langres.

Porte gallo-romaine
Set within the walls, this gate (1C) was used as a tower in medieval times.

Porte Neuve or Porte des Terreaux
This is the most recent of the gates (1855).

Tours de Navarre et d'Orval
◷ *Jul–Aug 10am–6.30pm; Apr–Jun and Sept 2–6pm (Sat–Sun and public holidays, 10.30am–6.30pm).*
◉€4. ℰ*03 25 87 67 67.*
This defensive complex, inaugurated by François I in 1521, was designed to guard the southern access to the town; the walls are 7m thick in places.

OLD TOWN
A slanting elevator links the Sous-Bie parking area, situated outside the walls, to the town centre, offering a panoramic view of the town, the Lac de la Liez and the Vosges mountains.

Rue Diderot
Lined with shops, the town's high street runs past the **theatre** housed since 1838 inside the former Chapelle des Oratoriens (1676).

Collège
This vast Baroque edifice is the former 18C Jesuit college.

Place Diderot
This is the town's main square, adorned with a statue of Diderot by Bartholdi famed for the Statue of Liberty.
As you walk down rue du Grand-Cloître, admire the view of the Lac de la Liez. Note the 15C timber-framed house at the beginning of rue Lhuillier.

◖ Walk along the south side of the cathedral.

Cloître de la cathédrale
♿◷*The exterior is accessible all year.*
The cloisters date from the early 13C.

◖ Walk across place Jeanne-Mance.

Note the bronze statue of **Jeanne Mance** (1606–73) by Jean Cardot.

Maison Renaissance
◷*Enquire at tourist office for details.*
ℰ*03 25 87 67 67.*
This 16C Renaissance house has a splendid façade overlooking the garden. Follow the side passage *(spiral staircase)* to in rue Cardinal-Morlot; turn left.

◖ Continue along rue Lambert-Payen and rue Gambetta leading to the charming place Jenson.

Église St-Martin
Built in the 13C and rebuilt following a fire in the 18C, when it was topped with an elegant campanile.

SIGHTS
Cathédrale St-Mammès★
The cathedral (94m long and 23m high) was built during the second half of the 12C, but it was subsequently remodelled many times. The vast **interior** is in Burgundian Romanesque style.

Tour sud
◷*Jul–Aug daily 2–6.30pm; Apr–Jun and Sept, Wed, Sat–Sun and public holidays, 4.30–5.30pm.* ◷*During services.*
◉€3. ℰ*03 25 87 67 67.*
From the top of the South tower (45m), there is a panoramic view.

Musée d'Art et d'Histoire
♿◷*Apr–Sept 9am–noon, 1.30–6.30pm; Oct–Mar 1.30–5.30pm.* ◷*Tue, 1 Jan, 1 May, 1 Nov, 25 Dec.* ◉€7 *(child 12–18, €4).* ℰ*03 25 86 86 86.*
The department of **prehistory and ancient history** includes items discovered during excavations made in the region (Farincourt, Cohons).
The **Gallo-Roman department★** displays stone fragments.
Painting from the 17C, 18C and 19C is represented by Gustave Courbet and Camille Corot as well as by local artists Jean Tassel and Edmé Bouchardon.

LAND OF THE FOUR LAKES

Four reservoirs were created in the late 19C and the early 20C in order to supply the Marne-Saône canal.

Lac de la Liez

5km/3mi E of Langres. This is the largest of the four lakes (270ha).

⚐ Take a walk along the earth dike (460m long and 16m high) to catch views of fortified Langres. A footpath runs round the lake. There is also a **boat hire** (⚑*See Addresses*) service.

Lac de la Mouche

6km/3.7mi W of Langres.
This is the smallest of the four lakes (94ha).

Lac de Charmes

8km/5mi N of Langres.
For more adventure, consider a trip on the lake aboard an electric-powered boat.

Lac de la Vingeanne

12km/7.5mi S along N 74.
⚐ A footpath (8km/5mi) runs all the way round this lake (190ha) which has the longest dike (1 254m).

Gorges de la Vingeanne

▷ From the Lac de Vingeanne, drive along D 141C towards Bayssey then Aprey (8km/5mi) and leave the car in the parking area.

⚐ A botanical trail leads from the village of Aprey to the source of the Vingeanne.

NORTHWEST OF LANGRES

Tuffière de Rolampont

▷ 14km/8.7mi along N 19 to 1km/0.6mi beyond Rolampont then left onto D 254; follow the arrows.

⚐ The cascade on this site has been formed over time as mineral spring water, rich in calcium, has made the rock porous through the deposit of microscopic algae and moss.

Mausolée gallo-romain de Faverolles

▷ 10km/6mi along N 19 to Rolampont, then left along D 155 and D 256.

The ruins of this mausoleum were discovered in 1980 in the forest, 3.5km/2.2mi outside the village. And, it is possible to visit the excavation site during the course of a walk through the forest.
Fragments of the mausoleum are displayed in a **Centre archéologique** (⚐*2.30–6pm: Jul–Aug Wed–Sun; May–Jun and Sept Sat–Sun and public holidays.* ✆*03 25 87 67 67*).

⚗DRIVING TOUR

80km/50mi round tour. Allow half a day.

▷ Leave Langres SE along N 74, then follow D 122 on the left towards Noidant-Chatenoy; 2.5km/1.5mi farther on, turn left onto D 290 towards Balesmes-sur-Marne; drive for another 1km/0.6mi and turn right towards the parking area; a path on the left leads down to the source of the River Marne (400m).

Source de la Marne

⚐ *45min on foot there and back.*
The Marne springs from a kind of vault closed by an iron door. Footpaths meander through the rocks. Picnic area.

▷ Return to Noidan-Chatenoy and turn left onto D 51.

Fort du Cognelot

⚐*Guided tours: May–Jun and Sept Sun and public holidays, 3.30pm; Jul–Aug Sat–Sun and public holidays 3.30pm.* ⚐*€3.50.* ✆*03 25 87 67 67.*
This is one of eight forts built round Langres after the 1870 war to defend France's eastern border.

▷ Continue along D 51 to Chalindrey and turn right onto D 17.

Château de Pailly

2.15–5.30pm: Jun Thu–Sun; Jul–Aug Tue–Sun; Apr–May and Sept, on specific dates; check website for details. €5. *06 03 84 45 12.* http://renaissancechateaudupailly.com. An elegant Renaissance residence was built in 1560 round a feudal castle by Marshal de Saulx-Tavannes.

▷ Return to Chalindrey and follow D 26 to Chaudenay then N 19 to Fayl-Billot.

Fayl-Billot

Famous for cane furniture and wicker-work, the tourist office is located inside the **basket-maker's house**. The **National School of Basket-making and Wickerwork** houses three exhibition rooms. Since 1906 this has been the place where students go to train to be professional basket-makers, working with willow and rattan. The institution is unique in France (*Jul–Aug 10am–noon, 2–5.30pm, Sat–Sun 2–5.30pm.* *20 Dec–3 Jan, 1 May.* €3. *03 25 88 19 62*).

▷ Follow D 17 to Bussières-lès-Belmont.

Bussières-les-Belmont

Daily except Sun and public holidays, 9am–noon, 2–6pm (Sat 2–6pm only). Basket-making demonstrations in Jul–Aug. No charge. *03 25 88 62 75.* Willow is grown in this area, and turned into reeds for local handicrafts, including baskets, bird cages, wine baskets. The local association presents a video of the made-by-hand techniques and display of finished willow articles.

▷ Take D 125 to Chaudenay then follow N19 back to Langres.

ADDRESSES

STAY

Chambre d'hôte Japiot – *52250 Flagey. 15km/9.4mi S of Langres on D 428 and D 6.* *03 25 84 45 23. www. fermedusoleildelangres.com. 4 rooms.* Hospitality and spontaneity are the name of the game in this B&B that has been run by the same family for four generations. The rooms are modernly furnished and the one with a terrace is especially nice. Hiding in the dining room are two 245-year-old box beds. The food served is made with produce from the farm, which is also open to visitors.

Chambre d'hôte L'Orangerie – *Pl. Adrien-Guillaume (formerly pl. de l'Église). 52190 Prangey. 16km/10mi S of Langres on N 74 and D 26.* *03 25 87 54 85. 3 rooms.* This charming ivy-clad B&B stands in a rural setting, between the castle and the village church. Its comfortable rooms have a romantic atmosphere.

Le Cheval Blanc – *4 r. de l'Estres.* *03 25 87 07 00. www.hotel-langres. com. Closed 15–30 Nov. 23 rooms. Restaurant.* This 9C abbey church was converted into a hotel in 1793 and some of the bedrooms have retained the typical vaulted ceilings. Behind the house, opposite the town ramparts, the remains of the old buildings enhance the pretty summer terrace. Traditional menu.

EAT

Aux Délices – Pâtisserie Henry – *6 r. Diderot.* *03 25 87 02 48.* This lovely building dating from 1580 is situated in the old town of Langres. Inside, recent frescoes depict some of the interesting features of the town. The quiches, meat pies and pastries make this a tempting option for a light meal or afternoon tea.

Hotel-Restaurant les Voiliers –
1 rue des Voiliers, 52210 Peigney (Lac de la Liez). 4km/2.5mi E of Langres on N 19 and D 284. ✆*03 25 87 05 74. www.lesvoiliers.fr. Closed Mon.* The Lac de la Liez is well known by sailors and windsurfers, and this lakeside inn is ideal for weekend breaks or short holidays.
The combination of comfy rooms and a skilled chef make this an agreeable place to stop off. The restaurant (⊜⊜) produces daily changing menus depending on availability of local produce.

Auberge des Trois Provinces –
14 Rue de Verdun, 52190 Vaux-sous-Aubigny. 25km/15.5mi S of Langres on N 74. ✆*03 25 88 31 98. www.levauxois.fr. Closed Sun evening from 15 Sept–22 Jun and Mon. 9 rooms.* The decor in this little inn is decidedly modern, with beams and painted ceilings and brightly coloured frescoes. Only the stone walls give it a country feel.

SPORT AND RECREATION
Lac de la Liez – ✆*03 25 87 09 03.*
Rent electric and pedal boats for your own excursions.

Montier-en-Der

Destroyed by intensive shelling in June 1940, Montier-en-Der was completely rebuilt. The town developed round a Benedictine monastery established on the banks of the River Voire. It is the capital of the Der (*Der* means oak copse in Celtic).

▸ **Population:** 2 144.
🛈 **Tourist Office:** 2B pl. Auguste-Lebon, 52220 Montieren-Der. ✆03 25 04 69 17. www.tourisme-paysduder.fr.
🜨 **Michelin Map:** Michelin Local map 313: I-3.

SIGHTS
Église Notre-Dame
This is the former church of the monastery founded in Montier in 672, which followed the rule of St Columba (an Irish monk who founded Luxeuil abbey, 🜨*see LUXEUIL-LES-BAINS*). The present edifice was built between the 10C and 13C. Damaged by fire in June 1940, it is remarkably well restored.
The **nave** (*36.5m long*) is the oldest part of the building: eight rounded arches rest on low rectangular piers.
The **chancel★** (12C–13C) is a splendid four-storey example of Early Gothic in the Champagne region. It includes main arches and an upper gallery both with twinned columns, a triforium with trefoil arches, and clerestory windows separated by colonnettes. A row of columns separates the radiating chapels from the ambulatory.

Haras national
♿🕐*Mon–Fri only 2.30–5.30pm.*
🕐*1 Jan and 25 Dec.* ✆*03 26 04 22 17.*
This stud farm, situated on the site of the former abbey, on the left of the

church, looks after some 40 stallions and 15 horses for various riding clubs.

🚗 DRIVING TOUR

60km/37mi round tour. Allow 4h.

The Lac du Der-Chantecoq (🜨*see Lac du DER-CHANTECOQ*) and the **timber-framed churches★** are the two main attractions of the Der region. Most of these churches are decorated with stained glass from the Troyes School.

🜨 Churches are floodlit every night from May to September and weekends only during the rest of the year.

◗ Drive out of Montier-en-Der along the Brienne road (D 400).

Ceffonds
The **Église St-Rémi**, rebuilt round its Romanesque belfry at the beginning of

16C church, Lentilles

the 16C, stands in the disused cemetery which has retained a 16C stone cross. The transept and the chancel are decorated with fine 16C **stained-glass windows★** made in the famous workshops of the city of Troyes: in the chancel you can see from left to right St Rémi's legend, Christ's Passion and Resurrection and the Creation.

▶ Turn back towards Montier-en-Der then left onto D 173.

Puellemontier
Timber-framed houses stand scattered in the fields. The **church** is surmounted by a slender pointed steeple; the nave dates from the 12C but the chancel is more recent (16C).

▶ Continue along D 173 then D 62 to Lentilles.

The road runs close to the peaceful **Étang de la Horre** (250ha), lined with tall grass.

Lentilles★
This is a typical Der village with a well-ordered street plan, low timber-framed and a fine 16C timber **church**.

▶ Follow D 2 to Chavanges.

Chavanges
The **church**, dating from the 15C and 16C, has a 12C doorway; it contains several 16C stained-glass windows (some made after drawings by Dürer).

▶ Drive E along D 56 to Bailly-le-Franc.

Bailly-le-Franc
Barely restored during the past centuries, the late 17C **church** has remained the simplest and most authentic of all the churches in the Der region.

▶ Follow D 121 west to Joncreuil. Follow D 127 then D 128 to Arrembécourt.

Arrembécourt
Note the **church**'s carved doorway.

▶ Continue along D 6 then D 58.

Drosnay
This village has retained a few timber-framed buildings and church.

▶ Drive along D 55 to Outines.

Outines
The **Maison de l'Oiseau et du Poisson** shows the changing aspects of the Lac du Der-Chantecoq and its varied bird population through the seasons (&*see Lac du DER-CHANTECOQ*).

▶ Continue east along D 55.

Châtillon-sur-Broué
&*See Lac du DER-CHANTECOQ.*

Droyes
The brick-built church comprises a Romanesque nave and a 16C chancel.

▶ Take D 13 to return to Montier-en-Der.

Balcony designed by Hector Guimard

St-Dizier

This iron and steel town was once a mighty stronghold with a garrison of 2 500 soldiers. In 1544, it withstood an attack by the Holy Roman Emperor, Charles V, and his army of 100 000 men. It was here that, in 1814, Napoleon won his last victory before being exiled to the island of Elba. In 1900, **Hector Guimard**, one of the initiators of Art Nouveau in France, used the St-Dizier ironworks for his ornamental creations, leaving the town with a heritage of fine balconies and banisters.

WALKING TOUR

IN SEARCH OF GUIMARD'S CAST-IRON ORNAMENTS
Many houses were decorated by Guimard, outside and inside, in Art Nouveau style: balconies, window sills, palmettes, door panels and banisters.

▶ Start from place de la Liberté (tourist office).

At the beginning of rue de la Commune-de-Paris, **No. 29** has a door panel decorated with tulips dating from 1900.

▶ Follow rue de l'Arquebuse.

Rue de l'Arquebuse
No. 1: railing, banisters and window sills dating from 1900; **Nos. 1bis** and **1ter**: window sills by Guimard; **No. 31**:

▶ **Population:** 26 634.
▶ **Michelin Map:** Michelin Local map 313: J-2.
▶ **Tourist office:** 4 avenue de Belle-Forêt-sur-Marne, 52100 St-Dizier.
  ✆ 03 25 05 31 84.
  www.tourisme-saintdizier deretblaise.com.
▶ **Location:** The biggest town in the Haute-Marne département, roughly equidistant between Troyes and Nancy.
▶ **See also:** The Lac du DER-CHANTECOQ artificial lake and bird reserve.

window sills, door panels, basement window by Guimard; **No. 33**: window sills from 1900.

▶ Turn left onto rue du Colonel-Raynal.

Rue du Colonel-Raynal
No. 4: window sills; **No. 6**: window sills and door panel by Guimard; **No. 8**: window sills. Before turning left onto rue du Général-Maistre, note the window sills of **No. 39**.

Rue du Général-Maistre
No. 24 on the street corner: window sills; **No. 15** and **No. 13**: door panels by Guimard and window sills dating from 1900.

▶ Return to the square via rue Robert-Dehault.

ADDITIONAL SIGHTS
Quartier de la Noue
This suburb west of the town centre was inhabited by boatmen who floated convoys of logs down the River Marne to Paris and returned on foot.
They lived in low houses built in cob, with a yard backing onto gardens and fields. Eighty tiny alleyways, known as *voyottes* and accessible to pedestrians, run at right angles.

Vignory ★

The picturesque village of Vigory is tiny, but worth visiting because of its Romanesque church, lying below the ruins of a medieval castle, for which it is known.

▶ **Population:** 273.
◔ **Michelin Map:** Michelin Local map 313: K-4.
◖ **Location:** Situated between Chaumont and Joinville at the junction of the D40 and the N67.

VISIT
Église St-Étienne★

Built c. 1000 by the lord of Vignory, this church is a rare example of mid-11C Romanesque architecture. Some say this is the oldest church in France that is still in regular use. The rectangular belfry is decorated with a storey of blind arcading beneath two storeys of twinned openings, topped by a stone cone with an octagonal roof.

Interior★

Although remodelled, the church has kept its original appearance with a nave extending over nine bays, separated from the aisles by three-storey elevations. The chancel has two parts: a front area with two-storey elevations and an oven-vaulted apse separated from the ambulatory by seven columns; some of which have capitals elaborately carved with lions, gazelles etc.

The church contains a wealth of sculpture from the 14C, 15C and 16C. Note the 14C monumental statue of the Virgin Mary carrying Jesus who is holding a bird in his hand. However, the most remarkable carvings are in the first chapel off the south aisle: an altarpiece and an altar front featuring the *Coronation of the Virgin* between St Peter and St Paul. The same regional workshop produced a series of small Nativity scenes to be found in the fourth chapel.

Castle ruins

The ruins are accessible by car up a narrow road leading to the keep.
Originally built in the 10C, the ruins that can be seen today are from the 12C rebuild.
From the esplanade laid out as a picnic area, there is a fine view of the town.

Altarpiece depicting the Passion, Église St-Étienne

© Gérard Labriet/Photononstop

Wassy

This quiet little town, at the heart of "wet Champagne," has retained the traditional ironworks which brought prosperity at a time when, before the First World War, Wassy was one of the main centres of iron-ore mining and metalwork in France. In 1562, Wassy was the setting for a massacre that marked the start of the Wars of Religion.

SIGHTS
Église Notre-Dame
Dating from the late 12C, the church has both Romanesque (belfry, capitals) and Gothic (doorway, vaulting) features.

Musée Protestant de la Grange
&. ○May–Sept Tue–Sun 2–5.30pm. Rest of the year by appointment. ○Public holidays. ℘03 25 07 64 47.
The Protestant museum illustrates the history of the reformed church of Wassy in the 16C and 17C and is located in a Protestant church, built on the site of the barn where the massacre took place. **Paul and Camille Claudel** lived opposite with their parents. Paul later became a poet and playwright and his sister Camille a talented sculptor and close friend of Rodin.

Paradis, Sommevoire
© Christian Goupi/age fotostock

- ▶ **Population:** 3 019.
- ⚲ **Michelin Map:** Michelin Local map 313: J 2-3.
- ▤ **Tourist Office:** R. du Gén.-Rignoux, 52130 Wassy. ℘03 25 07 64 47.
- ▶ **Location:** On the River Blaise, 19km from St-Dizier by D2.

🚗 DRIVING TOUR

Vallée de la Blaise
34km/21mi from Wassy to Cirey-sur-Blaise.

Between Juzennecourt and St-Dizier, the Blaise valley is a nature lovers' paradise. The river, abounding in trout, meanders through pastures between forested slopes. Hillside villages such as Lamothe-en-Blaisy or riverside ones like Daillancourt, are most attractive with their white-stone houses.

As early as 1157, monks from Clairvaux founded the first industrial forge in Wassy and smelting works and workshops gradually settled along the river, using wood from the nearby forests, water power and local iron ore.

In 1840, Osne-le-Val was the birthplace of ornamental cast iron. In 1900, Hector Guimard chose St-Dizier for his Art Nouveau creations.

Today, the area produces furniture, plus metalworks firms supply the aeronautical industry, the car industry and the chemical industry. An unmarked road, known as the Route du Fer, links the main sites.

▷ Drive S along D 2 to Dommartin-le-Franc.

Dommartin-le-Franc
The former **smelting works** built in 1834 are now used for exhibitions about metalwork and ornamental cast iron. (○mid-Jun–mid-Sept daily except Mon

Doulevant-le-Château

2–6.30pm; rest of the year Sat–Sun and public holidays. &03 25 04 07 07).

▶ Continue S along D 60 and turn right 2km/1.2mi farther on.

Sommevoire

In the 19C, this village specialised in the production of ornamental cast iron (fountains, lamps, vases, religious statues) initiated by Antoine Durenne. The **Paradis** (Ⓒ*mid-Jul–mid-Sept Fri–Sun 2.30–6pm, rest of the year by arrangement*, &06 88 15 11 82; www.fontesdart-sommevoire.org) houses a collection of his models, plaster casts, some of them by artists such as Bartholdi.

▶ From Sommevoire drive SE along D 229 and rejoin the River Blaise in the town of Doulevant-le-Château.

Doulevant-le-Château

This village, surrounded by beautiful forests, is well known for its wrought-iron and cast-iron workshops. The 13–16C church has a fine Renaissance doorway.

Cirey-sur-Blaise

From 1733 to 1749, Voltaire stayed for long periods in the **château** (Ⓒ*guided tours only, at 2.50pm, 4.05pm, 5.20pm: May–Jun Sun and public holidays; Jul–Aug afternoons; Sept Sun afternoon;* ⊛€8 (park only €3). &03 25 55 43 04; www.chateaudecirey.com) of his friend the Marquise du Châtelet, whom he called the "divine Émilie." He wrote several works here, including *Alzire* and *Mahomet.* The château consists of a 17C pavilion in the Louis XIII style and an 18C wing built by Madame du Châtelet and Voltaire. The tour takes in the library, the chapel, the kitchens, reception rooms adorned with tapestries and Voltaire's small theatre.

The Wassy Massacre

In 1562, François de Guise returned to Wassy one Sunday when the Protestant community was assembled in a vast barn. The duke's men began quarrelling with some of the Protestants and, having entered the barn, they massacred all those they could lay their hands on. The duke later disavowed the massacre although he had done nothing to stop it. This event deeply stirred the growing Protestant population of France and was one of the causes of the Wars of Religion which tore the country apart until 1598 when the Edict of Nantes was signed, granting religious freedom to all French subjects.

INDEX

INDEX

INDEX

INDEX

S

INDEX

INDEX

🏠 STAY

♀/EAT

MAPS AND PLANS

THEMATIC MAPS

MAPS AND PLANS

MAP LEGEND

	Sight	Seaside resort	Winter sports resort	Spa
Highly recommended	★★★	⚲⚲⚲	✳✳✳	♯♯♯
Recommended	★★	⚲⚲	✳✳	♯♯
Interesting	★	⚲	✳	♯

Additional symbols

🅸	Tourist information
═══ ═══	Motorway or other primary route
❶ ❶	Junction: complete, limited
⊨═══⊨ ═══	Pedestrian street
⊨=====⊨	Unsuitable for traffic, street subject to restrictions
▭▭▭▭ - - - -	Steps – Footpath
🚂 🚋	Train station – Auto-train station
🚌 SNCF	Coach (bus) station
—•—•—	Tram
ⓐ	Metro, underground
ℙℝ	Park-and-Ride
♿	Access for the disabled
✉	Post office
☏	Telephone
⬚	Covered market
⚔	Barracks
△	Drawbridge
⊔	Quarry
⚒	Mine
🅱 🅵	Car ferry (river or lake)
🚢	Ferry service: cars and passengers
⛴	Foot passengers only
③	Access route number common to Michelin maps and town plans
Bert (R.)...	Main shopping street
AZ B	Map co-ordinates

Sports and recreation

🏇	Racecourse
⛸	Skating rink
🏊 🏊	Outdoor, indoor swimming pool
🎥	Multiplex Cinema
⛵	Marina, sailing centre
⛺	Trail refuge hut
▭■▬■▭	Cable cars, gondolas
▭++++▭	Funicular, rack railway
🚂	Tourist train
◆	Recreation area, park
🎢	Theme, amusement park
⚥	Wildlife park, zoo
✿	Gardens, park, arboretum
🦅	Bird sanctuary, aviary
🚶	Walking tour, footpath
🧒	Of special interest to children

Abbreviations

A   Agricultural office
(Chambre d'agriculture)

C   Chamber of Commerce
(Chambre de commerce)

H   Town hall (Hôtel de ville)

J   Law courts (Palais de justice)

M   Museum (Musée)

P   Local authority offices
(Préfecture, sous-préfecture)

POL.   Police station (Police)

⊞   Police station (Gendarmerie)

T   Theatre (Théâtre)

U   University (Université)

Selected monuments and sights

Tour - Departure point

Catholic church

Protestant church, other temple

Synagogue - Mosque

Building

Statue, small building

Calvary, wayside cross

Fountain

Rampart - Tower - Gate

Château, castle, historic house

Ruins

Dam

Factory, power plant

Fort

Cave

Troglodyte dwelling

Prehistoric site

Viewing table

Viewpoint

Other place of interest

COMPANION PUBLICATIONS

travelguide.michelin.com
www.viamichelin.com

MAPS
Regional and local maps

To make the most of your journey, travel with **Michelin Regional maps nos 514 and 515** and the Local maps at a scale of 1:150 000, which are illustrated on the map of France below.

And remember to travel with the latest edition of the **map of France no 721** (1:1 000 000), also available in atlas format: spiral bound, hard back and mini-atlas – perfect for your glove compartment.

INTERNET

Michelin offers travellers a route-planning service on the internet:
travelguide.michelin.com
www.viamichelin.com

Choose the shortest route, a route without tolls, or the Michelin recommended route to your destination; you can also access information about hotels and restaurants from the *Michelin Guide France.*

MICHELIN IS CONTINUALLY INNOVATING FOR SAFER, CLEANER, MORE ECONOMICAL, MORE CONNECTED... BETTER ALL-ROUND MOBILITY.

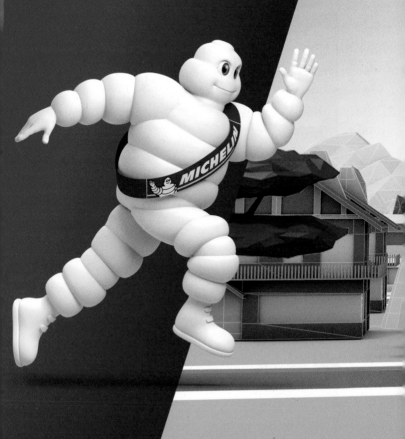

Tyres wear more quickly on short urban journeys.

?

TRUE!

You tend to accelerate and brake more often when driving around town so your tyres work harder!
If you are stuck in traffic, keep calm and drive slowly.

Tyre pressure only affects your car's safety.

?

FALSE!

Driving with underinflated tyres (0.5 bar below recommended pressure) doesn't just impact handling and fuel consumption, it will shave 8,000 km off tyre lifespan.
Make sure you check tyre pressure about once a month and before you go on holiday or a long journey.

*Fitting **2 winter tyres** on my car guarantees maximum safety.*

FALSE!

In the winter, especially when temperatures drop below 7°C, to ensure better road holding, all four tyres should be identical and fitted at the same time.

2 WINTER TYRES ONLY =
risk of compromised road holding.

4 WINTER TYRES =
safer handling when cornering, driving downhill and braking.

If you regularly encounter rain, snow or black ice, choose a **MICHELIN Alpin tyre**. This range offers you sharp handling plus a comfortable ride to safely face the challenge of winter driving.

MICHELIN
IS COMMITTED

▶ MICHELIN IS **GLOBAL LEADER IN FUEL-EFFICIENT TYRES** FOR LIGHT VEHICLES.

▶ **EDUCATING OF YOUNGSTERS IN ROAD SAFETY,** NOT FORGETTING TWO-WHEELERS. LOCAL ROAD SAFETY CAMPAIGNS WERE RUN IN **16 COUNTRIES** IN 2015.

QUIZ

1 TYRES ARE BLACK SO WHY IS THE MICHELIN MAN WHITE?

Back in 1898 when the Michelin Man was first created from a stack of tyres, they were made of natural rubber, cotton and sulphur and were therefore light-coloured. The composition of tyres did not change until after the First World War when carbon black was introduced. But the Michelin Man kept his colour!

2 FOR HOW LONG HAS MICHELIN BEEN GUIDING TRAVELLERS?

Since 1900. When the MICHELIN guide was published at the turn of the century, it was claimed that it would last for a hundred years. It's still around today and remains a reference with new editions and online restaurant listings in a number of countries.

3 WHEN WAS THE "BIB GOURMAND" INTRODUCED IN THE MICHELIN GUIDE?

The symbol was created in 1997 but as early as 1954 the MICHELIN guide was recommending "exceptional good food at moderate prices". Today, it features on the MICHELIN Restaurants website and app.

If you want to enjoy a fun day out and find out more about Michelin, why not visit the l'Aventure Michelin museum and shop in Clermont-Ferrand, France:
www.laventuremichelin.com

Michelin Travel Partner

Société par actions simplifiées au capital de 11 288 880 EUR
27 cours de l'Ile Seguin - 92100 Boulogne Billancourt (France)
R.C.S. Nanterre 433 677 721

No part of this publication may be reproduced in any form
without the prior permission of the publisher.

© Michelin Travel Partner
ISBN 978-2-067229-52-5
Printed: April 2018
Printed and bound in France : Imprimerie CHIRAT, 42540 Saint-Just-la-Pendue - N° 201804.0151

Although the information in this guide was believed by the authors and publisher to be accurate
and current at the time of publication, they cannot accept responsibility for any inconvenience,
loss, or injury sustained by any person relying on information or advice contained in this guide.
Things change over time and travellers should take steps to verify and confirm information,
especially time-sensitive information related to prices, hours of operation, and availability.

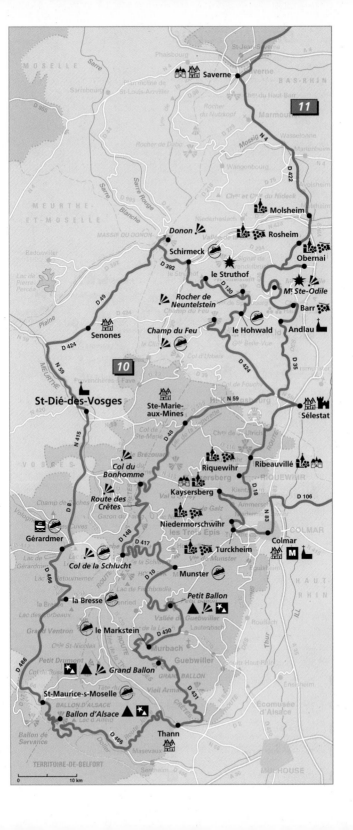

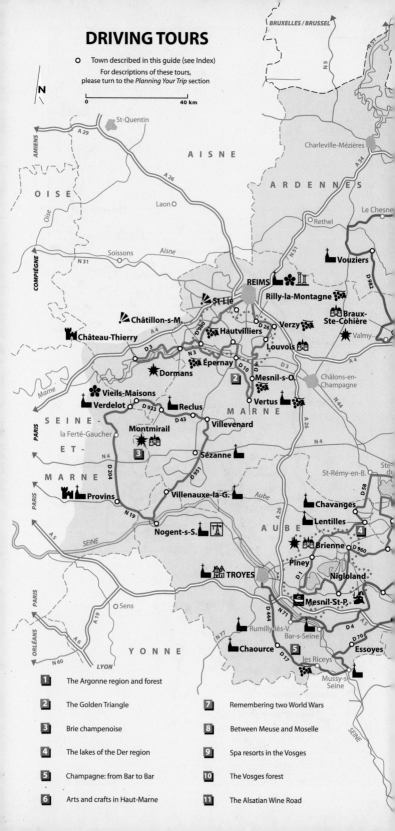

DRIVING TOURS

○ Town described in this guide (see Index)
For descriptions of these tours,
please turn to the *Planning Your Trip* section

0 ————————— 40 km

1 The Argonne region and forest

2 The Golden Triangle

3 Brie champenoise

4 The lakes of the Der region

5 Champagne: from Bar to Bar

6 Arts and crafts in Haut-Marne

7 Remembering two World Wars

8 Between Meuse and Moselle

9 Spa resorts in the Vosges

10 The Vosges forest

11 The Alsatian Wine Road